D1138176

Good
University
Guide
2019

John O'Leary

Published in 2018 by Times Books

An imprint of HarperCollins Publishers
Westerhill Road
Bishopbriggs
Glasgow G64 2QT
www.harpercollins.co.uk
times.books@harpercollins.co.uk

First published in 1993. Twenty-fourth edition 2018

© Times Newspapers Ltd 2018

The Times is a registered trademark of Times Newspapers Ltd

ISBN 978-0-00-827036-0

Patrick Kennedy was the lead consultant with Andrew Farquhar for UoE Consulting Limited, which has compiled the main university league table and the individual subject tables for this *Guide* on behalf of *The Times*, *The Sunday Times* and HarperCollins Publishers.

Please see chapters 1 and 12 for a full explanation of the sources of data used in the ranking tables. The data providers do not necessarily agree with the data aggregations or manipulations appearing in this book and are also not responsible for any inference or conclusions thereby derived.

Project editor: Alan Copps
Design and layout: Davidson Publishing Solutions

A catalogue record for this book is available from the British Library.

Printed and bound by CPI Group (UK) Ltd, Croydon, CR0 4YY.

MIX
Paper from
responsible sources
FSC **FSC™ C007454**
www.fsc.org

This book is produced from independently certified
FSC™ paper to ensure responsible forest management.

For more information visit: www.harpercollins.co.uk/green

Contents

About the Author

John O'Leary is a freelance journalist and education consultant. He was the Editor of *The Times Higher Education Supplement* from 2002 to 2007 and was previously Education Editor of *The Times*, having joined the paper in 1990 as Higher Education Correspondent. He has been writing on higher education for more than 30 years and is a member of the executive board of the QS World University Rankings. He is a member of the Higher Education Commission and the author of *Higher Education in England*, published in 2009 by the Higher Education Funding Council for England. He has a degree in politics from the University of Sheffield.

Acknowledgements

We would like to thank the many individuals who have helped with this edition of *The Times and Sunday Times Good University Guide*, particularly Rosemary Bennett, Education Editor of *The Times*, Alastair McCall, Editor of *The Sunday Times Good University Guide*, and Patrick Kennedy, the lead consultant with Andrew Farquhar, for UoE Consulting Limited, which has compiled the main university league table and the individual subject tables for this *Guide* on behalf of *The Times*, *The Sunday Times* and HarperCollins Publishers.

To the members of *The Times and Sunday Times Good University Guide* Advisory Group for their time and expertise: Patrick Kennedy, Consultant, Collective Intelligence Limited; Christine Couper, Head of Planning and Statistics, University of Greenwich; James Galbraith, Senior Strategic Planner, University of Edinburgh; Alison Hartrey, Head of Planning, SOAS, London; Mark Langer-Crame, Senior Planning Officer, Cardiff University; Daniel Monnery, Head of Corporate Strategy, Northumbria University; Aaron Morrison, Principal Planning Officer, De Montfort University; Jackie Njoroge, Head of Strategic Planning, Manchester Metropolitan University; Komal Patel, Strategic Planning Officer, Imperial College, London; Dr Sarah Taylor, Head of Strategy Development, Aberystwyth University; David Totten, Head of Planning, Queen's University, Belfast; Jenny Walker, Planning Officer, Loughborough University; to James McLaren, Denise Jones and Pip Day of HESA for their technical advice; to Alice Hancock, Matilda Curtis and Martin Ince for their contributions to the book.

We also wish to thank all the university staff who assisted in providing information for this edition.

Timeline to a University Place

This book is designed to help you find a university place in September 2019. That may seem a long time away, but a decision that can change your life needs a lot of consideration. Add to that the fact that the application process is somewhat long-winded and there is less time than you might think – for example, if you want to study medicine starting in September 2019 you will have to have had some practical experience of helping to care for people, have taken an aptitude test during the summer and completed your application by 15 October 2018, almost a year before your studies will start. Planning well ahead of application and decision deadlines will always give you greater flexibility and choice. The less time you give yourself, the more limited will become your choices.

So where to start? The dates below indicate the key staging points along the way to a university place.

Key dates
February to July 2018
This is the time to develop your thoughts on the subject you would like to study and on where you would like to be at university. See overleaf for where to find advice in this book on choosing a subject and a university.

March 2018 onwards
Attend university open days. Open Days are a good way to gain a personal impression of what a university feels like, where it is located, and what studying in a particular department or faculty would be like. You will only have the time and resources to attend a small number of Open Days, so careful planning is necessary, not least because Open Days at different universities can often clash. The calendar for Open Days for 2018 (as announced by the beginning of the year) appears alongside each university's profile in Chapter 14.

July 2018
Registration starts for UCAS Apply, the online application system through which you will make your application. You will have a maximum of five choices when you come to complete your application form.

September 2018
UCAS will begin to accept completed applications.

15 October 2018
Deadline for applications to Oxford or Cambridge (you can only apply to one of them), and for applications to any university to study medicine, dentistry or veterinary science. Note that for some courses you will need to have completed a pre-application assessment test by this date.

15 January 2019
Deadline for applications for all other universities and subjects (excluding a few art and design courses with a deadline of 24 March 2019). It is advisable to get your application in ahead of this deadline; aim for the end of November 2018.

End of March 2019

Universities should have given you decisions on your applications by now if you submitted them by 15 January 2019.

April onwards

Apply for student loans to cover tuition fees and living costs.

Early May 2019

You will need to have responded to all university decisions. You have to select first choice, if your first offer is conditional, a second choice, and reject all other offers. Once you have accepted an offer, apply for university accommodation if you are going to require it.

6 August 2019

Scottish examination results. If your results meet the offer from your first choice (or, failing that, your second choice), your place at university will be confirmed. If not, you can enter Clearing for Scottish universities in order to find a place on another course.

15 August 2019

A-level results announced. If your results meet the offer from your first choice (or, failing that, your second choice), your place at university will be confirmed. If not, you can enter Clearing to find a place on another course offered by any university.

Mid to late September 2019

Arrive at university for Freshers' Week.

How This Book Can Help You

The process of making a successful application to university has many stages. Fundamental to the whole process are your decisions on which subject to pick and where to study it.

How do I choose a course?
As you will be taking a course that will last three or sometimes four years, you will need enthusiasm for, and some aptitude in, the subject. The options of studying full-time or part-time also need to be considered.

» The first half of chapter 2 provides advice on choosing a subject area and selecting relevant courses within that subject.

» Chapter 12 provides details for 67 different subject areas (as listed on page 36). For each subject there is specific advice and a league table that provides our assessment of the quality of universities offering courses.

How will my choice of subject affect my employment prospects?
As the course you choose will also influence your job prospects at its conclusion, your initial subject decision will have an impact on your life long after you complete your degree.

» The employment prospects and average starting salaries for the main subject groups are given in chapter 3.

» The subject tables in chapter 12 give the employment prospects for each university offering a course.

» Universities are now doing more to increase the employability of their graduates. Some examples are given in chapter 3.

How do I choose a university?
While choosing your subject comes first, the place where you study will also play a major role. You will need to decide upon what type of university you wish to go to: campus, city or smaller town? How well does the university perform? How far is the university from home? Is it large or small? Is it specialist or general? Do you want to study abroad?

» Central to our *Guide* is the main *Times and Sunday Times* league table in chapter 1. This ranks the universities by assessing their performance not just according to teaching quality and the student experience but also through seven other factors, including research quality, the spending on services and facilities, and graduate employment prospects.

» The second half of chapter 2 provides advice on the factors to consider when choosing a university.

» Chapter 13, the largest chapter in the book, contains two pages on each university, giving a general overview of the institution as well as data on student numbers, contact details, accommodation provision, and the fees for 2018–19. Note that fees and student support for 2019–20 will not be confirmed until August 2018, and you must check these before applying.

» For those considering Oxford or Cambridge, details of admission processes and of all the undergraduate colleges can be found in chapter 13.

» If you are considering studying abroad, chapter 10 provides guidance and practical information.

» Specific advice for international students coming to study in the UK is given in chapter 11.

How do I apply?

» Chapter 5 outlines the application procedure for university entry. It starts by advising you on how to complete the UCAS application, and then takes you through the process that we hope will lead to your university place for autumn 2019.

Can I afford it?

Note that most figures in chapters 4 and 6 refer to 2018 and there will be changes for 2019, which you will need to check.

» Chapter 4 describes how the system of tuition fees works and what you are likely to be charged, depending upon where in the UK you plan to study.

» Chapter 6 provides advice on the tuition fee loans and maintenance loans that are available, depending upon where you live in the UK, other forms of financial support (including university scholarships and bursaries), and how to plan your budget.

» Chapter 7 provides advice on where to live while you are at university. University accommodation charges for each university are given in chapter 14.

How do I find out more?

The Times and Sunday Times Good University Guide website at **https://www.thetimes.co.uk/gooduniversityguide** will keep you up to date with developments throughout the year and contains further information and online tables (subscription required).

You can also find much practical advice on the UCAS website (**www.ucas.com**), and on individual university websites. There is a wealth of official statistical information on the Unistats website (**www.unistats.ac.uk**).

Introduction

There has seldom been a better time to apply for a degree place, with the number of 18-year-olds declining, fewer mature students coming forward, and universities reliant on undergraduate fees to stay afloat. As many struggle to fill their places, universities are making a growing number of unconditional offers and the rest are increasingly competitive.

Yet in this buyer's market, the value of higher education is being questioned as never before. Universities, which are more accustomed to being the critics than the criticised, have been under attack for everything from their vice-chancellors' salaries, to their position on Brexit, their students' attitudes to freedom of speech, academic standards and – crucially – the financial returns from a degree. From being seen as one of the country's most successful sectors, they have become a favourite target of pundits, politicians and many of the public.

The change in attitudes coincided with the first increase in fees for five years. While the near trebling of fees to £9,000 a year caused less disruption than expected, the addition of £250 brought immediate talk of cartels and wasteful spending. Interestingly, universities in the United States and Australia, two other countries with high fees, have been under political and public pressure at exactly the same time.

So far, the negative publicity surrounding universities has not put off teenage applicants, who were present in record numbers in 2017, despite a fall in the size of the age group. The numbers of mature and part-time applicants did fall, but they were already in decline. The first application figures for 2018 suggest continuing growth in full-time applications, but they cover only Oxford and Cambridge, and medicine, dentistry and veterinary science.

With some research showing up to 75 per cent of people believing university to be poor value for money and more than a third of recent graduates telling one pollster that their degree had been a 'waste of time', the focus on a degree as a career investment is bound to continue. So what does the evidence show? The most recent Government statistics say graduates were far more likely than non-graduates to be employed (87 per cent, compared with 70 per cent) in 2016 and, overall, graduates were earning £9,500 a year more than others.

However, not all subjects or universities provide an equal prospect of career success, as this *Guide* has demonstrated over the years. Even taking all graduates together, apprentices earn more at the age of 21 and those whose highest qualifications are good-grade GCSEs earn a similar amount. By the age of 24, however, graduates are ahead and by the age of 30, the gap is £5,000 – or £10,000 compared with the GCSE cohort.

Even then, there are further complications. The Institute for Fiscal Studies has reported that the male graduates of 23 institutions continued to earn less than non-graduates and the same was true for female graduates at nine institutions. At the other end of the scale, there were 36 institutions for men and 10 for women where graduates were earning more than £60,000 after ten years – far more than those with lower qualifications.

The statistics will continue to come thick and fast, with the Government now planning to use graduate salary averages in the next round of its Teaching Excellence Framework, but it is clear that university remains a good financial investment for most – but certainly not all – students. In international terms, the salary premium enjoyed by UK graduates is still higher than in most other parts of the world, even if it has declined somewhat with the sharp rise in the proportion of the working-age population with a degree – 42 per cent now, compared with 24 per cent in 2002.

With so many more graduates competing for jobs, a degree will never again be an automatic passport to a fast-track career. But it is a fair assumption that most of the better-paid jobs in the future will require post-school education, whether it is a traditional degree, a higher-level apprenticeship, or in-company training. Even for those who cannot or do not wish to afford the costs associated with three or more years of full-time education when they leave school, university remains a possibility. Degree apprenticeships are an attractive new option, while the modular courses adopted by most universities enable students to work through even a traditional degree at their own pace, dropping out for a time if necessary, or switching to part-time attendance. Distance learning is another option, and advances in information technology now mean that some nominally full-time courses are delivered mainly online.

Most graduates do not regret their decision to go to university. Students from all over the world flock to British universities, and they offer a valuable resource for those on their doorstep. No league table can determine which is the right university for any candidate, but this *Guide* should provide some of the information necessary to draw up a shortlist for further investigation and make the right choice in the end.

After small but important changes two years ago to the way our tables are compiled, the methodology for the new edition remains stable. The *Guide* has always put a premium on consistency in the way that it uses the statistics published by universities and presents the results. The overriding aim is to inform potential students and their parents and advisors, not to make judgments on the performance of universities. As such, it differs from the Government's Teaching Excellence Framework (TEF), which uses some of the same statistics but makes allowance for the prior qualifications of students and uses an expert panel to place the results in context. Our tables use the raw data produced by universities to reflect the undergraduate experience, whatever advantages or disadvantages those institutions might face. We also rank all 129 universities, while the TEF uses only three bands, leaving almost half of the institutions in our table on the same middle tier.

The TEF represents the first official intervention in this area since the Quality Assurance Agency's assessments of teaching quality were abolished more than a decade ago. Scores in those reports correlated closely with research grades, and the first discussions on the framework in the Coalition Government envisaged one comparison taking account of both teaching and research. This remains our approach, to look at a broad range of factors (including the presence of excellent researchers on the academic staff) that will impact on undergraduates.

An era of change

Higher education has undergone numerous changes in the 24 years that this book has been published, and more are on the way in 2018. In England, the Office for Students will take on the responsibilities for regulating universities that have been the province of the Higher Education Funding Council. Research will be overseen by a different body, bringing the likelihood that universities will be less able to juggle their finances between different budgets.

In the short term, fees of £9,250 are here to stay in England and Wales, following the Prime Minister's announcement of a three-year freeze and the adoption of a new system in the Principality. In Scotland, too, the current regime of free higher education for Scottish residents and those from other EU countries is unlikely to change. However, it is impossible to be sure how long Theresa May's minority government will last and Jeremy Corbyn's Labour Party is committed to abolishing fees if it wins power. Nor is there any certainty about the arrangements for EU students coming to English universities from 2019 onwards.

Already, the pattern of applications and enrolments has changed, however, since the introduction of higher fees. Students are plainly opting in larger numbers for subjects that they think will lead to well-paid jobs. While there has been a recovery in some arts and social science subjects, the trend towards the sciences and some vocational degrees is unmistakeable. Languages have suffered particularly – perhaps partly because they tend to be four-year degrees – and so have courses associated with parts of the economy that were hardest hit in the recession. Building is one example, where numbers are still well down even though the subject is in the top ten for employment prospects, with four out of five graduates going straight into a professional job.

The vast majority of students take a degree primarily to improve their career prospects, so some second-guessing of the employment market is inevitable. But most graduate jobs are not subject-specific and the best brains in the country are hard-pressed to predict employment hotspots four or five years ahead, when today's applicants will be looking for jobs. Computer science is a good example of the pitfalls. Demand for the subject plummeted when the "dotcom bubble" burst and courses closed. Now parts of the IT industry are booming again and there is a skills shortage. Applications for the subject have shot up, but no one can be certain of market conditions in such a fast-moving industry so far ahead.

Just as it may be unwise to second-guess employment prospects, the same goes for the competition for places in different subjects. Universities may close or reduce the intake to courses that have low numbers of applicants while some of the more selective institutions may make more places available, especially to candidates who achieve good grades at A-level. Bristol, Birmingham, Exeter and University College London have all taken hundreds more students than usual since the restrictions were relaxed for high-grade candidates. Now others plan to follow suit – as long as they can attract enough students.

Even before the increase to £9,250 fees in 2017, it seems that universities of all types saw the expansion of undergraduate provision as a sensible strategy. But even those that are expanding may do so only in areas where they are strong and extra students can be taught at reasonable cost. In the absence of clear announcements, applicants are still best advised to go for the courses and universities that meet their requirements, rather than trying to second-guess the system.

Using this *Guide*

The merger of *The Times and Sunday Times* university guides four years ago began a new chapter in the ranking of higher education institutions in the UK. The two guides had 35 editions between them and, in their new form, provide the most comprehensive and authoritative assessments of undergraduate education at UK universities.

There is one new institution in the main table this year. Birkbeck, University of London, though established in 1823, has not been included previously because its portfolio of part-time courses did not lend it to fair comparisons with traditional universities. In recent years, however, Birkbeck has developed a range of full-time degrees taught in the evening, which have encouraged it to join the table. In addition, Trinity Saint David, University of Wales, has rejoined after four years in which it boycotted league tables. Only two public universities with a focus on full-time undergraduate education are now absent. For different reasons, University College Birmingham and Wolverhampton have instructed the Higher Education Statistics Agency not to release data on their performance and are missing from the institutional and subject tables. Private universities such as the University of Law, Regent's University and BPP University, do not currently have the necessary data to be included.

Some famous names in UK higher education have never been ranked because they do not fit the parameters of a system that is intended mainly to guide full-time undergraduates. The Open University, for example, operates entirely through distance learning, while the London and Manchester Business Schools have no undergraduates. Other specialist institutions, including a number of university colleges, appear in relevant subject tables only.

There are now 67 subject tables, since the addition last year of Criminology. Other subject tables will be added in due course because there is growing demand for information at this level. Successive surveys have found that international students are more influenced by subject rankings than those for whole institutions, and there is no reason to believe that domestic applicants think differently.

Since the separation of NSS scores, outlined below, there has been no change in the basic methodology behind the tables, however. The nine elements of the main table are the same, with the approach to scores in the 2014 Research Excellence Framework mirroring as closely as possible those for previous assessments. In order to reflect the likelihood of undergraduates coming into contact with outstanding researchers, the proportion of eligible academics entered for assessment is part of the calculation, as well as the average grades achieved.

This year's tables

This year's results again show more movement than usual, perhaps reflecting the increased level of competition for undergraduates. The division of NSS scores continues to have an effect, with the four sections of the survey categorised as 'Teaching Quality' given more weight than the remaining four (student experience). The survey was extended and toughened up in 2017, causing a general decline in scores and making the results less comparable with 2016.

There were changes, too, in the graduate employment market, with slightly lower unemployment in 2016 – the year in which the latest available employment survey took place – but a significant increase in the number of students staying on to take postgraduate degrees.

As in last year's *Guide*, there was considerable variation in the amounts spent on student facilities and some universities (but by no means all) saw further increases in the proportion of students awarded good honours.

It seems, however, that nothing can shake the dominance of Cambridge and Oxford at the head of the main table – and the majority of the subject tables. Cambridge has maintained a clear lead over its ancient rival, although the gap has narrowed slightly. St Andrews remains the nearest challenger, with Imperial College London hot on its heels in fourth place. Cambridge tops 30 of the subject tables, compared with five at Oxford. Throughout all the years of the *Guide*, Oxford and Cambridge have seldom been challenged, especially in terms of the undergraduate education they offer.

St Andrews remains easily Scotland's top university in the table and Queen's, Belfast the same in Northern Ireland, while in Wales, Cardiff has won back the top spot, pipping last year's leader, Swansea, by a mere three points out of 1,000. Other movements in the upper reaches of the table have seen Lancaster and Leeds each rise three places and Loughborough four. Finishing sixth, Lancaster is in its highest-ever position and was rewarded with the title of *The Times and Sunday Times* University of the Year. A little further down, Glasgow is up nine places and back in the top 20 as Scottish University of the Year.

Harper Adams, in 33rd place, has recorded its third successive rise up the table, reaching the highest position ever achieved by a post-1992 university. But the biggest rises of all (29 places) are by Staffordshire and Leeds Trinity, in =63rd and =67th places respectively. Those going in the other direction include City (down 25 places to =75th) and Edinburgh Napier (down 23 places to 116th).

More modern universities than ever feature above some older foundations. The first edition of *The Times Good University Guide* predicted the development of a new pecking order in an era of growing competition between universities, many of which had just acquired that title. It has taken longer than many expected and the top 30 places in the table are still monopolised by old universities, but the previous binary division is breaking down.

Guide Award Winners

University of the year	**Lancaster**
Runner up	**Loughborough**
Shortlisted	**Essex**
	Glasgow
	Nottingham
Scottish University of the year	**Glasgow**
Welsh University of the year	**Cardiff**
Modern University of the year	**Nottingham Trent**
Sports University of the year	**Bath**
International University of the year	**Heriot Watt**
University of the year for	
Teaching quality	**Aberystwyth**
Student experience	**St Andrews**
Graduate employment	**London South Bank**
Student retention	**Edge Hill**

Making the right choices

Anyone hoping to embark on a degree in 2019 will be well advised to tread carefully and muster as much comparative information as possible before making their choices. This *Guide* is intended as a starting point, a tool to help navigate the statistical minefield that will face applicants, as universities present their performance in the best possible light. There is advice on fees and financial questions, as well as all-important employment issues, along with the usual ranking of universities and 67 subject tables.

While some of the leading universities have expanded considerably in recent years, most will remain selective, particularly in popular subjects. Even when the demand for places dropped in 2012, there were between five and six applications (not applicants) to the place across the whole higher education system. The demand for places is far from uniform, however; even within the same university the level of competition will vary between subjects. The entry scores quoted in the subject tables in Chapter 12 offer a reliable guide to the relative levels of selectivity, but the figures are for entrants' actual qualifications. The standard offers made by departments will invariably be lower.

Making the right choice for 2019 will require a mixture of realism and ambition. Most sixth-formers and college students have a fair idea of the grades they are capable of attaining, within a certain margin for error. Even with five choices of course to make, there is no point in applying for a degree where the standard offer is so far from your predicted grades that rejection is virtually certain. If your results do turn out to be much better than predicted, there will be an opportunity through the Adjustment system, or simply through Clearing, to trade up to an alternative university.

With the relaxation of recruitment restrictions, universities that once took pride in their absence from Clearing are now continuing to recruit after A-level results day. As a result, the use of insurance choices – the inclusion of at least one university with lower entrance standards than your main targets – is likely to decline further. It is still a dangerous strategy, but there is now more chance of picking up a place at a leading university if you aimed too high with all your first-round choices. Oxford and Cambridge will not be appearing in the Clearing lists, but there is now a wider range of universities to choose from than ever before. Some may even come to you if you sign up for the new arrangements introduced by UCAS last year, which allow universities to approach unplaced candidates on Results Day if their grades are similar to other entrants'.

The Adjustment Period that runs for five days after results have been published is reserved for those with better grades than the offer they have accepted to approach other universities. Although only 1,000 students found places this way in 2017, the numbers may rise as the system offers a valuable safety net for those in this happy position. Universities at the very top of the table may be full, but there should be more opportunities elsewhere.

The long view

School-leavers who enter higher education in 2019 were not born when our first league table was published and most will never have heard of polytechnics, even if they attend a university that once carried that title. But it was the award of university status to the 34 polytechnics, a quarter of a century ago, that was the inspiration for the first edition of *The Times Good University Guide*. The original poly, the Polytechnic of Central London, had become the University of Westminster, Bristol Polytechnic was now the University of the West of England and – most mysteriously of all – Leicester Polytechnic had morphed into De Montfort University. The new *Guide* charted the lineage of the new universities and offered the first-ever comparison of institutional performance in UK higher education.

The university establishment did not welcome the initiative. The vice-chancellors described the table as "wrong in principle, flawed in execution and constructed upon data which are not uniform, are ill-defined and in places demonstrably false." The league table has changed considerably since then, and its results are taken rather more seriously. While consistency has been a priority for the *Guide* throughout its 24 years, only six of the original 14 measures have survived. Some of the current components – notably the National Student Survey – did not exist in 1992, while others have been modified or dropped in consultation with the expert group of planning officers from different types of universities that meets annually to review the methodology and make recommendations for the future.

While ranking is hardly popular with academics, the relationship with universities has changed radically, and this *Guide* is quoted on numerous university websites. As Sir David Eastwood, now vice-chancellor of the University of Birmingham, said in launching an official report on university league tables that he commissioned as Chief Executive of the Higher Education Funding Council for England: "We deplore league tables one day and deploy them the next."

Most universities have had their ups and downs over the years, although Oxford and Cambridge have tended to pull away from the rest. Both benefited from the introduction of student satisfaction ratings and from the extra credit given to the top research grades – the two measures that carry an extra weighting in our table. They also have famously high entry standards, much the largest proportions of first and upper-second class degrees and consistently good scores on every other measure. Several other famous names have been among the chasing pack throughout. The London School of Economics, Imperial College and University College London have seldom been out of the top five, while Warwick and, in recent years, Durham and St Andrews have all been fixtures in the top ten.

There have been spectacular rises, however. Coventry, for example, was only 12 places off the bottom a decade ago and is now well inside the top 50, having reached the highest position ever for a modern university two years ago. Harper Adams, which now enjoys that distinction, was not even a university until 2012.

Since this book was first published, the number of universities has increased by a third and the full-time student population has rocketed. Individual institutions are almost unrecognisable from their 1993 forms. Nottingham, for example, had less than 10,000 students then, compared with more than 30,000 now. Manchester Metropolitan, the largest of the former polys, has experienced similar growth. Yet there are universities now which would have been too small and too specialist to qualify for the title in 1992. The diversity of UK higher education is celebrated as one of its greatest strengths, and the modern universities are neither encouraged nor anxious to compete with the older foundations on some of the measures in our table.

The coming years, let alone the next 20, may see another transformation in the higher education landscape, with the private sector competing strongly alongside established universities in some fields and distance learning becoming more popular as there is greater investment in Massive Open Online Courses (MOOCs) and the cost of full-time degrees rises. There may, indeed, be university closures and mergers, although they have been predicted before and seldom come about. Universities are among the most enduring of the UK's institutions, and will take some shifting.

1 The University League Table

The Top Universities

What distinguishes a top university? And who is to say that one course is better than another – especially when the university system has been reluctant to make any such comparison? Critics of league tables insist that this is because every university has different priorities, every course has a different way of approaching a subject and students must choose the one that suits them best. So they must. Not everyone would find the top universities to their taste, even if they were able to secure a place. But that does not mean that there are not important differences in the quality of universities and the courses they offer.

Universities publish reams of statistics about themselves – more than ever now that the Government insists on greater transparency. But even some of the official attempts to provide prospective students with better information can leave the reader more confused, rather than less. Some would say that the Teaching Excellence Framework falls into this category, with its use of benchmarks to allow for students' prior qualifications and an expert panel to put the results in context, yet still only placing universities and colleges in one of three bands.

The table in this chapter has been developed over 24 years to focus on the fundamentals of undergraduate education and make meaningful comparisons in an accessible way. The institutions will have their own ideas about what should go into comparisons of this type, but ours has stood the test of time because it uses the statistics that universities themselves employ to measure their own performance and combines them in a straightforward way that generations of students have found revealing.

Every element of the table has been chosen for the light it shines on the undergraduate experience and a student's future prospects. The selection of these measures and the way in which they are combined give a particular view of universities' overall strengths, and it is one that has stood the test of time. Unlike some others, *The Times and Sunday Times Good University Guide* has placed a premium on consistency, confident that the measures are the best currently available for the task. Some changes have been forced upon us. Universities stopped assessing teaching quality by subject, when this was the most heavily weighted measure in the table, for example. However, the arrival of the National Student Survey (NSS) 13 years ago has enabled the student experience to be reflected in the table. It is designed to inform prospective students and their advisers in choosing what and where to study. More than two thirds of final-year undergraduates give their views on the quality of their courses, a remarkable response rate that makes the results impossible to dismiss.

Two years ago, we split the student satisfaction measure in two while keeping the overall contribution of the NSS to the table unchanged, and we have retained this approach. The "teaching quality" indicator reflects the average scores of the survey's sections on teaching, assessment and feedback, learning opportunities and academic support, while the "student experience" indicator is drawn from the average of the sections on organisation and management, learning resources, the student voice and the learning community sections, as well as the final question on overall satisfaction. Teaching quality is favoured over student experience and accounts for 67 per cent of the overall student satisfaction score, with student experience making up the remaining 33 per cent.

The basic information that applicants need in order to judge universities and their courses does not change, however. A university's entry standards, staffing levels, completion rates, degree classifications and graduate employment rates are all vital pieces of intelligence for anyone deciding where to study. Research grades, while not directly involving undergraduates, bring with them considerable funds and enable a university to attract top academics.

Any of these measures can be discounted by an individual, but the package has struck a chord with readers. The ranking is the most-quoted of its type both in Britain and overseas, and has built a reputation as the most authoritative arbiter of changing fortunes in higher education. The measures used are kept under review by a group of university administrators and statisticians, which meets annually. The raw data that go into the table in this chapter and the 67 subject tables in chapter 12 are all in the public domain and are sent to universities for checking before any scores are calculated.

Indeed, while the various official bodies concerned with higher education do not publish league tables, several produce system-wide statistics in a format that invites comparisons. The Higher Education Funding Councils' Research Excellence Framework is one example of this. The Higher Education Statistics Agency (HESA), which supplies most of the figures used in our tables, also publishes annual "performance indicators" on everything from completion rates to research output at each university. To these must now be added the Teaching Excellence Framework, which uses several of the measures included in this *Guide*.

Any scrutiny of league table positions is best carried out in conjunction with an examination of the relevant subject table – it is the course, after all, that will dominate your undergraduate years and influence your subsequent career.

How *The Times and Sunday Times* league table works

The table is presented in a format that displays the raw data, wherever possible. In building the table, scores for student satisfaction (combining the teaching quality, student experience scores) and research quality were weighted by 1.5; all other measures were weighted by 1.

For entry standards, student/staff ratio, good honours and graduate prospects, the score was adjusted for subject mix. For example, it is accepted that engineering, law and medicine graduates will tend to have better graduate prospects than their peers from English, psychology and sociology courses. Comparing results in the main subject groupings helps to iron out differences attributable simply to the range of degrees on offer. This subject-mix adjustment means that it is not possible to replicate the scores in the table from the published indicators because the calculation requires access to the entire dataset.

The indicators were combined using a common statistical technique known as Z-scores, to ensure that no indicator has a disproportionate effect on the overall total for each university, and the totals were transformed to a scale with 1,000 for the top score. The Z-score technique makes it impossible to compare universities' total scores from one year to the next, although their relative positions in the table are comparable. Individual scores are dependent on the top performer: a university might drop from 60 per cent of the top score to 58 per cent but still have improved, depending on the relative performance of other universities.

Only where data are not available from HESA are figures sourced directly from universities. Where this is not possible scores are generated according to a university's average performance on other indicators, apart from the measures for research quality, student–staff ratio and services and facilities spend, where no score is created.

The organisations providing the raw data for the tables are not involved in the process of aggregation, so are not responsible for any inferences or conclusions we have made. Every care has been taken to ensure the accuracy of the tables and accompanying information, but no responsibility can be taken for errors or omissions.

The Times and Sunday Times league table uses nine important indicators of university activity, based on the most recent data available at the time of compilation:

» Teaching quality
» Student experience
» Research quality
» Entry standards
» Student staff ratio

» Services and facilities spend
» Completion
» Good honours
» Graduate prospects

Teaching quality and student experience

The student satisfaction measure has been divided into two components which give final-year undergraduates' views of the quality of their courses. The National Student Survey (NSS) published in 2017 was the source of the data, except where a boycott of the survey prevented the response rate reaching 50 per cent. This was the case at nine universities (Bristol, Cambridge, King's College London, Liverpool, Manchester, Oxford, Sheffield, SOAS London and University College London).

Where 2017 NSS data was not available, the 2016 scores for Teaching Quality and Student Experience were adjusted by the overall percentage point change between 2016 and 2017. The adjusted scores were used for z-scoring only, and do not appear in the final table.

» The National Student Survey covers eight aspects of a course, with an additional question gauging overall satisfaction. Students answer on a scale from 1 (bottom) to 5 (top) and the score in the table is the percentage of positive responses (4 and 5) in each section
» The teaching quality indicator reflects the average scores of the first four sections, which contain 14 questions
» The student experience indicator is drawn from the average scores of the remaining four sections, containing 12 questions, and the additional question on overall satisfaction.
» Teaching quality accounts for 67 per cent of the overall score covering student satisfaction, with student experience making up the remaining 33 per cent.
» The survey is based on the opinion of final-year undergraduates rather than directly assessing teaching quality. Most undergraduates have no experience of other universities, or different

courses, to inform their judgements. Although all the questions relate to courses, rather than other aspects of the student experience, some types of university – notably medium-sized campus universities – tend to do better than others.

Research quality

This is a measure of the quality of the research undertaken in each university. The information was sourced from the 2014 Research Excellence Framework (REF), a peer-review exercise used to evaluate the quality of research in UK higher education institutions undertaken by the UK Higher Education funding bodies. Additionally, academic staffing data for 2013–14 from the Higher Education Statistics Agency have been used.

» A research quality profile was given to every university department that took part. This profile used the following categories: 4* world-leading; 3* internationally excellent; 2* internationally recognised; 1* nationally recognised; and unclassified. The Funding Bodies have directed more funds to the very best research by applying weightings, and for the 2015 *Guide* we used the weightings adopted by HEFCE (the funding council for England) for funding in 2013–14: 4* was weighted by a factor of 3 and 3* was weighted by a factor of 1. Outputs of 2* and 1* carried zero weight. This meant a maximum score of 3. In the interests of consistency, the above weightings continue to be applied this year.

» The scores in the table are presented as a percentage of the maximum score. To achieve the maximum score all staff would need to be at 4* world-leading level.

» Universities could choose which staff to include in the REF, so, to factor in the depth of the research quality, each quality profile score has been multiplied by the number of staff returned in the REF as a proportion of all eligible staff.

Entry standards

This is the average score, using the new UCAS tariff (see page 32), of new students under the age of 21 who took A and AS Levels, Scottish Highers and Advanced Highers and other equivalent qualifications (eg, International Baccalaureate). It measures what new students actually achieved rather than the entry requirements suggested by the universities. The data comes from HESA for 2015–16 and has been converted into points from the new tariff because this is the system used by current applicants. The original sources of data for this measure are data returns made by the universities themselves to HESA.

» Using the UCAS tariff, each student's examination results were converted to a numerical score. HESA then calculated an average for all students at the university. The results have then been adjusted to take account of the subject mix at the university.

» A score of 144 represents three As at A-level. Although all but five of the top 40 universities in the table have average entry standards of at least 144, it does not mean that everyone achieved such results – let alone that this was the standard offer. Courses will not demand more than three subjects at A-level and offers are pitched accordingly. You will need to reach the entry requirements set by the university, rather than these scores.

Graduate prospects

This measure is the percentage of the total number of graduates undertaking further study or in a professional job six months after graduation. The professional employment marker is derived from the latest Standard Occupational Classification (SOC2010) codes. The data came from the HESA Destination of Leavers from HE (DLHE) Record for 2016 graduates.

The results have been adjusted for subject mix.

» HESA's survey of graduates six months after graduation is the only research to show what at least 80 per cent of them do immediately after leaving university.

Good honours

This measure is the percentage of graduates achieving a first or upper second class degree. The results have been adjusted to take account of the subject mix at the university. The data comes from HESA for 2015–16. The original sources of data for this measure are data returns made by the universities themselves to HESA.

» Four-year first degrees, such as an MChem, are treated as equivalent to a first or upper second.

» Scottish Ordinary degrees (awarded after three years of study) are excluded.

» Universities control degree classification, with some oversight from external examiners. There have been suggestions that since universities have increased the numbers of good honours degrees they award, this measure may not be as objective as it should be. However, it remains the key measure of a student's success and employability.

Completion

This measure gives the percentage of students expected to complete their studies (or transfer to another institution) for each university. The data comes from the HESA performance indicators published in March 2017 and based on students entering in 2014–15.

» This measure is a projection, liable to statistical fluctuations.

Student–staff ratio

This is a measure of the average number of students to each member of the academic staff, apart from those purely engaged in research. In this measure a low value is better than a high value. The data comes from HESA for 2015–16. The original sources of data for this measure are data returns made by the universities themselves to HESA.

» The figures, as calculated by HESA, allow for variation in employment patterns at different universities. A low value means that there are a small number of students for each academic member of staff, but this does not, of course, ensure good teaching quality or contact time with academics.

» Student/staff ratios vary by subject; for example the ratio is usually low for medicine. In building the table, the score is adjusted for the subject mix taught by each university.

» Adjustments are also made for students who are on industrial placements, either for a full year or for part of a year.

Services and facilities spend

The expenditure per student on staff and student facilities, including library and computing facilities. The data comes from HESA for 2014–15 and 2015–16. The original data sources for this measure are data returns made by the universities to HESA.

» This is a measure calculated by taking the expenditure on student facilities (including sports, grants to student societies, careers services, health services, counselling, etc.) and library and computing facilities (books, journals, staff, central computers and computer networks, but not buildings) and dividing this by the number of full-time-equivalent students. Expenditure is averaged over two years to even out the figures (for example, a computer upgrade undertaken in a single year).

2018 rank	2017 rank		Teaching quality (%)	Student experience (%)	Research quality (%)	Entry standards (UCAS pts)	Graduate prospects (%)	Good honours (%)	Completion rate (%)	Student-staff ratio	Services & facilities spend per student (£)	Total	Page
1	1	Cambridge	n/a	n/a	57.3	230	87.5	92.1	98.9	11	3,510	1000	350
2	2	Oxford	n/a	n/a	53.1	221	85.3	92.8	98.2	10.3	3,334	983	476
3	3	St Andrews	87.0	87.1	40.4	209	81.9	91.1	96.4	11.6	2,635	930	502
4	5	Imperial College London	77.1	80.9	56.2	222	90.7	88.6	96.2	11.3	3,423	872	418
5	4	Durham	82.5	79.4	39.0	201	84.1	89.5	95.9	14.5	2,726	851	378
6	=9	Lancaster	83.4	84.3	39.1	159	84.9	77.5	92.7	13	3,104	834	428
=7	6	University College London	n/a	n/a	51.0	193	82.1	88.8	94.8	10.4	2,805	812	544
=7	11	Loughborough	84.4	86.9	36.3	157	82.3	80.7	93.4	14.2	2,864	812	452
9	7	Warwick	78.6	79.4	44.6	186	80.8	83.4	95.1	12.9	2,605	792	546
10	13	Leeds	82.4	83.3	36.8	168	81.5	84.2	92.7	13.2	2,987	790	430
11	8	London School of Economics	67.5	65.7	52.8	203	87.1	86.1	95.4	11.4	2,990	787	448
12	12	Bath	81.4	81.5	37.3	186	85.2	85.9	94.8	15.7	2,371	778	318
13	15	East Anglia	81.6	81.6	35.8	157	77.5	86.4	89.7	13.2	3,153	774	380
14	=9	Exeter	80.6	81.7	38.0	179	84.1	85.1	95.5	16.4	2,446	770	392
15	16	Birmingham	81.1	79.7	37.1	167	86.4	84.9	94.5	14.1	2,665	759	326
=16	19	Bristol	n/a	n/a	47.3	187	80.2	87.0	95.9	13.4	2,094	741	342
=16	17	York	83.4	81.8	38.3	163	81.5	81.2	92.3	14.5	1,982	741	564
18	20	Nottingham	80.6	80.1	37.8	164	83.3	83.1	94.0	13.8	2,345	731	470
19	14	Surrey	81.7	81.4	29.7	169	76.8	83.6	90.6	15.4	2,734	718	532
20	29	Glasgow	79.4	80.7	39.9	200	83.0	83.1	88.6	14.6	2,300	714	396
21	24	Sheffield	n/a	n/a	37.6	161	82.6	80.0	94.4	14.6	2,276	711	510
22	30	Essex	79.9	81.3	37.2	130	79.6	72.0	87.9	16	3,262	708	390
23	28	Dundee	83.5	82.4	31.2	164	85.1	82.7	87.6	13.2	2,013	706	376
24	=37	Edinburgh	75.1	75.7	43.8	194	75.1	86.8	92.4	12.5	2,164	705	386

2019 rank	2018 rank		Teaching quality (%)	Student experience (%)	Research quality (%)	Entry standards (UCAS pts)	Graduate prospects (%)	Good honours (%)	Completion rate (%)	Student–staff ratio	Services & facilities spend per student (£)	Total	page
25	32	Manchester	n/a	n/a	39.8	170	82.5	78.4	93.1	13.3	2,700	703	454
26	22	Newcastle	80.5	81.2	37.7	163	80.7	81.0	93.9	14.6	2,097	696	460
27	18	Sussex	78.8	79.4	31.3	141	80.2	78.5	92.7	16.3	2,710	690	534
=28	27	King's College London	n/a	n/a	44.0	174	84.1	85.8	93.6	12	2,326	684	424
=28	34	Royal Holloway, London	81.2	80.0	36.3	148	72.0	76.0	91.0	14.8	2,265	684	500
30	21	Southampton	78.4	77.1	44.9	152	80.3	78.5	91.2	13.2	2,190	682	518
31	23	Kent	78.5	78.6	35.2	138	82.6	79.6	90.4	13.3	1,761	679	422
32	31	Reading	78.2	77.2	36.5	142	75.6	81.2	91.5	14.4	2,344	669	492
33	36	Harper Adams	86.5	86.0	5.7	133	69.5	61.4	86.7	15.1	3,174	666	406
34	25	Leicester	78.1	79.1	31.8	145	75.7	74.7	92.9	13	2,702	663	436
35	46	Cardiff	77.9	78.3	35.0	157	78.9	79.1	93.0	12.9	2,243	662	354
=36	35	SOAS, University of London	n/a	n/a	27.9	153	70.5	81.0	85.5	11.6	2,050	659	514
=36	=44	Swansea	81.1	81.3	33.7	129	82.6	78.0	89.6	15.2	2,336	659	536
38	26	Queen's, Belfast	79.9	79.7	39.7	153	79.9	77.9	91.2	15.6	2,171	647	490
39	=37	Heriot-Watt	77.0	77.4	36.7	167	76.8	77.4	87.6	16.6	2,775	646	408
40	=44	Aberdeen	78.9	79.8	29.9	178	77.6	82.6	85.8	14.9	2,290	645	302
41	48	Strathclyde	78.9	78.3	37.7	202	80.0	79.2	88.0	19.7	1,839	644	526
42	39	Liverpool	n/a	n/a	31.5	152	78.5	76.7	90.6	13.5	2,210	637	440
43	40	Queen Mary, London	76.0	76.8	37.9	155	73.6	76.6	91.6	12.5	2,604	630	488
44	47	Coventry	84.0	84.4	3.8	129	81.4	71.3	86.9	14.6	2,234	624	366
45	43	Stirling	79.7	76.6	30.5	158	74.8	81.3	87.0	15.8	1,814	619	524
46	33	Aston	82.8	82.0	25.8	137	79.7	75.8	90.5	20.9	2,132	618	314
=47	56	Aberystwyth	86.2	84.2	28.1	116	74.3	68.5	85.0	16.4	1,845	615	306
=47	41	Buckingham	87.2	85.9	n/a	122	75.0	62.0	78.1	10.4	2,185	615	346

2018 rank	2017 rank		Teaching quality (%)	Student experience (%)	Research quality (%)	Entry standards (UCAS pts)	Graduate prospects (%)	Good honours (%)	Completion rate (%)	Student-staff ratio (%)	Service & facilities spend per student (£)	Total	Page
=47	57	Nottingham Trent	84.8	83.1	6.5	136	76.7	69.9	87.4	15.8	2,061	615	472
50	42	Keele	82.9	83.1	22.1	134	79.5	67.5	90.7	13.9	2,018	609	420
51	64	Arts, Bournemouth	83.2	79.0	2.4	147	79.5	65.5	88.2	15.1	1,731	608	310
52	49	Liverpool Hope	86.9	85.8	9.2	117	80.5	63.8	78.7	15.5	2,080	603	442
53	59	Portsmouth	82.4	81.3	8.6	124	80.3	73.9	86.0	15.4	2,159	599	484
54	51	Lincoln	82.1	81.7	10.3	130	76.2	68.2	89.1	15.6	1,921	587	438
55	61	Bangor	83.9	83.4	27.2	134	69.5	66.7	85.4	16.2	1,704	579	316
56	84	West London	85.3	82.9	1.6	119	70.5	69.5	79.8	15.6	2,837	575	548
57	60	West of England	83.0	82.8	8.8	126	77.1	72.6	84.4	18.1	2,544	574	550
58	53	Creative Arts	80.7	76.9	3.4	128	61.2	72.5	81.3	12.6	2,701	573	368
59	=54	Brunel London	77.3	78.2	25.4	134	73.1	73.4	88.6	15.8	2,106	568	344
60	88	Norwich Arts	84.1	79.1	5.6	135	66.8	70.8	82.0	17.1	1,806	544	468
=61	81	Chester	82.7	79.6	4.1	119	69.5	64.0	80.7	13.5	2,640	543	360
=61	58	Edge Hill	81.7	79.0	4.9	128	70.4	69.4	84.2	14.2	2,147	543	384
=63	=54	Goldsmiths, London	76.3	72.0	33.4	134	55.4	81.3	80.0	14.1	2,337	541	402
=63	92	Staffordshire	84.1	80.3	16.5	115	79.8	65.8	76.0	15.2	1,766	541	522
65	77	Huddersfield	83.4	80.8	9.4	131	78.6	70.9	80.8	18.9	1,986	539	414
66	=65	Northumbria	80.0	79.5	9.0	144	72.5	74.6	86.1	17.1	1,944	536	466
=67	67	De Montfort	81.6	81.6	8.9	111	80.4	67.3	83.9	19.1	2,177	532	372
=67	96	Leeds Trinity	85.5	83.5	2.0	108	68.0	77.6	86.8	21.4	1,769	532	434
69	52	Falmouth	82.5	76.7	4.6	124	72.0	73.4	86.6	17.7	1,440	531	394
=70	=86	Liverpool John Moores	82.3	81.2	8.9	138	72.7	74.6	83.3	17.5	1,557	527	444
=70	79	Sheffield Hallam	82.0	80.0	5.4	120	69.3	73.5	86.1	16.6	2,101	527	512
72	82	Chichester	83.9	82.1	6.4	122	62.7	70.0	90.2	15.6	1,337	525	362

2008 rank	2007 rank		Teaching quality (%)	Student experience (%)	Research quality ($)	Entry standards (UCAS pts)	Graduate prospects (%)	Good honours (%)	Completion rate (%)	Student-staff ratio	Service & facilities spend per student (£)	Total	page
73	68	Ulster	80.5	79.2	31.8	126	67.8	71.6	83.5	18.8	1,835	519	542
74	78	Roehampton	76.7	76.6	24.5	108	69.3	68.2	82.2	14.3	2,126	518	496
=75	76	Bradford	78.2	79.3	9.2	128	80.8	74.6	83.5	16	2,108	517	338
=75	50	City, University of London	76.8	77.5	21.4	140	69.4	73.6	86.6	18	2,378	517	364
=75	=65	Hull	79.5	77.0	16.7	126	76.1	69.5	84.4	16.5	2,151	517	416
=75	70	St George's, London	74.3	75.3	22.2	162	93.6	72.4	94.6	12.5	2,552	517	504
79	62	Bournemouth	77.6	76.5	9.0	123	70.1	77.2	84.1	16.5	2,204	516	336
80	=72	Manchester Metropolitan	79.2	78.3	7.5	134	69.5	68.9	83.9	15.6	2,084	515	456
81	83	Derby	83.1	79.1	2.5	112	74.1	67.0	82.2	14.8	1,914	514	374
82	=86	Robert Gordon	80.5	78.6	4.0	164	77.8	69.5	85.1	18.1	1,474	509	494
83	71	Gloucestershire	82.1	80.7	3.8	121	68.8	70.9	85.7	19.1	1,866	508	400
84	69	Oxford Brookes	78.2	77.2	11.4	129	72.5	73.0	89.7	16.6	1,623	506	478
85	=72	Winchester	80.4	78.4	5.8	113	63.1	76.7	88.0	15.9	1,533	505	556
=86	80	Plymouth	80.9	79.7	15.9	125	71.5	70.6	84.5	16.1	1,659	501	480
=86	63	Royal Agricultural	78.4	78.8	1.1	114	64.5	68.9	94.5	21.8	2,705	501	498
88	98	Salford	81.1	79.0	8.3	127	71.1	73.1	81.5	16.6	1,814	494	508
89	91	Hertfordshire	78.9	78.6	5.6	119	78.8	66.0	86.5	17.6	2,278	492	410
90	89	Cardiff Metropolitan	80.6	80.0	3.9	128	63.8	63.7	80.8	17.2	2,512	481	356
91	74	Middlesex	78.1	77.2	9.7	117	59.2	65.9	77.6	16.5	3,140	477	456
92	=101	Teesside	81.3	76.7	3.6	119	79.6	63.8	79.8	16.6	2,152	474	538
93	=101	Central Lancashire	80.3	77.7	5.6	137	70.0	68.1	79.5	16.2	1,945	473	358
94	75	Bath Spa	80.0	75.8	7.9	120	64.0	73.2	85.0	18.7	1,592	465	320
95	95	Bishop Grosseteste	83.7	76.9	2.1	112	70.9	69.2	91.6	22.3	1,299	463	332
96	100	Sunderland	80.2	78.9	5.8	112	68.3	63.7	76.3	15.4	2,064	460	530

2018 rank	2017 rank		Teaching quality (%)	Student experience (%)	Research quality (%)	Entry standard (UCAS pts)	Graduate prospects (%)	Good honours (%)	Completion rate (%)	Student-staff ratio	Services & facilities spend per student (£)	Total	page
97	97	Northampton	79.8	77.0	3.2	108	63.4	69.4	83.4	18.5	2,577	458	464
98	85	Abertay	80.3	76.5	5.1	158	66.1	69.9	76.9	19.9	1,842	456	304
99	116	St Mary's, Twickenham	80.9	80.2	4.0	123	73.3	59.7	80.5	17.9	1,593	451	506
=100	=110	Southampton Solent	79.4	77.6	0.5	109	64.1	69.7	77.1	15.5	1,995	450	520
=100	106	West of Scotland	81.6	76.6	4.3	143	72.1	70.2	80.1	20.2	1,747	450	552
=102	=101	Queen Margaret, Edinburgh	74.9	71.3	6.6	139	76.7	77.8	79.2	18.1	1,569	449	486
=102	90	Worcester	81.7	80.0	4.3	120	66.5	63.0	84.3	16.4	1,450	449	560
104		Wales, Trinity St David	83.6	78.7	2.6	109	53.0	66.7	78.9	15.4	2,043	447	540
105	=93	Birmingham City	81.0	77.9	4.3	122	70.6	67.3	81.2	18.7	1,900	446	328
=106	120	London South Bank	79.0	77.5	9.0	107	82.1	63.9	74.6	17	2,248	443	450
=106	117	Westminster	75.5	76.5	9.8	123	67.2	70.4	81.7	17.9	1,917	443	554
108	121	Bedfordshire	80.1	78.9	7.0	97	68.6	65.8	75.3	16.9	2,201	439	322
=109	99	Glasgow Caledonian	76.1	74.5	7.0	165	69.7	74.4	82.6	19.4	1,565	436	398
=109	107	Greenwich	77.5	76.2	4.9	133	66.4	67.5	83.4	17.8	2,049	436	404
111	114	Canterbury Christ Church	79.8	74.9	4.5	113	63.9	70.0	83.3	16.3	1,658	433	352
112	104	Brighton	79.2	76.0	7.9	119	68.7	70.5	82.1	17.4	1,458	431	340
113	108	Anglia Ruskin	82.1	79.5	5.4	102	68.3	69.4	78.9	17.8	1,709	428	308
114	123	East London	81.3	79.3	7.2	116	62.1	61.7	71.4	16.8	2,277	424	382
115	109	Arts London	76.5	71.8	8.0	122	56.6	64.2	87.0	15.9	1,644	417	312
116	=93	Edinburgh Napier	76.5	75.4	4.6	148	65.7	74.4	79.2	19.1	1,578	416	388
117	122	Kingston	76.3	76.7	5.1	118	63.5	67.9	82.2	17.3	2,085	405	426
118	=110	York St John	80.8	78.8	4.1	120	55.8	56.4	86.4	17.4	1,692	401	566
=119	105	Plymouth Marjon	81.5	78.7	n/a	137	59.9	58.2	80.7	21.3	1,995	399	482
=119	115	South Wales	77.9	74.2	4.0	128	62.4	66.5	80.8	17.9	1,810	399	516

2018 rank	2017 rank		Teaching quality (%)	Student experience (%)	Research quality (%)	Entry standards (UCAS pts)	Graduate prospects (%)	Good honours (%)	Completion rate (%)	Student-staff ratio	Services & facilities spend per student (£)	Total	page
121	=112	Newman	78.9	76.2	2.8	117	63.4	62.8	78.6	16.1	1,627	393	462
122		Birkbeck, University of London	76.7	73.8	34.6	104	73.3	58.9	68.0	16	858	383	324
123	=112	Leeds Beckett	79.3	79.1	4.1	11<	62.9	64.6	75.6	19.9	1,591	375	432
124	124	Bolton	82.1	78.5	2.9	114	65.1	58.7	68.4	15.1	1,272	368	334
125	119	Cumbria	75.8	70.6	1.2	118	69.1	61.2	84.1	17.8	1,504	347	370
126	118	Buckinghamshire New	78.5	76.4	1.5	109	62.0	55.5	77.1	17.5	2,047	344	348
127	125	Wrexham Glyndŵr	81.9	76.5	2.3	107	62.9	64.0	67.7	20.9	1,490	332	562
128	127	London Metropolitan	78.5	75.0	3.5	105	65.1	50.2	72.7	18.1	1,417	307	446
129	126	Suffolk	77.7	74.9	n/a	113	65.9	56.9	72.5	19.2	683	263	528

Notes on the Table

Birkbeck, University of London, is included this year for the first time. Trinity Saint David, University of Wales, has returned after a four-year boycott of league tables.

University College Birmingham and Wolverhampton continue to block the release of their data and so do not appear in this year's table.

The following universities provided replacement data or requested modifications as follows:

» *Entry standards*: Loughborough, Trinity Saint David.
» *Student–staff ratio*: Central Lancashire, Edinburgh Napier, Exeter, Kingston, Queen Mary, South Wales.
» *Services and facilities spend*: Central Lancashire, Edinburgh Napier, Exeter, Manchester Metropolitan, Salford.
» *Graduate prospects*: Cardiff, Manchester, Nottingham, Surrey.

2 Choosing What and Where to Study

Choosing a degree course is a life-defining decision – and not just in terms of future earning power. Many graduates end up living and working near their university; they often make their closest friends in their student days and may even meet their future partner there. And that is without considering the three or four years you will spend as an undergraduate, which should develop your intellect and shape you as a person.

Of course, with fees now exceeding £9,000, no one is suggesting that you should ignore career prospects – although it is dangerous to read too much into employment statistics that are collected only six months after graduation. Whatever else they want out of a degree course, students all over the world are seeking an advantage in the labour market more than anything. This chapter will suggest some of the signs to take into account in selecting the course that is right for you, if indeed you are certain that your immediate future should be in higher education at all.

Most young people with the necessary qualifications to go to university decide that it is right for them – half the working age population of London are now graduates. But applications and enrolments since the introduction of much higher fees are beginning to show clear patterns that favour particular subjects and universities – and may make life increasingly difficult for others. It is not surprising that growing numbers should decide to play it safe, as they see it, in choosing what and where to study. Although most graduate jobs continue to be open to students of any discipline, some arts subjects may now seem more of a gamble, and there may be pressure at home to go for a science or business subject if you have the right qualifications.

Your choices must be realistic, however. The course must not only be within your capabilities, but will have to maintain your interest for at least three years – possibly much longer than that if it is then going to determine your field of employment. Ideally, higher education should broaden your options in later life, not narrow them. Most of today's graduates will work in several different fields during their careers. In any case, no one can be sure which skills will be required in four or more years' time, when today's applicants enter the graduate labour market.

Some subjects and universities will be more marketable than others, but which ones? This *Guide* may give some pointers – medicine is unlikely to go into decline, for example – but times do change.

Computer science, for instance, went through years of falling numbers after the dotcom bubble burst, before recovering strongly recently. Applications for the group of subjects that includes architecture and building are only now returning to the totals reached before the recession.

Why applicants have reached some of the conclusions they have remains a mystery. Languages, for example, have been hardest hit in terms of applications and enrolments. Yet business leaders are constantly stressing the need for linguists. In this case, decisions made on entry to the sixth-form may be the biggest factor behind falling applications – the numbers taking languages at A-level have been dropping for a number of years, perhaps because they are seen as more difficult than other arts subjects.

There will be a number of different factors influencing your choice of university and course, ranging from the limitations imposed by your qualifications to favoured geographical locations. You may want to stay within reach of home – or to get as far away as possible. You may have heard good things about a particular course from friends, or a teacher. This *Guide* – and the tables it contains – offers a reality check to supplement such opinions, and the opportunity to narrow down your options.

Key reasons for going to university

To improve job opportunities	71%
To improve knowledge in an area of interest	56%
To improve salary prospects	53%
To specialise in a certain subject/area	51%
Obtain an additional qualification	49%
Essential for my chosen profession	45%
To become more independent	43%
Meet new people	39%
It's the obvious next step – just what you do	36%
To experience a different way of life	33%
I didn't want to get a job straight away	24%
To have a good social life	21%
My parents expected me to	21%
Can live at home and still go to university	12%

Sodexo University Lifestyle Survey 2016

Is higher education for you?

Before you start, there is one important question to ask yourself: what do you want out of higher education? The answer will make it easier to choose where (and if) to be a student. With nearly three in ten school-leavers going on to university, it is easy to drift that way without much thought, opting for the subject in which you expect the best A-level grades, and looking for a university with a reasonable reputation and a good social life. Your career will look after itself – you hope.

With graduate debt soaring, however, and job prospects varying widely between subjects and universities, now is the time to look at your own motivation. Fewer young people than predicted have opted out of higher education since higher fees were introduced, but apprenticeships and big firms' training schemes are now offering attractive alternatives. Many of those who do choose higher education appear to be rethinking their choice of course to give themselves the best possible chance of a satisfying and lucrative career.

Love of a subject is an excellent reason for taking a degree, and one that allows you to focus almost exclusively on the search for a course that corresponds with your passions. If, however, higher education is a means to an end, you need to think about career ambitions and look carefully at employment rates for any courses you might consider. These are examined in more detail in chapter 3.

Many graduates look back on their student days as the best years of their lives, and there is nothing wrong with wanting to have a good time. Remember, though, that you will be paying for it later (literally) and there will be more studying than partying. If you have not enjoyed sixth-form or college courses, you may be better off in a job and possibly becoming one of the hundreds of thousands each year who return to education later in life.

Setting your priorities

Even in the world of £9,250 fees, there are good reasons to believe that the right degree will still be a good investment. Research by London Economics for the million+ group of universities suggested that, on average, a degree would add £115,000 to lifetime earnings. A more recent Labour Force Survey showed working-age graduates earning almost 50 per cent more on average than non-graduates – a bigger premium than graduates enjoy in most countries.

The majority of graduate jobs are not subject-specific; employers value the transferable skills that higher education confers. Rightly or wrongly, however, most employers are influenced by which university a graduate attended, so the choice of institution remains as important as ever. The Institute for Fiscal Studies found that the male graduates of 23 universities and the female graduates of nine were earning less than those without degrees after 10 years. Although most of the IfS report focused mainly on 2012–13, there is little reason to think that this has changed.

Those who want to add value to their degree in the jobs market will find that growing numbers of universities are offering employment-related schemes that are considered in more detail in chapter 3. In many cases, this will involve work experience or extra activities organised by the careers service. A growing number of universities now run certificated employability programmes, while others, such as Liverpool John Moores, have built such skills into degree courses. Such programmes are also highlighted in chapter 3 and in the university profiles in chapter 14.

Narrowing down the field

Once you have decided that higher education is for you, the good news is that, as long as you start early enough, finding the right university can be relatively straightforward. Media attention focuses on the scramble for places on a relatively small proportion of courses where competition is intense, but there are plenty of places at good universities for candidates with the basic qualifications – it's just a matter of finding the one that suits you best. For older applicants, relevant work experience and demonstrable interest in a subject may be enough to win a place.

If anything, the problem is that of too much choice, although universities have reduced the number of degree combinations in anticipation of tougher financial conditions. Students prepared to move away from home will still have more than 100 universities and numerous specialist colleges to consider, most with hundreds – even thousands – of course combinations on offer. Institutions come in all shapes and sizes, so there is work to do at the outset narrowing down your options.

Most applicants start by choosing a subject, rather than a university, and this may reduce the field considerably – there are only eight institutions offering veterinary medicine for example, although the total is around 100 in subjects such as law and English. By the time you have factored in personal preferences about the type or location of your ideal university, the list of possibilities may already be reduced to manageable proportions.

After that, you can take a closer look at what the courses contain and what life is really like for students. Prospectuses and university websites will give you an accurate account of course combinations, and important facts like the accommodation available to new students, but it is their job to sell the university. To get a true picture, you need more – preferably a visit not just to the university, but to the department where you would be studying. If that is not possible, there are plenty of other sources of objective information, such as the National Student Survey (which is available online, with a range of additional data about the main courses at each institution, at **www.unistats.com**).

Some students' unions publish alternative prospectuses, giving a "warts and all" view of the university, and those that do not provide this service may be able to arrange a brief discussion with a current student, either by phone or email. Your school or college may put you in contact with someone who went to a university that you are considering. Guides and collections of statistics may give you valuable information about a course or a university, but there is no substitute for personal experience.

What to study?

Most people seeking a place in higher education start by choosing a subject and a course, rather than a university. If you take a degree, you are going to spend at least three years immersed in your subject. It has to be one you will enjoy and can master – not to mention one that you are qualified to study. Many economics degrees require maths A-level, for example, while most medical schools demand chemistry or biology. The UCAS website (**www.ucas.com**) contains course profiles, including entrance requirements, which is a good starting point, while universities' own sites contain more detailed information. In chapter 12, we describe 67 subject areas and provide league tables for each of them.

Your school subjects and the UCAS tariff

The official yardstick by which your results will be judged is the UCAS tariff, which gives a score for each grade of most UK qualifications considered relevant for university entrance, as well as for the International Baccalaureate (IB). The tariff changed last year. The new points system is shown on Page 32, but most applicants are not affected – two thirds of offers are made in grades, rather than tariff points. This allows universities to stipulate the grades that they require in particular subjects, if they wish, and to determine which vocational qualifications are relevant to different degrees. In certain universities, some departments, but not others, will use the tariff to set offers. Course profiles on the UCAS website and/or universities' own sites should show whether offers are framed in terms of grades or tariff points. It is important to find out which, especially if you are relying on points from qualifications other than A-level or Scottish Highers, more of which are included in the new tariff.

Entry qualifications listed in the *Guide* relate not to the offers made by universities, but to the actual grades achieved by successful candidates who are under 21 on entry. For ease of comparison, a tariff score is included even where universities make their offers in grades.

"Soft" subjects

There is a related issue for many of the most selective universities about the subjects studied in the sixth-form or at college. Not only have growing numbers of students been applying with vocational (usually BTEC) qualifications, but the variety of A-level courses now available includes many subjects that top universities usually will not consider on a par with traditional academic subjects. For many years, a minority of universities have refused to accept General Studies as a full A-level for entrance purposes (although even some leading universities do). The growth of supposedly "soft" subjects, such as media studies and photography, has prompted a few universities to produce lists of subjects that will only be accepted alongside at least two traditional academic subjects.

UCAS tariff scores for main qualifications:

A-levels		AS levels	
Grade	Points	Grade	Points
A*	56	A	20
A	48	B	16
B	40	C	12
C	32	D	10
D	24	E	6
E	16		

Scottish Advanced higher		Scottish higher	
Grade	Points	Grade	Points
A	56	A	33
B	48	B	27
C	40	C	21
D	32	D	15

International Baccalaureate			
Higher level		Standard level	
H7	56	S7	28
H6	48	S6	24
H5	32	S5	16
H4	24	S4	12
H3	12	S3	6

The Extended Essay and Theory of Knowledge course are awarded A 12, B 10, C 8, D 6, E 4

For other qualifications see: ucas.com/ucas/ucas-tariff-points

The Russell Group of 24 leading universities publishes an extremely useful report, called *Informed Choices*, on the post-16 qualifications preferred by its members for a wide range of degrees (**www.russellgroup.ac.uk/for-students**). Although it names media studies, art and design, photography and business studies among the vocational subjects that would normally be given this label, it does not subscribe to the notion of a single list of "soft" subjects. The report suggests you choose at most a single vocational course and primarily select from a list of "facilitating subjects", which are required for many degrees and welcomed generally at Russell Group universities. The list comprises: maths and further maths, English, physics, biology, chemistry, geography, languages (classical and modern) and history. In addition, their guide indicates the "essential" and "useful" A-level subjects for 60 different subject areas studied at Russell Group universities.

For most courses at most universities, there are no such restrictions, as long as your main subjects or qualifications are relevant to the degree you hope to take. Nevertheless, when choosing A-levels, it would be wise to bear the Russell Group lists in mind if you are likely to apply to one or more of the leading universities. At the very least, it is an indication of the subjects that admissions tutors may take less seriously than the rest. Although only the London School of Economics has published a list of "non-preferred" subjects (see page 33), others may adopt less formal weightings.

Vocational qualifications

The Education Department downgraded many vocational qualifications in school league tables from 2014. This has added to the confusion surrounding the value placed on diplomas and other qualifications by universities. The engineering diploma has won near-universal approval from universities (for admission to engineering courses and possibly some science degrees), but some of the other diplomas are in fields that are not on the curriculum of the most selective universities. Regardless of the points awarded under the tariff, it is essential to contact universities direct to ensure that a diploma or another vocational qualification will be an acceptable qualification for your chosen degree.

Admission tests

The growing numbers of applicants with high grades at A-level have encouraged the introduction of separate admission tests for some of the most oversubscribed courses. There are national tests in medicine and law that are used by some of the leading universities, while Oxford and Cambridge have their own tests in a growing number of subjects. The details are listed on page 34. In all cases, the tests are used as an extra selection tool, not as a replacement for A-level or other general qualifications.

Making a choice

Your A-levels or Scottish Highers may have chosen themselves, but the range of subjects across the whole university system is vast. Even subjects that you have studied at school may be quite different at degree level – some academic economists actually prefer their undergraduates not to have taken A-level economics because they approach the subject so differently. Other students are disappointed because they appear to be going over old ground when they continue with a subject that they enjoyed at school. Universities now publish quite detailed syllabuses, and it is a matter of going through the fine print.

The greater difficulty comes in judging your suitability for the many subjects that are not on the school or college curriculum. Philosophy and psychology sound fascinating (and are), but you may have no idea what degrees in either subject entail – for example, the level of statistics

---

"Traditional academic" and "non-preferred" subjects

The London School of Economics expects applicants to offer at least two of the traditional subjects listed below, while any of the non-preferred subjects listed should only be offered with two traditional subjects.

Traditional subjects		Non-preferred subjects	
» Ancient history	» Law	» Any Applied A-level	» Health and social care
» Biology	» Mathematics	» Accounting	» Home economics
» Classical civilisation	» Modern or classical	» Art and design	» Information and
» Chemistry	languages	» Business studies	communication technology
» Computing	» Music	» Citizenship studies	» Leisure studies
» Economics	» Philosophy	» Communication and culture	» Media studies
» English	» Physics	» Creative writing	» Music technology
» Further mathematics	» Psychology	» Design and technology	» Physical education/
» Geography	» Religious studies	» Drama/theatre studies	Sports studies
» Government and politics	» Sociology	» Film studies	» Travel and tourism
» History			

General studies, critical thinking, thinking skills, knowledge and enquiry and project work A-levels will only be considered as fourth A-level subjects and will not therefore be accepted as part of a conditional offer.

Admissions tests

Some of the most competitive courses now have additional entrance tests. The most significant tests are listed below. Note that registration for many of the tests is before 15 October and you will need to register for them as early as possible. All the tests have their own websites. Institutions requiring specific tests vary from year to year and you must check course website details carefully for test requirements. In addition over 50 universities also administer their own tests for certain courses. Details are given at:
www.ucas.com/ucas/undergraduate/getting-started/entry-requirements/admissions-tests

Law
Law National Admissions Test (LNAT): for entry to law courses at Bristol, Durham, Glasgow, King's College London, Nottingham, Oxford, SOAS, University College, London. Register from August; tests held from September to January.

Mathematics
Mathematics Admissions Test (MAT): for entry to mathematics at Imperial College, London and mathematics and computer science at Oxford. Test held in early November.

Sixth Term Examination Papers (STEP): for entry to mathematics at Cambridge and Warwick (also encouraged by Bath, Bristol, Imperial College London, King's College London, Loughborough, Nottingham, Southampton and University College London). Register by end April; tests held in June.

Medical subjects
BioMedical Admissions Test (BMAT): for entry to medicine at Brighton and Sussex Medical School, Cambridge (also for veterinary medicine), Imperial College London, Keele (international applicants only), Lancaster, Leeds (also for dentistry), Oxford and University College London. Register by 1 October; test held early November.

Graduate Medical School Admissions Test (GAMSAT): for graduate entry to medicine and dentistry at Cardiff, Exeter, Liverpool, Nottingham, Plymouth, St. George's, University of London, Swansea, Keele and St Andrews and Dundee in partnership with University of the Highlands & Islands (Scotgem). Register by early August; test held mid-September

Health Professions Admissions Test (HPAT-Ulster): for certain health profession courses at Ulster.Register by start January; test held late January.

UK Clinical Aptitude Test (UKCAT): for entry to medical and dental schools at Aberdeen, Aston, Birmingham, Bristol, Cardiff, Dundee, East Anglia, Edinburgh, Exeter, Glasgow, Hull York Medical School, Keele, King's College London, Leicester, Liverpool, Manchester, Newcastle, Nottingham, Plymouth, Queen Mary, University of London, Queen's University Belfast, Sheffield, Southampton, St Andrews, St George's, University of London, Warwick. Register between May and mid-September; tests held between July and early October.

Cambridge University
Pre-interview or at-interview assessments take place for all subjects. Full details given on the Cambridge admissions website. See also STEP and BMAT above.

Oxford University
Pre-interview tests take place in many subjects that candidates are required to register for specifically by early October. Full details given on the Oxford admissions website. Tests held in early November, usually at candidate's educational institution. See also LNAT, MAT and BMAT above.

---

that may be required. Forensic science may look exciting on television – more glamorous than plain chemistry – but it opens fewer doors, as the type of work portrayed in *Silent Witness or Raising the Dead* is very hard to find.

Academic or vocational?

There is frequent and often misleading debate about the differences between academic and vocational higher education. It is usually about the relative value of taking a degree, as opposed to a directly work-related qualification. But it also extends to higher education itself, with jibes about so-called "Mickey Mouse" degrees in areas that were not part of the higher education curriculum when most of the critics were students.

Such attitudes ignore the fact that medicine and law are both vocational subjects, as are architecture, engineering and education. They are not seen as any less academic than geography or sociology, but for some reason social work or nursing, let alone media studies and sports science, are often looked down upon. The test of a degree should be whether it is challenging and a good preparation for working life. Both general academic and vocational degrees can do this.

Nevertheless, it is clear that the prospect of much higher graduate debt is encouraging more students into job-related subjects. This is understandable and, if you are sure of your future career path, possibly also sensible. But much depends on what that career is – and whether you are ready to make such a long-term commitment. Some of the programmes that have attracted public ridicule, such as surf science or golf course management, may narrow graduates' options to a worrying extent, but often boast strong employment records.

As you would expect, many vocational courses are tailored to particular professions. If you choose one of these, make sure that the degree is recognised by the relevant professional body (such as the Engineering Council or one of the institutes) or you may not be able to use the skills that you acquire. Most universities are only too keen to make such recognition clear in their prospectus; if no such guarantee is published, contact the university department running the course and seek assurances.

Even where a course has professional recognition, bear in mind that a further qualification may be required to practise. Both law and medicine, for example, demand additional training to become a fully qualified solicitor, barrister or doctor. Nor is either degree an automatic passport to a job: only about half of all law graduates go into the profession. Both law and medicine also provide a route into the profession for graduates who have taken other subjects. Law conversion courses, though not cheap, are increasingly popular, and there are a growing number of graduate-entry medical degrees.

One way to ensure that a degree is job-related is to take a "sandwich" course, which involves up to a year in business or industry. Students often end up working for the organisation which

Most popular subject areas by application 2017		Most popular subject areas by acceptance 2016	
1 Subjects allied to medicine	340,980	1 Business & Admin	67,655
2 Business & Admin	336,650	2 Subjects allied to medicine	55,450
3 Biological Sciences	278,800	3 Creative Arts & Design	54,485
4 Creative Arts & Design	259,600	4 Biological Sciences	54,200
5 Social Studies	254,440	5 Social Studies	47,935
6 Engineering	167,180	6 Engineering	30,775
7 Law	140,200	7 Computer Science	26,845
8 Computer Science	130,940	8 Law	25,050
9 Physical Sciences	105,630	9 Physical Sciences	20,210
10 Education	91,750	10 Education	20,165

UCAS applications by June 30 2017

UCAS end of cycle data 2016

Subject areas covered in this Guide

The list below gives each of the 67 subject areas that are covered in detail later in the book (in chapter 12). For each subject area in that chapter, there is specific advice, a summary of employment prospects and a league table of universities that offered courses in 2015–16, ranked on the basis of an overall score calculated from research quality, entry standards, teaching quality, student experience and graduate employment prospects.

Accounting and Finance
Aeronautical and Manufacturing
  Engineering
Agriculture and Forestry
American Studies
Anatomy and Physiology
Animal Science
Anthropology
Archaeology and Forensic Science
Architecture
Art and Design
Biological Sciences
Building
Business Studies
Celtic Studies
Chemical Engineering
Chemistry
Civil Engineering
Classics and Ancient History
Communication and Media Studies
Computer Science
Creative Writing
Criminology
Dentistry
Drama, Dance and Cinematics
East and South Asian Studies
Economics
Education
Electrical and Electronic Engineering
English
Food Science
French
General Engineering
Geography and Environmental Sciences

Geology
German
History
History of Art, Architecture and Design
Hospitality, Leisure, Recreation and Tourism
Iberian Languages
Italian
Land and Property Management
Law
Librarianship and Information Management
Linguistics
Materials Technology
Mathematics
Mechanical Engineering
Medicine
Middle Eastern and African Studies
Music
Nursing
Other Subjects Allied to Medicine
Pharmacology and Pharmacy
Philosophy
Physics and Astronomy
Physiotherapy
Politics
Psychology
Radiography
Russian
Social Policy
Social Work
Sociology
Sports Science
Theology and Religious Studies
Town and Country Planning and Landscape
Veterinary Medicine

---

provided the placement, while others gain valuable insights into a field of employment – even if only to discount it. The drawback with such courses is that, like the year abroad that is part of most language degrees, the period away from university inevitably disrupts living arrangements and friendship groups. But most of those who take this route find that the career benefits make this a worthwhile sacrifice.

Employers' organisations calculate that more than half of all graduate jobs are open to applicants from any subject, and recruiters for the most competitive graduate training schemes often prefer traditional academic subjects to apparently relevant vocational degrees. Newspapers, for example, often prefer a history graduate to one with a media studies degree; computing firms are said to take a disproportionate number of classicists. A good degree classification and the right work experience are more important than the subject for most non-technical jobs. But it is hard to achieve a good result on a course that you do not enjoy, so scour prospectuses, and email or phone university departments to ensure that you know what you are letting yourself in for. Their reaction to your approach will also give you an idea of how responsive they are to their students.

Studying more than one subject

You may find that more than one subject appeals, in which case you could consider Joint Honours – degrees that combine two subjects – or even Combined Honours, which will cover several related subjects. Such courses obviously allow you to extend the scope of your studies, but they should be approached with caution. Even if the number of credits suggests a similar workload to Single Honours, covering more than one subject inevitably involves extra reading and often more essays or project work.

The numbers taking such degrees are falling, but there are advantages to them. Many students choose a "dual" to add a vocational element to make themselves more employable – business studies with languages or engineering, for example, or media studies with English. Others want to take their studies in a particular direction, perhaps by combining history with politics, or statistics with maths. Some simply want to add a completely unrelated interest to their main subject, such as environmental science and music, or archaeology and event management – both combinations that are available at UK universities.

At most universities, however, it is not necessary to take a degree in more than one subject in order to broaden your studies. The spread of modular programmes ensures that you can take courses in related subjects without changing the basic structure of your degree. You may not be able to take an event management module in a single-honours archaeology degree, but it should be possible to study some history or a language. The number and scope of the combinations

---

Proportion of state-educated students

	Lowest		Highest
1 Royal Agricultural	46.8%	1 Ulster	100%
2 Oxford	55.7%	2 Wrexham Glyndŵr	99.7%
3 St Andrews	56.7%	3 Newman	99.6%
4 Durham	60.5%	4 Liverpool Hope	99.4%
5 Bristol	61.4%	5 Bolton	99.3%
6 Cambridge	61.9%	6 Bedfordshire	99.0%
7 Imperial College	65.5%	=7 Edge Hill	98.9%
=8 Buckingham	68.4%	=7 Suffolk	98.9%
=8 University College London	68.4%	=7 Teesside	98.9%
10 Exeter	68.5%	=7 Wales Trinity St David	98.9%

Hesa 2015–16

offered at many of the larger universities is extraordinary. Indeed, it has been criticised by academics who believe that "mix-and-match" degrees can leave a graduate without a rounded view of a subject. But for those who seek breadth and variety, close scrutiny of university prospectuses is a vital part of the selection process.

What type of course?

Once you have a subject, you must decide on the level and type of course. Most readers of this *Guide* will be looking for full-time degree courses, but higher education is much broader than that. You may not be able to afford the time or the money needed for a full-time commitment of three or four years at this point in your life.

Part-time courses

Tens of thousands of people each year opt for a part-time course – usually while holding down a job – to continue learning and to improve their career prospects. The numbers studying this way have dropped considerably, but loans are available for students whose courses occupy between a quarter and three-quarters of the time expected on a full-time course. Repayments are on the same conditions as those for full-time courses, except that repayments will begin after three years of study even if the course has not been completed by then. The downside is that many universities have increased their fees in the knowledge that part-time students will be able to take out student loans to cover fees and employers are now less inclined to fund their employees on such courses. At Birkbeck, University of London, for example, a compromise has been found with full-time courses taught in the evening. For courses classified as part-time, students pay fees in proportion to the number of credits they take.

Part-time study can be exhausting unless your employer gives you time off, but if you have the stamina for a course that will usually take twice as long as the full-time equivalent, this route should still make a degree more affordable. Part-time students tend to be highly committed to their subject, and many claim that the quality of the social life associated with their course makes up for the quantity of leisure time enjoyed by full-timers.

Distance learning

If you are confident that you can manage without regular face-to-face contact with teachers and fellow students, distance learning is an option. Courses are delivered mainly or entirely online or through correspondence, although some programmes offer a certain amount of local tuition. The process might sound daunting and impersonal, but students of the Open University (OU), all of whom are educated in this way, are among the most satisfied in the country, according to the results of the annual National Student Survey. Attending lectures or oversized seminars at a conventional university can be less personal than regular contact with your tutor at a distance.

Of course, not all universities are as good at communicating with their distance-learning students as the OU, or offer such high-quality course materials, but this mode of study does give students ultimate flexibility to determine when and where they study. Distance learning is becoming increasingly popular for the delivery of professional courses, which are often needed to supplement degrees. The OU now takes students of all ages, including a growing number of school-leavers, not just mature students.

In addition, there is now the option of Massive Open Online Courses (MOOCs) provided by many of the leading UK and American universities, usually free of charge. As yet, such courses are the equivalent of a module in a degree course, rather than the entire qualification. Some are assessed formally but none is likely to be seen by employers as the equal of a conventional degree, no matter how prestigious the university offering the course. That may change – some commentators see in MOOCs the beginning of the end of the traditional, residential university – but their main value at the moment is as a means of dipping a toe in the water of higher education. For those who are uncertain about committing to a degree, or who simply want to learn more about a subject without needing a high-status qualification, they are ideal.

A growing number of UK universities are offering MOOCs through the Futurelearn platform, run by the Open University (**www.futurelearn.com**). But the beauty of MOOCs is that they can come from all over the world. Perhaps the best-known providers are Coursera (**www.coursera.org**), which originated at Stanford University, in California, and now involves a large number of American and international universities including Edinburgh, and edX (**www.edx.org**), which numbers Harvard among its members. MOOCs are also being used increasingly by sixth-formers to extend their subject knowledge and demonstrate their enthusiasm and capability to admissions tutors. They are certainly worth considering for inclusion in a personal statement and/or to spark discussion at an interview.

Foundation degrees

Even if you are set on a full-time course, you might not want to commit yourself for three or more years. Two-year vocational Foundation degrees have become a popular route into higher education in recent years. Many other students take longer-established two-year courses, such as Higher National Diplomas or other diplomas tailored to the needs of industry or parts of the health service. Those who do well on such courses usually have the option of converting their qualification into a full degree with further study, although many are satisfied without immediately staying on for the further two or more years that completing a BA or BSc will require.

Other short courses

A number of universities are experimenting with two-year degrees, encouraged by the Government, squeezing more work into an extended academic year. The so-called "third semester" makes use of the summer vacation for extra teaching, so that mature students, in particular, can reduce the length of their career break. Several universities are offering accelerated degrees as part of a pilot project initiated under the last government. But only at the University of Buckingham, the UK's longest-established private university, is this the dominant pattern for degree courses. Other private institutions – notably BPP University – are following suit.

Other short courses, usually lasting a year, are designed for students who do not have the necessary qualifications to start a degree in their chosen subject. Foundation courses in art and design have been common for many years, and are the chosen preparation for a degree at leading departments, even for many students whose A-levels would win them a degree place elsewhere. Access courses perform the same function in a wider range of subjects for students without A-levels, or for those whose grades are either too low or in the wrong subjects to gain admission to a particular course. Entry requirements are modest, but students have to reach the same standard as regular entrants to progress to a degree.

Higher and Degree Apprenticeships

Apprenticeships have been a serious alternative to university for more than a decade. But now students can have the best of both worlds at a growing number of universities, with higher or degree apprenticeships, which combine study at degree level with extended work experience with a named industrial or business partner. The programmes are already popular, but are only available in a limited range of subjects, such as accountancy, healthcare sciences, management and some branches of engineering. Nevertheless, some 28,000 places were available in 2017 and more are certain to be added in future. Such apprenticeships take up to five years to complete and leave the graduate with a Bachelor's or even a Master's degree.

Employers including Deloitte, BMW and the BBC are offering higher-level apprenticeships, although naturally not all are with household names such as these. Students are a paid employee of the sponsoring company, with a contract of employment and holiday entitlement, as well as wages of up to £300 a week.

Further details of the structure of courses and the areas in which apprenticeships are available can be found at **www.gov.uk/government/publications/higher-and-degree-apprenticeships**. In addition, Which? University and the National Apprenticeship Service have produced a more detailed publication, *The Complete Guide to Higher and Degree Apprenticeships*, which is available online and in print.

Yet more choice

No single guide can allow for personal preferences in choosing a course. You may want one of the many degrees that incorporate a year at a partner university abroad, or to try a six-month exchange on the Continent through the European Union's Erasmus Programme. Either might prove a valuable experience and add to your employability. Or you might prefer a January or February start to the traditional autumn start – there are plenty of opportunities for this, mainly at post-1992 universities.

In some subjects – particularly engineering and the sciences – the leading degrees may be Masters courses, taking four years rather than three (in England). In Scotland, most degree courses take four years and some at the older universities will confer a Masters qualification. Those who come with A-levels may apply to go straight into the second year. Relatively few students take this option, but it is easy to imagine more doing so in future at universities that charge students from other parts of the UK the full £9,250 for all years of the course.

Universities with highest and lowest offer rates

Highest		Lowest	
1 Aberystwyth	98.3%	1 Oxford	24.7%
2 Portsmouth	96.3%	2 University of the Arts London	25.9%
3 Bangor	93.1%	3 Cambridge	33.8%
4 Sussex	92.3%	4 Stirling	36.1%
5 St Mary's Twickenham	91.7%	5 Arts University Bournemouth	36.5%
6 SOAS	91.5%	6 London School of Economics	37.1%
7 Roehampton	91.3%	7 Imperial College	46.2%
8 Lancaster	91.2%	8 Edinburgh	48.6%
=9 Lincoln	90.7%	9 St George's University of London	49.9%
=9 Swansea	90.7%	=10 Queen Margaret	54.7%
		=10 St Andrews	54.7%

Proportion of applicants who receive offers

UCAS 2016 18-year-old applicants

Where to study

Once you have decided what to study, there are still several factors that might influence your choice of university or college. Obviously, you need to have a reasonable chance of getting in, you may want reassurance about the university's reputation, and its location will probably also be important to you. On top of that, most applicants have views about the type of institution they are looking for – big or small, old or new, urban or rural, specialist or comprehensive. Campus universities tend to produce the highest levels of student satisfaction, but big city universities continue to attract sixth-formers in the largest numbers. You may surprise yourself by choosing somewhere that does not conform to your initial criteria, but working through your preferences is another way of narrowing down your options.

Best paid graduates

(Median salary six months after graduating)

1	Imperial College	£30,000
2	London School of Economics	£28,500
3	Cambridge	£27,000
=4	Bath	£25,000
=4	Durham	£25,000
=4	King's College London	£25,000
=4	Loughborough	£25,000
=4	Oxford	£25,000
=4	University College London	£25,000
=4	Warwick	£25,000

Hesa 201 –16

Entry standards

Unless you are a mature student or have taken a gap year, your passport to your chosen university will probably be a conditional offer based on your predicted grades, previous exam performance, personal statement, and school or college reference. A growing number of universities have followed Birmingham's lead in making unconditional offers to candidates in selected subjects who have a strong academic record and are predicted high grades. But in most subjects at most institutions, only those who already have their grades receive unconditional offers.

Supply and demand dictate whether you will receive an offer. Beyond the national picture, your chances will be affected both by the university and the subject you choose. A few universities (but not many) at the top of the league tables are heavily oversubscribed in every subject; others will have areas in which they excel, but may make relatively modest demands for entry to other courses. Even in many of the leading universities, the number of applicants for each place in languages or engineering is still not high. Conversely, three As at A-level will not guarantee a place on one of the top English or law degrees, but there are enough universities running courses to ensure that three Cs will put you in with a chance somewhere.

University prospectuses and the UCAS website will give you the "standard offer" for each course, but in some cases, this is

Most popular universities by applications 2016

1	Manchester	63,570
2	Edinburgh	61,650
3	Manchester Metropolitan	56,355
4	Leeds	52,110
5	Nottingham	51,185
6	Birmingham	49,365
7	King's College London	44,060
8	Bristol	43,930
9	Southampton	42,405
10	Exeter	42,335

UCAS 2016

pitched deliberately low in order to leave admissions staff extra flexibility. The standard A-level offer for medicine, for example, may not demand A*s, but nearly all successful applicants will have one or more.

As already noted, the average entry scores in our tables give the actual points obtained by successful applicants – many of which are far above the offer made by the university, but which give an indication of the pecking order at entry. The subject tables (in chapter 12) are, naturally, a better guide than the main table (in chapter 1), where average entry scores are influenced by the range of subjects available at each university.

Location

The most obvious starting point is the country you study in. Most degrees in Scotland take four years, rather than the UK norm of three. It goes without saying that four years cost more than three, especially given the loss of the year's salary you might have been earning after graduation. A later chapter will go into the details of the system, but suffice to say that students from Scotland pay no fees, while those from the rest of the UK do. Nevertheless, Edinburgh and St Andrews remain particularly popular with English students, despite charging them £9,250 a year for the full four years of a degree starting in 2018. The number of English students going to Scottish universities has increased almost every year since the fees went up, despite the fact that there would be no savings, perhaps because the institutions have tried harder to attract them. Fees – or the lack of them – are by no means the only influence on cross-border mobility: the number of Scots going to English universities rose sharply, in spite of the cost, probably because the number of places is capped in Scotland, but not any longer in England.

Close to home

Far from crossing national boundaries, however, growing numbers of students choose to study near home, whether or not they continue to live with their family. This is understandable for Scots, who will save themselves tens of thousands of pounds by studying at their own fees-free universities. But there is also a gradual increase in the numbers choosing to study close to home either to cut living costs or for personal reasons, such as family circumstances, a girlfriend or boyfriend, continuing employment or religion. Some simply want to stick with what they know.

Non-academic factors considered when choosing a university

Location-related

Close to transport links	35%
Able to live away from parental home but close enough for support	30%
Quality of accommodation	27%
Low cost of living	23%
Cost of accommodation	22%
Able to live at parental home	17%
Opportunities for part-time jobs	12%

University-related

Good impression from open days	46%
Campus university	36%
Attractive environment	33%
Active social life / good social facilities	28%
IT / Resource / study facilities	28%
Good links to business or other organisations	27%
Clubs and societies	27%
City centre university	24%
Careers advice / support	17%
Good sporting facilities	15%
Accommodation is located on campus	14%
Good catering and retail facilities	8%

Sodexo University Lifestyle Survey 2016

The trend for full-time students who do go away to study, is to choose a university within about two hours' travelling time. The assumption is that this is far enough to discourage parents from making unannounced visits, but close enough to allow for occasional trips home to get the washing done, have a decent meal and see friends. The leading universities recruit from all over the world, but most still have a regional core.

University or college?

This *Guide* is primarily concerned with universities, the destination of choice for the vast majority of higher education students. But there are other options – and not just for those searching for lower fees. A number of specialist higher education colleges offer a similar, or sometimes superior, quality of course in their particular fields. The subject tables in chapter 12 chart the successes of various colleges in art, agriculture, music and teacher training in particular. Some colleges of higher education are not so different from the newer universities and may acquire that status themselves in future years, as ten did in 2012–13 and one more in the following year.

Further education colleges

The second group of colleges offering degrees are further education (FE) colleges. These are often large institutions with a wide range of courses, from A-levels to vocational subjects at different levels, up to degrees in some cases. Although their numbers of higher education students have been falling in recent years, the new fee structure presents them with a fresh opportunity because they tend not to bear all the costs of a university campus. For that reason, too, they may not offer a broad student experience of the type that universities pride themselves on, but the best colleges respond well to the local labour market and offer small teaching groups and effective personal support.

FE colleges are a local resource and tend to attract mature students who cannot or do not want to travel to university. Many of their higher education students apply nowhere else. But, as competition for university places has increased, they also have become more of an option for school-leavers to continue their studies, as they always have done in Scotland.

Their predominantly local, mature student populations do FE colleges no favours in statistical comparisons with universities. But it should be noted that the proportion of college graduates unemployed six months after graduation is often lower than at universities, as are average graduate salaries. Indeed, 14 further education colleges secured 'gold' ratings in the Government's Teaching Excellence Framework (TEF) – although more than twice as many found themselves in the 'bronze' category.

Both further and higher education colleges are audited by the Quality Assurance Agency and appear in the National Student Survey, as well as the TEF. In all three, their results usually show wide variation. Some demonstrate higher levels of satisfaction among their students than most universities, for example, while others are at the bottom of the scale

Private universities and colleges

The final group of colleges that present an alternative to university was insignificant in terms of size until recently, but may also prosper under the current fee regime, as well as the most recent legislation. This is the private sector, seen mainly in business and law, but also in some other specialist fields.

By far the longest established – and the only one to meet the criteria for inclusion in our main table – is the University of Buckingham, which is profiled on pages 346–347. The best-known "newcomer" currently is BPP University, which became a full university in 2013 and offers degrees, as well as shorter courses, in both law and business subjects. Like Buckingham, BPP offers two-year degrees with short vacations to maximise teaching time – a model that other private providers are likely to follow. Fees are £9,000 a year for UK students taking BPP's three-year degrees in 2017–18 and £13,500 a year for the accelerated version. International students pay £12,500 and £18,750 respectively.

The New College of the Humanities, which graduated its first students in 2015, started out with fees of nearly £18,000 a year for all undergraduates, guaranteeing small-group teaching and some big-name visiting lecturers in economics, English, history, law and philosophy. The college reduced its fees to £12,000 for 2017 and it is now matching the 'public sector' at £9,250 a year. Many students are offered bursaries for University of London external degree courses and Combined Honours degrees validated by Southampton Solent.

Two other private institutions have been awarded university status. Regent's University, attractively positioned in London's Regent's Park, caters particularly for the international market with courses in business, arts and social science subjects priced at £16,400 a year for 2017–18. However, about half of the students at the not-for-profit university, which offers British and American degrees, are from the UK or other parts of Europe. The University of Law, as its name suggests, is more specialised. It has been operating as a college for more than 100 years and claims to be the world's leading professional law school. Law degrees, as well as professional courses, are available in London and Manchester, with fees for three-year degrees set at £9,250 in 2018–19 for UK and EU students and £12,500 for the two-year version. For non-EU students, the equivalent fees are £13,000 and £18,000 respectively.

There are also growing numbers of specialist colleges offering degrees, especially in the business sector. GSM London (formerly the Greenwich School of Management), with more than 3,500 students on two London campuses, is probably the largest in terms of full-time students, but there are others that have forged partnerships with universities or are going it alone. The ifs School of Finance, for example, also dates back more than 100 years and now has university college status (as ifs University College) for its courses in finance and banking.

Some others that rely on international students have been hit by tougher visa regulations, but the Government is keen to encourage the development of a private sector to compete with

---

The top universities for quality of teaching, feedback and support in the 2018 *Times and Sunday Times* table		The top universities for overall student experience in the 2018 *Times and Sunday Times* table	
1 Buckingham	87.2%	1 St Andrews	87.1%
2 St Andrews	87.0%	2 Loughborough	86.9%
3 Liverpool Hope	86.9%	3 Harper Adams	86.0%
4 Harper Adams	86.5%	4 Buckingham	85.9%
5 Aberystwyth	86.2%	5 Liverpool Hope	85.8%
6 Leeds Trinity	85.5%	6 Coventry	84.4%
7 West London	85.3%	7 Lancaster	84.3%
8 Nottingham Trent	84.8%	8 Aberystwyth	84.2%
9 Loughborough	84.4%	9 Leeds Trinity	83.5%
=10 Norwich Arts	84.1%	10 Bangor	83.4%
=10 Staffordshire	84.1%		

the established universities. Two newcomers will focus on engineering, for example. The Dyson Institute of Engineering and Technology, based at Malmesbury, in Wiltshire, welcomed its first 33 undergraduates in September. Funded entirely by Sir James Dyson, there are no fees, and students will work at the nearby Dyson headquarters for 47 weeks a year. The New Model in Technology and Engineering, in Hereford, has received more than £20m in Government funding and promises to "totally reimagine and redesign the higher education experience". It will take its first students in 2020. A list of private universities and other institutions appears on pages 569–571.

City universities

The most popular universities, in terms of total applications, are nearly all in big cities with other major centres of population within the two-hour travelling window. For those looking for the best nightclubs, top sporting events, high-quality shopping or a varied cultural life – in other words, most young people, and especially those who live in cities already – city universities are a magnet. The big universities also, by definition, offer the widest range of subjects, although that does not mean that they necessarily have the particular course that is right for you. Nor does it mean that you will actually use the array of nightlife and shopping that looks so alluring in the prospectus, either because you cannot afford to, because student life is focused on the university, or even because you are too busy working.

Campus universities

City universities are the right choice for many young people, but it is worth bearing in mind that the National Student Survey shows that the highest satisfaction levels tend to be at smaller universities, often those with their own self-contained campuses. It seems that students identify more closely with institutions where there is a close-knit community and the social life is based around the students' union rather than the local nightclubs. There may also be a better prospect of regular contact with tutors and lecturers, who may live on or near the campus. Few UK universities are in genuinely rural locations, but some – particularly among the more recently promoted – are in relatively small towns. Several longer-established institutions in Scotland and Wales also share this type of setting, where the university dominates the town.

Importance of Open Days

The only way to be certain if this, or any other type of university, is for you is to visit. Schools often restrict the number of open days that sixth-formers can attend in term-time, but some universities offer a weekend alternative. The full calendar of events is available at **www.opendays.com** and on universities' own websites. Bear in mind, if you only attend one or two, that the event has to be badly mismanaged for a university not to seem an exciting place to someone who spends his or her days at school, or even college. Try to get a flavour of several institutions before you make your choice.

How many universities to pick?

When that time comes, of course, you will not be making one choice but five; four if you are applying for medicine, dentistry or veterinary science. (Full details of the application process are given in chapter 5.) Tens of thousands of students each year eventually go to a university that did not start out as their first choice, either because they did not get the right offer or because they changed their mind along the way. UCAS rules are such that applicants do not list universities in order of preference anyway – universities are not allowed to know where else you have applied. So do not pin all your hopes on one course; take just as much care choosing the other universities on your list.

The value of an "insurance" choice

Until recently, nearly all applicants included at least one "insurance" choice on that list – a university or college where entry grades were significantly lower than at their preferred institutions. This practice has been in decline, presumably because candidates expecting high grades think they can pick up a lower offer either in Clearing or through UCAS Extra, the service that allows applicants rejected by their original choices to apply to courses that still have vacancies after the first round of offers. However, it is easy to miscalculate and leave yourself without a place that you want. You may not like the look of the options in Clearing, leaving yourself with an unwelcome and potentially expensive year off at a time when jobs are thin on the ground.

The lifting of recruitment restrictions in 2015 has increased competition between universities and seen more of the leading institutions taking part in Clearing. For those with good grades, this makes it less of a risk to apply only to highly selective universities. However, if you are at all uncertain about your grades, including an insurance choice remains a sensible course of action – especially since entry requirements have risen in recent years in response to increased demand for places. Even if you are sure that you will match the standard offers of your chosen universities, there is no guarantee that they will make you an offer. Particularly for degrees demanding three As or more at A-level, there may simply be too many highly qualified applicants to offer places to all of them. The main proviso for insurance choices, as with all others, is that you must be prepared to take up that place. If not, you might as well go for broke with courses with higher standard offers and take your chances in Clearing, or even retake exams if you drop grades. Thousands of applicants each year end up rejecting their only offer when they could have had a second, insurance, choice.

Reputation

The reputation of a university is something intangible, usually built up over a long period and sometimes outlasting reality. Before universities were subject to external assessment and the publication of copious statistics, reputation was rooted in the past. League tables are partly responsible for changing that, although employers are often still influenced by what they remember as the university pecking order when they were students.

The fragmentation of the British university system into groups of institutions is another factor: the Russell Group (**www.russellgroup.ac.uk**) represents 24 research-intensive universities, nearly all with medical schools; the million+ group (**www.millionplus.ac.uk**) contains many of the former polytechnics and newer universities; the University Alliance (**www.unialliance.ac.uk**) provides a home for 18 universities, both old and new, that did not fit into the other categories; while GuildHE (**www.guildhe.ac.uk**) represents specialist colleges and the newest universities. The Cathedrals Group (**www.cathedralsgroup.ac.uk**) is an affiliation of 16 church-based universities and colleges, some of which are also members of other groups.

Many of today's applicants will barely have heard of a polytechnic, let alone be able to identify which of today's universities had that heritage, but most will know which of two universities in the same city has the higher status. While that should matter far less than the quality of a course, it would be naïve to ignore institutional reputation entirely if that is going to

Checklist

Choosing a subject and a place to study is a major decision. Make sure you can answer these questions:

Choosing a course

» What do I want out of higher education?
» Which subjects do I enjoy studying at school?
» Which subject or subjects do I want to study?
» Do I have the right qualifications?
» What are my career plans and does the subject and course fit these?
» Do I want to study full-time or part-time?
» Do I want to study at a university or a college?

Choosing a university

» What type of university do I wish to go to: campus, city or smaller town?
» How far is the university from home?
» Is it large or small?
» Is it specialist or general?
» Does it offer the right course?
» How much will it cost?
» Have I arranged to visit the university?

---

carry weight with a future employer. Some big firms restrict their recruitment efforts to a small group of universities (see chapter 3), and, however short sighted that might be, it is something to bear in mind if a career in the City or a big law firm is your ambition.

Facilities

A 2015 survey commissioned by university directors of estates found that the quality of campus facilities was an important factor in choosing a university for two thirds of applicants. Only the course and the university's location had a higher priority. Accommodation is the main selling point for those living away from home, but sports facilities, libraries and computing equipment also play an important part. Even campus nightclubs have become part of the facilities race that has followed the introduction of top-up fees.

Many universities guarantee first-year students accommodation in halls of residence or university-owned flats. But it is as well to know what happens after that. Are there enough places for second or third-year students who want them, and if not, what is the private market like? Rents for student houses vary quite widely across the country and there have been tensions with local residents in some cities. All universities offer specialist accommodation for disabled students – and are better at providing other facilities than most public institutions. Their websites give basic information on what is provided, as well as contact points for more detailed inquiries.

Special-interest clubs and recreational facilities, as well as political activity, tend to be based in the students' union – sometimes known as the guild of students. In some universities, the union is the focal point of social activity, while in others the attractions of the city seem to overshadow the union to the point where facilities are underused. Students' union websites are included with the information found in the university profiles (chapter 14).

Sources of information

With more than 130 universities to choose from, the Unistats and UCAS websites, as well as guides such as this one, are the obvious places to start your search for the right course. Unistats now includes figures for average salaries at course level, as well as student satisfaction ratings and some information on contact hours, although this does not distinguish between lectures and seminars. The site does not make multiple comparisons easy to carry out, but it does contain a wealth of information for those who persevere. Once you have narrowed down the list of candidates, you will want to go through undergraduate prospectuses. Most are available online, where you can select the relevant sections rather than waiting for an account of every course to arrive in the post. Beware of generalised claims about the standing of the university, the quality of courses, friendly atmosphere and legendary social life. Stick, if you can, to the factual information.

If the material that the universities publish about their own qualities is less than objective, much of what you will find on the internet may be completely unreliable, for different reasons. A simple search on the name of a university will turn up spurious comparisons of everything from the standard of lecturing to the attractiveness of the students. These can be seriously misleading and are usually based on anecdotal evidence, at best. Make sure that any information you may take into account comes from a reputable source and, if it conflicts with your impression, try to cross-check it with this *Guide* and the institution's own material.

Useful websites

The best starting point is the UCAS website (**www.ucas.com**). On the site there is extensive information on courses, universities and the whole process of applying to university. UCAS has an official presence on Facebook (**www.facebook.com/ucasonline**) and Twitter (**@UCAS_online**) and now also has a series of video guides (**www.ucas.tv**) on the process of applying, UCAS resources and comments from other students.

For statistical information which allows limited comparison between universities (and for full details of the National Student Survey), visit: **www.unistats.com**.

On appropriate A-level subject choice, visit: **www.russellgroup.ac.uk/for-students/school-and-college-in-the-uk/subject-choices-at-school-and-college/**
Narrowing down course choices: **www.ukcoursefinder.com**.

For a full calendar of university and college open days: **www.opendays.com**.

Students with disabilities:
Disability Rights UK: **www.disabilityrightsuk.org/how-can-we-help**

3 Assessing Graduate Job Prospects

There is growing controversy, in the media, Parliament and elsewhere, about the financial value of higher education. Might a degree get less valuable as the foundation stone of a career if more and more of the working-age population have one? And is it worth the considerable cost?

The answer seems to be that so far, a degree is holding up as an investment in your future employment prospects. The UK Labour Force Survey, run by the Office for National statistics, finds that over 14 million working-age people in this country now have a degree or similar qualification, out of just over 34 million people in the possible workforce. But while 75 per cent of the overall workforce is employed, the figure rises to 82 per cent for graduates. They remain at an advantage even though the percentage of graduates in the workforce rose from 24 per cent to 40 per cent between 2002 and 2017.

And even these figures understate the advantages of a degree for your employment potential. Only 3 per cent of graduates were unemployed in mid-2017. For those with no qualifications, the figure was 8 per cent. The Labour Force survey also makes it clear that a degree is a growing expectation for certain lines of work, 40 per cent of graduates work in the public sector, health, or education, and a further 21 per cent in banking and finance. Energy, water, fisheries, agriculture and forestry attract only 2 per cent of all graduates, less than their share of the workforce as a whole.

Of course, what matters to readers of this book is how the market will look in four or five years' time, when this year's applicants graduate in a post-Brexit world, not the picture today. Although no one knows that, there would have to be seismic changes in the economy for graduates not to be in a much better position than those without a degree. That has been the case for several decades, and all projections suggest that a growing proportion of the jobs created in the coming years will require a degree.

This does not mean, however, that every degree will be a passport to a well-paid job, nor that it will be worth the debts that graduates are going to accrue in the current era of high fees. Recent salary figures for graduates five and ten years into their careers show startling differences between universities and subjects in the earning power of their graduates.

Graduate employment and underemployment

An average graduate earns at least £100,000 more than a non-graduate over a working lifetime. However, competition for graduate jobs remains stiff. As we have seen, there are 14 million graduates in the UK, and in Inner London they make up 56 per cent of the adult population. Even in the North East, Britain's region with the fewest graduates, 34 per cent of those over 20 have a degree.

Today's graduates may take longer than their predecessors to find the right opening, and may experiment with internships before committing themselves. The proportion of recent graduates in "non-graduate" jobs rose to 49 per cent in 2017 (it had hit over half in 2012). And regardless of their job title, many others felt that the skills and knowledge they had acquired at university were not being utilized in their current job. There has also been a steady growth in the number of less recent graduates doing non-graduate work. Here the figure has risen from 30 per cent in 2001 to 37 per cent in 2017.

This change in employment patterns explains why underemployment has come to the fore in the public debate about higher education. It is an important subject, but is also one with little precision and where the practice of collecting employment data only six months after graduation can be extremely misleading. This *Guide* uses the definition from the Higher Education Statistics Agency (HESA) of a graduate job. But employers' ideas of which jobs require a degree, and of the jobs for which they prefer graduates, change over time. Nurses now require a degree, partly because the job has changed and requires skills that were not needed 20 years ago. The same is true of many occupations. In others it may be possible to do the job without a degree, but having one makes it much easier to get hired in the first place.

Nevertheless, a survey by consultants Accenture found that 60 per cent of 2013 and 2014 graduates considered themselves underemployed or working in a job that did not require a degree. Eight out of ten said they had considered the availability of jobs in their intended field before selecting their degree course, but only 55 per cent were working in their chosen field. Almost 60 per cent said they would trade salary for a more fulfilling job.

The graduate labour market

Government reports take a longer-term view of the whole labour market. The findings continue

---

Median earnings by degree subject five years after graduation (2009 graduates)

Medicine and dentistry	£47,000	Law	£25,300
Economics	£36,600	Education	£24,700
Veterinary Science	£35,900	Historical & philosophical studies	£24,700
Mathematical Science	£31,900	Social studies	£24,600
Engineering & technology	£31,800	Combined subjects	£24,200
Architecture/building/planning	£29,300	Biological Sciences	£24,100
Nursing	£28,400	English studies	£23,800
Computer Science	£27,100	Mass communications/documentation	£22,300
Physical Sciences	£26,600	Psychology	£22,200
Subjects allied to medicine	£26,600	Agriculture and allied subjects	£21,800
Languages	£26,500	Creative arts & design	£20,000
Business & administration	£26,300		

Source: Department for Education, Graduate outcomes (June 2017)

to support the case for taking a degree if you have the opportunity. The first "experimental statistics" from its Longitudinal Education Outcomes (LEO) data were published at the end of 2016, showing average salaries and employment status three, five and ten years after graduation. You may be encouraged by the long-term effects of higher education that they revealed. Looking at 2003/04 graduates, it showed that 55 per cent of those a year out of college had steady employment, but that a decade after graduation, the figure had hit 69 per cent. In addition, the data shows that graduates are on a steadily ascending salary ladder, with median earnings rising from £16,500 a year after graduation to £31,000 after a decade. The figures also show predictable differences between subjects in employment and salary rates, some of which are shown in the table below. While the institutional comparisons would require more work to be consistent with other measures in the *Guide*, they illustrate the lasting impact of university choice. Among law graduates, for example, the top earners from Oxford and Cambridge average more than £75,000 (and the lowest some £35,000) after five years, compared with under £10,000 for low earners from the University of East London.

Overall, however, graduates continued to earn 43 per cent more than non-graduates in 2015. This may be a smaller premium than they enjoyed before the financial crash – it was over 50 per cent in 2006 – but it remains one of the biggest differentials in the Western world. Inevitably, national surveys average out the experiences of millions of people and often take no account of the mix of subjects at different universities. The material in this *Guide* – particularly in the subject tables – should help to create a more nuanced picture. A close examination of individual universities' employment rates in your subject – possibly supplemented by the salary figures on the Unistats website (**www.unistats.com**) – will tell you whether national trends apply to your chosen course.

Inevitably, future graduate expectations are clouded by the uncertainty caused by Brexit. But even without this big unknown, there would be swings in employment trends before anyone starting a degree course in 2018 manages to graduate.

However, current employment trends provide some grounds for optimism. The graduate recruitment specialist High Fliers said in its Graduate Market Report for 2017 that top employers were expecting to expand their graduate recruitment for the fifth year running in 2017, this time by 4.2 per cent. Particular growth areas were in online and physical retail, manufacturing, and the public sector. Only eight of 100 employers surveyed planned to cut graduate recruitment in 2017 because of Brexit uncertainty.

However, the High Fliers survey covers only the upper end of the market, with median starting salaries of a useful £30,000. For the boom years of graduate employment to return, there will have to be stronger recruitment by small and medium-sized companies as well. Increasingly, there will also be a greater proportion of self-employed graduates – and not simply because they cannot find the jobs they want. Many universities report growing demand for the services they provide for students who want to set up their own company.

Subject choice and career opportunities

For those thinking of embarking on higher education in 2018, the signs are still positive. But in any year, some universities and some subjects produce better returns than others.

The tables on the pages that follow give a more detailed picture of the differences between subjects, while the rankings in chapters 1 and 12 include figures for each university and subject area. There are a few striking changes, but mainly among subjects with relatively small and fluctuating numbers of graduates.

What graduates are doing six months after graduation by subject studied

Subject	Professional job %	Professional job and studying %	Studying %	Non-professional job and studying %	Non-professional job %	Unemployed %	Professional job and/or studying %
1 Medicine	93	1	5	0	0	1	99.1
2 Dentistry	95	2	0	0	1	1	97.9
3 Nursing	93	1	2	0	1	2	96.7
4 Physiotherapy	93	1	2	0	1	2	96.3
5 Veterinary Medicine	94	1	1	0	2	2	95.9
6 Radiography	91	2	1	0	3	3	94.4
7 Pharmacology & Pharmacy	74	8	11	1	4	3	93.3
8 Building	79	3	5	0	6	7	86.8
9 Land and Property Management	81	4	2	0	5	9	86.4
10 Civil Engineering	66	2	15	1	8	8	83.9
11 Other Subjects Allied to Medicine	63	3	15	2	11	7	82.6
12 Architecture	66	5	10	1	9	9	81.4
13 Anatomy & Physiology	39	4	34	3	12	8	79.6
14 Chemical Engineering	53	2	22	1	9	13	78.4
15 Town and Country Planning and Landscape	60	3	14	1	12	10	78.2
16 Chemistry	40	3	34	2	12	10	78.1
17 General Engineering	57	2	18	1	11	11	77.6
18 Physics & Astronomy	37	4	36	1	11	12	77.3
19 Electrical and Electronic Engineering	60	2	14	1	12	11	77.0
20 Mechanical Engineering	60	2	14	1	12	11	76.9
21 Librarianship & Information Management	65	1	10	1	15	9	76.2
22 Economics	55	5	15	1	12	12	75.9
23 Law	33	6	32	5	16	8	75.3
24 Mathematics	46	5	24	1	13	12	75.2
25 Computer Science	62	2	10	1	13	12	74.9
=26 Aeronautical and Manufacturing Engineering	56	2	16	1	14	12	74.5
=26 Materials Technology	48	2	22	2	15	10	74.5
28 Education	54	2	16	2	21	5	73.7
29 Food Science	54	3	15	1	18	9	73.5
30 Middle Eastern and African Studies	41	3	29	0	15	13	72.9
31 Social Work	58	3	10	2	19	8	72.7
32 German	43	4	23	2	17	11	72.4
33 Geology	31	1	37	2	19	10	71.3
34 French	45	3	21	3	19	10	71.1
=35 Theology & Religious Studies	29	4	33	4	21	9	70.3
=35 Italian	43	3	20	4	18	11	70.3
37 Politics	40	3	24	3	19	11	70.0
38 Russian	42	3	21	3	11	19	69.9
39 Iberian Languages	44	3	20	3	19	11	69.5

	Subject	Professional job %	Professional job and studying %	Studying %	Non-professional job and studying %	Non-professional job %	Unemployed %	Professional job and/or studying %
40	Accounting & Finance	50	9	9	2	21	10	**69.4**
41	Linguistics	37	4	24	4	22	9	**68.9**
=42	Biological Sciences	29	3	35	3	20	11	**68.8**
=42	Classics & Ancient History	31	3	31	4	19	12	**68.8**
=44	Business Studies	53	3	10	2	22	11	**67.0**
=44	Music	40	6	19	3	25	8	**67.0**
=46	Celtic Studies	19	4	40	3	29	5	**66.5**
=46	Sport Science	37	5	22	3	27	7	**66.5**
=46	Philosophy	33	3	27	4	21	13	**66.5**
=46	Geography & Environmental Sciences	39	3	22	3	22	11	**66.5**
50	English	33	3	25	4	26	9	**65.0**
51	East and South Asian Studies	41	2	20	2	18	18	**64.4**
=52	History	30	3	27	4	25	11	**63.9**
=52	Archaeology and Forensic Science	32	2	24	6	25	12	**63.9**
54	Anthropology	39	2	21	2	21	16	**63.3**
55	History of Art, Architecture and Design	35	1	23	4	24	13	**63.2**
56	Art & Design	52	1	8	2	28	10	**62.1**
57	Psychology	29	5	22	5	30	9	**61.3**
58	Communication and Media Studies	47	2	9	2	29	12	**58.9**
59	American Studies	31	2	21	4	31	11	**58.6**
60	Drama, Dance and Cinematics	45	2	9	2	33	9	**58.2**
61	Social Policy	30	4	19	5	30	12	**57.9**
62	Criminology	33	3	16	4	34	10	**56.3**
=63	Sociology	29	3	20	4	34	11	**55.7**
=63	Hospitality, Leisure, Recreation & Tourism	45	1	7	2	35	10	**55.7**
65	Creative Writing	31	3	16	6	30	15	**55.4**
66	Agriculture and Forestry	42	3	8	2	30	15	**55.3**
67	Animal Science	23	2	17	4	47	7	**46.1**
	Average	**50**	**3**	**17**	**2**	**19**	**9**	**71.8**

Note: The table is ranked on the proportion of graduates in professional jobs and/or further study six months after leaving university, this total shown in the final column in bold

This is the fourth year of a new classification developed by HESA to distinguish between "graduate-level" work and jobs that do not normally require a degree. In the employment table, subjects are ranked on "positive destinations", which include professional jobs and further study, whether or not combined with a job. Some similar tables do not make a distinction between different types of job. These tend to give the misleading impression that all universities and subjects offer uniformly rosy employment prospects.

The definition of a graduate job is a controversial one. The statistics include internships and temporary jobs, which may or may not lead to permanent employment. New universities

What graduates earn six months after graduation by subject studied

	Subject	Professional employment	Non-professional employment
1	Dentistry	31,000	–
2	Medicine	30,000	–
3	Veterinary Medicine	28,000	–
=4	Chemical Engineering	27,000	16,262
=4	Economics	27,000	18,000
=4	General Engineering	27,000	18,500
=7	Aeronautical and Manufacturing Engineering	26,000	17,108
=7	Electrical and Electronic Engineering	26,000	16,575
=7	Mechanical Engineering	26,000	16,000
=7	Social Work	26,000	15,327
11	Civil Engineering	25,500	17,420
=12	Building	25,000	17,160
=12	Land and Property Management	25,000	–
=12	Librarianship & Information Management	25,000	–
=12	Materials Technology	25,000	16,000
=12	Mathematics	25,000	16,500
=12	Physics & Astronomy	25,000	15,974
=18	Computer Science	24,000	16,000
=18	Russian	24,000	–
=20	Accounting & Finance	22,000	18,000
=20	Business Studies	22,000	17,500
=20	Chemistry	22,000	16,300
=20	East and South Asian Studies	22,000	18,000
=20	Education	22,000	15,000
=20	Geography & Environmental Sciences	22,000	15,834
=20	Iberian Languages	22,000	16,800
=20	Politics	22,000	16,500
=20	Town and Country Planning and Landscape	22,000	15,600
=20	Radiography	22,000	13,650
30	Physiotherapy	21,999	–
=31	Food Science	21,909	15,600
=31	Nursing	21,909	16,380
=31	Other Subjects Allied to Medicine	21,909	16,000
34	Anatomy & Physiology	21,900	16,380
35	Middle Eastern and African Studies	21,840	–
36	German	21,500	16,016
=37	Agriculture and Forestry	21,000	17,500
=37	Classics & Ancient History	21,000	16,000
=37	French	21,000	17,249
=37	Geology	21,000	15,500
=37	Italian	21,000	18,000

Subject	Professional employment	Non-professional employment
=37 Philosophy	21,000	15,600
43 Social Policy	20,900	16,600
44 History	20,500	16,000
=45 American Studies	20,000	16,000
=45 Anthropology	20,000	15,600
=45 Architecture	20,000	15,392
=45 Biological Sciences	20,000	15,542
=45 History of Art, Architecture and Design	20,000	16,800
=45 Sociology	20,000	16,000
=45 Theology & Religious Studies	20,000	15,600
52 Hospitality, Leisure, Recreation & Tourism	19,700	16,796
53 Criminology	19,500	16,000
54 Psychology	19,048	16,000
=55 English	19,000	15,600
=55 Sport Science	19,000	15,600
57 Archaeology and Forensic Science	18,800	16,000
58 Law	18,720	16,500
59 Animal Science	18,700	16,800
60 Pharmacology & Pharmacy	18,500	16,800
=61 Art & Design	18,000	15,470
=61 Celtic Studies	18,000	15,000
=61 Communication and Media Studies	18,000	15,717
=61 Drama, Dance and Cinematics	18,000	15,000
=61 Linguistics	18,000	15,600
=61 Music	18,000	15,600
=61 Creative Writing	18,000	15,000
Average	**22,000**	**16,000**

Note: The salaries table is ranked by the median salary of those in professional employment in each subject area.

Source: Higher Education Statistics Agency, Destination of Leavers from Higher Education survey, 2015–16

in particular often claim that the whole concept of a graduate job immediately after graduation fails to reflect reality for their alumni, especially in subjects such as media studies or art. In any case, a degree is about enhancing your whole career, your way of working and your view of the world, not just your first job out of college.

That said, these tables will help you assess whether your course will pay off in career terms, at least to start with. They show both the amount you might expect to earn with a degree in a specific subject, and the odds of being in work. They reflect the experience six months after graduation of those who completed their degrees in 2016, and the picture may have improved by the time you leave university. But there is no reason to believe that the pattern of success rates for specific subjects and institutions will have changed radically.

The table of employment statistics does reveal some unexpected results. For example, only 67 per cent of business studies graduates are working in graduate jobs or doing further study.

Accounting and finance graduates are only two percentage points better off. The librarians and the town and country planners fare a lot better. The figures also explode a few popular myths, such as the suggestion that young people avoid engineering because salaries are low. All six branches of engineering are in the top dozen subjects for graduate earnings, and in the top 30 for successful graduate destinations.

The employment table also shows that graduates in some subjects, especially sciences such as physics, chemistry and geology, are more likely to undertake further study than others, such as those in art and design or hospitality. In Celtic studies, 40 per cent of graduates continued to study, and the figure is above 30 per cent for several branches of science. A range of professions now regard a Master's degree as a basic entry-level qualification.

Those going into subjects such as art and design appreciate that it, too, has its own career peculiarities. Periods of freelance or casual work may be an occupational hazard at the start of a career, and perhaps later on as well. Less surprisingly, doctors and dentists are virtually guaranteed a job if they complete a degree, as are nurses. HESA found that only one graduate in 100 in medicine or dentistry was unemployed six months after graduating. The picture is pretty similar for vets and physiotherapists.

The second table, on pages 54–55, gives average earnings of those who graduated in 2016, recorded six months after leaving college. It contains interesting, and in some cases surprising, information about early career pay levels. Few would have placed social work in the top 10 for graduate pay. However, nursing is now in 31st place, having been in the top 20 a few years ago. The cause may be a general ban on big pay rises in the National Health Service, abandoned by the government in late 2017.

It is important of course to consider the differences between starting salaries and the long-term prospects of different jobs. After all, those years at university should teach you about the benefits of long-term strategic thinking. Over time, the accountants may well end up with bigger rewards, despite being only £91 a year better off than the nurses in our early-career snapshot.

In any case, it is important to realise that once you ignore the stellar incomes available to medics and other elite professionals, there does seem to be a general level of early graduate incomes that varies less than you might think from subject to subject. Ten subjects, ranging from accountancy to radiography and chemistry, tie for 20th spot in our salary ranking. A further six tie for 40th – to be exact, from 37 to 42. But the difference between these two groups is only £1,000 a year, with the first set on £22,000 and the second on £21,100. That's why you should consider the lifetime earnings you might derive from these subjects, and your own interests and inclinations, at least as much as this snapshot.

There are reasons for longer-term optimism in surveys by HESA on the occupations and views of graduates three and a half years into their careers. The last one, published in 2017, paints a more positive picture than surveys conducted six months after graduation. Of the UK graduates surveyed, 88 per cent were in employment, 6 per cent were studying full-time and 2.2 per cent were unemployed. The majority of those who had been unemployed six months after graduation were in work by this stage. The median salary of these 2013 graduates was £27,000, for those in full-time work, and £25,500 overall, and 87.5 per cent were fairly or very satisfied with their careers to date.

Enhancing your employability

Universities are well aware of the difficulties of graduate employment, and have been introducing all manner of schemes to try to give their graduates an advantage in the labour market. Many have incorporated specially designed employability modules into degree courses; some are certificating extra-curricular activities to improve their graduates' CVs; and yet others are stepping up their efforts to provide work experience to complement degrees.

Opinion is divided on the value of such schemes. Some of the biggest employers restrict their recruitment activities to a small number of universities, believing that these institutions attract the brightest minds and that trawling more widely is not cost-effective.

In 2015–16, High Fliers reported that the universities most targeted were Manchester, Nottingham, Warwick, Bristol, Cambridge and Oxford. These companies, often big payers from the City of London and including some of the top law firms, are not likely to change their ways at a time when they are more anxious than ever to control costs. Widening the pool of universities from which they set out to recruit is costly, and can seem unnecessary if employers are getting the people they think they need. They will expect outstanding candidates who went to other universities to come to them, either on graduation or later in their careers.

The best advice for those looking to maximise their employment opportunities (and who isn't?) must be to go for the best university you can. But most graduates do not work in the City and most students do not go to universities at the top of the league tables.

University schemes

If a university offers extra help towards employment, it is worth considering whether its scheme is likely to work for you. Some are too new to have shown results in the labour market yet, but they may have been endorsed by big employers or introduced at an institution whose graduates already have a record of success in the jobs market. They might involve classes in CV writing, interview skills, personal finance, entrepreneurship and negotiation skills, among many other topics. There can be guest lectures and demonstrations, or mock interviews, by real employers, to assess students' strengths and weaknesses. In time, these extras may turn into mandatory parts of a degree, complete with course credits.

Hertfordshire is one institution which has demonstrated a sustained focus on its students' job prospects. Employer groups are consulted on the curriculum and often supply guest lecturers on degree courses. Like some other universities, such as Derby, it offers career development support to graduates throughout their working life, and has an outstanding record for graduate employment. The University of Exeter is helping students to build their employability skills and certificating them. It believes that the Exeter Award will encourage employers to take more notice of graduate attainment beyond exam results. It says "Student Employability is a key resource for students, graduates and graduate recruiters. We have over 40 staff working to help improve student chances of getting a great job after they graduate."

The value of work experience

The majority of graduate jobs are open to applicants from any discipline. For these general positions, employers tend to be more impressed by a good degree from what they consider a prestigious university than by an apparently relevant qualification. Here numeracy, literacy and communications – the arts needed to function effectively in any organisation – are of vital importance. Specialist jobs, for example in engineering or design, are a different matter. Employers may be much more knowledgeable about the quality of individual courses, and less influenced by a university's overall position in league tables, when the job relies directly on knowledge and skills acquired as a student. That goes for medicine and architecture as well as computer games design or environmental management.

In either case, however, work experience has become increasingly important. It is common for major employers and smaller firms to hire graduates who have already worked for them, whether in holiday jobs, internships or placements. Sandwich degrees, extended programmes that include up to a year at work, have always boosted employment prospects. Graduates – often engineers – frequently end up working where they undertook their placement. And while a sandwich year will make your course longer, it will not be subject to a full year's fees.

Many conventional degrees now include shorter work placements that should offer some advantages in the labour market. Not all are arranged by the university, most big graduate employers offer some provision of this nature, although access to it can be competitive.

If your chosen course does not include a work placement, you may want to consider arranging your own part-time or temporary employment. The majority of supposedly full-time students now take jobs during term time, as well as in vacations, to make ends meet. But such jobs can boost your CV as well as your wallet. Even working in a bar or a shop shows some experience of dealing with the public and coping with the discipline of the workplace. Inevitably, the more prosperous cities are likely to offer more employment opportunities than rural areas or conurbations that have been hard hit in the recession.

The ultimate work-related degree is one sponsored by an employer or even taken in the workplace. Middlesex University provides tailored programmes for Asda and Halifax Bank, among other organisations, and has many students taking professional practice qualifications. Most such courses are for people already employed by the companies concerned, rather than being a route into the company. But they may become an alternative to entering full-time higher education straight from school or college.

Consider part-time degrees

Another option, also favoured by ministers in successive governments, is part-time study. Although enrolments have fallen sharply both before and since the big 2012 increases in fees, there are now loans available for most part-time courses. Employers may be willing to share the cost of taking a degree or another relevant qualification, and the chance to earn a wage while studying has obvious attractions. Bear in mind that most part-time courses take twice as long to complete as the full-time equivalent. If your earning power is linked to the qualification, it will take that much longer for you to enjoy the benefits.

Plan early for your career

Whatever type of course you choose, it is sensible to start thinking about your future career early in your time at university. There has been a growing tendency in recent years for students to convince themselves that there would be plenty of time to apply for jobs after graduation, and that they were better off focusing entirely on their degree while at university. In the current employment market, all but the most obviously brilliant graduates need to offer more than just a degree, whether it be work experience, leadership qualities demonstrated through clubs and societies, or commitment to voluntary activities. Many students finish a degree without knowing what they want to do, but a blank CV will not impress a prospective employer.

Half of the leading employers in the High Fliers survey mentioned above said that they are not interested in graduates without previous work experience and that any such applicants would have "little or no chance" of a place on their graduate programmes. Nearly half of all final year students in the survey had done course placements, internships, or vacation work with graduate employers whilst at university, completing an average of more than six months work experience. He may be overstating the case, but Martin Burchall, High Fliers' Managing Director, claimed that work placements and internships were now "just as important as getting a 2:1 or first-class degree".

However, nobody knows what the future holds, especially in today's turbulent times. You may not walk straight into your dream job upon graduation. But if you don't, the effects will not be terminal. A survey by graduate careers website magnet.me in 2017, found that 33 per cent of 2016 graduates left their first job after university within 12 months, up from 28 per cent a year earlier. Most said that the roles didn't match what they were told when applying.

It seems from the survey that the graduate recruitment market is an unsophisticated one, with too many generic applications for underspecified jobs. The rise of online job hunting may be part of the problem. Physical attendance at recruitment fairs, where the student and recruiter at least meet in the flesh, is on the way down. But despite these pressures, most graduates – as we saw in the three and a half-year survey mentioned above – do find their way through this baffling maze, and end up with satisfying and rewarding working lives.

Useful websites

Prospects, the UK's official graduate careers website: **www.prospects.ac.uk**
For career advice, internships and student and graduate jobs: **www.milkround.com**
High Fliers: **www.highfliers.co.uk**

4 University Tuition Fees

Politicians originally hoped that the introduction of a maximum fee of £9,000 per year of undergraduate study would produce price competition between universities. Very little happened, and any variation that there was will have practically disappeared when students start courses in 2018. None of the English or Welsh institutions in our table will charge less than £9,250 for Honours degree courses although bursaries and fee waivers will bring the actual cost down for those from low-income families.

At least fees will not be going any higher for the next three years, under the Government's latest commitment, and they could even be abolished if Labour were to come to power. Ministers have also promised a review of fees and other aspects of higher education funding, so even the medium-term scale of charges for degree courses is uncertain. But nothing is likely to change before new entrants arrive this autumn. The information in this chapter is based on the current system as it operates around the UK.

Bursaries, scholarships and fee waivers mean that the average fees charged in England, let alone other parts of the UK, will vary much more widely than media reporting might suggest. But this only matters to those who qualify for one of the awards, usually by virtue of family income or their academic performance; most students will pay the maximum. For 2018/19 entry, some universities are charging an average fee after bursaries that is quite a lot lower than the headline £9,250. The lowest for a mainstream university is £8,065 at Bournemouth. These discounts may or may not be enough to persuade you to apply there, but should obviously be viewed alongside the course offering from each institution and the lifetime earnings it might lead to. Some further education colleges will still be offering average fees of less than £6,000 after accounting for financial support, or £6,000–8,000 if you are paying the full price.

This *Guide* quotes the higher headline fees, but even these will vary according to whether you are from inside or outside the EU, studying full-time or part-time, and whether you are taking a Foundation degree or an Honours programme. Non-European medical students at Imperial College, London, will pay £40,000 a year for their clinical years, a figure that will rise with inflation. Meanwhile, Britons taking Foundation degrees at nearby Kingston University will pay £5,170. Here we focus on full-time Honours degrees for British and other EU undergraduates: these students make up the biggest group on any UK campus, and are the group for whom maximum fees shot up to £9,000 in 2012.

Fees and loans

Student numbers dropped in the first year of higher fees, but prospective students now appear to have resigned themselves to the new regime. In 2017, admissions body UCAS reported that applications from 18-year-olds had held firm even as the number of people in this age group fell a little. However, there were falls in applications from older people and in some subjects, as well as for part-time courses, which have been particularly badly hit.

There is little sign that applicants are basing their choices on the marginal differences in fee levels at different universities, and numbers from the poorest socio-economic groups are at record levels, although they remain severely under-represented compared with more affluent groups. Concern remains, however, over the impact on part-time courses and, in years to come, on the numbers prepared to continue to postgraduate study.

Most readers of *The Times and Sunday Times Good University Guide* will be choosing full-time undergraduate or Foundation degree courses. The fees for 2018–19 are listed alongside each university's profile in chapter 14, and access agreements for universities in England, including details of bursaries and scholarships, are on the website of the Office for Fair Access (OFFA). Institutions in Scotland, Wales and Northern Ireland will continue to have lower charges for their own residents, but will charge varying amounts to students from other parts of the UK. Only those living in Scotland and studying at Scottish universities will escape all fees, although there will be reduced fees for those living in Wales and Northern Ireland.

The number of bursaries and scholarships offered to reduce the burden on new students has been falling since OFFA has suggested that such initiatives do little to attract students from low-income households. As a result, the government has turned the grants paid to the poorest students into loans. While this decision may not affect many of those qualifying for the new loans, because repayment will only begin if and when they have paid off the loans for their tuition fees, there are signs that the fear of yet more debt may be the final straw that puts some off higher education.

Variations among universities

The lowest full-time fee at an English university in 2018/19 will probably be the £4,000 a year cost of a Foundation degree in education or theology at York St John University. But even there, Honours degree students will pay £9,250. At most university-level institutions, every course will cost £9,250 and at several others the only exceptions will be during work placements or years abroad, when fees cannot exceed £1,800 for work placements and £1,350 for a year abroad, and are often less.

Many universities will continue to devote a substantial proportion of the income they receive from higher fees to access initiatives, whether in the form of bursaries or outreach activities. In the case of the London School of Economics, half of all of its fee income above £6,000 was to be spent in this way in 2016/17. A more usual figure is in the 15–30 per cent range. Generosity is at its minimum in the West Midlands. The two lowest figures are for Wolverhampton and Newman Universities at 10.7 and 11.3 per cent respectively.

These measures appear to be having some success in attracting students from disadvantaged backgrounds. OFFA, the body set up to close this gap, says: "Currently, young people from the most advantaged neighbourhoods are nearly two-and-a-half times more likely to go to higher education than young people from the most disadvantaged neighbourhoods." The government has set a challenging target of getting 28 per cent of young people from the least privileged backgrounds in university by 2020.

Fees for students from other EU countries are the same as those for 'home' students at their chosen university, but charges will be higher, sometimes massively higher, for those from other countries.

The new fees regime has had less effect on the demand for higher education than many universities dared hope in the run-up to the fees hike, but financial considerations will still be important to the decision-making process for many students. In the current economic circumstances, students will want to keep their debts to a minimum and are bound to take the cost of living into account. They will also want the best possible career prospects. and may choose their subject accordingly.

Alternative options

Some further education colleges will offer substantial savings on the cost of a degree, or Foundation degree, but they tend to have very local appeal, and generally in a limited range of vocational subjects. Similarly, the private sector may be expected to compete more vigorously in future, following the success of two-year degrees at the University of Buckingham and BPP University in particular. Most will continue to undercut traditional universities, although Regent's University, one of the latest to be awarded that title, is charging £16,400 in the current year for all students, irrespective of their place of origin, although less for some foundation years. The New College of the Humanities, also in London, has surprisingly reduced its charges to the standard £9,250 for 2018/19, having originally come in at twice the price charged by mainstream institutions.

Impact on subject and university choice

Fee levels have had little impact on students' choices of university, but that is not the case for choices of subject. Predictions that old universities and/or vocational subjects would prosper at the expense of the rest have been shown to be too simplistic. Some, but not all, arts subjects have suffered, while in general science courses have prospered. For many young people, the options have not changed. If you want to be a doctor, a teacher or a social worker, there is no alternative to higher education. And, while there are now more options for studying post A-level, it remains to be seen whether they offer the same promotion prospects as a degree.

Even among full-time degrees, the pattern of applications and enrolments has varied considerably since the introduction of higher fees. In 2017, the big losers among subjects included history, philosophy and business, and major winners were medicine, computing and maths. Notably less popular were melange degrees such as combinations of the arts, sciences and social sciences, or combined arts and sciences. Perhaps these choices seem too indecisive for the modern age.

It will take time to be certain whether the new fees regime brings about more permanent changes in subject choice, starting at A-level or the equivalent or even earlier. Sixth formers studying English, history and French cannot suddenly switch to a chemistry degree, but those entering university in 2018 will at least have made choices after GCSE, knowing that the cost of a university education had risen considerably. Not all of the trends in undergraduate education are shaped by fee levels: there were signs in schools, well before the fees went up, of a renaissance in the sciences and a decline in languages. Between 2013 and 2017, UCAS placements for languages and literature fell from 5,320 to 4,520 people a year.

There is little doubt, however, that applicants are looking more carefully at future career prospects when choosing a degree, and they have decided (rightly or wrongly) that some careers are more secure, or more lucrative, than others. Applications for law remain buoyant and medicine is holding its own, despite a long and now much more expensive training. Law enrolments went up from 22,840 students to 25,320 between 2013 and 2017.

Anyone hoping to start a course in 2018 would be unwise to jump to conclusions about levels of competition in different subjects, or between whole universities. A drop in applications may mean less competition for places, or it may lead universities to close courses and possibly even intensify the race for entry. The only reliable forecast is that competition for places on the most popular courses will remain stiff, just as it has been since before students paid any fees.

Finally, there is enthusiasm in the current UK government for the radical idea of delivering degrees in two years. At the moment, support for this concept comes mainly from private institutions. The University of Law, for example, already does degrees in this way. It charges £12,500 per year, a saving of £2,750 on a three-year course. A two-year course also gets you into the workforce faster and means less spending on living costs. However, this approach also cuts out much chance of holiday earnings and of sandwich courses or placements, where students can often get paid and gain work experience. It remains to be seen whether the idea will catch on with traditional universities and if so, whether it will be applicable to the full range of academic subjects.

Getting the best deal

There will still be a certain amount of variation in student support packages in 2018–19, so it will be possible to shop around, particularly if your family income is low. But remember that the best deal, even in purely financial terms, is one that leads to a rewarding career. By all means compare the full packages offered by individual universities, but consider whether marginal differences in headline fees really matter as much as the quality of the course and the likely advantages it will confer in the employment market. Higher career earnings will soon account for more than £3,000 in extra fees to be repaid over 30 years. It is all a matter of judgement – Scottish students can save themselves £27,750 by opting to study north of the border. That is a very different matter to the much smaller saving that is available to students in England, particularly if the Scottish university is of comparable quality to the alternatives elsewhere.

Those who are eligible for means-tested bursaries may not be able to afford to ignore the financial assistance they offer. No one has to pay tuition fees while they are a student, but you still have to find thousands of pounds in living costs to take a full-time degree. In some cases, bursaries may make the difference between being able to afford higher education and having to pass up a potentially life-changing opportunity. Some are worth up to £3,000 a year, although most are less generous than this, often because large numbers of students qualify for an award.

Some scholarships are even more valuable, and are awarded for sporting and musical prowess, as well as academic achievement. Most scholarships are not means-tested, but a few are open only to students who are both high performers academically and from low-income families.

How the £9,250 fee system works

What follows is a summary of the position for British students at the start of 2018. While there are substantial differences between the four countries of the UK, there is one important piece of common ground. Up-front payment of fees is not compulsory, as students can take out a fee loan from the Student Loans Company to cover them (see chapter 6). This is repayable in instalments after graduation when earnings reach £21,000 for English students, rising soon to £25,000, a threshold set by the Government.

Undergraduate fees are remaining unchanged at £9,250, and this is the most you can borrow to pay fees, with lower sums for private colleges (up to £6,165) and part-time study, where the cap is £6,935. There are different levels of fees and support for UK students who are not from England. Students from other EU countries will pay the same rate as home students in the UK nation in which they study. Those from outside the EU are not affected by the changes, and may well have to pay quite a lot more than home and European students. The latest information on individual universities' fees at the time of going to press is listed alongside their profiles in chapter 14.

With changes, large or small, becoming almost an annual occurrence, it is essential to consult the latest information provided on the websites of the relevant Government agencies.

Fees in England

In England, the maximum tuition fee for full-time undergraduates from the UK or anywhere in the European Union will be £9,250 a year in 2018–19. As we have seen, most courses will demand fees of £9,250, or close to it, in order to recoup the money removed from their Government grants and leave room for further investment and student support.

In many public universities, the lowest fees will be for Foundation degrees and Higher National Diplomas. Although some universities have chosen to charge the same for all courses, in many universities and further education colleges, these two-year courses will remain a cost-effective stepping stone to a full degree or a qualification in their own right. Those universities that offer extended work placements or a year abroad, as part of a degree course, will charge much less than the normal fee for the "year out". The maximum cost for a placement year is 20 per cent of the full tuition fee (£1,850) and for a full year abroad, 15 per cent. If you spend only part of the year abroad, you will probably have to pay the whole £9,250.

Fees in Scotland

At Scottish universities and colleges, students from Scotland and those from other EU countries outside the UK pay no fees directly. The universities' vice-chancellors and principals have appealed for charges to be introduced at some level to save their institutions from falling behind their English rivals in financial terms, but Alex Salmond, when he was Scotland's First Minister, famously declared that the "rocks will melt with the sun" before this happens.

Tuition fees

The figures below show the maximum fees that students can be charged in 2018–19.

Domicile of student	Location of institution			
	England	Scotland	Wales	Northern Ireland
England	£9,250	£9,250[1]	£9,000	£9,250
Scotland	£9,250	No fee	£9,000	£9,250
Wales[2]	£9,250	£9,250	£9,000	£9,250
Northern Ireland	£9,250	£9,250[1]	£9,000	£4,160
European Union	£9,250	No fee	£9,000	£4,160
Other international	Variable	Variable	Variable	Variable

[1] Note that Honours degrees in Scotland take four years and some universities charge £9250 for each year.

[2] Students whose home is in Wales will be entitled to tuition fee loans and means-tested maintenance grants.

Students whose home is in Scotland and who are studying at a Scottish university apply to the Student Awards Agency for Scotland (SAAS) to have their fees paid for them. Note, too, that three-year degrees are rare in Scotland, so most students can expect to pay four years of living costs.

Students from England, Wales and Northern Ireland studying in Scotland will pay fees at something like the level that applies in England and will have access to finance at similar levels to those available for study in England. Several Scottish universities are offering a "free" fourth year to bring their total fees into line with English universities, but Edinburgh and St Andrews are charging £9,250 in all four years of their degree courses.

Fees in Wales

In previous years, Welsh universities have applied a range of fees up to £9,000, but for 2018–19 all have opted for £9,000. Students who live in Wales will be able to apply for a Tuition Fee Loan as well as a maintenance grant, wherever they study. You can get a combined loan and grant for up to £9,000 if you study in Wales, or £9,250 for Scotland, England or Northern Ireland, but only a loan, of up to £6,165, for study in a private institution.

Fees in Northern Ireland

The two universities of Northern Ireland are charging local students £4,160 a year for 2018–19. Students can receive a fee loan to postpone paying this until their earnings reach a certain level. In 2017/18 this was £17,775. For students from elsewhere in the UK, the fee is currently £9,000 a year at Ulster and £9,250 for new students at Queen's, Belfast. It is £4,160 for European students from outside the UK.

Useful websites

With changes, large or small, becoming almost an annual occurrence, it is essential to consult the latest information provided by Government agencies. It is worth checking the following websites for the latest information:
England: **www.gov.uk/student-finance**
Wales: **www.studentfinancewales.co.uk**
Scotland: **www.saas.gov.uk**
Northern Ireland: **www.studentfinanceni.co.uk**
OFFA: **www.offa.org.uk**

5 Making Your Application

Applying to university is deceptively simple. It all takes place online and there is abundant help available. But too many people take their eye off the ball at this crucial stage in the process. Surprising numbers of applicants each year spell their own name wrongly, or enter an inaccurate date of birth, or the wrong course code. And that is to say nothing of the damage that can be done in the personal statement and teachers' references.

While UCAS will decode misspelt names, other errors in grammar or spelling present admissions officers with an easy starting point in cutting applications down to a more manageable number. Of course, your grades will be the most important factor in winning a degree place, but what goes on the application form is more important than many students realise. The art of conveying knowledge of, and enthusiasm for, your chosen subject – preferably with supporting evidence from your school or college – can make all the difference.

In years to come, applications may be made after students have their results, but for the moment decisions have to be made well before that point. You will be able to make up to five choices, although you do not have to use all five if you do not want to. Some people make only a single application, perhaps because they do not want to leave home or they have very particular requirements – but you will give yourself the best chance of success if you go for the maximum.

At the time of writing, no major changes were planned for 2018 or 2019. There has been a trial of names-blind applications at 16 universities to test whether this would counter unconscious bias among admissions officers, but the results were inconclusive. Perhaps the most important recent change allowed candidates to submit a new personal statement if their initial applications are unsuccessful and they use the UCAS Extra process. This and other changes are outlined below.

The application process

Most applications for full-time higher education courses go through UCAS, although there is still a different process for the music conservatoires. The trend is towards the UCAS model even among specialist providers, however: recruitment to nursing and midwifery diploma and degree courses in Scotland switched to the UCAS system in 2010, and the art and design courses that used to recruit using the separate "Route B" scheme have also moved to the main system.

Some universities that have not filled all their places, even during Clearing, will accept direct applications up to and sometimes after the start of the academic year, but UCAS is both the official route and the only way into the most popular courses.

All UCAS applications are made online. The Apply electronic system is accessed via the UCAS website and is straightforward to use. For those who do not have the internet at home and prefer not to use school or college computers, the UCAS website lists libraries all over the UK where you can make your application. Apply is available 24 hours a day, and, when the time comes, information on the progress of your application may arrive at any time.

Registering with Apply

The first step in the process is to register. If you are at a school or college, you will need to obtain a "buzzword" from your tutor or careers adviser – it is used when you log on to register. It links your application to the school or college so that the application can be sent electronically to your referee (usually one of your teachers) for your reference to be attached. If you are no longer at a school or college, you do not need a "buzzword", but you will need details of your referee. More information is given on the UCAS website.

To register, go to the UCAS website and click on "Apply". The system will guide you through the business of providing your personal details and generating a username and password, as well as reminding you of basic points, such as amending your details in case of a change of address. You can register separate term-time and holiday addresses – a useful option for boarders, who could find offers and, particularly, the confirmation of a place, going to their school when they are miles away at home. Remember to keep a note of your username and password in a safe place.

Throughout the process, you will be in sole control of communications with UCAS and your chosen universities. Only if you nominate a representative and give them your unique nine-digit application number (sent automatically by UCAS when your application is submitted), can a parent or anyone else give or receive information on your behalf, perhaps because you are ill or out of the country.

Video guides on the application process are available on the UCAS website. Once you are registered, you can start to complete the Apply screens. The sections that follow cover the main screens.

Personal details

This information is taken from your initial registration, and you will be asked for additional information, for example, on ethnic origin and national identity, to monitor equal opportunities

---

The main screens to be completed in UCAS Apply

» Personal and contact details and some additional non-educational details for UK applicants.
» Student finance, a section for UK-resident applicants.
» Your course choices.
» Details of your education so far, including examination results and examinations still to be taken.
» Details of any jobs you have done.
» Your personal statement.
» A declaration that you confirm that the information is correct and that you will be bound by the UCAS rules.
» Pay for the application (applications for 2018 cost £24, or £13 to apply to just one course).
» A reference from one of your teachers.

in the application process. UK students will also be asked to complete a student finance section designed to speed up any loan application you might make.

Choices

In most subjects, you will be able to apply to a maximum of five universities and/or colleges. The exceptions are medicine, dentistry and veterinary science, where the maximum is four, but you can use your fifth choice as a back-up to apply for a different subject.

The other important restriction concerns Oxford or Cambridge, because you can only apply to one or the other; you cannot apply to both universities in the same year, nor can you apply for more than one course there. For both universities you may need to take a written test (see pages 33–34) and submit examples of your work, depending on the course selected. In addition, for Cambridge, many subjects will demand a pre-interview assessment once the university has received your application from UCAS, while the rest will set written tests to be taken at interview.

The deadline for Oxbridge applications – and for all medicine, dentistry and veterinary science courses – is 15 October. For all other applications the deadline is 15 January (or 24 March for some specified art and design courses). The other exceptions to this rule are the relatively small but growing number of courses that start in January or February. If you are considering one of these, contact the university concerned for application deadlines.

Most applicants use all five choices. But if you do choose fewer than five courses, you can still add another to your form up to 30 June, as long as you have not accepted or declined any offers. Nor do you have to choose five different universities if more than one course at the same institution attracts you – perhaps because the institution itself is the real draw and one course has lower entrance requirements than the other. Universities are not allowed to see where else you have applied, or whether you have chosen the same subject elsewhere. But they will be aware of multiple applications within their own institution. Remember that it is more difficult to write a convincing personal statement if it has to cover two subjects.

For each course you select, you will need to put the UCAS code on the form – and you should check carefully that you have the correct code and understand any special requirements that may be detailed on the UCAS description of the course. It does not matter what order you enter in your choices as all your choices are treated equally. You will also need to indicate whether you are applying for a deferred entry (for example, if you are taking a gap year – see page 77).

Education

In this section you will need to give details of the schools and colleges you have attended, and the qualifications you have obtained or are preparing for. The UCAS website gives plenty of advice on the ways in which you should enter this information, to ensure that all your relevant qualifications are included with their grades. While UCAS does not need to see qualification certificates, it can double-check results with the examination boards to ensure that no one is tempted to modify their results.

In the Employment section that follows, add details of any paid jobs you have had (unpaid or voluntary work should be mentioned in your personal statement).

Personal statement

As the competition for places on popular courses has become more intense, so the value attached to the personal statement has increased. Admissions officers look for a sign of potential beyond the high grades that growing numbers of applicants offer. Many academics responsible for admissions value success in extracurricular activities such as drama, sport or the Duke of Edinburgh's Award scheme. But your first priority should be to demonstrate an enthusiasm for and understanding of your subject beyond the confines of the exam syllabus.

This is not easy in a relatively short statement that can readily sound trite or pretentious. You should resist any temptation to exaggerate, let alone lie, particularly if there is any chance of an interview. A claim to have been inspired by a book that you have not read will backfire instantly under questioning and, even without an interview, academics are likely to see through grandiose statements that appear at odds with a teacher's reference.

Genuine experiences of after-hours clubs, lectures or visits, work experience or actual reading around the syllabus are much more likely to strike the right note. If you are applying for medicine, for example, any practical work experience or volunteering in medical or caring settings should be included. Take advice from teachers and, if there is still time before you make your application, look for some subject-related activities that will help fill out your statement.

UCAS top ten personal statement tips

1 Express interest in the subject and show real passion.
2 Go for a strong opening line to grab the reader's attention.
3 Relate outside interests to the course.
4 Think beyond university.
5 Get the basics right.
6 Don't try to sound too clever.
7 Take time and make it your best work.
8 Don't leave it until the last minute – remember the 15January deadline!
9 Get a second opinion.
10 Honesty is the best policy

Admissions officers are also looking for evidence of character that will make you a productive member of their university and, eventually, a successful graduate. Taking responsibility in any area of school or college life suggests this – leading activities outside your place of learning even more so. Evidence of initiative and self-discipline is also valuable, since higher education involves much more independent study than sixth-formers are used to.

Your overall aim in writing your personal statement is to persuade the admissions officer to pick yours out from the piles of applications. That means trying to stand out among an often rather dull and uniform set of statements based around the curriculum and the more predictable sixth-form activities. Everyone is going to say they love reading, for example; narrow your interest down to an area of (real) interest. Don't be afraid to include the unusual, but bear in mind that an academic's sense of humour may not be the same as yours.

Give particular thought to why you want to study your chosen subject – especially if it is not one you have taken at school or college. You need to show that your interests and skills are well suited to the course and, if it is a vocational degree, that you know how you envisage using the qualification. Admissions officers want to feel that you will be committed to their subject for the length of the course, which could be three, four or even five years, and capable of achieving good results. If your five choices cover more than one subject, be careful not to focus too much on one; try to make more general comments on your academic strengths and enthusiasms. And, since the same statement goes to all your chosen departments, avoid expressing any preference for an individual institution.

Your school or college should be the best source of advice, since they see personal statements every year, but there are others. The UCAS website has a useful checklist of themes that you may wish to address, while sites such as **www.studential.com** also provide tips. But do not fall into the trap of cutting and pasting from the model statements included on such sites – both UCAS and individual universities have software that will spot plagiarism immediately. In one year, no fewer than one in 20 applicants came to grief in this way. Plagiarists of this type are unlikely to be disqualified, but they destroy the credibility of their application.

Try not to cram in more than the limited space will allow – admissions officers will have many statements to go through, and judicious editing may be rewarded. As long as you write clearly – preferably in paragraphs and possibly with sub-headings – it will be up to you what to include. It is a *personal* statement. But consider the points listed below and make sure that you can answer all the questions raised. Once you have completed your statement show it to others you trust. It is really important to have others read your statement before submitting it – sometimes things that are clear to you may not be to fresh eyes.

The Apply system allows 4,000 characters (including spaces) or 47 lines for your statement. While there is no requirement to fill all the space, it should not look embarrassingly short. Indeed, your statement now has to be at least 1,000 characters long. UCAS recommends using a word-processing package to compile the statement before pasting it into the application system. This is because Apply will time-out after 35 minutes of inactivity, so there is a danger of losing valuable material. Working offline also has the advantage of leaving you with a copy and making it easier to show it to others.

References

Hand in hand with your personal statement goes the reference from your school, college or, in the case of mature students, someone who knows you well, but is not a friend or family member. Since 2014, even referees who are not your teachers have been encouraged to predict your grades, although they are allowed to opt out of this process. Whatever the source, the reference has to be independent – you are specifically forbidden to change any part of it if you send off your own application – but that does not mean you should not try to influence what it contains.

Most schools and colleges conduct informal interviews before compiling a reference, but it does no harm to draw up a list of the achievements that you would like to see included, and ensure your referee knows what subject you are applying for. Referees cannot know every detail of a candidate's interests and most welcome an aide-memoire.

The UCAS guidelines skirt around the candidate's right to see his or her reference, but it does exist. Schools' practices vary, but most now show the applicant the completed reference.

Key points to consider in writing your personal statement

» What attracts you to this subject (or subjects, in the case of dual or combined honours)?

» Have you undertaken relevant work experience or voluntary activities, either through school or elsewhere?

» Have you taken part in other extra-curricular activities that demonstrate character – perhaps as a prefect, on the sports field or in the arts?

» Have you been involved in other academic pursuits, such as Gifted and Talented programmes, widening participation schemes, or courses in other subjects?

» Which aspects of your current courses have you found particularly stimulating?

» Are you planning a gap year? If so, explain what you intend to do and how it will affect your studies. Some subjects – notably maths – actively discourage a break in studies.

» What other outside interests might you include that show that you are well-rounded?

Timetable for applications for university admission in 2019

At the time of writing UCAS had not confirmed the exact dates for the application schedule. Please check the UCAS website for the most recent information.

2018

January onwards	Find out about courses and universities. Check schedule of open days.
February onwards	Attend open days.
early July	Registration starts for UCAS Apply.
mid September	UCAS starts receiving applications.
15 October	Final day for applications to Oxford and Cambridge, and for most courses in medicine, dentistry and veterinary science.

2019

15 January	Final day for all other applications from UK and EU students including all art and design courses except those which have a 24 March deadline (specified in UCAS Course Search).
16 January–end June	New applications continue to be accepted by UCAS, but only considered by universities if the relevant courses have vacancies.
late February	Start of applications through UCAS Extra.
24 March	Final day for applications to art and design courses that specify this date.
end March	Universities should have sent decisions on all applications received by 15 January.
early May	Final time by which applicants have to decide on their choices if all decisions received by end March (exact date for each applicant will be confirmed by UCAS). **If you do not reply to UCAS, they will decline your offers.** UCAS must have received all decisions from universities if you applied by 15 January.
early June	Final time by which applicants have to decide on their choices if all decisions received by early May.
start of July	Any new application received from this time held until Clearing starts. End of applications through UCAS Extra.
5 July	International Baccalaureate results published.
7 August	SQA results published. Scottish Clearing starts.
16 August	A-level results published. Full Clearing and Adjustment starts.
end August	Adjustment closes. Last time for you to meet any offer conditions, after which university might not accept you.
late October	End of period for adding Clearing choices and last point at which a university can accept you through Clearing.

Where this is not the case, the candidate can pay UCAS £10 for a copy, although at this stage it is obviously too late to influence the contents. Better, if you can, to see it before it goes off, in case there are factual inaccuracies that can be corrected.

Timing

The general deadline for applications through UCAS is 15 January, but even those received up to 30 June will be considered if the relevant courses still have vacancies. After that, you will be limited to Clearing, or an application for the following year. In theory – and usually in practice – all applications submitted by the January deadline are given equal consideration. But the best advice is to get your application in early: before Christmas, or earlier if possible. Applications are accepted from mid-September onwards, so the autumn half-term is a sensible target date for completing the process. Although no formal offers are made before the deadline, many admissions officers look through applications as they come in and may make a mental note of promising candidates. If your form arrives with the deadline looming, you may appear less organised than those who submitted in good time; and your application may be one of a large batch that receives a more cursory first reading than the early arrivals. Under UCAS rules, last-minute applicants should not be at a disadvantage, but why take the risk?

Next steps

Once your application has been processed by UCAS, you will receive an email confirming that your application has been sent to your university choices and summarising what will happen next. The email will also confirm your Personal ID, which you can use to access "Track", the online system that allows you to follow the progress of your application. Check all the details carefully: you have 14 days to contact UCAS to correct any errors. Universities can make direct contact with you through Track, including arranging interviews.

After that, it is just a matter of waiting for universities to make their decisions, which can take days, weeks or even months, depending on the university and the course. Some obviously see an advantage in being the first to make an offer – it is a memorable moment to be reassured that at least one of your chosen institutions wants you – and may send their response almost immediately. Others take much longer, perhaps because they have so many good applications to consider, or maybe because they are waiting to see which of their applicants withdraw when Oxford and Cambridge make their offers. Universities are asked to make all their decisions by the end of March, and most have done so long before that.

Interviews

Unless you are applying for a course in health or education that brings you into direct contact with the public, the chances are you will not have a selection interview. For prospective medics, vets, dentists or teachers, a face-to-face assessment of your suitability will be crucial to your chances of success. Likewise in the performing arts, the interview may be as important as your exam grades. Oxford and Cambridge still interview most applicants in all subjects, and a few of the top universities see a significant proportion. But the expansion of higher education has made it impractical to interview everyone, and many admissions experts are sceptical about interviews.

What has become more common, however, is the "sales" interview, where the university is really selling itself to the candidate. There may still be testing questions, but the admissions staff have already made their minds up and are actually trying to persuade you to accept an offer. Indeed, you will probably be given a clear indication at the end of the interview that an offer is on its way. The technique seems to work, perhaps because you have invested time and nervous energy in a sometimes lengthy trip, as well as acquiring a more detailed impression of both the department and the university.

The difficulty can come in spotting which type of interview is which. The "real" ones require lengthy preparation, revisiting your personal statement and reading beyond the exam syllabus. Impressions count for a lot, so dress smartly and make sure that you are on time. Have a question of your own ready, as well as being prepared to give answers.

While you would not want to appear ignorant at a "sales" interview, lengthy preparation might be a waste of valuable time during a period of revision. Naturally, you should err on the side of caution, but if your predicted grades are well above the standard offer and the subject is not one that normally requires an interview, it is likely that the invitation is a sales pitch. It is still worth going, unless you have changed your mind about the application.

Offers

When your chosen universities respond to your application, there will be one of three answers:

» Unconditional Offer (U): This used to be a possibility only if you applied after satisfying the entrance requirements – usually if you are applying as a mature student, while on a gap year, after resitting exams or, in Scotland, after completing Highers. However, a growing number of universities competing for bright students have begun to make unconditional offers to those who are predicted high grades – just how high will depend on the university. If you are fortunate (and able) enough to receive one, do not assume that grades are no longer important because they may be taken into consideration when you apply for jobs as a graduate.

» Conditional Offer (C): The vast majority of students will still receive conditional offers, where each university offers a place subject to you achieving set grades or points on the UCAS tariff.

» Rejection (R): You do not have the right qualifications, or have lost out to stronger competition.

Unconditional offers have been the subject of considerable controversy in recent months, following evidence from UCAS that applicants who received them were much more likely than others to miss their predicted grades. Far from targeting only the brightest students, students with BBB at A-level were now the most likely to receive an unconditional offer, as the number grew by 40 per cent between 2016 and 2017.

One danger is that an unconditional offer might tempt a candidate to lower his or her sights and accept a place that would not have been their first choice otherwise. As long as this is not the case, however, there is no reason to spurn such an offer if it comes, as long as you do not take your foot off the pedal in the run-up to examinations.

If you have chosen wisely, you should have more than one offer to choose from, so you will be required to pick your favourite as your firm acceptance – known as UF if it was an unconditional offer and CF if it was conditional. Candidates with conditional offers can also accept a second offer, with lower grades, as an Insurance Choice (CI). You must then decline any other offers that you have.

You do not have to make an Insurance Choice – indeed, you may decline all your offers if you have changed your mind about your career path or regret your course decisions. But most people prefer the security of a back-up route into higher education if their grades fall short. Some 37,500 took up their Insurance Choice in 2017. You must be sure that your firm acceptance is definitely your first choice because you will be allocated a place automatically if you meet the university's conditions. It is no good at this stage deciding that you prefer your Insurance choice because UCAS rules will not allow a switch.

The only way round those rules, unless your results are better than your highest offer (see Adjustment, below), is through direct contact with the universities concerned. Your firm acceptance institution has to be prepared to release you so that your new choice can award you a place in Clearing. Neither is under any obligation to do so but, in practice, it is rare for a university to insist that a student joins against his or her wishes. Admissions staff will do all they can to persuade you that your original choice was the right one – as it may well have been, if your research was thorough – but it will almost certainly be your decision in the end.

UCAS Extra

If things do go wrong and you receive five rejections, that need not be the end of your higher education ambitions. From the end of February until the end of June, you have another chance through UCAS Extra, a listing of courses that still have vacancies after the initial round of offers. Extra is sometimes dismissed (wrongly) as a repository of second-rate courses. In fact, even in the boom years for applications, most Russell Group universities still have courses listed in a wide variety of subjects.

You will be notified if you are eligible for Extra and can then select courses marked as available on the UCAS website. In order to assist students who choose different subjects after a full set of rejections in their original application, you will be able to submit a new personal statement for Extra. Applications are made, one at a time, through UCAS Track. If you do not receive an offer, or you choose to decline one, you can continue applying for other courses until you are successful. About half of those applying through Extra normally find a place. More than 6,000 were successful this way in 2017.

Results Day

Rule Number One on results day is to be at home, or at least in easy communication – you cannot afford to be on some remote beach if there are complications. The day is bound to be stressful, unless you are absolutely confident that you achieved the required grades – more of a possibility in an era of modular courses with marks along the way. But for thousands of students, Track has removed the agony of opening the envelope or scanning a results noticeboard. On the morning of A-level results day, the system informs those who have already won a place on their chosen course. You will not learn your grades until later, but at least your immediate future is clear.

If you get the grades stipulated in your conditional offer, the process should work smoothly and you can begin celebrating. Track will let you know as soon as your place is confirmed and the paperwork will arrive in a day or two. You can phone the university to make quite sure, but it should not be necessary and you will be joining a long queue of people doing the same thing.

If the results are not what you hoped – and particularly if you just miss your grades – you need to be on the phone and taking advice from your school or college. In a year when results are better than expected, some universities will stick to the letter of their offers, perhaps refusing to accept your AAC grades when they had demanded ABB. Others will forgive a dropped grade to take a candidate who is regarded as promising, rather than go into Clearing to recruit an unknown quantity. Admissions staff may be persuadable – particularly if there are extenuating personal circumstances, or the dropped grade is in a subject that is not relevant to your chosen course. Try to get a teacher to support your case, and be persistent if there is any prospect of flexibility.

If your results are lower than predicted, one option is to ask for papers to be re-marked, as growing numbers do each year. The school may ask for a whole batch to be re-marked, and you should ensure that your chosen universities know this if it may make the difference to whether or not you satisfy your offer. If your grades improve as a result, the university will review its decision, but if by then it has filled all its places, you may have to wait until next year to start.

If you took Scottish Highers, you will have had your results for more than a week by the time the A-level grades are published. If you missed your grades, there is no need to wait for A-levels before you begin approaching universities. Admissions staff at English universities may not wish to commit themselves before they see results from south of the border, but Scottish universities will be filling places immediately and all should be prepared to give you an idea of your prospects.

Adjustment

If your grades are better than those demanded by your first-choice university, there is now an opportunity to "trade up". The Adjustment Period runs from when you receive your results until 31 August, and you can only use it for five 24-hour periods during that period, so there is no time to waste. First, go into the Track system and click on "Register for Adjustment" and then contact your preferred institutions to find another place. If none is available, or you decide not to move, your initial offer will remain open. The number of students switching universities in this way has not increased as much as many observers expected, perhaps because Clearing has become much more flexible, but there were still more than 1,000 successful candidates in 2017. The process has become an established part of the system and, without the previous restrictions on the number of students they could recruit, many leading universities see it as a good source of talented undergraduates. UCAS does not publish a breakdown of which universities take part – some, such as Oxford and Cambridge, simply do not have places available – but it is known that many students successfully go back to institutions that had rejected them at the initial application stage. Even if you are eligible for Adjustment, you may decide to stick with the offer you have, but it is worth at least exploring your options.

Clearing

If you do not have a place on Results Day, there will still be plenty of options through the UCAS Clearing scheme. A record 66,800 people –one successful applicant in eight – found a place through this route in 2017, despite a small drop in the number of applicants. With recruitment restrictions lifted, universities that used to regard their absence from Clearing as a point of pride are appearing in the vacancy lists. It is likely that this trend will continue in 2019, as more universities seek to expand, particularly in arts, social science and business subjects.

Although the most popular courses may still fill up quickly, many remain open up to and beyond the start of the academic year. And, at least at the start of the process, the range of courses with vacancies is much wider than in Extra. Most universities will list some courses, and most subjects will be available somewhere.

Clearing runs from A-level Results Day until the end of September, matching students without places to full-time courses with vacancies. As long as you are not holding any offers and you have not withdrawn your application, you are eligible automatically. You will be sent a Clearing number via Track to quote to universities.

There are now two ways of entering Clearing: the traditional method of ringing universities that still have vacancies, or by using the system introduced last year which allows universities to approach candidates with suitable grades for one of their courses. You will be given the option of signing up for this service in an email from UCAS and issued with a code word to be used by universities contacting you on Results Day or subsequently. You will be approached by a maximum of five universities or colleges. UCAS advises students to approach universities themselves in any case, but the new system does add an extra string to their bow and may take some of the anxiety out of Clearing.

Assuming you are making your own approaches, the first step is to trawl through the lists on the UCAS website, and elsewhere, before ringing the university offering the course that appeals most, and where you have a realistic chance of a place – do not waste time on courses where the standard offer is far above your grades. Universities run Clearing hotlines and have become adept at dealing with a large number of calls in a short period, but you can still spend a long time on the phone at a time when the most desirable places are beginning to disappear. If you can't get through send an email setting out your grades and the course that interests you.

The best advice is to plan ahead and not to wait for Results Day to draw up a list of possible Clearing targets. Many universities publish lists of courses that are likely to be in Clearing on their websites from the start of August. Think again about some of the courses that you considered when making your original application, or others at your chosen universities that had lower entrance requirements. But beware of switching to another subject simply because you have the right grades – you still have to sustain your interest and be capable of succeeding over three or more years. Many of the students who drop out of degrees are those who chose the wrong course in a rush during Clearing.

In short, you should start your search straight away if you do find yourself in Clearing, and act decisively, but do not panic. You can make as many approaches as you like, until you are accepted on the course of your choice. Remember that if you changed your personal statement for applications in Extra, this will be the one that goes to any universities that you approach in Clearing, so it may be difficult to return to the subjects in your original application.

Most of the available vacancies will appear in Clearing lists, but some of the universities towards the top of the league tables may have a limited number of openings that they choose not to advertise – either for reasons of status or because they do not want the administrative burden of fielding large numbers of calls to fill a handful of places. If there is a course that you find particularly attractive – especially if you have good grades and are applying late – it may be worth making a speculative call. Sometimes a number of candidates holding offers drop grades and you may be on the spot at the right moment.

What are the alternatives?

If your results are lower than expected and there is nothing you want in Clearing, there are several things you can do. The first is to resit one or more subjects. The modular nature of most courses means that you will have a clear idea of what you need to do to get better grades. You can go back to school or college, or try a "crammer". Although some colleges have a good success rate with re-takes, you have to be highly focused and realistic about the likely improvements. Some of the most competitive courses, such as medicine, may demand higher grades for a second application, so be sure you know the details before you commit yourself.

Other options are to get a job and study part-time, or to take a break from studying and return later in your career. You may have considered an apprenticeship before applying to university, but the number and variety are growing all the time, so it may be worth another look. The UCAS Progress service provides information on apprenticeship opportunities post-16 and a new search tool has been established for higher and degree apprenticeship vacancies.

The part-time route can be arduous – many young people find a job enough to handle without the extra burden of academic work. But others find it just the combination they need for a fulfilling life. It all depends on your job, your social life and your commitment to the subject you will study. It may be that a relatively short break is all that you need to rekindle your enthusiasm for studying. Many universities now have a majority of mature students, so you need not be out of place if this is your chosen route.

Taking a gap year

The other popular option is to take a gap year. In most years, about 7 per cent of applicants defer their entry until the following year while they travel, or do voluntary or paid work. A whole industry has grown up around tailor-made activities, many of them in Asia, Africa or Latin America. Some have been criticised for doing more for the organisers than the underprivileged communities that they purport to assist, but there are programmes that are useful and character-building, as well as safe. Most of the overseas programmes are not cheap, but raising the money can be part of the experience.

Various organisations can help you find voluntary work. Some examples include vInspired (**www.vinspired.com**), Lattitude Global Volunteering (**www.lattitude.org.uk**) and Plan my Gap Year (**www.planmygapyear.co.uk**). Voluntary Service Overseas (**www.vsointernational.org**) works mainly with older volunteers but has an offshoot, run with five other volunteering organisations, International Citizen Service (**www.volunteerics.org**), that places 18–25-year-olds around the world.

The alternative is to stay closer to home and make your contribution through organisations like Volunteering Matters (**http://volunteeringmatters.org.uk**) or to take a job that will make higher education more affordable when the time comes. Work placements can be casual or structured, such as the Year in Industry Scheme (**www.etrust.org.uk**). Sponsorship is also available, mainly to those wishing to study science, engineering or business. Buyer beware: we cannot vouch for any of these and you need to be clear whether the aim is to make money or to plump up your CV. If it is the second, you may end up spending money, not saving it.

Many admissions staff are happy to facilitate gap years because they think it makes for more mature, rounded students than those who come straight from school. The longer-term benefits may also be an advantage in the graduate employment market. Both university admissions officers and employers look for evidence that candidates have more about them than academic ability. The experience you gain on a gap year can help you develop many of the attributes they are looking for, such as interpersonal, organisational and teamwork skills, leadership, creativity, experience of new cultures or work environments, and enterprise.

There are subjects – maths in particular – that discourage a break because it takes too long to pick up study skills where you left off. From the student's point of view, you should also bear in mind that a gap year postpones the moment at which you embark on a career. This may be important if your course is a long one, such as medicine or architecture.

If you are considering a gap year, it makes sense to apply for a deferred place, rather than waiting for your results before applying. The application form has a section for deferments. That allows you to sort out your immediate future before you start travelling or working, and leaves you the option of changing your mind if circumstances change.

Useful websites

The essential website for making an application is, of course, that of UCAS:
www.ucas.com/ucas/undergraduate/apply-and-track

For applications to music conservatoires: **www.ucas.com/ucas/conservatoires**

For advice on your personal statement:
www.ucas.com/ucas/16-18-choices/search-and-apply/writing-ucas-progress-personal-statement

Gap years

To help you consider options and start planning: **www.gapadvice.org**
For links to volunteering opportunities in the UK: **www.do-it.org**
For links to many gap year organisations: **www.yearoutgroup.org**

6 The Cost of Studying

The cost of university study – and in particular the debts with which students leave college – have become an emotive and politically sensitive issue. But there is little agreement about the scale of the problem or the best way for an individual to minimise it. Unless you have tens of thousands of pounds per year to spend on student fees and living costs, you have little chance of avoiding debt altogether. But depending on your subsequent earnings, you might never have to repay most of any student loan you have taken out, particularly since the point at which you will begin repayments was raised from £21,000 to £25,000. The majority of students will not repay the full amount they borrow.

Even finance experts disagree about the best approach to your student loan upon graduation, however. One recent study described student loans as "one of the most expensive ways of funding a university education" because of the interest charged over the 30-year repayment period. The rate of interest is fixed at up to 3 per cent more than the Retail Price Index if you earn between £25,000 and £41,000, or at exactly 3 per cent more than RPI if you earn more than this. The problem is that the RPI is a measure of UK inflation. Partly because of the pressure on sterling stemming from Brexit, economists now expect inflation to rise after some quiescent years, and this may be reflected in future interest rates.

However, the good news is that nobody earning less than £25,000 a year pays anything on their student finance. When your income goes above this figure, you pay 9 per cent of the extra, via the tax system, to the Student Loans Company which, as its name implies, makes the loans in the first place. However much you owe, you will never have to pay more than that 9 per cent figure.

One constant, however, is that after 30 years in England (the figure varies elsewhere in the UK), the debt is written off. Because the repayments are modest for anyone with a normal income, and because of the 30-year rule, student debt is a lot more forgiving than debt such as a mortgage or a credit card, where the bills keep on coming even if you are out of work. And the Student Loans Company is, after all, probably the only lender in Britain who will give you tens of thousands of pounds of credit without a credit check.

The last significant change in this system was the abolition of grants for students from low-income families in England and their replacement by loans. As with the introduction of £9,000 fees, there is no immediate impact on students. Repayments still begin only after graduation and when the borrower's salary reaches £25,000, but the fear remains that the prospect of yet more debt will deter applicants from this already under-represented section of society. That did not happen when fees went up in 2012, but no one can be sure what will happen over time.

There are different arrangements in other parts of the UK, which are addressed later in this chapter. But wherever you study, there are two quite different timescales to consider: in the short term the calculations are all about having enough money to live on and maybe have some fun, while the long term is more about value for money. Most commentary on the subject conflates the two, focusing on the total debt that the average student will have at graduation. Although the total will be an intimidating figure and one that should not be ignored by those contemplating a degree, it has little to do with whether you can afford three or more years as an undergraduate.

Affordability

The introduction of £9,000 fees, now fixed at a maximum of £9,250 for three or four-year courses, added enormously to graduates' debts. But it makes no difference to the amount of money you will need as a student. That calculation is about bridging the gap between a maintenance loan, which in England will now be worth up to £8,700 (or £11,354 in London) in 2018–19, and the real cost of living. The figure falls to £7,324 if you are living with your parents, but with hall fees topping £5,000 a year at some universities, that might still seem an attractive option. Loans are also available if you are studying abroad for at least one term. This was up to £9,564 for 2017–18. The upshot is that there will be a financial gap for most students. But don't panic. Students have always had trouble making ends meet, typically through a combination of parental help, part-time employment and institutional bursaries.

How well you can live on these sums will vary from person to person. But analysis by the National Union of Students suggests that it is not possible to get by on student loans alone. Savings, earnings, and help from family and friends have to be added to the pot. The information provided here will help you understand how big your pot needs to be, and what you can expect to be added and taken away from it. But it takes careful budgeting to avoid adding credit card debt to the income-contingent variety offered by the Government and repaid (or not) over 30 years.

Value for money

Only when you are sure you can cope with the costs of student life should you move on to the longer-term question of whether your chosen degree will be worth repaying £40,000 or more in student loans. Even in purely financial terms, there are too many uncertainties to be sure of the answer. You may never earn the £25,000 a year which triggers repayments, although few students go to university with that expectation and in practice, very few will be in that position. At the other extreme, your degree may help you land such a well-paid job that university was cheap at the price. Most graduates will be somewhere in the middle, and the system is too new for any to have experienced the impact of loan repayments of 9 per cent of salary above the threshold for more than a few years.

Contrary to some alarmist media coverage of graduate employment prospects, most surveys suggest that on average, a degree is still a worthwhile investment in terms of future salary expectations, even after adding in the amount you might have earned while you were at university. A study by London Economics for the MillionPlus group of post-1992 universities put the average graduate premium at £115,000 over a working lifetime. And a 2015 analysis from the

Institute for Fiscal Studies found that women, in particular, benefit from a degree. While women in the workforce overall earn a third less than men on average, the difference is only 23 per cent for graduate women – hardly ideal, but something of an improvement. The IFS said: "Median earnings of English women around ten years after graduation were just over three times those of non-graduates. Median earnings of male graduates were around twice those of men without a degree. This advantage for graduates was maintained through the recent recession, although all groups saw significant falls in their earnings during this period."

The Government's decision to raise the threshold for starting repayments from £21,000 to £25,000 was announced after this study and is expected to mean that graduates pay back £15,700 less over a full career. The real advantage, obviously, will be for those on relatively low incomes.

This *Guide* should help to fill in some of the detail on employment rates on different courses at different universities, while salary data by course is available on the Unistats website. But no one can be certain of salary prospects over an entire career, which is increasingly likely to span several forms of employment. Many satisfying jobs are open only to graduates, while in others the majority of new entrants have degrees.

Planning your finances

This chapter will focus on the costs while at university and the support that is available to get you through your undergraduate years. Like maximum fees, national student support schemes are the responsibility of the devolved UK administrations. There are separate sections for Northern Ireland, Wales and Scotland that follow the advice given for English students below.

At the time of writing, the government had decided to keep the basic rate of fees at £9,250 per year for England, partly as a political response to its unpopularity with young people. This standstill is bad news for university finance managers, who might have expected an inflation-linked increase, but is excellent for you. Despite this stasis, it is essential to consult the

Maintenance loan for a first-year English student 2018–19

Household income	Living at home	Living away from home but not in London	Living away from home in London
£25,000 and below	£7,324	£8,700	£11,354
£30,000	£6,707	£8,076	£10,719
£35,000	£6,090	£7,452	£10,084
£40,000	£5,473	£6,828	£9,449
£42,875	£5,118	£6,469	£9,083
£45,000	£4,855	£6,204	£8,813
£50,000	£4,238	£5,579	£8,178
£55,000	£3,621	£4,955	£7,543
£58,215 and above	£3,224	–	–
£60,000	–	£4,331	£6,907
£62,215 and above	–	£4,054	–
£65,000	–	–	£6,272
£69,860 and above	–	–	£5,654

Figures subject to Parliamentary approval at time of writing

information provided by Government agencies. It is worth checking the following websites for the latest information:

» England: **www.gov.uk/student-finance**
» Wales: **www.studentfinancewales.co.uk**
» Scotland: **www.saas.gov.uk**
» Northern Ireland: **www.studentfinanceni.co.uk**

Student loans for English students

More than 80 per cent of students take out a student loan, and it is not difficult to see why. The National Union of Students estimates that undergraduates spend £12,000 a year outside London and £13,500 in the capital. While some other estimates are marginally lower, most students find it impossible to cover all their living costs on savings and earnings alone and require significant family support to cover the difference if they do not take out a loan.

Most experts such as Martin Lewis of moneysavingexpert.com, who writes regularly on student finance, agree that student loans are a good deal compared with other forms of borrowing. In particular, he counsels against using family savings to pay fees upfront, especially since the Government's own estimates suggest that most graduates will not repay the whole amount that they borrow.

There are two types of student loan – one to cover the cost of tuition fees, and another to help you cover the cost of living.

Tuition fees loan

You can borrow up to the full amount needed to cover the cost of your tuition fees wherever you study in the UK, and this loan is not dependent upon your household income.

Tuition fees loans for part-time students

The most that universities or colleges can charge for part-time courses in 2017–18 is £4,625 per year at private institutions and £6,935 per year at public ones. They cannot charge more than 75 per cent of the full-time course fee. New part-time students will be able to apply for a tuition fee loan that is not dependent on household income or on age, which has led to some courses having a surprising number of pensioner students. Eligibility depends on the "intensity" of the course being at least 25 per cent of a full-time course. This measure works by comparing the course to a full-time equivalent. So, if a course takes six years to complete and the full-time equivalent takes three, the intensity will be 50 per cent. In practice, most courses will manage more than 25 per cent intensity.

Maintenance loan

The second type of student loan, a maintenance loan, is means-tested. The amount you can borrow depends on several factors, including your family income, where you intend to study, and whether you expect to be living at home.

Although you are legally an adult, your student finance options depend heavily on your family income, frequently termed "household income", which in practice usually means your mother's and father's earning power. If your parents are separated, divorced or widowed, only the income of the parent with whom you normally live will be assessed. However, if that parent has married again, entered into a civil partnership, or has a partner of the opposite sex, then both their incomes will be taken into account. If you are over 25, married or in some other way visibly independent of your parents, you can avoid having their income taken into account.

If you have not been in contact with them for a year or more, you can apply as "estranged."

For 2018 entry, the maximum loan for those living at home is £7,324, but only if the combined household income is £25,000 or less. The size of the loan is then reduced on a sliding scale to £3,224 for incomes over £58,215. For students living away from home outside London, the maximum loan is £8,700, and for those living away from home in London, £11,354, but again these are rates for a household income of £25,000 or less. For students outside London, the loan is reduced on a sliding scale to £4,054 for those whose parents earn £62,215 and above, while for students in London the loan reduces to £5,654 for incomes of £69,860 and above.

You can also get a loan for a year studying abroad as part of a UK course. Final-year students receive less than those in earlier years. Of the maintenance loan, 65 per cent is available to you regardless of your family circumstances, while the remaining 35 per cent is means-tested. Note, too, that there is extra cash available for future teachers, social workers and healthcare workers, including doctors and dentists.

Students who would have qualified for maintenance grants and are studying away from home will be able to borrow up to £8,700, which is £1,269 more than they would have received in 2015–16. In London the maximum will be £11,354 or, for those living in the parental home, £7,324. Those who qualify for benefits and would have received a Special Supplementary Grant will receive an increased loan of £9,609 (studying away from home), £11,998 (in London) and £8,372 (at home) for 2018–19.

Repaying loans

As we have seen, full-time students will begin accumulating interest during their course and will start repaying in the April after graduation if they earn over £25,000. They will then pay 9 per cent of their income above £25,000, but repayments will stop during any period in which annual income falls below the threshold. Repayments are normally taken automatically through tax and National Insurance. If the loan has not been paid off after 30 years, no further repayments will be required. During the repayment period, the amount of interest will vary according to how much you earn. If you earn less than £25,000, interest will be at the rate of inflation as measured by the Retail Price Index (1.6 per cent for 2016–17); between £25,000 and £41,000 you will be charged inflation plus up to 3 per cent; and if you earn over £41,000, interest will be at inflation plus the full 3 per cent.

The Student Loan Company website (**www.studentloanrepayment.co.uk**) has information to guide prospective students through these arrangements and gives examples of levels of repayment.

Student loans and grants for Northern Ireland students

Maintenance loans in 2017–18 vary from a maximum of £3,750 for students living at home, £4,840 for those studying away from home, all the way to £5,770 for those living overseas and £6,780 for those studying in London (and only 25 per cent of the loan is means-tested). There are also extra sums for people taking courses longer than 30 weeks a year, worth up to £108 a week if you are in London. Tuition fee loans are available for the full amount of tuition fees, regardless of where you study in the UK. Maintenance grants range from £3,475 for students with household incomes of £19,203 or below, to zero if the figure is £41,066 or above. Your maximum loan is reduced by the size of any grant you receive. Loan repayments of 9 per cent of salary start once your income reaches £17,775, less than in England, and interest is calculated on the retail price index or 1 per cent above base rate, whichever is lowest and again less than for England. In 2016–17, the rate was 1.25 per cent. The loan will be cancelled after 25 years, also quicker than in England.

As in England, there are also special funds for people with disabilities and other special needs, and for those with children or adult dependants. Students studying in the Republic of Ireland can also borrow up to €3,000 a year to pay their Irish student fees and may be able to get a bursary to study there.

Student loans and grants for Welsh students

For 2018/19, the maximum maintenance award will be £7,650 for students living at home, £9,000 for those living away from home and outside London, and £11,250 for those living in London. The cunning part is that these sums are mainly an outright grant to those from less prosperous households (£8100 grant and £900 loan for the £9,000 figure if total household income is £18,370 or less), but then become steadily more repayable. If your household income is over £59,200, £8,000 of the £9,000 is repayable and only £1,000 is a grant. The same logic applies to other levels of support, while part-time students can get a loan or grant up to the precise figure of £4,987.50.

Tuition fee loans are available to cover the first £9,000 of tuition fees in Wales, or £9,250 in Scotland, England or Northern Ireland.

Repayment of loans starts once a graduate's income reaches £21,000. Interest repayments and the length of loan are as for England (see above). In addition, students in Wales are also able to apply for Welsh Government support for parents of young children, for adult learners, for those with adult dependants and for those with disabilities. This support can cover carer costs as well as equipment and general expenditure.

Student loans and grants for Scottish students

The Scottish Government has a commitment to a minimum income of £7,625 a year for students from poorer backgrounds – not bad in a setting where tuition is also free. In 2017/18, students from a family with an income below £19,000 can get a £1,875 Young Students' Bursary (YSB) as well as a loan of £5,750. The bursary component does not have to be repaid, but the loan does. It tapers off to zero for family incomes of £34,000, at which point the maximum loan also falls from £5,750 to £4,750. The loan does not vary in size depending on whether you live at home or where you are studying in the UK. Higher loans but more limited bursaries are available for "independent" students – those who are married, mature or without family support.

Note that you must be under 60 when you first apply for a loan. Repayment of the loan starts when your income reaches £17,775 and is set at 9 per cent of your income above that threshold. Interest is linked to the Retail Price Index. Repayments will continue until the loan is paid off, with any outstanding amount being cancelled after 35 years.

As elsewhere in the UK, there are also special funds for people with disabilities and other special needs, and for those with children or adult dependants. No tuition fee loans are required by Scottish students studying in Scotland, but such loans are available for Scottish students studying elsewhere in the UK.

A review of the student support system led by Jayne-Anne Gadhia, the CEO of Virgin Money, reported in November 2017. Its recommendations were being considered by ministers as this guide went to press.

Living in one country, studying in another

As each of the countries of the UK develops its own distinctive system of student finance, the effects on students leaving home in one UK nation to go and study in another have become knottier. UK students who cross borders to study pay the tuition fees of their chosen university

Scottish maintenance bursaries and loans 2017–18[1]

Young student (under 25 at start of course)				Independent student			
Income	Bursary	Loan	Total	Income	Bursary	Loan	Total
£0–£18,999	£1,875	£5,750	£7,625	£0–£18,999	£875	£6,750	£7,625
£19,000–£23,999	£1,125	£5,570	£6,875	£19,000–£23,999	0	£6,750	£6,750
£24,000–£33,999	£500	£5,750	£6,250	£24,000–£33,999	0	£6,250	£6,250
£34,000 and over	0	£4,750	£4,750	£34,000 and over	0	£4,750	£4,750

Repayments start at a salary above £17,775. Any outstanding amount will be written off after 35 years.

[1] At the time of writing the figures for 2018–19 had not been released by the Scottish Government.

and are eligible for a fee loan, and maybe a partial grant, to cover them. They are also entitled to apply for the scholarships or bursaries on offer from that institution. Any maintenance loan or grant will still come from the awarding body of their home country. If you are in this position, you must check with the authorities in your home country about the funding you are eligible for.

While the UK remains in the European Union, EU students from outside the UK must be charged the same tuition fees as those paid by nationals of the country where they are studying, rather than the higher fees paid by students from outside the EU. They can also apply for a fee loan and may be considered for some of the scholarships and bursaries offered by individual institutions. Only students who have been living and studying in the UK for at least three years

Funding timetable

It is vital that you sort out your funding arrangements before you start university. Each funding agency has its own arrangements, and it is very important that you find out the exact details from them. The dates below give general indications of key dates.

March/April
» Online and paper application forms become available from funding agencies.
» You must contact the appropriate funding agency to make an application. This will be the funding agency for the region of the UK that you live in, even if you are planning to study elsewhere in the UK.
» Complete application form as soon as possible. At this stage select the university offer that will be your first choice.
» Check details of bursaries and scholarships available from your selected universities.

May/June
» Funding agencies will give you details of the financial support they can offer.
» Last date for making an application to ensure funding is ready for you at the start of term (exact date varies significantly between agencies).

August
» Tell your funding agency if the university or course you have been accepted for is different from that originally given them.

September
» Take letter confirming funding to your university for registration.
» After registration, the first part of funds will be released to you.

can apply for a maintenance loan or grant. Those who haven't, will need to apply for such assistance from the authorities in their own country. Tuition fee rules for non-UK European Union students are the same in Scotland as for Scottish students – that is, they do not have to pay tuition fees. There are also no fees to pay for exchange students coming to the UK, including those on the Socrates Programme.

Applying for support

English students should apply for grants and loans through Student Finance England, Welsh students through Student Finance Wales, Scottish students through the Student Awards Agency for Scotland, and those in Northern Ireland through Student Finance NI or their Education and Library Board. You should make your application as soon as you have received an offer of a place at university. Maintenance loans are usually paid in three instalments a year into your bank or building society account. European Union students from outside the UK will usually be sent an application form for tuition fee loans by the university that has offered them a place. Don't expect things to happen automatically. For instance, you will have to tell the finance system to pay your fees to the college. You'll never see this money yourself, only the repayments you end up making.

University scholarships and bursaries

As well as taking out student loans for both tuition and living costs, you can shop around for university bursaries, scholarships and other sponsorship packages, and seek out supplementary support to which you may be entitled. There may be reductions for a range of other groups, including local students, which vary widely from university to university and which are usually detailed on university websites. The details of the financial support offered by all universities in England are listed in the access agreements published on the website of the Office for Fair Access (**www.offa.org.uk**).

Although English universities have continued to scale back their support for 2017–18, there is still a bewildering variety of bursaries and scholarships on offer at UK universities. Some awards are guaranteed depending on your financial circumstances, while scholarships are available through open competition. In general, bursaries that provide students with the money to make ends meet at university have (rightly) proved more popular than fee waivers giving relief from repayments that may stretch over 30 years. Some universities offer eligible students the choice of accommodation discounts, fee waivers or cash. Most also have hardship funds for those who find themselves in financial difficulties. Many charities for specific industries or professions have a remit to support education, and many have bursaries for anyone studying a related subject. It might be worth seeking out some options online.

Do take note of the application procedures for scholarships and bursaries. They vary from institution to institution, and even from course to course within individual institutions. There may be a deadline you have to meet to apply for an award. In some cases, the university will work out for you whether you are entitled to an award by referring to your funding agency's financial assessment. If your personal circumstances change part-way through a course, your entitlement to a scholarship or bursary may be reviewed.

If you feel you still need more help or advice on scholarships or bursaries, you can usually find it on a university's website or in its prospectus. Most institutions also maintain a helpline. Some questions you will need answered include whether the bursary or scholarship is automatic or conditional and, if the latter, when you will find out whether your application has been successful. For some awards, you won't know whether you have qualified until you get your exam results. Another obvious question is how the scholarship or bursary on offer compares with awards made by another university you might consider applying to. Watch out for institutions that list entitlements that others don't mention, but which you would get anyway.

Students with disabilities

Extra financial help is available to disabled students, whether studying full-time or part-time through Disabled Students' Allowances, which are paid in addition to the standard student finance package. They are available for help with education-related conditions such as dyslexia, and for other physical and mental disabilities. They do not depend on income and do not have to be repaid. The cash is available for extra travel costs, equipment and to pay helpers. For 2017–18 the maximum for students in England for a non-medical helper is £21,305 a year, or £15,978 a year for a part-time student. In addition, there is a maximum equipment allowance of £5,358 for the duration of the course and £1,790 for general expenses a year, although the government warns that most students get less than these amounts. For postgraduates, the maximum award is a flat payment of £10,652.

The National Health Service has its own Disabled Students Allowance system, worth a look if you are in the health field. On that theme, the NHS Business Services Authority has a Student Services Arm which runs the NHS Learning Support Grants and the NHS Education Support Grant, again worth investigating if you are planning to study health or social work.

Further sources of income

If you are feeling daunted by the potential costs of study, take comfort from this section, which outlines just some of the ways you can raise additional funds.

Taking a gap year

Gap years (see chapter 5) have become increasingly popular both for travelling and to earn some money to help pay for higher education. Many students will simply want to travel, but others will be more focused on boosting the bank balance in preparation for life as a student. Work opportunities can be structured or casual. An example of the structured variety is the Year in Industry Scheme (**www.etrust.org.uk**).

Further support

There are various types of support available for students in particular circumstances, other than the main loans, grants and bursaries.

» Undergraduates in financial difficulties can apply for help to their university's student hardship fund. These are allocated to provide support for anything from day-to-day study and living costs to unexpected or exceptional expenses. Many universities have committed to increasing the size of their hardship funds. The university decides which students need help and how much money to award them. These funds are often targeted at older or disadvantaged students, and finalists who are in danger of dropping out. The sums range up to a few thousand pounds, are not repayable and do not count against other income.

» Students with children can apply for a Childcare Grant, worth up to £159.59 a week if you have one child and up to £273.60 a week if you have two or more children under 15, or under 17 with special needs; and a Parents' Learning Allowance, for help with course-related costs, of between £50 and £1,617 a year.

» Any students with a partner, or another adult family member who is financially dependent on them, can apply for an Adult Dependants' Grant of up to £2,834 a year for 2017/18.

If you do not qualify for any of this kind of financial support you may still be able to apply for a Professional and Career Development Loan available from certain banks, in partnership with the National Careers Service. Students on a wide range of vocational courses can borrow from £300 to £10,000 at a fixed rate of interest to fund up to two years of learning, but the loans cannot be used for first full-time degrees.

Part-time work

The need to hold down a part-time job during term time is now a fact of life for almost half of students. Students from a working-class background are more likely to need to earn while they learn.

If you need to earn during term time, it is important to try to ensure that you do not work so many hours that it starts to affect your studies. A survey by the NUS found that 59 per cent of students who worked felt it had an impact on their studies, with 38 per cent missing lectures and over a fifth failing to submit coursework because of their part-time jobs. You may find that new universities are better geared-up to cope with working students than more traditional institutions.

Student employment agencies, which can now be found on many university campuses, can help you get the balance right. These introduce employers with work to students seeking work, sometimes even offering jobs within the university itself. But they also abide by codes of practice that regulate both minimum wages and the maximum number of hours worked in term time (typically 15 hours a week). Some firms, such as the big supermarkets, offer continuing part-time employment to their school part-time employees when they go to university. Some students make use of their expertise in areas like web design to earn some extra money, but most take on casual work in shops, restaurants, bars and call centres.

Most students, including those who don't work during term time, get a job during vacations. A Government survey found that 86 per cent of students in their second year of study or above worked during their summer vacation. Most of this kind of work is casual, but some is formalised in a scheme like STEP (**www.step.org.uk**) or may be part of a sponsorship programme. Many vacation jobs are mundane, but it is possible to find more interesting work. Some students broaden their experience by working abroad, others work as film extras, do tutoring, or do a variety of jobs at big events such as festivals. It is also a good idea to try to use the summer holidays to get some work experience in a field that has some relevance to your career aspirations. Even if you don't get paid, this can significantly enhance your chances of finding employment after graduation.

What you will need to spend money on
Living costs

Certain costs are unavoidable. You have to have a roof over your head, eat enough, clothe yourself, and probably do a certain amount of travelling. But the cost of even these essential items can be cut significantly through a mixture of shopping around and careful budgeting. If you set aside a certain amount of money a week for food, you will find it goes much further if you keep takeaways and ready-meals to a minimum, and stick to a shopping list when you go to a supermarket. Some catering outlets at your university or in the students' union may well offer good value meals, but probably the most economical way to eat is to cook and share meals with fellow students with whom you may be living in a shared house. Make sure you make full use of student travel cards and other offers and facilities available locally to help you cut the cost of travel. In certain locations, a bicycle is a worthwhile investment (as is buying a lock for it).

If you can keep your essential costs down, you will have more for what you would probably prefer to spend your money on – going out and personal items. Most students spend a proportion of their budget on socialising, and this is certainly an important part of the university experience. You can have plenty of fun and keep your leisure costs down by making the most of your student union's facilities and events.

It is easy to let "other costs" get out of hand to the extent that they start to eat into your budget for day-to-day living. A recent survey on behalf of the student housing app SPCE found that although students spend less than in the past on alcohol, and many spend no money on it, they are upping their gym bills and their travel spending. Mobile phone bills are a case in point: the latest edition of an annual survey of student life by RBS put average spending at £4.40 a week, but Sodexo found that some students were spending over £20 a week on their phones. Extras like downloading games or music, or sending pictures, can add significantly to your bill. Most of all, try to avoid getting tied up with an expensive and inflexible contract.

The SPCE survey also shows that students spend £157 a month on groceries and household items, but adds, more surprisingly, that they spend £179 on clothes, fashion and beauty products. An earlier survey by Sodexo suggested that half of all students have altered their eating and socialising habits for lack of money.

Studying costs

An NUS survey estimated that the average student spent about £1,000 a year on costs associated with course work and studying, mainly books and equipment. The amount you spend will be determined largely by the nature of your course and what you study. Additional financial support may be available for certain expenditure, but this is unlikely to cover you fully for spending on books, stationery, equipment, fieldwork or electives. A long reading list could prove very expensive if you tried to buy all the required books brand new. Find out as soon as possible which books are available either in your university library or local libraries. Another approach is to buy books second-hand from students who no longer need them. Your students' union or your university may run second-hand book sales or offer a service helping students to buy and sell books.

Overdrafts and credit cards

Other costs it is best to avoid are the more expensive forms of debt. Many banks offer free overdraft facilities for students, but if you go over the limit without prior arrangement, you can end up paying way over the odds for your borrowing. Credit cards can be useful if managed properly. The best way to manage a credit card is to set up a direct debit to pay off your balance in full every month, which means you will avoid paying any interest. One of the worst ways is just paying the minimum charge each month, which can cost you a small fortune over a long period. If you are the kind of person who spends impulsively and doesn't keep track of your spending, you are probably better off without a credit card. That way, you can't spend money you don't have.

Insurance

One kind of additional spending that can save you money is getting insurance cover for your possessions. Most students arrive at university with laptops and other goodies such as digital cameras, games consoles, mobile phones and bikes that are tempting to thieves. It is estimated that around a third of students fall victim to crime at some point during their time at university. If you shop around, you should be able to get a reasonable amount of cover for these kinds of items without it costing you an arm and a leg. It may also be possible to add this cover cheaply to your parents' domestic contents policy.

Planning your budget

One in four freshers spend their first student loan instalment in under a month, according to Endsleigh Insurance. But university websites, the National Union of Students and many others offer guidance on preparing a budget, usually with the basic headings provided for you to complete. First, list all your likely income (bursaries, loans, part-time work, savings, parental support) and then see how this compares with what you will spend. Try to be realistic, and not too optimistic, about both sides of the equation. With care, you will end up either only slightly in the red, or preferably far enough in the black for you to be able to afford things you would really like to spend your money on.

Above all, keep track of your finances so that your university experience isn't ruined by money worries, or finding you can't go to the ball because the cash machine has eaten your card. Spreadsheets make doing this simpler, and it is one skill you can learn at college that you are going to need for the rest of your life.

If all else fails, your campus almost certainly has a student money adviser who is a member of NASMA, the National Association of Student Money Advisers. You can find them via **www.nasma.org.uk**. NASMA reports that some students, especially those with children, are struggling financially. However, the bargains available in student shops can mean that you might not experience the most exorbitant prices on the high street.

More than two thirds of young people aged 18–24 say they received no financial education at school. This chimes with the experience of NASMA, which finds that many students have low levels of basic financial awareness and planning ability. In addition, advisers have noticed that students are increasingly likely to spend money they cannot afford on TV and online gambling, so make sure to avoid this temptation.

Useful websites

For the basics of fees, loans, grants and other allowances:
www.gov.uk/student-finance
www.gov.uk/browse/education/student-finance

UCAS provides helpful advice: **www.ucas.com/ucas/undergraduate/undergraduate-finance-and-support**

For England, visit Student Finance England: **www.sfengland.slc.co.uk**
Office for Fair Access: **www.offa.org.uk**
For Wales, visit Student Finance Wales: **www.studentfinancewales.co.uk**
For Scotland, visit the Student Awards Agency for Scotland: **www.saas.gov.uk**
For Northern Ireland, visit Student Finance Northern Ireland: **www.studentfinanceni.co.uk**

All UK student loans are administered by the Student Loans Company: **www.slc.co.uk**

For guidance on the tax position of students, visit HM Revenue and Customs:
www.gov.uk/student-jobs-paying-tax

For finding out about availability of scholarships: **www.scholarship-search.org.uk**

7 Finding Somewhere to Live

Choosing where to live is one of the first and most important decisions a student has to make. Getting it right will have an impact on your whole university experience – not only because it will determine how much money you have left for other activities, but because it will influence your work and whole state of mind. Particularly in your first year – and especially if it is your first time away from home – you are likely to be happier and more successful academically in accommodation of reasonable quality, preferably in a setting that helps you meet other students.

Fortunately, there is more choice than ever, with a number of private providers supplementing what universities and individual landlords provide. Many universities guarantee to provide accommodation for first-year undergraduates, and even those who cannot do this will offer help in finding somewhere of reasonable quality.

Of course, whatever you choose has to be affordable, but if your budget will stand it, you may well start off in a hall of residence or university flat. Three quarters of applicants hope to live in a hall of residence, but only 60 per cent actually do so, according to research by Unite Students. Indeed, the company's most recent UK survey showed halls gaining in popularity among second and third-year undergraduates, with the proportion opting for shared houses in their second year falling to little more than half.

With tastes apparently changing and the numbers going to university remaining high, student housing has become the biggest growth area in the property market. Rents have been rising at more than 3 per cent a year and billions of pounds have been committed to student residences.

Particularly in the big student cities, but increasingly in other university towns as well, student accommodation now comes in all shapes and sizes – and prices. Despite considerable expansion by universities themselves, property consultants JLL estimate that more than a third of residential places for students are now in private hands. Most of the developments are in big complexes, but there are also niche providers such as Student Cribs, which convert properties and rent them to students providing a rather higher spec than the traditional landlord.

Of the big providers, Unite Students has 50,000 beds in 28 towns and cities, some provided in partnership with universities and others in developments that serve more than one institution.

UPP manages over 32,000 residential places in complexes it has built for 15 universities, where rents are negotiated with the university, often in consultation with the students' union.

There is even an award for the best private halls of residence – won for the last four years by the Student Housing Company, which now has accommodation in 14 UK cities. The best university halls in 2017 were judged to be at Lancaster, with Edge Hill and Derby runners-up.

For most students, it will not matter whether the owner of their accommodation is the university, a private landlord or larger organisation if the quality and the price are right. But successive reports by the National Union of Students (NUS) have told a story of increasingly unaffordable rents, often poor facilities and rushed decisions by inexperienced students. While those who can afford it – or think they can – are living in luxury, NUS has found others coping with mice, slugs, mould, cold, or all of these. So it is worth putting some effort into basic decisions on this subject.

Living at home

Although student loan repayments start only after graduation, many undergraduates are understandably cautious about the debts they run up, so the option of avoiding big accommodation charges is a tempting one for those who are attracted by a local university. The pattern of recent applications shows that the trend towards studying at home is accelerating, albeit only gradually, and there is no reason to think that this will change in the near future. Indeed it may be a permanent shift, given the rising costs of student housing and the willingness of many young people to live with their parents well into their twenties.

The proportion of students living at home was already rising before undergraduate fees went up. Including mature students, many of whom live at home because of their family circumstances, the proportion is now close to 20 per cent. Among younger students, women are more likely than men to stay at home, and Asian women are particularly likely to take this option. Home study is also four times more common at post-1992 universities than older institutions, again reflecting the larger numbers of mature students at the newer universities and a generally younger and more affluent student population at the older ones.

Term-time type of accommodation of full-time and sandwich students

	2016/17
University maintained property	19.4%
Private-sector halls	7.8%
Parental/guardian home	18.8%
Own residence	16.7%
Other rented accommodation	29.8%
Other	3.4%
Not known	3.9%

HESA 2016 (adapted)

For those considering studying from home, there are important considerations, of which the relationship with your parents and the availability of quiet space are the most obvious ones. You will still be entitled to a maintenance loan, although for 2018–19 it is a maximum of £7,324 in England, rather than £8,700 if you were living away from home outside London. There may be advantages in terms of academic work if the alternative involves shopping, cooking and cleaning as well as the other distractions of a student flat. The downside is that you may miss out on a lot of the student experience, especially the social scene and the opportunity to make new friends.

A 2017 report by the Student Engagement Partnership found that students who live at home find life unexpectedly 'tiring, expensive and stressful'. Issues affecting their quality of life include travel, security and the lack of their own space. There is no evidence that students living at home do any worse academically, however. You can always move out at a later date if you think you are missing out – many initially home-based students do so in their second year.

Living away from home

Most of those who can afford it still see moving away to study as integral to the rite of passage that student life represents. Some have little option if, in spite of the expansion of higher education, the course they want is not available locally. Others are happy to travel to secure their ideal place and widen their experience.

For the lucky majority, the search for accommodation will be over quickly because the university can offer a place in one of its halls of residence or self-catering flats. The choice may come down to the type of accommodation and whether or not to do your own cooking. But for others, there will be an anxious search for a room in a strange city. Most universities will help with this if they cannot offer accommodation of their own.

Going to university will oblige those who take the "away" route to think for the first time about the practicalities of living independently. This can make the decision about where to live – in terms of location and the type of accommodation – doubly difficult. It may even influence your choice of university, since there are big differences across the sector and the country in the cost and standard of accommodation, and in its availability.

Most important factors for student accommodation

1	Location	39%
2	En suite facilities	36%
3	High speed Wifi	26%
4	Study space	18%
5	Overall cleanliness	16%
6	Multi-use outside games space	14%
=7	Security presence	12%
=7	On-site retail shop	12%
=7	24/7 helpdesk	12%
10	Gym	11%
=11	Environmentally friendly	10%
=11	Social space (café/bar)	10%
13	Cleaning service for room	8%
14	Laundrette	7%
15	Vending machines	5%

Sodexo University Lifestyle Survey, 2016)

How much will it cost?

Rents vary so much across the UK that national averages are almost meaningless. The 2017 NatWest Student Living Index found a range from £325 a month in Belfast to £560 in Exeter and £584 in London. All but five of the 35 student cities in the survey averaged more than £400 a month. However accurate such figures may be, they conceal a wide range of actual rents, particularly in London. This was always the case, but has become even more obvious with the rapid growth of a luxury market at the same time as many students are willing to accept sub-standard accommodation to keep costs down.

A series of recent reports suggest that the need for good Wi-Fi has overtaken reasonable rents as students' top priority in choosing accommodation. A big bedroom with a double bed was the other top priority for British students, according to a Europe-wide survey for the Uniplaces website. But obviously you have to be able to afford the rent in the first place. The last annual NUS/Unipol survey found a dwindling amount of "affordable" housing, judged against the loans available to students. Most universities with a range of accommodation find that their most expensive rooms fill up first, and that students appear to have higher expectations than they used to. More than half of all the rooms in the NUS survey had en-suite facilities.

It is important to remember that both your living costs and your potential earnings should be factored into your calculations when deciding where to live. While living costs in London are by far the highest, potential part-time earnings are also much higher than average. Taking account of both income and outgoings, the NatWest index made Cardiff the most affordable student city, followed by Aberdeen, where students were found to earn the most.

The choices you have

The NUS puts accommodation into 16 categories, ranging from luxurious university halls to a bedsit in a shared house. The choices include:

» University hall of residence, with individual study bedrooms and a full catering service. Many will have en-suite accommodation.
» University halls, flats or houses where you have to provide your own food.
» Private, purpose-built student accommodation.
» Rented houses or flats, shared with fellow students.
» Living at home.
» Living as a lodger in a private house.

This chapter will help you decide where you would like to live and whether you can afford it.

Making your choice

Finance is not the only factor you should consider when deciding where to live. It is worth investing time to find the right place, and to avoid the false economy of choosing somewhere cheap, where you may end up feeling depressed and isolated. Most students who drop out of university do so in the first few months, when homesickness and loneliness can be felt most acutely.

Being warm and well fed is likely to have a positive effect on your studies. Perhaps for these reasons, most undergraduates in their first year plump for living in university halls, which offer a convenient, safe and reliable standard of accommodation, along with a supportive community environment. The sheer number of students – especially first years – in halls also makes this form of accommodation an easy way of meeting people from a wide range of courses and making friends.

If meals are included, this extra adds further peace of mind both for students and their parents. The last NUS survey, which covered students in 2015–16, found that the difference in cost between full board and self-catering was less than £40 a week on average, not unreasonable for two hot meals a day. But only 7.6 per cent of places are now catered, compared with 27 per cent in 1994. Most are self-catering, with groups of students sharing a kitchen.

Wherever you choose to live, there are some general points you will need to consider, such as how safe the neighbourhood seems to be, and how long it might take you to travel to and from the university, especially during rush hour. A survey of travel time between term-time accommodation and the university found that most students in London can expect a commute of at least 30 minutes and often over an hour, while students living in Wales are usually much less than 30 minutes away from their university.

In chapter 14, we provide details of what accommodation each university offers, covering the number of places, the costs, and policy towards first-year students.

What universities offer

You might think that opting to live in university accommodation is the most straightforward choice, especially since first-year students are invariably given priority in the allocation of places in halls of residence, and it is possible to arrange university accommodation in advance and at a distance. Searching for private housing can often be a matter of having to be in the right place at the right time. However, you may still need to select from a range of options, because most universities will have a variety of accommodation on offer. You will need to consider which best suits your pocket and your preferred lifestyle.

New student accommodation

At the top end of the market, private firms usually lead the way, at least in the bigger student cities. Companies such as UPP, Unite Students and Liberty Living offer some of the most luxurious student accommodation the UK sector has ever seen, either in partnerships with universities or in their own right. Rooms in these complexes are nearly always en suite and with internet access and may include other facilities such as your own phone line and satellite TV. Shared kitchens are top-quality and fitted out with all the latest equipment.

This kind of accommodation naturally comes at a higher price, but offers the advantages of flexibility both in living arrangements and through a range of payment options. An earlier NUS survey found little difference between the rents charged by higher education institutions for their own accommodation and those for rooms managed by private companies under contract, but private providers operating outside institutional links charged over £20 a week more.

Halls of residence

Many new or recently refurbished university-owned halls offer a standard of accommodation that is not far short of the privately built residences. This is partly because rooms in these halls can be offered to conference delegates during vacations. Even though these halls are also at the pricier end of the spectrum, you will probably find that they are in great demand, and you may have to get your name down quickly to secure one of the fancier rooms. That said, you can often get a guarantee of some kind of university accommodation if you give a firm acceptance of an offered place by a certain date in the summer. If you have gained your place through Clearing, this option may not apply, although rooms in private halls might still be on offer at this stage.

While a few halls are single-sex, most are mixed, and often house over 500 students. Indeed, in student villages the numbers are now counted in thousands. They are therefore great places for making friends and becoming part of the social scene. Almost nine out of ten applicants surveyed for the Reality Check report by the Higher Education Policy Institute, in association with UNITE, said the ability to make friends was more important than the specification of the accommodation. Two-thirds put a priority on the availability of social events where they lived, particularly in their first term.

One possible downside is that such developments can also be noisy places where it can be difficult at times to get down to some work. Indeed, 44 per cent of those responding to another Unite survey identified noise as the biggest challenge in student accommodation. For those who had experienced it, peace and quiet was a higher priority than access to public transport or good nightlife. The more successful students learn, before too many essay deadlines and exams start to loom, to get the balance right between all-night partying and escaping to the library for some undisturbed study time. Remember that some libraries, especially new ones, are now open 24 hours a day.

University self-catering accommodation

An alternative to halls, now offered by most universities, are smaller, self-catering properties fitted out with a shared kitchen and other living areas. The Reality Check report found that almost half of all university applicants felt a degree of anxiety about the prospect of living with people they had never met. This applied particularly to those from lower socio-economic groups. But students looking for a more independent and flexible lifestyle often prefer this option, which is now the norm at many universities. As well as having to feed yourself, you may also have heating and lighting bills to pay. University properties are often on campus or nearby, so travel costs should not be a problem.

Catering in university accommodation

Many universities have responded to a general increase in demand from students for a more independent lifestyle by providing more flexible catering facilities. A range of eateries, from fast food outlets to more traditional refectories, can usually be found on campus or in student villages. Students in university accommodation may be offered pay-as-you-eat deals as an alternative to full-board packages.

What after the first year?

After your first year of living in university residences you may well wish, and will probably be expected, to move out to other accommodation. The main exceptions are the collegiate universities – particularly Oxford and Cambridge – which may allow you to stay on in college for another year or two, and particularly for your final year. Students from outside the EU are also often guaranteed accommodation. At a growing number of universities, where there is a sufficiently large stock of residential accommodation, it is not uncommon for students to move back in to halls for their final year.

Practical details

Whether or not you have decided to start out in university accommodation, you will probably be expected to sign an agreement to cover your rent. Contract lengths vary. They can be for around 40 weeks, which includes the Christmas and Easter holiday periods, or for just the length of the three university terms. These term-time contracts are common when a university uses its rooms for conferences during vacations, and you will be required to leave your room empty during these weeks. It is therefore advisable to check whether the university has secure storage space for you to leave your belongings. Otherwise you will have to make arrangements to take all your belongings home or to store them privately between terms. International students may be offered special arrangements by which they can stay in halls during the short vacation periods. Organisations like **www.hostuk.org** can arrange for international students to stay in a UK family home at holiday times such as Christmas.

Parental purchases

One option for affluent families is to buy a house or flat and take in student lodgers. This might not be the safe bet it once appeared, but it is still tempting for many parents. Agents Knight Frank have had a student division since 2007, mostly working with new developers to sell specially adapted homes. Those who are considering this route tend to do so from their first year of study to maximise the return on the investment.

Being a lodger or staying in a hostel

A small number of students live as a lodger in a family home, an option most frequently taken up by international students. The usual arrangement is for a study bedroom and some meals to be provided, while other facilities such as the washing machine are shared. Students with particular religious affiliations or those from certain countries may wish to consider living in a hostel run by a charity catering for a specific group. Most of these are in London.

Renting from the private sector

Around a third of students live in privately rented flats or houses. Every university city or town is awash with such accommodation, available via agencies or direct from landlords. Indeed, this type of accommodation has grown to the point where so-called "student ghettoes", in which local residents feel outnumbered have become hot political issues in some cities. Into this traditional market in rented flats and houses have come the new private-sector complexes and residences, adding to the options. Some are on university campuses, but others are in city centres and usually open to students of more than one university. Examples can be seen online; some sites are listed at the end of this chapter.

While there are always exceptions, a much more professional attitude and approach to managing rented accommodation has emerged among smaller providers, thanks to a combination of greater regulation and increasing competition. Nevertheless, it is wise to take certain precautions when seeking out private residences.

How to start looking for rented property

Contact your university's accommodation service and ask for its list of approved rented properties. Some have a Student Accommodation Accreditation Scheme, run in collaboration with the local council. To get onto an approved list under such schemes, landlords must show they are adhering to basic standards of safety and security, such as having an up-to-date gas and electric safety certificate. University accommodation officers should also be able to advise you on any hidden charges. For instance, you may be asked to pay a booking or reservation fee to secure a place in a particular property, and fees for references or drawing up a tenancy agreement are sometimes charged. The practice of charging a "joining fee", however, has been outlawed.

It would be wise to speak to older students with first-hand experience of renting in the area. Certain companies in the area may be notorious among second and third years and you can try to avoid them. In addition to websites and accommodation services designed for students, you can also use sites such as Gumtree that cater for the population at large.

Making a choice

Once you have made an initial choice of the area you would like to live in and the size of property you are looking for, the next stage is to look at possible places. If you plan to share, it is important that you all have a look at the property. If you will be living by yourself, take a friend with you when you go to view a property, since he or she can help you assess what you see objectively, and avoid any irrational or rushed on-the-spot decisions. Don't let yourself be pushed into signing on the dotted line there and then. Take time to visit and consider a number of options, as well as checking out the local facilities, transport and the general environment at various times of the day and different days of the week.

If you are living in private rented accommodation, it is likely that at least some of your neighbours will not be students. Local people often welcome students, but resentment can build up, particularly in areas of towns and cities that are dominated by student housing. It is important to respect your neighbours' rights, and not to behave in an anti-social manner.

Preparing for sharing

The people you are planning to share a house with may have some habits that you find at least mildly irritating. How well you cope with some of the downsides of sharing will be partly down to the kind of person you are – where you are on the spectrum between laid back and highly strung – but it will help a lot if you are co-habiting with people whose outlook on day-to-day living is not too far out of line with your own. According to Unite Students, 31 per cent of female students find sharing more difficult than they had expected, compared with 22 per cent of men.

Some students sign for their second year houses as early as November. While it is good to be ahead of the rush, you may not yet have met your best friends at this stage. If you have not selected your own group of friends, universities and landlords can help by taking personal preferences and lifestyle into account when grouping tenants together.

Potential issues to consider when deciding whether to move into a shared house include whether any of the housemates smoke or own a loud musical instrument. It will also be important to sort out broadband arrangements that will work for everyone in the house, and that you will be able to arrange access to the university system. It is a good idea to agree a rota for everyone to share in the household cleaning chores from the start. Otherwise, it is almost certain that you will live in a state of unhygienic squalor or that one or two individuals will be left to clear up everyone else's mess.

The practical details about renting

It is a good idea to ask whether your house is covered by an accreditation scheme or code of standards. Such codes provide a clear outline of what constitutes good practice as well as the responsibilities of both landlords and tenants. Adhering to schemes like the National Code of Standards for Larger Student Developments compiled by Accreditation Network UK (**www.anuk.org.uk**) may well become a requirement for larger properties, including those managed by universities, now that the Housing Act is in force.

At the very least, make sure that if you are renting from a private landlord, you have his or her telephone number and home address. Some can be remarkably difficult to contact when repairs are needed or deposits are due to be returned.

Multiple occupation

If you are renting a private house it may be subject to the 2004 Housing Act in England and Wales (similar legislation applies in Scotland and Northern Ireland). Licences are compulsory for all private Houses in Multiple Occupation (HMOs) with three or more storeys and that house five or more unrelated residents. The provisions of the Act also allow local authorities to designate whole areas in which HMOs of all sizes must be licensed. The regulations may be applied in sections of university towns and cities where most students live. This means that a house must be licensed, well-managed and must meet various health and safety standards, and its owner subject to various financial regulations.

Tenancy agreements

Whatever kind of accommodation you go for, you must be sure to have all the paperwork in order and be clear about what you are signing up to before you move in. If you are taking up residence in a shared house, flat or bedsit, the first document you will have to grapple with is a tenancy agreement or lease offering you an "assured shorthold tenancy". Since this is a binding legal document, you should be prepared to go through every clause with a fine-tooth comb. Remember that it is much more difficult to make changes or overcome problems arising from unfair agreements once you are a tenant than before you become one.

You would be well advised to seek help in the likely event of your not fully understanding some of the clauses. Your university accommodation office or students' union is a good place to start – they should know all the ins and outs, and have model tenancy agreements to refer to. A Citizens Advice Bureau or Law Advice Centre should also be able to offer you free advice. In particular, watch out for clauses that may make you jointly responsible for the actions of others with whom you are sharing the property. If you name a parent as a guarantor to cover any costs not paid by you, they may also be liable for charges levied on all tenants for damage that was not your fault. A rent review clause could allow your landlord to increase the rent at will, whereas without such a clause, they are restricted to one rent rise a year. Make sure you keep a copy of all documents, and get a receipt (and keep it somewhere safe) for anything you have had to pay for that is the landlord's responsibility.

Contracts with private landlords tend to be longer than for university accommodation. They will frequently commit you to paying rent for 52 weeks of the year. Leaving aside the cost, there are probably more advantages than disadvantages to this kind of arrangement. It means you don't have to move out during vacation periods, which you will have to in most university halls. You can store your belongings in your room when you go away (but don't leave anything really valuable behind if you can help it). You may be able to negotiate a rent discount for those periods when you are not staying in the property. The other advantage, particularly important for cash-strapped students, is that you have a base from which to find work and hold down a job during the vacations. Term dates are also not as dictatorial as they might be in halls; if you rent your own house then you can come back when you wish.

Security in rented accommodation

Students in private housing are twice as likely to be burgled as those in university halls. When looking at accommodation, use this NUS security checklist:

» Check that the front and back doors are fitted with five-lever mortise locks in addition to standard catch locks.
» Make sure the door to your room has a lock, and always lock up when you leave it, especially for long periods such as during vacations.
» Check the locks and catches on accessible windows, especially those at ground-floor level.
» Before you move in, try to talk to neighbours about how safe the area is and whether there have been many instances of burglary.
» Ask your landlord to ensure that all previous tenants and holders of keys no longer have copies.
» If you find a property that you like but have some security concerns, discuss these with the letting agency or landlord.

Deposits

On top of the agreed rent, you will need to provide a deposit or bond to cover any breakages or damage. This will probably set you back the equivalent of another month's rent. The deposit should be returned, less any deductions, at the end of the contract. However, be warned that disputes over the return of deposits are common, with the question of what constitutes reasonable wear and tear often the subject of disagreements between landlord and tenant. To protect students from unscrupulous landlords who withheld deposits without good reason, the 2004 Housing Act introduced a National Tenancy Deposit Scheme under which deposits are held by an independent body. This is designed to ensure that deposits are fairly returned, and that any disputes are resolved swiftly and cheaply.

Inventories and other paperwork

You should get an inventory and schedule of condition of everything in the property. This is another document that you should check very carefully – and make sure that everything listed is as described. Write on the document anything that is different. The NUS even suggests taking photographs of rooms and equipment when you first move in (setting the correct date on your camera), to provide you with additional proof should any dispute arise when your contract ends and you want to get your deposit back. If you are not offered an inventory, then make one of your own. You should have someone else witness and sign this, send it to your landlord, and keep your own copy. Keeping in contact with your landlord throughout the year and developing a good relationship with him or her will also do you no harm, and may be to your advantage in the long run.

You should ask your landlord for a recent gas safety certificate issued by a qualified CORGI engineer, a fire safety certificate covering the furnishings, and a record of current gas and electricity meter readings. Take your own readings of meters when you move in to make sure these match up with what you have been given, or make your own records if the landlord doesn't supply this information. This also applies to water meters if you are expected to pay water rates (although this isn't usually the case).

Finally, students are not liable for Council Tax. If you are sharing a house only with other full-time students, then you will not have to pay it. However, you may be liable to pay a proportion of the Council Tax bill if you are sharing with anyone who is not a full-time student. You may need to get a Council Tax exemption certificate from your university as evidence that you do not need to pay Council Tax.

Safety and security

Once you have arrived and settled in, remember to take care of your own safety and the security of your possessions. You are particularly vulnerable as a fresher, when you are still getting used to your new-found independence. This may help explain why so many students are burgled or robbed in the first six weeks of the academic year. Take care with valuable portable items such as mobile phones, tablet computers and laptops, all of which are tempting for criminals. Ensure you don't have them obviously on display when you are out and about and that you have insurance cover. If your mobile phone is stolen, call your network or 08701 123123 to immobilise it. Students' unions, universities and the police will provide plenty of practical guidance when you arrive. Following their advice will reduce the chance of you becoming a victim of crime, and help you to enjoy living in the new surroundings of your chosen university town.

Useful websites

For advice on a range of housing issues, visit: **www.nus.org.uk/en/advice/housing-advice**

The Shelter website has separate sections covering different housing regulations in England, Wales, Scotland and Northern Ireland: **www.shelter.org.uk**

As examples of providers of private hall accommodation, visit:
www.upp-ltd.com
http://www.unitestudents.com/
www.libertyliving.co.uk
http://thestudenthousingcompany.com

A number of sites will help you find accommodation and/or potential housemates, including:
www.accommodationforstudents.com
www.sturents.com,
www.studentpad.co.uk
www.let4students.com
http://student.spareroom.co.uk
http://uk.easyroommate.com

8 Enjoying University Sport

Some of the best and most extensive sports facilities in the UK are at universities. Such has been the scale of investment in recent years that nationally, they are said to be worth an astonishing £20 billion. Nottingham opened a £40-million sports complex in 2016 and Southampton Solent began work on a £28-million sports development last summer. Such facilities attract elite performers and are often used for high-level teaching, but they are also available for day-to-day use by undergraduates. Two thirds of students take part in sport of some sort while at university and more than half of all students now exercise at least once a week.

The quality of the sports facilities will not be the clinching factor in most applicants' choice of university – and nor should it be – but nearly a third say it played some part in their decision-making. Universities are well aware of this and have upgraded their provision accordingly. Most people will never again have as much opportunity to exercise and play different sports as they do in their undergraduate years. Even those whose timetable dictates long hours in the laboratory will find plenty of opportunities available in the evenings and at weekends.

Especially at the big universities – but also at many of the smaller ones – sporting provision is now both diverse and high quality. Half of all universities were chosen as training bases for Great Britain squads in the run-up to the 2012 Olympic Games and 30 hosted other nations' teams. Comparing such facilities is not easy, but most universities display them prominently on their websites. There are brief descriptions of the bigger developments in the university profiles in chapter 14.

At the elite level, university sport has never been stronger. At the Rio Olympics in 2016, more than half Team GB's medals were won by university students or alumni. Five of the gold medal-winning ladies hockey team (and the coach) were Loughborough graduates, for example. Indeed, Loughborough would have been 17th in the overall medal table in Rio, taking into account all its successes for Team GB and other countries. It was not the only successful university – St Mary's, Twickenham, would have been 25th in the table. Such successes are the result of considerable investment in sports scholarships and training programmes, as well as campus facilities.

Naturally, most students will never aspire to such heights, but may still welcome the chance to use top-grade facilities. Research for British Universities and Colleges Sport (BUCS) suggests that at least 1.7 million students take part in regular physical activity, from gym sessions to competitive individual or team sports. There are good reasons, beyond fitness, for doing so, according to the BUCS research. In 2013, graduates who had played and/or volunteered in sport were found to be earning between £4,624 and £5,616 more than those who had not, and were 25 per cent less likely to have been unemployed. Nine out of ten employers thought that participation in university sport helped to develop valuable skills in potential employees.

Sporting opportunities

Some specialist facilities may be reserved at times for elite performers, but all universities are conscious of the need for wider access. Surveys show that two-thirds of sessions at university sports facilities are taken by students, roughly a quarter by the local community and the rest by staff. Many institutions still encourage departments not to schedule lectures and seminars on Wednesday afternoons, to give students free time for sport. There are student-run clubs for all the major sports and – particularly at the larger universities – a host of minor ones. In addition, there are high-quality gyms, with staff on hand to devise personalised training regimes and to run popular activities such as Zumba and Pilates. The cost varies widely between universities, and membership fees can represent a large amount to lay out at the start of the year, but most provide good value if you are going to be a regular user.

Sport for all

For most universities, it is in the area of "sport for all" that most attention has been focused. Beginners are welcomed and coaching provided in a range of sports, from Ultimate Frisbee to tai-chi, that would be difficult to match outside the higher education system. Check on university websites to see whether your usual sport is available, but do not be surprised if you come across a new favourite when you have the opportunity to try out something different. Many universities have programmes designed to encourage students to take up a new sport, with expert coaching provided.

All universities are conscious of the need to provide for a spread of ability – and disability. Sports scholarships for elite performers are now commonplace, but there will be plenty of opportunities, too, for beginners. University teams demand a hefty commitment in terms of training and practice sessions – often several times a week – and in many sports standards are high. University teams often compete in local and national leagues.

For those who are looking for competition at a lower level, or whose interests are primarily social, there are thriving internal, or intramural, leagues. These provide opportunities for halls of residence or faculties, or even a group of friends, to form a team and participate on a regular basis. A recent BUCS survey found 41,000 participants in the intramural programmes of 41 institutions. The largest programme was at the University of Brighton, where more than 6,000 students were playing sports ranging from football, rugby and badminton to softball, orienteering and fencing. Nor is university sport a male preserve – student teams were among the pioneers in mixed sport and are still strong in areas such as women's cricket, football and rugby.

Some universities have cut back sports budgets, but representative sport continues to grow. There are plans for a home nations competition at international level and in London, 33 institutions take part in the London Universities Sport League. This now involves more than 450 teams – male, female and mixed – competing at a variety of levels in 14 different sports, not all of which are in the main national competitions.

First-year sport

Halls of residence and university-owned flats will often have their own sports teams. At some universities, these are part of the intramural network of leagues, while others have separate arrangements for first years. In such cases, a Sports Captain, elected the year previously as part of the Junior Common Room, takes responsibility for organising trials and picking the teams, as well as arranging fixtures for the year. Hall sport is a great way of meeting like-minded people from your accommodation and over the course of the years, friendly rivalries often develop with other halls or flats. Generally, there will be teams for football (both five and 11-a-side), hockey, netball, cricket, tennis, squash, badminton and even golf. If your lodgings are smaller, they are often twinned with similar flats to enable as many first-year students as possible to get involved in freshers' sport.

Other opportunities

You may end up wanting to coach, umpire or referee – and this is another area in which higher education has much to offer. Many university clubs and sports unions provide subsidised courses for students to gain qualifications that may be of use in later life, as well as benefiting university teams in the short term. Or you might want to try your hand at some sports administration, with an eye to your career. In most universities there is a sports (or athletic) union, with autonomy from the main students' union, which organises matches and looks after the wider interests of those who play. There are plenty of opportunities for those seeking an apprenticeship in the art of running a club, or larger organisation. Southampton Solent University, for example, deploy students on volunteer coaching placements in more than 70 local schools. These placements increase a university's community engagement as well as enhancing student employability with minimal investment.

Universities that excel

A few universities are known particularly for sport. Exeter and Loughborough men's teams have played national Premier League hockey, for example, while Bath, Loughborough and Northumbria have teams in the Netball Super League. The University of London women's volleyball team has won the English Volleyball Championships, and "Team Bath" have tasted success in the FA Cup. Several of this elite group had a head start as former physical education colleges. Loughborough is probably the best-known of them, but Leeds Beckett and Brunel are others with a similar pedigree. Other universities with different traditions, such as Bath and East Anglia, also have a variety of outstanding facilities, while the likes of Stirling and Cardiff Metropolitan have the same in a narrower range of sports.

As in so much else, Oxford and Cambridge are in a category of their own. The Boat Race and the Varsity Match (in rugby union) are the only UK university sporting events with a big popular following – although there are varsity matches in several university cities that have become big occasions for students – and there is a good standard of competition in other sports. But you should not assume that success in school sport will be a passport to an Oxbridge place, for the days of special consideration for sporty undergraduates are long since over.

Representative sport

Competitive standards have been rising in university sport, as have the numbers taking part in it. More than 6,000 students competed in ten sports at the 2017 BUCS Nationals in Sheffield. BUCS (**www.bucs.org.uk**) runs competitions in almost 50 sports, and ranks participating institutions based on the points earned in the competitive programme. Over 4,700 teams compete in BUCS leagues, making the organisation the largest provider of league sport across Europe. More than a third of those teams are female and many others mixed. There is also international competition in a number of sports, and the World Student Games have become one of the biggest occasions in the international sporting calendar.

BUCS is the national organisation for higher education sport in the UK, providing a comprehensive, multi-sport competition structure and managing the development of services and facilities for participative, grass-roots sport and healthy campuses, through to high-performance elite athletes. Its mission is to raise the profile of student sport and drive the university sport agenda by influencing government and key stakeholders in the sector.

British Universities and Colleges Sports (BUCS) league table positions

University	2016–17	2015–16	University	2016–17	2015–16
Loughborough	1	1	Bournemouth	31	30
Durham	2	2	Southampton	32	22
Edinburgh	3	3	Swansea	33	33
Nottingham	4	4	Essex	34	32
Exeter	5	5	Oxford Brookes	35	31
Bath	6	7	Manchester Metropolitan (MMU)	36	38
Birmingham	7	6	King's College London	37	37
Northumbria	8	8	Brunel	38	36
Bristol	9	13	Leicester	39	46
Newcastle	10	9	Gloucestershire	40	49
Cardiff	11	11	Sussex	41	43
Stirling	12	17	East London	42	48
Oxford	13	10	East Anglia	43	55
Leeds Beckett	14	12	Reading	44	39
Nottingham Trent	15	19	Hertfordshire	45	44
Leeds	16	14	York	46	40
Manchester	17	18	St Mary's, Twickenham	47	59
Cambridge	18	16	Kent	48	51
Sheffield	19	21	Lancaster	49	45
Sheffield Hallam	20	23	Aberdeen	50	42
Cardiff Metropolitan	21	15	Plymouth	51	53
Glasgow	22	26	Coventry	52	47
Warwick	23	20	LSE	53	62
Imperial College	24	24	Dundee	54	54
St Andrews	25	29	Portsmouth	55	41
Strathclyde	26	34	Chichester	56	57
University College London	27	27	Derby	57	64
West of England (UWE)	28	35	Southampton Solent	58	71
Surrey	29	28	South Wales	59	50
Liverpool	30	25	Worcester	60	61

University	2016–17	2015–16	University	2016–17	2015–16
Brighton	61	52	FXU (Falmouth and Exeter Students' Union)	104	104
Royal Holloway	62	56	Liverpool Hope	105	105
Bangor	63	66	Queen's, Belfast	106	102
Queen Mary, University of London	=64	58	Leeds Trinity	107	116
Heriot-Watt	=64	60	St George's, University of London	108	107
Liverpool John Moores	66	69	Birmingham City	109	117
Central Lancashire	67	63	Queen Margaret Edinburgh	110	115
Aberystwyth	=68	70	Bishop Burton College, Yorks	111	-
Hartpury University centre	=68	76	Highlands and Islands	112	110
Anglia Ruskin	70	65	Greenwich	113	111
University of London	71	77	Westminster	114	112
Chester (Chester)	72	72	Royal Agricultural University	115	118
Lincoln	73	67	UCFB (Football Business)	116	-
Robert Gordon	74	68	Cranfield University	117	
De Montfort	75	84	Newman	118	126
Hull	76	79	Bath Spa	119	119
Keele	77	73	Ulster	120	131
Canterbury Christ Church	78	73	Goldsmiths	121	138
Edinburgh Napier	79	83	West London	=122	135
Edge Hill	80	85	Universities at Medway	=122	
Middlesex	81	78	London Metropolitan	124	131
St Mark and St John (Marjon)	82	75	Trinity Saint David (Carmarthen)	125	108
Northampton	83	81	Royal Veterinary College	126	-
Kingston	84	80	Trinity Saint David (Swansea)	127	127
Abertay	85	93	University of the Arts London	=128	130
City	86	87	South Glos & Stroud College	=128	-
Bradford	87	89	Chester (Warrington)	130	124
Glasgow Caledonian	88	90	Guildford College (Merrist Wood)	131	-
Aston	89	97	SOAS	132	142
Staffordshire	90	99	BPP University	133	-
Roehampton	91	91	Dundee & Angus College	134	-
London South Bank	92	96	Doncaster College & Uni centre	135	-
Wolverhampton	93	98	Bolton	=136	143
York St John	94	86	Edinburgh College	=136	-
Bedfordshire	=95	82	Bishop Grosseteste	=138	135
West of Scotland	=95	109	Wrexham Glyndŵr	=138	125
Buckinghamshire New	97	94	University College Birmingham	=138	128
Harper Adams	98	103	Tottenham Hotspur Foundation	=138	-
Sunderland	99	92	Richmond, American University	=138	-
Wolverhampton (Walsall)	98		West College Scotland	=138	-
Winchester	100	100	North East College Scotland	=138	-
Salford	=101	88	Cumbria	145	121
Huddersfield	=101	95	Writtle University College	=146	-
Teesside	103	101	Borders College	=146	-

University	2016–17	2015–16	University	2016–17	2015–16
University of Law	=148	-	City of Liverpool, College	=154	
New College Lanarkshire	=148	-	Dumfries & Galloway College	=154	-
Glasgow Kelvin College	=148	-	Trinity Saint David (Lampeter)	=154	144
Eaton & Otley College	151	-	City of Glasgow College	=154	-
University for Creative Arts	152	144	West Lothian College	=154	-
Glasgow Clyde College	153	-	University Centre Peterborough	=154	-
Suffolk	=154	141	Leeds College of Art	=154	-
University of Chester (Shrewsbury)	=154	-			

University sports facilities

Even the smallest university should provide reasonable indoor and outdoor sports facilities – a sports hall, modern gym equipment and outdoor pitches (usually including an all-weather surface and floodlights). Many will also have a swimming pool and extras such as climbing walls, but some smaller universities make arrangements for students to use local sports centres and clubs when it is not feasible to provide for minority sports. The same goes for the really expensive sports, like golf, which is usually the subject of an arrangement with one or more local clubs that give students a discount. Specialist facilities, like boat houses and climbing huts, obviously depend on location, but the most landlocked university is likely to have a sailing club that organises regular activities away from campus, and a skiing club that runs at least annual trips to the mountains.

Developments at many universities have come in partnership with local authorities or national sporting bodies. University campuses are ideal locations for national coaching centres, and many have been established in recent years. Although elite coaching generally takes place in closed sessions, students may occasionally find themselves rubbing shoulders with star players.

Universities now boast a significant proportion of the UK's 50-metre pools, for example, the latest of which, at the University of Surrey, has some of the most advanced facilities in the country. Innovative schemes include Leeds Beckett's development of the Headingley cricket and rugby league grounds, providing teaching space for students during the week and improved facilities for players and spectators on match days.

Beyond scrutinising the website and prospectus for the extent of university facilities, there are two important questions to ask: how much do they cost and where are they? Neither is easy to track down on the average university website.

How much?

University prospectuses tend to major on the quality of the sports facilities without being so forthcoming about the prices. Students who are used to free (if inferior) facilities at school often get a nasty surprise when they find that they are expected to pay to join the Athletic Union and then pay again to use the gym or play football. Because most university sport is subsidised, the charges are reasonable compared to commercial facilities, but the best deal may require a considerable outlay at the start. Some campus gyms and swimming pools now charge more than £300 a year, for example, which is still considerably cheaper than paying per visit if you intend to use the facilities regularly (and provides an incentive to carry on doing so). Some universities are offering sports facility membership as part of the £9,250 fee, but most offer a variety of peak and off-peak membership packages – some for the entire length of your course.

Outdoor sports are usually charged by the hour, although clubs will also charge a membership fee. You may be required to pay up to £60 for membership of the Athletic Union (although not all universities demand this). Fees for intramural sport are seldom substantial; teams will usually pay a fee for the season, while courts for racket sports tend to be marginally cheaper per session than in other clubs.

How far away?

The other common complaint by students is that the playing fields are too far from the campus – understandable in the case of city-centre universities, but still aggravating if you have to arrange your own transport. This is where campus universities have a clear advantage. For the rest, there has to be some trade-off between the quality of outdoor facilities and the distance you have to travel to use them. But universities are beginning to realise that long journeys depress usage of important and expensive facilities, and some have tried to find suitable land closer to lectures and halls of residence. Indoor sports centres should all be within easy reach.

Sport as a degree subject

Sports science and other courses associated with sport had seen consistent increases in applications until the imposition of higher fees, and their popularity has now returned. Over 15,000 students started courses in 2017, and it is one of the ten most popular degree subjects for applicants. A separate ranking for the subject is on page 262. If you are hoping to be rewarded with an academic qualification for three years on the sports field, you will be disappointed because there is serious science involved.

However, sport is a growing employment field and one that demands qualifications like any other. It is even spawning whole new higher education institutions. The University College of Football Business (UCFB) is already offering undergraduate degrees at Wembley Stadium, its original home at Burnley's Turf Moor ground, and at the Etihad Stadium, in Manchester. And now Gary Neville, the former Manchester United captain and television pundit, is planning to open University Academy '92, in Manchester, in partnership with Lancaster University, offering sport, business and media degrees, from September 2019.

Many existing degrees in the sports area focus on management, with careers in the leisure industry in mind – golf course management, for example, has proved popular with students despite being a target of those who see anything beyond the traditional academic portfolio as "dumbing down". The question is not whether the courses are up to standard, but whether a less specialised one will offer more career flexibility if a decline in popularity for the particular sport limits future opportunities.

Sports scholarships

The number and range of sports scholarships have expanded just as rapidly as courses in the subject, but the two are usually not connected. Sports scholarships are for elite performers, regardless of what they are studying – indeed, they exist at universities with barely any degrees in the field. Imported from the USA, scholarships now exist in an array of sports. At Birmingham University, for example, there are specialist golf awards (as there are at a number of other universities) and a scholarship for triathletes, as well as others open to any sport.

The value of scholarships varies considerably – sometimes according to individual prowess. The Royal and Ancient scholarships for golfers, for example, range from £500 for promising handicap golfers to £10,000 for full internationals, and are available at 15 universities. All of them demand that you meet the normal entrance requirements for your course and maintain the necessary academic standards, as well as progressing in your sport. In practice, most departments will be flexible about attendance and deadlines, as long as you make your requests well in advance.

Many sports scholarships offer benefits in kind, in the form of coaching, equipment or access to facilities. The Government-funded Talented Athlete Scholarship Scheme (TASS), which is restricted to students at English universities who have achieved national recognition at under-18 level and are eligible to represent England in one of 30 different sports, is one such example. No fewer than 165 current or former TASS athletes took part in the Rio Olympics and Paralympics, winning 78 medals, 35 of them gold. The scholarships are worth £3,500 a year and can be put towards costs such as competition and training costs, equipment or mentoring. In 2017–18, more than 500 student athletes were supported across a wide range of sports. The Scottish equivalent, Winning Students Scotland awards scholarships worth up to £6,000 a year for training, competition fees and other expenses such as student accommodation. Further details of the two schemes are available at **www.tass.gov.uk** and **www.winningstudents-scotland.ac.uk**.

Leading performers in many sports still look first to US universities – often unfamiliar ones – for sports scholarships. In some sports, such as American football or basketball, this is the main route into professional sport, while in others it may provide bigger awards – and in some cases better coaching – than are available in the UK. Half of the UK's six-strong tennis team at the 2015 World Student Games were from US universities. The gold medal winners in the men's doubles, Darren Walsh and Joe Salisbury, were from the Southern Methodist University in Texas and the University of Memphis respectively – not household names on this side of the Atlantic. For the most promising athletes, US scholarships can cover the full cost of university; for others they may be worth only a few thousand dollars, but may make the difference in gaining admission. Further details are available at **www.fulbright.org.uk/study-in-the-usa/undergraduate-study/funding/sports-scholarships**.

Part-time work

University sports centres are an excellent source of term-time (and out-of-term) employment. You may also be trained in first aid, fire safety, customer care and risk assessment – all useful skills for future employment. The experience will help you secure employment in commercial or local authority facilities – and even for jobs such as stewarding at football grounds and music venues. Most universities also have a sabbatical post in the Athletic Union or similar body, a paid position with responsibility for organising university sport and representing the sporting community within the university.

9 How Parents Can Help

Parents are more involved in the higher education process than they have ever been. Many take an active role in selecting courses, may have their say subsequently on the student experience – and, of course, contribute large sums towards their children's time at university. Under such circumstances, there is a thin line between helping and meddling. But it is a balance that every parent wants to get right – and naturally the same applies to step-parents and guardians.

Nearly half of all parents in the UK think university is now poor value for money, according to a survey by HSBC. But a larger proportion also believe that higher education is essential to their children's career prospects and are willing to help them through it. Nine out of ten expect to make a financial contribution to their children's time at university – and to spend up to eight years paying off the debts they incur in the process.

The introduction of £9,000 fees was meant to make the student responsible for his or her higher education – including paying for it – but parents' involvement has, if anything, increased under the new system. That is because most parents are paying towards students' living costs, not their tuition. Maintenance loans may be larger than they were, but very few students will get by on them alone. For undergraduates outside London, they range from £8,700 for students with a family income below £25,000 to £4,054 with a family income above £62,215 for 2018–19. Those parents who can, are often anxious to spare their children yet more debt on top of the cost of tuition. Surprising numbers of students from affluent families are not taking out loans at all, and are relying instead on support from parents or sometimes grandparents. Up to half the students at some leading universities are doing without Government maintenance loans, although throughout England, well over 80 per cent are taking them up.

On average, according to HSBC, parents of university students in the UK spend more than £18,000 helping their children through higher education. This is considerably less than the average in the 15 countries in the bank's survey, which were mainly in Asia and North America. But it is still a tidy sum for the average family and one which, the survey suggested, often requires sacrifices on the part of the parents.

Operating the "bank of mum and dad" may be the most indispensable role played by parents, but there are plenty of others, from chauffeur on open days to cookery coach in anticipation of their first experience of living away from home. The scale of parental involvement naturally depends on individual relationships, but the right advice and encouragement before, during and after the selection process can be invaluable. Many parents have been to university themselves and will be more adept than a teenager at reading between the lines of a self-congratulatory prospectus or website. But it is important to remember who is going to be the student and not to allow your own (inevitably dated) preconceptions to muddy the waters. Those who are not graduates are just as capable of doing the necessary research to offer a second opinion on universities and courses.

Laying the ground

The first thing any parent can do to smooth the path to university is to be encouraging about the value of higher education. Ideally, this should have started long before the application process, but it is especially important at this point. Now that student debt and variable graduate employment prospects have become frequent media topics, it is only natural for sixth-formers and others to have second thoughts about higher education.

The lure of a regular wage packet will be tempting, should one be available, and there are plenty of young people who are not suited to full-time higher education. More big companies are choosing to employ promising 18-year-olds, rather than rely entirely on graduate recruitment, and there has been a rapid development of higher-level apprenticeships. Even after the years of enormous university expansion, most people still do not go to university. Nevertheless, those who are capable of going, generally do not regret the decision. Many people look back on their student days as the best period of their life, as well as the one that shaped their personality and their career. Time as a student should still pay off for the individual in terms of lifetime earnings, as well as personal development. A little reassurance at this stage may make all the difference.

There are important decisions to be made before the sixth-form even begins because the choice of A-levels or vocational qualifications – and even GCSEs – can close off avenues at degree level. A core of traditional academic subjects will help to keep options open, but there are specific requirements for some degrees that can easily be overlooked until it is too late. Maths A-level will be needed for many economics courses, for example, as well as for most sciences.

Making the choice

Any parent wants to help a son or daughter through the difficult business of choosing where and what to study. How big a role you play will depend on a number of factors, not the least of which is the extent to which your advice is wanted. If the quality of advice available at school or college is good, parental involvement may be marginal. But often that is not the case, and you may have to call on other resources, including your own research. Avoid second-hand opinions gleaned through the media or dinner party gossip. You may think that some subjects are a sure-fire route to lucrative employment, while others are shunned by employers, but are you right? And do you really know the strengths and weaknesses of more than 100 universities? Above all, do not try to rewind your own career decisions through your children. The fact that you enjoyed – or hated – a subject or a university does not mean that they will. You may have always regretted missing out on the chance to go to Oxbridge or to become a brain surgeon, but they have their own lives to lead. Students who switch courses or drop out frequently complain that they were pressured into their original choice by their parents. The tables in chapters 1 and 3 offer a reality check, but even they cannot take account of the differences within institutions. The subject tables in chapter 12 show that the best graduate employment rates are often not at the obvious universities.

Parents are encouraged by many schools and colleges to play an active role in the process of choosing a course. At the most basic (but vital) level, this means keeping an eye on deadlines, but it is also about acting as a sounding board and trying to guide your child towards the right university and course. Check that choices are being made for sensible reasons, not on the basis of questionable gossip or trivial criteria. But beyond that, you should stay in the background unless there is a very good reason to play a more substantive role. Make a point of looking for important aspects of university life that the applicant might miss. Security, for example, usually does not feature near the top of a teenager's list of priorities; likewise other practical issues, such as the proximity of student accommodation to lectures, the library and the students' union.

Many universities now publish guides specifically for parents and put on programmes for them at Open Days. The latter may be a way of separating prospective applicants from their more demanding "minders", but the programmes themselves can be interesting and informative. Do not worry that you will be an embarrassment by attending Open Days – many thousands of parents do so, and you may add a critical edge to the proceedings. Like prospectuses, Open Days are part of the sales process, and it is easy for a sixth-former to be carried away by the excitement surrounding a lively university campus. You are much more likely to spot the defects – even if they are ignored in the final decision. The Open Days in 2018 that had been announced at the time of going to press are included alongside each university's profile, in chapter 14. As Open Days at popular institutions are often on the same day, providing assistance in planning Open Day visits is important. Where there is a clash, universities and individual departments are always happy for prospective applicants to visit on another occasion. Ring ahead or email the department to see if an academic will be available to answer questions.

Most of today's sixth-formers and college students seem happy to have their parents' help and advice – even if they do not take it in the end. Research by the Knowledge Partnership consultancy found that more than half of the parents of first-year undergraduates felt they had exerted some influence on their children's choices of university and course, although only about 7 per cent characterised this as "a lot".

UCAS also publishes its own guide for parents, offering useful tips and outlining the deadlines that applicants will have to meet. The school should be on top of the timing and offering the necessary advice, but there is no harm in providing a little back-up, especially on parts of the process that take time and thought, such as writing the personal statement. There is little a parent can do as the offers and/or rejections come rolling in, other than to be supportive. If the worst happens and there is a full set of rejections, you may have to start the advice process all over again for a new round of applications through UCAS Extra. If so, a cool head is even more necessary, but the same principles apply.

Results Day

Then, before you know it, results day is upon you. Make sure you are at home, rather than in some isolated holiday retreat. Your son or daughter needs to have access to instant advice at school or college, and to be able to contact universities straight away if Clearing or Adjustment is required. And your moral support will be much more effective face to face, rather than down a telephone line. Whatever happens, try not to transmit the anxiety that you will inevitably be feeling to your son or daughter, especially if the results are not what was wanted. It is easy to make rash decisions about re-sitting exams or rejecting an insurance offer in the heat of the moment. Try to slow the process down and encourage clear and realistic thinking. Make sure you know in advance what might be required, such as where to access Clearing lists, and if Clearing or Adjustment is being used, you will need to be on hand to offer advice and help with visits to possible universities. For most applicants, Clearing or Adjustment is all but over in a week, so the agony should be short-lived.

Before they go

Little more than a month after the tension of results day, everything should be ready for the start of term. Unless your son or daughter chooses to stay at home to study – as one in five now does, according to NatWest – there will be forms to fill in to secure university accommodation, as well as student loans to sort out and registration to complete. You can perform useful services, like supplying recipe books if the first year is to be spent in self-catering accommodation, but now is the time for independence to become reality. Make sure that important details like insurance are not forgotten, but otherwise stand clear.

Then it is just a matter of agreeing a budget, assuming you are in a position to make a financial contribution. How large that contribution is will depend on family circumstances and your attitude to independent living. Some parents want to ensure that their children leave university debt-free; others could never afford to do that. The important thing is that students and parents know where they stand.

Student finance and parental involvement

After a mortgage, a university degree can be the most significant debt families have to repay, according to HSBC. The debt usually combines student loans for tuition fees and maintenance, and is repayable only when a graduate is paid £25,000 a year and can never amount to more than 9 per cent of his or her salary above that threshold. The immediate priority, however, is budgeting for the cost of living, which the National Union of Students puts at £12,000 a year, aside from course costs, outside London and some £13,400 in the capital. Other estimates are slightly lower – Manchester University puts average costs for its undergraduates at £9,255 for a 40-week year – but the final bill is still substantial.

Hundreds of thousands of undergraduates – particularly mature students – pay their own way through university. Many undergraduates of all ages supplement their income with term-time and vacation jobs. But every survey shows that families play an important (and growing) role where students move straight from school to higher education. More than half of all students consider the family contribution crucial to their ability to afford a university education. This may rise following the withdrawal of grants for students from the poorest families in 2016, although there will actually be more cash available through the replacement loan system.

Costs are likely to be higher if the choice is an overseas university, although most American institutions have generous scholarships and employment opportunities. Even so, HSBC found that most parents were prepared to pay more for the experience, although they would prefer that their children stayed closer to home.

A frank discussion on what the family can afford is essential before the student leaves home. It is all too easy for a young person who has never had to budget for themselves to get into financial difficulties in the social whirl that is the first term of a degree course. In the worst cases, this can lead to excessive term-time employment to keep up with spiralling debts and pressures that contribute towards a student dropping out.

After they've left

Any new student is going to be nervous if he or she is leaving home for the first time and having to settle into a strange environment. But in most cases it is not going to last long because everyone is in the same boat and freshers' weeks hardly leave time for homesickness. In any case, they will not want to let their apprehension show. The people who are most likely to be emotional are the parents – especially if they are left with an empty nest for the first time. It can take a while to get used to an orderly, quiet house after all those years of mayhem.

Resist any temptation to decorate their bedroom and turn it into an office – it is more common than you might think, and psychologists say it can do lasting damage to family relationships. Keep in touch by phone, text or email, but try not to pry. You're not going to be told everything anyway – which is probably just as well. They will be back soon enough and, just as you were getting used to having the place to yourself, a weekend visit or the Christmas vacation will remind you of how things used to be. If things are not going smoothly at university, this may be the time for more reassurance – more students drop out at Christmas of their first year than at any other time.

"Helicopter parents"

Growing numbers of parents now want to play their part in ensuring that their children get value for money at university, but there is a fine line between constructive involvement and unwelcome interference. Universities report that anxious mothers and fathers are more inclined than ever to question what their children are getting for their now substantial fees. There have been stories of parents challenging not just the amount and quality of tuition, but even the marking of essays and exams. The phenomenon, first reported in the USA, has given rise to the phrase "helicopter parents" – so called because they hover over their children's education when they should be letting go. No one wants to think of themselves in that category, but it is not surprising – or reprehensible – that parents are taking more of an interest.

One of the reasons that some overstep the mark is that they are shocked that the amount of teaching and size of seminar groups are not what they recall from their own "free" higher education. The new fees were meant to herald improvements in the student experience, including more contact hours, but these have been marginal in most universities so far. It may be that fewer and larger seminars are here to stay in the arts and social sciences, where almost all state support for teaching was withdrawn, and more learning opportunities will be provided online.

An associated reason for greater parental involvement is that family relationships have changed. Many teenage applicants are glad to accept a lift to an open day to get a second opinion on a university and their prospective course. They are also more likely than previous generations of students to come home at the weekend – or to live there in the first place – and to air any grievances. By all means, give advice, but leave direct contact with university administrators and academics to the student. Most universities will cite the Data Protection Act, in any case, to say they can only deal with students, not parents. What they really mean is that students are adults and should look after themselves.

Useful websites

Many universities have sections on their websites for parents of prospective students.

UCAS has a Parents section and a guide on its website:
www.ucas.com/ucas/undergraduate/getting-started/ucas-undergraduate-parents-and-guardians

To find out more about open days, visit: **www.opendays.com**

10 Going Abroad to University

One student in three is interested in studying abroad for at least part of their time at university, according to research by the British Council. And, good though UK universities are by international standards, other studies suggest that they are right to do so. Research by QS, publishers of the World University Rankings, found that 60 per cent of employers worldwide – and 42 per cent of those in the UK – gave extra weight to an international student experience when recruiting graduates.

Of course, everything will depend on how and where that experience is gained. An Ivy League university will naturally carry more weight than one that the employer knows nothing about. But leaving the UK to study, even for a short period, can confer advantages in the employment market. Some universities now have international summer schools and many degrees include the opportunity of a semester or a year abroad, either studying or with an employer. The numbers going abroad as part of a UK degree have grown by 50 per cent in recent years, topping 30,000.

This is a genuinely new trend. British students have been notoriously reluctant to go abroad even for part of their degree, let alone an entire course. Poor linguistic skills and good universities at home have encouraged them to stay in their own country, while students elsewhere in the world are travelling in unprecedented numbers. France has three times as many studying abroad, Germany more than four times as many, according to UNESCO. The Government and universities themselves have been encouraging students to take advantage of overseas opportunities – and finally there appears to be a response.

There has been speculation since £9,000 fees were introduced that more students would apply to universities on the Continent, where the equivalent charges are low or even non-existent. More sixth-formers – particularly at independent schools – do appear to be considering it, but the predicted surge has yet to materialise. There has been an increase in the numbers going to universities in the USA, where the fees gap has narrowed, at least with state universities, but it is still very much a minority pursuit. There were over 9,000 UK students at US universities last year, but many were postgraduates and/or the children of Britons working on that side of the Atlantic.

Some of the obstacles that have held British students back are now being removed. The maximum fee for a year abroad while studying at a UK university is £1,385 in 2017–18, for example, and many universities are charging less than that. The maximum for a sandwich placement outside the UK is £1,850. But there is still one important disincentive to taking a full degree overseas: although support from the Student Loans Company continues for a year abroad during a UK degree course, it is not available for degrees from non-UK institutions.

Universities in some countries – notably the Netherlands and the USA – now mount frequent recruitment campaigns in the UK. Numbers of British students have been rising sharply at Dutch universities, where fees in 2017/18 are €2,006 for most courses, but they still account for only about 2,000 of the 2.5-million UK student population. Leading independent schools report serious interest in American universities and attendance at the Fulbright Commission's recruitment fairs continues to rise, but the numbers enrolling remain modest, despite attractive incentives in the form of scholarships, bursaries and campus employment opportunities.

Nevertheless, it would be surprising if high fees at home and an increasingly international graduate labour market did not encourage continuing growth in overseas study. Most students who go abroad are motivated by a desire to study at a "world-class" institution, according to Government-sponsored research. Often the trigger is failure to win a place at a leading UK university and being unwilling to settle for second best. Other motivations include a desire for adventure and a belief that overseas study might lead to an international career. The question is how to judge a university that may be thousands of miles from home against more familiar names in the UK. This chapter will make some suggestions, including the use of the growing number of global rankings that are available online or in print.

It is possible to have your academic cake and eat it by going on an international exchange or work placement organised by a UK university, or even to attend a British university in another country. The University of Nottingham has campuses in China and Malaysia; Middlesex can offer Dubai or Mauritius, where students registered in the UK can take part or all of their degree. At Heriot-Watt, undergraduates can mix and match between Edinburgh, Malaysia and Dubai. Other universities, such as Liverpool, also have joint ventures with overseas institutions which offer an international experience (in China, in Liverpool's case) and degrees from both universities.

In most cases, however, an overseas study experience means a foreign university – usually through a partnership with a UK institution. Until recently, this tended to be for a postgraduate degree – and there are still strong arguments for spending your undergraduate years in the UK before going abroad for more advanced study. Older students taking more specialised programmes may get more out of an extended period overseas than those who go at 18 and, since first degrees in the UK are shorter than elsewhere, it may also be the more cost-effective option.

If cost is the main consideration, however, even the generally longer courses at Continental universities can work out cheaper than a degree in the UK. The main obstacle, apart from British students' traditional reluctance to take degrees anywhere else, concerns the language barrier. Although there are now thousands of postgraduate courses taught in English at Continental universities, first-degree programmes are still much thinner on the ground. A few universities, like Maastricht and most others in the Netherlands, are offering a wide range of subjects in English. But the vast majority of European universities teach undergraduates in the host language – and, up to now, that has always deterred UK students.

The obvious alternative lies in American, Australian and Canadian universities, all of which are keen to attract more international students. Here, cost and distance are the main obstacles. Four-year courses add considerably to the cost of affordable-looking fees, while the state of the pound has been another serious disadvantage. Add in the natural reluctance of most 18-year-olds to commit to life on the other side of the world (or even just the Atlantic), and the prospect of a dramatic increase in student emigration lessens considerably.

Where do students go to?

There is remarkably little official monitoring of how many students leave the UK, let alone where they go. But it seems that for all the economic advantages of studying in Continental Europe, the USA remains by far the most popular student destination. Most surveys put Canada, France and Germany, Ireland and Australia as the biggest attractions outside the USA.

A few British students find their way to unexpected locations, like South Korea or Slovakia, but usually for family reasons or to study the language. The figures suggest that British students are more attracted to countries that are familiar or close at hand, and where they can speak English. Many are doubtless planning to stay in their adopted country after they graduate, although visa regulations may make this difficult.

Studying in Europe

More than 12,000 UK students now attend Continental European universities and colleges, according to UNESCO. But international statistics pick up those whose parents emigrated or are working abroad, as well as those who actually leave the UK to take a degree. A minority are undergraduates, if only because the availability of courses taught in English is so much greater at postgraduate level.

The increased interest in Continental universities arises both from the generally low fees they charge and from the growth in the number of courses offered in English. Some countries charge no fees at all, even to international students, and public universities in the European Union are obliged to charge other member countries' students the same as local residents, as well as allowing them to get a job while studying. Of course, when the UK is no longer a member, students will not enjoy these advantages, but fee levels will remain lower than at home across most of Europe.

At present, undergraduates can study at a French university for £164 a year but, not surprisingly, nearly all first degrees are taught in French. Only 100 of the 1,337 programmes taught in English and listed on the Campus France website (**www.campusfrance.org/en**) are at the Licence (Bachelors equivalent) level – and 27 of them have some teaching in French. Germany is much the same, despite attracting large numbers of international students. The DAAD website (**www.daad.de/en**) lists 216 undergraduate programmes taught wholly or mainly in English, but many are at private universities like Jacobs University in Bremen, which charges up to €20,000 a year. There is gradual growth in teaching in English in the public sector, where tuition fees have been abolished, but they are still thin on the ground.

Any potential saving has to be considered with care. In spite of the Bologna process – an intergovernmental agreement which means that degrees across Europe are becoming more similar in content and duration – most Continental courses are longer than their UK equivalents, adding to the cost and to your lost earnings from attending university. And, of course, you will have higher travel costs. It is harder to generalise about the cost of living. It can be lower than the UK in southern Europe, but frighteningly high in Scandinavia.

Obviously, the cost of an international experience and the commitment involved is much reduced if you opt for an exchange scheme or other scheme arranged by a UK university, many of which have partners all over the world. There are opportunities for everything from a summer school of less than a month to a full year abroad, and a number of universities now have targets to increase the numbers taking advantage of such schemes.

The most common offering is the EU's Erasmus+ scheme, which funds exchanges of between three months and a year, the work counting towards your degree. More than two million students throughout Europe have used the scheme, and there are 2,000 universities to choose from in 30 countries. It is uncertain whether UK students will have access to the scheme beyond 2020, but the Government has promised to underwrite applications for the 2019–20 academic year. Erasmus+ membership may well be included in any eventual Brexit deal but, especially since the programme comes up for renewal as part of the EU budget process for 2020, it is difficult to speculate on what the conditions might be.

For the moment at least, applications are made through universities' international offices, and must be approved by the UK university as well as by the Erasmus administrators. Erasmus+ students do not pay any extra fees and they are eligible for grants to cover the extra expense of travelling and living in another country. During 2017–18 academic year, this amounts to €280–€330 a month for studying abroad, and €380–€430 a month for doing a traineeship abroad, depending on the cost of living in the country you choose to go to. There are extra grants for disadvantaged students of €120 a month for studying abroad and €20 a month for traineeships.

Studying in America

American universities remain the first choice of British students going abroad to take a degree, just as the UK is the first choice for Americans. Regardless of any special relationship, this is not surprising since international rankings consistently show US and UK universities to be the best in the world (as well as teaching in English).

Around half of the British students taking courses in the USA are undergraduates. Already by far the most popular student destination, the attractions of an American degree have multiplied since fees trebled in England. The Fulbright Commission, which promotes American higher education, has seen a 30 per cent increase in the number of Britons taking US university

---

Top Ten destinations for UK undergraduates studying abroad

1	United States	9,601
2	France	2,110
3	Netherlands	2,060
4	Germany	1,798
5	Australia	1,592
6	Ireland	1,579
7	Canada	1,337
8	United Arab Emirates	799
9	Denmark	789
10	Austria	674

Unesco statistics

Best Student Cities ranking

1	Montreal	Canada
2	Paris	France
3	London	United Kingdom
4	Seoul	South Korea
5	Melbourne	Australia
6	Berlin	Germany
7	Tokyo	Japan
8	Boston	United States
9	Munich	Germany
10	Vancouver	Canada

QS Best student cities in the World 2017

entrance exams. Even before the latest rise in UK fees, the top American universities had seen demand rise sharply, and this is spreading to universities further down the rankings.

The sheer depth of the US university system means that if you are thinking of studying abroad, the USA is almost bound to be on the list of possibilities. Tuition fees at Ivy League institutions are notoriously high – Harvard puts the full cost of attendance at $64,000 a year, but 60 per cent of students receive some financial aid. Outside the Ivy League, the fee gap for UK students has been narrowing, but fees at many state universities have shot up in the last four years as politicians have tried to balance the books. At Texas A&M University, for example, ranked in the top 200 in the world, international students now pay almost $37,000 a year for tuition, and the university put undergraduates' total costs at $54,742 before scholarships and bursaries. Fees are up to $25,845 at the State University of New York, although the university puts the total cost for those living on campus at up to $38,787. Only at much lower-ranked state universities do the costs compare with those in the UK – at South Dakota State University, for example, tuition fees are less than $12,000, although the yearly cost for an undergraduate is put at almost $24,000.

The individual systems of state universities and private universities mean that there is a great variation in the financial support given to international students. Fulbright advises students considering a US degree to assess and negotiate a funding package at the same time as pursuing their application. Otherwise, they may end up with a place they cannot afford, losing valuable time in the quest for a more suitable one.

The main rankings of US universities are published by US News and World Report, which also now publishes its own global ranking (**https://www.usnews.com/rankings**).

Which countries are best?

Anyone going abroad to study will be in search of a memorable and valuable all-round experience, not just a good course. Most international students are motivated by location – both the country and the city in which a university is based – as well as by the reputation of the institution. QS publishes an annual ranking of student cities, based on quality of life indicators as well as the number of places at world-ranked universities. Montreal topped the ranking in 2017, with Paris second and London third.

Many Asian countries are looking to recruit more foreign students, both as part of a broader internationalisation agenda and to compensate for falling numbers of potential students at home. Japan is a case in point. The high cost of living may put off many potential students, as may the unfamiliarity of its language, but more support is being offered to attract foreign students and more courses are being taught in English. However, as with any non-English speaking country, the language of instruction is only part of the story. You will need to know enough of the local language to manage the shops and the transport system, and, of course, to make friends and get the most out of being there.

Another option of growing interest is China, although Western students are often put off by the dormitory accommodation that is the norm at most universities. The country has already grown massively in importance. Its university system is growing in quality, with the leading institutions climbing the world rankings and improving their facilities. Familiarity with China is unlikely to be a career disadvantage for anyone in the 21st century. Some see Hong Kong, which has several world-ranked universities and a familiar feel for Britons, as the perfect alternative to mainland Chinese universities.

Will my degree be recognised?

Even in the era of globalisation, you need to bear in mind that not all degrees are equal. At one extreme is the MBA, which has an international system for accrediting courses, and a global admissions standard. But with many professional courses, study abroad is a potential hazard. To work as a doctor, engineer or lawyer in the UK, you need a qualification which the relevant professional body will recognise. It is understandable that to practise law in England, you need to have studied the English legal system. For other subjects, the issues are more to do with the quality and content of courses outside UK control.

There are ways of researching this issue in advance. One is to contact NARIC, the National Recognition Centre for the UK (**www.naric.org.uk**). NARIC exists to examine the compatibility and acceptability of qualifications from around the world. The other approach is to ask the UK professional body in question – maybe an engineering institution, the relevant law society or the general teaching, medical or dental councils – about the qualification you propose to study for.

Which are the best universities?

Going abroad to study is a big and expensive decision, and you want to get it right. Whether your ultimate aim is to become an internationally mobile high-flyer, or simply to broaden your experience, you will want to know that the university you are going to is taken seriously around the world.

At the moment there are three main systems for ranking universities on a world scale. One is run by QS (Quacquarelli Symonds), an educational research company based in London (www.topuniversities.com). Another is by Shanghai Ranking Consultancy, a company set up by Shanghai Jiao Tong University, in China, and is called the Academic Ranking of World Universities (ARWU) (**www.shanghairanking.com**). These two have been joined by *Times Higher Education* (**www.timeshighereducation.com/world-university-rankings**), a weekly magazine with no connection to *The Times*, which has been producing its own ranking since 2010, having previously published the QS version.

There are several more international ranking systems that an online search might throw up, but most are either specialist – like the Webometrics-ranking of universities' web activity – or limited in their readership and influence. Some are still developing: the European Commission's U-Multirank (**www.umultirank.org**), for example, is still limited in the subjects it covers, but may become a more widely used source of information in time.

The QS system uses a number of measures including academic opinion, employer opinion, international orientation, research impact and staff/student ratio to create its listing, while the ARWU uses measures such as Nobel Prizes and highly-cited papers, which are more related to excellence in scientific research. The *Times Higher Education* has added a number of measures to the QS model, including research income and a controversial global survey of teaching quality.

Naturally, the different methodologies produce some contrasting results – the three main rankings each have a different university at the top, for example. The table on the following pages is a composite of the three main rankings, which places Stanford at the top, as it was last year, and includes four UK universities in the top 20. In practice, however, if you go to a university that features strongly in any of the tables, you will be at a place that is well-regarded around the world. After all, even the 200th university on any of these rankings is an elite institution in a world with more than 5,000 universities.

These systems tend to favour universities which are good at science and medicine. Places that specialise in the humanities and the social sciences, such as the London School of Economics,

Top universities in the world, averaged from their positions in the QS World University Ranking (QS), the Academic Ranking of World Universities (ARWU) and *Times Higher Education* (THE) for 2018

Rank	Institution	Country
1	Stanford University	USA
=2	Massachusetts Institute of Technology	USA
=2	Harvard University	USA
=2	University of Cambridge	UK
5	University of Oxford	UK
=6	California Institute of Technology (Caltech)	USA
=6	Princeton University	USA
8	University of Chicago	USA
=9	UCL (University College London)	UK
=9	ETH Zurich (Swiss Federal Institute of Technology)	Switzerland
=9	Yale University	USA
12	Columbia University	USA
13	Imperial College London	UK
14	University of Pennsylvania	USA
15	Cornell University	USA
16	Johns Hopkins University	USA
17	University of California, Berkeley	USA
18	University of California, Los Angeles	USA
19	Duke University	USA
20	University of Michigan	USA
21	Northwestern University	USA
22	University of Toronto	Canada
23	University of Edinburgh	UK
24	University of California, San Diego	USA
25	The University of Tokyo	Japan
26	University of Washington	USA
27	Tsinghua University	China
28	King's College London	UK
29	New York University	USA
30	The University of Melbourne	Australia
31	University of British Columbia	Canada
32	The University of Manchester	UK
=33	Ecole Polytechnique Fédérale de Lausanne (EPFL)	Switzerland
=33	University of Wisconsin-Madison	USA
35	National University of Singapore	Singapore
36	Peking University	China
37	McGill University	Canada
38	Kyoto University	Japan
39	University of Illinois at Urbana-Champaign	USA
40	Carnegie Mellon University	USA

Rank	Institution	Country
=41	Technical University of Munich	Germany
=41	Ruprecht-Karls University Heidelberg	Germany
=43	Ludwig-Maximilian University of Munich	Germany
=43	London School of Economics and Political Science (LSE)	UK
45	Nanyang Technological University	Singapore
46	Australian National University	Australia
=47	University of Hong Kong	Hong Kong
=47	The University of Queensland	Australia
49	University of Texas at Austin	USA
50	The Hong Kong University of Science and Technology	Hong Kong

can appear in deceptively modest positions. In addition, the rankings tend to look at universities in the round, and contain only limited information on specific subjects. QS published the first 26 global subject rankings in 2011 and has since increased this to 42. One advantage of the QS ranking system is that ten per cent of a university's possible score comes from a global survey of recruiters. So you can look at this column of the table for an idea about where the major employers like to hire. Note that the author of this *Guide* has a role in developing the QS Rankings.

Other options for overseas studies

For the growing numbers who want to study abroad without committing themselves to a complete degree, a number of options are available. A language degree will typically involve a year abroad, and a look at the UCAS website will show many options for studying another subject alongside your language of choice. UK universities offer degrees in information technology, science, business and even journalism with a major language such as Chinese.

Many universities offer a year abroad, either studying or in a work placement, even to those who are not taking a language. At Aston University, for example, 70 per cent of students do a year's work placement and a growing number do so abroad. China and Chile have been among recent destinations. Other universities offer the opportunity to take shorter credit-bearing courses with partner institutions overseas. American universities are again the most popular choice. The best approach is to decide what you want to study and then see if there is a UK university that offers it as a joint degree or with a placement abroad. Make sure that all the universities involved are well-regarded, for example by looking at their rankings on one or other of the websites mentioned at the end of the table on the following pages.

Useful websites

Association of Commonwealth Universities: **www.acu.ac.uk**

Campus France: **www.campusfrance.org/en**

College Board (USA): **www.collegeboard.org**

DAAD (for Germany): **www.daad.de/en/**

Study in Holland: **www.studyinholland.co.uk**

Education Ireland: **www.educationinireland.com/en**

Erasmus+ Programme (EU): **www.erasmusplus.org.uk**

Finaid (USA): **www.finaid.org**

Fulbright Commission: **www.fulbright.org.uk**

Study in Australia: **www.studyinaustralia.gov.au**

Study in Canada: **www.studyincanada.com**

For information on the recognition in the UK of international degrees, visit the National Recognition Centre for the UK (NARIC): **www.naric.org.uk**

11 Coming to the UK to Study

Universities are still anxious about the long-term consequences of tougher visa controls and leaving the European Union but, for the moment at least, the referendum vote has helped to boost international recruitment. Students may be swayed by political decisions like Brexit, but there is nothing like a fall in the value of the pound to counteract negative attitudes. A degree at a UK university is better value for money than it has been for some years, thanks to the pound's fall since the Brexit vote. And, now that the Government has reassured European students that they will pay the same fees and remain eligible for loans if they come in 2018–19, applications from the continent are rising again. EU students will continue to pay no fees in Scotland.

The uncertainties following the referendum hit EU enrolments in 2017, but those from the rest of the world were already rising strongly, with a record 40,000 undergraduates starting degrees last year. The first application figures for 2018–19 cover only Oxford and Cambridge, medical, dental and veterinary courses, but they showed positive signs. Applications from the EU were up by 6 per cent, reversing much of the 9 per cent fall seen at this point in the 2017 cycle. Beyond the EU, the increase was 12 per cent. This could mean slightly tougher competition for places in 2018, but with the number of British school-leavers continuing to decline, universities will be keen to attract international students.

As yet, no decisions have been announced for 2019–20, by which time the UK will have left the EU. It would not be surprising if this encouraged an unusually high number of applications from European students this year, as those contemplating entry in 2019 bring forward their applications if they have the flexibility to do so.

Universities in the UK have been a magnet for international students for many years – only the huge higher education system in the USA attracts more. Global surveys have shown that UK universities are seen as offering high quality in a relatively safe environment, with the added advantage of allowing students to learn and immerse themselves in English. Even after the fall in the value of the pound, the UK remains an expensive destination by international standards, but shorter than average courses both at undergraduate and Master's level redress the balance to some extent. The UK's 11 per cent share of the world's young people who choose to study outside their own country is important to its universities and welcomed by British students.

More than four million people now travel abroad to study, and universities in many parts of the world compete aggressively to attract them. The students concerned may see other countries' universities as better than their own, or they may want to master another language and/or experience another culture, but most also see international study as a boost to their career prospects. Surveys in a number of countries have shown that employers – particularly those engaged in global markets – favour applicants with an international education.

While international students have continued to favour UK universities, the numbers of undergraduates coming from individual countries have varied considerably over recent years. The source of most stability has been China, which, including Hong Kong, sends four times as many students as any other country and increased the number of undergraduate entrants by another 10 per cent in 2017. Elsewhere, there has been more fluctuation, often due to economic or political factors. Most significant has been the decline in students coming from the Indian sub-continent, where tougher visa policies have hit hardest. But even here there was a significant upturn in 2017, with 12 per cent more Indian students accepting places. Universities in the UK continue to be extremely proactive in the recruitment of international students, participating in international fairs and sometimes opening their own offices in target countries.

The top countries for sending international students to the UK

EU countries (top 20)		%	Non-EU countries (top 20)		%
France	7,412	9.4	China	36,087	25.3
Cyprus (European Union)	7,011	8.9	Hong Kong (Special Administrative		
Italy	6,060	7.7	Region of China)	14,099	9.9
Romania	6,039	7.7	Malaysia	13,074	9.2
Germany	5,656	7.2	Nigeria	6,206	4.3
Bulgaria	5,406	6.9	Singapore	6,064	4.2
Ireland	5,028	6.4	India	5,579	3.9
Greece	4,668	6.0	United States	5,285	3.7
Spain	4,541	5.8	Norway	3,956	2.8
Poland	4,230	5.4	Korea (South)	2,900	2.0
Lithuania	3,523	4.5	Canada	2,882	2.0
Sweden	2,164	2.8	Saudi Arabia	2,799	2.0
Belgium	1,940	2.5	Russia	2,581	1.8
Portugal	1,900	2.4	Pakistan	2,371	1.7
Finland	1,531	2.0	United Arab Emirates	2,310	1.6
Hungary	1,489	1.9	Switzerland	2,019	1.4
Netherlands	1,435	1.8	Vietnam	1,937	1.4
Czech Republic	1,179	1.5	Kuwait	1,937	1.4
Latvia	1,154	1.5	Qatar	1,877	1.3
Slovakia	1,103	1.4	Thailand	1,686	1.2
Total	**78,439**		Oman	1,363	1.0
			Total	**142,813**	

Grand total **221,252**

Note: First degree non-UK students

Why study in the UK?

Aside from the strong reputation of UK degree courses and the opportunity to be taught and surrounded by English, research shows that most graduates are handsomely rewarded when they return home. A Government-sponsored report showed that UK graduates earn much higher salaries than those who studied in their own country. The starting salaries of UK graduates in China and India were more than twice as high as those for graduates educated at home, while even those returning to the USA enjoyed a salary premium of more than ten per cent.

Some premium is to be expected – you are likely to be bright and highly motivated if you are prepared to uproot yourself to take a degree. And, unless they have government scholarships, most students have to be from a relatively wealthy background to afford the fees and other expenses of international study. A higher salary will probably be a necessity to compensate for the cost of the course. But the scale of increase demonstrated in the report suggests that a UK degree remains a good investment. Three years after graduation, 95 per cent of the international graduates surveyed were in work or further study. More than 90 per cent had been satisfied with their learning experience and almost as many would recommend their university to others.

A popular choice

Nearly all UK universities are cosmopolitan places that welcome international students in large numbers. Almost one student in five is from outside the UK – 6 per cent from the EU and 14 per cent from the rest of the world. Recent surveys by i-graduate, the student polling organisation, put the country close behind the USA among the world's most attractive study destinations. More full-time postgraduates – the fastest-growing group – come from outside the UK than within it. In many UK universities you can expect to have fellow students from over 100 countries.

More than 90 per cent of international students declare themselves satisfied with their experience of UK universities in i-graduate surveys, although they are less enthusiastic in the Government's National Student Survey and more likely than UK students to make official complaints. Nevertheless, satisfaction increased by eight percentage points in four years, according to i-graduate, reflecting greater efforts to keep ahead of the global competition. International students are particularly complimentary about students' unions, multiculturalism, teaching standards and places of worship. Their main concerns tend to be financial, partly because of a lack of employment opportunities. In one survey, only 56 per cent were satisfied with the ability to earn money while studying, and statements from ministers in the UK Government suggest that controls on this, and particularly on the opportunity to work after completing a degree, are unlikely to be eased.

One way round this in a growing number of countries is to take a UK degree through a local institution, distance learning or a full branch campus of a UK university. Indeed, there are now more international students taking UK first degrees in their own country than there are in Britain – around 480,000 of them outside the EU. The numbers grew by 70 per cent in a decade and are likely to rise further if UK Government policies obstruct universities' efforts to increase the number of students coming to Britain. Most branch campuses are in Asia or the Middle East, but some universities, such as King's College London, are now planning campuses in other parts of the EU.

Where to study in the UK

The vast majority of the UK's universities and other higher education institutions are in England. Of the 133 universities profiled in this *Guide*, 108 are in England, 15 in Scotland, 8 in Wales and 2 in Northern Ireland. Fee limits in higher education for UK and EU students are determined separately in each administrative area, which in some cases has brought benefits for EU students. All undergraduates from other EU countries are currently charged the same fees as those from the part of the UK where their chosen university is located, which is why EU students currently pay no tuition fees in Scotland, for example. With the UK expected to leave the EU in March 2019, it is unclear whether these arrangements will continue for students starting in 2019–20 or what system might replace them.

Within the UK, the cost of living varies by geographical area. Although London is the most expensive, accommodation costs in particular can also be high in many other major cities. You should certainly find out as much as you can about what living in Britain will be like. Further advice and information is available through the British Council at its offices worldwide, at more than 60 university exhibitions that it holds around the world every year, or at its Education UK website **www.educationuk.org**. Another useful website for international students is provided by the UK Council for International Student Affairs (UKCISA) at **www.ukcisa.org.uk**.

Universities in all parts of the UK have a worldwide reputation for high quality teaching and research, as evidenced in global rankings such as those shown on page 121. They maintain this

The universities most favoured by EU and non-EU students

Institution (top 20)	EU students	Institution (top 20)	Non-EU students
The University of Glasgow	2,250	The University of Manchester	5,376
The University of Aberdeen	2,067	The University of Liverpool	4,777
University College London	2,030	University College London	4,360
King's College London	1,984	Coventry University	4,355
The University of Edinburgh	1,972	University of the Arts, London	4,301
University of the Arts, London	1,825	The University of Edinburgh	3,594
Coventry University	1,811	The University of Sheffield	3,200
The University of Manchester	1,586	University of Nottingham	3,068
The University of Westminster	1,541	Imperial College of Science, Technology and Medicine	2,769
The University of Essex	1,348	The University of Warwick	2,571
Middlesex University	1,311	King's College London	2,422
The University of Warwick	1,291	The University of Birmingham	2,215
The University of Kent	1,207	The University of St Andrews	2,197
Imperial College of Science, Technology and Medicine	1,198	Newcastle University	2,148
Queen Mary University of London	1,139	City, University of London	2,141
The University of Bath	1,133	The University of Southampton	2,118
The University of Southampton	1,057	The University of Exeter	2,071
The University of Greenwich	1,040	The University of Sussex	2,058
The University of Strathclyde	1,036	The University of Leeds	2,021
The University of Lancaster	1,035	The University of Portsmouth	2,002

Note: First degree non-UK students

standing by investing heavily in the best academic staff, buildings and equipment, and by taking part in rigorous quality assurance monitoring. The new Office for Students, which came into being at the start of this year, will be the chief regulatory body for higher education in England, overseeing organisations such as the Quality Assurance Agency for Higher Education (QAA), which remains the arbiter of standards.

Although many people from outside the UK associate British universities with Oxford and Cambridge, in reality most higher education institutions are nothing like this. Some universities still maintain ancient traditions, but most are modern institutions that place at least as much emphasis on teaching as on research and offer many vocational programmes, often with close links with business, industry and the professions. The table on the previous page shows the universities that are most popular with international students at undergraduate level. Although some of those at the top of the lists are among the most famous names in higher education, others achieved university status only in the last 25 years.

What subjects to study?

One of the reasons for such diversity is that strongly vocational courses are favoured by international students. Many of these in professional areas such as architecture, dentistry or

The most popular subjects for international students

Subject Group	EU students	Non-EU students	Total students	% of all international students
Business Studies	11,299	26,012	37,312	16.9
Accounting & Finance	2,432	14,290	16,722	7.6
Law	3,793	10,329	14,122	6.4
Art & Design	3,923	6,791	10,714	4.8
Economics	2,802	7,263	10,065	4.5
Computer Science	5,173	4,733	9,906	4.5
Mechanical Engineering	1,905	5,755	7,661	3.5
Politics	3,491	3,594	7,084	3.2
Biological Sciences	3,419	3,370	6,790	3.1
Electrical and Electronic Engineering	1,337	5,122	6,459	2.9
Psychology	3,401	2,965	6,365	2.9
Communication and Media Studies	2,806	3,010	5,815	2.6
Mathematics	1,478	4,252	5,730	2.6
Medicine	1,011	3,565	4,576	2.1
Drama, Dance and Cinematics	2,569	1,972	4,540	2.1
Architecture	1,646	2,805	4,451	2.0
Civil Engineering	877	3,523	4,400	2.0
Hospitality, Leisure, Recreation & Tourism	2,022	2,104	4,126	1.9
Chemical Engineering	538	2,755	3,293	1.5
Pharmacology & Pharmacy	625	2,482	3,108	1.4

Note: First degree non-UK students

Note: 4071 students (1.8%) recorded as 'Other'. Would be 19th.

smedicine take one or two years longer to complete than most other degree courses. Traditional first degrees are mostly awarded at Bachelor level (BA, BEng, BSc, etc.) and last three to four years. There are also some "enhanced" first degrees (MEng, MChem, etc.) that take four years to complete. The relatively new Foundation degree programmes are almost all vocational and take two years to complete as a full-time course, with an option to study for a further year to gain a full degree. The table opposite shows the most popular subjects studied by international students. Remember, though, that you need to consider the details of any university course that you wish to study and to look at the ranking of that university in our main league table in chapter 1 and in the subject tables in chapter 12.

English language proficiency

The universities maintain high standards partly by setting demanding entry requirements, including proficiency in English. For international students, this usually includes a score of at least 5.5 in the International English Language Testing System (IELTS), which assesses English language ability through listening, speaking, reading and writing tests. Under visa regulations introduced in 2011, universities are able to vouch for a student's ability in English. This proficiency will need to be equivalent to an "upper intermediate" level (level B2) of the CEFR (Common European Framework of Reference for Languages) for studying at an undergraduate level (roughly equivalent to an overall score of 5.5 in IELTS).

There are many private and publicly funded colleges throughout the UK that run courses designed to bring the English language skills of prospective higher education students up to the required standard. However, not all of these are Government approved. Some private organisations such as INTO (**www.intostudy.com**) have joined with universities to create centres running programmes preparing international students for degree-level study. The British Council also runs English language courses at its centres around the world.

Tougher student visa regulations were introduced in 2012 and have since been refined. Although under the current system, universities' international students should not be denied entry to the UK, as long as they are proficient in English and are found to have followed other immigration rules, some lower-level preparatory courses taken by international students have been affected. It is, therefore, doubly important to consult the official UK government list of approved institutions (web address given at the end of this chapter) before lodging an application.

How to apply

You should read the information below in conjunction with that provided in chapter 5, which deals with the application process in some detail.

Some international students apply directly to a UK university for a place on a course, and others make their applications via an agent in their home country. But most applying for a full-time first degree course do so through the Universities and Colleges Admissions Service (UCAS). If you take this route, you will need to fill in an online UCAS application form at home, at school or perhaps at your nearest British Council office. There is plenty of advice on the UCAS website about the process of finding a course and the details of the application system (**www.ucas.com/ucas/undergraduate/getting-started/ucas-undergraduate-international-and-eu-students**).

Whichever way you apply, the deadlines for getting your application in are the same. For those applying from within an EU country, application forms for most courses starting in 2019 must be received at UCAS by 15 January 2019. Note that applications for Oxford and Cambridge and for all courses in medicine, dentistry and veterinary science have to be received at UCAS by 15 October 2018, while some art and design courses have a later deadline of 24 March 2019.

If you are applying from a non-EU country to study in 2019, you can submit your application to UCAS at any time between 1 September 2018 and 30 June 2019. Most people will apply well before the 30 June deadline to make sure that places are still available and to allow plenty of time for immigration regulations, and to make arrangements for travel and accommodation.

Entry and employment regulations

Visa regulations have been the subject of continuing controversy in the UK and many new rules and regulations have been introduced, often hotly contested by universities. Recent governments have been criticised for increasing visa fees, doubling the cost of visa extensions, and ending the right to appeal against a refusal of a visa.

The current points system for entry – known as Tier 4 – came into effect in 2009. Under this scheme, prospective students can check whether they are eligible for entry against published criteria, and so assess their points score. Universities are also required to provide a Confirmation of Acceptance for Studies (CAS) to their international student entrants, who must have secured an unconditional offer, and the institutions must appear as a "Tier 4 Sponsor" on the Home Office's Register of Sponsors. Prospective students have to demonstrate that, as well as the necessary qualifications, they have English language proficiency and enough money for the first year of their specified course. This includes the full fees for the first year and, as at July 2016, living costs of £1,265 a month, up to a maximum of nine months, if studying in London or £1,015 a month in the rest of the UK. Under the new visa requirements, details of financial support are checked in more detail than before.

All students wishing to enter the UK to study are required to obtain entry clearance before arrival. The only exceptions are British nationals living overseas, British overseas territories citizens, British Protected persons, British subjects, and non-visa national short-term students who may enter under a new Student Visitor route. Visa fees have been increased again (to £335 for a Tier 4 visa, plus £150 a year healthcare surcharge). As part of the application process, biometric data will be requested and this will be used to issue you with a Biometric Residence Permit (BRP) once you have arrived in the UK. You will need a BRP to open a bank account, rent accommodation or establish your eligibility for benefits and services or to work part-time, for example. The details of the regulations are continually reviewed by the Home Office. You can find more about all the latest rules and regulations for entry and visa requirements at **www.gov.uk/tier-4-general-visa**.

The rules and regulations governing permission to work vary according to your country of origin and the level of course you undertake. If you are from a European Economic Area (EEA) country (the EU plus Iceland, Liechtenstein and Norway) or Switzerland, you do not need permission to work in the UK, although you will need to be ready to show an employer your passport or identity card to prove you are a national of an EEA country. However, the regulations that will apply after the UK leaves the EU are unknown at the time of writing and you will need to check for the latest information before making an application.

Students from outside the EEA who are here as Tier 4 students are allowed to work part-time for up to 20 hours a week during term time and full-time during vacations. These arrangements apply to students on degree courses; stricter limits were introduced in 2010 for lower-level courses. If you wish to stay on after you have graduated, you can apply for permission under Tier 2 of the points-based immigration system, but you will need a sponsor and the work must be considered "graduate level", commanding a salary of at least £21,600. The reforms abolished the Tier 1 two-year post-study period for graduates who do not have such a sponsor. They will be required to apply for a new visa from scratch. Full details are on the Home Office study visas website above.

The Tier 1 Graduate Entrepreneur Scheme enables up to 2,000 graduates to remain in the UK if they have "genuine and credible business ideas and entrepreneurial skills". Successful applicants, who will be selected by their university, will be allowed to stay in the UK for 12 months, with the possibility of a further 12-month extension.

Bringing your family

Since 2010, international students on courses of six months or less have been forbidden to bring a partner or children into the UK, and the latest reforms extend this prohibition to all undergraduates except those who are government sponsored. Postgraduates studying for 12 months or longer will still be able to bring dependants to the UK, and most universities can help to arrange facilities and accommodation for families as well as for single students. The family members you are allowed to bring with you are your husband or wife, civil partner (a same-sex relationship that has been formally registered in the UK or your home country) or long-term partner and dependent children. You can find out more about getting entry clearance for your family at **www.ukcisa.org.uk**.

Support from British universities

Support for international students is more comprehensive than in many countries, and begins long before you arrive in the UK. Many universities have advisers in other countries. Some will arrange to put you in touch with current students or graduates who can give you a first-hand account of what life is like at a particular university. Pre-departure receptions for students and their families, as well as meet-and-greet arrangements for newly-arrived students, are common. You can also expect an orientation and induction programme in your first week, and many universities now have "buddying" systems where current students are assigned to new arrivals to help them find their way around, adjust to their new surroundings and make new friends. Each university also has a students' union that organises social, cultural and sporting events and clubs, including many specifically for international students. Both the university and the students' union are likely to have full-time staff whose job it is to look after the welfare of students from overseas.

International students also benefit from free medical and subsidised dental and optical care and treatment under the UK National Health Service (non-EU students will have had to pay a healthcare surcharge when paying for their visa to benefit from this), plus access to a professional counselling service and a university careers service.

At university, you will naturally encounter people from a wide range of cultures and walks of life. Getting involved in student societies, sport, voluntary work, and any of the wide range of social activities on offer will help you gain first-hand experience of British culture, and, if you need it, will help improve your command of the English language.

Useful websites

The British Council, with its dedicated Study UK site designed for those wishing to find out more about studying in the UK:
https://study-uk.britishcouncil.org

The UK Council for International Student Affairs (UKCISA) provides a wide range of information on all aspects of studying in the UK:
www.ukcisa.org.uk

UCAS, for full details of undergraduate courses available and an explanation of the application process:
www.ucas.com/ucas/undergraduate/getting-started/ucas-undergraduate-international-and-eu-students

For the latest information on entry and visa requirements:
www.gov.uk/tier-4-general-visa

Register of sponsors for Tier 4 educational establishments:
www.gov.uk/government/publications/register-of-licensed-sponsors-students

For a general guide to Britain, available in many languages:
www.visitbritain.com

12 Subject by Subject Guide

The rankings of whole institutions capture all the headlines when university guides appear, but recent surveys suggest that students take more notice of the subject tables. Knowing where a university stands in the pecking order of higher education is a vital piece of information for any applicant, but the quality of the course is what matters most – particularly in the short term. Your chosen course, rather than the character of the whole university, will determine what you get out of taking a degree and may have a big bearing on your employment prospects. As the 2014 Research Excellence Framework confirmed, the most modest institution may have a centre of specialist excellence, and even famous universities have mediocre departments. This chapter offers some pointers to the leading universities in a wide range of subjects. With a number of universities reviewing the courses they will offer in the future, it is possible that not all institutions listed in a particular subject area will be running courses in 2019.

The subject tables in this *Guide* include scores from the National Student Survey (NSS). These distil the views of final-year undergraduates on various aspects of their course, with the results presented in two columns. The teaching quality indicator reflects the average scores of the sections of the survey focusing on teaching, assessment and feedback, learning opportunities and academic support. The student experience indicator is drawn from the average of the organisation and management, learning resources, student voice and learning community sections, as well as the overall satisfaction question. The three other measures used are research quality, students' entry qualifications and graduate employment prospects. None of the measures is weighted. A full explanation of the measures is given on the next page.

Many subjects, such as dentistry or sociology, have their own table, but others are grouped together in broader categories, such as "other subjects allied to medicine". Scores are not published where the number of students is too small for the outcome to be statistically reliable. Cambridge is again the most successful university. It tops 30 of the 67 tables, while Oxford leads in five subjects. Edinburgh, Glasgow, Loughborough, St Andrews and Strathclyde are all top in three subjects; Bath, Birmingham and Imperial College London in two. Eleven other universities are top in one subject.

Research quality

This is a measure of the quality of the research undertaken in the subject area. The information was sourced from the 2014 Research Excellence Framework (REF), a peer-review exercise used to evaluate the quality of research in UK higher education institutions, undertaken by the UK Higher Education Funding Bodies. The approach mirrors that in the main table, with the REF results weighted and then multiplied by the percentage of eligible staff entered for assessment.

For each subject, a research quality profile was given to those university departments that took part, showing how much of their research was in various quality categories. These categories were: 4* world-leading; 3* internationally excellent; 2* internationally recognised; 1* nationally recognised; and unclassified. The funding bodies decided to direct more funds to the very best research by applying weightings. The English, Scottish and Welsh funding councils have slightly different weightings. Those adopted by HEFCE (the funding council for England) for funding in 2012–13 are used in the tables: 4* is weighted by a factor of 3 and 3* is weighted by a factor of 1. Outputs of 2* and 1* carry zero weight. This results in a maximum score of 3. In the interest of consistency, the above weightings continue to be applied this year.

The scores in the table are presented as a percentage of the maximum score. To achieve the maximum score, all staff would need to be at 4* world-leading level.

Universities could choose which staff to include in the REF, so, to factor in the depth of the research quality, each quality profile score has been multiplied by the number of staff returned in the REF as a proportion of all eligible staff.

Entry standards

This is the average new UCAS tariff score for new students under the age of 21, based on A and AS Levels and Scottish Highers and Advanced Highers and other equivalent qualifications (including the International Baccalaureate), taken from HESA data for 2015–16. Each student's examination grades were converted to a numerical score using the new UCAS tariff to make the figures more accessible to those applying in 2019, who will be using the new system. The points used in the revised tariff appear on page 32.

Teaching quality and student experience

The student satisfaction measure is divided into two components. These measures are taken from the National Student Survey (NSS) results published in 2017 and 2016. A single year's figures are used when that is all that is available, but an average of the two years' results is used in all other cases. Students at some universities boycotted the 2017 NSS, leaving individual departments below the 50 per cent threshold for publication. Where 2017 NSS data was not available, the 2016 scores for Teaching Quality and Student Experience were adjusted by the percentage point change in each subject between 2016 and 2017. The adjusted scores were used for z-scoring only, and do not appear in the final table.

The NSS covers eight aspects of a course, with an additional question gauging overall satisfaction. Students answer on a scale from 1 (bottom) to 5 (top) and the score in the table is calculated from the percentage of positive responses (4 and 5) in each section. The teaching quality indicator reflects the average scores for the first four sections of the survey. The student experience indicator is drawn from the average scores of the remaining sections and the additional question on overall satisfaction. Teaching quality is favoured over student experience and accounts for 67 per cent of the overall student satisfaction score, with student experience making up the remaining 33 per cent.

Graduate prospects

This is the percentage of graduates undertaking further study or in a professional job ("positive destinations"), in the annual survey by HESA six months after graduation. Because of the relatively small numbers in some departments, two years of data (2015 and 2016 graduates) are aggregated to make the scores more reliable. A low score on this measure does not necessarily indicate unemployment – some graduates may have taken jobs that are not categorised as professional work. The averages for each subject are given at the foot of each subject table in this chapter and in two tables in chapter 3 (see pages 52–55).

The Education table uses a fifth indicator: Ofsted grades, a measure of the quality of teaching based on the outcomes of Ofsted inspections of teacher training courses.

Note that in the tables that follow, when a figure is followed by *, it refers solely to data from 2014–15 because no data for 2015–16 are available.

The subjects listed below are covered in the tables in this chapter:

Accounting and Finance
Aeronautical and
 Manufacturing Engineering
Agriculture and Forestry
American Studies
Anatomy and Physiology
Animal Science
Anthropology and Forensic
 Science
Archaeology
Architecture
Art and Design
Biological Sciences
Building
Business Studies
Celtic Studies
Chemical Engineering
Chemistry
Civil Engineering
Classics and Ancient
 History
Communication and Media
 Studies
Computer Science
Creative Writing
Criminology
Dentistry
Drama, Dance and
 Cinematics

East and South Asian Studies
Economics
Education
Electrical and Electronic
 Engineering
English
Food Science
French
General Engineering
Geography and
 Environmental Sciences
Geology
German
History
History of Art, Architecture
 and Design
Hospitality, Leisure,
 Recreation and Tourism
Iberian Languages
Italian
Land and Property
 Management
Law
Librarianship and
 Information Management
Linguistics
Materials Technology
Mathematics
Mechanical Engineering

Medicine
Middle Eastern and
 African Studies
Music
Nursing
Other Subjects Allied to
 Medicine (see page 236
 for subjects included in
 this category)
Pharmacology and Pharmacy
Philosophy
Physics and Astronomy
Physiotherapy
Politics
Psychology
Radiography
Russian and East European
 Languages
Social Policy
Social Work
Sociology
Sports Science
Theology and Religious
 Studies
Town and Country Planning
 and Landscape
Veterinary Medicine

Accounting and Finance

Record numbers of students started degrees in accounting and finance in 2016, after a second successive year of growth in enrolments. Neither subject could match the scale of increases in 2015, but accounting topped 7,000 entrants for the first time and finance passed 2,300. In both subjects, there were more than five applications to every place.

It is all change at the top of the table, with Strathclyde moving up two places to lead for the first time. Leeds, last year's top university, has dropped to fourth, while Bath, a previous leader, has moved up five places to second. Strathclyde has the highest entry standards, benefiting from the conversion rate for Scottish qualifications in the UCAS tariff, and has not been out of the top three overall during the current decade.

The most satisfied students are at universities outside the top 50, however. Only 2 per cent of final-year undergraduates were less than satisfied with the quality of teaching at Central Lancashire, but the university was restricted to 58th place because it had the poorest graduate prospects of the 100 institutions in the table. Perhaps significantly, four of the five universities scoring more than 90 per cent for teaching quality had not entered the Research Excellence Framework in these subjects.

Employment rates in both areas again come a surprisingly long way down the table of subjects – only 40th of 67 subjects. Those who do find graduate jobs are relatively well paid, however. At an average of £22,000 in 2016, they just made it to the top 20.

The table again shows huge variation in graduates' employment prospects. Every accountancy graduate at Sussex went straight into a professional job or further study, but at nine universities the proportion was below 50 per cent.

Some of the leading universities demand maths A-level and all welcome it, but there is considerable variation in entry standards. Almost 150 institutions expect to offer accounting, either alone or in combination, in 2018.

Accounting and Finance	Teaching quality %	Student experience %	Research quality %	Entry standards (UCAS points)	Graduate prospects %	Overall score
1 Strathclyde	85.2	86.8	44.3	213	79.1	100.0
2 Bath	86.0	87.2	41.8	183	83.1	98.1
3 Lancaster	86.7	89.2	42.6	161	88.9	97.9
4 Leeds	86.4	89.5	39.3	175	84.5	97.7
5 Loughborough	84.7	89.7	32.6	155	95.3	96.3
6 Warwick	75.3	77.7	40.4	184	86.8	94.8
7 Queen's, Belfast	81.5	82.9	32.7	160	92.8	94.7
8 London School of Economics	64.1	64.0	52.3	194	90.3	93.9
9 Nottingham	80.6	85.5	32.6	158	86.5	93.6
10 Glasgow	71.1	81.2	22.1	210	89.3	93.5
11 Exeter	80.1	82.8	24.4	175	88.9	93.4
12 Durham	78.9	81.1	23.1	166	91.8	92.5
13 Birmingham	78.4	81.0	29.1	155	89.5	92.1
14 Aberdeen	76.4	82.7	24.9	182	80.5	91.7
15 Stirling	82.1	84.1	25.2	166	78.2	91.6
=16 Sussex	77.6	82.2	23.7	133	100.0	91.2

=16 Ulster	80.6	81.5	40.4	130	80.5	91.2
18 East Anglia	82.2	86.2	28.1	146	79.9	91.1
=19 Dundee	81.6	77.7	12.1	169	92.2	91.0
=19 Sheffield	79.7	80.7	26.8	149	86.7	91.0
=19 Swansea	84.0	83.4	22.0	131	91.9	91.0
22 Newcastle	77.4	79.9	20.7	165	88.6	90.9
23 Queen Mary, London	77.3	83.9	31.3	159	74.9	90.4
=24 Kent	77.0	79.4	24.8	149	88.6	90.2
=24 Reading	75.8	76.8	29.3	150	87.3	90.2
26 Manchester	75.5	78.2	33.3	167	74.0	90.1
27 Heriot-Watt	78.7	81.7	18.8	154	86.6	89.9
28 Robert Gordon	88.5	86.6	2.6	180	72.8	89.7
29 Nottingham Trent	88.8	90.2	4.6	135	82.0	88.6
30 Leicester	78.5	81.8	24.3	137	79.2	88.2
=31 Aston	83.4	84.5	19.7	141	72.4	88.1
=31 Southampton	74.7	79.0	24.0	146	82.3	88.1
33 Liverpool	81.0	82.7	20.1	151	71.4	87.9
34 Surrey	79.1	81.4	15.8	168	70.7	87.8
35 Liverpool John Moores	94.7	92.5	n/a	128	74.8	87.7
36 City	74.9	78.0	27.8	164	66.7	87.4
37 Bristol	70.5	71.0	32.1	174	67.9	87.3
38 Aberystwyth	88.8	85.9	14.5	116	75.8	87.2
39 Bangor	85.5	85.9	23.4	121	68.0	87.1
=40 Cardiff	70.7	73.0	32.0	154	71.9	86.7
=40 Edinburgh	65.6	75.6	25.8	184	69.2	86.7
42 Royal Holloway	82.7	77.4	27.0	126	n/a	86.6
43 Portsmouth	84.0	85.4	9.5	126	77.9	86.3
44 Essex	76.4	83.3	25.1	127	70.7	85.7
45 De Montfort	80.2	83.0	10.7	107	86.5	85.2
46 Hull	82.1	87.5	10.2	115	76.7	85.1
47 Bradford	82.3	85.3	11.8	136	65.0	84.8
48 Northumbria	83.3	85.7	4.0	137	70.0	84.7
49 Lincoln	84.1	85.2	4.8	117	76.4	84.5
=50 Abertay	90.7	85.9	n/a	166	48.3	84.4
=50 Buckingham	89.5	93.2	n/a	105	73.1	84.4
=50 Oxford Brookes	87.0	88.2	5.1	122	67.2	84.4
53 Chester	87.6	86.8	0.5	104	79.4	84.3
54 Huddersfield	80.9	82.1	4.1	131	74.9	84.1
=55 Glasgow Caledonian	77.7	77.6	1.8	165	67.3	83.7
=55 Worcester	90.0	87.4	0.9	111	69.1	83.7
57 Coventry	84.7	86.4	1.6	121	71.0	83.6
58 Central Lancashire	98.0	96.3	4.4	128	38.5	83.5
59 West of Scotland	86.3	83.4	2.9	131	63.2	83.3
60 Keele	77.7	82.6	10.2	127	69.7	83.1
61 Bolton	96.9	97.5	n/a	93*	56.3	82.8
=62 Brunel	70.3	76.4	23.0	118	71.3	82.4

Accounting and Finance cont

		Teaching quality %	Student experience %	Research quality %	Entry standards (UCAS points)	Graduate prospects %	Overall score
=62	Plymouth	84.1	85.6	13.1	121	54.0	82.4
=62	West of England	79.8	83.4	5.5	113	72.6	82.4
65	West London	90.4	93.2	n/a	100	62.1	82.3
=66	Manchester Metropolitan	82.5	82.7	4.7	127	62.2	82.1
=66	Middlesex	82.9	86.7	10.5	106	62.5	82.1
=68	Edge Hill	82.9	84.5	n/a	116	69.6	82.0
=68	Westminster	81.0	85.4	2.4	134	60.7	82.0
70	South Wales	77.4	78.0	0.2	122	76.6	81.6
71	Teesside	87.5	84.5	2.0	103	63.8	81.4
72	London South Bank	82.6	85.0	2.1	91	74.4	81.2
73	Gloucestershire	76.6	75.7	n/a	116	79.7	81.1
74	Sheffield Hallam	82.7	83.6	0.6	113	64.7	80.9
75	Birkbeck	75.7	75.6	16.1	92	73.4	80.7
76	Hertfordshire	79.0	79.4	0.9	115	68.8	80.4
77	Derby	84.3	74.8	0.9	99	71.4	80.3
78	Leeds Beckett	81.2	84.3	0.8	105	65.0	80.1
79	Salford	84.6	84.9	5.9	108	51.2	79.7
=80	Edinburgh Napier	74.6	75.5	2.3	139	60.3	79.5
=80	Greenwich	77.5	77.4	3.3	131	57.1	79.5
82	London Metropolitan	83.8	80.4	0.6	97	60.4	78.7
83	Staffordshire	89.2	88.4	2.6	104	39.3	78.3
84	Birmingham City	82.8	83.5	1.3	99	54.9	78.2
85	East London	80.4	79.9	0.8	93	62.0	77.8
86	Cardiff Metropolitan	70.0	72.8	n/a	113	69.9	77.2
87	Roehampton	73.6	72.7	4.5	105	63.6	77.1
=88	Bournemouth	71.7	73.2	8.8	112	57.2	77.0
=88	Kingston	75.1	79.0	9.2	114	47.1	77.0
90	Liverpool Hope	71.1	61.3	n/a	108	75.5	76.6
91	Northampton	79.3	79.2	1.0	98	51.8	76.2
92	Chichester	77.5	78.9	n/a	95	56.7	76.1
93	Winchester	83.3	88.0	n/a	99	38.7	75.9
=94	Anglia Ruskin	81.6	82.6	3.4	84	47.9	75.7
=94	Southampton Solent	78.7	74.0	n/a	90	58.5	75.7
96	Sunderland	75.9	74.3	0.4	107	53.5	75.6
97	Buckinghamshire New	79.5	82.0	1.8	106	40.0	75.3
98	Brighton	60.5	61.7	6.5	111	68.9	74.4
99	Canterbury Christ Church	69.5	74.7	n/a	103	49.7	73.1
100	Bedfordshire	66.4	71.4	3.1	82	46.4	70.2

Employed in professional job	50%	Employed in non-professional job and Studying	2%
Employed in professional job and studying	9%	Employed in non-professional job	21%
Studying	9%	Unemployed	10%
Average starting professional salary	£22,000	Average starting non-professional salary	£18,000

Aeronautical and Manufacturing Engineering

Most of the courses in this ranking focus on aeronautical or manufacturing engineering, but the category includes some with a mechanical title. In addition, manufacturing degrees often go under the rubric of production engineering. Although they do not feature in this table, degree apprenticeships at leading firms like Rolls-Royce provide an attractive alternative to a conventional degree in this area.

Both applications and enrolments for traditional degree courses in aeronautical engineering have risen in each of the last four years, however. The numbers starting degrees were close to 3,500 in 2016. The smaller field of production and manufacturing engineering had been growing but the latest figures show a decline.

The subjects share seventh place out of the 67 subject groups for starting salaries and are just outside the top 25 for the proportion of graduates going straight into professional jobs or further study, despite a relatively high unemployment rate. Almost 60 per cent of the 2016 graduates went straight into high-level work, and there was less variation between institutions than in many subjects. Although Newcastle saw over 95 per cent of its graduates go straight into graduate jobs or further study and Manchester Metropolitan (for the second year in a row) less than 40 per cent, good scores were distributed throughout the table.

Cambridge remains well clear at the top of the table overall, registering by far the best scores for research and entry standards. Imperial is now the nearest challenger, although the University of the West of Scotland has much the most satisfied students. Nine out of ten undergraduates had a positive view both of teaching quality and the broader student experience.

Many universities demand maths and physics at A-level, and give extra credit for further maths, computing and/or design technology. Entry grades are high at the leading universities, with Cambridge averaging more than 240 points on the new UCAS tariff and Imperial almost 230. Only one university with enough entrants to compile a score averaged less than 100 points. Coventry and the West of Scotland are the only post-1992 universities in this year's top 20, but the University of the West of England is again just one place off it.

Aeronautical and Manufacturing Engineering	Teaching quality %	Student experience %	Research quality %	Entry standards (UCAS points)	Graduate prospects %	Overall score
1 Cambridge	75.5	77.6	67.0	241	93.0	100.0
2 Imperial College	69.6	75.7	59.6	228	86.7	95.0
3 Bristol	84.7	87.4	52.3	200	74.5	94.0
4 Bath	80.3	82.1	37.4	206	81.8	92.1
5 Leeds	83.0	86.0	40.9	175	83.4	91.8
=6 Glasgow	75.8	78.4	47.2	205	75.5	90.7
=6 Southampton	71.6	75.8	52.3	180	86.0	90.7
8 Newcastle	75.1	75.5	30.2	n/a	95.5	90.3
9 Nottingham	80.9	84.5	40.8	166	80.0	89.8
=10 Loughborough	75.6	75.7	41.8	162	86.2	88.7
=10 Surrey	81.6	84.3	30.8	180	76.9	88.7
12 Sheffield	76.7	75.6	36.0	163	86.7	88.3
13 Strathclyde	71.9	71.2	37.2	206	74.6	87.3

	Teaching quality %	Student experience %	Research quality %	Entry standards (UCAS points)	Graduate prospects %	Overall score
=14 Liverpool	77.0	79.7	32.1	157	77.3	85.7
=14 Queen's, Belfast	76.7	78.7	36.7	155	75.6	85.7
16 Queen Mary, London	70.3	76.6	46.7	148	76.5	85.3
17 Coventry	86.7	86.3	10.3	131	82.2	84.7
18 Swansea	66.1	67.8	45.5	148	81.3	84.1
19 West of Scotland	90.4	90.0	9.0	157	61.8	83.2
20 Ulster	78.2	78.3	n/a	126	93.8	82.3
21 West of England	72.7	74.6	10.6	127	91.6	81.8
=22 Brunel	66.6	69.7	23.7	157	80.2	81.6
=22 Staffordshire	86.7	86.5	5.7	115	76.9	81.6
24 Aston	77.0	76.7	20.6	141	71.4	81.3
25 Manchester	55.2	56.3	35.1	172	82.1	80.6
=26 Hertfordshire	75.1	75.4	16.5	118	78.3	79.9
=26 Sheffield Hallam	79.3	80.3	17.8	122	69.1	79.9
28 Teesside	78.0	77.1	5.8	127	n/a	79.0
29 Sussex	69.2	70.1	n/a	129	87.5	78.2
30 Plymouth	73.1	77.9	15.7	102	75.6	77.8
31 Portsmouth	74.1	78.0	9.1	111	70.0	76.5
32 Central Lancashire	69.1	67.1	7.1	124	n/a	73.9
33 City	70.1	73.5	20.2	121	50.0	73.1
34 Buckinghamshire New	78.2	75.3	n/a	84	65.4	72.8
35 Salford	66.0	68.7	4.4	124	62.5	72.2
36 Kingston	69.3	70.0	2.9	116	61.6	72.1
37 South Wales	64.3	59.4	n/a	133	66.2	71.5
38 Brighton	55.9	59.9	7.4	118	56.1	67.5
39 Manchester Metropolitan	62.3	64.3	16.3	n/a	37.5*	63.0

Employed in professional job	56%	Employed in non-professional job and Studying	1%
Employed in professional job and studying	2%	Employed in non-professional job	14%
Studying	16%	Unemployed	12%
Average starting professional salary	£26,000	Average starting non-professional salary	£17,108

Agriculture and Forestry

Agriculture and forestry have dropped into the bottom two subject groups this year for the proportion of graduates going straight into high-level work or continuing their studies. The 15 per cent unemployment rate was one of the highest among the 67 sub groupings. But the rewards for those who find professional work are higher than those figures might suggest: a mean salary of £21,000 at the end of 2016 put the subjects in the top 40.

Nottingham has regained the position it last held four years ago at the top of the table, replacing Lincoln (now fourth), which shot up the ranking and into the lead in the last edition.

Nottingham has the highest entry standards, while neighbouring Nottingham Trent has the most satisfied students but is restricted to tenth place by a low research score.

Reading and Newcastle share the best score for graduate prospects, although even there 20 per cent of students failed to find professional jobs or a postgraduate course within six months of graduating. At 4 of the 16 institutions in the table, fewer than 40 per cent of graduates enjoyed such positive destinations.

With little more than 2,000 undergraduates starting degrees in the two subjects across the UK, this table tends to be volatile. Queen's Belfast, which achieved much the best score in the Research Excellence Framework, achieves the biggest rise this year, from sixth to second. There are two specialist institutions in the table: the Royal Agricultural University and Harper Adams, which is the leading modern university in the overall table but still only eighth for agriculture and forestry.

Both subjects saw a dip in applications and enrolments in 2016, although they remain at historically high levels. But with fewer than four applicants to the place in agriculture and only two in forestry and arboriculture, entry standards remain low. Only Nottingham averages more than 150 points on the new UCAS tariff, although no university drops below 100 points.

Agriculture and Forestry	Teaching quality %	Student experience %	Research quality %	Entry standards (UCAS points)	Graduate prospects %	Overall score
1 Nottingham	78.9	82.9	36.4	164	66.7	100.0
2 Queen's, Belfast	78.5	79.8	56.3	142	76.3	99.4
3 Glasgow	84.3	87.5	42.3	144*	n/a	99.2
4 Lincoln	95.4	94.0	31.1	n/a	77.3*	98.1
5 Reading	73.3	75.1	50.7	139	80.0	97.1
6 Bangor	90.3	87.0	29.7	139	73.1	96.9
7 Newcastle	71.4	74.2	28.4	144	80.0	94.0
8 Harper Adams	86.2	86.8	5.7	135	76.4	91.5
9 Aberystwyth	81.0	75.3	38.2	125	68.6	91.4
10 Nottingham Trent	91.7	88.1	4.1	125	65.5	88.4
11 Kent	76.0	63.1	n/a	141	68.4	86.6
12 Greenwich	n/a	n/a	19.5	138	36.7	84.0
13 Royal Agricultural University	77.7	78.6	2.1	122	57.4	82.5
14 Plymouth	80.5	77.5	17.4	n/a	30.8*	82.0
15 Oxford Brookes	68.3	65.9	n/a	132	38.5	78.3
16 Cumbria	54.9	44.9	n/a	111	34.3	68.1

Employed in professional job	42%	Employed in non-professional job and Studying		2%
Employed in professional job and studying	3%	Employed in non-professional job		30%
Studying	8%	Unemployed		15%
Average starting professional salary	£21,000	Average starting non-professional salary		£17,500

American Studies

Applications for degrees in American Studies dropped by almost 30 per cent in 2016, taking them to their lowest level for more than a decade. Fewer than 400 students embarked on a course in the subject, which has become a fixture in the bottom 10 of our employment table. Only a third of graduates in 2016 went straight into professional jobs, although another quarter continued their studies. Starting salaries for those who did find graduate-level work put the subject higher up the earnings table, at 45th out of the 67 groupings.

Sussex is back on top of the American Studies table, after surrendering that position to Birmingham last year. There is barely more than a point between the two universities, with Sussex benefiting from the highest score in the table for graduate prospects, while Birmingham has the highest entry standards. Warwick, which topped the ranking for almost a decade and achieved the best results in the Research Excellence Framework, has dropped out of the ranking this year.

The small numbers inevitably make for some volatility. Kent and Essex have each jumped ten places up the latest table. Ironically, the highest scores in the National Student Survey for satisfaction with teaching quality are to be found at the university that is bottom of the table overall – York St John. And students at Derby, only two places higher, were the most satisfied with other aspects of the student experience.

With fewer than four applications to the place, entry qualifications are relatively modest. – only Birmingham, Manchester and East Anglia average more than 150 points on the new UCAS tariff. No university reached 80 per cent positive destinations among those graduating in 2016, although Sussex came within a point of that mark. Four others were below 40 per cent on this criterion.

More than 50 universities and colleges expect to offer degrees classified by UCAS as American studies in 2018, although they include a variety of courses such as international relations and black studies. Most concentrate on the culture and politics of the USA and Canada. A growing number of courses offer the opportunity of a year at an American or Canadian university as part of a four-year degree. The leading universities are likely to expect English or history at A-level or the equivalent.

American Studies	Teaching quality %	Student experience %	Research quality %	Entry standards (UCAS points)	Graduate prospects %	Overall score
1 Sussex	84.3	84.6	45.6	138	79.2	100.0
2 Birmingham	73.6	71.1	48.8	159	78.9	98.9
3 Manchester	n/a	n/a	49.1	157	65.5	98.6
4 Kent	89.1	84.8	47.3	112	59.5	95.1
5 East Anglia	79.8	78.1	33.1	157	50.1	93.0
6 Essex	74.0	75.1	46.9	131	52.2	91.2
7 Portsmouth	88.6	85.6	32.2	105	59.6	91.1
8 Goldsmiths, London	81.6	70.3	34.9	140*	51.6*	91.0
9 Nottingham	65.6	64.4	39.9	141	71.9	90.8
10 Hull	84.3	81.0	26.1	120	64.2	90.7
11 Leicester	71.4	68.0	34.3	125	68.9	89.2
12 Swansea	81.4	77.0	18.5	117	69.5	88.4
13 Keele	78.7	77.7	29.8	125	50.9	88.1
14 Liverpool	n/a	n/a	33.4	n/a	39.3	87.6
15 Winchester	86.1	81.0	n/a	111	53.1	82.7

16 Derby		83.3	89.1	13.5	108	32.0	82.1
17 Canterbury Christ Church		88.0	77.2	16.3	96	35.8	81.5
18 York St John		90.9	83.5	n/a	100	32.0	79.4

Employed in professional job	31%	Employed in non-professional job and Studying	4%
Employed in professional job and studying	2%	Employed in non-professional job	31%
Studying	21%	Unemployed	11%
Average starting professional salary	£20,000	Average starting non-professional salary	£16,000

Anatomy and Physiology

Cambridge is back on top of the table for anatomy and physiology, after giving way to St Andrews last year. But for really stellar graduate prospects, it is necessary to look outside the top 20. Cardiff Metropolitan, Northampton and the University of the West of England all saw every graduate go straight into professional employment or continue their studies at the end of 2016.

The subjects do well in the employment table, moving up ten places to 13th this year, but they are less competitive in terms of early career salaries, which are (just) in the bottom half of the 67 subject groups. Nevertheless, applications and enrolments rose for the fourth year in a row in 2016, with the numbers starting courses passing 4,500 for the first time. At well over eight applications to the place, it is one of the most competitive areas, with four of the leading universities averaging more than 200 points at entry.

The table covers a broad range of courses, including the biomedical science degrees that have been growing in popularity over recent years. Very few actually have the title of anatomy or physiology, but they include degrees in cell biology, neurosciences and pathology. Entry requirements often include at least two science subjects – usually biology and chemistry – although some post-1992 universities will accept just one science. In some cases, the courses are used as a fall-back for candidates whose real target was medical school, but partly because the courses in this category range so widely, there is also a broad spread of entry grades.

Student satisfaction levels are generally high, with the top scores both for teaching quality and the broader student experience coming at Westminster, even though it only appears in 30th place overall. Cambridge has by far the highest entry standards, while the top research score is shared between University College London, in 13th place, and Dundee, which just makes the top 20 this year. Four more universities have joined the table since last year. The total of 44 is almost 50 per cent more than there were a decade ago. Older universities dominate the leading positions, but two post-1992 institutions appear in the top 20: Huddersfield and Glasgow Caledonian.

Anatomy and Physiology	Teaching quality %	Student experience %	Research quality %	Entry standards (UCAS points)	Graduate prospects %	Overall score
1 Cambridge	n/a	n/a	52.5	244	84.8	100.0
2 St Andrews	87.7	89.5	37.6	212	n/a	98.5
3 Newcastle	88.8	89.5	47.8	181*	85.5	95.9
4 Oxford	n/a	n/a	50.9	226	74.8	93.6
=5 Leeds	84.2	87.2	40.9	168	82.5	92.2
=5 Loughborough	87.7	94.6	52.1	143	75.4	92.2
=5 Sussex	88.6	86.7	46.8	139	83.4	92.2

Anatomy and Physiology cont

		Teaching quality %	Student experience %	Research quality %	Entry standards (UCAS points)	Graduate prospects %	Overall score
8	Glasgow	78.9	83.1	33.4	208	81.8	92.1
9	Bristol	85.9	82.2	49.7	175	74.5	92.0
10	University College London	71.9	75.0	55.4	192	83.9	91.7
=11	Huddersfield	93.5	92.2	7.8	130	98.2	91.3
=11	Queen Mary, London	n/a	n/a	26.1	166	85.7	91.3
13	Liverpool	91.3	92.2	31.7	155	72.8	90.4
14	Aberdeen	83.3	82.9	34.7	189	69.8	89.5
15	Glasgow Caledonian	83.7	87.6	8.1	153	94.5	89.4
16	Salford	91.1	90.1	12.7	127	88.8	89.1
17	King's College London	76.7	80.4	38.0	172	79.8	89.0
18	Brighton	94.9	91.5	4.8	125	88.1	88.8
19	Manchester	n/a	n/a	38.3	174	71.4	88.6
20	Dundee	77.0	82.6	55.4	n/a	77.5	88.5
21	Leicester	78.5	82.7	36.5	157	78.2	88.3
=22	Cardiff Metropolitan	82.8	78.7	n/a	149	100.0	88.0
=22	Edinburgh	68.9	75.7	52.8	195	68.9	88.0
24	Queen's, Belfast	79.0	76.8	33.3	160	80.2	87.8
25	West of England	88.2	87.4	n/a	110	100.0	87.6
26	Coventry	92.6	94.1	4.5	113	86.4	87.4
=27	Manchester Metropolitan	83.9	84.5	12.0	131	90.3	87.2
=27	Queen Margaret, Edinburgh	85.5	79.5	n/a	135	97.5	87.2
29	Nottingham	84.6	80.2	26.5	159	71.5	86.8
30	Westminster	95.3	95.6	21.2	113	68.4	86.6
31	Central Lancashire	86.3	88.6	8.3	147	78.9	86.5
32	Northampton	81.8	76.4	n/a	128	100.0	86.0
33	Portsmouth	91.6	83.1	8.1	122	81.1	85.8
34	Keele	87.3	89.3	16.5	134	68.6	85.0
35	St George's, London	73.6	68.4	20.0	124	96*	84.7
36	East London	87.5	87.6	n/a	133	77.9	84.5
37	Plymouth	86.0	85.4	n/a	135	77.2	83.9
=38	Bangor	80.7	77.6	n/a	130	81.3	82.2
=38	Derby	89.1	81.5	1.6	106	n/a	82.2
40	Ulster	75.3	78.7	n/a	124	83.8	81.3
41	Reading	72.9	75.8	26.6	147	63.3	81.1
42	Anglia Ruskin	82.8	80.3	2.2	98	n/a	79.1
43	Greenwich	73.9	77.3	2.2	106	n/a	76.4
44	Oxford Brookes	72.8	74.0	21.3	124	45.8	75.2

Employed in professional job	39%	Employed in non-professional job and Studying	3%
Employed in professional job and studying	4%	Employed in non-professional job	12%
Studying	34%	Unemployed	8%
Average starting professional salary	£21,900	Average starting non-professional salary	£16,380

Animal Science

Animal Science remains rooted to the bottom of the employment table, with more than half of all 2016 graduates starting out in non-professional jobs. At only 7 per cent, the unemployment rate was among the lowest outside the leading subjects, but only a quarter went straight into graduate-level work. Despite this, applications and enrolments dropped only slightly from the record numbers reached in 2015. There are still twice as many undergraduates taking animal science as there were a decade ago.

The Animal Science table was first published only three years ago and was a reflection of growing interest in the group of subjects under this heading. Degree courses range from animal behaviour to equine science and veterinary nursing, all of which previously appeared in our Agriculture category.

Glasgow has retained the leadership it won for the first time last year, with Nottingham moving up to second place. Glasgow has the highest entry standards, but the top scores on the other measures are spread around the table. Reading recorded the best performance in the Research Excellence Framework, while Nottingham Trent, in fifth place, has the most satisfied students, as it did last year. At most of the 18 universities in the table, satisfaction with teaching, feedback and academic support has fallen in the new edition.

Most surprising, in view of the overall employment record of animal science graduates, is Middlesex's outstanding score for graduate prospects. Every one of its graduates found professional employment or continued studying in 2016, placing Middlesex almost 20 percentage points ahead of its nearest rival, Nottingham. Many of the other employment scores are worryingly low. Five universities are below 25 per cent for positive destinations, one of them below 5 per cent.

The subject is a little further up the pecking order for graduate salaries, although still in the bottom ten. The mean salary in professional jobs six months after graduation has dropped by almost £600, to less than £19,000, since the last edition, but other subjects near the foot of the table have seen a larger fall.

Animal Science	Teaching quality %	Student experience %	Research quality %	Entry standards (UCAS points)	Graduate prospects %	Overall score
1 Glasgow	83.2	86.7	42.3	189	75.0	100.0
2 Nottingham	75.8	79.3	36.4	146	80.3	90.4
3 Aberystwyth	87.3	84.5	38.2	120	65.7	88.4
4 Reading	77.0	79.6	50.7	123	50.0	86.7
5 Nottingham Trent	91.6	89.7	4.1	149	52.7	86.2
6 Liverpool	n/a	n/a	32.9	144	65.7	85.4
7 Lincoln	85.0	83.6	n/a	147	56.0	83.2
8 Middlesex	73.4	62.1	n/a	143	100.0	82.5
9 Bristol	n/a	n/a	33.2	168	23.5	81.3
10 Royal Veterinary College	79.9	80.4	n/a	143	57.6	81.2
11 Harper Adams	84.5	81.7	5.7	140	36.8	80.8
12 Plymouth	80.5	77.5	n/a	141	27.4	77.3
13 Edinburgh Napier	78.9	66.8	n/a	164	3.2	76.6
14 Chester	74.6	77.5	7.9	134	25.9	76.2
15 Greenwich	n/a	n/a	19.5	131	21.8	75.9

Animal Science cont	Teaching quality %	Student experience %	Research quality %	Entry standards (UCAS points)	Graduate prospects %	Overall score
16 Anglia Ruskin	63.6	62.7	24.6	123	30.0	74.2
17 Oxford Brookes	68.3	65.9	21.3	n/a	12.2	72.3
18 Canterbury Christ Church	n/a	n/a	n/a	103	20.8	68.0

Employed in professional job	23%	Employed in non-professional job and Studying	4%
Employed in professional job and studying	2%	Employed in non-professional job	47%
Studying	17%	Unemployed	7%
Average starting professional salary	£18,700	Average starting non-professional salary	£16,800

Anthropology

Anthropology continues to set records for applications and enrolments – 2016 saw the fifth successive year of growth, during which time the numbers starting courses have more than doubled. Anthropologists themselves warned that £9,000 fees could be disastrous for the subject, but instead there has been an extraordinary increase in demand, with more than five applications to the place.

Some attribute the subject's rise in popularity to television series, but there has been no firm explanation. Much of the growth has come in joint Honours degrees, pairing the subject with everything from accountancy to linguistics or law. Although small numbers of students on some courses have led to six universities dropping out of the table this year, it still contains six more than it did three years ago. More than 40 institutions expect to offer the subject in 2018.

There have been a number of changes in the latest table, which has been affected more than most by the boycott of the National Student Survey. Brunel achieved the best satisfaction ratings of those with enough responses to be included. Overall, Birmingham has jumped seven places to take over from Cambridge at the top. Exeter has joined the ranking in third place, while Roehampton has gone up five places to become the only post-1992 university in the top 20.

There are no subject-specific requirements for most degree courses, although some Russell Group universities favour candidates with biology or another science, at least at AS level. Employment prospects will be the main concern of those considering a degree in anthropology. The subject is well inside the bottom 20 for the proportion of graduates going straight into professional jobs or continuing their studies. Only one subject has a higher unemployment rate than the 16 per cent for anthropologists and nearly a quarter of graduates start out in lower-level jobs. The picture is a little better in salary terms, with the £20,000 average for recent graduates in professional jobs placing the subject 45th out of the 67 groupings.

Anthropology	Teaching quality %	Student experience %	Research quality %	Entry standards (UCAS points)	Graduate prospects %	Overall score
1 Birmingham	84.4	88.3	50.9	152	87.6*	100.0
2 Cambridge	n/a	n/a	40.4	210	81.7	98.7
3 Exeter	86.7	86.3	41.0	174	76.2	98.6
4 Oxford	n/a	n/a	38.8	207	72.8	97.8

5 University College London	n/a	n/a	49.3	182	68.9	97.4
6 St Andrews	87.7	88.1	25.0	199	66.7	96.6
7 Sussex	85.8	84.5	34.4	145	83.5	96.2
8 Manchester	n/a	n/a	36.7	159	79.9	95.9
9 SOAS London	n/a	n/a	31.1	162	68.0	93.9
10 Edinburgh	78.3	76.6	42.2	179	65.0	93.6
11 London School of Economics	71.1	65.1	41.3	188	77.8	92.4
12 Durham	75.7	72.3	29.1	180	75.2	91.7
13 Brunel	91.8	92.7	29.3	132	45.5	91.6
14 Aberdeen	83.3	79.5	31.8	160	56.3	91.2
15 Bristol	n/a	n/a	11.2	157	68.8	90.1
16 Roehampton	85.7	89.4	27.7	101*	61.5	89.4
17 Goldsmiths, London	n/a	n/a	34.5	130	56.3	89.2
18 Queen's, Belfast	77.1	72.9	49.0	137	48.9	88.8
19 Kent	75.8	71.6	20.5	140	78.5	88.1
20 Liverpool John Moores	78.8	76.6	15.1	134	66.7	86.6
21 Leeds	80.0	80.6	n/a	147	70.4	86.3
22 Bournemouth	80.1	76.9	19.9	117	63.8*	86.2
23 Oxford Brookes	83.1	76.2	17.3	118	51.7	85.0
24 East London	85.1	81.9	13.7	99*	50.9	84.2
25 Wales Trinity St David	78.4	74.3	17.3	91	38.5	79.5
26 Birmingham City	78.0	79.5	3.8	n/a	32.3*	77.6

Employed in professional job	39%	Employed in non-professional job and Studying	2%
Employed in professional job and studying	2%	Employed in non-professional job	71%
Studying	21%	Unemployed	16%
Average starting professional salary	£20,000	Average starting non-professional salary	£15,600

Archaeology and Forensic Science

Archaeology and forensic science have moved out of the bottom ten subjects both for employment and salary levels this year, although they are never going to be near the top of either table. Some undergraduates are not looking for career advancement – degrees in archaeology attract retired people as well as younger students – while others are well aware that archaeologists are not highly paid.

Only 420 students started archaeology degrees in 2016, but enrolments for forensic and archaeological science remained healthy, at 2,245.

In both areas, applications have yet to regain the levels seen before £9,000 fees arrived, but the decline appears to have ended. There are no specific subject requirements for a degree in archaeology, although geography, history and science subjects are all considered relevant.

The top two in the table are unchanged, with Cambridge extending its lead over Durham. Birmingham enjoys the biggest rise in the leading positions – up eight places to sixth – while Huddersfield has done even better, jumping 22 places to become the only post-1992 university in the top 20, thanks mainly to its student satisfaction ratings, which are easily the best in the table where teaching quality is concerned. Cambridge has the highest entry standards, while third-placed Dundee has the best graduate prospects and achieved the best results in the Research Excellence Framework.

The growing number of universities offering archaeology or forensic science has had the effect of spreading out entry scores, which now range from less than 100 points on the new UCAS tariff to more than 200 at Oxford and Cambridge. Almost a third of all archaeologists and forensic scientists stay on for a postgraduate qualification, either full or part-time, but a similar proportion starts work in a "non-professional" job.

Archaeology and Forensic Science	Teaching quality %	Student experience %	Research quality %	Entry standards (UCAS points)	Graduate prospects %	Overall score
1 Cambridge	n/a	n/a	47.2	210	82.4	100.0
2 Durham	89.2	85.7	41.2	178	75.6	97.3
3 Dundee	74.2	76.9	55.4	175	85.6	96.8
4 University College London	88.3	88.7	51.4	171	66.1	96.6
5 Oxford	n/a	n/a	42.9	201	69.6	96.5
6 Birmingham	90.2	90.2	40.3	154	77.1	96.1
7 Glasgow	86.2	84.4	16.4	195	81.3	95.2
=8 Exeter	80.6	83.1	33.6	168	82.2	94.3
=8 Liverpool	n/a	n/a	33.5	152	79.2	94.3
10 Southampton	95.5	94.1	43.5	132	62.0	93.4
11 Newcastle	90.1	85.8	25.8	156	75.3	93.1
12 York	87.3	87.1	35.1	152	71.7	93.0
=13 Leicester	81.6	79.9	37.2	147	78.1	92.1
=13 Sheffield	n/a	n/a	31.6	143	77.8	92.1
15 Reading	92.1	81.0	44.7	136	58.6	90.9
16 Huddersfield	96.7	91.8	n/a	138	80.7	90.7
17 Swansea	86.0	85.1	39.4	117	67.9	89.4
18 Manchester	88.5	82.6	24.7	136	68.5	89.1
19 Nottingham	84.1	79.7	23.7	146	70.2	88.7
20 Queen's, Belfast	87.7	87.4	36.9	131	56.1	88.4
21 Kent	81.1	78.4	33.1	142	65.3	88.1
22 Aberdeen	85.9	79.3	29.4	n/a	63.3	87.9
23 Bangor	94.3	85.1	24.3	109	n/a	87.7
24 Hull	85.5	79.7	31.7	123	65.4	87.4
25 Bradford	79.4	75.4	23.6	119	77.8	86.3
26 Greenwich	84.9	89.1	n/a	145	68.9	85.8
27 Worcester	87.3	77.1	8.1	113	77.8	85.3
28 De Montfort	92.9	95.1	n/a	106	65.9	84.5
29 Robert Gordon	72.8	77.5	8.8	152	72.4	84.4
30 Glasgow Caledonian	71.9	69.3	4.7	174	70.3	84.1
31 Coventry	88.6	88.6	n/a	121	64.4	83.6
=32 Cardiff	82.4	79.3	31.1	127	48.7	83.4
=32 Keele	73.4	74.1	n/a	166	69.7	83.4
=32 Liverpool John Moores	83.7	84.0	n/a	138	64.0	83.4
=32 Staffordshire	90.5	87.7	n/a	122	60.8	83.4
36 Bournemouth	82.4	82.3	19.9	117	58.6	83.2

37	Winchester	88.2	82.4	7.5	97	68.9	82.9
38	Central Lancashire	83.1	78.9	9.8	139	55.5	82.6
=39	Lincoln	81.2	83.3	n/a	118	71.4	82.5
=39	West of England	81.6	84.2	n/a	134	63.8	82.5
41	Edinburgh	74.2	70.9	20.9	179	43.4	82.4
=42	Chester	89.2	88.0	15.4	107	50.3	82.2
=42	Derby	89.0	88.6	3.6	103	61.5	82.2
44	West London	86.7	87.8	n/a	120	59.7	82.1
45	West of Scotland	78.3	74.7	n/a	135	67.3	81.4
46	Anglia Ruskin	74.0	77.9	24.6	117	57.1	81.1
47	Nottingham Trent	76.2	72.4	4.1	140	63.5	81.0
48	Manchester Metropolitan	78.2	75.4	n/a	143	57.8	80.3
49	Teesside	78.0	74.1	n/a	125	63.0	79.6
50	Canterbury Christ Church	80.4	75.7	16.3	116	49.5	79.4
51	South Wales	81.4	80.5	n/a	128	51.3	79.0
=52	Abertay	70.5	68.6	n/a	161	50.0	77.6
=52	Kingston	79.5	72.8	6.9	n/a	52.4*	77.6
54	Wales Trinity St David	88.6	72.7	17.3	99	35.5	76.8
55	London South Bank	77.6	78.6	n/a	112	52.0	76.6
56	Birmingham City	64.4	63.7	n/a	122	64.3	75.1
57	Cumbria	n/a	n/a	1.5	89*	35.7	72.8

Employed in professional job	32%	Employed in non-professional job and Studying	6%
Employed in professional job and studying	2%	Employed in non-professional job	25%
Studying	24%	Unemployed	12%
Average starting professional salary	£18,800	Average starting non-professional salary	£16,000

Architecture

Three years into their careers, architects are among the least likely of all graduates to say that they wished they had taken a different degree or chosen another profession. It is not a matter of money, at that stage at least – architecture is not in the top 40 subjects for starting salaries, although earning potential is much greater later for successful architects. The workload on degree courses is above average (16 hours a week, compared to 14 for all subjects) but initial employment prospects are good: architecture has moved into the top 12 of the 67 subject groups for the proportion of graduates finding high-level work or continuing to study. Seven out of ten graduates went straight into a professional role in 2016.

Applications and enrolments were up for the second year in a row in 2016, but the subject is yet to recover the popularity it had established before £9,000 fees were introduced. The length of courses may be one reason that architecture is yet to share fully in the recovery taking place in other subjects. Qualification usually takes seven years, in which the first degree is but a step on the way. That is a considerable financial commitment, especially when course materials can add another £1,000 to the burden. Nevertheless, there were still close to six applications per place in 2016 and satisfaction rates are higher after graduation than during the course itself.

The top four universities for architecture have remained the same since last year, when Bath took over the leadership from Cambridge. But there is plenty of movement further down the table, with Strathclyde climbing five places into fifth place and Queen's Belfast enjoying a six-place rise to eighth. Derby has done even better, jumping 24 places to 18th. Bath has the best graduate prospects and good scores on all the other measures, but the most satisfied students – both in relation to teaching quality and the broader student experience – are at the University for the Creative Arts, where the subject is taught at the Canterbury School of Architecture. The table contains one name that may be unfamiliar: Manchester School of Architecture is a joint enterprise between Manchester and Manchester Metropolitan universities.

There are no particular subjects required for entry to most degrees in architecture, although some universities prefer candidates with art A-level or equivalent, and most welcome maths. Entry standards at the leading universities are relatively high – more than 220 points average at Cambridge – but five universities towards the bottom of the table average less than 100 points on the new UCAS tariff.

Architecture

		Teaching quality %	Student experience %	Research quality %	Entry standards (UCAS points)	Graduate prospects %	Overall score
1	Bath	92.9	92.8	52.9	215	96.8	100.0
2	Cambridge	81.3	76.5	49.0	221	93.2	94.9
3	Sheffield	n/a	n/a	36.6	169	95.4	94.5
4	University College London	n/a	n/a	54.1	199	94.2	92.8
5	Strathclyde	88.8	81.4	23.0	196	94.5	91.7
6	Cardiff	86.8	81.2	40.7	174	89.8	91.1
7	Newcastle	77.5	76.4	43.7	184	94.1	90.9
8	Queen's, Belfast	82.1	78.4	35.2	159	93.4	88.9
9	Edinburgh	74.8	72.8	35.1	195	87.8	87.8
10	Nottingham	84.5	85.3	14.8	172	90.7	87.1
11	Kent	77.6	81.9	33.3	153	91.8	87.0
12	Manchester School of Architecture	83.0	84.6	12.6	171	91.8	86.6
13	West of England	95.3	94.2	10.6	137	87.3	86.3
14	Liverpool	78.1	77.6	43.5	150	83.7	86.0
15	Oxford Brookes	86.1	86.3	17.6	154	86.7	85.7
16	Robert Gordon	90.4	88.1	8.3	167	81.7	85.0
17	Dundee	83.9	77.0	8.7	161	88.6	84.0
18	Derby	85.3	82.8	6.7	119	93.4	82.8
=19	De Montfort	77.2	75.2	35.9	110	87.5	82.6
=19	Westminster	91.0	88.8	10.7	138	78.2	82.6
=21	Cardiff Metropolitan	90.1	89.3	n/a	123	88.2	82.4
=21	Central Lancashire	93.2	87.4	3.0	140	80.0	82.4
=21	University for the Creative Arts	96.8	96.5	3.4	119	79.0	82.4
24	Northumbria	87.4	87.9	5.9	149	79.2	82.0
25	Plymouth	84.5	83.0	13.2	118	86.5	81.8
26	Liverpool John Moores	80.3	76.9	4.9	156	80.7	80.2
27	Ulster	72.2	63.8	28.6	128	85.4	80.1
=28	Birmingham City	83.6	80.1	9.6	126	81.3	80.0

=28 University of the Arts London	82.8	85.4	n/a	122	86.7	80.0
30 Coventry	86.5	87.1	10.3	125	74.8	79.6
31 Arts University, Bournemouth	84.2	86.4	2.4	119	81.6	79.2
=32 Nottingham Trent	81.4	83.5	3.4	126	82.1	79.1
=32 Portsmouth	80.4	81.9	n/a	125	85.8	79.1
34 Edinburgh Napier	72.5	73.8	5.7	167	80.0	79.0
35 Lincoln	79.6	79.2	3.2	124	84.2	78.7
36 Northampton	91.0	84.5	n/a	101*	78.9	78.2
=37 Huddersfield	80.8	73.6	n/a	131	82.7	78.1
=37 Kingston	81.5	82.0	10.1	124	75.3	78.1
39 Leeds Beckett	86.9	83.2	5.6	106	76.8	77.8
40 Greenwich	82.2	69.8	2.0	122	82.8	77.7
=41 Brighton	80.8	73.3	13.1	116	76.7	77.4
=41 Southampton Solent	90.2	86.8	n/a	91	78.6	77.4
43 London Metropolitan	80.0	72.1	7.2	136	73.6	76.9
44 Salford	76.8	80.6	19.6	118	68.6	76.2
45 Bolton	78.3	79.2	2.5	n/a	75*	75.5
46 Sheffield Hallam	77.1	77.4	13.4	111	67.6	74.3
47 London South Bank	74.3	73.7	19.6	99	70.8	74.2
48 Norwich University of the Arts	81.8	66.4	n/a	98	76.9	73.8
49 Middlesex	81.6	85.4	13.3	97	62.5	73.6
50 Anglia Ruskin	68.4	61.9	5.2	89*	80.0	71.4
51 East London	80.6	73.5	8.1	107	54.1	70.1
52 Glasgow Caledonian	61.4	46.2	9.1	n/a	68.0	63.9

Employed in professional job	66%	Employed in non-professional job and Studying	1%
Employed in professional job and studying	5%	Employed in non-professional job	9%
Studying	10%	Unemployed	9%
Average starting professional salary	£20,000	Average starting non-professional salary	£15,392

Art and Design

The numbers starting courses in both fine art and design dropped slightly in 2016, although design, in particular, remains one of the biggest recruiters in higher education. There were still more than 19,000 entrants to design degree courses and 4,600 for fine art.

Only nursing attracts more applications than art and design, taken together, despite the fact that the subjects always feature in the lower reaches of the tables for employment and earnings. They remain just outside the bottom ten for the numbers going into graduate-level jobs or further study, but in the bottom seven for starting salaries. However, artists and designers have always accepted that they are likely to have a period of lowly paid self-employment early in their career while they find a way to pursue their vocation.

Brunel, in seventh place, was the only university to see more than 80 per cent of 2016 graduates achieve positive destinations. However, Newcastle retains the leadership of the table that it assumed last year for the first time. University College London remains second, beaten in the sections of the National Student Survey devoted to teaching quality, only by Bangor, which is just outside the top ten and which also has the highest satisfaction levels in other areas of the survey. Lancaster has moved up four places to third.

Most courses in art and design are at post-1992 institutions – including several specialist arts universities – but older foundations fill the top 14 places. Higher entry standards are partly responsible, although most artists would argue that entry grades are of less significance than in other subjects. Selection in art and design rests primarily on the quality of candidates' portfolios and many undergraduates enter through a one-year Art Foundation course. Predictably, Oxford has the highest entry grades, although Glasgow is not far behind. Nottingham Trent is the highest-placed modern university, after a 13-place rise.

Art and Design	Teaching quality %	Student experience %	Research quality %	Entry standards (UCAS points)	Graduate prospects %	Overall score
1 Newcastle	83.5	85.3	37.3	191	73.1	100.0
2 University College London	94.9	89.7	44.7	161	60.7	99.3
3 Lancaster	84.6	87.2	48.0	165	65.6	98.3
4 Oxford	n/a	n/a	39.7	215	71.4	98.2
5 Loughborough	80.0	80.9	35.3	192	69.9	97.7
6 Glasgow	71.6	65.3	37.2	210	75*	96.5
7 Brunel	82.6	79.5	32.8	145	80.6	96.2
8 Leeds	80.7	78.7	33.6	170	71.4	95.8
9 Aberystwyth	94.0	92.5	21.6	120	71.3	95.0
10 Kent	76.2	78.3	44.3	132	79.5	94.7
=11 Bangor	95.7	95.0	n/a	123	75.5	93.7
=11 Dundee	82.0	80.7	39.9	156	60.4	93.7
13 Heriot-Watt	78.3	76.6	31.1	158	69.1	93.0
14 Ulster	81.7	73.3	57.2	118	63.2	92.8
15 Nottingham Trent	84.7	83.7	4.7	148	77.3	92.7
16 Goldsmiths, London	79.9	76.9	25.9	189	55.6	92.3
17 Essex	89.3	87.5	46.9	102*	56.4	92.0
=18 Arts University, Bournemouth	84.6	79.6	2.4	150	76.7	91.9
=18 De Montfort	91.3	89.4	10.2	115	71.7	91.9
=18 West of England	91.0	89.4	15.0	125	65.7	91.9
21 Reading	74.4	67.4	38.9	142	72.2	91.4
22 Coventry	82.6	79.3	18.1	134	72.2	91.3
23 Edinburgh	82.4	79.2	27.9	169	53.0	91.2
24 Manchester Metropolitan	81.4	80.0	9.7	155	68.6	90.7
=25 Kingston	85.3	81.9	10.1	152	63.3	90.6
=25 Lincoln	86.7	84.8	7.1	131	70.0	90.6
=27 Bournemouth	80.5	83.2	15.0	116	78.1	90.5
=27 Middlesex	88.7	86.1	13.3	118	67.4	90.5
=29 Liverpool Hope	86.8	79.6	n/a	131	75.2	90.1
=29 Robert Gordon	86.5	81.1	11.5	158	56.8	90.1
31 Falmouth	84.5	77.6	3.0	126	78.6	90.0
32 Southampton	79.4	73.5	35.4	145	57.8	89.9

33 Portsmouth	84.4	80.4	n/a	127	75.2	89.3
34 Northumbria	79.4	77.0	13.3	150	64.3	89.0
35 Wales Trinity St David	85.3	81.5	39.2	114	50.4	88.8
36 Sheffield Hallam	88.9	84.1	15.5	115	59.5	88.7
=37 Edinburgh Napier	80.6	79.8	n/a	166	62.4	88.5
=37 Staffordshire	88.0	83.0	2.3	112	70.5	88.5
=39 Abertay	80.7	74.7	n/a	177	59.6	88.4
=39 Norwich University of the Arts	85.0	79.9	5.6	140	62.4	88.4
41 Huddersfield	83.6	79.8	4.8	129	67.9	88.2
42 Chichester	92.3	89.5	n/a	115	60.0	88.0
43 Westminster	80.1	75.6	22.5	119	65.1	87.9
44 Liverpool John Moores	84.2	81.9	7.2	151	54.1	87.7
45 Winchester	88.9	87.6	n/a	115	63.2	87.6
=46 Brighton	85.2	79.0	13.1	125	58.0	87.2
=46 Cardiff Metropolitan	87.8	84.7	7.9	118	57.9	87.2
=46 Central Lancashire	84.8	77.9	3.9	143	58.1	87.2
=46 Oxford Brookes	89.8	83.4	10.4	139	46.7	87.2
=50 Hertfordshire	83.6	77.8	5.8	113	69.4	87.1
=50 London Metropolitan	83.7	76.1	4.7	119	68.5	87.1
=52 Plymouth	85.5	82.2	14.7	125	51.9	86.6
=52 Salford	89.3	84.4	8.0	135	47.0	86.6
54 Teesside	78.8	79.9	2.9	122	69.0	86.3
55 Suffolk	88.7	87.2	n/a	127	52.9	86.2
56 Anglia Ruskin	87.9	84.3	8.5	111	55.4	86.1
57 Hull	81.9	81.3	11.2	109	61.5	85.9
58 University for the Creative Arts	82.1	77.7	3.4	132	58.4	85.5
59 Derby	83.3	81.3	3.1	125	56.1	85.4
60 London South Bank	80.3	73.7	12.8	108	64.4	85.3
61 West London	84.9	76.9	4.5	118	56.5	84.7
62 Bolton	87.6	79.1	n/a	118	54.7	84.6
63 Birmingham City	79.3	75.4	9.6	133	52.6	84.2
64 Glasgow Caledonian	78.3	75.0	1.8	171	43.8	84.0
65 Bath Spa	76.3	69.2	9.6	124	61.6	83.9
66 Sunderland	78.8	73.0	9.8	118	57.5	83.7
67 University of the Arts London	76.3	71.1	8.0	125	60.0	83.6
68 Greenwich	77.9	70.7	3.5	137	56.0	83.5
=69 Chester	76.1	70.7	6.2	130	57.9	83.2
=69 Worcester	83.2	78.2	11.1	110	49.8	83.2
71 Wrexham Glyndŵr	88.1	83.8	7.8	95	46.4	82.7
72 Leeds Beckett	83.1	78.7	1.2	113	52.4	82.6
73 Canterbury Christ Church	85.4	76.8	7.3	108	48.2	82.5
74 South Wales	76.1	69.7	3.3	120	60.5	82.4
75 Northampton	85.7	82.8	2.9	110	45.3	82.2
=76 Buckinghamshire New	77.2	69.8	6.1	110	57.2	81.6
=76 Cumbria	81.6	78.8	6.1	109	47.9	81.6
78 Southampton Solent	79.9	77.6	1.6	104	53.9	81.2

		Teaching quality %	Student experience %	Research quality %	Entry standards (UCAS points)	Graduate prospects %	Overall score
79	York St John	81.6	77.7	n/a	118	44.4	80.5
80	East London	76.6	69.9	9.8	107	50.3	80.1
81	Gloucestershire	75.6	69.7	n/a	118	53.2	80.0
82	Bedfordshire	65.4	64.3	n/a	94	43.2	72.4

Employed in professional job	52%	Employed in non-professional job and Studying	2%
Employed in professional job and studying	1%	Employed in non-professional job	28%
Studying	8%	Unemployed	10%
Average starting professional salary	£18,000	Average starting non-professional salary	£15,470

Biological Sciences

Only zoology, of the biological sciences, failed to register another increase in enrolments in 2016, although the signs are that there may have been a marginal decline in the current academic year. Applications for biology itself and for genetics were running at record levels in 2016, with more than five of them to each place. The group as a whole remains the most popular in the sciences.

Cambridge and Oxford (in that order) make it 13 years in a row at the head of the Biological Sciences table. But there is plenty of movement elsewhere, notably at Lancaster, which has jumped 14 places to fifth, and Bristol, which has come from outside the top 20 to enter the top ten. Once again, the students most satisfied with the quality of teaching are at Lincoln, which is outside the top 40 overall, having chosen not to enter the 2014 Research Excellence Framework in this category.

Satisfaction rates are high generally – only five of the 100 universities dropped below 70 per cent in the sections relating to teaching quality. Graduates are less enthusiastic, however: three years after graduation a third of biologists wish they had chosen a different subject – one of the biggest proportions in the arts or sciences. Employment rates and graduate salaries are surprisingly modest, with the biological sciences outside the top 40 for both. More than 40 per cent of graduates stay on for a postgraduate qualification, either full or part-time, but the 11 per cent unemployment rate is above average for all subjects.

Cambridge's Natural Sciences degree boasts some of the highest entry grades in any subject, averaging 244 points on the new UCAS tariff. Nationally, microbiology provides the stiffest competition, with almost six applications to the place, but the leading universities' requirements can be tough across all the subjects in this category. Many will demand two sciences at A-level, or the equivalent – usually biology and chemistry – for any of the biological sciences.

		Teaching quality %	Student experience %	Research quality %	Entry standards (UCAS points)	Graduate prospects %	Overall score
Biological Sciences							
1	Cambridge	80.6	77.4	52.5	244	84.9	100.0
2	Oxford	n/a	n/a	50.9	218	83.3	98.7
3	Imperial College	74.6	76.8	61.6	210	87.1	97.8

4 St Andrews	87.8	91.8	37.6	210	73.0	97.6
5 Lancaster	86.4	88.4	46.5	163	82.7	96.9
6 Durham	82.4	80.7	32.9	208	81.0	95.6
=7 Dundee	81.9	84.9	55.4	165	77.0	95.4
=7 University College London	75.2	85.8	55.4	193	76.1	95.4
=7 York	84.7	82.7	41.9	185	77.0	95.4
10 Bristol	82.3	85.2	46.8	189	73.5	95.2
11 King's College London	n/a	n/a	38.0	172	82.7	94.8
12 Warwick	84.2	85.0	37.1	163	82.7	94.7
13 Exeter	83.0	84.3	39.7	179	76.7	94.5
14 Strathclyde	73.8	79.3	52.2	193	78.9	94.3
15 Sheffield	77.5	81.2	57.4	169	76.2	94.1
=16 Edinburgh	74.8	80.1	62.9	200	66.2	93.9
=16 Kent	83.6	84.3	39.1	135	87.4	93.9
18 Birmingham	82.0	79.4	38.1	168	81.0	93.5
=19 Glasgow	80.8	82.6	33.4	202	71.4	93.3
=19 Sussex	78.5	80.2	46.8	148	85.3	93.3
21 Surrey	83.1	82.2	37.5	169	75.8	93.2
22 Leeds	79.3	81.9	40.9	166	76.5	92.5
23 Swansea	85.0	87.1	38.6	134	74.8	92.1
=24 Leicester	83.8	85.1	36.5	153	72.6	92.0
=24 Manchester	79.3	75.6	38.3	173	77.5	92.0
26 Southampton	83.3	85.5	34.2	147	74.7	91.7
27 Liverpool	84.1	82.2	33.9	156	73.0	91.6
28 Aston	81.7	82.2	39.1	134	78.3	91.3
29 Nottingham Trent	85.3	85.8	24.1	132	80.0	91.1
30 Aberdeen	84.3	84.8	34.7	172	62.0	91.0
31 Bath	76.7	78.5	31.5	176	76.7	90.9
32 Nottingham	80.9	82.8	26.5	156	75.0	90.4
33 East Anglia	75.5	81.4	38.8	151	75.3	90.1
34 Royal Holloway	84.4	85.1	25.7	135	73.9	90.0
=35 Newcastle	80.1	81.2	28.4	151	73.4	89.6
=35 Portsmouth	85.7	83.1	24.3	121	77.0	89.6
37 Brunel	n/a	n/a	18.2	131	68.5	89.5
38 Aberystwyth	87.0	86.8	38.2	117	62.5	89.1
=39 Cardiff	76.3	77.4	33.3	159	70.4	88.7
=39 Essex	88.2	86.9	17.8	124	69.3	88.7
41 Robert Gordon	79.8	76.0	4.9	179	77.8	88.5
=42 Abertay	86.6	85.0	4.3	161	67.2	88.3
=42 Huddersfield	85.8	85.4	7.8	130	76.1	88.3
44 Liverpool Hope	84.9	85.9	n/a	117	85.5	88.2
45 Lincoln	89.4	91.2	n/a	130	69.4	87.8
46 Teesside	89.2	86.4	n/a	96	83.0	87.6
=47 Reading	80.0	79.9	26.6	143	67.3	87.5
=47 Sheffield Hallam	85.7	85.1	10.4	119	73.9	87.5
49 Keele	82.4	83.2	16.5	136	69.9	87.4

Biological Sciences cont

		Teaching quality %	Student experience %	Research quality %	Entry standards (UCAS points)	Graduate prospects %	Overall score
50	Queen's, Belfast	69.3	75.3	47.3	141	69.8	87.1
51	Birkbeck	74.4	73.9	41.0	109	78.3	87.0
52	Glasgow Caledonian	75.7	74.3	8.1	173	73.5	86.5
53	Stirling	75.4	76.8	49.0	163	48.8	86.4
54	Plymouth	84.9	84.8	17.4	132	59.5	86.2
55	Staffordshire	86.9	80.7	n/a	128	71.3	86.0
=56	Oxford Brookes	77.7	79.8	21.3	129	69.7	85.9
=56	Queen Margaret, Edinburgh	87.9	77.3	n/a	140	67.9	85.9
58	Chester	88.6	84.6	12.0	120	60.3	85.8
=59	Bangor	80.8	83.1	31.5	138	52.4	85.7
=59	Cardiff Metropolitan	82.7	81.6	n/a	126	75.4	85.7
=61	Bradford	78.2	81.6	9.5	119	76.1	85.5
=61	Hull	77.4	77.0	31.7	126	64.4	85.5
=61	Queen Mary, London	n/a	n/a	26.1	149	76.9	85.5
64	St George's, London	69.3	71.0	20.0	151	77.9	85.4
65	Heriot-Watt	69.1	68.7	26.3	148	76.8	85.3
66	Coventry	77.3	75.6	4.5	112	86.2	85.2
67	Leeds Beckett	79.5	84.6	3.5	121	72.2	84.9
=68	Central Lancashire	75.5	79.6	8.3	138	72.5	84.8
=68	West of England	78.7	80.5	8.2	116	74.7	84.8
=68	West of Scotland	83.2	82.9	29.0	149	42.7	84.8
71	Ulster	85.5	82.5	n/a	119	66.7	84.5
72	Worcester	82.9	83.3	10.9	116	62.2	84.2
73	Northumbria	70.4	73.6	14.0	139	75.5	84.0
74	Middlesex	75.6	79.1	10.0	106	73.7	83.3
=75	Edinburgh Napier	78.7	76.8	8.9	156	55.5	83.2
=75	Roehampton	77.8	79.9	20.6	110	61.7	83.2
77	Brighton	82.0	80.3	4.8	117	63.2	83.1
78	Bath Spa	79.9	76.0	n/a	102	76.0	82.9
=79	Liverpool John Moores	81.5	79.7	15.1	135	50.0	82.8
=79	Westminster	71.6	77.1	21.2	112	68.9	82.8
81	Hertfordshire	75.8	72.9	10.9	111	72.2	82.6
=82	Derby	83.6	81.3	1.6	112	61.1	82.5
=82	Manchester Metropolitan	76.5	77.0	12.0	130	61.0	82.5
84	Bolton	85.4	80.4	n/a	86*	68.0	82.4
=85	Greenwich	73.0	77.9	7.4	146	61.7	82.3
=85	Salford	80.3	77.6	12.7	126	55.7	82.3
=87	Gloucestershire	77.2	83.9	14.5	114	55.2	81.8
=87	Kingston	78.9	83.6	2.6	107	63.0	81.8
89	Sunderland	79.8	81.8	7.5	96	63.0	81.7
90	Suffolk	76.7	80.5	n/a	140*	56.3	81.3
91	Bedfordshire	74.8	75.7	25.1	90	58.6	80.6

92 Edge Hill	74.2	77.0	6.2	119	60.8	80.5
93 London Metropolitan	76.0	80.4	n/a	89	64.9	79.6
94 London South Bank	68.0	74.8	35.0	95	54.7	79.5
95 Anglia Ruskin	84.4	81.6	2.2	103	44.5	79.2
96 Bournemouth	77.4	78.5	4.7	112	48.8	78.7
97 Canterbury Christ Church	72.3	67.9	11.9	101	57.3	77.7
98 Northampton	81.2	72.4	n/a	99	49.6	77.5
99 South Wales	69.3	67.1	n/a	125	58.1	77.1
100 East London	72.7	72.7	n/a	116	40.2	74.8

Employed in professional job	29%	Employed in non-professional job and Studying	3%
Employed in professional job and studying	3%	Employed in non-professional job	20%
Studying	35%	Unemployed	11%
Average starting professional salary	£20,000	Average starting non-professional salary	£15,542

Building

Both applications and enrolments on degrees in building are recovering at last, but the numbers starting courses are still down by more than a third since the recession of 2008, when the decline set in. Building is among the top eight subjects for employment prospects – and only just outside the top 10 for starting salaries in professional jobs – and yet there are still only four applications per place. There may be better times ahead, however: 2016 saw the fourth increase in a row in the demand for places.

More than 80 per cent of those completing building degrees in 2016 went straight into graduate-level employment, and only four of the 34 universities in our table dropped below this mark. Third-placed Heriot Watt registered a rare 100 per cent score for graduate prospects and several other universities came close to emulating this feat. Loughborough tops this year's table, after exchanging positions with University College London. Loughborough achieved the best grades in the Research Excellence Framework, while students on UCL's Project Management for Construction degree have the highest entry grades. In general, grades are lower than for most subjects – the average of 64 points per student at Trinity, Wales, is one of the lowest in the *Guide*.

The relatively low numbers of students on many building courses make for fluctuations in the scores, especially where satisfaction levels are concerned. Nottingham Trent, which has this year's highest score in the sections of the National Student Survey concerned with teaching quality, has gone up ten places to seventh overall. The University of Nottingham has the highest score for the broader student experience, but has dropped 12 places to 18th because of a poor year for graduate prospects.

Courses in this category include surveying and building services engineering, as well as construction. The table is dominated by post-1992 universities, although older foundations take five of the top six places. In addition to the universities in our table, many colleges offer courses in building, most of them focusing on foundation degrees and Higher National Diplomas.

Building	Teaching quality %	Student experience %	Research quality %	Entry standards (UCAS points)	Graduate prospects %	Overall score
1 Loughborough	85.3	90.6	58.3	142	96.8	100.0
2 University College London	83.3	79.3	54.1	176	88.2	99.6
3 Heriot-Watt	69.5	71.4	38.1	173	100.0	95.7
4 Reading	83.0	82.2	40.0	138	93.9	94.3
5 Oxford Brookes	84.5	82.9	17.6	113	98.0	88.9
6 Ulster	77.0	79.5	28.6	121	93.0	88.5
7 Nottingham Trent	89.5	87.6	3.4	119	97.6	88.4
8 West of England	80.7	81.2	10.6	132	94.3	88.0
9 Aston	79.9	74.7	20.6	136	84.6	86.9
10 Liverpool John Moores	84.2	84.5	4.9	135	87.0	86.5
11 Northumbria	76.7	78.9	5.9	139	90.7	85.9
12 Glasgow Caledonian	77.1	75.6	9.1	144	84.5	85.2
13 Coventry	86.8	87.2	10.3	115	83.3	85.0
14 Portsmouth	82.6	84.6	n/a	109	96.7	84.8
15 Edinburgh Napier	76.3	78.8	5.7	144	84.1	84.7
16 Sheffield Hallam	79.3	81.6	13.4	112	88.5	84.4
17 Westminster	81.0	79.0	10.7	127	82.7	84.2
=18 Anglia Ruskin	86.7	85.6	5.2	107	87.8	84.1
=18 Nottingham	85.7	92.5	14.8	131	68.8*	84.1
20 Robert Gordon	67.2	68.9	8.3	136	94.0	84.0
21 Salford	76.9	76.9	19.6	116	83.6	83.8
22 South Wales	76.5	70.5	n/a	136	88.6	83.2
23 Brighton	78.6	76.4	n/a	112	94.2	82.8
24 Derby	88.2	85.2	5.6	81	91.7	82.5
25 Birmingham City	83.1	81.8	2.7	112	82.1	81.7
26 Plymouth	72.3	67.6	13.2	115	85.5	81.2
=27 East London	68.8	75.3	8.1	n/a	83.3	79.2
=27 Kingston	68.7	74.9	n/a	112	88.4	79.2
29 London South Bank	69.1	73.8	19.6	94	81.6	78.8
=30 Greenwich	71.1	65.8	2.0	123	81.0	78.6
=30 Leeds Beckett	76.1	70.7	5.6	86	89.4	78.6
32 Central Lancashire	59.7	53.9	3.0	126	70.7	72.9
33 Bolton	74.7	76.2	2.5	n/a	47.6	66.5
34 Wales Trinity St David	51.0	43.0	n/a	64	68.0	61.7

Employed in professional job	79%	Employed in non-professional job and Studying	0%
Employed in professional job and studying	3%	Employed in non-professional job	6%
Studying	5%	Unemployed	7%
Average starting professional salary	£25,000	Average starting non-professional salary	£17,160

Business Studies

The Business Studies table is the biggest in our *Guide*, with 120 universities – two more than last year. The various branches of business and management are the largest recruiters of undergraduates in the UK, with more than 50,000 students starting courses in 2016. For the first time in four years, fewer students embarked on business degrees, but management continued its rise, with another 10 per cent increase in enrolments. Taking account of the many students who take combined honours including business or management, applications have risen by more than 40,000 during the current decade.

The subjects are the mainstay of many modern universities, but some of the most famous business schools are absent from this ranking because they do not offer undergraduate courses. Manchester Business School provides Manchester's undergraduate courses, as well as MBAs and executive education. Oxford is back on top of the table for the first time in three years, taking over from St Andrews, which is now in second place. Only two of the top dozen universities have moved by more than one place, but you do not have to look much further down the table to find real volatility. East Anglia, in 14th place, has jumped no fewer than 22 places after recovering from a poor year for graduate prospects.

Student satisfaction levels have dipped with the introduction of more focused questions in the National Student Survey. Only Leeds Trinity, just outside the top 50, scored 90 per cent in the sections relating to teaching quality, and only Buckingham – compared with ten universities last year – reached this level for the broader student experience. Three years after graduation, almost a third of respondents say they would have chosen a different subject. Disappointments in the graduate employment market may be partly responsible. Although more than half of 2016 graduates went straight into a professional job, the subjects are outside the top 40 overall. Salary levels for those who do find professional employment are much better – business studies is among a large group of subjects sharing 20th place.

Graduate prospects vary considerably between universities. The top two and two others saw 90 per cent of graduates go straight into professional employment or postgraduate study, while the rate dropped below 50 per cent at six lowly-ranked institutions – and below 40 per cent at two of them. St Andrews had the best score of all, as it did last year.

Business Studies	Teaching quality %	Student experience %	Research quality %	Entry standards (UCAS points)	Graduate prospects %	Overall score
1 Oxford	n/a	n/a	32.0	237	90.6	100.0
2 St Andrews	85.8	85.3	43.8	226	94.1	99.8
3 Bath	81.5	84.2	41.8	189	84.3	94.4
4 Lancaster	84.3	85.8	42.6	152	89.5	93.9
5 Strathclyde	80.6	81.6	44.3	206	75.3	93.8
6 Loughborough	83.7	88.2	32.6	158	92.9	93.6
7 Warwick	77.6	81.7	40.4	187	89.1	93.5
8 University College London	74.0	74.2	43.9	193	86.4	92.0
9 King's College London	n/a	n/a	38.2	189	88.8	91.9
10 Leeds	78.9	81.9	39.3	166	85.6	91.8
11 Durham	78.4	79.8	23.1	174	90.8	90.5

Business Studies cont

	Teaching quality %	Student experience %	Research quality %	Entry standards (UCAS points)	Graduate prospects %	Overall score
12 London School of Economics	69.7	74.8	52.3	188	77.0	90.4
13 York	84.9	87.5	24.0	145	81.8	90.0
14 East Anglia	82.5	87.2	28.1	150	74.8	89.1
15 Exeter	74.8	81.5	24.4	176	81.2	88.6
16 Manchester	75.2	77.8	33.3	164	80.1	88.5
=17 Aston	83.0	84.5	19.7	143	80.5	88.2
=17 Birmingham	73.5	73.9	29.1	161	89.1	88.2
19 Sheffield	75.1	80.4	26.8	149	86.5	88.0
20 Queen's, Belfast	80.1	78.7	32.7	146	72.4	87.4
21 Nottingham	73.3	77.4	32.6	154	80.7	87.3
=22 Kent	75.3	77.1	24.8	143	87.4	87.1
=22 Newcastle	72.6	78.0	20.7	159	88.3	87.1
24 Liverpool	81.0	82.8	20.1	152	73.5	87.0
25 Reading	73.4	75.0	29.3	148	84.7	86.8
26 Stirling	78.1	77.0	25.2	162	72.9	86.7
27 Glasgow	66.8	75.5	22.1	188	83.4	86.6
28 Cardiff	76.1	77.9	32.0	153	71.7	86.5
=29 Sussex	72.7	75.4	23.7	143	87.9	86.1
=29 Ulster	82.6	81.7	40.4	123	60.2	86.1
31 Aberdeen	69.1	80.2	24.9	165	77.4	85.8
32 Swansea	78.7	81.0	22.0	130	77.1	85.6
=33 Buckingham	89.9	90.8	n/a	116	75.3	85.5
=33 Leicester	77.0	80.0	24.3	138	74.9	85.5
=33 Surrey	74.9	78.2	15.8	169	74.6	85.5
36 Edinburgh	70.9	77.5	25.8	182	66.0	85.3
=37 Heriot-Watt	74.5	78.4	18.8	166	71.5	85.2
=37 Nottingham Trent	81.3	82.2	4.6	134	82.8	85.2
=37 Robert Gordon	81.8	80.6	2.6	179	67.5	85.2
40 Dundee	76.4	79.0	12.1	156	77.4	85.1
41 Southampton	72.8	75.4	24.0	146	77.5	84.7
42 SOAS London	n/a	n/a	25.0	142	67.9	84.6
43 Coventry	83.2	83.8	1.6	125	79.9	84.4
=44 Portsmouth	78.8	80.7	9.5	128	81.0	84.3
=44 Royal Holloway	72.7	76.3	27.0	156	67.5	84.3
=46 Bristol	65.4	68.0	32.1	181	66.7	83.5
=46 Essex	73.6	76.3	25.1	125	75.0	83.5
=46 Hull	79.7	81.4	10.2	118	77.4	83.5
49 Bangor	75.4	78.5	23.4	139	65.8	83.4
50 Falmouth	80.7	77.7	n/a	118	85.1	83.1
=51 Aberystwyth	78.2	78.1	14.5	118	75.3	82.9
=51 Leeds Trinity	90.1	89.7	n/a	106	63.9	82.9
=53 De Montfort	77.7	81.9	10.7	105	79.6	82.7

=53	Derby	86.9	83.3	0.9	110	70.9	82.7
=55	City	68.2	73.3	27.8	138	73.0	82.6
=55	Lincoln	77.4	79.3	4.8	121	80.6	82.6
57	Abertay	80.8	81.1	n/a	146	67.2	82.5
58	Northumbria	75.7	79.8	4.0	141	73.8	82.3
59	Brunel	71.5	76.6	23.0	138	66.1	82.1
60	Queen Mary, London	67.2	72.4	23.5	156	67.2	81.8
=61	Bradford	77.2	78.4	11.8	130	65.3	81.6
=61	Liverpool John Moores	80.4	80.0	n/a	135	67.2	81.6
=63	Bournemouth	76.7	76.7	8.8	124	71.8	81.4
=63	Oxford Brookes	74.6	77.5	5.1	123	77.7	81.4
65	West of England	77.2	79.1	5.5	120	72.5	81.3
=66	Central Lancashire	78.2	76.9	4.4	130	69.0	81.1
=66	Harper Adams	77.2	76.5	n/a	122	77.8	81.1
68	Gloucestershire	79.1	79.6	n/a	117	73.5	81.0
69	Huddersfield	75.3	75.2	4.1	137	70.9	80.9
70	Bath Spa	79.7	79.4	n/a	110	72.0	80.5
71	Keele	72.1	76.3	10.2	126	70.7	80.4
72	Liverpool Hope	80.9	81.0	n/a	112	67.2	80.3
73	Plymouth	76.0	77.8	13.1	107	66.9	80.1
=74	Sheffield Hallam	76.8	77.2	0.6	118	71.5	80.0
=74	Sunderland	81.4	82.6	0.4	104	65.9	80.0
76	Edinburgh Napier	72.6	74.8	2.3	150	65.7	79.9
77	Brighton	78.3	74.8	6.5	118	63.5	79.5
78	Edge Hill	79.6	74.7	n/a	126	62.0	79.4
=79	Manchester Metropolitan	70.3	72.8	4.7	133	70.4	79.1
=79	Staffordshire	81.2	74.8	2.6	113	62.1	79.1
=79	West London	83.3	80.3	n/a	103	60.2	79.1
82	West of Scotland	76.8	72.7	2.9	145	56.7	79.0
83	Birmingham City	79.6	80.8	1.3	113	59.0	78.9
=84	Chichester	79.6	79.0	n/a	104	64.6	78.8
=84	Glasgow Caledonian	70.3	71.1	1.8	176	55.2	78.8
=86	Birkbeck	74.3	74.5	16.1	92	66.5	78.7
=86	Hertfordshire	73.5	76.5	0.9	121	68.1	78.7
=88	Anglia Ruskin	81.5	79.8	3.4	90	61.8	78.5
=88	Winchester	78.7	75.7	n/a	108	65.4	78.5
90	London South Bank	79.7	81.9	2.1	95	61.1	78.4
=91	Chester	75.2	73.7	0.5	112	67.5	78.0
=91	Royal Agricultural University	72.8	76.7	n/a	109	69.8	78.0
93	Leeds Beckett	74.1	76.0	0.8	107	67.3	77.8
94	Middlesex	75.1	77.2	10.5	109	54.5	77.6
95	East London	81.2	82.3	0.8	110	48.1	77.5
=96	Bolton	76.9	76.9	n/a	101	62.2	77.3
=96	Buckinghamshire New	81.1	79.2	1.8	109	49.2	77.3
=98	Greenwich	73.1	73.7	3.3	133	54.3	77.1
=98	University of the Arts London	75.1	72.8	n/a	135	54.2	77.1

Business Studies cont

		Teaching quality %	Student experience %	Research quality %	Entry standards (UCAS points)	Graduate prospects %	Overall score
=98	Worcester	70.6	73.4	0.9	119	65.6	77.1
101	York St John	79.1	79.0	0.8	106	52.5	77.0
102	Wrexham Glyndŵr	78.1	76.3	n/a	93	62.0	76.9
103	Southampton Solent	72.9	74.4	n/a	99	68.0	76.7
=104	Cardiff Metropolitan	70.7	73.8	n/a	118	63.8	76.6
=104	Wales Trinity St David	88.7	85.5	n/a	93	35.9	76.6
=106	St Mary's, Twickenham	80.2	78.5	n/a	108	47.2	76.3
=106	Westminster	67.6	72.1	2.4	135	58.7	76.3
108	Suffolk	78.0	79.2	n/a	96	51.9	75.9
109	Bedfordshire	78.9	78.0	3.1	85	52.6	75.8
=110	London Metropolitan	76.8	70.5	0.6	97	59.3	75.7
=110	Teesside	69.1	69.2	2.0	109	66.5	75.7
112	South Wales	70.8	69.4	0.2	130	54.4	75.3
=113	Canterbury Christ Church	74.5	74.0	n/a	104	54.3	75.2
=113	Queen Margaret, Edinburgh	72.8	72.4	n/a	117	52.7	75.2
115	Salford	69.3	68.9	5.9	118	54.6	75.0
116	Northampton	72.8	73.7	1.0	95	56.8	74.7
117	Roehampton	67.3	71.5	4.5	98	62.4	74.6
118	Kingston	68.5	73.9	9.2	108	49.9	74.5
119	Cumbria	81.1	77.2	5.6	95	31.3	73.8
120	Newman	56.3	60.8	n/a	109	53.9	69.2

Employed in professional job	53%	Employed in non-professional job and Studying	2%
Employed in professional job and studying	3%	Employed in non-professional job	22%
Studying	10%	Unemployed	11%
Average starting professional salary	£22,000	Average starting non-professional salary	£17,500

Celtic Studies

Applications for Celtic Studies degrees dropped by more than a third in 2016, after two years of encouraging increases. Only 95 students started full-time degrees, compared with 175 in the previous year. The small numbers inevitably make for exaggerated swings in percentage terms, but the table itself is surprisingly stable. Only one of the eight universities has moved more than one place, and half – including table-topping Cambridge – occupy the same positions as last year. Two universities – Liverpool and the University of the Highlands and Islands – have dropped out of the table this year, but both expect to offer courses in the Celtic Studies category in 2018–19.

The ranking is split between four universities from Wales, which naturally major in Welsh, and the remaining four, which focus on Irish or Gaelic studies. Ironically, it is the only one from England that tops the table for the sixth year in a row. Cambridge's average entry grades are well ahead of its nearest rival, although Queen's Belfast ran it close in the 2014 Research Excellence

Framework. Student satisfaction is high across the board, although it cannot be quantified at Cambridge because of the boycott of the National Student Survey (NSS) there. Second-placed Bangor scored at least 96 per cent on each of the measures derived from the NSS.

Third-placed Aberystwyth has the best graduate prospects in a year when Celtic Studies has dropped into the group of six subjects sharing last place in the comparison of graduate salaries in professional jobs. The subjects do rather better when judged on the proportion of graduates going straight into professional employment or continuing to study, where they tie for 46th out of the 67 subject groups. Only 23 per cent were in professional employment six months after graduating, the smallest proportion of all, but just 5 per cent were unemployed and, for the third year in a row, Celtic Studies had the largest share of graduates continuing their studies.

Celtic Studies	Teaching quality %	Student experience %	Research quality %	Entry standards (UCAS points)	Graduate prospects %	Overall score
1 Cambridge	n/a	n/a	54.0	205	78.4	100.0
2 Bangor	97.1	96.0	39.6	176	72.5	96.6
3 Aberystwyth	93.6	91.7	23.7	159	83.7	93.3
4 Queen's, Belfast	95.6	93.5	53.6	139	56.1	93.2
5 Cardiff	89.2	91.2	32.5	170	73.5	92.7
6 Glasgow	87.8	84.3	41.1		75.0	91.9
7 Swansea	83.6	80.4	19.4	129	75.9	85.6
8 Ulster	85.3	83.4	35.7	124	44.2	84.0

Employed in professional job	19%	Employed in non-professional job and Studying	3%
Employed in professional job and studying	4%	Employed in non-professional job	29%
Studying	40%	Unemployed	5%
Average starting professional salary	£18,000	Average starting non-professional salary	£15,000

Chemical Engineering

The numbers starting chemical engineering degrees dropped for the first time in six years in 2016, but the total of 3,300 was still double the 2008 figure. A decline of almost 3,000 applications was a surprise, given that the subject remains among the top four subjects for starting salaries in professional jobs. Indeed, it was even higher last year, when sixth-formers were selecting courses. At the time, it was also in the top ten for positive destinations among graduates, although it is down to 14th this year.

Like other branches of the discipline, chemical, process and energy engineering remains in a healthy state, with more than six applications to the place. But the latest dip has seen it overtaken by civil and general engineering courses in terms of applications. Degree courses normally demand chemistry and maths A-levels, or their equivalent, and often physics as well. Most courses offer industrial placements in the final year and lead to Chartered Engineer status.

Cambridge tops the table for the 16th year in a row, with the highest entry standards, the best employment record and the top research score. Cambridge is ranked by QS among the top four universities in the world for chemical engineering. The most satisfied students both with teaching quality and the broader student experience are those at Bradford, although the university is only just inside the top 20 overall. Swansea is the biggest riser – up 10 places to sixth.

The degrees on offer for 2018 include specialist options such as petroleum engineering at Leeds and chemistry with green nanotechnology at Glyndŵr. Four out of five chemical engineers come with A-levels or equivalent qualifications, and average entry grades are the highest for any engineering subject – more than half of the 28 universities in the table average at least 150 points at entry. This helps produce engineering's largest proportion of Firsts and 2:1s.

Chemical Engineering	Teaching quality (%)	Student experience (%)	Research quality (%)	Entry standards (UCAS points)	Graduate prospects (%)	Overall score
1 Cambridge	85.0	90.6	62.0	239	93.8	100.0
2 Imperial College	80.8	83.9	59.6	235	86.8	95.8
3 Birmingham	76.4	79.5	47.0	186	89.1	90.6
4 Manchester	73.0	77.6	48.4	198	84.3	89.2
5 Heriot-Watt	78.4	79.7	47.8	176	82.2	88.5
=6 Edinburgh	76.9	80.8	50.3	207	73.9	87.8
=6 Swansea	77.8	82.9	45.5	136	88.2	87.8
=8 Bath	79.7	81.3	37.4	201	77.8	87.5
=8 Sheffield	73.6	80.9	36.8	171	87.7	87.5
10 Nottingham	80.4	82.9	40.8	173	80.3	87.4
11 Loughborough	82.6	93.2	41.8	160	76.9	87.2
12 Strathclyde	63.7	63.8	37.2	222	85.6	86.3
13 Lancaster	67.7	75.8	41.6	145	90.0	85.7
14 Leeds	66.0	74.4	30.7	192	85.3	85.1
15 University College London	62.4	67.2	44.6	193	81.9	84.6
16 Newcastle	73.4	71.6	30.2	167	82.8	84.0
17 Queen's, Belfast	70.4	69.1	36.7	153	83.1	83.3
18 Bradford	88.3	92.7	7.7	122	80.6	82.6
19 Surrey	83.6	87.0	30.8	164	66.7	82.4
=20 Chester	88.1	86.2	7.1	116	n/a	81.8
=20 London South Bank	81.1	78.9	19.6	110	84.0	81.8
22 West of Scotland	87.6	85.5	9.0	156	71.4	81.1
23 Hull	70.2	74.5	16.5	114	90.0	80.9
24 Huddersfield	83.9	78.9	10.2	124	n/a	80.7
25 Aston	77.0	76.7	20.6	129	78.9	80.5
26 Portsmouth	72.8	76.8	9.1	137	83.3	79.9
27 Teesside	82.1	79.0	5.8	101	77.6	77.6
28 Aberdeen	61.6	66.2	28.4	170	62.5	74.8

Employed in professional job	53%	Employed in non-professional job and Studying	1%
Employed in professional job and studying	2%	Employed in non-professional job	9%
Studying	22%	Unemployed	13%
Average starting professional salary	£27,000	Average starting non-professional salary	£16,262

Chemistry

The days when universities were closing down chemistry departments, attracting critical headlines, are now a distant memory. But seven years of growth in applications and enrolments came to an end in 2016, with small declines in both. Nevertheless, entry standards at the leading universities remain high – seven universities average more than 200 points. Some courses require maths as well as chemistry, and most successful candidates for the leading universities take more than one science at A-level.

The top four are unchanged, leaving Cambridge as the leader, with the highest entry standards and the best research grades – 97 per cent of the work submitted for the Research Excellence Framework was considered world-leading or internationally excellent. Both Cambridge and second-placed Oxford are among the top six universities in the world for chemistry, according to QS. Five of our leading universities, including Cambridge and Oxford, have no satisfaction ratings because their students boycotted the National Student Survey (NSS). The best scores on both of our measures derived from the NSS are outside the top 20, at Loughborough.

The prospects for chemistry graduates have improved in the new edition, with four universities, including Liverpool John Moores, only seven places off the bottom of the table, seeing over 90 per cent going straight into professional jobs or continuing their studies. Overall, the subject is up to 16th in the employment table, with 12th placed Aston recording positive destinations for almost 95 per cent of its graduates. The subject is a little lower for salaries in professional jobs, sharing 20th place with nine other subjects.

Chemistry is mainly old university territory, but Nottingham Trent has broken into the top 20 this year, 20 places ahead of its nearest challenger among the 13 post-1992 universities in the table. Nearly nine out of ten chemistry undergraduates come with A-levels or their equivalent. More than 100 universities and colleges plan to offer the subject in 2018.

Chemistry	Teaching quality %	Student experience %	Research quality %	Entry standards (UCAS points)	Graduate prospects %	Overall score
1 Cambridge	n/a	n/a	70.3	244	84.8	100.0
2 Oxford	n/a	n/a	63.1	231	91.4	98.4
3 Durham	84.0	84.3	49.1	224	82.0	95.0
4 York	88.6	89.0	44.6	186	84.1	94.3
5 Liverpool	n/a	n/a	55.6	152	86.7	93.3
6 St Andrews	75.6	81.6	50.3	212	82.6	92.6
7 Warwick	84.1	82.0	50.8	174	83.0	92.4
8 Manchester	n/a	n/a	46.0	177	81.5	92.2
9 Lancaster	90.8	87.2	37.5	153	n/a	91.8
10 Imperial College	69.1	70.3	54.6	212	87.2	91.7
11 Nottingham	84.1	85.1	48.5	164	82.0	91.6
12 Aston	91.5	83.8	20.6	140	94.9	91.4
13 Birmingham	86.7	87.7	37.3	162	83.3	91.3
=14 Bristol	n/a	n/a	56.6	193	75.0	91.1
=14 Edinburgh	79.9	76.4	48.4	204	78.7	91.1
16 Nottingham Trent	90.5	92.3	24.1	116	93.5	90.9

Chemistry cont

		Teaching quality %	Student experience %	Research quality %	Entry standards (UCAS points)	Graduate prospects %	Overall score
17	University College London	74.3	72.1	56.0	188	82.7	90.6
18	Keele	87.9	87.7	41.1	125	84.2	90.1
19	Glasgow	71.9	75.8	41.1	205	83.3	89.8
=20	Bath	80.4	82.0	43.0	172	79.5	89.6
=20	Southampton	85.5	85.9	50.7	139	77.6	89.6
22	Loughborough	91.9	92.4	23.9	137	82.3	89.4
23	East Anglia	82.8	82.7	39.2	156	81.6	89.3
24	Heriot-Watt	84.0	81.3	34.2	172	79.2	89.1
=25	Strathclyde	78.4	75.2	40.1	195	78.4	89.0
=25	Surrey	89.1	89.6	30.8	164	74.6	89.0
=27	Leeds	80.5	82.2	35.9	165	79.7	88.4
=27	Leicester	90.0	87.7	32.8	140	76.9	88.4
29	Sheffield	82.3	84.3	38.9	156	77.5	88.3
30	Sheffield Hallam	91.5	91.2	17.8	112	81.6	86.8
31	Queen's, Belfast	67.7	71.8	34.7	155	89.7	86.4
32	Cardiff	77.8	82.4	30.9	140	81.0	86.1
33	Sussex	81.6	82.0	25.8	137	79.2	85.6
34	Newcastle	76.5	81.1	28.5	154	76.2	85.0
35	Bangor	75.6	83.4	19.1	128	84.1	84.4
=36	Huddersfield	86.9	83.7	11.0	127	79.0	84.3
=36	Queen Mary, London	77.9	78.1	37.0	136	73.8	84.3
=38	Aberdeen	77.0	80.6	31.6	186	64.1	84.1
=38	Hull	80.3	79.7	24.2	116	81.1	84.1
40	Plymouth	80.6	77.0	25.3	120	79.7	83.9
41	Central Lancashire	85.4	83.0	11.7	113	80.9	83.8
42	South Wales	86.1	85.9	n/a	110	84.6	83.5
43	Kent	81.5	79.2	27.5	132	71.6	83.2
44	Reading	77.4	76.1	27.3	129	76.3	83.0
45	Manchester Metropolitan	78.8	80.5	16.3	128	74.6	81.8
46	Brighton	76.3	75.0	4.8	123	82.6	81.1
47	Liverpool John Moores	65.0	64.8	6.0	127	92.3	80.5
=48	Bradford	75.0	76.6	9.5	111	80.5	80.3
=48	Kingston	94.4	93.4	2.6	102	62.9	80.3
50	London Metropolitan	90.9	88.3	n/a	107	66.7	79.9
51	Greenwich	72.3	76.5	7.4	108	80.3	79.3
52	West of Scotland	80.2	76.5	29.0	147	53.3	78.9
53	Northumbria	76.9	76.3	14.0	141	60.8	77.8

Employed in professional job	40%	Employed in non-professional job and Studying	2%
Employed in professional job and studying	3%	Employed in non-professional job	12%
Studying	34%	Unemployed	10%
Average starting professional salary	£22,000	Average starting non-professional salary	£16,300

Civil Engineering

Civil engineering saw its first increase in enrolments in five years in 2015, and continued the trend since then, with moderate growth both in applications and the numbers starting courses. Graduate prospects that are in the top ten for all subjects are one obvious attraction; two thirds of leavers go straight into professional jobs, earning average salaries of £25,500, which places civil engineering just outside the top ten of the 67 subject groups.

The plentiful employment opportunities are reflected in the table, where 22 of the 54 universities saw at least nine out of ten graduates go straight into professional jobs or on to postgraduate study. Ironically, top-placed Imperial College London was not one of them, although it could hardly have been closer to this mark. Both Imperial and second-placed Cambridge are rated among the top five universities in the world by QS.

Cambridge has the highest entry standards and the best research score, while Southampton, in sixth place, had the best graduate prospects, with 98 per cent positive destinations among the 2016 graduates.

Undergraduates at West London were the most satisfied with the quality of teaching and the broader student experience, but the university is only just inside the top 40 because it did not enter the Research Excellence Framework in this subject. Scores in the National Student Survey are high throughout most of the table, although down a little on last year.

Some of the top degrees in civil engineering are four-year courses leading to an MEng; others are sandwich courses incorporating a period at work. The leading departments will expect physics and maths A-levels, or their equivalent. Fewer than half of all civil engineering undergraduates are admitted with A-levels, however, reflecting the popularity of BTEC. Almost half of the universities in the table are post-1992 institutions. Although none reaches the top 20, the University of the West of Scotland is on the verge of it after an eight-place rise.

Civil Engineering	Teaching quality %	Student experience %	Research quality %	Entry standards (UCAS points)	Graduate prospects %	Overall score
1 Imperial College	85.7	91.2	61.5	222	89.7	100.0
2 Cambridge	75.5	77.6	67.0	241	93.0	98.9
3 Glasgow	83.5	86.4	47.2	210	97.4	98.4
4 Bath	87.9	83.8	52.9	195	94.3	98.0
5 Bristol	82.5	86.2	52.3	202	89.2	96.2
6 Southampton	80.5	81.2	52.3	181	98.0	96.1
=7 Aberdeen	84.2	86.4	28.4	195*	93.1	94.4
=7 Leeds	92.6	92.8	32.0	167	88.3	94.4
9 Strathclyde	82.9	81.4	35.7	197	91.2	94.1
10 Loughborough	87.4	91.1	26.9	148	97.0	93.5
11 Nottingham	82.0	86.6	40.8	159	91.3	92.7
12 Birmingham	86.1	82.0	21.9	163	95.1	92.1
=13 Heriot-Watt	81.4	84.2	47.8	174	81.1	91.5
=13 Sheffield	74.8	80.8	43.1	166	92.5	91.5
=15 Dundee	77.4	79.1	46.2	156	92.0	91.4
=15 Queen's, Belfast	83.7	79.9	31.3	143	96.0	91.4

	Teaching quality %	Student experience %	Research quality %	Entry standards (UCAS points)	Graduate prospects %	Overall score
17 Edinburgh	75.7	83.2	50.3	194	79.5	91.3
18 Manchester	76.8	81.6	36.4	174	90.5	91.2
19 Cardiff	77.1	80.9	35.0	168	92.2	91.1
20 Swansea	78.1	78.7	45.5	139	93.9	90.9
21 West of Scotland	93.7	91.8	9.0	151	87.2	90.7
22 Newcastle	76.7	78.8	40.9	160	90.8	90.6
23 Surrey	80.1	82.4	30.8	158	89.2	90.1
24 University College London	70.2	75.0	23.1	187	97.7	90.0
25 Brunel	83.7	85.1	23.7	142	87.9	89.0
26 Abertay	88.9	86.2	16.3	133	87.1	88.6
27 Northumbria	84.6	81.3	30.7	138	83.3	88.2
28 Edinburgh Napier	85.8	88.0	7.7	147	87.5	88.1
29 Coventry	80.7	86.2	10.3	132	93.7	87.8
30 Liverpool	77.0	79.7	32.1	143	86.4	87.6
31 Greenwich	79.1	82.9	5.5	156	89.7	87.0
=32 Exeter	64.9	64.3	36.4	169	91.3	86.5
=32 London South Bank	87.6	89.5	19.6	106	83.3	86.5
34 Nottingham Trent	79.5	81.0	n/a	127	97.2	86.2
35 Glasgow Caledonian	85.3	83.9	9.1	157	78.0	86.0
=36 Bradford	75.8	79.0	17.8	124	90.4	85.4
=36 Ulster	80.0	79.5	n/a	113	97.6	85.4
38 West London	96.9	93.4	n/a	116	73.9	85.0
39 Plymouth	73.1	77.9	15.7	113	89.0	83.4
40 Portsmouth	75.2	79.2	9.1	117	87.0	83.0
=41 Salford	78.7	80.7	19.6	115	78.0	82.8
=41 West of England	80.6	80.5	10.6	109	82.4	82.8
43 Liverpool John Moores	77.3	75.5	n/a	138	84.9	82.7
44 South Wales	81.6	78.7	n/a	134	77.4	82.0
45 East London	84.5	89.6	2.3	119	70.4	81.4
46 Kingston	85.8	87.8	2.9	116	69.4	81.1
47 Teesside	71.7	74.3	5.8	122	84.4	80.9
48 Central Lancashire	69.1	67.1	7.1	154	n/a	80.4
49 Anglia Ruskin	77.8	73.6	5.2	106	81.0	80.3
50 City	75.3	75.8	20.2	132	68.6	80.2
51 Derby	76.0	76.4	6.7	92	82.8	80.0
52 Brighton	76.9	78.7	5.1	119	73.4	79.6
53 Bolton	75.8	82.1	n/a	130	63.9	77.5
54 Leeds Beckett	69.7	70.9	5.6	101	78.3	77.2

Employed in professional job	66%	Employed in non-professional job and Studying	1%
Employed in professional job and studying	2%	Employed in non-professional job	8%
Studying	15%	Unemployed	8%
Average starting professional salary	£25,500	Average starting non-professional salary	£17,420

Classics and Ancient History

Applications and enrolments for classics both rose for the third year in a row in 2016, as modern languages continued to struggle. The numbers starting degrees are now in excess of 1,000 and applications are running at record levels. Ancient history was already sharing in the increases enjoyed by other history departments. Independent schools dominate provision of Latin and Greek at A-level, producing some of the highest average grades of any subjects. However, most universities offering classics teach the subject from scratch, as well as to more practised students.

Cambridge has topped the table with Oxford in second place for the last 12 years, although, like five other universities, neither has satisfaction scores this year because of the boycott of the National Student Survey (NSS). Indeed, the top six positions are unchanged compared with the last edition of the *Guide*. Cambridge has the highest scores in the table for research and entry grades, and is only a fraction of a point behind Oxford for the top employment score.

Roehampton has the most satisfied students, despite being only one place off the bottom of the table because it was the only one of the 22 universities not to enter the Research Excellence Framework. NSS scores are high throughout the table, with only one university failing to satisfy at least three quarters of undergraduates on the quality of teaching. Several universities teach the subjects as part of a modular degree scheme, but not as degrees in their own rights, while most providers now broaden their offering with degrees in classical studies or classical civilisation that range beyond Latin or Greek.

Graduate prospects for classicists vary from year to year more than in many subjects. In the new edition, starting salaries in graduate-level employment have dropped eight places to 38th, while the proportion going into such jobs or on to further study has improved to 43rd. More than a third of graduates opt for postgraduate courses, but the unemployment rate of 12 per cent was above average in 2016.

Classics and Ancient History	Teaching quality (%)	Student experience (%)	Research quality (%)	Entry standards (UCAS points)	Graduate prospects (%)	Overall score
1 Cambridge	n/a	n/a	65.0	222	80.5	100.0
2 Oxford	n/a	n/a	58.3	210	80.6	96.3
3 St Andrews	92.3	88.3	43.2	190	80.0	94.9
4 Durham	88.4	78.4	54.3	197	68.4	93.2
5 Exeter	84.3	84.1	45.0	180	76.7	91.5
6 Warwick	n/a	n/a	45.0	157	66.3	90.1
7 Glasgow	87.1	83.1	32.7	155	84.6	89.6
8 Nottingham	84.6	76.1	52.0	148	71.4	88.9
9 University College London	76.1	70.7	42.7	185	79.5	88.5
10 Birmingham	81.6	81.8	40.3	149	73.8	87.0
=11 King's College London	n/a	n/a	43.6	164	67.8	85.8
=11 Newcastle	79.1	75.7	44.7	156	66.7	85.8
13 Edinburgh	86.1	80.8	34.9	177	54.2	85.2
14 Liverpool	n/a	n/a	28.9	164	62.5	84.8
15 Bristol	n/a	n/a	42.2	184	68.1	84.2
16 Leeds	84.8	83.3	29.1	151	60.2	83.4

Classics and Ancient History cont

	Teaching quality (%)	Student experience (%)	Research quality (%)	Entry standards (UCAS points)	Graduate prospects (%)	Overall score
17 Reading	86.8	77.9	45.2	132	50.7	83.3
18 Manchester	n/a	n/a	31.0	144	62.2	82.2
19 Royal Holloway	81.9	79.3	20.4	153	66.1	82.0
20 Swansea	85.7	79.7	25.0	114	61.0	80.2
21 Kent	70.0	59.6	33.1	117	71.7	78.0
22 Roehampton	93.1	88.8	n/a	96	51.2	75.2
23 Wales Trinity St David	89.5	77.8	15.7	95	35.0	72.9

Employed in professional job	31%	Employed in non-professional job and Studying	4%
Employed in professional job and studying	3%	Employed in non-professional job	19%
Studying	31%	Unemployed	12%
Average starting professional salary	£21,000	Average starting non-professional salary	£16,000

Communication and Media Studies

There is not just one new leader, but two, in Communication and Media Studies, where Loughborough and Sheffield cannot be separated at the top. Like six other universities in the table, Sheffield's satisfaction scores are generated from their performance on the other measures because their students boycotted the National Student Survey (NSS). Undergraduates at Northumbria are the most satisfied with the quality of teaching, while those at neighbouring Newcastle, last year's leader, gave the top score for the broader student experience. Exeter has moved up to sixth in the table, a rise of 14 places this year.

Graduate prospects are the weak suit of many universities in these subjects – fewer than half of the 2016 graduates at 18 of the 92 universities in the table had professional jobs or places on a postgraduate course by the end of the year. For the third year in a row, Kent, despite only just making the top 40 because it did not enter the Research Excellence Framework in this area, recorded an exceptional 92 per cent score for graduate prospects. But the subjects were in the bottom ten on this measure nationally and tied for last place for starting salaries in professional jobs. The division of jobs into professional and non-graduate fields of employment hits communication and media studies harder than most other subjects. Academics in the field argue that it is normal for students completing media courses to take "entry level" work that is not classified as a graduate job.

Nevertheless, courses in media studies continue to confound the sceptics who believed that a combination of £9,000 fees and poor employment prospects would bring about the collapse in recruitment long predicted in the media itself. Although journalism did see a small decline in the numbers starting degrees in 2016, both applications and enrolments for media studies were up by 10 per cent.

Communication and media studies used to be the preserve of post-1992 universities, but older institutions have been moving in and now occupy the top 19 places. Liverpool Hope is the one modern university in the top 20. Entry standards are generally modest, with seven universities averaging less than 100 points on the new UCAS tariff.

Communication and Media Studies

	Teaching quality %	Student experience %	Research quality %	Entry standards (UCAS points)	Graduate prospects %	Overall score
=1 Loughborough	81.7	84.9	62.3	148	77.6	100.0
=1 Sheffield	n/a	n/a	37.9	148	86.8	100.0
3 Leeds	78.9	76.5	54.5	162	79.7	99.1
4 Newcastle	88.3	93.2	37.8	148	77.4	98.7
5 Lancaster	85.9	86.6	51.4	147	70.8	98.0
6 Exeter	86.3	85.1	46.2	163	65.0	97.8
7 Warwick	n/a	n/a	61.7	172	54.2	97.5
8 Cardiff	83.2	88.9	55.4	146	63.4	96.6
9 East Anglia	78.3	73.3	43.8	158	75.2	95.6
10 Stirling	82.4	80.8	36.0	177	59.1	95.2
11 Southampton	86.5	86.3	42.7	142	63.0	94.6
12 King's College London	n/a	n/a	55.8	168	53.1	94.5
13 Leicester	74.1	75.3	46.1	141	80.0	94.1
14 Queen's, Belfast	n/a	n/a	38.3	159	44.6	93.8
15 Sussex	74.5	75.4	43.6	140	78.4	93.4
=16 Goldsmiths, London	n/a	n/a	60.0	140	62.5	93.2
=16 Surrey	72.8	73.5	30.2	154	82.7	93.2
18 Queen Mary, London	n/a	n/a	35.1	143	61.0	93.1
19 Salford	85.4	83.3	36.9	132	62.4	91.8
20 Liverpool Hope	87.8	91.6	nn	110	91.1	91.0
21 Birkbeck	88.9	82.0	34.7	94	76.9	90.8
22 Swansea	88.5	82.9	18.5	115	76.5	90.6
23 Royal Holloway	77.2	70.8	38.1	155	58.1	90.3
24 Strathclyde	73.5	66.1	39.4	196	40.0*	90.0
25 Northumbria	90.4	83.8	22.2	140	52.4	89.8
26 Liverpool	n/a	n/a	27.5	139	60.3	89.4
27 Glasgow Caledonian	77.4	73.4	15.2	172	56.2	88.6
28 Keele	78.8	77.9	25.0	123	69.6	88.1
=29 Coventry	77.6	77.6	18.1	132	69.1	87.7
=29 Nottingham Trent	84.2	80.5	10.0	127	68.8	87.7
31 Robert Gordon	76.3	72.3	7.5	166	61.3	87.4
32 Brunel	74.1	76.7	23.0	126	70.2	87.0
33 Portsmouth	85.5	82.8	12.8	110	68.3	86.7
34 Oxford Brookes	79.1	81.3	25.3	127	57.3	86.6
35 De Montfort	76.6	76.3	31.2	103	68.9	86.0
36 Bangor	87.3	85.5	24.7	126	42.7	85.9
=37 Kent	64.1	64.9	n/a	139	92.3	85.6
=37 Lincoln	75.7	75.8	4.0	137	70.2	85.6
=39 Manchester Metropolitan	76.6	74.5	29.0	129	53.6	85.3
=39 Sunderland	81.3	80.0	13.0	111	67.0	85.3
=41 Bournemouth	74.7	73.8	15.1	130	64.5	84.9
=41 Falmouth	79.2	72.6	n/a	120	76.6	84.9

Communication and Media Studies
cont

		Teaching quality %	Student experience %	Research quality %	Entry standards (UCAS points)	Graduate prospects %	Overall score
43	Leeds Beckett	85.3	85.8	11.0	108	60.2	84.8
44	Edge Hill	88.8	84.3	10.2	125	46.8	84.7
=45	Liverpool John Moores	78.0	77.7	6.2	129	64.3	84.6
=45	Plymouth Marjon	90.3	89.2	n/a	112	57.1	84.6
=47	Edinburgh Napier	70.5	70.7	9.5	163	55.3	84.5
=47	Queen Margaret, Edinburgh	72.7	67.8	14.0	155	55.7	84.5
=47	Roehampton	80.9	79.2	26.4	97	62.2	84.5
=47	Westminster	67.6	66.7	28.3	135	62.2	84.5
=51	Bath Spa	79.8	75.3	13.9	120	60.2	84.1
=51	City	66.1	56.7	30.1	126	71.9	84.1
=51	Derby	87.2	81.3	13.5	107	55.5	84.1
54	Staffordshire	78.5	76.1	6.7	107	71.5	83.6
55	Greenwich	78.0	79.3	3.5	129	60.0	83.5
56	Leeds Trinity	87.2	83.0	3.9	102	60.3	83.3
57	Southampton Solent	83.6	81.5	0.8	110	62.2	83.0
58	Huddersfield	78.1	75.6	n/a	118	67.8	82.9
59	Teesside	81.3	74.4	2.9	111	66.2	82.8
=60	East London	84.3	82.7	13.9	109	50.2	82.7
=60	University for the Creative Arts	88.7	87.9	3.4	95	57.7	82.7
=60	West of England	77.8	76.8	18.6	117	53.1	82.7
63	London Metropolitan	83.0	73.7	5.9	100	66.3	82.5
=64	Aberystwyth	81.4	80.0	9.2	107	56.0	82.0
=64	Central Lancashire	76.2	74.3	7.9	124	57.1	82.0
=64	London South Bank	86.1	82.7	12.8	97	51.8	82.0
=67	Ulster	73.0	72.3	34.0	126	39.7	81.7
=67	West of Scotland	69.2	59.9	11.3	152	53.5	81.7
69	Gloucestershire	77.3	77.0	9.3	115	54.5	81.2
70	University of the Arts London	77.8	74.7	n/a	110	64.2	81.1
=71	Birmingham City	75.6	70.0	6.0	119	59.2	80.9
=71	Hull	84.3	80.7	11.2	113	41.9	80.9
=73	Middlesex	71.9	70.6	11.0	110	62.0	80.4
=73	Worcester	78.6	73.2	8.2	110	54.2	80.4
75	Sheffield Hallam	75.7	74.3	14.4	114	49.9	80.2
76	Winchester	71.4	73.5	15.8	111	55.0	80.0
77	Chester	80.2	72.1	4.3	109	54.5	79.9
=78	Canterbury Christ Church	73.6	74.2	7.3	110	57.1	79.6
=78	Kingston	72.9	68.2	15.7	118	50.0	79.6
80	York St John	88.8	83.7	4.4	108	35.3	79.3
=81	Anglia Ruskin	81.0	76.8	26.4	93	38.1	79.0
=81	Bradford	79.9	75.4	n/a	120	45.3	79.0
83	Brighton	72.7	70.0	16.2	113	48.8	78.9
84	Bedfordshire	80.4	81.8	8.2	91	46.3	77.9

85 Chichester	83.1	79.6	n/a	112	38.1	77.8
86 Cumbria	92.0	84.6	n/a	98	29.2	77.2
=87 South Wales	73.6	68.7	n/a	124	42.1	76.5
=87 St Mary's, Twickenham	71.7	70.1	9.1	107	46.5	76.5
89 Northampton	75.7	73.5	n/a	105	46.2	76.2
90 Wrexham Glyndŵr	66.8	58.0	7.8	105	58.1	75.8
91 Buckinghamshire New	68.1	66.8	n/a	109	40.2	72.7
92 West London	55.6	53.1	4.5	106	57.0	71.8

Employed in professional job	47%	Employed in non-professional job and Studying	2%
Employed in professional job and studying	2%	Employed in non-professional job	29%
Studying	9%	Unemployed	12%
Average starting professional salary	£18,000	Average starting non-professional salary	£15,717

Computer Science

Computer science is the ultimate example of students reacting to their perception of the jobs market when they choose courses. Applications declined for a decade after the dot.com bubble burst but, with the exception of a single year when £9,000 fees were introduced, they have risen strongly throughout this decade. There have been further substantial rises in applications and enrolments both in 2016 and 2017. The latest survey showed almost two-thirds of graduates going straight into professional roles and the subject was 18th in the salary league, averaging £24,000 in graduate-level jobs.

Cambridge, which has the highest entry standards, has retained the leadership of the table. It is rated in the top five in the world for computer science by QS, with Oxford only two places lower.

However, it is Imperial College, which produced the best grades in the Research Excellence Framework and whose students were only two points behind Cambridge's on entry standards, which has moved up to second in our table. The students most satisfied with their teaching, feedback and academic support, are at West London, while Loughborough is the top university for the broader student experience.

Although computer science has a good employment record overall, the table shows the advantage of winning a place at one of the leading universities. All but three of the top 20 universities registered positive destinations for at least 90 per cent of graduates, whereas only three of the bottom 20 reached 70 per cent. Bath had the best record in 2016, with almost 97 per cent of graduates going straight into professional employment or continuing their studies. Entry standards also vary more widely than in most subjects, with average scores on the new UCAS tariff ranging from more than 200 points at six universities to less than 100 points at another six.

Some of the leading universities demand maths at A-level, or the equivalent, while others want computing or computer science. The most competitive area is the small field of artificial intelligence, where there were only 109 places in 2016, while the strongest growth has been in computer games courses.

Computer Science

	Teaching quality %	Student experience %	Research quality %	Entry standards (UCAS points)	Graduate prospects %	Overall score
1 Cambridge	n/a	n/a	57.1	234	93.7	100.0
2 Imperial College	77.9	84.3	64.1	232	94.8	99.1
3 Warwick	91.1	90.1	54.8	194	92.6	98.6
4 Oxford	n/a	n/a	60.6	222	91.8	98.0
5 St Andrews	89.6	89.4	33.4	204	93.2	96.4
6 Durham	84.3	83.5	38.8	210	89.3	94.8
7 Surrey	91.4	86.2	25.3	180	94.7	93.9
8 Birmingham	79.5	82.9	46.4	181	94.6	93.4
9 Southampton	81.0	84.3	48.2	174	90.3	92.8
10 Manchester	78.7	81.0	50.7	179	91.0	92.7
11 Bath	79.7	79.8	33.3	188	96.4	92.3
12 Sheffield	81.6	83.5	51.1	152	90.7	91.7
=13 Exeter	78.6	85.3	40.7	168	93.3	91.6
=13 Swansea	82.8	85.1	47.5	140	94.4	91.6
=15 Lancaster	80.2	80.4	44.8	158	95.0	91.5
=15 University College London	63.7	68.9	62.7	201	94.9	91.5
=17 Glasgow	73.4	77.0	50.3	197	85.8	91.2
=17 Loughborough	90.4	91.3	18.7	152	92.8	91.2
=17 Nottingham	83.3	83.2	45.4	164	85.3	91.2
20 Royal Holloway	88.1	83.3	35.1	149	91.1	91.1
21 Bristol	n/a	n/a	49.2	196	91.0	91.0
22 York	78.0	74.3	46.9	165	94.6	90.9
=23 Edinburgh	69.9	69.4	54.3	197	88.7	90.5
=23 King's College London	n/a	n/a	47.6	167	91.2	90.5
25 Leeds	76.5	83.1	41.6	165	91.1	90.3
26 Liverpool	n/a	n/a	40.5	149	89.0	89.5
27 Newcastle	76.5	77.4	49.7	156	87.7	89.3
28 Strathclyde	78.6	79.4	21.1	193	85.6	88.9
=29 East Anglia	77.2	79.1	35.9	150	90.5	88.1
=29 Heriot-Watt	75.9	76.2	39.5	166	85.2	88.1
31 Stirling	81.6	83.7	14.0	150	93.4	87.5
32 Dundee	76.7	82.6	29.4	160	85.4	87.4
33 Kent	72.6	75.1	37.8	149	93.0	87.2
34 Essex	77.4	79.4	34.3	135	88.7	86.5
35 Aberystwyth	80.0	79.7	38.4	108	91.9	86.4
36 Cardiff	73.9	75.3	25.0	162	89.1	86.1
37 Aston	80.5	79.8	21.7	133	90.0	85.9
38 Liverpool Hope	90.0	88.4	8.8	126	83.0	85.8
39 Sussex	79.3	75.9	21.6	137	91.6	85.7
40 Nottingham Trent	87.7	87.4	5.2	141	81.8	85.5
41 Lincoln	85.8	86.9	13.6	130	82.7	85.4
42 Queen's, Belfast	72.6	74.3	29.5	147	88.6	85.1

43 Leicester	73.4	73.7	30.2	150	84.5	84.7
44 Aberdeen	65.9	70.6	37.4	154	89.1	84.6
45 Brunel	n/a	n/a	25.2	136	84.8	84.1
46 Queen Mary, London	67.9	73.6	37.4	141	84.2	83.6
=47 Plymouth	78.5	73.6	21.8	134	80.6	83.0
=47 West London	93.0	90.8	1.2	111	73.6	83.0
49 Hull	77.7	73.3	22.2	126	84.2	82.9
=50 Bangor	79.2	75.7	17.6	131	80.2	82.6
=50 Keele	77.7	79.6	10.8	133	83.2	82.6
=52 Abertay	82.1	77.0	3.4	146	78.7	82.5
=52 Robert Gordon	80.8	80.9	4.3	148	76.4	82.5
54 Huddersfield	77.4	76.9	7.4	145	81.8	82.4
55 West of England	77.2	76.6	5.9	138	82.2	81.7
56 City	78.0	79.0	19.2	151	65.2	81.6
57 Portsmouth	81.7	79.2	7.2	126	77.6	81.5
58 Reading	69.9	67.3	16.3	138	87.9	81.2
59 Staffordshire	81.4	79.8	0.4	121	80.6	80.9
60 Sheffield Hallam	79.7	78.9	14.4	117	75.2	80.8
61 Derby	81.9	75.5	5.0	120	79.1	80.7
=62 Coventry	73.3	75.6	3.3	135	84.1	80.5
=62 East London	90.7	91.3	2.3	117	60.0	80.5
64 Cardiff Metropolitan	80.3	81.5	n/a	113	81.5	80.3
65 Central Lancashire	81.6	79.7	n/a	142	69.3	80.2
66 De Montfort	74.7	73.7	13.4	108	85.2	80.1
67 Goldsmiths, London	74.7	75.1	29.2	125	65.9	79.8
=68 Bradford	77.9	78.2	n/a	128	73.3	79.0
=68 Salford	77.7	77.2	15.3	133	62.5	79.0
=70 Bournemouth	72.1	71.1	8.5	125	80.5	78.9
=70 Liverpool John Moores	78.4	77.4	3.2	138	66.8	78.9
72 Edinburgh Napier	71.7	71.1	5.2	135	78.9	78.8
73 Wales Trinity St David	88.8	85.0	1.0	104	62.4	78.7
74 Worcester	82.4	75.6	n/a	105	75.5	78.4
75 South Wales	79.5	77.2	3.6	128	66.2	78.3
=76 Sunderland	82.7	76.7	1.8	112	69.3	78.2
=76 Ulster	73.5	72.8	16.6	123	69.3	78.2
78 Anglia Ruskin	83.8	82.8	n/a	101	68.6	78.0
=79 Greenwich	75.3	73.7	7.3	141	63.9	77.9
=79 Middlesex	79.2	80.3	14.2	124	57.2	77.9
=81 Northumbria	73.2	69.4	4.0	148	67.6	77.7
=81 Oxford Brookes	63.6	72.2	13.0	120	83.3	77.7
=83 Gloucestershire	78.0	76.9	n/a	121	69.6	77.6
=83 Leeds Beckett	79.0	76.6	0.2	112	71.7	77.6
85 West of Scotland	75.2	70.4	3.2	133	68.3	77.2
86 Manchester Metropolitan	71.6	71.2	5.6	137	68.8	77.1
87 Glasgow Caledonian	70.9	68.4	4.0	151	66.8	77.0
88 Hertfordshire	64.6	70.3	7.8	121	81.6	76.9

Computer Science cont

		Teaching quality %	Student experience %	Research quality %	Entry standards (UCAS points)	Graduate prospects %	Overall score
89	Teesside	78.3	72.8	3.4	120	65.2	76.7
=90	Edge Hill	71.6	74.0	0.3	122	71.7	76.2
=90	Westminster	73.4	77.7	2.9	120	65.8	76.2
=92	Kingston	75.7	76.4	5.3	112	64.7	76.1
=92	Wrexham Glyndŵr	87.8	84.2	3.9	98	50.6	76.1
94	Brighton	69.6	70.4	6.4	116	73.4	75.9
95	Chester	77.1	68.6	1.3	113	67.5	75.6
96	London South Bank	n/a	n/a	19.6	90*	66.7	75.3
97	Southampton Solent	77.2	73.7	n/a	103	66.8	75.2
98	Birmingham City	69.7	69.1	4.9	124	63.0	74.3
=99	Buckinghamshire New	78.6	76.8	n/a	94	59.9	73.9
=99	Northampton	73.5	66.8	n/a	110	66.5	73.9
101	Canterbury Christ Church	79.6	72.3	n/a	107	55.8	73.8
102	London Metropolitan	79.4	78.7	0.7	96	54.9	73.7
103	Bolton	68.7	59.2	n/a	116	66.0	72.2
104	Bedfordshire	69.3	69.1	9.1	89	61.7	71.9
105	Suffolk	78.6	73.0	n/a	91	46.4	70.7
106	Birkbeck	56.9	59.7	28.7	106	n/a	70.0

Employed in professional job	62%	Employed in non-professional job and Studying	1%
Employed in professional job and studying	2%	Employed in non-professional job	13%
Studying	10%	Unemployed	12%
Average starting professional salary	£24,000	Average starting non-professional salary	£16,000

Creative Writing

Creative writing is locked together with six other subjects at the bottom of the salaries table and only three places off it for the proportion of graduates going straight into professional jobs or continuing their studies. But the demand for places was steady in 2016, with 3,250 applications and 815 students taking up places. Some 90 universities and colleges plan to offer undergraduate courses in the subject starting in 2018. Many will be part of a joint honours programme or are still too small to qualify for our table, which is now in its fourth year. Creative writing is paired with subjects as diverse as ceramics, business and biology, but more normally with English.

The top two in the table are unchanged since last year, with Warwick leading the way, with the highest entry grades and the best performance in the 2014 Research Excellence Framework. Chichester, in 33rd place, posted the best scores for teaching, feedback and academic support in the National Student Survey, while Coventry and Manchester Metropolitan tied for the highest levels of satisfaction with other elements of the student experience.

Only one university – Lancaster, in third place – saw more than 80 per cent of graduates go straight into professional jobs or further study. Indeed, only five managed 70 per cent and the rate was below 20 per cent at two universities. But most applicants recognise that professional employment will be uncertain and some are not even aiming for a full-time job on graduation. Nevertheless, creative writing – or imaginative writing, as it is known by UCAS – has been a significant, but little-noticed area of growth in higher education over recent years. With only four applications to the place, entry standards are generally low – only seven of the 50 universities averaged more than 150 points on the new UCAS tariff. The table is largely composed of post-1992 universities, although the top ten are all older foundations.

Creative Writing	Teaching quality %	Student experience %	Research quality %	Entry standards (UCAS points)	Graduate prospects %	Overall score
1 Warwick	n/a	n/a	59.8	196	60.6	100.0
2 Newcastle	87.3	79.4	54.3	166	n/a	96.8
3 Lancaster	75.4	74.5	47.0	164	84.6	93.9
4 Birmingham	84.1	78.2	37.0	164	76.8	93.5
5 Nottingham	80.4	75.7	56.6	172	57.1	93.1
6 Queen's, Belfast	83.3	80.3	53.1	155*	57.1	92.1
7 Royal Holloway	79.1	72.7	49.9	149	73.7	91.7
8 Bangor	86.3	83.2	46.3	137	64.1	91.4
9 East Anglia	77.5	78.8	36.2	176	57.9	90.2
10 Surrey	76.7	75.9	39.1	145*	69.0	88.7
11 Coventry	87.7	85.7	18.1	124	71.9	87.5
12 Brunel	80.0	77.0	30.9	141	62.1	86.8
13 Manchester Metropolitan	90.0	85.7	29.0	119	52.9	86.2
14 Bath Spa	87.9	78.0	23.5	126	62.1	86.0
=15 Hull	88.8	79.9	22.7	120	63.2	85.9
=15 Portsmouth	80.1	80.8	17.1	123	78.4	85.9
17 West of England	84.5	78.9	35.4	126	52.9	85.8
18 Reading	77.8	71.2	36.3	n/a	66.7*	85.7
19 Aberystwyth	86.0	82.8	31.2	109	55.8	84.7
20 Birmingham City	78.9	76.1	30.9	108	69.7	84.2
21 Liverpool John Moores	82.5	77.0	17.9	135	53.3	83.2
22 Gloucestershire	87.5	84.1	9.3	123	51.4	82.4
=23 De Montfort	75.8	74.3	24.1	107	68.9	82.0
=23 Middlesex	88.0	83.6	11.0	107	56.5	82.0
25 Westminster	78.8	79.4	28.9	106	52.1	81.3
26 London South Bank	85.4	82.3	12.8	86	65.6	80.8
27 Plymouth	70.1	75.8	30.5	120	51.4	80.4
=28 Chester	80.2	76.9	10.7	114	56.9	80.0
=28 Winchester	87.2	85.6	n/a	125	43.4	80.0
30 St Mary's, Twickenham	79.8	68.1	14.6	110	62.5	79.9
31 Falmouth	89.6	72.0	n/a	116	53.8	79.6
32 York St John	82.3	73.8	9.7	117	n/a	79.5
33 Chichester	92.6	83.1	16.3	96	36.3	79.4
34 Derby	81.4	76.8	13.5	113	48.1	79.2
=35 Central Lancashire	70.8	67.7	9.9	127	63.2	78.9

	Teaching quality %	Student experience %	Research quality %	Entry standards (UCAS points)	Graduate prospects %	Overall score
=35 Edge Hill	79.6	78.7	12.1	120	43.9	78.9
=37 Bolton	75.8	68.6	14.4	105*	63.0	78.6
=37 Roehampton	76.3	75.8	20.8	109	48.0	78.6
39 Northampton	89.2	79.6	15.3	103	35.0	78.5
40 South Wales	79.9	73.0	12.8	117	40.0	77.4
41 Worcester	85.9	75.7	8.2	111	28.8	76.0
42 Southampton Solent	81.9	78.8	n/a	95*	48.3	75.6
43 Salford	72.8	69.9	7.8	121	42.9	75.4
44 Bedfordshire	75.7	72.8	45.8	90	17.6	75.3
45 Sheffield Hallam	77.6	72.8	14.6	110	30.9	74.9
46 Bournemouth	62.6	58.3	15.1	123	50.0	74.0
47 Kingston	67.5	61.9	15.7	111	44.2	73.6
48 Greenwich	60.9	63.7	14.4	114	47.8	73.0
49 East London	85.5	77.3	n/a	94	23.5	72.2
50 Canterbury Christ Church	72.8	69.0	8.0	101	18.8	69.4

Employed in professional job	31%	Employed in non-professional job and Studying	6%
Employed in professional job and studying	3%	Employed in non-professional job	30%
Studying	16%	Unemployed	15%
Average starting professional salary	£18,000	Average starting non-professional salary	£15,000

Criminology

The Criminology table has seen a considerable shake-up in only its second year of publication, with 11 universities joining, one of them going straight to the top. That university is Lancaster, which is the clear leader even though it did not register the top score on any of the individual measures, while last year's leader, York, has dropped 11 places. Fourth-placed Birmingham is another new entrant, while Swansea has moved up six places to third.

Criminology is the latest discipline to be added to our subject tables. The data previously appeared in the sociology and law tables, but the growth in demand for degrees in criminology justified a ranking of its own. In 2016, that growth was stronger, in percentage terms, than in any other subject, as more universities began to offer criminology or policing, partly in response to moves towards a graduate-entry police force. The number of students aged 21 or under shot up from 3,700 to 4,700, with more than 130 universities and colleges teaching criminology, albeit in some cases only as part of a broader social science degree.

Sociology or psychology A-level will be welcomed by some departments, but there are no specific entry requirements for criminology degrees apart, possibly, from a GCSE in maths since the course is likely to involve the use of statistics. Durham has the highest entry standards and Kent the best research score. Students at third-placed Swansea are the most satisfied, both with the quality of teaching and with the broader student experience.

Criminology is in the bottom six subjects for the proportion of graduates going straight into professional employment or further study and only a little better in the comparison of salaries. Although the unemployment rate is a respectable 10 per cent, almost 40 per cent of graduates start out in lower-level jobs. Not one of the 59 universities with enough criminology graduates to compile a score saw three-quarters of the 2016 cohort achieve positive destinations. Liverpool Hope came closest, but the proportion dropped below half at 16 universities. Many criminology graduates eventually find employment in the police force, prison service, the Home Office, charities or law practices.

Criminology	Teaching quality %	Student experience %	Research quality %	Entry standards (UCAS points)	Graduate prospects %	Overall score
1 Lancaster	78.9	74.8	51.4	154	73.3	100.0
2 Sussex	85.8	84.5	27.9	145	n/a	98.6
3 Swansea	87.3	88.4	20.4	136	69.6	98.4
4 Birmingham	82.9	78.6	40.1	149	n/a	98.1
5 Manchester	n/a	n/a	27.2	153	68.4	97.5
6 Leeds	78.9	79.6	40.1	155	60.4	97.1
7 Essex	76.4	78.1	44.3	139	70.5	97.0
8 Stirling	83.4	77.0	33.8	161	52.3	96.5
9 Kent	74.3	73.0	59.0	124	72.4	96.4
10 Durham	74.2	71.5	28.7	172	67.4	96.1
11 Surrey	84.4	82.5	n/a	165	64.3	96.0
12 York	75.3	73.9	47.5	161	55.6	95.8
13 Nottingham	78.6	77.9	43.5	139	n/a	95.1
14 Portsmouth	84.7	80.9	12.1	127	67.2	94.4
15 Liverpool Hope	86.5	81.4	8.6	112	73.5	94.3
16 Plymouth	86.0	81.8	16.0	116	63.4	93.6
=17 Nottingham Trent	82.5	80.5	5.1	131	68.2	93.4
=17 Southampton	72.9	70.8	52.8	143	53.8	93.4
19 Leicester	81.7	82.4	26.3	138	47.9	92.9
20 City	81.0	80.2	19.2	132	n/a	92.8
21 Aberystwyth	84.6	82.1	14.3	115	61.3	92.6
=22 Huddersfield	83.1	78.7	9.5	126	62.9	92.4
=22 Queen's, Belfast	75.8	75.7	39.3	139	50.9	92.4
24 Northumbria	79.2	80.1	12.7	145	54.1	92.0
25 Liverpool John Moores	79.9	79.2	5.8	132	63.0	91.7
26 Coventry	85.9	85.1	n/a	121	57.3	91.6
27 Abertay	83.1	76.4	5.0	160	44.4	91.4
=28 Cardiff	72.9	69.6	30.8	153*	51.3	91.1
=28 Lincoln	79.3	78.1	5.8	126	64.8	91.1
30 Edinburgh Napier	79.1	75.9	n/a	163	50.0	90.8
31 Hull	73.5	72.3	14.3	131	68.3	90.6
32 Sheffield Hallam	82.5	79.6	14.4	117	53.7	90.5
33 Bradford	81.1	79.6	10.6	124	51.9	89.9
34 Gloucestershire	85.9	86.1	n/a	117	47.9	89.7

	Teaching quality %	Student experience %	Research quality %	Entry standards (UCAS points)	Graduate prospects %	Overall score
=35 Birmingham City	81.7	82.2	3.8	118	53.8	89.5
=35 De Montfort	76.2	73.2	11.2	115	66.9	89.5
37 East London	83.9	81.6	10.6	103*	n/a	89.4
38 West of England	80.5	79.9	10.9	127*	47.1	89.3
=39 Manchester Metropolitan	80.0	76.7	6.9	131	50.7	89.2
=39 Royal Holloway	78.7	76.6	n/a	142	52.0	89.2
41 Wrexham Glyndŵr	83.1	81.9	n/a	97	62.5	89.0
42 Central Lancashire	78.5	75.6	11.8	139	44.6	88.9
43 Middlesex	75.7	75.6	14.9	129	52.0	88.7
44 London Metropolitan	78.9	76.2	8.8	112	56.7	88.3
45 Bangor	86.9	82.8	n/a	124*	36.9	88.2
=46 Southampton Solent	81.5	83.5	n/a	100	55.4	87.8
=46 West London	76.6	70.6	n/a	117	65.1	87.8
48 Westminster	82.9	83.6	n/a	107	48.8	87.7
49 Northampton	83.9	82.4	n/a	106	46.9	87.4
=50 Edge Hill	78.8	74.2	12.1	119	44.1	86.9
=50 Greenwich	74.6	70.7	2.1	134	53.4	86.9
=52 Anglia Ruskin	84.6	82.4	5.4	93	44.4	86.6
=52 South Wales	78.1	76.2	15.4	129	34.8	86.6
54 Canterbury Christ Church	87.1	81.2	3.2	106	34.7	86.4
55 Kingston	78.0	76.4	n/a	109	53.3	86.2
56 Brighton	75.7	73.0	12.4	117	46.6	86.1
=57 Derby	78.5	74.3	2.4	103	54.2	85.9
=57 Teesside	75.8	69.5	15.0	97	56.5	85.9
59 London South Bank	70.0	69.9	20.1	95	59.4	85.2
60 Chester	81.6	74.8	0.3	107	41.1	84.8
61 Suffolk	81.3	78.4	n/a	101	39.3	84.3
62 Winchester	78.7	77.2	4.4	106	38.0	84.1
63 Roehampton	76.3	73.6	n/a	96	52.7	84.0
64 Leeds Beckett	75.0	74.3	6.4	107	34.2	82.3

Employed in professional job	33%	Employed in non-professional job and Studying		4%
Employed in professional job and studying	3%	Employed in non-professional job		34%
Studying	16%	Unemployed		10%
Average starting professional salary	£19,500	Average starting non-professional salary		£16,000

Dentistry

Applications for degrees in dentistry continue to fall, despite the fact that graduates in the subject are the best-paid in higher education. The numbers seeking places were down by another 8 per cent in 2016, leaving them 30 per cent lower than at the start of the decade. Even so, there were more than eight applications to the place and entry standards are high – nowhere averages less than 175 points on the new UCAS tariff. Most schools demand chemistry and biology, and some also require maths or physics.

For the fifth year in a row, dentistry is the only subject whose graduates were paid more than £30,000 in "professional" jobs six months after leaving university. There is no figure for less skilled work because virtually everyone who completes a degree goes on to become a dentist, so the subject is also in the top two in the employment table. None of the 15 undergraduate dental schools saw less than 98 per cent of graduates going into professional jobs or further study. This measure is not used to determine positions so as not to exaggerate the impact of tiny numbers delaying their entry into the profession.

Most degrees last five years, although several universities offer a six-year option for those without the necessary scientific qualifications. The number of places has been increased in recent years to tackle shortages of dentists, but there are still more applications to the place than in any subject except medicine.

Scores in the subject are so close that the ranking changes frequently, but Glasgow has held on to the lead it assumed last year. Glasgow has the highest entry standards and good scores for student satisfaction and employment. Second-placed Dundee did best in the sections of the National Student Survey concerned with teaching quality, while Newcastle and Sheffield tied for the best scores on the broader student experience. Student satisfaction remains high at almost all the dental schools. Fourth-placed Manchester produced the best results in the Research Excellence Framework, as it did in the 2008 assessments.

Dentistry

	Teaching quality %	Student experience %	Research quality %	Entry standards (UCAS points)	Graduate prospects %	Overall score
1 Glasgow	93.1	90.2	29.3	225	98.4	100.0
2 Dundee	97.4	94.6	22.1	216	100.0	98.3
3 Newcastle	97.0	95.2	43.6	193	98.6	97.5
4 Manchester	87.8	85.6	57.1	193	98.5	95.9
5 Queen's, Belfast	91.2	91.1	50.7	184	98.8	94.5
6 King's College London	89.6	88.7	40.9	187	98.2	92.1
7 Bristol	82.9	80.1	47.1	195	99.0	92.0
8 Queen Mary, London	74.5	76.0	48.3	206	98.1	91.6
9 Cardiff	88.2	88.2	36.8	189	99.2	91.2
10 Liverpool	n/a	n/a	31.7	179	99.2	90.2
11 Sheffield	95.6	95.2	28.5	177	98.3	89.9
12 Birmingham	88.4	85.8	19.2	197	99.2	88.9
13 Central Lancashire	93.6	91.8	8.3	n/a	100.0	86.9
14 Leeds	76.0	78.6	31.7	190	98.5	85.1
15 Plymouth	80.9	81.4	9.5	191	98.3	82.6

Employed in professional job	95%	Employed in non-professional job and Studying		0%
Employed in professional job and studying	2%	Employed in non-professional job		1%
Studying	0%	Unemployed		1%
Average starting professional salary	£31,000	Average starting non-professional salary		–

Drama, Dance and Cinematics

Exeter has taken over at the top of the table for Drama, Dance and Cinematics in a year when all three subjects show a drop in the number of students starting degrees. Applications for dance and cinematics remained broadly stable in 2016, but drama saw its first decline for four years. As a group, the three main subjects attracted almost 95,000 applications – enough to maintain a table of 97 universities.

There are more than six applications to the place in drama and in cinematics and photography, although the ratio is nearer 5:1 in dance. The subjects' popularity has never been reflected in high entry grades – quality of performance is a more important criterion on many courses. No university averages 200 points at entry and three average less than 100. Edinburgh Napier has the highest score, at 188 points, but is restricted to seventh place overall. The majority of institutions offering drama, dance or cinematics are post-1992 universities, but Napier and Coventry are their only representatives in the top 20.

Students on Teesside's performing arts degree are the most satisfied in the country, with at least 94 per cent responding positively about both teaching quality and their broader experience in the National Student Survey. The Royal Conservatoire of Scotland has by far the best of a generally poor set of employment figures, with 84 per cent of leavers going straight in to professional jobs or further study. Overall, drama, dance and cinematics are in the bottom ten for graduate prospects, despite an unemployment rate of 9 per cent that is no higher than the average for all subjects, and they tie with six others for last place in the salaries table. As in other performing arts, freelancing and periods of temporary employment are common for new graduates – more than a third started out in low-level jobs in 2016.

Drama, Dance and Cinematics	Teaching quality %	Student experience %	Research quality %	Entry standards (UCAS points)	Graduate prospects %	Overall score
1 Exeter	89.3	88.2	46.3	183	74.6	100.0
2 Lancaster	87.5	86.9	48.0	166	72.5	97.4
3 Essex	89.7	87.9	37.7	160	78.9	97.3
4 Sheffield	n/a	n/a	60.0	161	72.1	97.2
5 Birmingham	84.5	85.8	36.9	181	73.9	97.0
6 Warwick	n/a	n/a	61.7	167	63.6	96.7
7 Edinburgh Napier	89.2	82.7	37.9	188	63.1	96.5
8 Sussex	93.4	83.0	45.6	143	75.0	96.1
9 Manchester	n/a	n/a	58.6	180	60.0	95.1
10 Glasgow	74.5	75.8	53.9	184	67.0	94.6
11 Central School of Speech and Drama	n/a	n/a	47.7	145	71.9	94.2
12 Queen Mary, London	81.5	76.8	68.4	156	60.2	94.0
13 Leeds	83.8	82.7	28.0	159	70.0	92.1
14 East Anglia	80.9	79.8	43.8	184	50.5	91.9
=15 Bristol	n/a	n/a	48.7	185	57.1	90.4
=15 Coventry	86.3	84.7	18.1	134	77.9	90.4
=15 Royal Conservatoire of Scotland	n/a	n/a	11.3	145	84.8	90.4
18 Loughborough	84.0	87.8	32.4	148	61.3	90.3
19 Royal Holloway	75.2	70.6	50.6	155	63.8	89.9

20 Kent	78.3	76.0	44.3	139	68.3	89.6
21 Surrey	73.9	70.2	27.2	173	66.7	89.0
22 York	80.3	81.4	26.0	163	57.4	88.6
23 Nottingham Trent	85.1	79.4	10.0	157	65.3	88.4
24 Edinburgh	74.6	69.8	48.0	164	54.0	88.3
25 Arts University, Bournemouth	82.0	78.7	2.4	147	76.6	87.8
26 Nottingham	78.7	76.5	45.8	138	58.1	87.7
27 Huddersfield	86.0	82.0	28.0	124	64.0	87.5
28 Oxford Brookes	81.0	80.1	27.8	130	63.0	86.4
=29 Robert Gordon	86.8	81.6	11.5	n/a	56.3	86.1
=29 Ulster	90.7	86.4	40.0	123	42.3	86.1
=31 Chichester	89.1	87.7	9.7	136	55.6	85.9
=31 Middlesex	79.7	79.0	16.1	130	70.5	85.9
33 Reading	77.8	71.2	34.8	145	54.3	85.5
34 Aberystwyth	84.1	82.0	30.3	117	58.1	85.3
35 East London	84.5	79.9	11.2	144	56.1	85.2
36 De Montfort	79.4	79.0	14.5	121	72.4	85.1
37 Queen Margaret, Edinburgh	78.5	71.5	14.0	164	54.5	85.0
=38 Liverpool Hope	n/a	n/a	3.0	118	73.7	84.8
=38 Roehampton	79.6	74.7	46.6	124	50.7	84.8
40 Chester	88.2	85.0	4.3	128	58.8	84.5
=41 Falmouth	79.1	75.5	6.2	128	73.4	84.4
=41 Hertfordshire	79.2	76.1	5.3	129	72.6	84.4
43 Birmingham City	86.2	82.2	11.6	134	53.1	84.3
44 Hull	86.3	85.5	11.2	132	52.7	84.2
45 Goldsmiths, London	73.9	74.4	28.3	136	58.2	83.8
46 Brunel	73.6	70.0	32.0	134	56.5	83.3
47 Portsmouth	80.9	82.1	n/a	130	64.0	83.1
=48 Aberdeen	81.5	70.5	29.3	171*	28.1*	83.0
=48 Manchester Metropolitan	82.8	77.9	7.5	138	54.1	83.0
=48 Newman	91.1	85.0	9.6	109	54.8	83.0
51 Northumbria	84.7	82.2	13.3	143	42.7	82.9
=52 Norwich University of the Arts	82.2	78.7	n/a	131	62.4	82.8
=52 Queen's, Belfast	74.6	73.4	38.3	142	43.7	82.8
=52 Teesside	96.7	94.0	2.9	124	38.7	82.8
55 Lincoln	85.1	81.8	6.5	132	51.8	82.7
56 Liverpool John Moores	83.6	83.7	n/a	140	51.9	82.5
57 Staffordshire	85.3	82.6	n/a	117	60.2	82.1
58 Westminster	80.6	78.9	n/a	118	67.1	82.0
=59 Gloucestershire	86.8	84.5	n/a	124	52.5	81.9
=59 London South Bank	85.9	80.5	n/a	113	61.8	81.9
61 Bath Spa	78.6	73.2	10.7	131	57.3	81.7
=62 Edge Hill	83.5	82.7	3.8	135	47.6	81.5
=62 Sunderland	81.8	80.0	4.2	120	58.7	81.5
64 Central Lancashire	77.0	72.7	3.9	138	57.7	81.3
65 West of England	79.2	76.4	n/a	128	60.6	81.2

Drama, Dance and Cinematics cont	Teaching quality %	Student experience %	Research quality %	Entry standards (UCAS points)	Graduate prospects %	Overall score
66 St Mary's, Twickenham	88.0	82.8	n/a	126	44.8	80.5
67 Plymouth	76.3	78.4	20.2	129	44.4	80.2
68 Derby	77.8	71.3	5.1	118	60.4	79.8
69 West London	82.2	73.6	2.3	118	53.7	79.4
70 Cardiff Metropolitan	88.1	84.6	n/a	125	38.1	79.3
71 York St John	80.9	75.9	10.5	123	42.9	78.8
=72 London Metropolitan	85.3	80.2	n/a	113	46.4	78.6
=72 University for the Creative Arts	75.9	72.8	3.4	126	52.7	78.6
74 Southampton Solent	81.3	76.6	n/a	112	51.9	78.2
75 Suffolk	85.8	90.1	n/a	114	36.7	77.8
76 Sheffield Hallam	78.6	74.5	14.4	114	43.4	77.6
=77 South Wales	75.3	69.5	6.4	134	43.7	77.5
=77 Winchester	76.0	73.0	11.2	118	46.6	77.5
=79 Bedfordshire	83.0	78.6	5.6	97	49.7	77.4
=79 Kingston	74.2	70.6	15.7	127	41.5	77.4
81 Salford	76.8	72.8	7.2	128	41.5	77.2
82 Northampton	79.4	73.2	n/a	122	44.9	77.0
83 Greenwich	65.0	67.9	3.5	146	49.5	76.9
84 University of the Arts London	76.3	71.3	n/a	122	49.0	76.8
85 Leeds Beckett	76.4	70.7	1.7	123	45.7	76.4
86 Wales Trinity St David	81.6	73.6	n/a	113	43.8	76.3
87 West of Scotland	65.2	52.9	n/a	139	59.5	76.2
88 Canterbury Christ Church	72.8	71.3	15.2	116	42.7	76.0
89 Brighton	71.2	61.3	13.1	121	46.3	75.6
90 Bournemouth	56.3	52.5	15.1	140	54.5	75.0
91 Bishop Grosseteste	81.0	76.1	n/a	94	44.8	74.6
92 Worcester	81.4	82.1	3.5	112	29.0	74.5
93 Anglia Ruskin	73.7	72.7	16.9	101	39.7	74.4
94 Cumbria	71.6	66.7	n/a	116	42.1	73.1
95 Bolton	70.4	63.4	n/a	117	43.1	72.8
96 Buckinghamshire New	68.3	66.8	n/a	113	36.8	70.9
97 Wrexham Glyndŵr	69.0	56.8	n/a	80	56.4	70.4

Employed in professional job	45%	Employed in non-professional job and Studying	2%
Employed in professional job and studying	2%	Employed in non-professional job	33%
Studying	9%	Unemployed	9%
Average starting professional salary	£18,000	Average starting non-professional salary	£15,000

East and South Asian Studies

The apparent surge in interest in China, including the promotion of Mandarin in some sixth forms, has barely impacted on higher education. Indeed, the numbers starting degrees dropped in 2016 and the total for East and South Asian Studies slipped back below 500. Both applications and enrolments for non-European languages as a group have fallen by more than 4 per cent since 2008. Japanese is the main draw among East and South Asian subjects, although only 215 students started degrees in 2016. The figure for Chinese was only 140.

Most undergraduates learn their chosen language from scratch, although universities expect to see evidence of potential in other modern language qualifications. East and South Asian studies are often included in broader modern languages or area studies degrees, but the School of Oriental and African Studies, in London, offers a range of languages, including Burmese, Indonesian, Thai, Tibetan and Vietnamese. South Asian Studies is available at only four universities.

Degrees in these subjects are afforded extra protection by the Government because of their small size and their economic and cultural importance. Despite the low numbers, this year's table is extremely stable, however, with Cambridge retaining the lead and registering the highest entry grades and the best employment score. Students at second-placed Durham are the most satisfied with the quality of teaching, although there are no scores for the other three universities in the top four because of the boycott of the National Student Survey (NSS) there. Nottingham Trent did best in the remaining sections of the NSS.

The small numbers make for exaggerated swings, especially in the employment table. As a group, East and South Asian studies remain well outside the bottom ten this year, but still have the second-highest unemployment rate in our table, at 18 per cent. Those who secured professional employment in 2016 did much better, however. The subjects share 20th place in the earnings table with nine others.

East and South Asian Studies	Teaching quality %	Student experience %	Research quality %	Entry standards (UCAS points)	Graduate prospects %	Overall score
1 Cambridge	n/a	n/a	45.0	224	86.0	100.0
2 Durham	84.6	75.3	34.6	188	n/a	96.4
=3 Manchester	n/a	n/a	48.9	166	68.9	96.3
=3 Oxford	n/a	n/a	36.2	218	82.4	96.3
5 Leeds	77.2	78.1	30.6	161	67.0	90.7
6 Edinburgh	76.2	76.5	30.1	188	58.5	90.4
7 SOAS London	n/a	n/a	26.3	165	60.8	89.9
8 Hull	82.8	72.6	22.7	130	n/a	87.1
9 Nottingham	65.7	64.0	27.3	140	78.1	85.7
10 Nottingham Trent	83.6	83.5	10.0	113	n/a	85.4
11 Sheffield	73.5	69.7	16.7	149	66.1	84.9
12 Westminster	84.1	77.6	11.3	n/a	46.2*	84.4
13 Oxford Brookes	83.6	79.7	n/a	129	52.3	81.9
14 Central Lancashire	72.7	62.4	n/a	120	51.0	75.8

Employed in professional job	41%	Employed in non-professional job and Studying	2%
Employed in professional job and studying	2%	Employed in non-professional job	18%
Studying	20%	Unemployed	18%
Average starting professional salary	£22,000	Average starting non-professional salary	£18,000

Economics

Students have flocked to economics degrees since higher fees were introduced, attracted by excellent prospects for graduates. There was another 5 per cent increase in the numbers starting courses in 2016, contributing to growth of almost 20 per cent since £9,000 fees arrived in 2012. The subject remains in the top four for graduate starting salaries, reflecting the value that employers place on a subject that they see combining the skills of the sciences and the arts. Surprisingly, it has dropped out of the top 20 for the proportion of graduates going straight into professional jobs or continuing their studies, but it is still in the top third.

The number of applications topped 55,000 for the first time in 2016 and the 8,670 enrolments also constituted a record. With more than six applications for every place, competition is stiff: Oxford and Cambridge entrants average more than 230 points on the new UCAS tariff and another six universities average more than 200. Many of those considering a degree in economics underestimate the mathematical skills required. Most of the leading universities demand maths at A-level or its equivalent as part of offers that are consistently high. The range of entry scores has been widening, however, as more universities have joined the table: nine have averages of less than 100 points in the latest table.

Cambridge has won back the top position it lost to Oxford two years ago, with the highest entry grades and the best graduate prospects. The London School of Economics took the laurels in the Research Excellence Framework, while Central Lancashire, in 45th place, had the best score in the sections of the National Student Survey (NSS) concerned with teaching quality. Coventry did best in the remaining sections of the NSS. The leading universities invariably produce some of the highest graduate salaries of the year. While the average for 2016 in "professional" jobs was £27,000, Cambridge economists averaged £45,000 six months after graduation and £61,000 five years later.

Economics	Teaching quality %	Student experience %	Research quality %	Entry standards (UCAS points)	Graduate prospects %	Overall score
1 Cambridge	n/a	n/a	45.0	252	94.3	100.0
2 Oxford	n/a	n/a	58.0	231	87.6	99.8
3 University College London	75.3	74.3	70.2	205	88.7	99.5
4 Warwick	77.0	82.6	49.6	206	89.7	98.0
5 London School of Economics	62.4	61.3	70.7	214	88.4	95.4
6 Leeds	82.2	85.8	39.3	169	87.9	95.2
7 St Andrews	80.6	80.4	23.6	214	89.6	95.1
8 Loughborough	84.1	88.4	32.6	153	90.7	94.6
9 Nottingham	78.6	83.4	31.7	184	87.7	93.9
10 Bath	70.6	70.2	41.8	190	92.0	93.3
11 Aberdeen	86.0	86.4	16.0	168	87.9	92.6
12 Durham	72.7	72.6	23.1	209	91.8	92.3
13 Surrey	81.5	83.1	33.0	170	79.1	91.9
14 Strathclyde	79.7	80.7	44.3	203	65.5	91.8
15 Lancaster	76.6	79.9	42.6	154	82.7	91.6
=16 Bristol	68.7	69.9	43.6	190	84.5	91.4

=16 York	82.2	83.3	22.6	161	85.7	91.4
18 Exeter	72.3	78.1	26.9	185	88.7	91.3
19 Queen Mary, London	79.0	81.4	31.3	174	77.5	90.7
=20 East Anglia	86.6	85.5	25.7	146	77.9	90.4
=20 Heriot-Watt	81.2	82.4	18.8	159	86.3	90.4
22 Essex	79.9	83.0	43.6	118	80.8	90.2
23 Royal Holloway	81.8	83.6	31.3	134	80.0	89.6
=24 Aston	81.3	80.1	19.7	130	89.2	89.2
=24 Coventry	92.3	93.9	1.6	120	85.7	89.2
26 Sussex	77.4	79.2	25.1	136	86.2	88.6
27 Stirling	78.5	76.9	25.2	150	80.7	88.3
28 Kent	80.5	79.9	14.6	137	87.6	88.2
29 Manchester	71.3	74.8	26.8	168	81.4	87.9
30 Birmingham	73.8	70.9	26.6	162	81.9	87.7
=31 Queen's, Belfast	76.3	78.0	32.7	150	74.3	87.6
=31 Southampton	73.4	79.5	23.4	146	84.0	87.6
33 Portsmouth	86.4	85.5	9.5	121	83.0	87.4
=34 De Montfort	88.7	88.0	10.7	98	83.8	87.2
=34 Sheffield	73.7	78.2	16.6	152	85.5	87.2
36 Glasgow	62.9	73.8	26.4	176	84.6	87.0
37 Newcastle	65.0	72.5	20.7	163	89.5	86.7
38 Goldsmiths, London	83.9	81.0	16.8	119	n/a	86.3
=39 Nottingham Trent	87.1	87.2	4.6	124	77.9	86.1
=39 Reading	76.2	75.5	29.3	142	73.9	86.1
41 Edinburgh	66.1	69.4	30.2	192	72.1	85.9
42 Dundee	81.5	79.9	12.1	143	75.6	85.7
43 Huddersfield	84.6	80.0	4.1	130	n/a	85.6
44 SOAS London	69.9	74.3	22.9	150	77.0	84.8
45 Central Lancashire	92.7	91.2	4.4	110	67.8	84.7
=46 Liverpool	73.4	76.7	20.1	145	74.0	84.5
=46 West of England	82.1	86.1	5.5	113	79.0	84.5
48 Cardiff	65.6	62.6	32.0	153	77.9	84.1
49 Hertfordshire	90.4	92.7	0.9	112	67.2	83.8
50 Oxford Brookes	81.4	79.5	5.1	121	76.4	83.4
51 Swansea	71.0	72.1	22.0	124	78.5	83.3
52 Hull	75.8	75.6	10.2	119	80.2	83.1
53 Bradford	73.5	79.5	12.7	104	82.5	83.0
54 Manchester Metropolitan	81.8	79.1	4.7	120	74.0	82.7
55 Bangor	76.6	74.6	23.4	112	71.1	82.6
56 Leicester	70.1	76.0	21.4	136	70.4	82.4
57 Middlesex	73.7	77.8	10.5	97	83.3	82.3
58 Plymouth	80.5	82.1	13.1	103	70.2	82.1
59 Aberystwyth	89.7	82.5	14.5	95	61.4	82.0
60 Keele	74.4	81.0	10.2	121	72.4	81.8
61 Buckingham	81.9	81.7	n/a	108	73.5	81.5
62 Cardiff Metropolitan	69.4	63.1	n/a	103	90.0	79.7

	Teaching quality %	Student experience %	Research quality %	Entry standards (UCAS points)	Graduate prospects %	Overall score
63 Ulster	73.8	70.3	n/a	123	75.5	79.6
64 Brunel	74.3	73.8	9.9	113	68.6	79.5
65 Birkbeck	70.6	70.8	19.1	106	n/a	78.9
66 Kingston	80.6	80.5	9.2	94	59.6	78.4
67 Birmingham City	74.8	78.1	1.3	104	69.1	78.3
=68 Anglia Ruskin	89.5	87.4	3.4	82	53.6	78.2
=68 City	63.4	68.1	15.1	134	68.1	78.2
=68 Salford	72.7	72.0	5.9	121	66.4	78.2
71 Sheffield Hallam	76.0	80.6	n/a	111	63.0	77.8
72 London Metropolitan	85.5	84.1	n/a	72*	61.9	77.7
73 Greenwich	71.3	72.9	3.3	120	60.9	76.3
74 Leeds Beckett	73.2	79.8	0.8	98	59.5	75.5
75 East London	77.6	78.4	0.8	92	46.4	73.0
76 Northampton	68.8	72.7	n/a	88	48.9	70.4

Employed in professional job	55%	Employed in non-professional job and Studying	1%
Employed in professional job and studying	5%	Employed in non-professional job	12%
Studying	15%	Unemployed	12%
Average starting professional salary	£27,000	Average starting non-professional salary	£18,000

Education

More than six women started courses in education for every man in 2017, which helps to explain the shortage of male teachers in primary schools. Degrees in the education category are not confined to teacher training; some are classified as Academic Studies in Education. But the majority are BEd courses which remain the most common route into primary teaching. Secondary school teachers are more likely to take the Postgraduate Certificate in Education, or train through the Teach First or Schools Direct programme. Applications for BEd courses are now back to the levels seen before higher fees were introduced in 2012, and enrolments were the highest ever.

Entry standards are not high – even Cambridge does not average 200 points on the new UCAS tariff – but there are almost six applicants to every place. However, the ratio in the Academic Studies in Education category, which includes training for early years and outdoor education, is below 4:1. Glasgow tops the Education table this year, taking over from Cambridge despite not leading on any individual measure. The Cambridge course is an example of those that do not offer Qualified Teacher Status, but combines the academic study of education with other subjects. The table includes Ofsted inspection data for universities in England. Nine institutions – all in the top 20 overall – tie for the best scores.

Students at Glyndŵr are the most satisfied with the quality of teaching on their course, but the university remains outside the top 50 because it did not enter the Research Excellence Framework and it is in the bottom ten for graduate prospects. Employment scores at different universities are influenced by the variations in demand for new staff between primary and secondary schools, as well as between different parts of the UK – the top seven are all Scottish.

Universities that specialise in primary training and are at an advantage at the moment in terms of employment. Some of the best-known education departments are absent from the table because they offer only postgraduate courses. University College London's Institute of Education, which is ranked top in the world in this field by QS, and Oxford, which achieved the top grades in the 2014 Research Excellence Framework, are two examples.

Morale is often said to be low in the teaching profession, but the official survey of graduates three years into their careers shows that those who studied education are among the least likely to wish they had taken a different subject. Only those who took medicine or dentistry are more satisfied. Competitive salaries in the early years of teaching may be one reason – education is in the top 20 of our 67 subject groups. The subject is also in the top 30 for the proportion going straight into professional jobs or continuing to study.

Education	Teaching quality %	Student experience %	Ofsted rating	Research quality %	Entry standards (UCAS points)	Graduate prospects %	Overall score
1 Glasgow	85.8	84.5	..	32.5	186	96.2	100.0
2 Cambridge			4.0	36.6	196	85.5	99.5
3 Durham	85.8	78.2	4.0	38.9	175	87.0	98.3
4 West of Scotland	89.1	87.4	..	7.5	180	94.9	97.4
5 Birmingham	88.0	86.5	4.0	40.9	142	83.6	96.9
6 Dundee	83.3	79.7	..	11.7	173	97.5	95.0
7 Manchester			4.0	46.0	153	75.7	94.9
8 Stirling	79.5	73.8	..	29.2	173	94.6	94.7
9 Edinburgh	75.0	74.9	,,	23.1	185	97.2	94.6
10 Royal Conservatoire of Scotland			..	..	188	97.4	93.6
=11 Brighton	89.1	85.5	4.0	1.6	134	89.5	92.4
=11 Strathclyde	76.6	70.9	..	19.8	188	85.6	92.4
13 Brunel	86.2	84.7	4.0	20.4	139	65.1	91.0
14 St Mary's, Twickenham	85.9	86.5	4.0	1.8	115	89.5	90.4
15 Chichester	87.6	85.3	4.0	..	122	84.1	90.3
=16 Keele	89.2	86.2	3.5	25.0	135	67.4	90.2
=16 Southampton	86.1	84.6	3.0	41.1	148	67.7	90.2
18 Northumbria	77.7	80.7	4.0	..	143	86.6	89.8
19 Reading	85.1	80.0	3.0	25.8	137	87.3	89.6
=20 West of England	93.7	92.7	3.0	5.3	133	84.7	89.5
=20 York	79.2	82.5	3.0	43.3	141	76.0	89.5
22 Sheffield			3.0	32.9	160	51.5	88.9
=23 Bangor	77.2	77.6	..	39.6	142	73.7	88.8
=23 Coventry	87.3	89.3	..	18.1	117	78.3	88.8
25 Gloucestershire	89.1	88.4	3.7	..	121	77.4	88.6
=26 East Anglia	82.7	84.8	3.0	27.2	151	70.2	88.4
=26 University College London			3.5	40.2	137	60.8	88.4
28 Liverpool Hope	91.6	91.3	3.0	7.3	121	81.3	87.8
29 Winchester	85.3	84.3	3.5	2.2	127	79.6	87.6
=30 Chester	83.5	79.8	3.7	1.4	128	79.4	87.5

Education cont

		Teaching quality %	Student experience %	Ofsted rating	Research quality %	Entry standards (UCAS points)	Graduate prospects %	Overall score
=30	Warwick			3.7	43.6	140	65.1	87.5
32	Aberdeen			..	7.6	167	96.1	87.4
33	Liverpool John Moores	82.8	82.3	3.5	3.0	140	72.2	87.0
34	Nottingham Trent	83.9	82.5	3.3	2.6	144	73.9	86.8
35	Huddersfield	88.5	84.7	3.1	5.9	127	77.9	86.7
36	Aberystwyth	91.4	89.2	..	..	120	69.4	86.4
37	Birmingham City	88.1	82.5	3.0	1.8	120	82.9	85.6
38	Derby	86.2	83.9	3.4	1.1	117	73.2	85.4
=39	Bath Spa	78.5	77.8	3.7	3.2	124	72.2	85.2
=39	Oxford Brookes	76.5	72.4	3.5	3.3	141	75.5	85.2
41	Portsmouth	82.6	80.3	3.5	..	132	68.2	85.1
=42	Middlesex	85.7	84.7	3.0	14.9	121	68.1	85.0
=42	York St John	79.7	78.6	3.3	1.5	130	78.6	85.0
44	Hertfordshire	85.9	85.2	3.0	..	117	81.9	84.9
45	Worcester	87.5	86.6	3.0	2.5	121	72.9	84.7
46	Leeds	72.7	73.2	3.0	31.6	145	65.3	84.6
47	Cardiff	75.8	77.7	..	35.3	140	55.8	84.4
48	Sheffield Hallam	83.2	80.4	3.3	2.0	121	71.6	84.3
=49	De Montfort	78.6	79.5	..	11.2	121	75.5	84.2
=49	Sunderland	79.2	78.5	2.7	3.8	130	90.6	84.2
51	Wrexham Glyndŵr	94.1	87.7	..	..	116	56.0	84.1
52	Roehampton	74.4	75.2	3.0	20.2	119	81.3	84.0
53	Manchester Metropolitan	82.4	77.7	2.7	5.8	136	79.5	83.9
=54	Canterbury Christ Church	81.0	76.8	3.0	2.8	123	81.5	83.7
=54	Staffordshire	90.6	83.2	3.0	7.6	119	60.0	83.7
56	Edge Hill	79.8	76.3	3.0	1.4	127	81.6	83.6
57	Leeds Trinity	81.8	82.9	3.0	..	114	81.3	83.5
58	Greenwich	79.0	77.0	3.3	0.8	135	65.7	83.2
59	Plymouth Marjon	77.6	72.6	3.3	..	130	72.4	82.9
60	Plymouth	75.8	76.6	3.0	9.4	119	78.3	82.7
=61	Bishop Grosseteste	83.1	77.6	3.1	1.4	118	69.9	82.5
=61	Bolton			..	3.1	90	73.7	82.5
=61	Kingston	87.3	82.5	3.0	..	110	68.3	82.5
64	Bedfordshire	89.2	87.3	2.4	3.1	113	73.9	82.1
65	London South Bank	84.0	79.1	3.0	..	100	77.9	82.0
66	Cumbria	76.8	70.7	3.0	0.4	121	82.2	81.9
67	Leeds Beckett	79.9	78.7	3.0	2.3	112	73.3	81.7
68	South Wales	80.8	74.3	..	..	136	60.0	81.5
69	Wales Trinity St David	87.9	83.3	..	..	121	50.6	81.4
70	Northampton	79.9	77.2	3.0	1.8	116	67.9	81.1
71	Goldsmiths, London	84.0	76.2	3.0	17.4	108	52.6	80.9
=72	Central Lancashire	77.1	75.0	..	..	134	62.1	80.8

	Teaching quality %	Student experience %	Research quality %	Entry standards (UCAS points)	Graduate prospects %	Overall score
=72 Newman	76.5	74.1	3.0	2.2	122	70.0	80.8
=74 Anglia Ruskin	88.1	84.8	3.0	0.8	111	48.1	80.3
=74 Teesside	79.3	76.0	..	15.0	120	54.2	80.3
76 East London	79.2	78.2	3.0	2.8	120	56.0	79.8
77 London Metropolitan	82.5	79.4	3.1	3.3	100	55.9	79.5
78 Hull	68.6	65.4	3.0	5.0	124	73.3	79.3
79 Cardiff Metropolitan	80.7	77.4	..	..	118	55.8	79.2
80 Ulster	76.6	74.7	..	27.5	116	39.1	77.7

Employed in professional job	54%	Employed in non-professional job and Studying	2%
Employed in professional job and studying	2%	Employed in non-professional job	21%
Studying	16%	Unemployed	5%
Average starting professional salary	£22,000	Average starting non-professional salary	£15,000

Electrical and Electronic Engineering

The demand for places in electrical and electronic engineering dipped slightly in 2016, when other branches of the discipline were still growing. The numbers starting courses were still marginally lower than in 2010, the last year unaffected by higher fees, and the signs are that there may have been a further small decline in 2017. Some natural applicants have been diverted into courses such as computer science or games design and, at around five applications to the place, selection is less competitive than in most other branches of engineering. Nevertheless, only mechanical courses attract more students. The subject has moved into the top 20 for employment prospects and the top seven for salaries in graduate-level jobs.

Cambridge maintains its lead in electrical and electronic engineering, with the best research grades and a lead of more than 20 points over second-placed Imperial College on entry standards. The scores are close together for much of the top 20, allowing some big moves. Essex has jumped 20 places to 17th, for example, while University College London is down 10 places to 14th. Anglia Ruskin's students are the most satisfied with the quality of teaching, although the university is still outside the top 50 overall, while those at Northumbria gave the best score for other aspects of the student experience. Northumbria, Robert Gordon and Coventry are the only post-1992 institutions in the top 30.

Most of the top courses demand maths and physics at A-level, or the equivalent. There are considerable variations in employment rates, with 12 universities seeing at least 90 per cent of their 2016 graduates find professional work or continue their studies, while at three universities the rate was below 60 per cent. Three-quarters of graduates go straight into professional jobs or continue their studies, but the 11 per cent unemployment rate is above the average for all subjects.

Electrical and Electronic Engineering	Teaching quality %	Student experience %	Research quality %	Entry standards (UCAS points)	Graduate prospects %	Overall score
1 Cambridge	75.5	77.6	67.0	241	93.0	100.0
2 Imperial College	79.1	84.9	65.0	219	90.6	98.8
3 Southampton	87.1	88.4	53.3	184	92.7	97.0
4 Strathclyde	83.8	82.8	41.7	218	84.3	94.8
5 Bristol	n/a	n/a	52.3	178	89.2	93.6

	Teaching quality %	Student experience %	Research quality %	Entry standards (UCAS points)	Graduate prospects %	Overall score
6 Edinburgh	75.5	81.2	50.3	195	88.4	93.2
7 Surrey	87.9	87.4	36.3	187	83.7	92.8
8 Glasgow	69.5	73.5	47.2	209	92.6	92.7
9 Leeds	83.1	87.3	41.8	161	88.4	91.6
10 Manchester	78.9	85.1	37.0	176	90.5	91.4
11 Bath	84.0	89.3	28.6	170	90.4	91.3
12 Queen's, Belfast	80.8	79.7	47.3	146	94.2	91.2
13 Nottingham	82.6	84.8	40.8	155	90.3	91.0
=14 Sheffield	81.5	83.1	42.6	151	92.0	90.9
=14 University College London	68.7	72.6	59.0	188	86.0	90.9
16 Newcastle	83.9	83.6	39.4	151	86.8	89.8
17 Essex	88.2	87.0	34.3	125	90.5	89.2
18 Exeter	77.8	81.7	36.4	166	86.7	89.0
19 Lancaster	73.9	80.8	41.6	162	87.8	88.8
=20 Birmingham	80.6	83.9	32.1	149	89.7	88.6
=20 Loughborough	83.8	87.2	23.8	146	91.0	88.6
=22 Cardiff	82.1	85.1	30.2	151	84.2	87.7
=22 Swansea	75.8	79.6	45.5	132	89.7	87.7
24 Northumbria	89.0	90.4	30.7	151	75.0	87.6
25 Heriot-Watt	69.5	71.7	47.8	171	82.7	87.3
26 York	85.1	83.3	21.4	150	81.9	86.3
27 Brunel	81.5	79.6	26.4	136	83.3	85.0
28 Kent	75.5	78.0	27.3	141	85.4	84.6
29 Robert Gordon	80.9	83.9	8.8	183	72.6	84.0
30 Coventry	84.0	89.2	10.3	128	83.8	83.8
31 Bedfordshire	83.2	86.7	9.1	n/a	76.9*	83.5
=32 Queen Mary, London	64.8	69.5	41.9	148	81.7	83.1
=32 West of England	85.1	79.0	10.6	136	81.6	83.1
=34 Liverpool	81.2	82.2	30.4	135	72.0	83.0
=34 Liverpool John Moores	86.3	85.4	8.7	148	74.5	83.0
=36 Aberdeen	67.1	73.3	28.4	170*	77.3	82.8
=36 Bangor	80.2	81.3	31.9	117	77.4	82.8
38 Brighton	85.0	82.1	7.4	124	82.4	82.1
=39 Huddersfield	85.6	84.8	10.2	126	76.6	81.7
=39 Sheffield Hallam	78.2	78.7	17.8	119	83.6	81.7
41 Plymouth	81.7	84.4	13.3	122	78.8	81.5
=42 City	77.8	80.5	20.2	140	73.5	81.4
=42 Portsmouth	76.3	76.6	7.2	126	89.0	81.4
44 Aston	76.2	76.4	25.8	134	74.8	81.2
45 Ulster	73.4	70.9	22.8	121	83.3	80.7
46 Glasgow Caledonian	79.2	79.1	4.7	164	68.5	80.0
=47 Derby	80.3	80.9	6.7	121	78.4	79.7

=47 Sunderland	84.5	80.7	n/a	80	92.3	79.7
=49 Central Lancashire	74.4	71.8	11.7	127*	80.0	79.1
=49 Reading	68.7	64.1	16.3	133	83.8	79.1
51 Sussex	66.0	66.4	24.0	133	78.9	78.7
52 East London	84.8	88.8	2.3	n/a	61.9	78.1
53 Hull	71.7	67.9	16.5	118	78.6	77.7
54 Anglia Ruskin	90.6	86.3	9.1	107*	60.0	77.3
55 Westminster	88.7	88.2	2.9	116	59.6	76.9
=56 Bolton	73.6	75.8	n/a	127*	75.0	76.4
=56 De Montfort	73.0	73.3	12.5	99	78.1	76.4
58 Hertfordshire	80.2	82.4	16.5	121	56.3	76.0
=59 Greenwich	76.1	77.5	7.5	130*	62.7	75.6
=59 London South Bank	68.0	71.5	19.6	111	72.0	75.6
61 Birmingham City	80.3	77.8	n/a	125	63.2	75.2
62 Teesside	76.5	73.3	5.8	121	64.4	74.7
63 Salford	73.5	70.4	4.4	135	62.3	74.2
64 Manchester Metropolitan	59.0	62.2	16.3	135	70.3	73.8
65 Bradford	73.3	78.3	n/a	115*	57.1	71.5
66 Staffordshire	56.6	57.5	5.7	140	63*	69.9
67 South Wales	56.5	54.3	n/a	125*	69.4	69.1

Employed in professional job	60%	Employed in non-professional job and Studying	1%
Employed in professional job and studying	2%	Employed in non-professional job	12%
Studying	14%	Unemployed	11%
Average starting professional salary	£26,000	Average starting non-professional salary	£16,575

English

Degrees in English are a perennial favourite of university applicants, despite the fact that they are usually in the bottom 20 subjects for employment prospects or starting salaries in professional jobs. Both applications and enrolments declined in 2016, however. Applications were at their lowest for at least a decade, but were still close to 50,000, and the table remains one of the largest in the *Guide*. Entry standards are high at the leading institutions, although only three universities (led by Durham) have averages of more than 200 points.

St Andrews and Durham, which have swapped places at the top of the table for the last two years, are now tied for the leadership. For once, Cambridge is not in the top five, not helped, perhaps, by the boycott of the National Student Survey (NSS), which deprived ten universities of satisfaction scores. The best scores across our two measures derived from the NSS were at Bolton in 35th place, followed closely by Southampton Solent, which is only just in the top 80 overall, having chosen not to enter the Research Excellence Framework (REF) in English. Queen Mary, University of London, in 15th place, produced much the best results in the REF.

Almost one English graduate in three goes on to a postgraduate course, and unemployment has been no higher than average for all subjects for the last two years, but three in ten graduates start out in lower-level jobs. Employment rates have improved recently, but only Lancaster, Durham, Birmingham, Loughborough and Exeter saw eight out of ten graduates go straight into graduate-level work or further study. The rate was below 50 per cent at 18 universities. English has produced consistently good levels of student satisfaction, however. In the 2017 survey, all but four of the 94 universities with enough NSS responses to compile a score had satisfied at least three-quarters of the final-year undergraduates on teaching quality.

English	Teaching quality %	Student experience %	Research quality %	Entry standards (UCAS points)	Graduate prospects %	Overall score
=1 Durham	88.4	80.4	57.9	211	82.6	100.0
=1 St Andrews	89.7	87.3	60.4	199	78.8	100.0
3 Oxford	n/a	n/a	50.7	209	75.6	97.4
4 University College London	n/a	n/a	61.7	195	71.8	97.2
5 Exeter	88.4	85.4	46.2	183	80.9	96.9
6 Cambridge	n/a	n/a	50.0	210	79.1	95.7
=7 Newcastle	86.1	84.3	54.3	165	74.5	94.9
=7 York	82.8	79.3	61.5	170	75.5	94.9
9 Nottingham	84.8	78.1	56.6	163	79.6	94.8
10 Warwick	n/a	n/a	59.8	183	71.5	93.9
11 King's College London	n/a	n/a	47.6	181	76.1	93.5
12 Lancaster	82.3	78.8	47.0	161	82.8	93.4
13 Birmingham	85.5	82.9	37.0	165	80.3	93.3
14 Glasgow	81.2	78.2	52.0	181	69.5	92.7
15 Queen Mary, London	84.9	79.4	64.0	152	64.1	92.5
16 Manchester	n/a	n/a	49.1	161	78.8	92.4
17 Sussex	83.4	80.4	45.6	145	79.2	92.1
18 Loughborough	84.8	86.2	32.4	147	81.3	91.9
19 Surrey	87.0	85.2	39.1	159	67.9	91.8
20 Leeds	80.8	79.9	38.6	171	76.4	91.6
21 Sheffield	n/a	n/a	42.2	155	73.6	91.2
22 Bristol	n/a	n/a	30.0	193	76.5	90.9
23 Aberystwyth	93.1	89.5	31.2	115	71.2	90.5
24 Royal Holloway	83.9	79.4	49.9	152	63.7	90.4
25 Swansea	84.5	81.3	43.6	122	76.6	90.2
=26 Aberdeen	83.0	80.3	46.3	158	62.0	89.9
=26 Kent	80.0	79.3	47.3	135	75.2	89.9
28 Bangor	85.9	87.3	46.3	131	61.0	89.6
29 Edinburgh	76.8	73.9	43.6	188	64.5	89.5
30 Southampton	83.0	81.2	38.4	146	69.1	89.4
31 Edinburgh Napier	90.3	84.0	37.9	162	47.5	89.0
32 Birkbeck	86.6	85.5	36.7	103	75.0	88.9
33 Liverpool	n/a	n/a	47.8	148	63.2	88.8
34 Brunel	88.5	87.7	30.9	126	64.7	88.7
=35 Bolton	94.2	92.4	14.4	87	79.2	88.6
=35 Leicester	79.7	76.5	45.4	134	72.2	88.6
37 Coventry	92.3	90.4	18.1	117	68.6	88.5

=38 De Montfort	91.4	89.1	24.1	105	69.3	88.2
=38 Stirling	79.6	70.4	29.8	169	72.5	88.2
=40 Cardiff	84.6	79.9	35.1	150	60.0	88.0
=40 Queen's, Belfast	81.8	78.5	53.1	150	52.1	88.0
42 East Anglia	79.0	77.8	36.2	166	62.5	87.8
43 Northumbria	89.7	80.7	27.2	140	59.4	87.7
44 Plymouth	89.3	84.7	30.5	124	59.8	87.5
45 Bedfordshire	85.1	82.5	45.8	83	71.8	87.4
=46 Nottingham Trent	86.1	81.8	30.0	130	63.7	87.3
=46 Teesside	92.2	89.8	15.6	98	71.7	87.3
=46 West of England	91.5	90.3	35.4	120	49.2	87.3
49 Sunderland	90.4	87.6	15.3	104	72.9	87.1
50 Reading	n/a	n/a	36.3	138	59.4	87.0
51 Aston	83.0	84.9	23.4	128	69.6	86.8
=52 Dundee	81.8	78.2	32.8	148	59.4	86.5
=52 Edge Hill	89.8	81.1	12.1	125	68.9	86.5
=52 Strathclyde	77.9	75.7	39.4	196	44.0	86.5
55 Middlesex	87.5	87.2	11.0	n/a	60.3	86.0
56 Buckingham	94.5	91.5	n/a	96	71.2	85.9
=57 Huddersfield	81.5	77.8	29.9	123	68.2	85.8
=57 Manchester Metropolitan	87.3	83.0	29.0	117	58.1	85.8
59 Lincoln	86.6	82.2	16.2	120	66.2	85.5
=60 Essex	73.1	75.7	37.7	127	73.0	85.4
=60 Portsmouth	84.8	82.0	17.1	117	69.3	85.4
62 Derby	82.5	86.7	17.5	102	61.7	85.3
63 Newman	89.5	87.5	9.6	107	66.1	85.2
64 Keele	81.7	79.6	29.8	131	58.6	85.0
65 Staffordshire	94.2	87.9	n/a	91	70.0	84.9
66 Oxford Brookes	79.9	77.0	27.8	126	65.4	84.8
67 Birmingham City	85.0	80.8	30.9	114	53.3	84.1
68 Liverpool Hope	72.0	69.9	26.9	104	86.5	83.9
69 Northampton	90.1	80.8	15.3	112	55.6	83.8
70 Westminster	84.0	78.4	28.9	111	57.0	83.7
=71 Liverpool John Moores	85.7	81.1	17.9	127	53.5	83.6
=71 Ulster	86.5	87.6	35.1	124	36.3	83.6
73 Hull	82.0	76.8	22.7	124	59.0	83.5
74 Roehampton	83.1	81.2	20.8	101	64.3	83.4
75 Chichester	n/a	n/a	16.3	109	54.1	83.0
76 Salford	87.6	78.8	7.8	121	57.7	82.9
77 Leeds Beckett	87.8	86.6	11.0	105	55.4	82.8
78 Bath Spa	85.5	77.4	23.5	123	48.0	82.6
=79 Leeds Trinity	93.7	86.0	6.2	96	51.0	82.4
=79 Southampton Solent	94.9	91.4	n/a	99	49.0	82.4
=81 Falmouth	81.0	70.3	n/a	121	76.2	82.3
=81 St Mary's, Twickenham	85.4	80.2	14.6	97	61.1	82.3
83 Greenwich	83.9	79.2	14.4	121	54.9	82.2

		Teaching quality %	Student experience %	Research quality %	Entry standards (UCAS points)	Graduate prospects %	Overall score
84	Bournemouth	79.7	77.8	15.1	125	58.6	82.0
=85	Central Lancashire	79.0	75.1	9.9	120	65.2	81.6
=85	Gloucestershire	84.1	85.3	9.3	125	48.9	81.6
87	Goldsmiths, London	74.6	67.7	34.9	131	53.0	81.3
88	Suffolk	94.3	87.2	n/a	109	41.4	81.1
89	Chester	85.0	80.7	10.7	116	49.7	81.0
90	South Wales	86.0	84.5	12.8	120	41.4	80.9
91	Canterbury Christ Church	83.7	78.9	8.0	98	57.8	80.4
92	Winchester	80.5	80.4	n/a	122	58.3	80.2
=93	Hertfordshire	80.6	78.8	7.8	108	58.0	80.1
=93	York St John	84.3	80.5	9.7	112	47.6	80.1
95	Brighton	77.5	73.8	16.2	107	57.6	79.6
=96	Kingston	79.8	77.0	15.7	106	50.8	79.3
=96	Sheffield Hallam	78.3	72.1	14.6	115	53.3	79.3
98	London Metropolitan	88.6	85.2	n/a	88*	49.0	79.2
99	Cardiff Metropolitan	83.9	84.8	n/a	104	49.4	79.0
100	London South Bank	85.4	87.8	12.8	86	42.1	78.9
101	Anglia Ruskin	82.3	77.6	16.3	94	44.1	78.2
102	Bishop Grosseteste	74.4	58.0	6.7	115	67.0	77.9
103	Worcester	76.6	67.4	8.2	112	51.9	77.0
104	East London	76.9	68.2	13.7	96	44.6	75.5
105	Plymouth Marjon	n/a	n/a	n/a	122	41.3	75.2
106	Cumbria	84.5	82.4	n/a	96*	30.8	75.1

Employed in professional job	33%	Employed in non-professional job and Studying	4%
Employed in professional job and studying	3%	Employed in non-professional job	26%
Studying	25%	Unemployed	9%
Average starting professional salary	£19,000	Average starting non-professional salary	£15,600

Food Science

The hope that the courses classified by UCAS as Food and Beverage Studies might be the next big thing in higher education, thanks to television's obsession with cookery, lasted only a year. The 33 per cent increase in the numbers starting degrees in 2015 had turned into a 13 per cent drop 12 months later. Nevertheless, the 670 enrolments were still twice as many as the total for 2007, and the number of universities offering the subjects continues to grow. There are three new universities in this year's table.

Employment levels are healthy, too – food science remains in the top 30 for positive destinations in the latest table, with 57 per cent of graduates finding "professional" jobs within six months of completing a course. The subject does almost as well in the earnings table, with a median salary of close to £22,000 in graduate-level employment securing a place on the verge of the top 30 out of 67 subjects. Eight universities, led for the second year in a row by Hertfordshire, saw more than 90 per cent of their 2016 graduates secure professional employment or continue studying.

Degrees range from professional cookery to food manufacturing and nutrition. Almost a third of entrants to food science courses arrive with alternative qualifications to A-levels, usually BTECs. Entry standards have been rising – none of the universities in this year's ranking averages less than 100 points – but there were still little more than three applications per place in 2016.

Surrey is enjoying its third year at the top of the food science table, with Leeds remaining in second place.

Neither is top on any of the individual measures. Worcester has the most satisfied students on both of the measures derived from the National Student Survey, but is still outside the top 30 overall because it did not enter the Research Excellence Framework (REF) in this area and it is in the bottom four for graduate prospects. Queen's, Belfast produced the best results in the REF. Most of the institutions offering food science are post-1992 universities, but only third-placed Robert Gordon, Plymouth and Glasgow Caledonian feature in the top ten.

Food Science	Teaching quality %	Student experience %	Research quality %	Entry standards (UCAS points)	Graduate prospects %	Overall score
1 Surrey	89.0	88.0	37.5	167	92.2	100.0
2 Leeds	79.4	84.9	36.8	174	91.1	98.3
=3 Nottingham	84.8	84.5	36.4	157	86.1	96.0
=3 Robert Gordon	89.8	86.8	4.9	177	92.0	96.0
5 Queen's, Belfast	75.7	83.9	56.3	141	87.5	95.5
=6 King's College London	76.5	77.0	46.8	171	77.1	95.4
=6 Reading	76.2	80.0	50.7	150	86.6	95.4
8 Plymouth	92.3	88.2	17.4	158	80.0	93.9
9 Glasgow Caledonian	87.0	86.8	8.1	n/a	93.8	93.1
10 Ulster	87.4	86.3	42.5	133	76.5	92.8
11 Hertfordshire	90.6	87.2	14.8	127	96.9	92.2
12 Newcastle	77.9	77.7	28.4	149	86.2	91.5
13 Central Lancashire	82.0	87.6	8.3	152	80.8	89.6
14 London Metropolitan	80.9	81.0	n/a	154	88.0	88.9
15 Coventry	83.0	85.3	n/a	139	93.7	88.8
16 Lincoln	84.1	84.4	31.1	n/a	70*	88.7
17 Greenwich	83.0	80.8	19.5	n/a	78.6	88.3
18 Manchester Metropolitan	87.5	85.4	12.0	137	76.4	88.2
19 Huddersfield	89.3	84.6	n/a	134	83.6	87.5
20 Bath Spa	91.5	89.8	n/a	123	78.2	86.0
=21 Harper Adams	85.2	85.1	5.7	120	83.6	85.8
=21 Northumbria	79.7	79.8	14.0	137	73.3	85.8
23 Liverpool John Moores	90.8	91.9	6.0	139	59.6	85.7
24 Leeds Beckett	86.2	86.2	n/a	118	83.7	85.0
25 Cardiff Metropolitan	86.8	83.9	n/a	123	76.2	84.1
=26 Sheffield Hallam	85.6	83.1	3.7	124	70.9	83.4
=26 Teesside	94.1	88.4	n/a	110	71.4	83.4

Food Science cont

		Teaching quality %	Student experience %	Research quality %	Entry standards (UCAS points)	Graduate prospects %	Overall score
28	Chester	66.7	67.8	12.0	117	91.8	82.3
29	Royal Agricultural University	77.2	78.5	2.1	103	91.7	82.2
30	Roehampton	84.1	86.0	20.6	110	58.3	81.8
31	Abertay	70.0	65.2	n/a	146	76.5	81.7
32	Edge Hill	89.2	91.0	n/a	132	50.0	81.4
33	Worcester	94.9	94.7	n/a	112*	54.5	81.2
34	St Mary's, Twickenham	84.6	85.7	n/a	114	68.8	81.1
35	Leeds Trinity	85.5	74.7	n/a	105	68.0	78.8
36	Bournemouth	73.5	80.3	4.7	113	59.3	77.1
37	Queen Margaret, Edinburgh	60.0	56.4	n/a	149	56.0	75.0
38	Suffolk	70.1	71.7	n/a	120*	56.0	74.9
39	Kingston	73.4	70.7	2.6	116	50.0	74.2
40	Oxford Brookes	58.9	57.8	3.0	126	64.0	73.9
41	London South Bank	80.5	71.4	n/a	102	44.4	72.5
42	Westminster	65.1	72.5	n/a	105	56.5	72.1

Employed in professional job	54%	Employed in non-professional job and Studying	1%
Employed in professional job and studying	3%	Employed in non-professional job	18%
Studying	15%	Unemployed	9%
Average starting professional salary	£21,909	Average starting non-professional salary	£15,600

French

Languages have suffered a well-publicised decline in recent years – enrolments were dropping before the introduction of £9,000 fees and the process has accelerated since. Applications were down for the seventh year in a row in 2016, and the numbers starting courses have fallen again in 2017. Some universities are now closing their language departments, but more than 70 of them are offering full-time undergraduate courses in or including French starting in 2018. Only 390 students embarked on a degree in French in 2016 – 40 fewer than in the previous year – although another 2,400 opted for broader modern language courses. French remains the most popular language at degree level, but a continuing decline at A-level suggests more tough times ahead.

Entry standards remain relatively high, however. In spite of the falling numbers, there were almost six applications to the place in 2016 and many of the candidates came from high-achieving independent schools. Five universities average 200 points or more on the new UCAS tariff and another 12 of the 49 universities in the table averaged 170 or more. Only one dropped below 110. Perhaps not surprisingly, nine out of ten undergraduates enter with A-levels or their equivalents, although many universities will teach the language from scratch, especially as part of joint degrees.

The top three are unchanged since last year, with Cambridge well clear at the top of the table. It has the best research grades and the highest entry standards, but the top performers on the other measures are spread through the table. Sixth-placed Surrey had the best scores in all aspects of the National Student Survey (NSS), with an unusually high 98 per cent approving of the quality of teaching. Lancaster, in second place, has much the best score for graduate prospects and was the only university to see nine out of ten graduates find professional jobs or continuing studying at the end of 2016. French is outside the top 30 subjects for employment and earnings.

French	Teaching quality %	Student experience %	Research quality %	Entry standards (UCAS points)	Graduate prospects %	Overall score
1 Cambridge	n/a	n/a	54.0	216	85.1	100.0
2 Lancaster	84.2	87.7	47.0	158	92.9	95.7
3 Warwick	n/a	n/a	45.2	175	79.3	95.1
4 Durham	86.1	75.6	34.6	205	86.8	94.5
5 Oxford	n/a	n/a	41.3	211	75.4	94.4
6 Surrey	98.4	93.3	39.1	175	64.7	94.2
7 King's College London	n/a	n/a	42.1	170	88.8	93.6
8 St Andrews	90.0	89.2	26.4	193	79.3	93.5
9 Strathclyde	85.9	81.9	42.0	208	66.7	93.0
10 Exeter	88.3	88.3	35.1	176	76.0	92.7
11 York	85.4	82.5	37.3	172	78.9	92.0
12 Newcastle	84.3	86.0	36.3	164	79.5	91.6
13 Nottingham	83.2	80.3	39.4	161	81.8	91.5
14 Queen's, Belfast	83.9	79.1	53.6	152	70.3	91.2
15 Southampton	81.8	84.4	42.7	154	78.5	91.1
16 Bangor	97.5	90.6	39.6	133	64.0	90.9
=17 Birmingham	85.2	76.8	33.7	161	82.5	90.6
=17 Stirling	87.0	83.4	29.8	176	74.6	90.6
=19 Manchester	n/a	n/a	48.9	153	73.1	90.5
=19 University College London	n/a	n/a	43.7	182	78.2	90.5
21 Bristol	n/a	n/a	36.0	178	79.0	90.4
22 Sheffield	n/a	n/a	41.2	156	76.8	90.1
23 Bath	81.7	83.3	27.4	166	83.8	90.0
24 Leeds	85.1	85.3	30.6	169	73.5	89.9
25 Queen Mary, London	90.5	88.8	35.1	133	71.0	89.5
26 Liverpool	n/a	n/a	33.4	152	70.7	89.0
27 Aberdeen	78.3	79.7	29.3	191	72.1	88.6
28 Glasgow	86.9	83.0	26.3	200	56.2	88.1
29 Kent	76.5	76.3	41.9	130	81.6	87.8
30 Cardiff	84.1	85.7	32.5	152	66.7	87.6
31 Royal Holloway	80.7	78.6	48.3	138	64.7	87.4
32 Edinburgh	71.2	69.1	30.3	195	73.7	86.4
33 Portsmouth	91.6	88.7	32.2	101	66.7	86.3
34 Leicester	89.0	89.1	16.9	149	62.3	85.3
35 Heriot-Watt	70.7	67.2	26.3	179	76.1	84.7
36 Aberystwyth	77.8	76.9	16.6	128*	87.6	84.6
37 Swansea	85.2	81.6	22.8	123	69.3	84.2
=38 Aston	88.6	84.5	23.4	131	58.4	84.0

French cont

	Teaching quality %	Student experience %	Research quality %	Entry standards (UCAS points)	Graduate prospects %	Overall score
=38 Reading	79.0	71.4	41.7	128	62.4	84.0
40 Manchester Metropolitan	86.8	89.2	29.0	117	49.6	82.5
41 Hull	81.5	75.6	22.7	119	68.6	82.3
42 Coventry	89.9	87.6	n/a	104	76.0	82.0
43 Chester	81.3	80.8	17.3	113	67.4	81.2
44 Nottingham Trent	85.0	81.9	7.6	115	68.5	80.8
45 Ulster	84.5	83.2	22.4	127	46.0	80.1
46 Oxford Brookes	89.9	86.7	n/a	117	60.9	79.9
47 Central Lancashire	78.1	72.3	15.2	n/a	62.4*	78.8
48 Edinburgh Napier	83.4	79.2	n/a	152	46.3	77.1
49 Westminster	72.7	75.3	2.0	112	52.0	72.8

Employed in professional job	45%	Employed in non-professional job and Studying	3%
Employed in professional job and studying	3%	Employed in non-professional job	19%
Studying	21%	Unemployed	10%
Average starting professional salary	£21,000	Average starting non-professional salary	£17,249

General Engineering

There has been a surprise change at the top of the general engineering table, which has been headed by Cambridge for as long as it has been published. This year, Bristol has jumped five places to take over the leadership and Cambridge has dropped to third, behind Imperial College London. There is movement further down the table, too, with Liverpool John Moores going up 19 places and Greenwich 14 to share 17th place. Cambridge still has the highest entry grades and research score, but its downfall came with two mediocre student satisfaction scores. Bristol, by contrast, registered unusually high levels of satisfaction, exceeding 95 per cent on both of the measures derived from the National Student Survey.

The numbers starting general engineering courses dropped slightly in 2016 and the same applied to engineering as a whole in 2017. But this followed four years of increases, and enrolments are well above the levels seen before £9,000 fees were introduced. Although they do not yet draw as many applications as the specialist branches of engineering, the general courses attract students who are looking for maximum career flexibility. It may also help that general engineering has become a fixture in the top five of the graduate earnings table, with median salaries of £27,000 in professional jobs. The subject has been falling in the overall employment table, however. Having been in the top 10 only two years ago, it is now only just inside the top 20.

Fourth-placed Nottingham scored a rare 100 per cent for graduate prospects, with all of the 2016 graduates finding professional jobs or moving on to a postgraduate course within six months of completing their degree. More than half of the top 13 universities registered such positive destinations for at least 90 per cent of leavers. Oxford, which has dropped to fifth, had the best results in the 2014 Research Excellence Framework, while Lincoln, in 13th place, is back as the highest-placed post-1992 university for general engineering. Most of the leading universities will require both maths and physics at A-level, with further maths, design technology and/or computing welcome additions.

General Engineering

		Teaching quality %	Student experience %	Research quality %	Entry standards (UCAS points)	Graduate prospects %	Overall score
1	Bristol	96.6	95.1	52.3	203	95.1	100.0
2	Imperial College	82.8	87.3	60.1	231	90.2	97.3
3	Cambridge	75.5	77.6	67.0	241	93.0	96.6
4	Nottingham	84.9	79.6	40.8	n/a	100.0	96.0
5	Oxford	n/a	n/a	68.7	228	87.3	94.7
6	Glasgow	83.5	86.4	47.2	214	85.7	93.9
7	Durham	77.6	79.7	39.4	225	90.5	92.6
8	Heriot-Watt	80.5	82.8	47.8	178	n/a	91.1
9	Warwick	75.6	80.8	47.2	173	87.8	89.7
10	Sheffield	74.8	80.8	51.4	165	82.1	88.3
11	King's College London	74.7	73.8	56.6	169	n/a	87.8
12	Exeter	65.4	75.6	36.4	177	95.7*	87.7
13	Lincoln	87.2	84.1	12.4	128*	90.9	87.0
14	Cardiff	80.7	79.6	30.2	175	76.7	86.2
15	Liverpool	77.0	79.7	32.1	164	78.6*	85.5
16	Swansea	77.9	81.0	45.5	145	73.9	85.2
=17	Greenwich	79.1	82.9	5.5	n/a	84.6	85.1
=17	Liverpool John Moores	85.6	81.5	14.3	160	77.8	85.1
19	Aberdeen	65.3	69.5	28.4	218*	n/a	84.7
20	West of England	85.8	83.6	10.6	123	83.2	84.3
21	Bournemouth	81.5	80.5	8.5	115	86.5	83.1
22	Coventry	80.7	86.2	10.3	107	84.8	83.0
23	Leicester	70.5	73.6	34.4	132	81.2	82.4
24	Aston	77.0	76.7	20.6	126	n/a	81.5
=25	Bradford	81.6	85.4	7.7	127	72.1	80.8
=25	Queen Mary, London	67.9	72.3	46.7	n/a	75.0	80.8
27	London South Bank	69.7	67.8	19.6	108	87.5	80.1
28	Ulster	78.8	71.0	n/a	120	82.1	79.6
29	City	75.3	75.8	20.2	130	70.5	79.5
30	West of Scotland	91.2	89.2	9.0	n/a	52.9	79.3
31	Central Lancashire	73.5	75.7	7.1	151	71.4	79.0
32	Glasgow Caledonian	67.7	68.7	4.7	154	77.0	78.1
33	Edinburgh Napier	75.6	77.7	n/a	133	71.2	77.8
34	Derby	76.0	76.4	6.7	96	n/a	77.1
35	Northampton	69.8	67.3	n/a	101	76.4	74.8

Employed in professional job	57%	Employed in non-professional job and Studying	1%
Employed in professional job and studying	2%	Employed in non-professional job	11%
Studying	18%	Unemployed	11%
Average starting professional salary	£27,000	Average starting non-professional salary	£18,500

Geography & Environmental Sciences

Geography and environmental sciences are holding their own in terms of applications and enrolments, as they continue to benefit from strong interest in "green" issues among young people. It was the human geography courses that saw more students enrolling in 2016, however, while physical and environmental were static. The subjects' attractions do not seem to be related to immediate career prospects since geography and environmental science are only just in the top 50 in the employment table. They fare rather better in the comparison of earnings, where an average starting salary of £22,000 in professional jobs places them in the top 20, tied with ten other subject groups.

The top four in the table are unchanged, with Cambridge holding on to the leading position it secured last year. It has the highest entry grades, while Bristol was the top university in the Research Excellence Framework (REF). Winchester, which was one of two universities with a 90 per cent score for graduate prospects in last year's guide, is the only one to score so highly this year. A low research score and entry standards in the bottom ten restricted it to 38th place overall. Like last year, too, Coventry has the highest levels of satisfaction on both of the measures derived from the National Student Survey.

Physical geography courses may give preference to candidates with a science or maths A-level in addition to geography, while for environmental science, most of the leading universities will ask for two from biology, chemistry, maths, physics and geography at A-level or the equivalent. Average entry scores range from over 200 points at three of the top four universities to less than 100 at seven of the institutions in the table. Satisfaction ratings are generally good in both branches of geography and in environmental science, and the unusually low graduate prospects at some universities in last year's guide have gone, although there are still six where fewer than half of the 2016 graduates found professional jobs or postgraduate courses by the end of the year.

Geography and Environmental Sciences	Teaching quality %	Student experience %	Research quality %	Entry standards (UCAS points)	Graduate prospects %	Overall score
1 Cambridge	n/a	n/a	57.3	216	85.3	100.0
2 Durham	86.3	83.6	55.0	199	81.8	99.2
3 Oxford	n/a	n/a	41.1	211	83.6	98.7
4 St Andrews	87.4	87.7	44.2	206	73.1	97.2
5 Glasgow	89.2	84.1	42.4	178	78.2	95.9
6 Bristol	75.7	74.2	61.3	188	81.3	95.4
7 Exeter	84.1	85.1	43.7	173	79.7	94.9
8 Lancaster	83.1	83.3	46.5	159	84.3	94.7
9 Leeds	83.0	86.2	42.3	161	82.4	94.3
10 Newcastle	86.2	84.7	43.1	154	78.5	93.7
11 Royal Holloway	88.8	85.6	45.8	142	75.1	93.2
12 Loughborough	87.8	88.6	24.3	142	88.7	93.0
13 London School of Economics	68.1	63.2	46.9	197	89.0	92.4
14 Aberdeen	81.9	84.0	38.2	189	67.9	92.3
15 Manchester	81.6	83.7	36.6	167	77.3	92.2

16 Southampton	85.2	83.7	45.8	149	71.0	91.8
17 Sussex	82.8	87.1	35.8	143	79.6	91.5
18 Aberystwyth	87.1	86.4	38.6	116	80.6	91.1
=19 Birmingham	80.7	76.7	42.0	157	75.9	90.9
=19 East Anglia	81.8	83.6	47.4	151	68.7	90.9
21 Nottingham	78.6	81.8	39.6	153	76.7	90.5
22 Leicester	87.4	89.0	29.7	140	71.1	90.1
23 Bangor	90.0	89.3	31.5	125	68.9	89.4
24 Coventry	94.1	94.5	2.0	122	81.4	89.2
25 Cardiff	81.3	83.0	36.8	153	67.1	89.0
26 Liverpool Hope	92.3	87.6	1.6	117	88.2	88.9
27 Reading	83.8	82.8	35.0	137	70.2	88.8
28 Edinburgh	75.6	73.1	38.2	181	67.4	88.7
=29 Queen Mary, London	83.4	81.6	45.1	136	62.9	88.4
=29 York	82.9	77.8	23.9	153	74.5	88.4
31 Queen's, Belfast	85.9	85.4	36.9	140	61.0	88.3
=32 Dundee	83.9	82.3	28.3	155	65.4	88.2
=32 University College London	60.3	63.2	52.3	179	80.1	88.2
=34 King's College London	n/a	n/a	40.0	157	67.9	88.0
=34 Liverpool	n/a	n/a	26.3	145	69.1	88.0
36 Sheffield	75.4	80.0	31.1	162	71.5	87.9
37 Hull	88.1	88.5	31.7	118	63.3	87.3
38 Winchester	n/a	n/a	7.5	102	90.6*	87.0
39 Stirling	77.5	76.9	30.3	159	64.6	86.4
40 Swansea	75.8	79.7	39.4	129	68.8	86.2
=41 Birkbeck	72.6	73.3	34.7	n/a	76.2	85.1
=41 Nottingham Trent	90.8	90.4	4.1	119	66.9	85.1
43 Greenwich	80.4	85.5	7.4	127	76.9	85.0
44 Keele	85.9	85.5	16.4	121	64.3	84.7
45 West of England	89.0	88.2	6.4	119	65.4	84.4
=46 Northumbria	87.1	86.2	15.4	134	54.7	84.0
=46 Portsmouth	84.9	85.2	14.9	109	67.8	84.0
48 Central Lancashire	92.2	93.0	9.8	124	50.0	83.6
49 South Wales	87.3	89.9	n/a	138	57.9	83.2
50 Plymouth	81.0	81.2	25.8	117	58.2	82.8
51 Bournemouth	79.3	81.1	19.9	112	64.9	82.5
52 Oxford Brookes	83.2	84.7	17.3	116	57.8	82.4
53 Gloucestershire	88.6	93.2	14.5	116	47.7	82.3
54 Salford	n/a	n/a	16.7	102	69.8	82.0
55 Worcester	83.8	83.1	8.1	99	66.0	81.5
=56 Chester	86.8	87.1	6.4	115	55.0	81.4
=56 Liverpool John Moores	90.7	89.6	n/a	118	52.1	81.4
58 Derby	86.9	83.3	3.6	96	64.3	81.0
59 Manchester Metropolitan	80.8	77.8	14.9	114	59.7	80.9
60 Brighton	86.2	80.9	5.1	109	52.8	79.4
61 Kingston	79.3	74.1	6.9	104	65.0	79.3

Geography and Environmental Sciences cont

		Teaching quality %	Student experience %	Research quality %	Entry standards (UCAS points)	Graduate prospects %	Overall score
62	Sheffield Hallam	77.3	77.8	13.4	113	56.3	79.0
63	Hertfordshire	76.1	71.8	n/a	98	75.0	78.8
64	Staffordshire	84.6	82.2	n/a	93	57.7	78.3
=65	Northampton	86.0	81.2	7.7	95	47.1	77.7
=65	Southampton Solent	89.8	87.7	n/a	89	46.3	77.7
=65	Ulster	85.0	82.6	n/a	111	47.1	77.7
68	Leeds Beckett	74.8	78.1	5.6	104	60.8	77.6
69	Edge Hill	72.1	72.1	6.2	110	60.4	76.7
70	Bath Spa	73.7	72.9	n/a	106	53.1	74.6
71	St Mary's, Twickenham	66.4	73.6	n/a	99	59.6	73.7
72	Canterbury Christ Church	72.9	75.6	n/a	101	49.7	73.6
73	Cumbria	77.8	64.0	1.5	111	40.0	72.5

Employed in professional job	39%	Employed in non-professional job and Studying	3%
Employed in professional job and studying	3%	Employed in non-professional job	22%
Studying	22%	Unemployed	11%
Average starting professional salary	£22,000	Average starting non-professional salary	£15,834

Geology

There was a big drop – 14 per cent – in applications for geology in 2016, taking them back to the level seen in the year when £9,000 fees were introduced. The numbers starting courses fell as a consequence, although there were still five applications to the place and entry standards remained high at the leading universities. Six of the 32 universities in the table averaged at least 200 points on the new UCAS tariff. Cambridge recorded among the highest grades in any subject (244 on average) but was still no nearer to overhauling Imperial College London at the head of the table, where the top three are unchanged compared with last year. Some of the leading universities expect candidates to have two scientific or mathematical subjects at A-level, or the equivalent.

Competitive graduate salaries and the prospect of an international career have contributed to the subject's popularity, although it has slipped 22 places and into the bottom half of the salaries table this year. Geology is higher in the overall employment ranking, but still only just in the top half. More of those graduating in 2016 opted for a postgraduate course than went straight into professional jobs.

Imperial College continued to demonstrate impressive strength across the board, with the best research grades and exceptional scores in all aspects of the National Student Survey for the fifth year in a row. With this year's best graduate prospects as well, Imperial became one of the few universities in any subject to be top on every measure except entry points. No university saw 90 per cent of graduates find professional jobs or a postgraduate course within six months of leaving, but only one dropped (marginally) below 60 per cent on this measure. Portsmouth is the leading post-1992 university, four places outside the top 20.

Geology

		Teaching quality %	Student experience %	Research quality %	Entry standards (UCAS points)	Graduate prospects %	Overall score
1	Imperial College	95.3	95.8	59.6	208	89.0	100.0
2	Cambridge	n/a	n/a	58.0	244	84.8	97.6
3	Oxford	n/a	n/a	52.1	227	85.7	95.8
=4	Durham	84.9	86.3	42.2	186	86.2	92.2
=4	St Andrews	80.2	83.7	44.2	200	86.4	92.2
6	Royal Holloway	90.3	87.4	43.4	150	85.5	91.2
7	Exeter	79.3	75.6	45.7	164	87.0	89.4
8	Glasgow	81.6	85.7	38.5	206	74.1	88.6
9	Bristol	77.8	79.3	55.8	176	75.4	88.4
10	Birmingham	90.2	88.8	38.6	147	77.0	87.9
11	Southampton	84.3	86.3	58.3	143	69.6	87.2
12	Leeds	85.0	87.4	41.9	169	71.4	87.1
13	East Anglia	83.2	82.7	47.4	143	73.5	86.1
14	Edinburgh	78.3	81.9	38.2	201	63.8	84.4
15	Aberystwyth	81.3	78.8	34.9	116	82.6	84.3
16	Liverpool	n/a	n/a	30.3	148	67.5	83.9
17	Hull	86.3	89.5	31.7	115	n/a	83.3
18	Aberdeen	72.5	78.7	38.2	166	72.4	83.2
19	University College London	74.3	72.1	47.9	171	65.0	82.6
20	Leicester	81.7	83.3	37.2	143	67.4	82.5
21	Manchester	n/a	n/a	44.5	155	73.2	82.1
22	Bangor	78.9	83.0	31.5	122	75.0	82.0
23	Newcastle	76.3	80.6	35.4	141	n/a	81.9
24	Portsmouth	81.6	78.5	19.8	114	80.2	81.2
=25	Cardiff	78.5	80.0	21.3	139	68.2	79.0
=25	Derby	91.9	92.9	3.6	102	71.8	79.0
27	Keele	84.2	84.4	12.2	120	67.7	77.9
28	Plymouth	83.5	85.2	25.3	116	61.1	77.8
29	South Wales	82.7	81.8	n/a	98*	66.7	73.9
30	Edge Hill	61.3	60.7	n/a	115	73.7	70.5
31	Brighton	72.8	68.3	5.1	104	59.4	69.6
32	Kingston	59.7	60.9	6.9	92	67.7	68.2

Employed in professional job	31%	Employed in non-professional job and Studying	2%
Employed in professional job and studying	1%	Employed in non-professional job	19%
Studying	37%	Unemployed	10%
Average starting professional salary	£21,000	Average starting non-professional salary	£15,500

German

The decline of German as a degree subject continues. Having seen the number of students starting degrees in German drop below 200 for the first time in 2015, there have been further small drops in the two subsequent years. Many students are learning the language through broader modern languages degrees, but German has suffered more than other European languages from the decline in the numbers taking courses in the sixth-form, or even earlier. The introduction of £9,000 fees undoubtedly contributed to falling numbers, but there has been a worldwide decline in the language that has been worrying the German government, as well as academic linguists.

Cambridge makes it 12 years in a row at the top of the table for German and has a big lead in the new *Guide*, with the highest entry standards and the best score from the Research Excellence Framework (REF). Lancaster retains second place, but the best scores for student satisfaction and graduate prospects are to be found further down the table. St Andrews, in 15th place, registered the best graduate prospects, while Chester, in the bottom10, had the most satisfied students, heading both measures derived from the National Student Survey (NSS). Chester was the highest-placed of just four post-1992 universities in the ranking. Most universities scored well in the NSS, although overall satisfaction levels were down on last year.

Most universities in the table offer German from scratch as well as catering for those who took the subject at A-level. Employment prospects are better than in other modern languages, although the small numbers mean that the differences can be slight. German is just outside the top 30 for the proportion of graduates going into professional jobs or onto postgraduate courses, but four places lower in the salary table.

German	Teaching quality %	Student experience %	Research quality %	Entry standards (UCAS points)	Graduate prospects %	Overall score
1 Cambridge	n/a	n/a	54.0	216	85.1	100.0
2 Lancaster	84.0	87.2	47.0	172*	88.5	96.6
3 Oxford	n/a	n/a	41.3	214	82.9	95.0
4 Durham	86.1	75.6	34.6	205	86.8	94.9
5 King's College London	n/a	n/a	42.1	172	76.7	93.2
6 Warwick	n/a	n/a	45.2	172	75.7	93.1
7 Newcastle	87.9	87.5	36.3	169	80.8	92.6
8 Leeds	88.6	90.0	30.6	166	85.1	92.5
=9 Exeter	88.3	88.3	35.1	176	76.0	91.7
=9 University College London	n/a	n/a	43.7	182	84.6	91.7
11 Nottingham	82.4	76.1	39.4	157	82.8	90.8
12 Manchester	n/a	n/a	48.9	151	82.1	90.4
13 York	80.0	76.8	37.3	177*	n/a	90.0
14 Birmingham	89.3	75.8	33.7	142*	83.1	89.7
=15 Bath	82.0	82.0	27.4	168	84.1	89.6
=15 St Andrews	70.3	73.0	26.4	197*	88.9	89.6
17 Sheffield	n/a	n/a	41.2	153	76.9	89.5
18 Glasgow	78.7	84.8	26.3	207	74.7*	89.4
19 Bristol	n/a	n/a	36.0	172	77.0	89.1
20 Royal Holloway	81.6	76.9	48.3	n/a	70.2	88.6
21 Liverpool	n/a	n/a	33.4	146	n/a	88.2
22 Reading	79.0	71.4	41.7	137	80.8	88.1
23 Aberystwyth	88.5	86.6	16.6	n/a	78.3	87.8

24 Kent	90.3	82.5	41.9	124*	69.2	87.6
25 Southampton	86.2	87.9	42.7	160	58.8	87.3
26 Cardiff	79.7	81.2	32.5	139	79.7	86.9
27 Aston	89.1	83.8	23.4	135	76.8	85.8
28 Bangor	85.5	83.1	39.6	115	70.0	85.6
29 Queen Mary, London	72.3	71.1	35.1	145	79.6	85.5
30 Chester	96.2	93.3	17.3	113*	77.6	85.3
31 Portsmouth	91.7	89.1	32.2	102	69.3	84.5
32 Heriot-Watt	70.7	67.2	26.3	179	75.3	84.1
33 East Anglia	87.9	85.1	n/a	156	80.0	82.6
34 Edinburgh	74.4	77.6	30.3	174	57.1	81.7
35 Manchester Metropolitan	86.1	83.1	29.0	n/a	56.4*	80.8
36 Swansea	64.4	73.9	22.8	107	78.4	78.2
37 Aberdeen	70.2	67.2	29.3	n/a	61.8*	75.9
38 Nottingham Trent	68.5	62.7	7.6	105*	68.2	71.4
39 Hull	64.4	59.1	22.7	106	58.4	71.3

Employed in professional job	43%	Employed in non-professional job and Studying	2%
Employed in professional job and studying	4%	Employed in non-professional job	17%
Studying	23%	Unemployed	11%
Average starting professional salary	£21,500	Average starting non-professional salary	£16,016

History

Four years of growth in applications for history came to an end in 2016, but there was still a small increase in the numbers starting degrees. In contrast to many other arts subjects, the demand for places is well above the period before the arrival of £9,000 fees. Yet the subject is in the bottom 20 for employment, with almost as many graduates starting out in low-level jobs as in those categorised as professional occupations. History is also outside the top 40 subjects in the earnings table, although surveys have suggested that historians often rise to the top later in their careers.

Durham and Cambridge took it in turns to lead the history table for seven years, but Cambridge is now top for the third time in a row. The two leaders still tie for the highest entry standards, but Cambridge recorded the top score in the 2014 Research Excellence Framework (REF). The leading scores for our other measures are all to be found outside the top 20. Liverpool Hope has by far the best graduate prospects, as the only institution over 90 per cent on this measure, while undergraduates at Chichester are the most satisfied with the broad student experience.

History illustrates some of the paradoxes surrounding the National Student Survey (NSS), especially where teaching quality is concerned. The top eight universities for student satisfaction with teaching quality – and 15 of the top 16 – are all post-1992 institutions; yet the top 23 in our table, even including the NSS results, are older foundations. Two universities share the top score for teaching quality: Leeds Trinity and Suffolk, which are 77th and 91st respectively out of 94 in the table. At Suffolk, less than one graduate in five went straight into professional employment or a postgraduate course, the lowest score in this table and most others.

Employment scores are disappointing at many of the 94 universities in the table, although still an improvement on last year. More than 20 institutions saw less than half of those graduating in 2016 go into professional jobs or start postgraduate courses by the end of the year, and the figure was below 40 per cent at three of them.

History

		Teaching quality %	Student experience %	Research quality %	Entry standards (UCAS points)	Graduate prospects %	Overall score
1	Cambridge	n/a	n/a	56.3	216	81.0	100.0
2	Durham	88.3	80.0	41.4	216	84.8	97.3
3	St Andrews	91.5	86.7	46.7	198	74.6	97.1
4	Oxford	n/a	n/a	56.1	213	81.1	96.9
5	Exeter	85.9	82.8	45.6	184	77.9	94.6
6	Warwick	n/a	n/a	51.7	182	73.3	93.9
7	Lancaster	88.7	85.8	37.0	164	82.2	93.8
8	Sheffield	n/a	n/a	53.7	159	78.6	93.7
9	Birmingham	83.9	79.2	48.8	165	80.1	93.2
=10	Leeds	86.3	83.4	43.6	172	71.0	92.7
=10	University College London	n/a	n/a	51.9	187	75.8	92.7
12	King's College London	n/a	n/a	45.3	170	79.9	92.3
13	York	84.9	79.1	43.3	168	71.8	91.6
14	London School of Economics	74.1	69.6	46.8	195	82.4	91.3
15	East Anglia	86.4	82.9	47.4	160	62.5	91.1
16	Royal Holloway	88.9	83.0	40.6	144	70.6	91.0
17	Nottingham	83.6	80.5	36.9	158	78.1	90.8
18	Southampton	84.6	81.4	50.6	142	67.9	90.7
19	Sussex	82.4	77.7	41.3	141	84.1	90.6
20	Glasgow	82.3	78.5	47.7	186	57.9	90.5
21	Manchester	n/a	n/a	39.8	161	68.9	90.4
22	Bristol	n/a	n/a	40.6	190	75.0	90.3
23	Kent	83.5	78.9	41.3	138	78.3	90.0
24	Hertfordshire	91.4	89.1	46.7	113	60.7	89.9
25	Loughborough	89.0	89.4	22.5	142	75.8	89.8
26	Aberdeen	85.9	79.3	36.1	170	63.6	89.7
27	Dundee	88.2	85.2	30.4	148	63.7	88.8
28	Huddersfield	94.1	87.4	22.3	123	67.8	88.5
29	Liverpool	n/a	n/a	38.9	149	61.2	88.4
30	Newcastle	82.0	78.8	29.0	165	68.4	88.0
31	Queen Mary, London	80.5	74.2	43.7	144	67.9	87.8
=32	Essex	84.5	78.6	34.8	126	72.4	87.6
=32	Strathclyde	79.9	77.9	42.0	195	45.1	87.6
34	Edinburgh	72.6	70.9	46.9	190	59.6	87.4
=35	Keele	83.0	80.6	32.8	125	73.8	87.3
=35	Lincoln	89.7	84.2	25.9	125	65.8	87.3
=37	Northumbria	87.2	82.7	30.7	138	59.9	87.1
=37	Teesside	91.7	87.2	27.9	104	65.5	87.1
=39	Coventry	93.8	89.0	5.6	120	75.0	87.0

=39 Portsmouth	89.5	84.7	32.2	111	63.8	87.0
41 Queen's, Belfast	80.6	80.0	46.3	141	55.0	86.8
42 SOAS London	n/a	n/a	20.8	147	69.2	86.6
=43 De Montfort	89.1	83.4	23.4	98	76.4	86.5
=43 Stirling	84.7	76.5	28.5	163	57.5	86.5
45 Liverpool Hope	84.0	76.1	15.7	112	91.7	86.3
46 Hull	88.5	85.0	26.1	122	60.9	86.2
47 Swansea	85.6	84.5	25.0	120	67.5	86.1
=48 Liverpool John Moores	91.6	86.0	15.9	127	59.7	85.7
=48 Reading	84.2	76.5	35.4	136	57.7	85.7
50 Leicester	78.1	72.4	34.3	137	69.0	85.2
=51 Bangor	87.8	81.2	24.3	126	57.4	85.0
=51 Brunel	85.7	81.8	32.4	118	56.3	85.0
=51 Newman	91.0	80.7	12.0	114	69.7	85.0
=54 Aberystwyth	88.8	85.8	19.5	115	60.2	84.9
=54 Edge Hill	87.2	82.3	23.6	116	61.6	84.9
56 Birkbeck	85.8	75.2	48.4	106	48.4	84.7
57 Cardiff	78.6	72.4	31.4	152	59.9	84.5
58 Oxford Brookes	84.1	80.5	35.0	128	49.5	84.4
59 West of England	85.0	82.2	28.9	121	53.7	84.1
60 Plymouth	88.8	84.3	22.6	112	53.7	83.9
61 Chichester	93.9	91.6	15.8	101	46.3	83.4
62 Goldsmiths, London	82.2	74.3	34.5	119	53.8	83.2
63 Nottingham Trent	84.5	77.8	17.5	126	56.4	82.5
64 Northampton	88.7	83.9	21.5	93	52.4	82.3
65 Sheffield Hallam	84.6	74.7	38.3	113	41.0	82.1
66 Derby	92.9	86.8	13.5	94	47.2	81.9
67 Manchester Metropolitan	85.2	78.3	18.0	121	50.9	81.7
68 St Mary's, Twickenham	87.4	84.2	11.0	101	57.0	81.6
69 Bath Spa	n/a	n/a	8.3	108	61.9	81.2
70 Canterbury Christ Church	90.2	84.1	16.3	96	43.4	80.8
71 Leeds Beckett	88.0	86.8	11.0	105	45.8	80.7
=72 Roehampton	77.7	74.8	21.4	98	66.3	80.6
=72 Wales Trinity St David	89.4	76.0	17.3	103	46.0	80.6
=74 Central Lancashire	82.3	75.1	12.0	113	60.1	80.5
=74 South Wales	89.0	86.0	15.8	118	33.1	80.5
76 Westminster	81.6	76.8	11.8	110	59.4	80.2
77 Leeds Trinity	94.3	85.7	10.3	87	40.0	80.1
78 Bishop Grosseteste	77.4	67.3	7.0	101	81.1	79.9
=79 Anglia Ruskin	88.5	87.0	15.3	86	40.0	79.4
=79 Chester	84.0	83.6	9.1	107	47.8	79.4
81 Gloucestershire	76.6	76.8	11.2	123	54.4	78.9
82 East London	77.9	76.4	13.9	84*	65.7	78.8
83 Greenwich	82.0	79.0	8.6	119	43.8	78.4
84 Worcester	81.3	75.7	19.5	110	40.3	78.3
85 Winchester	80.1	72.6	19.1	111	44.3	78.1

		Teaching quality %	Student experience %	Research quality %	Entry standards (UCAS points)	Graduate prospects %	Overall score
86	York St John	85.3	79.9	n/a	104	46.6	77.5
87	Ulster	80.8	73.3	24.0	119	29.0	77.4
88	Staffordshire	83.6	85.0	n/a	89	48.4	77.0
89	Bradford	n/a	n/a	12.7	n/a	72.0	76.8
90	Salford	76.9	69.0	n/a	116	60.3	76.7
91	Suffolk	94.3	86.2	n/a	92	18.9	75.8
=92	Brighton	n/a	n/a	13.1	99	59.3	74.9
=92	Kingston	79.5	72.8	n/a	97	48.4	74.9
94	Sunderland	78.1	72.8	7.7	101	40.6	74.8

Employed in professional job	30%	Employed in non-professional job and Studying	4%
Employed in professional job and studying	3%	Employed in non-professional job	25%
Studying	27%	Unemployed	11%
Average starting professional salary	£20,500	Average starting non-professional salary	£16,000

History of Art, Architecture and Design

More than 40 institutions are offering history of art at degree level in 2018, and student numbers continue to recover after a decline that coincided with the introduction of £9,000 fees. Entry standards are high: more than half of the universities in the table average at least 150 points on the new UCAS tariff, and only two have averages of less than 120 points. Cambridge, whose entrants had the highest of those grades, retains the leadership it won two years ago. However, it is the only one of the 28 universities in the table to occupy the same position as last year. Aberdeen is the biggest mover, with a rise of 14 places to 13th.

St Andrews is up to second place, with the best graduate prospects and the highest scores on both of our measures derived from the National Student Survey. Liverpool John Moores, although only four places off the bottom of the table, is only fractions of a point behind St Andrews on both measures of student satisfaction. The Courtauld Institute, an independent college of the University of London based in Somerset House, and previously the only specialist institution to top any of our league tables, has dropped to third. It had the best results in the Research Excellence Framework, when 95 per cent of its submission was rated as world-leading or internationally excellent.

Last year's improvement in employment levels has not been maintained, and the subjects have slipped out of the top 50 of the 67 subject groups. No university saw 80 per cent of their 2016 graduates go straight into professional jobs or postgraduate study, and the proportion was below 50 per cent at four of them. The relatively small numbers taking degrees in the history of art, architecture or design make for considerable volatility in the statistics; the subjects still have a better employment record than they did two years ago. The subjects have actually moved six places up the earnings table, despite a small decline in average salaries in graduate-level jobs.

History of Art, Architecture and Design

		Teaching quality %	Student experience %	Research quality %	Entry standards (UCAS points)	Graduate prospects %	Overall score
1	Cambridge	n/a	n/a	49.0	215	78.8	100.0
2	St Andrews	91.7	86.6	42.1	185	79.3	98.5
3	Courtauld	n/a	n/a	66.0	171	69.6	96.1
4	Warwick	n/a	n/a	53.0	180	71.2	95.6
5	Oxford	n/a	n/a	39.7	201	79.2*	95.5
6	Exeter	85.3	82.9	35.1	184	n/a	94.3
7	Essex	83.7	78.4	46.9	n/a	74.4*	93.9
8	Birmingham	84.3	79.8	43.7	157	79.2	93.8
=9	University College London	n/a	n/a	44.7	189	73.1	93.4
=9	York	85.5	80.9	53.2	154	66.9	93.4
11	Manchester	n/a	n/a	54.0	136	65.9	92.3
12	Leeds	86.1	82.6	30.0	163	69.7	91.7
13	Aberdeen	85.9	79.3	36.1	n/a	65.1	91.3
14	East Anglia	86.4	82.9	36.9	154	62.8	91.1
15	SOAS London	n/a	n/a	40.9	154	62.5	90.8
16	Nottingham	83.9	80.4	30.9	140	72.2	89.8
17	Leicester	77.9	72.8	42.0	n/a	73.0	89.4
18	Oxford Brookes	84.1	80.5	35.0	133	68.2	89.3
19	Sussex	82.4	77.7	25.2	146	75.0	89.1
20	Kent	83.1	78.4	44.3	127	63.6	88.9
21	Goldsmiths, London	82.2	74.3	25.9	150	68.2	88.0
22	Bristol	n/a	n/a	28.3	174	59.6	87.8
23	Glasgow	82.4	78.8	37.2	163	41.2	86.8
24	Edinburgh	73.0	71.1	27.9	184	62.6	86.7
25	Liverpool John Moores	91.6	86.0	7.2	132*	50.0	85.5
26	Plymouth	88.8	84.3	14.7	108	48.8	83.7
27	Manchester Metropolitan	85.2	78.3	9.7	132	39.3*	81.4
28	Brighton	n/a	n/a	13.1	106	36.4	74.1

Employed in professional job	35%	Employed in non-professional job and Studying	4%
Employed in professional job and studying	1%	Employed in non-professional job	24%
Studying	23%	Unemployed	13%
Average starting professional salary	£20,000	Average starting non-professional salary	£16,800

Hospitality, Leisure, Recreation & Tourism

This group of subjects covers a variety of courses directed towards management in the leisure and tourism industries, mainly delivered at modern universities. Taken together with sports studies, it remains close to the top 20 for applications, although the numbers dropped a little in 2016, as they did in the previous year. Because so many graduates begin their careers in low-level jobs, the subjects are never far from the foot of the employment table. Although they escaped the bottom four in the last edition, they are back in it now. The subjects do better in the earnings table, but are still outside the top 50.

Applications and enrolments have never returned to the level seen in 2010, the last year unaffected by the move to £9,000 fees. Entry standards are modest – only five universities average more than 150 points on the new UCAS tariff. They are led by Glasgow Caledonian, in 12th place, but the overall leader, for the third year in a row, is Birmingham, which produced by far the best results in the Research Excellence Framework, when 90 per cent of its submission was considered world-leading or internationally excellent. Manchester, in 11th place, has the best graduate prospects, one of only two universities to see eight out of ten graduates go straight into professional employment or onto a postgraduate course. At six universities the proportion was below 40 per cent.

Only ten of the 61 institutions in the table are pre-1992 universities, but they include five of the top ten. The leading modern universities are making progress, however, with Liverpool John Moores and Lincoln moving up to third and fourth places respectively. Students at eighth-placed Sunderland are the most satisfied with the quality of teaching, while those at Lincoln gave the best ratings for the broader student experience. Satisfaction rates are invariably high in the hospitality group: only three universities failed to achieve at least 70 per cent approval in the National Student Survey. More than 100 universities and colleges are offering courses in one or more of the hospitality, leisure, recreation and tourism subjects in 2018.

Hospitality, Leisure, Recreation and Tourism	Teaching quality %	Student experience %	Research quality %	Entry standards (UCAS points)	Graduate prospects %	Overall score
1 Birmingham	71.9	71.0	63.7	159	78.1	100.0
2 Exeter	74.8	81.5	24.4	176	81.2	97.8
3 Liverpool John Moores	84.0	86.4	45.3	143	55.7	94.9
4 Lincoln	96.8	97.5	11.4	119	79.4	94.3
5 Strathclyde	83.7	81.2	44.3	n/a	61.8	93.8
6 Surrey	79.4	84.1	33.6	160	55.1	93.6
7 Ulster	91.3	91.5	31.0	130	54.8	92.7
8 Sunderland	97.9	96.2	2.4	126	70.3	92.1
9 Huddersfield	90.6	88.2	n/a	133	67.7	89.5
10 Coventry	80.7	82.3	1.6	141	73.9	89.1
11 Manchester	76.9	79.8	n/a	140	81.8	89.0
12 Glasgow Caledonian	74.9	75.4	15.2	177	45.8	88.9
13 West of Scotland	86.3	84.7	9.1	141	53.9	88.2
14 Edinburgh	68.5	70.2	26.1	149	62.5	88.1
15 Staffordshire	89.8	87.4	19.1	112*	58.7	88.0
16 Westminster	83.9	85.6	10.7	132	58.2	87.5
17 Plymouth	85.3	83.3	13.1	122	56.6	86.4
18 Manchester Metropolitan	80.4	80.9	4.7	133	62.5	86.1
=19 Bournemouth	79.0	79.7	9.0	120	67.4	85.6
=19 Oxford Brookes	83.8	83.7	5.1	132	54.9	85.6
=21 Falmouth	86.2	81.9	n/a	114	68.5	85.4
=21 Robert Gordon	80.1	80.4	2.6	148	51.0	85.4

23	Arts University, Bournemouth	77.6	68.9	n/a	125	77.8	85.2
24	Aberystwyth	83.9	81.9	14.5	119	53.3	85.1
25	Edinburgh Napier	77.9	77.6	2.3	152	49.5	84.9
26	Leeds Beckett	79.2	79.8	12.6	115	63.4	84.8
=27	Hertfordshire	83.4	85.3	0.9	124	58.8	84.7
=27	Liverpool Hope	75.0	76.8	10.9	128	61.9	84.7
29	South Wales	73.4	70.8	10.8	133*	63.6	84.6
=30	Central Lancashire	79.6	79.8	5.1	134	54.7	84.4
=30	Gloucestershire	77.0	74.4	6.0	110	77.0	84.4
=30	Sheffield Hallam	80.3	79.1	8.5	124	57.8	84.4
33	Cardiff Metropolitan	77.0	78.2	7.7	126	59.4	84.0
34	London South Bank	76.4	75.3	35.0	113	45.2	83.9
=35	Greenwich	77.6	77.7	3.3	130	59.1	83.8
=35	Salford	81.0	86.7	5.9	131	47.1	83.8
=35	Winchester	80.0	80.4	n/a	120	64.9	83.8
=38	University of the Arts London	75.0	72.4	n/a	141	60.0	83.7
=38	West of England	84.6	87.2	n/a	113*	59.3	83.7
40	Portsmouth	70.9	72.6	8.1	122	70.1	83.6
41	Canterbury Christ Church	80.1	80.3	19.0	106	55.3	83.4
42	Southampton Solent	82.5	82.7	0.6	118	56.1	82.7
43	Chester	78.0	77.9	6.6	121	53.4	82.2
44	Brighton	80.3	75.8	10.9	115	52.1	82.1
45	West London	84.7	83.7	n/a	114	50.6	81.7
46	Derby	80.9	77.0	0.9	122	50.4	81.3
47	De Montfort	75.0	70.9	n/a	108	68.7	80.7
=48	Middlesex	77.1	78.1	10.5	132	33.2	80.3
=48	Suffolk	71.2	71.4	n/a	137*	50.5	80.3
50	St Mary's, Twickenham	88.0	93.0	4.8	109	31.8	80.0
=51	Cumbria	84.3	78.8	3.2	125	33.3	79.8
=51	Hull	80.7	83.7	10.2	n/a	36.4*	79.8
53	Chichester	70.0	72.1	n/a	113	64.9	79.5
54	Anglia Ruskin	90.0	90.1	3.4	99*	30.8	78.4
55	Northampton	78.6	78.4	n/a	113	41.3	77.7
56	Queen Margaret, Edinburgh	64.1	64.3	n/a	118	60.2	77.2
57	London Metropolitan	72.8	71.1	n/a	107	52.1	76.8
58	Wales Trinity St David	82.1	81.1	n/a	104	34.5	76.3
59	East London	64.4	65.2	0.8	114	52.5	75.4
60	Buckinghamshire New	74.8	69.0	0.9	105	40.0	74.7
61	Bedfordshire	66.3	68.3	6.7	81	43.7	71.0

Employed in professional job	45%	Employed in non-professional job and Studying	2%
Employed in professional job and studying	1%	Employed in non-professional job	35%
Studying	7%	Unemployed	10%
Average starting professional salary	£19,700	Average starting non-professional salary	£16,796

Iberian Languages

Spanish was the only language to have more students starting courses at degree level in 2016 than in the previous year. The increase was only 25 students, but it was the second year in a row that numbers had grown, and it came as other modern languages continued to decline. Indeed, although only 350 students embarked on Spanish degrees, this was just 40 fewer than the total for French. Those statistics do not capture the much larger number of students who learn the language as part of a broader modern languages programme, but even they continued to decline both in 2016 and 2017.

The table also includes Portuguese, but not a single student has started an honours degree in the language since 2012. Nevertheless, Portuguese will still be available – either alone or as part of a modern languages degree – at 28 universities in 2018. It can even be combined with Czech and Slovak at Oxford.

Cambridge has a clear lead at the top of the table, with Durham retaining second place, but there are new challengers moving up behind them. Lancaster has jumped 11 places to third, while Kent is up 17 places to sixth. For the moment, however, Cambridge has the highest entry grades and the top results in the Research Excellence Framework, while University College London and Kent tie for the best graduate prospects together with Aberystwyth which is down in 32nd place. Surrey has the top scores for student satisfaction – unusually high ones at that – although Bangor, which is only just inside the top 30 overall, is not far behind on satisfaction with teaching quality.

The relatively small numbers of students can cause volatility in the statistics. Iberian Languages are tied with nine other subjects for 20th place on graduate salaries in professional jobs, having been in the bottom half of the table last year. They still are in the bottom half for overall graduate prospects, although most universities offering the languages have a reasonable employment record. Only two in the table fell below 55 per cent for the proportion of graduates going straight into professional jobs or further study.

Iberian Languages	Teaching quality %	Student experience %	Research quality %	Entry standards (UCAS points)	Graduate prospects %	Overall score
1 Cambridge	n/a	n/a	54.0	216	85.1	100.0
2 Durham	86.1	75.6	34.6	205	86.8	94.4
3 Lancaster	82.3	89.2	47.0	164	83.8	93.8
4 Oxford	n/a	n/a	41.3	211	76.8	93.3
5 Warwick	84.7	87.9	45.2	173	n/a	93.1
=6 Kent	86.4	86.5	41.9	133	88.7	92.0
=6 University College London	n/a	n/a	43.7	183	88.7	92.0
8 Exeter	88.3	88.3	35.1	176	76.0	91.6
9 Bristol	n/a	n/a	36.0	173	85.3	91.3
=10 King's College London	n/a	n/a	42.1	167	74.9	90.9
=10 Newcastle	82.0	82.7	36.3	163	84.4	90.9
12 St Andrews	81.9	82.8	26.4	197	81.0	90.6
13 Strathclyde	81.5	73.2	42.0	193	72.1	90.5
14 Surrey	98.4	93.3	39.1	178	54.5*	90.4
15 Queen's, Belfast	83.9	79.1	53.6	151	69.8	90.3
16 Nottingham	80.5	76.4	39.4	153	83.3	89.5

=17 Southampton	83.2	84.9	42.7	155	71.8	89.2
=17 Stirling	88.6	82.5	29.8	165	76.3	89.2
=19 Bath	80.7	81.2	27.4	169	84.6	89.1
=19 Manchester	n/a	n/a	48.9	154	65.9	89.1
21 Birmingham	88.6	76.9	33.7	153*	78.8	89.0
22 Royal Holloway	86.7	80.4	48.3	146	67.3	88.9
23 Glasgow	82.2	78.2	26.3	202	71.2	88.4
24 East Anglia	87.9	85.1	33.1	156	71.0	88.1
25 Leeds	79.5	82.2	30.6	167	77.9	88.0
26 York	80.0	76.8	37.3	163	n/a	87.1
27 Sheffield	n/a	n/a	41.2	152	70.7	87.0
28 Bangor	96.4	91.9	39.6	111	56.8	85.3
=29 Aston	92.6	91.6	23.4	134	65.9	84.9
=29 Edinburgh	71.9	74.3	30.3	188	68.0	84.9
31 Portsmouth	91.7	89.1	32.2	102	69.2	84.5
32 Aberystwyth	85.8	86.7	16.6	104*	88.7	84.4
33 Heriot-Watt	70.7	67.2	26.3	179	76.4	84.3
34 Coventry	93.8	89.7	18.1	113	75.0	84.2
35 Liverpool	n/a	n/a	33.4	137	59.5	84.1
36 Queen Mary, London	87.4	83.7	35.1	128	59.0	83.4
37 Reading	79.0	71.4	41.7	129	n/a	83.0
38 Manchester Metropolitan	89.2	81.7	29.0	126	60.0	82.4
39 Cardiff	74.9	80.9	32.5	145	61.1	81.8
40 Leicester	85.5	86.6	16.9	146	60.0	81.1
41 Swansea	80.5	78.3	22.8	111	73.5	80.8
42 Chester	86.7	84.5	17.3	100	73.1	80.7
=43 Aberdeen	51.5	37.3	29.3	187	71.0	79.2
=43 Sussex	85.5	80.3	n/a	144*	70.9	79.2
45 Hull	78.7	73.6	22.7	107	69.2	78.6
46 Nottingham Trent	83.1	82.4	7.6	120	62.8	76.9
=47 Central Lancashire	78.1	72.3	15.2	n/a	61.4*	76.4
=47 Northumbria	72.1	78.9	n/a	136	74.2	76.4
49 Ulster	84.7	84.1	22.4	123	38.0	75.1
50 Westminster	68.1	58.8	2.0	113	63.7	69.7

Employed in professional job	44%	Employed in non-professional job and Studying	3%
Employed in professional job and studying	3%	Employed in non-professional job	19%
Studying	20%	Unemployed	11%
Average starting professional salary	£22,000	Average starting non-professional salary	£16,800

Italian

Only 20 students started degrees in Italian in 2016, even fewer than in 2015 and only a quarter of the total in 2009. Even allowing for the much larger numbers of students who included Italian in broader language degrees or as one or more modules in another subject, demand is worryingly low.

Forty universities offered the language in 2016, compared with only 28 in 2017. Most students have no previous knowledge of Italian, although they are likely to have taken another language at A-level.

Cambridge is well clear at the top of the table, with the top research score and the highest entry grades. St Andrews, its nearest challenger in the previous *Guide*, has dropped out of the table this year, along with Glasgow and Central Lancashire. Durham is now in second place, with good scores across the board. Kent has the highest levels of student satisfaction in both of the measures derived from the National Student Survey, while Birmingham was the only university to see 90 per cent of 2016 graduates go straight into professional jobs or continue studying. More than a quarter of those completing degrees in Italian go on to postgraduate courses.

As in Iberian languages, the small numbers can make for exaggerated swings in the graduate employment statistics, but this year Italian remains in the bottom half of the earnings and employment tables. Entry standards remain surprisingly high, given the small numbers of applicants. Only six of the 17 universities with enough students to compile an entry score average less than 150 points on the new UCAS tariff. There is a high response rate and scores have generally been good in the National Student Survey. Only one university failed to satisfy at least three quarters of final-year undergraduates taking Italian.

Italian

	Teaching quality %	Student experience %	Research quality %	Entry standards (UCAS points)	Graduate prospects %	Overall score
1 Cambridge	n/a	n/a	54.0	216	85.1	100.0
2 Durham	86.1	75.6	34.6	205	86.8	93.6
3 Oxford	n/a	n/a	41.3	199	77.3	92.6
4 Warwick	n/a	n/a	45.2	167*	66.9	92.4
5 Manchester	n/a	n/a	48.9	148	73.8	92.1
=6 Exeter	88.3	88.3	35.1	176	76.0	91.8
=6 Kent	96.4	93.2	41.9	123	n/a	91.8
8 Bangor	94.3	91.1	39.6	n/a	56.4	90.7
=9 Birmingham	83.1	77.5	33.7	164	90.3	90.6
=9 University College London	n/a	n/a	43.7	180	83.3	90.6
11 Bristol	n/a	n/a	36.0	172	78.8	90.0
12 Bath	77.8	81.9	27.4	165	88.5	88.1
13 Leeds	86.1	87.7	30.6	157	67.8	87.4
14 Edinburgh	82.6	84.8	30.3	183	60.8	86.9
15 Portsmouth	91.7	89.1	32.2	102	69.4	85.7
16 Manchester Metropolitan	86.1	83.1	29.0	n/a	56.8*	84.1
17 Cardiff	80.7	82.9	32.5	134*	62.3	83.5
18 Hull	80.1	75.4	22.7	n/a	67.0*	81.8
19 Royal Holloway	73.1	64.3	48.3	n/a	56.1	80.5
20 Nottingham Trent	90.7	92.6	7.6	108*	67.2	80.4
21 Reading	80.6	70.6	41.7	139	35.0	80.0

Employed in professional job	43%	Employed in non-professional job and Studying	4%
Employed in professional job and studying	3%	Employed in non-professional job	18%
Studying	20%	Unemployed	11%
Average starting professional salary	£21,000	Average starting non-professional salary	£18,000

Land and Property Management

Graduate salaries and employment levels continue to rise in land and property management, which is now in the top 12 of our 67 subject groups on both measures. Some 85 per cent of graduates go straight into professional employment and median salaries in such jobs reached £25,000 in 2016, after four successive increases. Like last year, there were too few graduates in lower-level jobs to compile a national average. In the main, the subject table reflects those high employment rates: almost 98 per cent of graduates at second-placed Reading found high-level work or continued to study, and only one university dropped below 80 per cent on this measure.

The table is still less than half the size it was in 2006, however, with no representation from Scotland or Wales, and one university less than last year. Nevertheless, more than 20 universities and colleges are offering courses in this area in 2018. They include degrees in woodland ecology and conservation, and property management and valuation, as well as the real estate degrees that are the largest recruiters. Cambridge has a predictably big lead, with the best research score and entry grades that are more than 60 points ahead of the nearest challenger.

The subjects have acquired a reputation for recruiting disproportionate numbers from independent schools, but property firms donated more than £500,000 to support a "Pathways to Property" scheme to try to widen participation. Those who take the courses appear to enjoy the experience: although there are no outstandingly high scores from the National Student Survey, only one university in the table recorded less than 70 per cent satisfaction with the teaching or broader student experience. Nottingham Trent, in sixth place, had the highest levels of satisfaction with teaching quality, but was pipped to the top score for course organisation, learning resources and personal development by Birmingham City, which is one place lower in the table.

Land and Property Management	Teaching quality %	Student experience %	Research quality %	Entry standards (UCAS points)	Graduate prospects %	Overall score
1 Cambridge	78.3	72.4	49.0	220	93.8	100.0
2 Reading	74.5	76.2	40.0	157	97.9	96.7
3 Ulster	79.5	79.0	28.6	118	96.0	94.9
4 Sheffield Hallam	76.6	77.1	13.4	118	95.9	92.4
5 Oxford Brookes	76.7	77.9	17.6	128	90.1	92.1
6 Nottingham Trent	80.9	81.6	3.4	122	90.4	92.0
7 Birmingham City	80.5	81.7	2.7	101	85.7	89.8
8 Greenwich	71.1	72.4	2.0	139	80.0	86.4
9 Westminster	67.3	72.0	10.7	112	77.9	84.5

Employed in professional job	81%	Employed in non-professional job and Studying	0%
Employed in professional job and studying	4%	Employed in non-professional job	5%
Studying	2%	Unemployed	9%
Average starting professional salary	£25,000	Average starting non-professional salary	–

Law

The numbers starting law degrees have risen for six years in a row, passing 25,000 in 2016. It remains one of the most popular subjects, with more than 100,000 applications, unaffected by the move to higher fees. Entry standards reflect this: only in medicine do so many universities make such testing demands. Nine of the 100 universities in the table average at least 200 points and more than a third average more than 150 points. However, so many universities now offer law that there are still six where the average was below 100 points in 2016.

The top three are unchanged since last year, with Cambridge extending its lead over Oxford. Like four other Russell Group universities in the table, neither has scores for teaching quality or the student experience because of the boycott of the National Student Survey in these institutions. The students who are most satisfied with the quality of teaching are again at Abertay, which remains the only post-1992 university in the top 20, despite recording one of the lowest scores in the Research Excellence Framework (REF). Cumbria, which is down in 84th place, is only a fraction of a point behind on this measure, and has the highest score for satisfaction with the broader student experience.

Glasgow, which has leapt 18 places up the table into fourth has the highest entry standards, benefiting from the boost given to Scottish secondary qualifications in the new UCAS tariff. The London School of Economics, in third place, achieved the best results in the REF, while Aberdeen just pips Cambridge to the best score for graduate prospects. Although most of these scores are good, the proportion enjoying "positive destinations" was below half at three universities.

Law is just outside the top 20 in the employment table, but it is 58th out of the 67 subjects for early career earnings. Only about half of all graduates go on to practise law, and training contracts for those who do keep the median in graduate-level jobs down to £18,720. Those in lower-level employment are little more than £2,000 behind, although the later rewards in professional jobs can be considerable. Aspiring solicitors in England go on to take the Legal Practice Course, while those aiming to be barristers take the Bar Vocational Course, so it is no surprise that 43 per cent of all law graduates are engaged in postgraduate study six months after completing a degree. Note that in Scotland, most law courses are based on the distinctive Scottish legal system, which also has different professional qualifications.

Law	Teaching quality %	Student experience %	Research quality %	Entry standards (UCAS points)	Graduate prospects %	Overall score
1 Cambridge	n/a	n/a	58.7	222	92.4	100.0
2 Oxford	n/a	n/a	51.8	216	85.6	95.2
3 London School of Economics	75.9	72.3	64.5	209	84.6	94.1
4 Glasgow	79.1	83.1	33.8	227	83.6	92.8
5 University College London	71.3	68.6	57.7	204	87.1	91.9
6 Nottingham	82.9	83.8	45.2	184	80.5	91.8
7 Durham	82.8	78.7	32.8	208	83.6	91.7
=8 Leeds	87.3	89.1	40.1	170	78.9	91.5
=8 York	87.3	90.6	30.3	166	85.2	91.5
10 Aberdeen	81.5	80.9	20.9	193	92.5	91.0
11 Edinburgh	70.0	75.0	40.8	216	86.5	90.6
12 Bristol	78.0	76.4	50.5	189	78.6	90.5

13 Dundee	86.3	86.4	16.3	174	90.4	90.4
14 Kent	83.4	83.1	43.9	143	85.1	90.0
15 King's College London	n/a	n/a	39.2	211	83.1	89.4
16 Strathclyde	77.1	76.4	29.4	211	77.8	88.6
17 Queen's, Belfast	76.6	73.2	40.3	158	88.1	88.5
=18 Abertay	93.6	90.1	1.2	146	88.0	88.1
=18 Lancaster	77.0	78.5	38.9	154	85.1	88.1
20 Warwick	n/a	n/a	41.9	182	80.6	88.0
=21 Keele	81.6	79.9	30.5	127	88.4	87.1
=21 Portsmouth	83.6	82.3	32.2	130	82.9	87.1
=21 Queen Mary, London	76.0	74.2	23.7	194	82.1	87.1
24 Exeter	78.5	78.8	21.4	179	82.6	87.0
25 Birmingham	78.1	68.6	33.6	159	83.5	86.4
26 East Anglia	81.9	81.2	26.5	157	77.0	86.2
27 Sheffield	75.7	77.6	31.9	155	82.2	86.1
28 Sussex	79.3	81.2	23.3	141	84.6	85.8
29 Reading	73.7	76.8	31.2	146	85.7	85.7
30 Swansea	82.4	82.3	20.4	126	85.9	85.5
31 Ulster	86.6	82.2	48.5	127	62.6	85.4
32 Heriot-Watt	76.8	73.4	18.8	165	84.7	85.2
33 Newcastle	77.6	75.0	25.4	177	73.3	84.8
34 Leicester	75.8	75.5	26.4	153	80.6	84.6
35 Stirling	85.1	78.8	19.4	145	75.2	84.5
=36 Birkbeck	73.3	69.5	37.9	124	86.7	84.4
=36 Cardiff	77.3	77.0	27.2	161	74.3	84.4
38 Manchester Metropolitan	88.3	87.8	14.9	123	75.3	84.3
39 Manchester	n/a	n/a	27.2	161	83.0	83.9
40 London South Bank	86.8	86.2	20.1	93	76.5	82.8
41 Southampton	75.5	69.2	18.2	154	80.0	82.6
42 Essex	65.0	68.5	31.6	122	91.9	82.5
43 Robert Gordon	76.5	77.7	3.9	165	78.9	82.3
=44 Bangor	81.9	81.6	12.0	141	72.5	82.2
=44 Liverpool	n/a	n/a	19.6	151	76.6	82.2
=46 Buckingham	84.5	79.9	n/a	122	81.4	81.7
=46 Lincoln	82.5	81.0	5.0	123	79.6	81.7
48 Nottingham Trent	82.3	78.6	2.3	133	79.3	81.6
49 Glasgow Caledonian	70.8	68.0	1.8	178	83.9	81.5
50 Bradford	79.9	78.5	11.8	128	76.4	81.4
51 Greenwich	86.5	85.6	2.1	139	68.3	81.3
=52 Aston	84.1	78.7	19.7	135	64.2	81.2
=52 Middlesex	77.9	83.1	21.4	108	75.0	81.2
54 West London	90.3	88.2	n/a	101	72.4	80.7
=55 Huddersfield	82.7	77.6	n/a	125	79.0	80.6
=55 Salford	87.1	88.8	5.9	116	67.1	80.6
57 Sheffield Hallam	86.9	83.9	14.4	112	64.8	80.4
58 SOAS London	66.1	67.5	26.7	154	75.2	80.3

Law cont

	Teaching quality %	Student experience %	Research quality %	Entry standards (UCAS points)	Graduate prospects %	Overall score
59 St Mary's, Twickenham	82.6	81.4	n/a	105	80.6	80.2
=60 Bedfordshire	92.4	90.3	3.6	88	68.0	80.1
=60 West of England	79.5	81.8	3.5	120	77.0	80.1
62 Hull	75.7	74.1	12.6	123	78.1	80.0
=63 Brunel	73.1	72.7	20.3	129	74.3	79.9
=63 Southampton Solent	89.8	90.2	n/a	94	70.7	79.9
65 Plymouth	85.2	84.9	16.0	117	60.7	79.8
66 De Montfort	79.5	81.3	5.2	108	77.6	79.7
=67 Coventry	79.9	78.8	5.6	115	75.7	79.6
=67 Surrey	75.9	68.7	8.5	161	70.1	79.6
69 Liverpool John Moores	82.3	77.2	2.7	134	69.7	79.4
70 Aberystwyth	73.7	75.5	14.3	117	76.2	79.2
71 Sunderland	79.9	81.8	0.7	106	76.8	78.8
=72 Gloucestershire	79.5	73.5	n/a	108	80.4	78.7
=72 Hertfordshire	80.5	79.5	n/a	107	76.6	78.7
=72 Northumbria	75.2	74.4	2.5	139	74.3	78.7
=75 Central Lancashire	78.2	75.5	5.3	141	67.1	78.5
=75 Edinburgh Napier	74.5	74.2	n/a	161	69.1	78.5
77 South Wales	86.5	83.1	n/a	128	60.6	78.3
78 Buckinghamshire New	89.7	86.0	n/a	113	58.3	78.0
79 City	72.4	73.3	9.1	137	70.2	77.9
80 Edge Hill	77.6	78.2	12.1	112	66.3	77.6
=81 Oxford Brookes	76.5	73.6	5.1	126	69.4	77.4
=81 Westminster	71.4	72.5	7.5	120	75.6	77.4
83 Staffordshire	82.9	80.0	n/a	114	65.2	77.2
84 Cumbria	93.5	92.3	n/a	101	48.9	76.7
85 Teesside	84.0	77.0	15.0	107	54.5	76.4
86 East London	79.9	77.5	8.6	101	63.8	76.3
87 Bournemouth	73.9	68.7	8.8	116	69.6	76.2
88 Chester	73.4	68.4	n/a	116	75.5	76.1
89 Leeds Beckett	78.3	79.0	n/a	102	68.7	76.0
90 Birmingham City	77.0	78.2	2.8	105	65.6	75.6
91 Anglia Ruskin	82.9	82.0	5.2	95	58.5	75.5
92 Bolton	77.8	77.2	n/a	105	61.3	74.3
93 Kingston	69.5	69.0	n/a	118	68.6	73.9
94 Derby	64.1	61.8	2.4	108	79.4	73.8
95 Northampton	74.3	76.1	n/a	97	59.5	72.4
=96 Brighton	66.4	68.7	6.5	115	61.8	72.3
=96 Winchester	76.9	71.5	n/a	103	57.0	72.3
98 West of Scotland	75.0	69.1	n/a	134	48.9	71.8
99 Canterbury Christ Church	80.7	71.4	3.2	115	40.9	70.9
100 London Metropolitan	65.3	59.3	0.3	86	68.1	69.7

Employed in professional job	33%	Employed in non-professional job and Studying	5%
Employed in professional job and studying	6%	Employed in non-professional job	16%
Studying	32%	Unemployed	8%
Average starting professional salary	£18,720	Average starting non-professional salary	£16,500

Librarianship and Information Management

Only five universities are left in the table for librarianship and information management – half the number of a decade ago – and none of them has a degree with librarianship in the title. Librarianship is now more normally studied at Masters level; indeed, some postgraduate training is required to enter the profession after completing a first degree. Most of the courses in this category focus on broader information services, but only 120 students started undergraduate courses in 2016 – 20 fewer than in the previous year.

As in other subjects with small enrolments, there can be huge swings in some of the statistics. But that certainly does not apply to the subject table, where an exchange of places between the bottom two universities is the only change since last year. It does apply to the national comparisons with other subjects, however. Librarianship and Information Management has jumped 17 places to the verge of the top 20 for the proportion of graduates in professional jobs or further study, and is sharing 12th place with five other subjects in the earnings table, with median salaries of £25,000 in graduate-level jobs. There are real contrasts among universities in our table, with top-placed Loughborough scoring 90 per cent for graduate prospects, but three of the five less than 55 per cent.

Only three universities, led by Loughborough, attracted enough students to meet our threshold for the publication of entry scores. Leeds, in second place, produced the best score in the Research Excellence Framework, while undergraduates at third-placed Northumbria were the most satisfied with the quality of teaching on their course. Loughborough which has extended its already considerable lead at the top of the table this year, also had the best score in the National Student Survey for our measure encompassing course management, learning resources, students' influence and the learning community.

Librarianship and Information Management	Teaching quality %	Student experience %	Research quality %	Entry standards (UCAS points)	Graduate prospects %	Overall score
1 Loughborough	83.6	87.5	45.1	156	90.5	100.0
2 Leeds	80.8	82.5	54.5	n/a	52.4*	92.1
3 Northumbria	84.6	82.2	21.0	124	82.4	91.0
4 Aberystwyth	78.0	78.5	9.2	n/a	40.9*	83.2
5 Manchester Metropolitan	67.1	69.1	4.7	133	53.8	81.2

Employed in professional job	65%	Employed in non-professional job and Studying	1%
Employed in professional job and studying	1%	Employed in non-professional job	15%
Studying	10%	Unemployed	9%
Average starting professional salary	£25,000	Average starting non-professional salary	–

Linguistics

Applications for courses in linguistics are running at record levels and grew for the fourth year in a row in 2016. The same number of students – 585 – started degrees as in the previous year, but the number of universities in our table is still going up, with two more joining this year. In its pure form, linguistics examines how language works, and can lead to work in speech therapy or the growing field of teaching English as a foreign language. The subject has fared much better than might have been expected since the introduction of £9,000 fees, with both applications and enrolments running well ahead of the levels seen at the start of the decade.

Almost three quarters of the students are female. There are about five applications for each place and entry standards are comparatively high, with nine of the top 10 universities averaging more than 150 points on the new UCAS tariff. Third-placed Cambridge has by far the highest entry standards, averaging over 220 points, but Oxford retains the leadership of the table as a whole. Students at SOAS London, in 16th place, are the most satisfied with the quality of teaching, while those at the University of the West of England, which is in the bottom ten, gave the highest rating to the broader student experience. Bangor was only a fraction of a point behind the leaders on both measures

Linguistics is just outside the top 40 in the employment table, an improvement on last year. But the subject shares last place in the earnings table with six others. A median salary of £18,000 in professional jobs is only £2,400 higher than the equivalent for lower-level employment. More than a quarter of graduates start off in such jobs and only Kent saw eight out of ten of those completing a linguistics degree go straight into professional work or onto a postgraduate course.

Linguistics	Teaching quality %	Student experience %	Research quality %	Entry standards (UCAS points)	Graduate prospects %	Overall score
1 Oxford	n/a	n/a	41.3	209	77.2	100.0
2 University College London	83.9	84.5	43.7	187	69.0	97.0
=3 Cambridge	n/a	n/a	54.0	224	76.9	96.5
=3 Lancaster	85.5	82.8	47.0	157	75.0	96.5
5 Newcastle	89.3	86.2	36.3	162	73.3	96.1
6 Leeds	87.4	87.2	30.6	157	77.9	95.4
7 Aberdeen	82.3	80.1	46.3	162	72.7	95.2
=8 Edinburgh	76.4	76.1	57.7	189	60.7	94.9
=8 Warwick	n/a	n/a	45.2	170	n/a	94.9
10 Kent	81.8	82.6	41.9	129	84.3	94.5
11 Manchester	n/a	n/a	48.9	154	75.8	94.1
12 Sheffield	n/a	n/a	42.2	148	77.3	93.9
13 King's College London	n/a	n/a	42.1	163	68.8	93.3
=14 Queen Mary, London	83.9	83.4	50.3	131	65.6	92.4
=14 York	83.6	80.5	37.3	153	68.9	92.4
16 SOAS London	94.2	88.9	26.0	153*	60.0	91.8
17 Glasgow	81.2	78.2	26.3	n/a	75.0	91.3
=18 Bangor	93.2	93.1	39.6	128	50.0	89.9
=18 Queen's, Belfast	81.8	78.5	53.1	n/a	57.2*	89.9

20 Cardiff	84.6	79.9	35.1	n/a	59.3	88.7
21 Central Lancashire	81.3	72.0	15.2	148	72.2	87.5
22 Manchester Metropolitan	90.8	90.3	29.0	110	55.1	86.9
23 Greenwich	83.9	79.2	8.2	n/a	65.2*	85.9
=24 Essex	64.1	66.0	36.0	130	74.8	85.4
=24 West of England	91.6	93.7	9.5	122	55.8	85.4
26 Nottingham Trent	84.3	80.5	10.0	123	67.9	85.1
27 Roehampton	79.1	70.2	21.8	104	72.7	84.2
28 York St John	83.8	82.3	9.7	117	56.3	81.9
29 Hertfordshire	82.4	80.9	n/a	111	63.4	80.9
30 Salford	87.6	78.8	4.8	111	53.3	80.4
31 Westminster	84.6	76.1	2.0	110	53.7	78.8
32 Brighton	81.7	78.5	16.2	108	44.8	78.7
33 Huddersfield	60.5	61.6	29.9	122	n/a	75.7
34 Ulster	67.5	81.6	22.4	121	32.6	75.0

Employed in professional job	37%	Employed in non-professional job and Studying	4%
Employed in professional job and studying	4%	Employed in non-professional job	22%
Studying	24%	Unemployed	9%
Average starting professional salary	£18,000	Average starting non-professional salary	£15,600

Materials Technology

Courses in this table cover four distinct areas: materials science, mining engineering, textiles technology and printing, and marine technology. The various subjects are highly specialised and attract relatively small numbers – fewer than 500 started courses in all of these areas combined in 2016 – with applications and enrolments falling after both had rallied in recent years. Only polymers and textiles drew more applications, and even they saw fewer students actually start courses. Although there are only 13 universities in the table – one less than last year – more than 50 institutions are offering courses in this area in 2018. The leading universities demand chemistry and sometimes also physics, maths or design technology at A-level or its equivalent.

Cambridge remains well ahead of the rest at the top of the table, with much the highest scores for entry standards and research: only 3 per cent of the university's submission to the Research Excellence Framework was considered less than world-leading or internationally excellent. However, Sheffield has the best graduate prospects and the top scores on both of the measures derived from the National Student Survey – successes that have helped the university jump six places into second.

Materials technology has moved into the top 12 subject groups for salaries in graduate-level jobs, with an average that reached £25,000 in 2016. But the subjects have slipped slightly in the table based on graduate destinations, after moving up nine places last year. They are now just outside the top 25, with more than a quarter of graduates continuing their studies, either full or part-time, and nearly half in professional jobs six months after graduation.

Materials Technology	Teaching quality %	Student experience %	Research quality %	Entry standards (UCAS points)	Graduate prospects %	Overall score
1 Cambridge	78.5	81.2	78.3	244	84.8	100.0
2 Sheffield	90.5	91.1	41.0	168	95.1	99.5
3 Oxford	n/a	n/a	70.8	242	77.2	96.7
=4 Imperial College	75.9	82.5	62.3	212	79.9	96.0
=4 Loughborough	85.0	84.2	41.8	152	92.0	96.0
6 Exeter	87.1	81.3	36.4	168	88.5	95.7
7 Birmingham	80.4	82.8	49.3	159	90.4	95.3
8 Swansea	82.4	84.0	45.5	119	95.0	94.6
9 Manchester	82.0	83.3	36.4	172	74.7	93.0
10 Queen Mary, London	77.3	83.7	40.0	146	71.0	90.5
11 De Montfort	82.9	82.9	12.5	106	64.7	86.8
12 Huddersfield	81.2	77.8	10.2	122	55.6	84.7
13 Sheffield Hallam	75.1	74.2	17.8	122	57.9	83.5

Employed in professional job	48%	Employed in non-professional job and Studying	2%
Employed in professional job and studying	2%	Employed in non-professional job	15%
Studying	22%	Unemployed	10%
Average starting professional salary	£25,000	Average starting non-professional salary	£16,000

Mathematics

Maths is one of the most popular subjects for those going on to higher education. The third increase in a row took the number of applications for the mathematical sciences group over the 50,000 mark for the first time in 2017, and the 9,200 enrolments also set a new record. With rising numbers taking A-level and universities in England receiving funding for new teaching facilities in maths, engineering and the sciences, further increases must be likely in future years. Entry standards are already high: the top six in this year's table all average at least 215 points. The scores are boosted by the fact that most successful candidates for the leading universities have taken two A-levels in the subject, as well as two or three others. But the table also covers a wide spread of entry scores: 11 universities average less than 120 points.

Maths is often cited as one of the subjects most likely to lead to a lucrative career, and our earnings table seems to bear this out. The subject is one of six sharing twelfth place for average salaries in professional jobs six months after graduation. However, it has dropped out of the top 20 this year in the table based on the proportion of graduates going straight into professional jobs or becoming postgraduate students.

Three graduates in ten continue their studies after graduation, while more than half find high-level employment. Employment scores in the table reflect this, with only 11 of the 73 universities failing to reach 70 per cent positive destinations for their 2016 graduates and none dropping below 50 per cent. Like last year, Sussex has the best score on this measure, with almost 95 per cent of graduates finding professional jobs or continuing to study.

Cambridge remains ahead of Oxford at the top of the table. Cambridge leads on entry grades, while Oxford produced the best results in the Research Excellence Framework. Aberystwyth, in 34th place, had the highest scores in the teaching sections of the National Student Survey, while Greenwich, 12 places lower, was the start performer in the sections relating to the student experience.

Mathematics

	Teaching quality %	Student experience %	Research quality %	Entry standards (UCAS points)	Graduate prospects %	Overall score
1 Cambridge	n/a	n/a	60.7	248	89.9	100.0
2 Oxford	n/a	n/a	67.5	235	88.3	98.3
3 St Andrews	82.9	84.1	44.2	237	90.4	97.1
4 Warwick	79.3	80.0	55.8	215	84.0	94.7
5 Durham	79.8	79.5	44.0	221	85.6	93.9
6 Imperial College	71.6	75.7	59.7	228	84.9	93.7
7 Nottingham	83.4	83.2	44.8	183	83.4	93.0
8 Dundee	88.6	89.3	48.2	142	81.7	92.9
=9 Lancaster	84.8	82.8	45.8	166	83.9	92.6
=9 Loughborough	88.2	89.9	31.0	157	86.8	92.6
11 Heriot-Watt	85.1	83.6	42.3	174	81.9	92.3
12 Edinburgh	80.1	79.8	43.7	202	80.3	91.9
13 Bath	80.0	78.5	35.7	198	86.3	91.8
14 Bristol	n/a	n/a	57.3	198	78.4	91.7
15 University College London	72.8	70.5	42.0	201	93.6	91.5
16 Leeds	79.8	81.6	42.0	178	84.0	91.4
17 Southampton	78.5	82.2	41.9	167	86.1	91.1
18 Birmingham	81.0	82.0	34.1	180	82.9	90.6
19 Surrey	83.3	81.2	31.5	174	83.2	90.5
20 Sheffield	n/a	n/a	34.0	158	85.4	90.2
=21 Exeter	78.8	81.3	37.9	185	79.7	90.1
=21 Glasgow	80.9	80.6	41.4	200	72.1	90.1
23 Essex	86.5	79.0	34.3	128	88.2	90.0
24 York	88.3	86.3	27.0	164	76.0	89.8
25 Manchester	n/a	n/a	44.3	189	75.1	89.4
26 Sussex	77.8	78.7	28.5	137	94.8	89.0
27 Strathclyde	78.7	79.4	34.6	184	76.9	88.7
28 Reading	87.4	84.1	35.3	136	73.8	88.4
29 Newcastle	83.4	86.3	32.0	158	73.1	88.3
=30 Queen's, Belfast	78.2	74.8	25.0	169	85.2	87.8
=30 Swansea	80.8	80.7	20.7	129	91.3	87.8
32 Royal Holloway	83.8	81.2	35.5	147	72.4	87.5
33 Keele	88.9	89.8	19.5	132	73.8	87.3
■34 Aberystwyth	92.8	85.6	19.4	123	72.8	87.0
=34 East Anglia	79.6	82.8	33.7	146	75.0	87.0
36 Hull	77.0	76.3	24.2	128	91.5	86.9
37 King's College London	n/a	n/a	37.1	177	81.5	86.4
38 Cardiff	78.4	82.7	31.6	163	70.2	86.3

	Teaching quality %	Student experience %	Research quality %	Entry standards (UCAS points)	Graduate prospects %	Overall score
39 London School of Economics	65.3	64.8	28.7	213	84.8	86.1
40 Liverpool Hope	82.9	80.3	8.8	103	93.3	85.9
41 Central Lancashire	88.9	88.7	19.8	152	60.4	85.5
42 South Wales	92.4	89.6	10.1	131	66.9	85.4
=43 Liverpool John Moores	88.2	88.1	3.2	127	77.3	85.3
=43 Nottingham Trent	85.9	84.5	18.4	133	71.0	85.3
=43 Stirling	83.2	77.7	14.0	141	79.3	85.3
46 Greenwich	89.9	90.9	5.1	121	73.6	85.2
=47 Brunel	84.4	83.0	25.8	124	70.6	85.1
=47 Coventry	85.3	86.1	9.4	120	78.7	85.1
=49 Aberdeen	n/a	n/a	32.0	177	61.5	85.0
=49 Kent	75.9	72.8	28.2	134	82.1	85.0
51 West of England	85.1	82.8	10.6	136	74.7	84.8
52 Northumbria	81.4	84.5	16.7	138	72.5	84.6
53 Sheffield Hallam	78.2	81.4	17.8	110	81.7	84.1
54 Plymouth	89.4	84.6	9.3	136	63.9	83.6
55 Portsmouth	83.7	84.1	11.2	109	75.2	83.5
56 Leicester	70.9	76.1	25.0	147	76.8	83.4
57 Chester	77.4	78.4	7.1	117	85.1	83.2
58 Liverpool	n/a	n/a	29.8	144	72.2	83.0
59 Queen Mary, London	73.4	74.1	30.3	147	67.5	82.5
60 City	81.7	75.7	30.2	141	58.5	82.4
61 Hertfordshire	76.5	82.2	20.2	106	74.0	82.3
62 Manchester Metropolitan	85.7	84.7	5.6	120	67.1	82.1
63 Aston	74.7	77.9	21.7	130	70.1	81.9
64 Salford	77.7	80.6	4.4	113	76.0	81.1
65 London Metropolitan	81.8	81.1	13.5	72	69.5	79.9
66 Brighton	74.3	79.5	6.4	112	71.8	79.5
67 Derby	84.2	83.4	5.0	93	63.2	79.4
68 Oxford Brookes	81.3	85.1	13.9	119	50.9	78.8
69 Kingston	77.3	74.6	n/a	96	57.5	74.9

Employed in professional job	46%	Employed in non-professional job and Studying	1%
Employed in professional job and studying	5%	Employed in non-professional job	13%
Studying	24%	Unemployed	12%
Average starting professional salary	£25,000	Average starting non-professional salary	£16,500

Mechanical Engineering

Mechanical engineering is by far the biggest branch of engineering, attracting twice as many applicants as any of the other subjects. Indeed, it is only just outside the top ten for all degree choices. The introduction of higher fees only increased the subject's popularity, as students looked for a sure route to well-paid employment. Although there were small declines in both applications and enrolments in 2017, the numbers remained at least 50 per cent up on a decade ago. It is not hard to see why. Mechanical engineering is among the top 20 subjects for early career prospects and in the top ten for starting salaries in graduate-level employment. Almost two-thirds of graduates go straight into such jobs.

Cambridge remains well clear of Imperial College London at the top of the table. Cambridge is ranked in the top three in the world for the subject by QS, with both Imperial and Oxford in the top ten. Cambridge has the highest entry standards and the best research grades in our table. But South Wales, which is outside the top 50 after choosing not to enter the Research Excellence Framework in this subject, has the best graduate prospects, with almost 95 per cent of graduates finding professional work or beginning a postgraduate course within six months of graduating. Student satisfaction with the quality of teaching is relatively low, compared with other subjects, however. No university had a rating of more than 90 per cent on this measure – Harper Adams came closest – and 17 universities were below 70 per cent. Scores were better in the sections of the National Student Survey dealing with the broader student experience, with De Montfort the highest scorer.

More than 120 universities and colleges are offering mechanical engineering in 2018. Most of the leading universities demand maths – preferably with a strong component of mechanics – and another science subject (usually physics) at A-level or its equivalent. With more than six applications to the place, entry standards are high at the leading universities, five of which averaged more than 200 points in 2016. Even so, three institutions averaged less than 100 points, and one less than 80.

Mechanical Engineering	Teaching quality %	Student experience %	Research quality %	Entry standards (UCAS points)	Graduate prospects %	Overall score
1 Cambridge	83.4	85.8	67.0	241	93.0	100.0
2 Imperial College	86.6	85.8	59.6	233	86.6	97.5
3 Bristol	83.1	86.4	52.3	199	85.1	93.2
4 Bath	82.9	85.8	37.4	204	92.0	92.9
5 Leeds	81.8	84.2	40.9	193	89.1	91.6
6 Southampton	81.3	81.3	52.3	178	86.0	91.0
7 Loughborough	83.3	83.2	41.8	160	89.6	89.8
=8 Heriot-Watt	85.3	85.5	47.8	165	80.5	89.6
=8 Strathclyde	75.0	76.8	37.2	224	83.5	89.6
=10 Sheffield	78.3	82.1	36.0	178	88.7	88.8
=10 Surrey	85.7	83.8	30.8	175	85.2	88.8
12 University College London	67.9	73.6	44.6	193	90.5	88.3
13 Birmingham	79.1	79.8	37.7	161	89.1	87.9
=14 Glasgow	67.8	72.9	47.2	209	81.8	87.6
=14 Nottingham	77.7	79.8	40.8	169	84.9	87.6
16 Lancaster	74.8	79.7	41.6	154	90.1	87.2
17 Swansea	73.9	75.9	45.5	145	87.4	85.9
18 Edinburgh	63.5	67.4	50.3	198	81.3	85.6

Mechanical Engineering cont

	Teaching quality %	Student experience %	Research quality %	Entry standards (UCAS points)	Graduate prospects %	Overall score
19 Newcastle	77.4	80.0	30.2	157	85.7	85.4
20 Coventry	83.1	85.8	10.3	147	89.7	84.8
21 Manchester	64.6	68.4	35.1	181	87.8	84.2
22 Queen's, Belfast	72.2	75.0	36.7	148	84.2	83.7
23 Exeter	67.7	71.7	36.4	166	81.9	83.0
24 Liverpool	74.0	76.3	32.1	152	77.0	82.2
25 Aberdeen	67.7	75.6	28.4	182	75.7	82.0
26 Harper Adams	88.9	87.8	n/a	127	83.1	81.9
=27 Greenwich	85.0	87.1	29.5	133	66.7	81.7
=27 Lincoln	87.2	84.1	n/a	140	81.8	81.7
29 Cardiff	64.8	72.5	30.2	156	83.8	81.4
=30 De Montfort	87.6	93.7	12.5	100	78.1	81.0
=30 Huddersfield	75.9	78.5	10.2	126	89.9	81.0
=32 Brunel	73.5	75.2	23.7	154	77.0	80.9
=32 Dundee	71.9	76.9	34.1	159	69.9	80.9
34 Aston	74.8	73.3	20.6	135	83.8	80.8
35 Plymouth	78.7	77.9	15.7	119	84.5	80.6
=36 London South Bank	76.2	72.7	19.6	121	85.7	80.4
=36 Teesside	82.0	79.9	5.8	126	83.3	80.4
=38 Liverpool John Moores	79.0	78.4	4.7	147	79.6	79.9
=38 Queen Mary, London	65.4	68.8	46.7	145	72.2	79.9
40 Northumbria	69.5	74.3	30.7	143	73.8	79.4
41 Derby	81.4	77.7	6.7	114	83.1	79.2
=42 Portsmouth	81.0	81.5	9.1	121	77.6	79.1
=42 Sussex	70.5	71.7	24.0	130	80.4	79.1
=44 Oxford Brookes	70.6	72.1	13.9	150	78.7	78.7
=44 West of Scotland	70.7	73.9	9.0	151	80.5	78.7
46 Robert Gordon	68.8	71.1	8.8	178	74.3	78.4
47 Sunderland	79.1	79.3	8.8	82	86.4	77.8
48 Hull	73.1	72.3	16.5	112	81.3	77.7
49 Bradford	75.7	78.0	7.7	115	79.4	77.4
=50 Hertfordshire	74.5	76.6	16.5	118	74.8	77.3
=50 Sheffield Hallam	70.8	71.4	17.8	121	78.8	77.3
=50 West of England	73.9	74.0	10.6	126	77.9	77.3
53 Ulster	72.6	71.2	n/a	121	83.8	76.3
54 South Wales	65.0	64.3	n/a	117	94.7	76.2
55 Northampton	78.8	74.6	4.1	109	n/a	75.7
56 Salford	76.7	78.4	4.4	124	69.2	75.4
57 Manchester Metropolitan	63.6	65.3	16.3	126	75.8	74.5
58 Wales Trinity St David	80.9	81.4	1.0	99	67.7	74.1
59 City	69.4	69.7	20.2	131	58.8	73.1
60 Kingston	71.9	77.4	2.9	118	61.1	71.8

61 Glasgow Caledonian	65.0	69.4	4.7	152	59.2	71.5
62 Central Lancashire	66.2	60.0	7.1	126	68.1	71.4
63 Birmingham City	70.1	69.6	n/a	116	66.0	71.1
64 Anglia Ruskin	85.2	86.0	9.1	79	48.0	70.7
65 Staffordshire	67.1	61.6	5.7	122	61.3	69.7
66 Brighton	54.0	57.9	7.4	114	70.0	68.2
67 Bolton	73.3	69.3	n/a	107	48.3	67.0

Employed in professional job	60%	Employed in non-professional job and Studying		1%
Employed in professional job and studying	2%	Employed in non-professional job		12%
Studying	14%	Unemployed		11%
Average starting professional salary	£26,000	Average starting non-professional salary		£16,000

Medicine

There will be 500 additional places available to study medicine in 2018, with new schools opening at Anglia Ruskin, Aston and Ulster. The news may have helped to spark the 8 per cent increase in applications for courses starting this autumn, which reversed a three-year decline. There were still nine applications to the place in 2017 and the highest entry standards in any subject. Eighteen of the 32 schools in the table average 200 points or more at entry and none less than 180. In spite of this – and the fact that you can only apply to four medical schools – medicine is in the top eight subjects for the volume of applications. Nearly all schools demand chemistry and most biology. Physics or maths is required by some, either as an alternative or addition to biology. Universities will want to see evidence of commitment to the subject through work experience or voluntary work. Almost all schools interview candidates, and several use one of the two specialist aptitude tests (see chapter 1)

The subject carries unique prestige and tops the employment table again this year. Employment scores for individual schools are not used in the ranking (although they are still shown for guidance) to avoid small differences distorting positions in a subject where virtually all graduates become junior doctors or researchers. Fifteen schools reported full employment in 2016, and none dropped below 98 per cent. The average starting salary of £30,000 for junior doctors was exceeded only by dentists.

Oxford has topped the table for the last seven years, but Cambridge has slipped to third for the first time in that period, overtaken by Glasgow, which is up six places this year. Edinburgh has enjoyed an even bigger rise, of eight places, to fourth. Brighton and Sussex, although in the bottom half of the table overall, has much the most satisfied students, with the top scores in both of the measures derived from the National Student Survey. There was little to choose between the top scorers in the Research Excellence Framework, but Lancaster produced the best results.

Undergraduates have to be prepared to work long hours, particularly towards the end of the course, which will usually be five years long. Many students are now opting for the postgraduate route into the medical profession instead, although this is even longer.

Medicine

	Teaching quality %	Student experience %	Research quality %	Entry standards (UCAS points)	Graduate prospects %	Overall score
1 Oxford	90.4	89.6	48.9	236	98.8	100.0
2 Glasgow	85.3	86.3	42.3	237	99.3	96.1
3 Cambridge	75.3	68.2	52.0	241	98.8	94.7
4 Edinburgh	77.8	74.3	49.8	233	98.5	94.0
5 Swansea	87.3	84.3	44.7	n/a	100.0	93.7
6 Imperial College	77.6	84.2	54.6	215	99.6	93.4
7 Queen Mary, London	85.6	88.1	40.2	222	99.5	93.0
8 Newcastle	87.6	85.3	44.8	211	99.6	92.3
9 Bristol	83.7	84.4	47.5	207	99.8	91.2
10 University College London	n/a	n/a	53.3	215	100.0	90.9
11 Lancaster	85.2	84.0	55.2	186	n/a	90.0
12 Keele	86.2	84.5	50.0	192	99.5	89.8
13 Exeter	81.6	80.5	41.6	214	100.0	89.5
14 Dundee	85.1	85.6	25.1	231	99.6	89.4
15 Leeds	87.1	89.0	32.1	209	99.8	88.3
16 Aberdeen	86.4	88.5	20.2	229	100.0	88.0
17 St Andrews	87.8	91.5	19.8	224	98.1	87.7
=18 Brighton and Sussex Medical School	94.3	94.6	34.3	183	100.0	86.7
=18 Sheffield	n/a	n/a	36.5	193	100.0	86.7
20 Queen's, Belfast	85.8	85.8	34.6	199	100.0	86.2
21 Birmingham	82.1	82.5	31.5	207	99.7	85.4
22 East Anglia	82.2	83.5	31.8	198	100.0	83.8
23 Hull-York Medical School	80.7	75.2	36.2	197	100.0	83.6
24 Cardiff	75.8	77.6	34.5	200	100.0	82.6
25 Southampton	81.0	77.9	35.6	190	100.0	82.3
26 Manchester	72.6	71.9	34.6	201	99.6	81.1
27 Plymouth	81.6	80.5	23.1	198	100.0	80.5
28 Nottingham	67.9	64.7	36.8	205	100.0	80.3
29 Leicester	70.1	73.1	33.3	199	99.5	79.7
30 King's College London	61.3	63.4	48.3	187	99.5	78.4
31 St George's, London	76.1	78.5	22.4	189	100.0	76.7
32 Liverpool	n/a	n/a	31.7	188	99.8	75.8
33 Warwick	n/a	n/a	26.2	n/a	100.0	72.5

Employed in professional job	93%	Employed in non-professional job and Studying	0%
Employed in professional job and studying	1%	Employed in non-professional job	0%
Studying	5%	Unemployed	1%
Average starting professional salary	£30,000	Average starting non-professional salary	–

Middle Eastern and African Studies

This is one of the smallest categories in the *Guide* in terms of student numbers at degree level. Only 100 students started courses in Middle Eastern Studies and African Studies combined in

2017, although larger numbers will have included modules from this group in a broader degree. Arabic shared in a small increase in enrolments for non-European languages, only 100 students started degrees in the entire group. The subjects enjoy some official protection because they are classed as "vulnerable" and of national importance. It is just as well because applications remain well down on the norm before the introduction of £9,000 fees.

St Andrews remains top of the table without leading on any of the individual measures. It is offering joint degrees with Middle East Studies in 16 different subjects, as well as single honours, in 2018. Cambridge, in second place, has the highest entry standards, while fourth-placed Durham, boasts the highest levels of satisfaction with the quality of teaching. As last year, Leeds has the best scores for the broader student experience in the National Student Survey, although it has slipped one place to eighth overall. Also like last year, third-placed Birmingham has much the best scores for graduate prospects, as well as for research.

Again, the small numbers can make for big swings even in the national statistics. But, having seen the average starting salary in professional jobs rise by £3,000 in the last edition of the *Guide* and the unemployment rate drop five percentage points, both figures are fairly stable this year. The subjects are just in the top half of the earnings table and for employment. Applicants for courses in Arabic or African languages are not expected to have previous knowledge of the language, although they would normally be expected to demonstrate an aptitude for learning other languages.

Middle Eastern and African Studies	Teaching quality %	Student experience %	Research quality %	Entry standards (UCAS points)	Graduate prospects %	Overall score
1 St Andrews	82.4	82.5	46.7	203	85.3*	100.0
2 Cambridge	n/a	n/a	45.0	224	86.0	00.2
3 Birmingham	84.1	75.2	50.9	143	91.1*	97.2
4 Durham	84.6	75.3	34.6	175	83.3*	94.5
5 Edinburgh	76.0	75.9	30.1	198	87.1	94.2
6 Oxford	n/a	n/a	36.2	206	83.3	90.5
7 SOAS London	n/a	n/a	26.3	154	80.1	90.1
8 Leeds	74.1	83.8	30.6	162	70.0	87.9
9 Exeter	69.9	67.2	36.0	175	68.9	87.0
10 Manchester	n/a	n/a	48.9	148	62.2	85.3
11 Westminster	73.5	68.8	11.3	117	60.7	76.1

Employed in professional job	41%	Employed in non-professional job and Studying	0%
Employed in professional job and studying	3%	Employed in non-professional job	15%
Studying	29%	Unemployed	13%
Average starting professional salary	£21,840	Average starting non-professional salary	–

Music

Four years of healthy increases in applications for music degrees came to an abrupt halt in 2017 with a decline of almost 5,000. However, the numbers starting courses are still running at approaching twice the level of enrolments before £9,000 fees arrived. The expansion of provision has meant that there are now fewer than four applications per place. Entry grades were already relatively low at most universities – 23 of the 79 universities in this year's table average less than 120 UCAS points –

although music grades and the quality of auditions carry more weight in selecting students. Nine out of ten applicants come with A-levels and most university departments expect music to be among them, although they may accept a distinction or merit in Grade 8 music exams.

The character of courses varies considerably, from the practical and vocational programmes in conservatoires to the more theoretical degrees in some of the older universities, and everything from creative sound design and new media to sonic arts elsewhere. Almost 200 universities, colleges and other providers are offering undergraduate courses in 2018.

Durham has retained the lead it established last year, although this time it does not top any individual measure. The most satisfied students are at City University, which topped both of our measures derived from the National Student Survey and scored 100 per cent for overall satisfaction.

The Royal Academy of Music has this year's best employment score, taking over from the Royal College of Music, with an impressive 94 per cent of graduates going straight into professional work or postgraduate study. The four specialist institutions are all in the top six on this measure. Music invariably finishes ahead of the other performing arts in the employment table, although it is still only just outside the bottom 20 subjects overall. The 8 per cent unemployment rate is one of the best in the table, but 28 per cent of leavers were in non-graduate occupations six months after graduation. Music has slipped back into a share of last place in this year's earnings table, however.

Music

	Teaching quality %	Student experience %	Research quality %	Entry standards (UCAS points)	Graduate prospects %	Overall score
1 Durham	88.9	85.4	64.9	215	92.5	100.0
2 Oxford	n/a	n/a	66.3	203	80.8	95.2
3 Manchester	n/a	n/a	56.3	214	78.3	95.1
4 Birmingham	84.7	81.5	50.7	194	85.9	93.8
5 Edinburgh	82.3	81.5	48.0	233	72.5	93.4
6 Nottingham	90.8	84.3	55.4	174	76.0	92.9
7 Bristol	n/a	n/a	48.0	191	71.6	92.3
8 Cardiff	87.0	88.8	47.0	188	73.7	92.1
9 Leeds	82.6	83.9	44.2	194	78.9	91.5
10 Southampton	83.3	81.5	70.7	152	77.2	91.3
11 Surrey	91.9	87.6	27.2	180	81.2	91.2
12 Glasgow	76.0	80.2	46.0	210	74.6	90.2
13 York	88.9	86.5	37.1	171	76.4	90.1
14 Cambridge	n/a	n/a	48.0	206	91.2	89.5
15 Royal Holloway	77.4	74.9	55.0	197	69.1	89.1
16 Sheffield	n/a	n/a	60.0	147	72.4	88.6
17 SOAS London	n/a	n/a	60.0	118	77.3*	88.3
18 Royal Academy of Music	84.6	82.0	23.9	133	94.3	87.1
19 Queen's, Belfast	89.3	87.9	38.3	153	64.9	87.0
20 King's College London	n/a	n/a	43.5	191	71.1	86.7
21 Aberdeen	83.1	79.0	32.0	172	72.5	86.5
22 Liverpool Hope	92.5	86.4	15.5	118	85.6	85.7
23 Huddersfield	88.3	84.3	28.0	134	75.1	85.4

24 City	94.3	92.1	34.0	121	63.6	85.3
25 Royal Northern College of Music	84.8	82.9	12.3	134	86.7	84.4
=26 Bangor	87.9	86.8	24.7	148	64.3	84.2
=26 Newcastle	76.9	69.5	40.8	155	74.4	84.2
28 Kent	76.8	74.0	44.3	126	78.8	83.7
29 Keele	79.7	76.7	41.7	125	74.3	83.5
30 Royal College of Music	80.2	76.2	10.9	136	90.7	83.3
=31 Birmingham City	92.3	82.4	11.6	121	76.2	83.1
=31 Chester	93.3	85.7	4.3	134	72.5	83.1
33 De Montfort	84.2	84.5	14.5	120	83.3	83.0
34 Edinburgh Napier	81.4	82.9	n/a	182	71.2	82.9
35 Goldsmiths, London	n/a	n/a	51.1	143	71.1	82.1
36 Sussex	77.0	65.0	30.2	137	79.7	81.9
37 Ulster	89.8	85.9	40.0	133	43.0	81.6
38 Oxford Brookes	81.3	80.8	30.2	127	65.7	81.4
39 Brunel	80.0	77.0	32.6	133	64.3	81.1
40 Royal Conservatoire of Scotland	n/a	n/a	11.3	151	90.0	80.9
41 Bath Spa	84.9	83.3	10.7	129	69.1	80.7
42 West London	87.7	86.6	2.3	135	65.1	80.3
43 Falmouth	85.2	77.1	6.2	126	73.8	80.1
44 Edge Hill	83.3	82.7	3.8	133	n/a	79.3
45 Essex	92.4	89.9	n/a	99*	59.4	77.6
46 Salford	87.2	84.2	7.2	123	50.4	77.0
47 Liverpool	n/a	n/a	31.4	152	38.6	76.9
=48 Coventry	73.5	66.1	18.1	130	65.9	76.5
=48 Manchester Metropolitan	80.3	79.4	7.5	130	56.5	76.5
=50 Hull	75.0	78.0	11.2	133	59.0	76.4
=50 Leeds Beckett	82.5	83.4	1.7	118	60.0	76.4
52 Greenwich	71.9	72.7	n/a	152	66.7	76.3
53 Plymouth	78.1	72.8	20.2	124	55.2	76.2
54 York St John	79.2	79.4	10.5	125	55.7	76.1
55 Hertfordshire	76.5	76.1	5.3	124	63.4	75.7
56 Sunderland	79.3	74.4	4.2	114	63.9	75.4
57 Central Lancashire	81.0	74.4	3.9	110	62.5	75.2
58 Middlesex	76.0	69.6	16.1	116	59.6	75.0
59 Westminster	71.1	71.9	22.5	122	55.9	74.7
60 Chichester	79.3	74.2	9.7	135	47.3	74.6
61 Bournemouth	72.4	67.3	15.0	116	63.5	74.5
62 West of Scotland	67.0	63.5	11.3	150	61.1	74.4
=63 Brighton	83.8	80.4	13.1	110	43.8	74.3
=63 South Wales	72.7	67.9	6.4	128	63.1	74.3
=65 Gloucestershire	80.2	77.7	n/a	116	55.2	73.9
=65 London South Bank	69.5	60.6	12.8	99	76.9	73.9
67 Northampton	89.6	89.8	n/a	93	42.1	73.4
68 Bolton	81.6	73.8	n/a	113*	51.1	72.8
=69 Canterbury Christ Church	72.8	67.4	15.2	113	54.5	72.7

Music cont

		Teaching quality %	Student experience %	Research quality %	Entry standards (UCAS points)	Graduate prospects %	Overall score
=69	Derby	87.7	79.7	6.7	98	40.3	72.7
71	Winchester	76.6	73.8	11.2	108	48.4	72.3
72	Southampton Solent	83.2	79.8	n/a	113	42.1	72.2
73	Plymouth Marjon	83.0	77.3	n/a	116	41.7	72.1
74	University of the Arts London	76.3	71.3	n/a	103	50.0	70.4
75	Kingston	72.2	71.2	n/a	108	51.6	70.0
76	Buckinghamshire New	72.4	62.9	n/a	109*	54.7	69.8
77	East London	68.0	63.1	11.2	102	54.1	69.6
78	Cumbria	70.2	67.2	n/a	124	46.6	69.4
79	Anglia Ruskin	66.0	63.4	16.9	94	46.3	67.8

Employed in professional job	40%	Employed in non-professional job and Studying	3%
Employed in professional job and studying	6%	Employed in non-professional job	25%
Studying	19%	Unemployed	8%
Average starting professional salary	£18,000	Average starting non-professional salary	£15,600

Nursing

The scrapping of bursaries for nursing degrees prompted an 18 per cent decline in applications in 2017. The total was 5,000 lower than at any time in the current decade. But, since nursing is by far the most popular subject in the UCAS system, there were plenty of places to go round, and the numbers starting courses were still the second-highest on record. The chances of winning a place were also the highest ever, as the acceptance rate shot up, from 43 per cent to 52 per cent. With no sign of bursaries returning, the trend may well continue in 2018.

Entry requirements were already comparatively low. Although only five universities averaged less than 120 points in 2016, the highest aggregate was Glasgow's 183 points and Edinburgh was the only other university to average more than 160 points. The two Scottish rivals have swapped places at the top of the table this year, with Edinburgh taking over the leadership. Almost two-thirds of nursing students arrive without A-levels, many of them upgrading other health-related qualifications.

Queen Margaret, Edinburgh in ninth place has the students most satisfied with teaching quality, although, ironically, second on this measure is the bottom university of the 71 in the table – Bolton. The top one – Edinburgh – gets the highest rating for other aspects of the student experience. Bolton suffers for not entering the Research Excellence Framework (REF) in nursing, but it also has much the lowest score for graduate prospects. Six universities, including Derby, in 61st place, saw all their 2016 graduates go straight into professional jobs or further study. Nursing is in the top three for graduate destinations, but just outside the top 30 for salaries in professional jobs.

As another of the universities with a 100 per cent employment record, as well as student satisfaction exceeding 90 per cent, Portsmouth remains the highest-placed post-1992 university, holding on to fourth place. Southampton, in 14th place, produced much the best results in the REF, when 94 per cent of its work was rated as world-leading or internationally excellent.

Nursing

		Teaching quality %	Student experience %	Research quality %	Entry standards (UCAS points)	Graduate prospects %	Overall score
1	Edinburgh	91.1	93.0	53.4	176	97.9	100.0
2	Glasgow	91.6	89.5	42.3	183	97.9	99.6
3	Liverpool	89.5	85.3	35.3	152	100.0	96.1
4	Portsmouth	91.5	92.8	24.3	n/a	100.0	96.0
5	Birmingham	88.0	83.4	37.0	152	98.6	95.4
6	Surrey	81.4	81.8	37.5	159	98.4	95.1
7	Leeds	83.4	78.6	31.7	157	99.5	94.9
8	Brunel	87.3	89.0	18.2	n/a	100.0	94.2
9	Queen Margaret, Edinburgh	96.7	91.0	1.5	160	97.3	94.0
10	Bangor	81.3	76.2	34.7	144	100.0	93.6
11	Queen's, Belfast	84.5	83.8	34.7	144	97.9	93.5
12	Manchester	n/a	n/a	57.1	148	97.8	93.4
13	York	80.0	74.6	40.2	153	96.6	93.2
=14	Keele	87.6	85.5	20.9	139	99.6	93.1
=14	Southampton	60.9	54.3	65.7	153	99.6	93.1
=16	City	87.9	84.7	19.2	142	99.1	93.0
=16	East Anglia	79.4	76.3	24.9	152	99.3	93.0
=18	Manchester Metropolitan	87.9	87.8	12.0	142	99.6	92.8
=18	Nottingham	76.8	68.7	31.4	155	98.9	92.8
20	Huddersfield	85.5	82.3	13.2	152	98.1	92.5
21	King's College London	76.5	77.0	34.6	146	98.2	92.3
=22	Northumbria	82.6	77.6	14.0	148	99.2	92.1
=22	South Wales	89.8	87.0	2.2	147	99.1	92.1
24	Coventry	89.3	87.1	4.5	143	98.8	92.0
=25	Cardiff	72.9	66.0	36.8	149	98.7	91.9
=25	Ulster	82.5	83.0	27.7	135	98.3	91.9
27	Swansea	88.2	86.4	14.5	139	97.2	91.6
28	Birmingham City	86.7	79.8	1.5	147	98.7	91.3
29	Liverpool John Moores	84.7	84.2	6.0	144	98.3	91.2
30	Bradford	86.3	83.6	9.5	138	98.4	91.1
31	Leeds Beckett	91.3	88.1	3.5	131	99.0	91.0
32	Chester	85.8	82.1	12.0	132	99.2	90.9
33	Hull	83.8	78.6	16.7	138	97.7	90.8
=34	De Montfort	80.7	76.0	13.0	135	100.0	90.6
=34	West of Scotland	86.4	80.7	29.0	124	96.9	90.6
36	West London	90.7	87.7	2.5	132	97.6	90.4
=37	Glasgow Caledonian	80.3	75.7	8.1	141	99.1	90.3
=37	Worcester	86.7	84.5	2.6	138	97.6	90.3
39	West of England	81.0	82.0	8.2	135	99.0	90.1
=40	Essex	87.9	82.8	n/a	130	99.3	90.0
=40	London South Bank	80.1	78.8	13.7	129	99.6	90.0
42	Central Lancashire	75.0	73.8	8.3	150	97.8	89.8

		Teaching quality %	Student experience %	Research quality %	Entry standards (UCAS points)	Graduate prospects %	Overall score
=43	Salford	77.5	74.3	3.8	146	98.5	89.7
=43	Teesside	84.1	80.2	2.4	137	98.1	89.7
45	Bournemouth	81.1	74.9	4.7	137	99.0	89.5
46	Stirling	77.3	71.9	34.1	119	98.3	89.4
47	Lincoln	71.3	70.1	22.6	132	99.4	89.3
=48	Dundee	82.4	80.1	22.1	116	98.2	89.2
=48	Staffordshire	86.4	77.4	n/a	137	97.1	89.2
=50	Edge Hill	88.1	83.9	2.0	133	95.9	89.1
=50	Hertfordshire	81.4	79.3	4.0	129	99.3	89.1
=52	Canterbury Christ Church	82.8	73.0	2.2	131	99.2	88.9
=52	Sheffield Hallam	79.6	75.6	3.7	135	98.4	88.9
=52	Sunderland	72.1	74.0	7.5	147	n/a	88.9
=55	Bedfordshire	76.3	72.5	25.1	114	99.7	88.5
=55	Plymouth	77.3	73.2	9.5	136	97.2	88.5
=57	Brighton	76.8	69.8	4.8	133	98.8	88.2
=57	Oxford Brookes	79.7	74.4	3.0	132	97.9	88.2
59	Anglia Ruskin	81.4	78.4	3.1	123	98.7	88.1
60	Greenwich	79.2	75.5	2.2	126	98.5	87.8
61	Derby	80.9	73.4	7.3	114	100.0	87.7
=62	Middlesex	76.6	72.7	10.0	127	97.4	87.6
=62	Northampton	82.7	76.5	1.6	121	98.1	87.6
64	Robert Gordon	72.6	65.7	4.9	132	98.0	87.0
65	Edinburgh Napier	77.8	73.9	5.3	121	97.3	86.7
66	Cumbria	73.6	70.1	0.7	128	98.3	86.6
67	Suffolk	68.6	64.4	n/a	123	99.5	85.6
68	Kingston/St George's, London	69.7	72.7	2.6	113	99.0	85.3
69	Buckinghamshire New	76.9	77.7	1.0	129	90.9	84.5
70	Abertay	61.0	64.2	n/a	120*	98.1	83.6
71	Bolton	92.8	89.3	n/a	128	74.2	79.7

Employed in professional job	93%	Employed in non-professional job and Studying	0%
Employed in professional job and studying	1%	Employed in non-professional job	1%
Studying	2%	Unemployed	2%
Average starting professional salary	£21,909	Average starting non-professional salary	£16,380

Other Subjects Allied to Medicine

The withdrawal of NHS bursaries hit applications in virtually all the subjects in this group, which includes audiology, complementary therapies, counselling, health services management, health sciences, nutrition, occupational therapy, optometry, ophthalmology, orthoptics, osteopathy, podiatry and speech therapy. Physiotherapy and radiography now have rankings of their own.

As in nursing, however, universities upped the offer rate in 2017 to the point where there were increases in enrolments for medical technology and some of the smaller subjects.

Most of the institutions in the table are post-1992 universities, but only Robert Gordon and Northumbria make the top 20 – in 19th and 20th place respectively. Strathclyde has extended its lead over Aston at the top of the table, while Liverpool has leapt 17 places into third, with the aid of high student satisfaction scores. The highest of all, where teaching quality is concerned, is at Worcester, which is just outside the top 40 overall. Cambridge, not surprisingly, has much the highest entry grades, but did not enter the Research Excellence Framework (REF) in the relevant category, so shares sixth place. Southampton, in eighth place, was the star performer in the REF.

The choice of specialism naturally affects graduate employment rates, which range from better than 90 per cent positive destinations at 26 of the 80 universities to less than 60 per cent at five others. Kingston (for the second year in a row) and Leeds both reached 100 per cent. Overall, the subjects are just outside the top ten for employment prospects, with two-thirds of graduates going straight into professional jobs and only 7 per cent unemployed. As a group, the subjects are level with nursing for median salaries in professional jobs, just outside the top 30, having arrested two years of decline in the earnings table.

Subjects allied to Medicine	Teaching quality %	Student experience %	Research quality %	Entry standards (UCAS points)	Graduate prospects %	Overall score
1 Strathclyde	91.6	89.2	52.2	207	89.2	100.0
2 Aston	91.6	89.5	39.1	154	98.3	94.9
3 Liverpool	93.9	95.7	35.3	148	96.1	94.6
4 Manchester	83.8	81.0	57.1	159	94.5	94.5
5 University College London	75.2	79.7	48.4	195	93.5	94.3
=6 Cambridge	n/a	n/a	n/a	244	84.8	94.2
=6 Dundee	83.2	86.5	31.3	191	93.6	94.2
8 Southampton	79.1	68.9	65.7	147	97.1	92.6
9 Lancaster	83.0	85.9	55.2	150	87.6	92.4
=10 East Anglia	88.2	91.5	24.9	162	92.5	92.1
=10 Newcastle	83.8	85.3	47.8	166	82.0	92.1
=12 Leeds	81.0	82.2	31.7	156	100.0	91.1
=12 Surrey	83.3	82.7	37.5	168	85.3	91.1
14 Reading	78.4	72.0	42.3	175	86.5	90.3
15 Swansea	85.5	76.6	44.7	138	91.4	90.2
16 Cardiff	76.2	74.2	36.8	157	98.2	89.7
17 Birmingham	84.9	85.4	31.5	156	82.1	89.2
18 City	86.8	85.0	19.2	142	95.5	89.0
19 Robert Gordon	91.4	90.5	4.9	164	85.4	88.9
20 Northumbria	88.1	85.8	14.0	150	92.1	88.8
21 Sheffield	75.9	80.4	38.3	157	83.8	87.9
22 King's College London	76.2	82.3	34.6	158	n/a	87.8
=23 Glasgow Caledonian	75.6	78.2	8.1	187	91.5	87.7
=23 Warwick	80.7	81.3	25.3	167	81.0	87.7
25 West of Scotland	80.9	83.9	29.0	160	78.3	87.4

Subjects allied to Medicine

		Teaching quality %	Student experience %	Research quality %	Entry standards (UCAS points)	Graduate prospects %	Overall score
26	Oxford Brookes	87.4	84.6	3.0	145	96.0	87.2
27	Huddersfield	89.9	84.9	13.2	139	87.7	87.1
28	Brunel	79.7	85.2	18.2	147	90.8	86.9
29	Hull	83.8	78.6	16.7	n/a	88.2	86.6
30	Exeter	82.0	79.6	n/a	173	89.7	86.5
31	Brighton	84.7	81.0	4.8	146	94.4	86.3
32	Portsmouth	87.7	81.5	24.3	130	n/a	86.2
33	Birmingham City	85.4	83.8	1.5	150	91.3	86.1
34	Plymouth	83.9	79.2	9.5	138	95.7	86.0
35	Manchester Metropolitan	88.3	83.0	12.0	153	77.7	85.9
=36	London South Bank	89.0	84.7	13.7	126	87.5	85.7
=36	Teesside	91.3	81.5	2.4	140	87.5	85.7
38	Sheffield Hallam	92.4	91.0	3.7	131	83.6	85.6
39	South Wales	84.0	78.3	2.2	149	90.9	85.1
40	London Metropolitan	80.9	81.0	5.2	n/a	90.0	84.9
=41	Coventry	89.5	89.2	4.5	128	84.7	84.8
=41	Worcester	95.5	92.0	2.6	133	74.4	84.8
43	West of England	87.3	88.9	8.2	137	79.1	84.6
=44	Bournemouth	79.9	77.1	4.7	147	91.4	84.3
=44	Ulster	81.0	80.5	27.7	137	76.0	84.3
46	Lincoln	83.1	84.8	22.6	135	72.3	83.7
47	Anglia Ruskin	88.7	88.6	3.1	111	89.5	83.6
48	De Montfort	84.3	85.3	13.0	119	84.2	83.4
49	Kingston	73.4	70.7	2.6	n/a	100.0	83.0
50	Wrexham Glyndŵr	89.4	84.4	3.6	129	77.8	82.9
=51	Bedfordshire	76.3	72.5	25.1	109	94.6	82.7
=51	Bradford	76.7	78.8	9.5	135	88.2	82.7
=51	Cardiff Metropolitan	80.0	74.2	3.6	141	88.2	82.7
54	Bangor	75.8	78.0	34.7	134	70.0	82.5
55	Salford	84.1	81.7	3.8	140	76.4	82.2
56	Essex	87.8	89.1	n/a	113	82.1	81.9
57	Greenwich	82.9	80.3	2.2	132	81.8	81.8
58	Liverpool John Moores	79.0	81.6	6.0	139	78.5	81.7
59	Northampton	78.6	75.4	1.6	130	89.5	81.4
60	York St John	81.1	81.1	1.9	131	81.1	81.3
61	Canterbury Christ Church	77.7	71.3	2.2	119	95.9	81.0
62	Derby	80.3	74.8	7.3	126	79.9	80.4
=63	Queen Margaret, Edinburgh	76.4	71.5	6.7	144	75.3	80.0
=63	Sunderland	69.5	64.5	7.5	n/a	95.2	80.0
65	Hertfordshire	75.1	75.4	4.0	121	87.8	79.9
66	Nottingham	80.1	77.6	31.4	106	65.8	79.6
=67	Central Lancashire	83.7	79.6	8.3	138	59.6	79.4

=67 Westminster	81.4	81.1	21.2	113	65.1	79.4
69 Leeds Beckett	79.3	80.0	3.5	117	79.3	79.3
70 Chester	79.7	75.9	12.0	119	70.2	78.7
71 Middlesex	76.2	76.2	10.0	126	70.7	78.4
72 Edge Hill	89.2	91.0	2.0	n/a	50.0*	78.1
73 St Mary's, Twickenham	64.5	63.0	n/a	139	87.4	77.2
=74 Abertay	61.0	64.2	n/a	149*	82.6	76.6
=74 East London	83.3	84.6	7.6	113	55.4	76.6
76 Cumbria	57.1	59.3	0.7	141	91.3	76.2
77 Plymouth Marjon	82.6	79.6	n/a	138	38.9	74.3
78 Newman	75.0	74.0	n/a	117	61.5	74.0
79 Staffordshire	78.2	76.7	n/a	86	67.7	73.3
80 Wales Trinity St David	86.8	76.8	n/a	117	39.1	72.9

Employed in professional job	63%	Employed in non-professional job and Studying	2%
Employed in professional job and studying	3%	Employed in non-professional job	11%
Studying	15%	Unemployed	7%
Average starting professional salary	£21,909	Average starting non-professional salary	£16,000

Pharmacology and Pharmacy

Applications for pharmacy, pharmacology and toxicology degrees were down for the sixth year in a row in 2017, having dropped 25 per cent in that time. However, as in other health subjects, changes in the offer rate have ensured that the numbers starting courses have not fluctuated to the same extent. Enrolments in 2017 were within ten of the previous year, but there were fewer than 5,4 applications per place, compared with seven in 2011. Entry standards have fallen accordingly.

Pharmacology and pharmacy are quite different courses, leading to different careers. Departments in England are evenly split between those specialising in the two disciplines, with only four covering both. While the MPharm degree, which is the only direct route to professional registration as a pharmacist, takes four years, pharmacology is available either as a three-year BSc or as an extended course. The MPharm is now offered at 30 institutions, while another 18 are running a BSc in the subject or as part of a broader degree. Most degrees in either area require chemistry and another science or maths at A-level or the equivalent.

Cambridge remains top of the table, the university's normal high entry standards making the difference. Queen's, Belfast, which produced the best results in the Research Excellence Framework, was the nearest challenger last year, but has dropped to fifth in the latest table. Bristol has moved up to second. Although only just in the top 30 overall, Westminster has the highest student satisfaction ratings, topping both of the measures derived from the National Student Survey.

The employment table does not suggest subjects that should be struggling to attract applicants – pharmacology and pharmacy remain seventh out of 67 subject groups, with 82 per cent of graduates going straight into professional jobs and only 3 per cent unemployed. At three universities – Ulster, Robert Gordon and Reading – the rate was 100 per cent. The earnings table is a different matter, however: partly because of the training structure for pharmacists, the subjects are seldom in the top 40. In the latest edition, they remain in the bottom 10.

Pharmacology and Pharmacy

	Teaching quality %	Student experience %	Research quality %	Entry standards (UCAS points)	Graduate prospects %	Overall score
1 Cambridge	n/a	n/a	52.5	244	84.8	100.0
2 Bristol	96.6	94.8	47.0	171	87.5	98.3
3 Strathclyde	77.8	76.7	52.2	226	95.6	98.0
4 Nottingham	83.7	84.9	51.2	180	98.9	97.5
5 Queen's, Belfast	84.3	86.6	60.0	161	98.5	97.4
6 Ulster	91.1	91.3	42.5	151	100.0	96.9
7 Bath	82.0	80.0	56.2	165	96.7	95.6
8 Glasgow	80.1	82.4	33.4	208	90.0	94.5
=9 East Anglia	86.4	85.6	38.1	147	99.1	94.2
=9 Manchester	78.2	76.1	57.1	169	94.3	94.2
11 Birmingham	90.6	89.4	19.2	159	n/a	94.0
12 Leeds	83.9	87.4	40.9	173	87.5	93.9
13 Cardiff	80.6	84.9	36.8	166	97.9	93.8
14 Aston	86.6	85.1	39.1	140	98.4	93.6
15 University College London	71.6	75.2	51.3	186	95.7	93.4
16 Robert Gordon	84.5	83.6	4.9	196	100.0	93.1
17 Keele	87.6	88.0	20.9	148	97.9	92.4
18 Liverpool	89.2	89.3	31.7	159	83.0	92.3
=19 Kent	n/a	n/a	42.3	130	99.3	92.1
=19 King's College London	75.9	79.9	46.8	161	93.1	92.1
21 Reading	83.4	81.4	34.2	139	100.0	92.0
22 Dundee	77.0	82.6	55.4	n/a	90.0	91.9
23 Newcastle	81.4	77.3	47.8	171	80.0	91.3
24 Aberdeen	86.3	84.1	34.7	172	75.4	90.8
25 Huddersfield	87.8	87.2	13.2	129	98.1	90.0
26 Hertfordshire	87.9	87.9	10.9	120	95.1	88.6
27 Liverpool John Moores	82.7	82.8	6.0	139	97.2	88.0
28 Westminster	97.5	95.3	21.2	114	69.0	87.6
29 De Montfort	77.2	79.6	13.0	126	98.0	86.4
30 Hull	83.8	78.6	16.7	n/a	81.1	86.1
=31 Coventry	83.4	88.5	4.5	136	84.2	86.0
=31 Portsmouth	73.6	75.8	24.3	129	94.2	86.0
33 Central Lancashire	68.0	70.6	8.3	154	99.4	84.9
34 Brighton	74.8	75.9	4.8	125	98.1	84.3
35 Glasgow Caledonian	79.3	86.1	8.1	169	66.7	84.2
36 Leicester	78.0	84.0	n/a	157*	77.8	83.9
=37 Kingston	81.2	82.6	2.6	118	85.0	83.3
=37 Sunderland	71.9	74.7	7.5	121	96.8	83.3
39 Greenwich	73.9	77.3	2.7	129	92.3	83.2
40 Bradford	67.3	69.1	9.5	138	95.8	82.9
41 Queen Margaret, Edinburgh	78.8	75.0	1.5	127	74.1	80.2
42 Anglia Ruskin	82.8	80.3	3.1	74	n/a	78.3

43 Lincoln	66.0	60.8	22.6	136	n/a	78.2
44 London Metropolitan	77.5	79.4	5.2	92	61.4	76.0
45 East London	83.9	84.3	7.6	103	39.9	75.1

Employed in professional job	74%	Employed in non-professional job and Studying	1%
Employed in professional job and studying	8%	Employed in non-professional job	4%
Studying	11%	Unemployed	3%
Average starting professional salary	£18,500	Average starting non-professional salary	£16,800

Philosophy

Oxford is back on top of the philosophy table for the first time in three years, taking over from St Andrews by dint of the highest entry standards and the best grades in the Research Excellence Framework. There has been more movement further down the table, notably by Essex, which has shot up 14 places and into the top ten. But the highest levels of student satisfaction, especially where teaching quality is concerned, are all in the bottom third of the table. Bangor, in 38th place, topped both of the measures derived from the National Student Survey, the teaching and support satisfying over 98 per cent of final-year undergraduates.

Philosophy continues to grow in popularity; both applications and enrolments are now higher than in the years before £9,000 fees were introduced. There was another 5 per cent increase in applications in 2017, even though the subject sits in the bottom half of the table for both graduate salaries and employment. The median salary of £21,000 is £3,000 lower than in the last edition of the *Guide*, when philosophy was in the top 20. The best graduate prospects in 2016 were at Sussex and the London School of Economics, where more than 86 per cent of graduates went straight into professional jobs or continued studying. However, the proportion was below 50 per cent at seven of the 54 universities in the table.

Relatively few philosophy undergraduates studied the subject at A-level – some departments actively discourage it. Degrees can require more mathematical skills than many candidates expect, especially when there is an emphasis on logic in the syllabus. There is wide variation in entry standards, with four of the top 10 universities averaging more than 200 points in 2016, but two dropping below 100 and another seven averaging less than 110 points.

Philosophy	Teaching quality %	Student experience %	Research quality %	Entry standards (UCAS points)	Graduate prospects %	Overall score
1 Oxford	n/a	n/a	61.3	221	83.2	100.0
2 St Andrews	86.0	89.1	52.7	205	75.9	98.9
3 Cambridge	n/a	n/a	51.6	210	81.5	98.6
4 Birmingham	83.2	77.5	52.8	157	83.9	94.9
5 Lancaster	83.7	83.9	53.0	156	79.1	94.7
6 Durham	79.8	75.1	30.1	205	81.7	93.2
7 Warwick	79.1	76.8	47.7	187	72.9	93.0
8 London School of Economics	69.3	63.8	48.6	197	86.1	92.9
9 University College London	n/a	n/a	55.6	188	84.4	92.8
10 Essex	84.2	80.2	44.0	140	78.3	91.5
11 Sussex	81.7	77.8	34.2	149	86.3	91.3
=12 Bristol	n/a	n/a	40.9	185	70.4	91.1
=12 Exeter	75.4	71.9	41.0	182	77.9	91.1

Philosophy cont

	Teaching quality %	Student experience %	Research quality %	Entry standards (UCAS points)	Graduate prospects %	Overall score
=12 King's College London	n/a	n/a	53.9	177	65.1	91.1
=12 York	85.4	82.7	30.7	158	77.8	91.1
16 Newcastle	81.9	81.9	54.3	148	64.0	90.5
17 Sheffield	n/a	n/a	48.3	158	71.8	90.3
18 Manchester	n/a	n/a	31.9	161	70.7	89.6
=19 Kent	84.5	81.1	31.0	129	79.8	89.0
=19 Leeds	81.8	77.8	39.5	159	67.1	89.0
21 Edinburgh	68.3	67.3	49.7	179	67.7	87.9
=22 Birkbeck	82.8	76.5	37.4	103	79.0	86.9
=22 Nottingham	81.3	77.4	28.2	152	69.7	86.9
24 Southampton	81.3	77.8	31.7	135	71.2	86.6
25 Aberdeen	84.8	82.4	39.1	151	52.2	86.5
26 Hertfordshire	88.3	82.9	32.9	104	67.6	86.0
27 East Anglia	81.6	76.4	28.6	156	60.7	85.4
28 Cardiff	82.9	77.1	36.3	140	56.0	84.9
29 Keele	87.2	80.1	23.7	127	62.9	84.6
30 Liverpool	n/a	n/a	28.4	141	64.3	84.0
31 Royal Holloway	75.2	75.1	30.5	138	66.0	83.8
32 Reading	83.5	79.9	28.6	132	54.9	83.3
33 Glasgow	76.5	72.0	18.9	172	60.3	83.2
34 West of England	94.2	94.6	18.6	113	46.3	82.5
35 St Mary's, Twickenham	93.4	87.7	7.0	103	61.7	82.0
=36 Bath Spa	96.7	93.9	n/a	109	57.2	81.9
=36 Liverpool Hope	92.8	90.7	n/a	111	62.9	81.9
38 Bangor	98.5	96.5	n/a	109	52.9	81.7
39 Dundee	82.3	76.0	27.7	141	48.0	81.6
40 Queen's, Belfast	71.2	66.5	40.3	147	45.8	80.0
41 Stirling	76.9	73.7	22.7	147	47.1	79.5
42 Hull	83.5	78.0	10.5	111	59.6	79.3
43 Manchester Metropolitan	82.7	79.6	12.5	118	54.1	79.0
44 Nottingham Trent	87.3	80.2	10.0	118	50.0	78.9
45 Central Lancashire	92.1	85.7	8.3	103*	43.2	77.9
46 Gloucestershire	81.5	83.2	6.9	110	52.9	77.3
47 Brighton	n/a	n/a	13.1	106	55.9	77.0
48 Anglia Ruskin	90.0	80.8	n/a	90	48.9	75.6
49 Oxford Brookes	75.8	68.5	8.4	126	48.2	74.8
50 Winchester	70.5	60.1	n/a	112	66.7	73.9
51 Roehampton	69.6	67.8	n/a	99	66.2	73.5

Employed in professional job	33%	Employed in non-professional job and Studying	4%
Employed in professional job and studying	3%	Employed in non-professional job	21%
Studying	27%	Unemployed	13%
Average starting professional salary	£21,000	Average starting non-professional salary	£15,600

Physics and Astronomy

Physics degrees have among the highest entry grades in the university system, with 10 of the 47 institutions in our latest table averaging at least 200 points and another 10 at least 170. No university drops below 110 points, the equivalent of BBC at A-level. Cambridge, the perennial leader of the table, averages 244 points, with Oxford and Imperial not far behind. Overall, there are almost six applications to the place. Most universities demand physics and maths at A-level for both physics and astronomy, as well as good grades overall.

The long decline in the numbers taking physics in the sixth-form and at university was being reversed before higher fees arrived. Eight successive increases in the numbers starting physics degrees came to a halt in 2016, but growth had resumed 12 months later, as had the volume of applications. The much smaller numbers taking astronomy or astrophysics also grew, with over 30 universities offering the subjects.

The "Brian Cox effect" has been credited with the current boom in popularity of physics and astronomy, in recognition of the engaging Manchester University professor's many television appearances.

The top four are unchanged in the latest table. Cambridge is in the top four universities in the world for physics, according to QS, and also produced the best grades in the Research Excellence Framework. St Andrews' strength in the National Student Survey keeps it in second place, although the highest scores in the sections on teaching quality were at Nottingham Trent, which is in the bottom ten overall. Swansea, which also scored well on this measure and Heriot Watt have both jumped 16 places into the top 20.

More than 40 per cent of those completing degrees in physics or astronomy stay on for a postgraduate course, helping the subjects to a place in the top 20 for graduate prospects. They are higher still in the earnings table, sharing 12th place with five other subject groupings However, no university saw 90 per cent of graduates go straight into professional jobs or continue studying in 2016. Sixth-placed Birmingham came closest, with 89 per cent, but the proportion dropped below 50 per cent at two universities.

Physics and Astronomy	Teaching quality %	Student experience %	Research quality %	Entry standards (UCAS points)	Graduate prospects %	Overall score
1 Cambridge	n/a	n/a	55.7	244	84.8	100.0
2 St Andrews	89.8	89.0	51.0	225	81.3	98.8
3 Oxford	n/a	n/a	52.1	237	88.4	97.6
4 Durham	83.0	80.3	46.2	221	88.4	96.7
5 Nottingham	89.8	90.5	48.3	185	79.2	95.7
=6 Birmingham	84.3	83.9	33.8	212	89.0	94.8
=6 Warwick	84.5	83.2	46.1	199	82.6	94.8
8 Lancaster	90.4	88.7	37.6	176	84.7	94.3
9 Manchester	n/a	n/a	44.9	210	83.8	93.6
10 Bath	84.9	80.7	40.0	200	81.2	93.2
11 Strathclyde	88.4	88.3	45.3	188	70.1	92.7
12 Exeter	85.5	86.9	42.4	178	78.4	92.6
=13 Bristol	n/a	n/a	43.7	181	83.2	92.2

Physics and Astronomy cont

	Teaching quality %	Student experience %	Research quality %	Entry standards (UCAS points)	Graduate prospects %	Overall score
=13 Edinburgh	78.0	73.1	48.7	214	76.5	92.2
15 Imperial College	64.8	66.3	49.6	236	86.5	91.9
=16 Leeds	84.4	83.7	41.8	169	80.4	91.8
=16 Southampton	85.7	86.7	44.1	159	77.9	91.8
18 Glasgow	77.8	76.8	42.0	199	79.8	91.2
19 York	79.7	79.1	35.8	169	86.9	90.5
=20 Heriot-Watt	82.4	82.4	44.1	167	75.0	90.3
=20 Swansea	89.6	92.3	33.0	134	80.5	90.3
22 Leicester	89.0	87.7	40.8	142	73.9	90.2
23 Surrey	81.8	82.4	39.6	170	77.5	90.1
24 University College London	66.7	65.0	45.1	201	88.1	89.8
=25 King's College London	n/a	n/a	35.8	179	80.8	89.1
=25 Queen's, Belfast	78.0	81.0	44.4	163	75.6	89.1
27 Liverpool	n/a	n/a	31.5	162	80.2	89.0
28 Royal Holloway	84.7	82.9	31.5	145	80.7	88.6
29 Sheffield	82.0	83.8	36.8	169	72.0	88.5
30 Loughborough	86.2	85.4	19.0	142	84.9	87.7
31 Sussex	81.6	80.4	24.7	143	86.9	87.6
32 Northumbria	84.4	86.2	30.7	143	n/a	87.5
33 Dundee	82.6	86.7	34.1	166	68.0	87.4
34 Cardiff	79.4	86.1	34.9	147	71.8	86.5
35 Queen Mary, London	82.0	81.7	27.6	144	76.4	86.1
36 Aberdeen	78.6	79.2	32.0	174	68.8	85.9
37 Portsmouth	88.4	80.9	21.8	123	75.0	85.0
38 Nottingham Trent	92.1	90.6	20.1	123	66.8	84.8
39 Hertfordshire	86.4	84.9	20.2	126	74.6	84.7
40 Keele	87.1	89.7	31.8	124	59.0	84.0
41 Hull	79.5	76.0	24.2	130	74.4	83.0
42 Kent	68.4	67.9	30.7	132	76.5	81.3
43 Central Lancashire	78.5	72.2	19.8	134	71.4	81.2
=44 Aberystwyth	76.9	77.3	12.4	114	78.5	80.4
=44 West of Scotland	90.6	85.5	19.1	142	46.7	80.4
46 Salford	88.2	88.5	4.4	114	65.2	79.9
47 South Wales	82.7	81.8	n/a	128*	46.2	73.7

Employed in professional job	37%	Employed in non-professional job and Studying	1%
Employed in professional job and studying	4%	Employed in non-professional job	11%
Studying	36%	Unemployed	12%
Average starting professional salary	£25,000	Average starting non-professional salary	£15,974

Physiotherapy

Robert Gordon has shot to the top of the physiotherapy table, moving up five places with the top entry grades, high levels of student satisfaction and as one of eight universities where all the 2016 graduates found professional jobs or continued studying. Southampton, last year's leader and the holder of the best results in the Research Excellence Framework, has dropped to fourth, mainly because of a fall in student satisfaction. Physiotherapy students are among the most satisfied in any subject; only eight of the 34 universities in the table fell below 80 per cent approval on the two measures drawn from the National Student Survey. Third-placed Bradford scored 99 per cent for teaching quality and 97 per cent on the broader student experience.

More than nine out of ten physiotherapy graduates go straight into professional jobs – enough to take the subject into the top four in the employment table this year and close to the top 20 for graduate salaries. Applications are well above the level before £9,000 fees arrived and the numbers starting courses rose again in 2017. As a result, over 50 universities and colleges are offering undergraduate courses in physiotherapy, or a related subject such as osteopathy or chiropractic, starting in 2018. Most of the leading courses demand biology A-level or equivalent, but some may also want another science or maths. The Chartered Society of Physiotherapy accredits all degrees in the subject in the UK.

The ranking is in its fifth year, the subject having appeared previously as part of the table for "other subjects allied to medicine". Entry standards have been rising and vary less than in most subjects. Although only Robert Gordon averages more than 200 points, aided by the conversion rate for Scottish qualifications in the new UCAS tariff, only East London, at the bottom of the table, averages (just) less than 130 points. Two-thirds of the universities in the table are post-1992 institutions, but only four feature in the top ten.

Physiotherapy	Teaching quality %	Student experience %	Research quality %	Entry standards (UCAS points)	Graduate prospects %	Overall score
1 Robert Gordon	94.7	94.8	4.9	206	100.0	100.0
2 Birmingham	93.9	91.8	63.7	159	96.6	98.6
3 Bradford	99.1	97.3	9.5	172	100.0	98.2
4 Southampton	79.1	75.8	65.7	175*	96.7	97.7
5 Nottingham	84.6	80.2	40.6	174	98.5	97.5
6 Liverpool	91.3	92.2	35.3	154	98.4	96.8
7 Cardiff	88.4	91.4	36.8	169	95.9	96.5
8 Plymouth	86.0	85.4	9.5	173	100.0	96.3
9 Coventry	92.6	94.1	4.5	159	99.3	95.5
10 Worcester	96.1	95.5	2.6	148	100.0	95.2
11 Keele	87.3	89.3	20.9	148	98.8	94.8
12 Leeds Beckett	93.5	95.7	3.5	143	100.0	94.7
13 Brunel	94.0	92.4	18.2	148	97.1	94.6
14 Huddersfield	93.5	92.2	13.2	144	98.5	94.5
15 Northumbria	91.0	89.7	14.0	161	96.1	94.2
16 West of England	88.2	87.4	8.2	154	98.0	93.9
=17 Brighton	94.9	91.5	4.8	140	98.7	93.8

Physiotherapy cont	Teaching quality %	Student experience %	Research quality %	Entry standards (UCAS points)	Graduate prospects %	Overall score
=17 Glasgow Caledonian	83.7	87.6	8.1	180	94.8	93.8
=19 King's College London	76.7	80.4	34.6	170	94.4	93.7
=19 Queen Margaret, Edinburgh	85.5	79.5	1.5	175*	96.8	93.7
21 Salford	91.1	90.1	3.8	134	100.0	93.4
22 Teesside	93.2	92.3	2.4	139	98.2	93.1
=23 Oxford Brookes	72.8	74.0	3.0	163	100.0	92.9
=23 Sheffield Hallam	89.3	79.9	3.7	151	97.9	92.9
=25 Central Lancashire	86.3	88.6	8.3	163	94.0	92.3
=25 East Anglia	70.5	77.9	24.9	167	95.2	92.3
27 Bournemouth	90.9	90.8	4.7	132	97.6	92.0
28 Manchester Metropolitan	83.9	84.5	12.0	163	93.4	91.9
29 Kingston/St George's, London	73.6	68.4	2.6	153	98.5	91.0
30 Ulster	75.3	78.7	27.7	148	93.8	90.8
31 Cumbria	65.3	73.5	0.7	146	100.0	90.6
32 York St John	72.2	69.5	1.9	155	96.6	90.1
33 Hertfordshire	81.8	80.4	4.0	144	94.2	89.6
34 East London	87.5	87.6	7.6	129	90.0	87.4

Employed in professional job	93%	Employed in non-professional job and Studying	0%
Employed in professional job and studying	1%	Employed in non-professional job	1%
Studying	2%	Unemployed	2%
Average starting professional salary	£21,999	Average starting non-professional salary	–

Politics

Applications to study politics have doubled in 10 years and the numbers starting degrees have risen by almost 1,000 – or 14 per cent – since 2015. It is a trend that has continued for most of the decade, with both applications and enrolments growing by around 5 per cent in 2017. The introduction of £9,000 fees barely had an impact and, even after considerable expansion of provision, there are still almost six applications to every place.

Oxford has been ousted from its accustomed top place by St Andrews in a photo finish. The scores could hardly be closer and Oxford may have suffered for the boycott of the National Student Survey, which meant that it and nine other Russell Group universities had to have student satisfaction scores generated from their performance on other measures. Oxford, which is rated by QS in the top two in the world for politics, had led our table in all but its inaugural year, in 2003. It still has the highest entry grades, but Essex, in fifth place, was well ahead of the field in the Research Excellence Framework, with 87 per cent of its work considered world-leading or internationally excellent.

For the second year in a row, final-year undergraduates at Huddersfield, just inside the top 30, were the most satisfied with the teaching, feedback and academic support they had received, while the University of the West of England again did best in other sections of the

National Student Survey (NSS), joined this time by Greenwich on 90 per cent approval. Politics students are generally satisfied with their courses: only two universities – the London School of Economics and Edinburgh – dropped below 70 per cent on the teaching quality measure.

Employment scores are less impressive, however. Politics is only just in the top 40 of the employment table, with three politics graduates in ten going on to take postgraduate courses, but close to a quarter starting their careers in low-level employment. Eight of the bottom 12 universities were under the 50 per cent mark for graduate prospects, with University College London, in fourth place, again boasting the best score in 2016. Politics does much better in the comparison of early-career salaries in professional jobs, however. The subject is one of 10 sharing 20th place.

Politics	Teaching quality %	Student experience %	Research quality %	Entry standards (UCAS points)	Graduate prospects %	Overall score
1 St Andrews	90.4	86.3	38.4	·207	83.2	100.0
2 Oxford	n/a	n/a	61.1	226	85.6	99.8
3 Warwick	83.5	83.0	52.7	186	80.7	98.0
4 University College London	n/a	n/a	57.0	195	91.2	97.9
5 Essex	78.4	81.7	69.6	129	85.7	96.4
6 Cambridge	n/a	n/a	38.2	210	82.4	96.3
7 Sheffield	n/a	n/a	48.3	159	81.2	94.5
8 Lancaster	79.6	79.1	53.0	153	79.4	94.3
9 York	84.5	81.2	36.9	156	83.6	94.2
10 London School of Economics	64.6	62.3	54.6	199	90.7	93.4
11 Exeter	80.0	79.3	29.8	179	84.2	93.3
=12 Bristol	n/a	n/a	30.4	184	71.0	92.9
=12 Sussex	84.8	85.5	33.6	142	80.8	92.9
14 Loughborough	88.6	89.1	22.5	138	81.7	92.6
15 Bath	77.2	76.8	27.4	174	88.4	92.3
16 Durham	73.2	64.2	27.0	199	85.4	90.7
17 Aberystwyth	87.2	81.7	40.2	111	72.3	90.6
18 Reading	83.3	75.7	37.0	142	71.9	90.2
19 Leeds	79.5	78.5	25.1	158	79.3	90.1
=20 Birmingham	75.8	72.3	31.1	153	83.9	89.8
=20 Manchester	n/a	n/a	28.4	162	78.1	89.8
=22 Edinburgh	69.9	69.8	44.5	188	69.4	89.6
=22 Strathclyde	74.8	76.9	41.6	198	56.3	89.6
=24 Glasgow	74.4	74.5	30.5	190	70.1	89.5
=24 Kent	81.7	80.1	27.8	135	77.9	89.5
=24 King's College London	n/a	n/a	29.0	183	76.0	89.5
=24 Surrey	87.6	83.5	12.5	174	65.6	89.5
=28 Aston	83.4	81.3	38.6	122	69.2	89.4
=28 Huddersfield	97.2	88.5	9.5	119	70.1	89.4
30 East Anglia	79.7	76.7	35.5	156	67.7	89.3
31 Nottingham	75.1	70.2	30.8	157	81.4	89.1

Politics cont

	Teaching quality %	Student experience %	Research quality %	Entry standards (UCAS points)	Graduate prospects %	Overall score
=32 Newcastle	80.7	76.8	22.0	158	75.2	89.0
=32 SOAS London	n/a	n/a	30.5	157	69.8	89.0
34 Dundee	86.0	88.0	10.8	176	62.1	88.9
=35 Birkbeck	85.5	75.5	31.3	91	83.1	88.6
=35 Stirling	83.7	81.0	33.8	158	55.8	88.6
37 Royal Holloway	80.6	78.4	30.5	142	69.9	88.5
=38 Portsmouth	83.5	79.7	32.2	107	74.0	88.1
=38 West of England	90.7	90.0	13.8	123	65.9	88.1
40 Keele	83.3	81.9	24.0	126	71.3	87.8
=41 Queen Mary, London	75.4	71.7	28.1	145	79.1	87.7
=41 Southampton	75.9	74.9	37.0	132	73.1	87.7
43 Swansea	85.2	86.3	18.5	113	73.5	87.6
44 Coventry	89.0	86.9	5.6	117	76.4	87.4
45 Queen's, Belfast	80.0	74.8	35.0	147	59.2	87.0
46 Greenwich	92.2	90.0	8.6	122	61.7	86.8
=47 Bradford	79.7	81.5	12.7	131	77.3	86.4
=47 Cardiff	76.5	72.3	30.4	146	67.3	86.4
49 Aberdeen	74.6	72.9	18.4	176	68.2	86.2
=50 Brunel	76.8	74.2	32.4	119	71.8	86.0
=50 De Montfort	85.2	87.7	10.7	99	75.5	86.0
52 Oxford Brookes	82.4	78.2	17.8	122	66.5	85.0
=53 Leicester	78.1	73.6	20.0	134	68.6	84.8
=53 Lincoln	86.0	84.1	7.7	120	64.9	84.8
55 Plymouth	84.9	78.6	25.8	103	60.1	84.6
56 Manchester Metropolitan	84.7	78.5	18.0	126	57.1	84.3
57 Chichester	87.0	84.7	15.8	84	n/a	84.1
58 Bournemouth	82.7	79.1	15.1	108	n/a	83.6
=59 Liverpool	n/a	n/a	12.0	146	55.3	83.4
=59 Salford	90.8	77.9	4.8	113	60.0	83.4
=61 Sheffield Hallam	81.7	79.3	14.4	109	61.4	82.7
=61 Westminster	83.4	82.7	14.3	111	55.8	82.7
63 Northumbria	79.9	73.0	12.7	138	59.0	82.6
64 Nottingham Trent	84.2	79.2	n/a	118	65.6	82.4
65 Hull	71.7	67.2	10.8	135	75.3	82.1
66 Liverpool Hope	82.3	84.6	7.0	108	57.1	81.5
=67 City	75.3	73.4	24.6	111	57.0	81.1
=67 Middlesex	78.1	81.4	14.9	89	63.6*	81.1
=69 Central Lancashire	81.6	78.9	12.0	115*	51.0	80.7
=69 East London	83.3	81.5	13.7	n/a	45.5	80.7
71 Ulster	88.1	78.5	20.9	107	36.6	80.6
72 Goldsmiths, London	n/a	n/a	16.8	111	63.8	79.9
73 London Metropolitan	84.7	80.2	1.2	84	61.3	79.8

74 Leeds Beckett	80.8	80.5	n/a	93	61.4	79.3
75 Derby	76.5	65.2	13.5	109*	n/a	78.4
76 Winchester	83.5	80.1	n/a	114	44.6	78.3
77 Canterbury Christ Church	84.0	78.4	3.2	94	46.5	77.7
78 Kingston	75.9	70.7	n/a	101	49.3	75.1
79 Chester	74.5	69.2	n/a	108	48.8	74.9
80 Northampton	79.1	78.4	n/a	80	43.6	74.5
81 Brighton	71.0	66.4	13.1	98	45.5	74.4

Employed in professional job	40%	Employed in non-professional job and Studying	3%
Employed in professional job and studying	3%	Employed in non-professional job	19%
Studying	24%	Unemployed	11%
Average starting professional salary	£22,000	Average starting non-professional salary	£16,500

Psychology

Psychology was one of only three subjects to attract more than 100,000 applications in 2017. In spite of the first decline in the demand for places for four years, there were still some 115,000 applications. The numbers starting degrees continued to rise, and were 50 per cent higher than in 2008. It is the biggest table in the *Guide*, with yet another university joining this year, bringing the total to 114.

Psychology's popularity endures in spite of poor performances in the graduate employment market: it is only just outside the bottom ten for the proportion of graduates with "positive destinations", and is only three places higher for average starting salaries in professional-level jobs. Although unemployment is no higher than the average for all subjects, more than a third of graduates begin their careers in low level jobs.

Most undergraduate programmes are accredited by the British Psychological Society, which ensures that key topics are covered, but the clinical and biological content of courses still varies considerably. Some universities require maths and/or biology A-levels among three high-grade passes, but others are much less demanding. The contrast is obvious in the ranking, with 36 universities averaging more than 150 points at entry but three falling below 100 points and several others coming close to that mark. Oxford has the highest entry grades in the table and remains top. Bath has the best graduate prospects and has moved up to second place as one of only five universities where more than 80 per cent of 2016 graduates found professional employment or continued studying.

Fourth-placed Loughborough achieved the highest scores in the Research Excellence Framework. Aberystwyth, still only just in the top 40 after a 17-place rise, has the highest satisfaction ratings in both of our indicators derived from the National Student Survey and is the only university scoring 90 per cent in each case. Nevertheless, satisfaction levels are high at most universities in the table, as they have been in previous years.

Psychology

	Teaching quality %	Student experience %	Research quality %	Entry standards (UCAS points)	Graduate prospects %	Overall score
1 Oxford	87.4	86.8	58.6	222	72.8	100.0
2 Bath	83.1	84.4	56.2	196	84.9	98.9
3 St Andrews	86.8	88.6	45.4	207	75.6	98.0
4 Loughborough	86.4	87.3	62.3	156	74.7	95.9
5 Durham	84.9	85.2	37.1	193	74.8	94.9
6 University College London	75.1	75.1	57.0	192	78.2	94.3
7 Birmingham	75.4	81.2	55.8	167	82.7	94.1
8 Cambridge	72.4	67.5	57.5	208	79.1	94.0
9 York	84.0	86.3	46.7	168	69.8	93.3
10 Kent	78.1	85.4	38.8	157	83.2	92.7
=11 Exeter	75.8	79.2	43.3	179	77.7	92.3
=11 Newcastle	79.0	85.7	50.0	162	71.8	92.3
13 Glasgow	71.0	81.0	52.9	191	72.2	92.2
=14 Bristol	n/a	n/a	49.4	183	69.7	92.1
=14 Cardiff	83.2	84.5	55.7	166	62.2	92.1
16 Sussex	78.1	83.2	42.3	146	82.3	91.9
=17 Lancaster	79.9	83.1	38.5	154	74.9	90.9
=17 Warwick	79.7	84.6	43.1	166	67.2	90.9
19 Nottingham	78.5	84.9	36.4	168	70.7	90.7
20 Leeds	79.1	82.2	33.0	167	71.6	90.2
21 Royal Holloway	79.5	84.5	37.8	163	66.1	89.8
22 Aberdeen	78.5	79.4	38.7	168	67.1	89.5
23 Bangor	84.4	85.6	32.0	133	71.4	89.3
24 Swansea	74.1	75.4	44.7	134	81.4	89.1
25 Strathclyde	80.6	80.4	23.5	199	58.6	88.9
26 Aston	80.8	81.1	39.1	135	71.2	88.8
=27 Southampton	76.0	77.0	47.8	154	67.3	88.7
=27 Surrey	78.2	80.9	22.0	168	72.2	88.7
29 East Anglia	83.9	84.3	33.2	153	60.8	88.5
30 Stirling	78.1	77.5	40.1	158	63.8	88.0
=31 Essex	77.9	82.0	41.0	126	71.9	87.9
=31 Nottingham Trent	86.0	84.6	19.3	139	68.4	87.9
33 Edinburgh	66.2	72.7	52.8	204	56.4	87.7
=34 Leicester	82.1	84.2	29.6	146	62.6	87.5
=34 Manchester	n/a	n/a	44.9	163	62.8	87.5
36 Portsmouth	84.4	82.5	21.0	129	71.0	87.4
=37 Dundee	84.7	86.5	22.7	150	58.3	87.0
=37 Queen's, Belfast	80.7	80.5	40.2	147	58.0	87.0
39 Aberystwyth	91.9	90.3	n/a	116	69.2	86.4
=40 Northumbria	84.0	86.3	18.7	142	60.9	86.3
=40 Sheffield	n/a	n/a	38.8	156	71.1	86.3
42 Lincoln	84.9	87.8	7.9	133	66.7	86.0

=43	De Montfort	87.7	88.9	11.2	111	67.9	85.9
=43	Reading	75.8	76.1	42.3	153	57.9	85.9
45	Coventry	81.2	82.3	7.8	130	72.3	85.3
46	Liverpool Hope	79.3	81.6	5.5	117	79.0	84.9
47	Manchester Metropolitan	83.1	83.8	12.0	130	63.2	84.6
48	Birkbeck	71.0	74.0	59.9	113	60.5	84.1
=49	Bolton	87.9	83.4	3.6	121	62.3	83.9
=49	Edge Hill	85.5	82.5	18.8	127	54.9	83.9
51	Keele	79.5	82.5	17.7	130	61.4	83.8
52	West of England	86.2	84.3	8.2	132	55.0	83.4
53	Brunel	79.1	80.6	26.6	128	55.6	83.2
=54	Glasgow Caledonian	79.9	79.7	8.1	181	45.9	83.0
=54	Huddersfield	79.9	78.7	9.5	129	64.2	83.0
=56	City	77.5	79.1	23.5	129	58.4	82.9
=56	West London	85.9	83.0	7.6	108	62.2	82.9
=58	Abertay	73.0	73.4	15.1	172	56.4	82.8
=58	Liverpool	n/a	n/a	34.6	147	58.3	82.8
=58	Plymouth	77.6	80.2	33.8	126	52.1	82.8
61	Oxford Brookes	79.4	80.4	18.1	132	56.4	82.7
=62	Central Lancashire	78.5	77.6	12.2	128	63.4	82.6
=62	Liverpool John Moores	82.2	80.6	7.8	131	58.4	82.6
64	Staffordshire	84.1	83.6	8.2	113	59.6	82.4
65	Goldsmiths, London	76.6	73.7	40.4	131	48.5	82.1
66	Leeds Trinity	88.9	85.6	n/a	106	57.5	82.0
67	Roehampton	75.0	77.3	26.4	106	63.2	81.8
=68	Hull	72.0	67.2	26.8	125	65.6	81.6
=68	Teesside	75.2	71.1	15.0	107	72.2	81.6
70	Derby	87.4	84.1	8.4	104	53.5	81.4
71	Heriot-Watt	66.9	70.0	26.9	161	55.7	81.2
72	Wrexham Glyndŵr	84.9	80.3	3.6	136	48.9	81.1
=73	Bedfordshire	78.2	76.9	25.1	91	62.1	81.0
=73	Chester	85.6	80.9	7.9	116	51.6	81.0
75	West of Scotland	82.4	73.8	9.4	160	43.1	80.9
76	Gloucestershire	78.3	79.6	n/a	119	63.8	80.8
77	Sheffield Hallam	83.1	82.5	3.7	120	53.5	80.7
78	Queen Mary, London	n/a	n/a	26.1	154	62.7	80.6
=79	Bournemouth	81.2	79.2	13.0	119	51.1	80.4
=79	Buckingham	79.4	80.5	n/a	108	63.7	80.4
=81	Cumbria	88.0	87.2	n/a	94	52.4	80.1
=81	East London	80.2	77.2	8.3	108	58.4	80.1
83	Birmingham City	81.9	82.4	n/a	117	53.3	79.8
84	Sunderland	77.3	76.6	7.5	112	59.4	79.7
85	Edinburgh Napier	69.5	72.4	5.3	159	55.8	79.6
86	Hertfordshire	76.8	76.6	6.0	111	60.5	79.5
87	Worcester	78.5	78.2	7.1	114	54.3	79.3
=88	London South Bank	72.0	70.8	8.6	108	67.6	79.2

Psychology

		Teaching quality %	Student experience %	Research quality %	Entry standards (UCAS points)	Graduate prospects %	Overall score
=88	Ulster	76.8	79.0	23.2	125	42.5	79.2
=88	York St John	78.9	81.0	11.0	116	49.1	79.2
91	Suffolk	80.5	81.2	n/a	110	55.1	79.1
92	Salford	79.6	76.8	3.8	120	52.8	79.0
=93	Bath Spa	77.9	76.5	n/a	115	58.1	78.9
=93	Canterbury Christ Church	79.8	76.7	2.2	112	55.3	78.9
=95	Middlesex	75.0	70.8	7.6	113	60.9	78.8
=95	St Mary's, Twickenham	80.4	81.6	n/a	117	50.8	78.8
=97	Brighton	77.2	76.3	12.4	122	48.3	78.7
=97	Chichester	82.9	85.4	10.3	105	43.4	78.7
99	Buckinghamshire New	85.2	82.7	n/a	104	47.3	78.5
100	Bradford	72.2	75.1	9.5	121	55.2	78.3
=101	Greenwich	72.3	73.4	6.7	132	53.8	78.2
=101	Kingston	81.0	81.2	6.5	110	46.1	78.2
=101	South Wales	81.6	77.5	0.9	132	43.3	78.2
=104	Cardiff Metropolitan	76.9	68.3	n/a	124	57.5	78.1
=104	Westminster	70.6	73.2	9.3	117	59.1	78.1
=106	Leeds Beckett	77.3	77.8	6.5	110	47.7	77.2
=106	Queen Margaret, Edinburgh	67.7	71.8	8.6	137	52.8	77.2
108	Winchester	70.1	70.4	6.5	114	58.5	76.9
109	Anglia Ruskin	81.2	78.4	12.6	102	39.9	76.8
=110	London Metropolitan	72.1	67.9	n/a	108	59.1	76.1
=110	Wales Trinity St David	80.4	76.1	n/a	113	42.5	76.1
=112	Newman	69.8	70.7	0.8	106	57.4	75.5
=112	Southampton Solent	72.1	78.6	n/a	96	53.4	75.5
114	Northampton	67.1	71.6	0.4	105	48.8	73.1

Employed in professional job	29%	Employed in non-professional job and Studying	5%
Employed in professional job and studying	5%	Employed in non-professional job	30%
Studying	22%	Unemployed	9%
Average starting professional salary	£19,048	Average starting non-professional salary	£16,000

Radiography

Radiography was among the top six subjects for employment in 2016. An impressive 93 per cent of graduates went straight into professional jobs and just 3 per cent were unemployed six months after completing a degree. The subject is also back in the top 20 for salaries in those professional jobs, although it shares the position with nine other groupings. Diagnostic courses usually involve two years of studying anatomy, physiology and physics followed by further training in sociology, management and ethics, and the practice and science of imaging. The therapeutic branch covers much of the same scientific content in the first year, but follows this with training in oncology, psycho-social studies and other modules. Degrees require at least one science subject, usually biology, among three A-levels or the equivalent.

The table is in its fifth year, radiography having been listed previously among "other subjects allied to medicine" in the *Guide*. Bangor, which has the highest entry qualifications, is top for the third year in succession. It is one of six institutions, compared with five last year, to record 100 per cent employment among its radiographers in 2016. Leeds, Robert Gordon, Bradford, Salford and Derby were the others. Exeter, which remains in second place, was the clear leader in the Research Excellence Framework. Teesside, in ninth place, had the most satisfied students in the teaching sections of the National Student Survey, while City, only four places off the bottom of the table, did best on the student experience.

The scores for graduate prospects reflect the subject's elevated position in the employment table. City was the only university where fewer than nine out of ten graduates went straight into professional jobs or further study – and its rate of 86.7 per cent would have been the top score in some subjects. Entry grades are not high, but they have been rising: only one university averaged (marginally) less than 120 points in the latest survey, and the top four plus Glasgow Caledonian in 15th place were all above 160 points.

Radiography	Teaching quality %	Student experience %	Research quality %	Entry standards (UCAS points)	Graduate prospects %	Overall score
1 Bangor	84.7	80.7	34.7	186	100.0	100.0
2 Exeter	80.5	83.9	42.4	161	97.7	97.0
3 Leeds	81.8	79.4	31.7	162	100.0	96.9
4 Robert Gordon	85.8	89.2	4.9	177	100.0	96.4
5 Liverpool	88.0	88.6	35.3	143	97.0	95.5
=6 Bradford	82.9	86.6	9.5	150	100.0	93.9
=6 West of England	95.3	93.2	8.2	138	98.3	93.9
8 Derby	92.7	94.5	n/a	137	100.0	93.4
9 Teesside	96.9	95.0	2.4	135	97.7	92.9
10 Cumbria	89.2	78.7	0.7	148	98.9	92.6
11 Salford	92.0	83.3	3.8	130	100.0	92.4
12 Cardiff	74.7	72.2	36.8	138	96.3	92.2
13 Portsmouth	87.7	81.5	24.3	143	93.5	92.1
14 Sheffield Hallam	90.9	87.3	3.7	138	96.5	91.6
15 Glasgow Caledonian	74.4	73.8	8.1	176	92.6	90.8
=16 Hertfordshire	82.2	86.0	4.0	136	96.8	90.3
=16 Suffolk	91.8	90.4	n/a	119	97.8	90.3
18 Queen Margaret, Edinburgh	83.7	79.8	1.5	153	93.9	90.1
19 Ulster	74.9	76.1	27.7	145	91.1	89.6
20 City	96.7	96.4	19.2	134	86.7	89.5
21 Canterbury Christ Church	67.7	69.0	2.2	137	98.1	88.0
22 Birmingham City	76.6	68.5	1.5	130	97.1	87.9
23 Kingston/St George's, London	74.0	74.8	2.6	129	96.6	87.7
24 London South Bank	74.9	61.2	13.7	121	94.0	86.3

Employed in professional job	91%	Employed in non-professional job and Studying	0%
Employed in professional job and studying	2%	Employed in non-professional job	3%
Studying	1%	Unemployed	3%
Average starting professional salary	£22,000	Average starting non-professional salary	£13,650

Russian and Eastern European Languages

Applications to study Russian have grown for the past two years, but there were still only 300 in 2017 – little more than half the number at the start of the decade. Only 55 students embarked on degrees in the current academic year, although many others are learning Russian as part of a broader modern languages programme. Only 14 universities are advertising single honours Russian degrees in 2018.

As in other subjects, the small numbers inevitably make for exaggerated swings in the statistics. Having gained almost 20 places in last year's employment table, Russian has dropped 10 places in the latest edition.

Whereas only 8 per cent of 2015 graduates were unemployed six months after completing their course, 19 per cent of the next cohort were in that position, the highest figure in the table. Average starting salaries for those who did find professional jobs were in the top 20.

Top for the fourth year in a row, Cambridge has the highest entry standards and the best research score. Oxford has been joined in a share of second place by Durham, which has the best graduate prospects.

Almost a third of the universities in the table have no scores for student satisfaction, owing to the boycott of the National Student Survey (NSS) in those institutions. St Andrews, in fourth place, again has the top scores in both of the measures derived from the NSS. Portsmouth is the sole representative of the post-1992 universities and there are no institutions from Wales or Northern Ireland.

Most undergraduates learn Russian or another Eastern European language from scratch. Despite the small numbers, entry standards remain high throughout the table: the top three all average more than 200 points on the new UCAS tariff and only Portsmouth has an average of less than 130 points. Satisfaction levels are also high. Every university with an NSS score satisfied at least three-quarters of its final-year undergraduates overall.

Russian and Eastern European languages	Teaching quality %	Student experience %	Research quality %	Entry standards (UCAS points)	Graduate prospects %	Overall score
1 Cambridge	n/a	n/a	54.0	216	85.1	100.0
=2 Durham	83.9	76.0	34.6	205	86.8	93.7
=2 Oxford	n/a	n/a	41.3	207	84.8	93.7
4 St Andrews	94.5	89.6	26.4	186*	76.7	91.7
5 Sheffield	n/a	n/a	41.2	n/a	72.1	91.6
6 Exeter	88.3	88.3	35.1	176	76.0	91.5
7 Birmingham	83.1	77.5	33.7	164	85.6	90.4
8 Leeds	85.4	81.9	30.6	165	82.9	90.0
9 University College London	n/a	n/a	43.7	182	82.8	89.6
10 Bristol	n/a	n/a	36.0	173	68.0	89.2
11 Manchester	n/a	n/a	48.9	157	65.7	88.1
12 Bath	81.3	82.1	27.4	159	73.9	85.8
13 Glasgow	78.3	75.6	26.3	169	76.2	85.4
=14 Nottingham	81.0	71.6	39.4	130	70.7	85.0
=14 Portsmouth	91.7	89.1	32.2	102	69.4	85.0
16 Edinburgh	76.6	75.7	30.3	177	55.7	82.0

Employed in professional job	42%	Employed in non-professional job and Studying			3%
Employed in professional job and studying	3%	Employed in non-professional job			11%
Studying	21%	Unemployed			19%
Average starting professional salary	£24,000	Average starting non-professional salary			–

Social Policy

There are big changes in the Social Policy table, with Strathclyde coming straight in at the top, sharing the lead with the London School of Economics, while last year's leader, Leeds, drops seven places after a decline in student satisfaction. Strathclyde's social policy programmes, which are offered mainly as joint degrees at undergraduate level, are too new to have graduates, but the entry standards are the highest in the table. LSE has the top research score and the best graduate prospects, but is handicapped by low student satisfaction. Students at Staffordshire, just outside the top 20, are much the most satisfied at any university in the table, both in relation to teaching quality and the broader student experience.

The demand for places on social policy degrees fluctuated in the aftermath of £9,000 fees, but both applications and enrolments grew for the third year in a row in 2017. There were less than four applications for every place, however. Yet there are three new universities in the latest table, as there were last year, taking the total to 41. Nor are entry standards especially low: while only three universities average more than 180 points on the new UCAS tariff, just one dropped below 100 points.

Nationally, the subject is firmly in the bottom ten for employment, with more than a third of graduates starting out in low-level jobs. This is reflected in the table for social policy, where less than half of the graduates at 11 of the 41 universities found professional work or continued studying, and only four universities reached 80 per cent on this measure. The picture is more positive in the summarisation of starting salaries to graduate-level jobs, where social policy is just outside the top 40 of the 67 subject groupings.

Social Policy	Teaching quality %	Student experience %	Research quality %	Entry standards (UCAS points)	Graduate prospects %	Overall score
=1 London School of Economics	69.9	60.3	74.9	175	87.0	100.0
=1 Strathclyde	78.9	78.5	31.9	204	n/a	100.0
3 Glasgow	84.9	79.2	41.8	188	69.8	99.7
4 Edinburgh	83.4	71.2	53.4	188	63.9	98.8
5 York	81.2	77.9	47.5	145	79.1	96.9
6 Bangor	86.7	82.8	39.6	n/a	67.7	96.6
7 Bristol	n/a	n/a	47.9	150	69.8	96.4
=8 Aston	84.1	85.6	38.6	127	78.2	95.4
=8 Leeds	80.7	77.4	47.6	158	64.9	95.4
10 Nottingham	73.1	80.1	43.5	139	85.0	95.1
11 Stirling	84.0	73.0	33.8	162	n/a	95.0
12 Birmingham	74.7	68.1	40.1	153	81.8	94.2
13 Liverpool Hope	90.9	89.5	8.6	119	81.5	93.2

		Teaching quality %	Student experience %	Research quality %	Entry standards (UCAS points)	Graduate prospects %	Overall score
14	Kent	72.9	68.3	59.0	129	74.7	92.8
15	Lincoln	80.5	78.9	5.8	n/a	79.2	91.8
=16	Bath	71.7	68.8	43.4	155	66.7	91.5
=16	Sheffield	n/a	n/a	26.8	139	71.7	91.5
18	Bolton	n/a	n/a	1.0	n/a	60.0	90.8
19	Loughborough	69.8	71.3	40.6	144	68.8	90.2
20	Cardiff	84.1	85.0	30.8	142	42.9	89.4
=21	Staffordshire	96.3	90.6	n/a	100	68.4	89.3
=21	Swansea	87.2	79.7	22.7	131	54.3	89.3
23	Southampton	73.4	70.9	52.8	131	n/a	88.7
24	Keele	80.5	79.5	25.0	134	57.1	88.6
25	Ulster	90.3	90.6	39.2	118	30.8	88.4
26	Queen's, Belfast	77.6	77.0	26.2	n/a	61.1	88.3
27	Central Lancashire	82.4	77.3	11.8	154	49.7	87.6
28	Salford	77.3	73.8	27.7	114	59.1	85.9
29	Plymouth	85.8	81.8	16.0	n/a	41.7	85.7
30	Middlesex	76.9	77.0	14.9	129	53.1	84.8
31	West of Scotland	83.1	73.8	9.4	n/a	47.6	83.7
32	Canterbury Christ Church	87.1	81.2	3.2	110*	48.3	83.5
33	Chester	80.3	75.3	0.3	118	n/a	82.8
34	Birmingham City	70.8	77.0	3.8	114	60.6	81.7
35	Wales Trinity St David	83.7	79.3	n/a	117	40.6	81.3
36	Bedfordshire	73.8	78.3	16.3	102	48.9	81.0
37	London Metropolitan	70.5	73.7	8.8	113	55.5	80.7
38	Northampton	78.6	75.8	n/a	120	40.0	79.7
39	Brighton	73.2	71.2	12.4	113	43.3	79.4
40	Anglia Ruskin	83.8	81.4	5.4	80	42.9	79.1
41	Goldsmiths, London	61.0	63.9	13.5	107	n/a	73.6

Employed in professional job	30%	Employed in non-professional job and Studying	5%
Employed in professional job and studying	4%	Employed in non-professional job	30%
Studying	19%	Unemployed	12%
Average starting professional salary	£20,900	Average starting non-professional salary	£16,600

Social Work

Edinburgh has shot up six places to the top of a much-changed Social Work ranking. Swansea is up 11 places to join the top ten and there are even bigger rises (and falls) further down the table. Edinburgh has the highest entry standards, while Bedfordshire, another university joining the top ten, has the best scores on both of our satisfaction measures drawn from the National Student Survey. Kent, which has dropped 12 places after a decline in student satisfaction, produced the best results in the Research Excellence Framework, but 18 of the 78 universities in the table did not enter the assessments.

The Frontline programme, modelled on Teach First, is trying to attract graduates of other subjects to train as social workers but, for the moment, social work degrees remain the main route into the profession.

Record numbers of students are taking them, in spite of the fact that applications have dropped from 80,000 to 52,500 over the course of the decade. A combination of falling demand and increasing provision has seen the number of applications per place drop from more than seven in 2010 to only four in 2017. Although no university averages less than 100 points at entry, only Edinburgh and Strathclyde have averages of more than 160 points.

Surprisingly, social work does better in the comparison of earnings in professional jobs than in the table based on overall graduate prospects. A median salary of £26,000 in graduate-level employment has taken the subject into the top seven, whereas it is outside the top 30 for the proportion of graduates going straight into such jobs or continuing to study. Unemployment is relatively low, at 8 per cent, but one graduate in five started out in low-level employment in 2016. A total of 23 universities saw positive destinations for over 90 per cent of their 2016 graduates, but the rate was under 60 per cent at seven others.

Social Work	Teaching quality %	Student experience %	Research quality %	Entry standards (UCAS points)	Graduate prospects %	Overall score
1 Edinburgh	90.2	88.7	53.4	169	90.5	100.0
2 Lancaster	85.8	87.6	51.4	152	90.0	96.2
3 East Anglia	93.5	78.8	45.8	148	92.9	96.1
4 Nottingham	81.7	79.9	43.5	160	96.7	95.7
5 Glasgow	87.7	74.2	41.8	n/a	91.7*	93.5
6 Stirling	87.0	74.2	33.8	n/a	95.0	93.1
7 Strathclyde	85.4	79.6	31.9	171	77.1	92.7
8 Swansea	87.6	82.2	22.7	n/a	93.8	92.4
9 Queen's, Belfast	78.6	79.9	39.3	148	94.1	92.3
=10 Bedfordshire	94.6	90.1	16.3	n/a	83.3	92.0
=10 Dundee	80.3	69.1	31.1	158	95.5	92.0
12 Bath	80.7	74.1	43.4	157	81.4	91.7
13 Leeds	77.0	74.0	47.6	156	81.3	91.3
14 York	84.1	66.5	47.5	137	89.7	91.1
15 Birmingham	73.8	72.1	40.1	150	90.8	90.3
16 Kent	76.3	77.1	59.0	122	91.7	90.2
=17 Keele	81.5	80.9	25.0	140	96.2	90.1
=17 West of England	81.1	82.3	10.9	154	96.5	90.1
19 Robert Gordon	84.1	78.5	18.0	143	91.8	89.1
=20 Bournemouth	91.9	85.3	4.7	138	93.2	89.0
=20 Salford	84.0	83.7	27.7	154	73.0	89.0
22 Portsmouth	84.3	75.9	12.1	149	90.8	88.7
23 West of Scotland	84.8	75.5	9.4	159	85.0	88.6
24 Hull	76.4	70.6	14.3	159	91.5	88.2

Social Work cont

		Teaching quality %	Student experience %	Research quality %	Entry standards (UCAS points)	Graduate prospects %	Overall score
25	East London	88.6	86.0	10.6	146	79.9	87.9
26	Glasgow Caledonian	79.1	73.0	8.1	158	88.4	87.5
27	Ulster	81.4	79.1	39.2	123	83.2	87.2
=28	Plymouth	90.5	81.9	16.0	133	81.1	87.1
=28	Sussex	77.6	72.7	27.9	138	88.1	87.1
30	Central Lancashire	83.0	81.3	11.8	158	70.7	86.4
31	Middlesex	83.1	79.9	14.9	142	79.2	86.1
32	Bolton	n/a	n/a	1.0	n/a	90.9	85.1
33	Brunel	69.8	56.9	28.5	156	80.0	85.0
34	London South Bank	81.8	75.0	20.1	138	76.2	84.9
35	Oxford Brookes	84.8	78.3	n/a	137	83.9	84.2
36	Huddersfield	82.7	81.2	9.5	141	73.8	84.1
37	Liverpool John Moores	90.1	90.4	5.8	135	67.2	84.0
38	Coventry	85.2	81.8	5.6	139	74.3	83.9
=39	Lincoln	69.7	64.3	5.8	140	97.6	83.3
=39	Nottingham Trent	81.4	78.3	5.1	141	76.2	83.3
=41	Staffordshire	84.0	81.5	n/a	120	90.7	83.2
=41	West London	88.0	76.1	n/a	140	73.5	83.2
43	Brighton	85.2	80.3	12.4	125	75.8	83.1
44	Hertfordshire	81.3	75.6	4.0	127	86.0	82.8
=45	Northumbria	79.8	76.9	12.7	146	62.3	82.2
=45	Sheffield Hallam	81.7	79.2	n/a	127	83.8	82.2
47	Kingston/St George's, London	81.0	78.6	n/a	124	86.8	82.1
48	Suffolk	75.0	68.9	n/a	133	90.8	81.9
=49	Greenwich	90.5	83.7	2.2	n/a	61.8	81.7
=49	Manchester Metropolitan	83.7	79.7	6.9	139	63.6	81.7
51	Liverpool Hope	74.4	81.3	8.6	123*	80.8	80.9
=52	Anglia Ruskin	72.2	61.9	5.4	130	89.7	80.8
=52	De Montfort	66.6	60.6	11.2	131	91.7	80.8
54	Teesside	68.1	58.9	15.0	126	87.5	80.0
55	Winchester	85.3	80.2	n/a	111	78.1	79.8
56	Goldsmiths, London	78.5	70.5	13.5	105	81.0	79.1
57	Bradford	75.9	78.0	10.6	129	64.4	79.0
58	Edge Hill	73.8	73.3	5.7	132	69.1	78.7
59	South Wales	84.0	76.3	15.4	118	58.1	78.6
60	Bangor	81.5	78.0	n/a	139	55.6	78.5
61	Cardiff Metropolitan	78.8	74.4	n/a	121	73.6	78.3
=62	Buckinghamshire New	88.7	86.1	n/a	101*	70.0	78.2
=62	Chichester	87.0	86.2	n/a	113	63.4	78.2
=64	Derby	75.2	67.2	5.6	117	76.5	77.7
=64	Sunderland	82.7	79.2	1.9	121	61.8	77.7
66	London Metropolitan	65.2	63.5	8.8	130	77.1	77.5

67 Gloucestershire	70.4	68.0	n/a	115	83.2	76.9
68 Birmingham City	74.1	67.4	3.8	115	75.0	76.7
69 Leeds Beckett	80.2	78.1	6.4	113	61.3	76.6
70 Chester	73.3	75.1	0.3	121	68.3	76.3
71 Plymouth Marjon	89.8	84.2	n/a	109	53.1	76.2
72 Northampton	75.6	69.5	n/a	119	68.8	76.0
73 Newman	77.2	73.7	2.2	129	51.6	75.3
74 Canterbury Christ Church	74.0	72.6	2.2	119	61.4	74.9
75 Southampton Solent	54.8	40.9	n/a	113	91.5	72.0
=76 Cumbria	75.3	70.1	n/a	107	54.6	71.7
=76 Essex	69.4	61.2	n/a	119*	57.7	71.7
78 Worcester	70.1	73.3	n/a	104	52.3	69.9

Employed in professional job	58%	Employed in non-professional job and Studying	2%
Employed in professional job and studying	3%	Employed in non-professional job	19%
Studying	10%	Unemployed	8%
Average starting professional salary	£26,000	Average starting non-professional salary	£15,327

Sociology

Sociology's spectacular renaissance continued in 2017, when universities filled 1,000 more places than they had two years earlier – and 3,000 more than when £9,000 fees were introduced in 2012. For the first time, more than 8,000 students started sociology degrees in 2017, prompting even more universities and colleges to offer the subject. Immediate job prospects cannot be responsible for the boom: sociology remains in the bottom five for the proportion of graduates finding professional work or continuing their studies. Almost half of those graduating in 2016 were in low-level jobs or unemployed at the end of the year. Those who did find professional work did rather better, but their median salary of £20,000 was still close to the bottom 20.

Cambridge remains at the top of the table, with the highest entry standards and the best graduate prospects. It was the only university to see 80 per cent of sociologists go straight into professional jobs or begin postgraduate courses. The proportion was under 40 per cent at seven universities, and under 30 per cent at one. The best performance in the Research Excellence Framework was at Kent, just outside the top ten. As in the 2008 assessments, the sociology panel was no respecter of reputations: neither Cambridge nor the London School of Economics is among the top eight universities on this measure.

Courses starting in 2018 will include subjects such as urban studies, women's studies and some communication studies, as well as sociology itself, and a large number of institutions teach the subject as part of a combined studies or modular programme. Entry standards are moderate: eight of the 95 universities in the table average less than 100 points on the new UCAS tariff and another 32 less than 120 points. Students at Plymouth, in 34th place overall, were the most satisfied with the quality of teaching, while Lincoln, only three places higher, did best on the broader student experience.

Sociology

	Teaching quality %	Student experience %	Research quality %	Entry standards (UCAS points)	Graduate prospects %	Overall score
1 Cambridge	n/a	n/a	39.2	210	82.4	100.0
2 Bristol	86.7	81.1	46.7	167	70.5	97.8
3 Exeter	83.4	78.8	41.0	167	73.2	96.4
4 Bath	79.8	75.7	43.4	161	77.3	95.4
5 Glasgow	78.3	81.5	41.8	199	56.5	95.1
6 Edinburgh	76.3	73.4	48.8	193	61.9	94.9
7 Manchester	n/a	n/a	50.4	148	68.6	94.4
8 Birmingham	82.6	76.9	31.1	154	77.4	94.2
9 Surrey	84.4	82.5	30.2	162	63.9	93.8
10 Loughborough	84.3	85.7	40.6	136	65.0	93.7
11 Kent	73.9	73.5	59.0	127	80.4	93.4
=12 Leeds	78.9	79.6	47.6	154	62.1	93.3
=12 Sheffield	n/a	n/a	26.8	144	72.5	93.3
14 Warwick	78.8	82.2	31.7	164	67.5	93.1
15 Sussex	83.3	82.1	29.7	136	72.8	92.8
16 Keele	86.0	84.1	25.0	127	73.7	92.6
17 Bangor	86.9	82.8	39.6	130	59.5	92.5
18 King's College London	76.2	82.3	42.2	158	n/a	92.2
=19 London School of Economics	71.1	65.1	45.2	174	72.1	92.0
=19 York	75.3	73.9	45.1	141	73.5	92.0
21 Aberdeen	81.0	78.4	31.0	186	49.3	91.9
22 Lancaster	78.9	74.8	51.4	149	56.6	91.8
23 Nottingham	78.6	77.9	43.5	143	62.0	91.5
24 Aston	82.7	79.8	38.6	130	58.0	90.6
25 Essex	76.4	78.1	44.3	132	63.4	90.4
26 Newcastle	79.3	78.6	30.3	146	61.9	90.2
27 Coventry	85.9	85.1	5.6	119	76.4	90.1
=28 Leicester	81.7	82.4	18.4	130	69.7	89.9
=28 Portsmouth	85.1	81.4	32.2	115	61.1	89.9
30 East Anglia	86.2	83.5	45.8	n/a	38.8*	89.5
31 Lincoln	87.0	90.0	n/a	126	67.8*	89.4
32 Stirling	82.4	75.7	33.8	159	42.8	89.1
33 Southampton	72.9	70.8	52.8	138	53.8	88.4
34 Plymouth	93.7	84.5	16.0	97	55.6	88.3
35 Bradford	81.1	79.6	10.6	129	67.1	87.8
36 Durham	70.4	69.6	28.7	167	58.7	87.5
=37 Huddersfield	83.8	77.4	9.5	113	69.1	87.2
=37 Newman	91.0	86.7	2.2	101	n/a	87.2
=37 Oxford Brookes	78.3	76.0	17.8	122	68.2	87.2
40 Northumbria	79.2	80.1	12.7	141	57.4	87.0
41 Nottingham Trent	84.1	81.3	5.1	125	60.3	86.7
42 Liverpool	n/a	n/a	24.5	140	51.2	86.6

43 Gloucestershire	85.9	86.1	14.5	115	48.3	86.4
44 Abertay	82.8	73.2	5.0	141	59.0	86.3
45 Central Lancashire	78.5	75.6	11.8	121	67.7	86.2
46 Glasgow Caledonian	80.2	72.9	12.7	178	38.5	86.0
47 Edinburgh Napier	79.1	75.9	5.3	150	55.0	85.7
=48 Cardiff	72.9	69.6	30.8	143	52.4	85.6
=48 Queen's, Belfast	73.9	79.5	26.2	132	51.9	85.6
50 West of Scotland	82.7	75.2	9.4	140	50.0	85.5
=51 Brunel	75.3	73.7	26.0	124	56.9	85.3
=51 Queen Margaret, Edinburgh	82.5	78.4	n/a	118	64.0	85.3
=53 Goldsmiths, London	n/a	n/a	33.4	116	42.8	85.2
=53 Strathclyde	78.9	78.5	31.9	n/a	45.0*	85.2
=55 Robert Gordon	75.4	76.7	4.9	163	51.2	85.1
=55 West of England	80.5	79.9	10.9	121	54.6	85.1
57 Staffordshire	87.1	84.5	n/a	113	50.8	84.8
=58 City	81.0	80.2	19.2	124	42.9	84.6
=58 Salford	82.3	77.4	27.7	116	39.9	84.6
60 Bedfordshire	86.1	82.3	16.3	81	54.5	84.5
=61 East London	83.9	81.6	13.7	111	46.7	84.4
=61 Hull	73.5	72.3	14.3	126	63.0	84.4
63 Manchester Metropolitan	80.0	76.7	14.9	121	49.0	84.1
64 Royal Holloway	78.7	76.6	n/a	137	55.2	84.0
65 Bournemouth	79.1	77.0	4.7	110	62.5	83.9
66 Liverpool John Moores	80.0	79.5	5.8	124	50.0	83.7
67 Roehampton	74.9	71.3	24.9	94	63.7	83.5
68 Sheffield Hallam	82.5	79.6	14.4	115	41.7	83.4
69 Westminster	82.9	83.6	n/a	111	48.7	83.3
=70 Anglia Ruskin	84.6	82.4	26.4	98	32.8	83.1
=70 Bath Spa	86.6	80.4	13.9	110	35.2	83.1
=72 Chester	81.6	74.8	6.4	114	50.8	82.9
=72 De Montfort	76.2	73.2	11.2	107	60.6	82.9
=74 Derby	78.5	74.3	13.5	91	60.9	82.7
=74 Northampton	88.3	84.6	n/a	99	42.7	82.7
76 Teesside	75.8	69.5	15.0	109	56.7	82.4
=77 Birmingham City	82.7	83.0	3.8	116	39.7	82.3
=77 Sunderland	82.9	77.6	1.9	112	47.1	82.3
=77 Winchester	78.7	77.2	4.4	116	50.7	82.3
80 Canterbury Christ Church	87.1	81.2	n/a	106	40.4	82.1
=81 South Wales	76.9	74.4	n/a	125	53.4	82.0
=81 Ulster	84.7	83.1	n/a	113	39.3	82.0
83 Liverpool Hope	86.5	81.4	8.6	110	30.4*	81.7
84 Brighton	77.8	73.8	12.4	111	46.4	81.5
85 Leeds Beckett	77.5	75.1	6.4	108	51.4	81.4
86 Edge Hill	78.8	74.2	5.7	114	45.3	81.1
87 Middlesex	74.1	74.2	14.9	105	49.8	81.0
88 Suffolk	81.6	77.3	n/a	114	40.2	80.6

	Teaching quality %	Student experience %	Research quality %	Entry standards (UCAS points)	Graduate prospects %	Overall score
89 London Metropolitan	78.9	76.2	n/a	85	55.0	79.9
90 Kingston	78.0	76.4	n/a	111	41.1	79.4
=91 London South Bank	70.0	69.9	20.1	99	43.5	78.5
=91 St Mary's, Twickenham	69.6	75.5	n/a	113	48.8	78.5
93 Buckinghamshire New	72.8	67.8	n/a	104	43.5	76.7
94 Greenwich	74.6	70.7	n/a	122	28.2	76.5
95 Worcester	69.0	62.2	n/a	114	43.8	75.8

Employed in professional job	29%	Employed in non-professional job and Studying	4%
Employed in professional job and studying	3%	Employed in non-professional job	34%
Studying	20%	Unemployed	11%
Average starting professional salary	£20,000	Average starting non-professional salary	£16,000

Sports Science

Both applications and enrolments for sports and exercise science degrees dipped in 2017, but student numbers were still well ahead of every year before 2015. Sports science has been one of the big growth areas of UK higher education over the past decade, with a 50 per cent increase in undergraduate entrants. It is now among the top 10 subjects for applicants, and over 160 universities and colleges are offering courses.

Sports and exercise science covers more than 40 specialisms, from sports therapy to equestrian sport studies and marine sport technology. Many courses contain more science and less physical activity than candidates may expect. Essex, for example, requires maths or one of the sciences at A-level. Many universities now offer sports scholarships for elite performers, but most are not tied to a particular course and, officially at least, they do not mean that the normal entry requirements are waived.

All the universities at the top of the table have excellent sports facilities and successful teams, but it is their performance in research and sports degree courses that counts here. Competition at the top of the table is as fierce as it would be in a major championship. Less than one point covers the top four universities, with Bath leading without claiming the top score for any of the measures. Birmingham, last year's leader is down to fifth, while Loughborough, the most famous name in university sport, remains in sixth place, less than three points off the top.

The students who are most satisfied with the quality of teaching are at Kingston, although the university is only just inside the top 50, while third-placed Leeds has the best score for satisfaction with other aspects of the student experience. Glasgow, which has moved up to second, again has the highest entry grades, while Swansea, in ninth place, has the best graduate prospects. Sports science remains in the top 50 subjects, out of 67, for graduate prospects, but is only just outside the bottom 10 for starting salaries in professional jobs. Only 7 per cent of 2016 graduates were unemployed at the end of the year, but 30 per cent started out in low-level jobs.

Sport Science

		Teaching quality %	Student experience %	Research quality %	Entry standards (UCAS points)	Graduate prospects %	Overall score
1	Bath	88.5	85.5	54.0	171	80.1	100.0
2	Glasgow	81.0	83.4	42.3	206	78.9	99.6
3	Leeds	92.5	94.7	50.5	153	79.1	99.5
4	Exeter	81.4	86.5	50.8	180	80.8	99.1
5	Birmingham	81.4	81.7	63.7	157	83.4	98.6
6	Loughborough	82.7	87.0	52.1	162	80.1	97.7
7	Edinburgh	84.5	86.3	26.1	179	84.6	97.4
8	Durham	88.7	88.5	28.7	164	81.6	96.8
9	Swansea	85.5	86.4	38.8	133	86.0	95.2
10	Surrey	82.0	82.8	33.6	170	n/a	94.2
11	Nottingham	90.3	87.7	31.4	141	n/a	93.6
12	Bradford	94.4	84.8	9.5	153	n/a	93.3
13	Essex	92.3	92.3	25.8	147	67.0	92.8
14	Liverpool Hope	94.1	94.4	10.9	122	79.0	91.9
=15	Bangor	87.1	87.9	30.6	146	66.4	91.4
=15	Stirling	76.8	80.0	33.6	160	73.2	91.4
17	Aberdeen	82.3	83.4	34.7	180	56.3	91.3
18	Coventry	84.6	86.0	4.5	147	82.7	91.1
19	Liverpool John Moores	78.4	77.2	45.3	147	69.2	90.8
20	Lincoln	83.4	83.5	11.4	163	70.8	90.2
21	Portsmouth	85.9	83.8	8.1	137	79.8	90.0
22	Brunel	n/a	n/a	46.4	142	61.9	89.4
23	Robert Gordon	81.6	85.5	4.9	149	77.3	89.1
24	East Anglia	75.4	80.4	27.2	169	64.6	89.2
25	Bournemouth	88.5	89.5	9.0	128	72.2	88.7
=26	Kent	74.5	72.6	21.0	147	78.5	88.4
=26	Salford	90.4	89.1	3.8	140	66.7	88.4
28	Huddersfield	91.4	85.3	n/a	132	72.5	88.2
29	Central Lancashire	89.1	87.7	5.1	153	61.1	88.1
30	Nottingham Trent	81.6	82.5	7.3	152	69.8	87.9
=31	Cardiff Metropolitan	82.4	84.3	7.7	143	70.2	87.6
=31	Staffordshire	88.9	85.3	19.1	119	66.7	87.6
33	Gloucestershire	85.8	84.0	6.0	135	70.3	87.4
34	West of Scotland	85.4	81.6	9.1	151	63.2	87.3
35	Chester	91.0	90.1	6.6	129	62.8	87.1
36	Brighton	82.3	83.2	10.9	143	66.5	87.0
37	Ulster	74.5	72.9	31.0	150	64.9	86.9
=38	Abertay	81.1	75.9	8.9	157	65.9	86.8
=38	Hull	86.2	85.3	14.2	140	59.6	86.8
40	London South Bank	77.5	75.7	35.0	96	79.4	86.6
41	Northumbria	81.7	81.6	4.4	154	65.0	86.5
42	Roehampton	79.7	78.6	20.6	105	76.8	85.9

Sport Science cont

		Teaching quality %	Student experience %	Research quality %	Entry standards (UCAS points)	Graduate prospects %	Overall score
43	Sheffield Hallam	84.3	82.9	8.5	135	64.1	85.8
44	London Metropolitan	88.6	86.0	n/a	114	70.6	85.5
45	St Mary's, Twickenham	75.1	75.3	4.8	143	74.2	85.4
46	Aberystwyth	83.8	82.7	23.5	115	62.3	85.3
47	Leeds Beckett	80.1	80.9	12.6	131	66.1	85.2
48	Kingston	97.4	93.5	2.6	118	53.0	85.1
49	Plymouth Marjon	80.3	81.3	n/a	153	61.8	84.8
=50	Chichester	80.2	81.9	15.2	126	64.2	84.7
=50	East London	82.1	74.7	7.6	129	68.4	84.7
=50	Edge Hill	83.0	80.6	7.7	145	58.2	84.7
=50	Edinburgh Napier	80.9	81.3	5.3	152	58.3	84.7
54	Bolton	82.4	76.0	n/a	121	74.4	84.6
55	Worcester	77.9	79.2	4.9	132	69.6	84.4
56	Greenwich	72.6	74.5	7.4	142	68.8	83.8
57	Teesside	82.6	74.4	2.4	130	66.0	83.6
=58	Anglia Ruskin	89.0	89.4	n/a	107	62.0	83.3
=58	Bedfordshire	81.0	81.3	6.7	107	70.1	83.3
=60	Manchester Metropolitan	76.2	78.0	12.0	131	62.2	83.0
=60	Winchester	83.1	81.3	n/a	97	74.5	83.0
62	Hertfordshire	76.9	74.9	0.9	127	70.1	82.8
63	Canterbury Christ Church	79.6	77.9	19.0	119	58.3	82.6
64	Newman	77.8	78.8	2.8	120	67.7	82.4
65	Derby	81.0	84.0	1.7	114	63.4	82.1
66	Southampton Solent	80.4	80.6	0.6	125	60.3	81.8
67	South Wales	77.3	78.8	10.8	130	55.8	81.6
=68	Leeds Trinity	77.1	78.5	0.8	119	64.6	81.3
=68	Middlesex	65.9	62.6	10.0	131	74.5	81.3
=70	Oxford Brookes	76.5	79.4	3.0	138	55.2	81.1
=70	Wrexham Glyndŵr	79.5	75.1	3.6	136	54.5	81.1
=72	Suffolk	84.3	80.8	n/a	92	61.0	79.6
=72	Sunderland	78.9	80.2	2.4	127	50.6	79.6
74	York St John	73.3	74.2	5.5	126	54.5	78.8
75	Wales Trinity St David	73.8	70.8	n/a	109	65.3	78.6
76	Buckinghamshire New	73.9	73.1	0.9	111	61.6	78.5
77	Bishop Grosseteste	73.4	69.2	n/a	108	59.4	77.0
78	Cumbria	74.6	71.9	3.2	111	50.8	76.3
79	Northampton	76.8	71.6	n/a	111	43.1	74.6

Employed in professional job	37%	Employed in non-professional job and Studying	3%
Employed in professional job and studying	5%	Employed in non-professional job	27%
Studying	22%	Unemployed	7%
Average starting professional salary	£19,000	Average starting non-professional salary	£15,600

Theology and Religious Studies

Just over 1,000 students began degrees in theology or religious studies in 2017 – slightly fewer than in the previous year and about a third down on the period before higher fees were introduced. Applications have followed a similar downward path, and this year will see the closure of Heythrop College, part of the University of London, after 400 years of teaching theology. There are now little more than four to the place nationally. There are still 36 universities in the table, however, and many more offering the subject as part of a broader degree. Religious studies can be combined with computing at Glasgow, film and media at Stirling, or applied psychology at Trinity Saint David.

The top two in the table remain unchanged from last year, with Cambridge extending its lead over Durham. Cambridge has the highest entry standards and the best graduate prospects, while Durham produced the best results in the Research Excellence Framework. Competition is particularly keen in Scotland, which has five universities in the top 20. They are led by St Andrews, in sixth place, which has the highest levels of satisfaction in both of the measures taken from the National Student Survey. Although only five places off the bottom overall, Bath Spa almost matches St Andrews on perceptions of teaching quality and the broader student experience.

By no means all graduates go into the church, but the vocation has helped to maintain relatively healthy employment records up until now. The two subjects are only just in the bottom half of the table for graduate prospects, although they have slipped a little in this year's earnings table and now share 45th place with six other subjects. More than 40 per cent of those completing courses take postgraduate degrees, either full or part-time.

Theology and Religious Studies	Teaching quality %	Student experience %	Research quality %	Entry standards (UCAS points)	Graduate prospects %	Overall score
1 Cambridge	n/a	n/a	44.6	201	91.7	100.0
2 Durham	85.1	77.5	56.6	190	87.6	98.6
3 Lancaster	94.5	87.3	53.0	160	85.1	97.9
4 Exeter	89.5	86.1	38.9	176	85.8	95.7
5 Oxford	n/a	n/a	46.7	200	84.8	95.1
6 St Andrews	96.7	93.3	28.9	169	75.9	93.7
7 Bristol	n/a	n/a	36.0	179	82.4	93.4
8 Edinburgh	85.8	85.1	43.2	172	71.9	92.4
9 Leeds	85.4	87.1	44.4	158	76.1	92.3
10 Nottingham	94.0	90.0	43.9	157	64.1	91.9
11 Birmingham	87.3	79.1	36.2	151	84.3	91.5
12 Stirling	78.1	73.5	29.8	170*	83.0*	89.0
13 King's College London	n/a	n/a	37.1	161	68.9	87.2
=14 Glasgow	89.4	91.5	21.4	n/a	66.0	86.6
=14 Sheffield	n/a	n/a	25.3	146	74.2	86.6
=14 SOAS London	n/a	n/a	34.1	141	75.4	86.6
17 Manchester	n/a	n/a	37.2	141	66.4	86.0
18 Kent	78.8	75.6	44.1	122	70.8	85.3
19 Aberdeen	72.0	66.9	39.9	145	74.1	84.7

Theology and Religious Studies
cont

	Teaching quality %	Student experience %	Research quality %	Entry standards (UCAS points)	Graduate prospects %	Overall score
20 Liverpool Hope	85.9	85.3	17.7	110	75.5	83.1
21 Leeds Trinity	89.2	86.1	9.9	102	72.6	81.2
22 Newman	94.6	85.2	3.5	105	70.0	81.0
23 Queen's, Belfast	77.8	78.9	n/a	141	79.0	80.8
24 Cardiff	77.6	74.3	33.5	142	51.3	80.7
25 St Mary's, Twickenham	86.2	80.2	9.4	107	74.3	80.6
=26 Chester	88.7	83.0	11.1	109	61.6	79.4
=26 Roehampton	75.7	75.2	24.3	110	68.8	79.4
28 Chichester	86.5	88.1	n/a	105	72.4	79.2
=29 Bishop Grosseteste	77.0	65.7	n/a	102	88.9	77.8
=29 Canterbury Christ Church	92.8	83.7	16.3	97	49.2	77.8
31 Bath Spa	96.5	93.2	8.3	108	42.0	77.7
32 York St John	85.6	80.9	4.8	116	52.6	76.1
33 South Wales	84.1	80.4	n/a	132	49.0	75.5
34 Wales Trinity St David	71.6	57.9	30.0	124	47.2	74.7
35 Winchester	61.9	52.4	18.0	116	70.7	73.7
36 Gloucestershire	82.7	78.2	6.9	110	45.0	73.4

Employed in professional job	29%	Employed in non-professional job and Studying	4%
Employed in professional job and studying	4%	Employed in non-professional job	21%
Studying	33%	Unemployed	9%
Average starting professional salary	£20,000	Average starting non-professional salary	£15,600

Town and Country Planning and Landscape

Three universities have dropped out of the table for town and country planning and landscape this year, reflecting the small pool of candidates seeking places in the subjects at undergraduate level. Many students considering a career in these areas opt for a postgraduate course. There were increases in applications and enrolments for both planning and landscape degrees in 2017, however, although the combined total starting courses remained below 1,000. Applications were 20 per cent higher before the arrival of £9,000 fees.

Almost two-thirds of graduates in the planning and landscape groups go straight into professional jobs, placing the subjects in the top 15 in the employment table. They are also in the top 20 for starting salaries in graduate-level employment. The subject table reflects these successes, with six of the top seven universities seeing at least nine out of ten graduates go straight into professional jobs or further study in 2016. At University College London, the rate was 100 per cent.

Cambridge, the perennial leader of the table, has by far the highest entry standards, although it is in the bottom ten for student satisfaction. Sheffield has moved up four places to second, although Ulster's students are the most satisfied with the quality of teaching and those at Queen's, Belfast gave the highest rating to other aspects of their experience.

Entry standards are lower on landscape and garden design courses, where there are only three applications to the place, than for planning, where the ratio is closer to five per place. But only six of the 25 universities in the table average more than 150 points. About 40 universities and colleges are offering courses in landscape or garden design in 2018, some of them as an element of a broader degree in geography or architecture. Over 70 expect to run courses in various areas of planning, including disaster management and emergency planning, rural enterprise and land management, and coastal safety management.

Town and Country Planning and Landscape	Teaching quality %	Student experience %	Research quality %	Entry standards (UCAS points)	Graduate prospects %	Overall score
1 Cambridge	78.3	72.4	49.0	220	93.8	100.0
2 Sheffield	85.8	91.0	36.6	150	96.6	96.8
3 University College London	71.0	71.7	54.1	175	100.0	96.2
4 Birmingham	86.6	85.4	42.0	135	96.2	95.8
5 Queen's, Belfast	92.5	94.0	35.2	138	86.8	95.7
6 Edinburgh	80.0	71.6	35.1	184	95.0	95.6
7 Loughborough	77.4	76.7	58.3	149	90.7	94.9
8 Heriot-Watt	84.7	77.7	38.1	159	87.1	94.1
9 Cardiff	86.4	88.8	36.8	152	78.8	93.3
10 Reading	82.4	81.5	40.0	147	n/a	92.4
11 Manchester	74.7	76.6	36.5	150	92.6	91.6
12 Gloucestershire	87.3	90.2	20.6	127	80.0	89.5
13 Liverpool	81.4	81.8	26.3	140	80.0*	89.1
14 Ulster	93.8	88.4	28.6	126	64.2	88.9
15 Dundee	83.9	77.4	8.7	n/a	85.2	88.6
16 Newcastle	72.0	72.5	43.7	134	83.9	88.4
17 Glasgow Caledonian	89.7	85.2	9.1	173	61.5	88.3
18 West of England	86.3	86.1	10.6	120	85.4	88.0
19 Nottingham Trent	86.2	86.0	3.4	n/a	75.0*	87.1
20 Manchester Metropolitan	83.0	84.6	9.7	n/a	75.0	86.5
21 Leeds Beckett	82.4	78.3	5.6	105	77.1	82.5
22 Birmingham City	80.4	73.1	2.7	91*	78.9	80.2
23 Oxford Brookes	69.5	71.8	17.6	120	69.4	80.0
24 Greenwich	76.3	67.4	2.0	n/a	68.2	78.0
25 Westminster	73.8	77.3	10.7	119	51.5	77.0

Employed in professional job	60%	Employed in non-professional job and Studying	1%
Employed in professional job and studying	3%	Employed in non-professional job	12%
Studying	14%	Unemployed	10%
Average starting professional salary	£22,000	Average starting non-professional salary	£15,600

Veterinary Medicine

The table for veterinary medicine is the most static in this year's *Guide*. The only change among the seven schools has seen Nottingham moving up from fourth into a share of third place with Cambridge. Nottingham again has much the most satisfied students – more than ten percentage points ahead of its nearest rival in both of the measures derived from the National Student Survey. Edinburgh remains ahead of Glasgow at the top of the table, however, benefiting from the best results in the Research Excellence Framework.

Only medicine itself has higher entry standards than veterinary medicine, where successful candidates had an average of more than 200 points on the new UCAS tariff in 2016 and, even after a fourth successive drop in applications, there were almost seven of them to every place. An eighth veterinary school opened in 2013 at the University of Surrey, but there is not enough data yet to include it in this table.

Veterinary medicine is another of the rankings in which employment scores have been removed from the calculations that determine universities' positions. The scores are still shown in the table, but the review group of academic planners consulted on the *Guide* agreed that employment rates in the subject were so tightly bunched that small differences could distort the overall ranking. Veterinary medicine is in the top three subjects for earnings in professional jobs, although it has dropped to fifth in this year's employment table.

The number of places in veterinary medicine is centrally controlled. Most courses demand high grades in chemistry and biology, with some accepting physics or maths as one alternative subject. Cambridge and the Royal Veterinary College also set applicants a specialist aptitude test that is used by a number of medical schools. Few candidates win places without evidence of practical commitment to the subject through work experience, either in veterinary practices or laboratories. The norm for veterinary science degrees is five years, but the Cambridge course takes six years and both Bristol and Nottingham offer a "gateway" year. Edinburgh and the Royal Veterinary College also run four-year courses for graduates. There are no degrees in the subject in Wales or Northern Ireland, or in the post-1992 universities, although a number of them and several colleges offer veterinary nursing.

Veterinary Medicine	Teaching quality %	Student experience %	Research quality %	Entry standards (UCAS points)	Graduate prospects %	Overall score
1 Edinburgh	86.0	83.7	46.8	216	95.6	100.0
2 Glasgow	85.0	82.0	42.3	225	98.8	98.1
=3 Cambridge	66.5	63.2	43.1	226	97.8	91.9
=3 Nottingham	96.8	97.0	36.4	182	99.2	91.9
5 Royal Veterinary College	82.0	84.1	40.8	188	97.4	90.3
6 Bristol	78.8	80.0	33.2	194	95.1	85.1
7 Liverpool	n/a	n/a	32.9	176	98.1	84.0

Employed in professional job	94%	Employed in non-professional job and Studying	0%
Employed in professional job and studying	1%	Employed in non-professional job	2%
Studying	1%	Unemployed	2%
Average starting professional salary	£28,000	Average starting non-professional salary	–

13 Applying to Oxbridge

Oxbridge (as Oxford and Cambridge are called) not only dominates UK higher education; the two universities are recognised as among the best in the world, regularly featuring among the top five in global rankings. But that is not why they merit a separate chapter in this *Guide*.

The two ancient universities have different admissions arrangements from the rest of the higher education system. Although part of the UCAS network, they have different deadlines from other universities, you can only apply to one or the other, and selection is in the hands of the colleges rather than the university centrally. Most candidates apply to a specific college, although you can make an open application if you are happy to go anywhere.

There have been reforms to the admissions system at both universities in recent years, in order to make the process more user-friendly to those who do not have school or family experience to draw upon. Most significantly, in 2017, Cambridge reintroduced 'pre-interview written assessments' in most subjects, with tests on the day of interview in the rest. Both universities have also changed the way applicants are matched to colleges. Candidates are now distributed around colleges more efficiently, regardless of the choices they make initially.

There is little to choose between the two universities in terms of entrance requirements, and a formidable number of successful (and even unsuccessful) applicants have the maximum possible grades. However, that does not mean that the talented student should be shy about applying: both have fewer applicants per place than many less prestigious universities, and admissions tutors are always looking to extend the range of schools and colleges from which they recruit. For those with a realistic chance of success, there is little to lose except the possibility of one wasted space out of five on the UCAS application.

Overall, there are about five applicants to every place at Cambridge and six at Oxford, but there are big differences between subjects and colleges. As the tables in this chapter show, competition is particularly fierce in subjects such as medicine and law, but those qualified to read earth sciences or modern languages have a much better chance of success. The pattern is similar to that in other universities, although the high degree of selection (and self-selection) that precedes an Oxbridge application means that, even in the less popular subjects, the field of candidates is certain to be strong.

The two universities' power to intimidate prospective applicants is based partly on myth.

Both have done their best to live down the *Brideshead Revisited* image, but many sixth-formers still fear that they would be out of their depth there, academically and socially. In fact, the state sector produces about 60 per cent of entrants to Oxford and Cambridge, and the dropout rate is lower than at almost any other university. The "champagne set" is still present and its activities are well publicised, but most students are hard-working high achievers with the same concerns as their counterparts on other campuses.

State school applicants

Both universities and their student organisations have put a great deal of effort into trying to encourage applications from state schools, and many colleges have launched their own campaigns. Such has been the determination to convince state school pupils that they will get a fair crack of the whip that a new concern has grown of possible bias against independent school pupils. In reality, however, the dispersed nature of Oxbridge admissions rules out any conspiracy. Some colleges set relatively low standard offers to encourage applicants from the state sector, who may reveal their potential at interview. Some admissions tutors may give the edge to well-qualified candidates from comprehensive schools over those from highly academic independent schools because they consider the former to have made a greater achievement in the circumstances. Others stick with tried and trusted sources of good students. The independent sector still enjoys a degree of success out of proportion to its share of the school population.

Choosing the right college

Simply in terms of winning a place at Oxford or Cambridge, choosing the right college is not quite as important as it used to be. Both universities have got better at assessing candidates' strengths and finding a suitable college for those who either make an open application or are not taken by their first-choice college.

Cambridge: The Tompkins Table 2017

College	2017	2016	College	2017	2016
Trinity	1	1	Magdalene	16	9
Christ's	2	3	Sidney Sussex	17	16
St John's	3	5	Lucy Cavendish	18	26
Pembroke	4	2	St Catherine's	19	17
Churchill	5	11	Downing	20	12
Emmanuel	6	4	Fitzwilliam	21	23
Queens'	7	6	St Edmund's	22	28
King's	8	14	Newnham	23	21
Selwyn	9	15	Girton	24	27
Peterhouse	10	8	Robinson	25	22
Gonville & Caius	11	19	Hughes Hall	26	29
Corpus Christi	12	10	Wolfson	27	20
Clare	13	18	Homerton	28	24
Jesus	14	7	Murray Edwards	29	25
Trinity Hall	15	13			

At Oxford, subject tutors from around the university put candidates into bands at the start of the selection process, using the results of admissions tests as well as exam results and references. Applicants are spread around the colleges for interview and may not be seen by their preferred college if the tutors think their chances of a place are better elsewhere. Over a quarter of successful candidates are offered places by a college other than the one to which they applied.

Cambridge relies on the "pool", which gives the most promising candidates a second chance if they were not offered a place at the college to which they applied. Those placed in the pool are invited back for a second round of interviews early in the new year. The system lowers the stakes for those who apply to the most selective colleges – typically around 20 per cent of offers come via the pool. Cambridge still interviews more than 80 per cent of applicants, whereas the system at Oxford has resulted in more immediate rejections in some subjects. Overall around 60 per cent of Oxford applicants are interviewed, but there is great variation by subject.

Most Oxbridge applicants still apply direct to a particular college, however, not only to maximise their chances of getting in, but because that is where they will be living and socialising, as well as learning. Most colleges may look the same to the uninitiated, but there are important differences. Famously sporty colleges, for example, can be trying for those in search of peace and quiet.

Thorough research is needed to find the right place. Even within colleges, different admissions tutors may have different approaches, so personal contact is essential. The tables in this chapter give an idea of the relative academic strengths of the colleges, as well as the varying levels of competition for a place in different subjects. But only individual research will suggest where you will feel most at home. For example, women may favour one of the few remaining single-sex colleges (Murray Edwards, Newnham and Lucy Cavendish at Cambridge). Men have no such option.

Oxford: The Norrington Table 2017

College	2017	2016	College	2017	2016
New College	1	18	Corpus Christi	16	15
Merton	2	1	Christ Church	17	24
Pembroke	3	13	Jesus	18	14
Worcester	4	9	St Anne's	19	26
Queen's	5	30	Oriel	20	2
St John's	6	12	St Hugh's	21	22
Brasenose	7	7	Hertford	22	20
University	8	4	Somerville	23	16
Trinity	9	5	St Edmund Hall	24	21
Balliol	10	8	Exeter	25	25
Magdalen	11	3	St Catherine's	26	10
Keble	12	17	Harris Manchester	27	11
Wadham	13	6	St Hilda's	28	27
Lady Margaret Hall	14	23	St Peter's	29	28
Mansfield	15	29	Lincoln	30	19

Oxford applications and acceptances by course

Arts	Applications			Acceptances			Acceptances to Applications %		
	2016	2015	2014	2016	2015	2014	2016	2015	2014
Ancient and modern history	92	77	73	22	18	18	24	23	25
Archaeology and anthropology	97	93	72	18	27	24	19	29	33
Classical archaeology and ancient history	108	79	84	19	20	24	18	25	29
Classics	325	291	291	121	111	106	37	38	36
Classics and English	40	42	37	8	11	12	20	26	32
Classics and modern languages	26	24	30	6	6	9	23	40	30
Computer science and philosophy	75	45	50	10	5	8	13	11	16
Economics and management	1,116	1,127	1,149	83	87	86	7	8	8
English	1,025	1,044	1,100	235	227	231	23	22	21
English and modern Languages	100	128	115	17	24	18	17	19	16
European and Middle Eastern languages	39	41	37	11	17	3	28	42	8
Fine art	251	255	193	27	28	27	11	11	14
Geography	347	321	322	70	82	76	20	26	24
History	1,003	1,004	1,001	227	237	234	23	24	23
History and economics	130	114	84	15	13	16	12	11	19
History and English	81	72	85	11	9	9	14	13	11
History and modern languages	109	87	106	24	18	23	22	21	22
History and politics	355	317	288	45	41	33	13	13	12
History of art	123	137	122	14	14	13	11	10	11
Law	1,403	1,298	1,262	211	195	185	15	15	15
Law with law studies in Europe	269	279	287	25	31	34	9	11	12
Mathematics and philosophy	111	100	83	18	14	15	16	14	18
Modern languages	483	491	515	159	173	172	33	35	33
Modern languages and linguistics	90	70	61	29	23	27	32	33	44
Music	188	195	208	71	72	66	38	37	32
Oriental studies	167	163	148	44	40	45	26	25	30
Philosophy and modern languages	61	60	66	17	17	15	28	28	23
Philosophy and theology	129	103	121	29	23	25	22	22	21
Physics and philosophy	108	104	135	12	16	16	11	15	12
Philosophy, politics and economics (PPE)	1,820	1,691	1,651	248	239	240	14	14	15
Theology	93	117	120	31	35	40	33	30	33
Theology and oriental studies	9	3	4	3	2	1	33	66	25
Total Arts	**10,373**	**9,972**	**9,778**	**1,880**	**1,875**	**1,851**	**20.8**	**18.6**	**18.9**

The ranking of colleges in the Tompkins Table (see page 270) is not officially endorsed by Cambridge University, but Oxford University now produces the Norrington Table (page 271). Sanctioned or not, both tables give an indication of where the academic powerhouses lie – information which can be as useful to those trying to avoid them as to those seeking the ultimate

Oxford applications and acceptances by course cont

Sciences	Applications			Acceptances			Acceptances to Applications %		
	2016	2015	2014	2016	2015	2014	2016	2015	2014
Biochemistry	558	511	424	103	98	102	18	19	24
Biological sciences	512	541	424	114	114	103	22	21	24
Biomedical sciences	339	266	229	39	31	36	12	12	16
Chemistry	659	750	684	174	189	187	26	25	27
Computer science	384	335	238	27	30	22	7	9	9
Earth sciences (Geology)	92	110	111	31	31	26	34	28	23
Engineering sciences	890	1,029	922	177	154	159	20	15	17
Experimental psychology	251	257	238	49	51	46	20	20	19
Human science	177	254	178	28	27	25	16	11	14
Materials science (including MEM)	155	145	118	35	32	33	23	22	28
Mathematics	1,333	1,145	1,015	189	176	178	14	15	18
Mathematics and computer science	226	199	153	28	29	28	12	10	18
Mathematics and statistics	210	229	143	17	16	13	8	7	9
Medicine	1,675	1,375	1,433	154	146	152	9	11	11
Physics	1,124	1,064	1,113	186	184	176	17	17	16
Psychology and philosophy (PPL)	186	195	161	30	33	24	16	17	15
Total Sciences	**8,771**	**8,405**	**7,584**	**1,381**	**1,341**	**1,310**	**17.1**	**16.0**	**17.3**
Total Arts and Sciences	**19,144**	**18,377**	**17,362**	**3,261**	**3,216**	**3,161**	**18.9**	**17.5**	**18.2**

challenge. Although there can be a great deal of movement year by year, both tables tend to be dominated by the rich, old foundations. Both tables are compiled from the degree results of final-year undergraduates. A first is worth five points; a 2:1, four; a 2:2, three; a third, one point. The total is divided by the number of candidates to produce each college's average.

In both universities, teaching for most students is based in the colleges. In practice, however, in the sciences this arrangement holds good only for the first year. One-to-one tutorials, which are Oxbridge's traditional strength for undergraduates, are by no means universal. Teaching groups remain much smaller than in most universities, and the tutor remains an inspiration for many students.

The applications procedure

Both universities will have a UCAS deadline of 15 October 2018 (at 6pm) for entry in 2019 or deferred entry in 2020. For Cambridge, you may then take admissions tests at the beginning of November at your school or college, or other authorised centre, while some subjects will continue to administer tests when you attend for interview. The Cambridge website lists the subjects setting the pre-interview assessments, which may include reading comprehension, a problem solving test, or a thinking skills assessment, in addition to a paper on the subject itself. At Oxford, a number of subjects (but not all) also require applicants to take a written test,

Cambridge applications and acceptances by course

Arts, Humanities and Social Sciences	Applications			Acceptances			Acceptances to Applications %		
	2016	2015	2014	2016	2015	2014	2016	2015	2014
Anglo-Saxon, Norse and Celtic	65	59	58	21	20	25	32.3	33.9	43.1
Architecture	360	384	403	44	49	43	12.2	12.8	10.7
Asian and Middle Eastern studies	121	121	114	38	43	49	31.4	35.5	43
Classics	146	136	155	78	74	74	53.4	54.4	47.7
Classics (4 years)	32	45	40	11	15	13	34.4	33.3	32.5
Economics	1,183	1,136	1,105	164	160	152	13.9	14.1	13.8
Education	105	80	113	31	31	35	29.5	38.8	31.0
English	726	714	767	190	197	193	26.2	27.6	25.2
Geography	322	345	314	97	108	101	30.1	31.3	32.2
History	607	625	607	199	197	198	32.8	31.5	32.6
History of art	102	101	87	26	23	26	25.5	22.8	29.9
Human, social and political sciences	1,070	1,012	898	182	208	186	17.0	20.6	20.7
Land economy	248	246	206	56	50	53	22.6	20.3	25.7
Law	1,048	1,015	1,047	217	208	204	20.7	20.5	19.5
Linguistics	113	88	100	38	27	30	33.6	30.7	30.0
Modern and medieval languages	385	387	383	176	173	169	45.7	44.7	44.1
Music	130	151	151	61	63	66	46.9	41.7	43.7
Philosophy	200	203	235	48	46	42	24.0	22.7	17.9
Theology and religious studies	100	87	89	43	41	43	43.0	47.1	48.3
Total Arts, Humanities and Social Sciences	**7,063**	**6,935**	**6,872**	**1,720**	**1,733**	**1,702**	**24.4**	**25.0**	**24.8**

Sciences	2016	2015	2014	2016	2015	2014	2016	2015	2014
Computer science	719	642	583	99	91	101	13.8	14	17.3
Engineering	2,351	2,089	2,161	337	312	326	14.3	14.9	15.1
Mathematics	1,312	1,308	1,336	256	247	236	19.5	18.9	17.7
Medical sciences	1,274	1,300	1,861	269	265	287	21.1	20.4	15.4
Natural sciences	2,943	3,036	3,170	618	652	660	21.0	21.5	20.8
Psychological and behavioural sciences	497	392	422	75	61	66	15.1	16	15.6
Veterinary medicine	228	251	347	60	64	70	26.3	26	20.2
Total Science and Technology	**9,687**	**9,018**	**9,880**	**1,737**	**1,692**	**1,746**	**17.9**	**18.1**	**17.7**
Total	**16,750**	**15,953**	**16,752**	**3,457**	**3,425**	**3,448**	**20.6**	**21.5**	**20.6**

Note: the dates refer to the year in which the acceptances were made.
Mathematics includes mathematics and mathematics with physics. Medical sciences includes medicine but does not include the graduate course in medicine.

either before or at the time of interview. In addition, once Cambridge receives your UCAS form, you will be asked to complete an online Supplementary Application Questionnaire (SAQ) by 22 October in most cases. For international applications to Cambridge, you must also submit a Cambridge Online Preliminary Application (COPA), by 20 September or 15 October, depending on where interviews are held; check the Cambridge website for full details.

You may apply to either Oxford or Cambridge, but not both in the same admissions year, unless you are seeking an Organ award at both universities. Interviews take place in December for those shortlisted (for international applicants, Cambridge holds some interviews overseas while Oxford holds some interviews over the internet, though medicine interviewees must come to Oxford, as must EU interviewees). Applicants will receive either a conditional offer or a rejection early in the new year.

For more information about the application process and preparation for interviews, visit **www.undergraduate.study.cam.ac.uk/** or **www.ox.ac.uk/admissions/undergraduate**.

Oxford College Profiles

Balliol

Oxford OX1 3BJ   01865 277777   www.balliol.ox.ac.uk
Undergraduates: 380   Postgraduates: 311   undergrad.admissions@balliol.ox.ac.uk

Balliol is one of the most academic colleges at the university, and usually falls in the top ten of the Norrington Table. This year it ranked tenth. Famous as the alma mater of many prominent, post-war politicians, Balliol has maintained a strong presence in university life and is usually well represented in the Union and most other societies. The college has an impressive medieval library, which allows students 24-hour access to over 70,000 books and periodicals. Balliol began admitting overseas students in the 19th century and recently students voted unanimously to establish a scholarship for a student with refugee status. The college has cultivated an attractively cosmopolitan atmosphere with a thriving music and drama scene. It is also one of the few colleges to run an annual charity musical. "Bruce's Brunch", organised by the Welfare Officer, brings a steady stream of interesting speakers to Balliol. Undergraduates are offered guaranteed accommodation in college for their first and final years. Graduate students are usually lodged in the Graduate Centre at Holywell Manor, a ten-minute walk from the main site. Hall food is good quality and cheap (around £3 for a meal) and the JCR has its own student-run café, Pantry. The student-run bar, the cheapest in Oxford, now sells its own brew, *BalliAle*. It is known for its well-attended 'Crazy Tuesday' nights with excellent drink deals.

Brasenose

Oxford OX1 4AJ   01865 277510 (admissions)   www.bnc.ox.ac.uk
Undergraduates: 356   Postgraduates: 209   admissions@bnc.ox.ac.uk

Nestled beside the stunning Radcliffe Camera, Brasenose has an advantageous city-centre position. The alma mater of David Cameron, the college was one of the first to admit women in the 1970s, and now has a near-even split. BNC, as the college is often known, has a strong rugby reputation, having won the rugby cuppers 14 times over the years. Overall, however, sport isn't taken too seriously at Brasenose and is usually more about participation. Named after the doorknocker on the 13th-century Brasenose Hall, the college has a pleasant, intimate atmosphere conducive to study and maintained its high place on the Norrington Table this year, moving from eighth to seventh. Law, PPE, medicine and modern history are traditional strengths and the library is open 24 hours – there is also a separate law library. Owing to the college's central location, there is little need for a bike to get around, although Brasenose does offer a free bike rental scheme for those who may need to travel further away. The annexe at Frewin Court, five minutes from the main site, means nearly all undergraduates can live in, and postgraduates are offered accommodation at the St Cross Hollybush Row sites. Wellbeing is taken seriously at Brasenose, with a baking fund and weekly yoga classes.

Christ Church

Oxford OX1 1DP   01865 276196 (admissions)   www.chch.ox.ac.uk
Undergraduates: 433   Postgraduates: 195   admissions@chch.ox.ac.uk

The college, founded by Cardinal Wolsey in 1525, boasts the largest quad in Oxford, complete with an ornamental pond full of Japanese koi carp, donated by the Empress of Japan. Around half of offers tend to be made to state school pupils, which leaves Christ Church with one of the highest proportions of private school students. Christ Church has its own art gallery, hosting a collection of Old Master paintings and drawings. The magnificent 18th-century library is one of the best in Oxford and is supplemented by a separate law library. The river is close by for the aspiring oarsman and the college has two excellent squash courts inside St Aldate's Quad. The sports ground is one of the best in Oxford, and students enjoy free membership of the gym on Iffley. Accommodation, provided for all three years, is rated by college undergraduates as excellent and includes flats off Iffley Road as well as a number of beautifully panelled shared sets (double rooms) in college. A three-course dinner (served daily in the "Hogwarts" hall) costs less than £3, providing exceptional value. The college has a formal approach to dining, with informal and formal sittings taking place every night, and twice-termly Guest Dinners. The chapel is also the cathedral of the Diocese of Oxford – England's smallest medieval cathedral. The constant stream of tourists is mildly disruptive to collegiate life, although college porters regularly check for student cards before allowing entry into the grounds.

Corpus Christi

Oxford OX1 4JF   01865 276693 (admissions)   www.ccc.ox.ac.uk
Undergraduates: 249   Postgraduates: 91   admissions.office@ccc.ox.ac.uk

Corpus is one of Oxford's smallest colleges, making it a tight-knit support network. It is naturally overshadowed by its gigantic neighbour, Christ Church, but makes the most of its intimate, friendly atmosphere and exquisite beauty. Although the college has only around 350 students including postgraduates, it has an admirable 24-hour library. Academic expectations are high and English, Classics, PPE and Medicine are especially well established. Corpus can offer accommodation to all its undergraduates, one of its many attractions to those seeking a smaller community in Oxford. Because of the college's small size, sports teams usually pair up with other colleges. First-years recently moved into the newly refurbished Jackson and Hugh Oldham Buildings, and rooms in the off-site Lampl building are modern and en-suite. The college is also one of the most generous with bursaries, giving travel, book and vacation grants at an almost unparalleled level across the university. Scholars are particularly well rewarded. The MBI Al-Jaber Auditorium is a large, modern and pleasant space built into a bastion of the medieval city wall and is used for music and drama, as well as for parties, art exhibitions and film screenings. Corpus's drama club, 'The Owlets', is highly regarded in Oxford. The college hosts an annual charity 'Tortoise Fair' every summer, where around 1500 people come to hear live music and watch the famous tortoise race.

Exeter

Oxford OX1 3DP   01865 279661   www.exeter.ox.ac.uk
Undergraduates: 323   Postgraduates: 180   admissions@exeter.ox.ac.uk

Exeter boasts one of the most spectacular views of the city from its Fellow's Garden, overlooking Radcliffe Square and All Souls' College. Nestled between the High Street and Broad Street, Exeter is located in the heart of town. Most undergraduates are guaranteed three years of college accommodation, although many second-year students currently live out. The rooms are graded in price, but tend to be of good standard. Graduate students are housed off-site on the Exeter House campus. The Cohen Quad, located on Walton Street, opened this year after some delay and provides a further 90 en-suite bedrooms. Exeter students are known to be lively and outspoken, having recently staged a successful campaign to abolish an £840 catering charge on food in halls. Exeter's student-run charity, ExVac, is a big part of the JCR's identity. The college also boasts a number of other societies. The John Ford Society exists to fund dramatic ventures; the Fortescue Society to talk about the law; the PPE Society to bring in high-profile speakers. The annual arts festival, in partnership with neighbours Lincoln and Jesus, brings a week of live music, theatre and poetry to Turl Street during Hilary Term. Exeter is one of the only colleges to have a ball every year, at a very competitive price.

Harris Manchester

Oxford OX1 3TD   01865 271009 (admissions tutor)   www.hmc.ox.ac.uk
Undergraduates: 03   Postgraduates: 159   enquiries@hmc.ox.ac.uk

As the university's only college for mature students (21 or older), Harris Manchester can appear out of step with the rest of the university. Students are proud, however, of its closely-knit college community. Founded in Manchester in 1786 to provide education for non-Anglican students, Harris Manchester finally settled in Oxford in 1889 after spells in both York and London. A full university college since 1996, its central location with fine buildings and grounds in Holywell Street is very convenient for the Bodleian, although the college also has an excellent library. All meals are provided – indeed the college encourages its members to dine regularly in-hall. Its food is among the finest in Oxford and Harris Manchester is one of the only colleges to serve students the same food as academics on the high table. Most members live in, and the Siew-Sngiem Clock tower provides five hotel-worthy rooms. The college has renovated most of its accommodation on the main site and a new student building opened in 2017, providing a further eight en-suite student rooms, a lecture hall, new music practice rooms and a gymnasium.

Hertford

Oxford OX1 3BW   01865 279404 (admissions)   www.hertford.ox.ac.uk
Undergraduates: 397   Postgraduates: 198   admissions@hertford.ox.ac.uk

Though tracing its roots to the 13th century, Hertford is determinedly modern. The college was one of the first colleges to admit women and is popular with state school applicants, thanks to its strong commitment to access. Hertford offers a £1,000 bursary to students from low income families and was the first college to become a living wage employer, further cementing its progressive reputation. The Principal, Will Hutton, a former editor of *The Observer*, has helped foster a dynamic atmosphere since his appointment in 2011. His popular panel discussions draw in large audiences and touch on a range of topical issues. Past events include a discussion on the Leveson inquiry with Hugh Grant. The college can lodge undergraduates for the entire course of their study. All first-years live in the main college site. Second- and third-years live in Abingdon House and Warnock House annex near Folly Bridge. Those who achieve a first in their preliminary examinations are given preference in the housing ballot. Music is very strong at Hertford, with a Jazz Band, Wind Band, Choir and Orchestra. Hertford has a fun reputation, hosting regular parties or bops at the club "Plush". Open mic nights and lunchtime recitals are popular. The quality of food in-hall is mediocre. Instead, some students choose to cycle to Warnock House to feast on the fine meals served up by its much loved chef, Nigel.

Jesus

Oxford OX1 3DW   01865 279721 (admissions)   www.jesus.ox.ac.uk
Undergraduates: 335   Postgraduates: 189   admissions.officer@jesus.ox.ac.uk

Alma mater to T.E. Lawrence and Harold Wilson, Jesus consistently ranks highly for student satisfaction. It is known for being one of the friendliest colleges in the university. Founded at the request of a Welsh churchman in 1571, the college continues to maintain strong links with the country. Welsh students form 15% of the student body and chalk drawings of welsh dragons sit proudly at the entrances to staircases in Second Quad, earning Jesus a reputation for being "the Welsh college." The college's JCR is well equipped with snacks throughout the day. Sporting success has tailed off in recent years but the college has squash courts and extensive playing fields with hockey, cricket, football and rugby pitches, hard grass tennis courts, netball courts, and a sports pavilion. Students can use the university's gym free of charge. The college also has a symphony orchestra shared with St Peter's. Accommodation is almost universally excellent and relatively inexpensive. Self-catering flats in north and east Oxford have enabled every graduate to live in throughout his or her Oxford career. The Ship Street Centre contains 33 en-suite rooms for first-year students and a lecture theatre. The college offers a number of generous bursaries and grants, including a book grant and a vacation grant, enabling students to study in Oxford outside of term time.

Keble

Oxford OX1 3PG   01865 272711 (admissions)   www.keble.ox.ac.uk
Undergraduates: 425   Postgraduates: 246   college.office@keble.ox.ac.uk

Keble is one of Oxford's most distinct colleges, built of brick in unmistakably extravagant Victorian Gothic style. With 425 undergraduates, it is one of the biggest colleges in Oxford, and with guaranteed college accommodation for most undergraduates for three years, its vibrant community spirit provides Keble students with a coveted social life. Graduates are currently housed in the Acland site on Banbury Road, a two-minute walk from the main college. Thanks to a £25 million grant, the largest donation in Keble's history, the new H B Allen Centre will house 230 graduate students – more than double the current capacity – from October 2018. The site will also boast a 120-seat lecture theatre and an exhibition space. The college's sporting record remains exemplary, with rugby and rowing traditional strengths. On the river, both the men's and women's crews performed strongly in division one this year. The college also has thriving music and drama societies, which make use of the modern O'Reilly Theatre, and hosts a successful Arts Week every Hilary term. The college hall, where students wishing to dine must wear gowns six nights a week, is one of the most impressive in the university. The annual Keble Ball is one of the most popular and best value black tie events in Oxford. Keble is usually ranked around the middle of the Norrington Table, this year coming in 12th.

Lady Margaret Hall

Oxford OX2 6QA   01865 274310 (admissions)   www.lmh.ox.ac.uk
Undergraduates: 391   Postgraduates: 201   admissions@lmh.ox.ac.uk

Lady Margaret Hall, Oxford's first college for women, has been co-educational since 1978 and now enjoys an equal gender balance. For many students, LMH's comparative isolation – the college is three quarters of a mile north of the city centre – is a real advantage, providing welcome refuge from tourists. For others it means a long journey to central facilities. The college's beautiful gardens back onto the Cherwell River, allowing LMH to have its own punt house and tennis courts. The college has a 24-hour library, with particularly strong collections in the arts and humanities and individual study booths prized among finalists seeking solitary working conditions. Accommodation is guaranteed for first-, second- and third-year students since the opening of the Pipe Partridge Building, which also houses a new JCR, dining hall and lecture theatre. The Clore Graduate Centre and Donald Fothergill building, opened in 2016, provides just over 40 en-suite study bedrooms for graduate students. Sporting successes include victory in athletics cuppers and blades on the river for the women's firsts. The JCR welfare team is very active and offers a subsidised mindfulness course. There is a wide range of social events at the college, including an annual gender equality week.

Lincoln

Oxford OX1 3DR   01865 279836 (admissions)   www.lincoln.ox.ac.uk
Undergraduates: 293   Postgraduates: 304   admissions@lincoln.ox.ac.uk

Lincoln's 15th-century buildings and beautiful library – a converted Queen Anne church – combine to produce a delightful environment in which to spend three years. The college's relaxed atmosphere is justly celebrated and city-centre accommodation is provided by the college for all undergraduates throughout their careers. Lincoln is known for the best dining hall food in Oxford, and its popular Deep Hall bar. Graduate students are housed a few minutes' walk away in Bear Lane, at the EPA Science Centre close to the university science area and at a new site on Little Clarendon Street. Lincoln has one of the largest number of scholarships available for graduate students and rewards undergraduates who perform well in examinations. However, the college plummeted 11 places in the Norrington table this year from 19th to 30th (last) place. The recently refurbished Garden Building is a stylish addition to the college, providing much-needed space for music practice, dining and teaching. In particular, Oakeshott room is a popular venue for screenings and performances and hosted many of the shows in this year's Turl Street Arts Festival. The college JCR is highly proactive. Among several recent initiatives is the JCR Art Scheme, in which the JCR purchases artworks for its collection, loaning the pieces to students who wish to hang them in their rooms.

Magdalen

Oxford OX1 4AU   01865 276063 (admissions)   www.magd.ox.ac.uk
Undergraduates: 402   Postgraduates: 177   admissions@magd.ox.ac.uk

Perhaps the most beautiful Oxbridge college, Magdalen is known around the world for its tower, its deer park and its May morning celebrations. C. S. Lewis is said to have dreamt up Narnia whilst on a walk around the awe-inspiring grounds. In recent years, the college has worked hard to shake off its public school image, with a large intake from overseas and one of the highest proportions of state school pupils. Undergraduates tend to be studious and ferociously competitive. The college consistently performs strongly in the Norrington Table, though it slipped from the top spot to third place this year, and has won University Challenge a record four times over the years. In 2016, the Longwall library at Magdalen re-opened after a £10.5 million refurbishment, providing three times the number of reader spaces. First-year students are accommodated in the Waynflete Building and all undergraduates can be housed in college for the full length of their course. Rents are not cheap compared to other colleges but the college has agreed to freeze rents for next year. Over 25% of students receive some type of financial support during their studies, ranging from travel grants to funding for creative projects. The college has had a lot of sporting success on the river in recent years and offers students free punting in the summer. Drama is strong in the college, and the well-regarded Magdalen Players host a production in the gardens every summer.

Mansfield

Oxford OX1 3TF   01865 270920 (admissions)   www.mansfield.ox.ac.uk
Undergraduates: 231   Postgraduates: 158   admissions@mansfield.ox.ac.uk

Formally becoming an Oxford College in 1995, Mansfield's attractive site is fairly central, close to the English faculty and social science library. Its proximity to University Parks facilitates collegiate sporting enthusiasm, most notably for croquet and Quidditch. Taking just over 70 undergraduate students per year, the community is close-knit and the atmosphere relaxed. Mansfield has a strong representation of state school students and over 10% of its students are BME. First- and third-year students live in college accommodation, either on site or in an annex in east Oxford. First-year postgraduates are also housed by the college in off-site accommodation. The college boasts four libraries, which are open 24 hours, and the JCR and Crypt Cafe are popular for socialising and casual study, as is the sun terrace during the summer months. The university's new Centre for Islamic Studies is situated next to the college. The recently completed Hands building provides additional accommodation, a new lecture building and a home for Oxford's Institute of Human Rights.

Merton

Oxford OX1 4JD   01865 286316 (admissions)   www.merton.ox.ac.uk
Undergraduates: 291   Postgraduates: 244   admissions@admin.merton.ox.ac.uk

Founded in 1264 by Walter de Merton, Bishop of Rochester and Chancellor of England, Merton is one of Oxford's oldest and most prestigious colleges. It has an enduring reputation for academic excellence reflected in its position usually at or near the top of the Norrington Table. After a surprise fall to 27th place two years ago, it is now in second place, after New. The medieval library is the envy of other colleges. Accommodation is some of the cheapest in the university, of good standard and offered for all three years. Merton's food is well priced and among the best in the university; formal hall is served six times a week. The college provides generous support to students, having awarded over £120,000 to students last academic year. Merton's many diversions include the Merton Floats, its dramatic society, the Bodley Club for literary speakers, and an excellent Christmas Ball every three years. Following the establishment of its choral foundation, both its choir and the organ have an ever-growing reputation. The college recently established a scheme inviting local school girls to form a choir at the college, enabling them to participate in Merton's musical tradition.

New College

Oxford OX1 3BN   01865 279512 (admissions)   www.new.ox.ac.uk

Undergraduates: 426   Postgraduates: 277   admissions@new.ox.ac.uk

New College is extremely academic, topping the Norrington Table this year. In spite of its name, the college is extremely old (founded in 1379 by William of Wykeham), large and much more relaxed than most expect behind its daunting facade. It is a bustling place, as proud of its excellent music and its bar as of its academic prestige. Musical students flourish here thanks to the choir, orchestra and chamber groups. There is a band room and a new music building on Mansfield Road is currently under construction. Traditionally poor at attracting state school students, the college has been making particular efforts to change this. It recently established a new bursary for students from the lowest income backgrounds, amounting to £4,500 a year. All first-, second- and fourth-year students can live in college and almost all of the third-years can, at a squeeze. Ninety per cent of the rooms at New College are en-suite. The college is hoping to add much needed off-site accommodation. New College boasts an enchanting common room and the college gardens are a memorable sight, especially the other-worldly mound in the heart of the college. The grounds provide the perfect setting for the Commemoration Ball, held every three years – a highlight of Oxford's social calendar. The college also hosts an annual boat party in London, which is popular with students from across the university. Students also benefit from summer access to the college chalet (shared with Balliol and University) near Mont Blanc. The college is currently building a philanthropy tower, above the height of Carfax Tower, which will overlook neighbouring Mansfield College.

Oriel

Oxford OX1 4EW   01865 276522 (admissions)   www.oriel.ox.ac.uk

Undergraduates: 324   Postgraduates: 179   admissions@oriel.ox.ac.uk

Oriel is a friendly, centrally-located college. Unlike its neighbour Christ Church, which is inundated with tourists, the college successfully keeps a low profile. Behind this, however, are some impressive achievements. The college is traditionally described as having "a strong crew spirit", reflecting its traditions on the river; the Oriel men's crew retained their position as Head of the River in 2016, for the third year in a row. The 2017 race had to be cancelled. Academically, the college celebrated its best ever performance this year, with just under half of its finalists achieving firsts. Oriel has a strong sporting reputation and facilities include a boathouse, impressive sports ground, squash courts and multiple gyms. Meal and rent costs are some of the lowest in Oxford. Accommodation is variable, but is available for the duration of an undergraduate course and extensive (mainly graduate) accommodation is provided one mile away off the popular Cowley Road. Several flats have recently been completed at a former industrial site on Rectory Road, providing some limited facilities for couples. The annual Summer Garden Party is a highlight of Trinity term.

Pembroke

Oxford OX1 1DW   01865 276412 (admissions)   www.pmb.ox.ac.uk

Undergraduates: 365   Postgraduates: 242   admissions@pmb.ox.ac.uk

Tucked away off St Aldate's, Pembroke is a welcoming and inclusive community with an improving state school intake. It is known as the 'pink college', with The Pink Panther as its official mascot. The college is historically impoverished but the JCR is among the wealthiest, thanks to the savvy purchase of a Francis Bacon painting for £150 in 1953. It was subsequently sold in 1997 for £400,000.

The college, formerly among the weakest academically, languishing at the bottom of the Norrington table for two years in a row, is now in third place. History is a traditionally strong subject, with several students winning university-wide prizes over the years. Pembroke is able to accommodate all undergraduates after a new quad was opened in April 2013, and the Sir Geoffrey Arthur Building on the river, ten minutes' walk away, offers excellent facilities; in addition to 100 student rooms there is a concert room, computer room and a multi-gym. The JCR successfully secured a rent decrease last year but college food is among the most expensive in Oxford and students must pre-pay for a minimum of six dinners a week. Rowing is strong, with Pembroke men and women traditionally performing well on the river and several going on to represent the university crews. They are often Cuppers finalists in men's and women's football.

Queen's

Oxford OX1 4AW   01865 279161   www.queens.ox.ac.uk
Undergraduates: 339   Postgraduates: 165   admissions@queens.ox.ac.uk

With its beautiful neoclassical dome and bell-tower, Queen's is one of the most striking sights of the High Street. Despite this, it is one of Oxford's least dynamic colleges. Its academic record is average and the college sank five places to last place this year. All students are offered accommodation. Unlike most other colleges, Queen's houses first-years away from the main site, in modernist annexes in east Oxford. The college has converted a large number of these rooms into en-suite facilities. Finalists are housed in the main college site, closer to the college and university libraries. Postgraduates are accommodated in St Aldate's House, a modern building close to the town centre. Queen's can be insular and is largely apolitical, but has a strong college enthusiasm for sport. The two refurbished squash courts are said to be the best in Oxford and the college is one of the few to have its own gym. Queen's also provides a generous grant for those participating in university-level sport, alongside its book and travel grants. The beer cellar is one of the most popular in the university and the JCR facilities are also better than average; the daily JCR afternoon tea is a must.

St Anne's

Oxford OX2 6HS   01865 274840 (admissions)   www.st-annes.ox.ac.uk
Undergraduates: 428   Postgraduates: 341   enquiries@st-annes.ox.ac.uk

Architecturally uninspiring, St Anne's makes up in community spirit what it lacks in awesome grandeur. The dining hall, with its sky-light and absence of portraits, is underwhelming but the food is some of the best in Oxford thanks to "Chef of the Year," Ray Killick. The new library and academic centre, on Woodstock Road, is an impressive sight and with 2000 books added to its shelves every year, library facilities are among the best across the colleges. The college coffee shop, STACS, is quaint and a hit with students wanting to take a break from their studies. The college has recently had a strong presence in the university journalism scene, and its rugby team tends to do well in the inter-college league. St Anne's is situated in North Oxford, ten minutes from the city centre. Accommodation is guaranteed to undergraduates for three years, and the college also operates an equalisation scheme, giving grants to students wishing to live out. The college JCR recently passed a motion for mandatory donation to homelessness charities in the students' fees. Graduates are housed in an 82-room hall of residence in Summertown, a five-minute cycle ride away. St Anne's students benefit from exclusive access to a number of internships organised by the college. St Anne's is not known for its academic excellence within Oxford, usually placing near the bottom of the Norrington Table.

St Catherine's

Oxford OX1 3UJ   01865 271703 (admissions)   www.stcatz.ox.ac.uk
Undergraduates: 497   Postgraduates: 409   admissions@stcatz.ox.ac.uk

St Catherine's strikes an immediate chord with those seeking to avoid the grandiosity of some other colleges. Arne Jacobsen's modernist design for "Catz", one of Oxford's youngest and largest undergraduate colleges, has attracted much attention as the most striking contrast to the lofty spires of Magdalen and New College. The student body describes itself as "Oxford without the stereotypes." Close to the law, English and social science faculties, the university science area and the pleasantly rural Holywell Great Meadow, St Catherine's is a lot nearer to the city centre than it feels. The Wolfson library is open until midnight. Rooms are small but tend to be warmer than in other, more venerable, colleges, and are now available on site for first-, second- and third-year students. Catz has the largest bar in Oxford and their "bops" are always very popular. There is an excellent theatre, as well as an on-site punt house, gym and squash courts. Like many of the larger colleges, sporting success is high – the women's football team topped the league this year. The JCR recently created a new constitution and has agreed to fly the rainbow flag during LGBTQ month. Six portraits of female college members have been commissioned and are due to be hung in the library's (currently all male) collection. The college hosts the Cameron Mackintosh Chair of Contemporary Theatre, whose incumbents have included Arthur Miller, Meera Syal and Sir Ian McKellen. With almost 500 undergraduate students this year, St Catherine's has the highest undergraduate population in Oxford.

St Edmund Hall

Oxford OX1 4AR   01865 279009 (admissions)   www.seh.ox.ac.uk
Undergraduates: 409   Postgraduates: 294   admissions@seh.ox.ac.uk

St Edmund Hall – "Teddy Hall" – has one of Oxford's smallest college sites but one of its most populous. The college offers students the chance to live in its medieval quads right in the heart of the city. Despite a near equal male/female ratio, the college still has an enduring image as a home for "hearties". The sporting culture is vigorous, with both the men's and women's teams securing victory in this year's rugby cuppers. Teddy Hall has a generous sporting fund for students who play at university level as well as four annual prizes for journalism. The college recently established a discussion group allowing students to talk freely about a range of topical issues and has created posts for a disabilities officer and black and minority ethnic officer. Academically, Teddy Hall tends to yo-yo between the middle and the bottom of the Norrington Table. This year, it came in 24th place out of 30 colleges. College accommodation is reasonable and can be offered for three years, either on the main site or in three annexes. The college also owns a house adjacent to the existing Norham Gardens site. The food is more expensive than most colleges but the quality is very high.

St Hilda's

Oxford OX4 1DY   01865 286620 (admissions)   www.st-hildas.ox.ac.uk
Undergraduates: 400   Postgraduates: 154   college.office@st-hildas.ox.ac.uk

October 2008 marked a milestone for St Hilda's and the university as a whole, as the college welcomed its first mixed-sex intake. Although the college, founded in 1893, lasted more than 100 years as an all-female institution, the governing body voted in 2006 to admit men. There are now equal numbers of males and females. The college prides itself on its commitment to fostering an inclusive and laid-back atmosphere, introducing the post of 'Class Liberation Officer' to support working class students. The college has long languished at the lower end of the Norrington Table, placing 28th this year. Like the other originally female colleges, St Hilda's boasts an impressive library, which is particularly well stocked for English. The college has beautiful riverside gardens, allowing students to go punting from the college site, and is close to the lively social scene in multi-ethnic Cowley Road, east Oxford. The college has a purpose-built music building and a recording studio and the drama society puts on termly plays in the theatre. Accommodation is guaranteed to first years and finalists, and the common room and student-run bar have been renovated and enlarged. Many of the rooms offer some of the best river views in Oxford, with the city's spires as a backdrop. St Hilda's commitment to music is particularly strong and its facilities world class.

St Hugh's

Oxford OX2 6LE   01865 274910 (admissions)   www.st-hughs.ox.ac.uk
Undergraduates: 432   Postgraduates: 336   admissions@st-hughs.ox.ac.uk

St Hugh's, alma mater of current Prime Minister Theresa May, is well liked for its pleasantly bohemian atmosphere and splendid grounds. It was criticised by students in 1986 when it began admitting men, but there is now an equal male/female ratio and it has a large student body. St Hugh's is a bicycle ride from the city centre. It is an ideal college for those seeking a place to live and study away from the madding crowd, and its gardens provide the perfect backdrop for the college's springtime outdoor cinema, launched last year. Despite having one of the biggest and best college libraries, open 24 hours, academic pressure remains comparatively low. St Hugh's guarantees on-site accommodation to undergraduates for the duration of their degree, although the standard of rooms is variable. The quality of food is high and meals are subsidised. The college also boasts an on-site café and kitchen facilities are among the best in Oxford. The Dickson Poon Building, a recently constructed China Centre, provides an additional place to work and socialise. As the college enjoys extensive grounds compared to most colleges, there is space for a croquet lawn and tennis courts. Elish Angiolini, former Lord Advocate of Scotland, has been a well-liked Principal of the college since 2012.

St John's

Oxford OX1 3JP   01865 277317 (admissions)   www.sjc.ox.ac.uk
Undergraduates: 386   Postgraduates: 215   admissions@sjc.ox.ac.uk

St John's is one of Oxford's powerhouses, excelling in almost every field and boasting arguably the most beautiful gardens in the university. Founded in 1555 by a London merchant, it is Oxford's wealthiest college, and makes the most of its resources by providing guaranteed college accommodation at a subsidised rate for all its undergraduates in addition to generous annual book grants and prizes. The college recently voted to provide £400 for the purchase of items that 'aid gender expression'. Academic standards are high, with English, chemistry and history among the traditional strengths. All students benefit from the impressive library and work has begun on a new study centre and library extension, allowing for double the number of reader seats. The college is usually challenging for the top spot of the Norrington Table, this year securing sixth place. St John's has a strong sporting tradition with a particular strength in women's rowing. As befits such an all-round strong college, entry is fiercely competitive.

St Peter's

Oxford OX1 2DL   01865 278863 (admissions)   www.spc.ox.ac.uk
Undergraduates: 350   Postgraduates: 198   admissions@spc.ox.ac.uk

Opened as St Peter's Hall in 1929, St Peter's has been an Oxford college since 1961. Its medieval, Georgian and 19th-century buildings are in the city centre and close to most of Oxford's main facilities. Though still young, St Peter's is well represented in university life and has pockets of academic excellence, despite being towards the bottom of the Norrington Table, this year coming second-to-last. History tutoring is particularly good and the college Master, Mark Damazar, former controller of BBC Radio 4, regularly invites high-profile speakers to the college. Nick Robinson and David Mitchell are among recent examples. Accommodation is offered to students in their first and third years, varying from traditional rooms in college to new, purpose-built rooms a few minutes' walk away. The college's facilities are impressive, including a recently upgraded JCR and a popular student bar, one of the few that are entirely student run. They host popular open mic nights every two weeks, along with documentary and film showings, art trips and shows. Linton Quad and the chapel have also undergone recent refurbishment. The college has a proud sporting heritage, being particularly strong at rugby and rowing. Thanks to a partnership with Laura Ashley, a generous bursary scheme will be available for the next five years.

Somerville

Oxford OX2 6HD   01865 270619 (admissions)   www.some.ox.ac.uk
Undergraduates: 400   Postgraduates: 184   secretariat@some.ox.ac.uk

Named after the astronomer Mary Somerville (1780–1872), one of the most celebrated scientific writers of her day, Somerville was one of the first two colleges at Oxford founded to admit women. Members of the college celebrated the news that the pioneering academic would become the first woman, other than a royal, to grace a British bank note. Since 1994, Somerville has admitted men and women equally, while retaining its pioneering and inclusive ethos. Alma mater to Margaret Thatcher, Indira Gandhi and Nobel prize winner Dorothy Hodgkin, Somerville is one of the most international and diverse colleges. Rooms in college are provided for three years to most undergraduates and all first-year postgraduates. There are kitchens in all buildings and subsidised food in-hall. There are a number of clubs from BakeSoc to Boat Club, and there is a new Arts Budget in place to fund various creative projects. Somerville usually ranks towards the bottom of the Norrington Table, this year coming in at 23rd. The library, one of the most beautiful and largest, is 24-hour. Students dominate university journalism and Somerville secured their third President of the Oxford Union in January 2016.

Trinity

Oxford OX1 3BH   01865 279860 (admissions)   www.trinity.ox.ac.uk
Undergraduates: 292   Postgraduates: 147   admissions@trinity.ox.ac.uk

Architecturally impressive and boasting beautiful lawns (which you can actually walk on), Trinity is one of Oxford's least populous colleges. The college admits some 80 undergraduates each year and is among the strongest academically. It usually places in the top 10 of the Norrington Table, this year coming ninth. It is ideally located, beside the Bodleian, Blackwell's bookshop and the White Horse pub, a short stroll from University Parks and the town centre. Whilst members are active in all walks of university life, the college has its own debating and drama societies. The Trinity Players stage at least two productions a year, including one on the signature Trinity lawn which is popular across the university. Facilities are impressive, with a well-stocked college gym and squash courts. Trinity Boat Club and the chapel choir are the largest societies. Journalism is popular at Trinity, and students produce a termly newsletter called 'The Broadsheet'. The 17th-century chapel re-opened last year after a year-long restoration project. Usually, all undergraduates are given a room on the main site in their first and second years, with the majority of third and fourth-years living in a purpose-built block a mile and a half north of the main site. Trinity Students rate the food highly for both its quality and price. Trinity's Commemoration Ball, held once every three years, has one of the biggest budgets in Oxford and is a popular event.

University

Oxford OX1 4BH   01865 276677 (admissions)   www.univ.ox.ac.uk
Undergraduates: 364   Postgraduates: 209   admissions@univ.ox.ac.uk

"Univ," as it is popularly known, is the first Oxford college to be able to boast a former student in the Oval Office. The former President Clinton was a Rhodes Scholar at University in the late 1960s. The college is probably Oxford's oldest – a claim fought over with Merton – and has made a significant effort to shake off its public school image. After a report revealed it to be one of the worst performing colleges for state school intake, University took the unprecedented step of reserving up to ten places each year for students from disadvantaged backgrounds. It adds to a generous bursary scheme, and an access programme that is among the best in Oxford. Academic expectations are high and the college prospers in most subjects. Thanks to a newly refurbished accommodation block, first- and third-year undergraduates are guaranteed a college room. University is particularly well represented on the river, with both men's and women's crews doing well in recent years. The college also has access to a chalet in the foothills of Mont Blanc, with student parties welcome in the summer. The bar has been recently refurbished and has a stylish and relaxed atmosphere. University College usually scores in the top 10 of the Norrington Table, this year ranking eighth.

Wadham

Oxford OX1 3PN   01865 277545 (admissions)   www.wadham.ox.ac.uk
Undergraduates: 462   Postgraduates: 189   admissions@wadh.ox.ac.uk

Wadham is known in about equal measure for its progressive and liberal atmosphere and its leftist politics. The JCR – or student union (SU) as it has rebranded itself – is famously dynamic and politically active, although the breadth of political opinion is greater than its left-wing stereotype suggests. The college is very strong on admitting students from state schools, owing to its successful Student Ambassador Scheme. Its gardens are beautiful and host Shakespearian performances each summer. The college has a good 24-hour library, with a well-stocked Persian history section. Wadham is the only college with no formal hall and accommodation is guaranteed in first year and at least one further year. Fourth years and graduates are offered accommodation in Merifield, the college's modern development of shared flats in Summertown. Wadham is planning to develop a new site on Iffley Road, which will enable the college to house all of its students for the duration of their degrees. Highlights in the social calendar are Queer Week, a riotous celebration of LGBTQ culture, and Wadstock, the college's open-air spring music festival. Student welfare is a big priority at Wadham. The Student Union has four welfare officers, along with a women's officer, an LGBTQIA officer, a people of colour and racial equality officer, a disabled students officer and a trans rep. The women's rowing team have been

Head of the River for three years and the men's 1st VIII are in the top division. The college also contributes to the local community through a new scheme, which delivers food that is not eaten in-hall to a local homeless centre.

Worcester

Oxford OX1 2HB   01865 278391 (admissions)   www.worc.ox.ac.uk
Undergraduates: 420   Postgraduates: 153   admissions@worc.ox.ac.uk

Worcester is to the west of Oxford what Magdalen is to the east: a spacious contrast to the urban rush of the city centre. The college's rather mediocre exterior conceals a delightful environment, including some striking Baroque architecture, extensive gardens and a lake. It is one of Oxford's most beautiful colleges. The college gardeners even post horticultural updates to their own blog and the Buskins dramatic society makes use of the beautiful grounds, with annual summer Shakespeare performances in the gardens. Worcester has a great reputation for sport; it is the only college with its sports grounds on site. Arts Week is an annual highlight and includes a delightful mix of plays, concerts and recitals. Accommodation, guaranteed for three years, is either within the college grounds or less than 300 metres away. The college boasts good quality food, with a Michelin-star chef every Wednesday. College chefs have even created an *Instagram* account to exhibit their fine dishes. Periodic "sustainable halls" feature local produce and the Edible Garden project encourages students to grow their own food in Oxford's only student-run vegetable patch. Like Magdalen and New, it is home to the Commemoration Ball once every three years, a highlight of the Oxford social calendar. Students hold the "Worcester in the Park" event every summer term, with music and Pimms.

Cambridge College Profiles

Christ's

Cambridge CB2 3BU   01223 334900   www.christs.cam.ac.uk

Undergraduates: 438   Postgraduates: 182   admissions@christs.cam.ac.uk

Through a gate on Saint Andrew's Street you will find the tranquility of Christ's College over whose quads have passed the feet of many illustrious alumni including Charles Darwin, John Milton and more recently Sacha Baron Cohen (of *Borat* fame). In front of the college is the bustle of Cambridge's main shopping centre, while behind lies Christ's Pieces with its popular tennis courts and lawns. Students can have rooms close to or in the college itself for all three years of their undergraduate degrees and 40 per cent of rooms are en-suite. Thanks to its proximity to the geography and national sciences faculties, it is strong in these subjects but also has a streak for the arts helped by its enviable Visual Arts Centre, theatre and annually-appointed artist-in-residence. Societies abound from amateur dramatics to one of the university's best-attended student film groups. On the sports front, Christ's is particularly strong on the football pitch and is one of only five Oxbridge colleges to have its own swimming pool, which is thought to be the oldest still in use in the UK. The college is strong academically and came second in the recent Tompkins ratings with over a third of degrees achieving a first. Last year it came third.

Churchill

Cambridge CB3 0DS   01223 336202   www.chu.cam.ac.uk

Undergraduates: 471   Postgraduates: 245   admissions@chu.ac.uk

Churchill is situated to the west of Cambridge city centre; a little way out of town but closest to the West Cambridge Site, which houses many of the University's science departments. It is Cambridge's largest college and though the brutalist architecture may not be to everyone's taste, it houses some of the best on-site facilities of any college: a gym, theatre-come-cinema, music room and recording studio, squash and tennis courts, grass pitches and the largest dining hall in Cambridge. A new court, housing 68 en-suite rooms (reputed to be the plushest undergraduate offerings in town), was completed in 2016, as was a new boathouse. Nearly 40 per cent of the college's rooms are now en-suite. Churchill is one of the least traditional Cambridge colleges: students are welcome to walk on the grass and they don't wear academic gowns when dining formally in-hall. It is also one of the few colleges not to charge a fixed bill for catering in addition to meal charges – a move popular with Churchillians. It has a very diverse student body, with one of Oxbridge's highest state undergraduate intakes (typically 70 per cent of UK entrants), and a relatively large number of postgraduate and overseas students. The college performs well academically (fifth in the most recent Tompkins Table), a success sometimes attributed to what students have called its 'dangerously comfortable' library.

Clare

Cambridge CB2 1TL   01223 761612   www.clare.cam.ac.uk

Undergraduates: 492   Postgraduates: 184   admissions@clare.cam.ac.uk

Clare, with its central location on the Backs and elegant courts and gardens, is popular with applicants. Amongst the oldest colleges in Cambridge, it has a strong reputation for music and a world-renowned choir. The student bar is in Clare Cellars, which often plays host to DJ and live music nights that draw students from across the university. For accommodation, Old Court offers a traditional experience, while Memorial Court, across the river, is close to the University Library and both humanities and science departments. 'The Colony', closer to the boathouse on the slopes of Castle Hill, provides diverse accommodation including flats and converted houses. The college has an enthusiastic boat club with the highest participation rate in Cambridge, and very good sports facilities just beyond the university's botanic garden (a ten-minute cycle ride away). It is particularly known for being musical, however, and has a thriving musical society as well as regular recitals. Clare is evenly balanced in terms of arts and sciences, and at Tripos over a quarter of finalists achieved Firsts last year. The college also has a good gender split – at last count it was almost 50:50 among undergraduates. An arts-heavy list of notable alumni includes David Attenborough and the journalist Matthew Parris.

Corpus

Cambridge CB2 1RH   01223 338056   www.corpus.cam.ac.uk
 Undergraduates: 294   Postgraduates: 161   admissions@corpus.cam.ac.uk

For those who prefer a more intimate atmosphere, consider Corpus. The college is one of Cambridge's smallest with an undergraduate population that hovers just below 300. Steeped in history, it is the only Oxbridge college to have been founded by townspeople (in 1352) and is home to the oldest court in either of the universities, which has been in continuous use since the 14th century. That said, there is plenty that is up-to-date. Accommodation is both in ancient college rooms (beware that walking to the bathroom may mean a quick trip outside) and modern buildings at the college's Leckhampton site just over a mile away where a gym, playing fields and an open-air swimming pool can also be found. Students can be housed for all three years in college accommodation though rooms are allocated on the basis of exam results, which is not always popular. Many in Cambridge know Corpus for its unusual clock, donated by an alumnus in 2008, which sits on the corner of Trumpington Street and is only correct every five minutes. Students pass it on their way to Kwee Court where one of Corpus' two libraries is found as well as the all-important college bar. To expand the sports offering, Corpus joins up with King's and Christ's Colleges to form collaborative 'CCK' sports teams. It also has a small but much-used theatre: the Corpus Playroom.

Downing

Cambridge CB2 1DG   01223 334826   www.dow.cam.ac.uk
 Undergraduates: 453   Postgraduates: 155   admissions@dow.cam.ac.uk

Downing students are rightly proud of the spacious quadrangle around which the college's neoclassical architecture is set. It opens onto a paddock where many a summer garden party livens up exam term. The college was originally founded for the study of law and natural sciences in 1800 and while it is still popular with scientists, lawyers and geographers thanks to its fall-out-of-bed-and-into-lectures proximity to their faculties, it is now home to an eclectic body of students studying all Tripos. Extra-curricular strengths lie on the sports field (Downing is known to be a fearsome opponent on both the rugby field and the river) and in the arts thanks to the Howard Theatre, a 120-seat space opened in 2010, a vibrant Drama Society that hosts a yearly festival of student writing, and the new Heong Gallery dedicated to modern and contemporary art that opened in 2016 with a small but acclaimed show of Ai Weiwei's works. All students, both graduate and undergraduate, can be housed on the college's main site, which helps to foster a solid sense of community. Its most recently built accommodation block was unveiled in 2014 and rooms are generally of a high standard.

Emmanuel

Cambridge CB2 3AP   01223 334290   www.emma.cam.ac.uk
Undergraduates: 516   Postgraduates: 123   admissions@emma.cam.ac.uk

'Emma' as Emmanuel is fondly known, prides itself on an open, friendly atmosphere that is underpinned (though you may not realise it) by a strong academic ethic. It regularly comes in the top ten in the Tompkins Table (sixth in the 2017 ratings) and has fielded a couple of successful years' worth of University Challenge teams. Students love it for its central location, busy and cheap bar, well-subsidised accommodation (which includes a free weekly load of washing in the rent) and the spacious grounds where ducks roam and barbecues are held in summer. Founded by Puritans in the 1580s, it tries to maintain a forward-thinking and egalitarian atmosphere. It has a virtually equal gender split, a female master and two thirds of the current undergraduate intake hails from the state sector. Societies and sports focus more on inclusion than competition with a diverse array of activities to choose from: its most recent sporting success was a win in the inter-college wind-surfing competition. Its understated yet beautiful Christopher Wren chapel hosts a number of concerts organised by the music society and societies also exist for art, mountaineering and even ice cream. As one of the better-endowed colleges, Emmanuel offers a number of bursaries and scholarships and accommodation for all undergraduates, some of which was refurbished last year.

Fitzwilliam

Cambridge CB3 0DG   01223 332030   www.fitz.cam.ac.uk
Undergraduates: 458   Postgraduates: 224   admissions@fitz.cam.ac.uk

Founded in the 19th century to increase access to Cambridge, Fitzwilliam College is proud of its heritage as a college committed to widening participation. It moved to its current location (in the grounds of a Regency estate) in 1963 and while it doesn't have the archetypal ancient architecture, the college gardens are some of the most beautiful and well tended in town. If you climb to the top of its library, designed by award-winning architect Edward Cullinan, you will be standing at the highest point in the city. The atmosphere in college is one of a tight-knit community and students are accommodated throughout their degrees in one of 400 rooms in college or in houses minutes from the main campus. The friendly feel is also helped by the busy café where students and staff alike indulge in the well-reputed homemade cakes. As well as extensive renovations to its Central Building and dining hall, the accommodation of 'Fitz', as the college is fondly known, is also undergoing a facelift. Thus far half the freshers' accommodation has been revamped and now includes large communal areas for socialising. On the academic front, Fitz ranges from mid-Tompkins Table to around 20th place, and it does well on the sports field – recent success includes winning the inter-college cricket two years on the trot – thanks to its well-kept pitches (five minutes from college) and a new gym.

Girton

Cambridge CB3 0JG   01223 338972   www.girton.cam.ac.uk
Undergraduates: 487   Postgraduates: 173   admissions@girton.cam.ac.uk

Girton is as far out to the west of Cambridge as Homerton is to the east, but for some the distance out of town is a good reason to apply there. Its grounds, which include lawns, orchards, sports pitches and courts, majestic brick buildings and an indoor swimming pool, amount to some 50 acres. Girton students either live on this tranquil campus in rooms that range from atmospheric Victorian bedrooms to modern en-suites, or at Swirles Court on the university's new North West Cambridge Development at Eddington. This court, which opened in September 2017, has 325 exclusively en-suite rooms though it is currently only for graduates. Founded as a women's college in 1869, it was the first college to go co-educational and now has an equal gender balance that at time of going to press was slightly weighted in favour of men. Being out of town fosters a familial feel and many at Girton would argue that they are Girtonian first and Cambridge students second. Academically, Girton tends towards the bottom of the ratings but this may be mostly to do with its vibrant extra-curricular scene. It is known for the arts and has its own museum, dark room for photography and permanent 'Peoples' Portraits' exhibition.

Gonville & Caius

Cambridge CB2 1TA   01223 332413   www.cai.cam.ac.uk

Undergraduates: 579   Postgraduates: 172   admissions@cai.cam.ac.uk

Hard to believe that Gonville & Caius (pronounced 'keys') is steps away from Cambridge's main thoroughfare and market place. It is one of the university's oldest colleges, having been founded as Gonville Hall in 1348, and is a haven of ancient courts and old world traditions. Students wear distinctive blue gowns for formal hall each week night (though often with jeans or sports kit underneath), and pass through symbolic gates in college on matriculation and graduation. Freshers sometimes question the need to pay for a minimum number of dinners in hall every term (it is the only college to do this) but by graduation many appreciate what regular communal eating does for Caius' familial feel. On other fronts, Caius is relatively forward looking. The £13-million Stephen Hawking Building offers well-kept, modern, en-suite accommodation (it's named in honour of the physicist who celebrates 53 years as a Fellow at the college this year and is often seen at High Table), as does Harvey Court, which was renovated in 2011. A brand new boathouse and gym has been welcomed by rowers and the college holds imaginative events for potential applicants such as its pioneering 'Women in Economics' day. New academic prizes for sixth formers were launched in 2017, no doubt with an eye to keeping up an impressive line-up of alumni: the College now boasts no fewer than 14 Nobel Laureates. It sits solidly in the upper half of the Tompkins table (11th this year), and for those keen on study, the college library is a treat. It used to be the university library and is set under the arched roof of the Cockerell Building just outside the college.

Homerton

Cambridge CB2 8PH   01223 747252   www.homerton.cam.ac.uk

Undergraduates: 557   Postgraduates: 326   admissions@homerton.cam.ac.uk

Homerton celebrates the 250th anniversary of its foundation in the London district of Homerton next year, yet it is the newest Cambridge College as well as the largest. That is because it only moved to Cambridge in 1894 and formally became a college in 2010. The College has 1,200 students – half undergraduates and half graduates – who live on a large, landscaped site in southeast Cambridge. Close to the railway station (convenient for some) it is a 15-minute cycle ride from town. The benefit is space. Accommodation is offered to students in all years with largely en-suite study bedrooms of a high standard. The College also has tennis courts, a gym, a squash court and a football pitch (with plans to soon have brand new sports facilities close by). There is also an orchard and extensive lawns that can be walked on – Homerton students are quick to talk of the college's friendly and unstuffy atmosphere. It still holds a feeling of history in its striking neo-Gothic Great Hall, built in 1889, which is used for daily student meals and for candlelit formal dinners. That said, this is set to be updated with a £7m project for a new, more capacious dining hall announced this year. It has a near 50:50 gender split and hosts all courses except veterinary medicine and architecture. It is particularly known for being home to the largest number of students studying the education Tripos in line with its history as a teaching training college. The arts abound and honorary fellows include Dame Carol Ann Duffy, Sir Andrew Motion and Dame Evelyn Glennie.

Hughes Hall

Cambridge CB1 2EW   01223 334897   www.hughes.cam.ac.uk
Undergraduates: 118   Postgraduates: 389   admissions@hughes.cam.ac.uk

Hop off the train and walk down Cambridge's vibrant Mill Road, and tucked-away you will find Hughes Hall. Founded in 1885, Hughes Hall is the oldest graduate college in the University of Cambridge and today welcomes applications for postgraduate courses and from undergraduates over 21 in all subjects. Two thirds of the students come from outside the UK with over 80 nationalities represented at the college, and the college has particular flair for sciences, law and business. Although just around the corner from a busy high street, the College has a peaceful setting around the University's cricket ground, with the two terraces above the dining hall providing a great view. This is also one of many reasons that the college boasts a strong record on the sports pitch and on the river. It had eight Blues rowers in 2016, one of whom rowed in the Rio Olympics. Accommodation is provided to all single undergraduates and affiliated students and, 85 new en-suite rooms were built in 2016 along with a bike store and study rooms in the new Gresham Court building.

Jesus

Cambridge CB5 8BL   01223 339455   www.jesus.cam.ac.uk
Undergraduates: 531   Postgraduates: 232   undergraduate-admissions@jesus.cam.ac.uk

Jesus is the envy of many a Cantabrigian for its spacious grounds near both the river and the centre of town. Its red brick buildings are iconic and many date to Jesus' founding in the 1500s. Its chapel is believed to be the oldest university building in Cambridge. Not all is old though. The college has just opened a development at West Court with new student common rooms, games room, café and James Bond-esque bar and terrace. It also has on-site football, rugby and cricket pitches as well as three squash courts and five tennis courts. As one of the biggest colleges (around 500 undergraduates and 400 postgraduates at last count), it is home to an eclectic student population that is as strong on the sports field as it is in music and art. Despite the size, all undergraduates are happily accommodated for all years of their degrees. The much-loved grounds are often punctuated by modern sculpture exhibitions (the college's collection contains work by the likes of Anthony Gormley and John Bellany) and students are allowed to roam on most of the grass – popular in summer. Also in summer is the hotly touted May Ball, which is known for its party-hard atmosphere. Despite all that is going on, students still find time for their degrees and Jesus regularly features in the top half of the Tompkins Table, coming 14th in 2017.

King's

Cambridge CB2 1ST   01223 331255   www.kings.cam.ac.uk
Undergraduates: 411   Postgraduates: 179   undergraduate-admissions@kings.cam.ac.uk

King's is the Cambridge of TV programmes and postcards. The iconic chapel (home to the famous Christmas Carol service that is broadcast on TV on Christmas Eve) and elegant facades back onto the River Cam, giving King's an enviable location that is ideal for both arts and science students – and popular with tourists. Despite its appearance and the fact that it was originally founded in 1441 as a college for boys from Eton, King's is proudly the most anti-establishment of the colleges. It hosts an 'affair' rather than a May Ball that is highly popular and always has a left-field theme, has done away with the Fellows' 'High Table' in the dining hall and hangs a hammer and sickle flag in its bar – though its presence there is hotly debated each year. A high state school intake (85 per cent of its offers were made to maintained sector students in the last application cycle) is aided by the college actively seeking out those from disadvantaged backgrounds. Accommodation ranges from the archetypally Cambridge (think mullioned windows overlooking the river) to en-suite rooms in newer hostels. It has climbed up the Tompkins Table this year coming eighth and two of its alumni, Zadie Smith and Fiona Mozley, were on the Man Booker shortlist. On the sports field, it joins up to some success with Corpus Christi and Christ's.

Lucy Cavendish

Cambridge CB3 0BU   01223 330280   www.lucy-cav.cam.ac.uk
Undergraduates: 126   Postgraduates: 139   admissions@lucy-cav.cam.ac.uk

Unlike any other Oxbridge college, Lucy Cavendish ('Lucy' to its members) takes only female students over the age of 21. This encourages a slightly more staid and studious atmosphere than other colleges but one that is highly supportive. Academic performance is rising fast; this year the college moved up eight places in the Tompkins Table to 18th – a record for a mature college. Founded in 1965 by female academics who believed that opportunities for women at the university were too restricted, Lucy holds strong to its founding remit. The eighth College President is political journalist and broadcaster Jackie Ashley, and guest speakers invited to the college last year included Dame Margaret Hodge, Dr Lorna Williamson OBE, novelists Nicci Gerrard and Sean French and the French Ambassador, Sylvie Berman. Accommodation is provided for all students either in college or in nearby houses, close to those of St Edmund Hall and Fitzwilliam making for easy intermingling with these other 'hill' colleges. The active students' union arranges frequent Formal Hall swaps and bops. The college has a growing reputation for sport, and is represented on many of the university's first teams, including two consecutive captains of the Blues female rugby team, two players on the Blues football team and three rowers in the Boat Club. Internally sport is also strong, and the Lucy Cavendish Boat Club persuades a third of the student community to give rowing a try at some point. The college is also known for its Fiction Prize, which has helped to launch the publishing career of many successful authors including Gail Honeyman and Laura Marshall.

Magdalene

Cambridge CB3 0AG   01223 332135   www.magd.cam.ac.uk
Undergraduates: 395   Postgraduates: 120   admissions@magd.cam.ac.uk

Magdalene rejoices in the longest river frontage of any Cambridge college and is renowned for its ancient and beautiful grounds. Students are often found revising on 'The Beach' during the summer exam term. It is one of the smaller colleges but this means that students tend to know each other and despite a reputation for being more traditional than some – it famously hosts one of the university's few white-tie balls every two years – it has a 50:50 gender balance and one of the cheapest formal halls in Cambridge. It also owns its own punts, which are a popular fixture in the summer term. The college's sports pitches are shared with St John's (both colleges have a sporty reputation) and it has its own Eton Fives court on site. Accommodation varies and is found across the college or in 21 houses and hostels nearby. Unlike many colleges, students are mixed together which helps inter-year socialising. The college's most famous alumnus, Samuel Pepys, is immortalised in its famous Pepys Building that houses a collection of 3,000 of the diarist's books preserved on their original shelves. Magdalene tends toward the middle of the Tompkins ratings and came 16th in the last list. Its renowned studious Master, former Archbishop of Canterbury Rowan Williams who arrived in 2013, has done much to raise the profile of the college's academic side and in March 2017 the college announced a big fundraising campaign in aid of more undergraduate bursaries, a new library and art gallery, and renovation of the Pepys Building.

Murray Edwards

Cambridge CB3 0DF   01223 762229   www.murrayedwards.cam.ac.uk
Undergraduates: 374   Postgraduates: 124   admissions@murrayedwards.cam.ac.uk

One of Cambridge's three colleges for women, Murray Edwards is possibly the most gregarious of them. It is an informal, relaxed college whose students spend as much time mingling with students from other colleges in town as taking advantage of their calm and spacious campus at the top of Castle Hill. It hosts a renowned garden party during May Week to which tickets sell fast and the Saturday brunch, served up in 'The Dome' dining hall is legendary – it has been voted best in Cambridge. Unsurprisingly for an all-female college it does much to promote women in the workplace, most notably running a programme on academic, leadership and career development called Gateway that runs once a week during term. It also has a strong population of women in STEM subjects and a high state school intake – around 70 per cent at last count. Its laid-back atmosphere extends to the gardens where students can grow herbs and vegetables as well as, unusually for a Cambridge college, walk on the grass. Sport is strong and everything from climbing to hockey is catered for. The college often provides Blues players to the university teams. Murray Edwards is also home to the second largest collection of women's art in the world, which is displayed around the college, and includes work by Barbara Hepworth, Tracey Emin and Paula Rego.

St Catharine's

Cambridge CB2 1RL   01223 338319   www.caths.cam.ac.uk
Undergraduates: 480   Postgraduates: 156   undergraduate.admissions@caths.cam.ac.uk

Despite its unusual open court frontage 'Catz', as St Catharine's is fondly known, is one of the least assuming of the colleges strung along Cambridge's famous King's Parade. It is one of the mid-sized colleges (around 500 undergraduates) and has not one but two college libraries thanks to the remit for learning instilled by its original benefactor, Robert Woodlark. Catz students live on site in first year before moving out to the popular St Chad's complex in second year, where accommodation is split into flats with octagonal bedrooms. Other recent improvements include the McGrath Centre, which houses an auditorium, junior common room and bar, and a refurbished boathouse and hockey pitch (the only collegiate Astroturf pitch in Cambridge). St Catharine's came 19th in the Tompkins Table in 2017 and its students are enthusiastic on the extra-curricular front. It fields strong rowing and hockey teams, and in the tradition of one of its most illustrious alumnus, Sir Peter Hall, The Shirley Society (the college's drama group) is a popular troupe.

Newnham

Cambridge CB3 9DF   01223 335783   www.newn.cam.ac.uk
Undergraduates: 374   Postgraduates: 170   admissions@newn.cam.ac.uk

Newnham was the first college established for women to attend lectures at Cambridge in 1871 (though it was another 77 years before they were admitted as full members of the university) and it prides itself on academic excellence and creating a supportive atmosphere for women to achieve their potential. Seminars in conjunction with organisations such as Women of the Year are common. Alumni include Germaine Greer (who is still a fellow at the college), Sylvia Plath, Mary Beard and Emma Thompson. This year Newnham came 23rd in the Tompkins Table though this still meant that a fifth of students achieved a first. For arts students it is ideally located for the Sidgwick Site and for those who like to socialise, Newnham often joins up with nearby Selwyn for socials, formals and for its choir (Newnham has no chapel). The grounds of the college are much loved by Newnhamites and stretch to 18-acres of space that includes sports pitches, tennis courts and an on-site arts centre known as 'The Old Labs'. Extensive work to build 90 en-suite rooms for students as well as a new Porters' Lodge, gym, café and rooms for conferences and supervisions reached the halfway stage last year and is expected to open in September 2018. It will be named after Cambridge's first ever female professor: Dorothy Garrod.

Pembroke

Cambridge CB2 1RF   01223 338154   www.pem.cam.ac.uk
Undergraduates: 473   Postgraduates: 173   adm@pem.cam.ac.uk

Duck your head through the gate of Pembroke College at the corner of Pembroke and Trumpington Streets and you'll find yourself in an historic oasis. Given its position, Pembroke is surprisingly large and is home to extensive gardens and a Christopher Wren chapel. Though most famous for its poets, including Ted Hughes and Edmund Spenser, Pembroke has been excelling in the sciences of late, hosting panels with business leaders and a cohort of its engineers has just won a national competition. Loyal Pembroke students love the college for the cheap rents (reports are that for some rooms the rents do reflect the quality somewhat), a lively café and facilities that include an on-site gym and Europe's oldest bowling green. While performing well academically – in 2017 Pembroke came fourth position in the Tompkins Table, down from second the year before – there is a strong extra-curricular ethos too. There are dozens of clubs and societies, including the Pembroke College Music Society, the Stokes Scientific Society, Pembroke Politics and the drama group the Pembroke Players, who regularly take productions to the Edinburgh Festival. In sport, the College is currently strong in football, hockey and rowing. The women's football team are the current champions. It is well endowed (hence the cheap rents) and in 2015 the college received what is thought to be the largest bequest ever given to a Cambridge college.

Peterhouse

Cambridge CB2 1RD   01223 338223   www.pet.cam.ac.uk
Undergraduates: 259   Postgraduates: 119   admissions@pet.cam.ac.uk

It may be Cambridge's most diminutive college – hovering around 260 undergraduates in recent years – but Peterhouse's influence belies its size and it boasts five Nobel Prize winners. It is also Cambridge's oldest college and it remains home to some quirky traditions and a famously old-world formal hall. That said, it is modern in outlook with a good gender balance and welcomed its first female master in 2016. Just under two thirds of the most recent intake are from state schools. It is also one of the richer colleges and has a roster of travel grants and academic awards available and accommodation standards are high. Students are housed either on site or not more than five minutes away for all years of their degree. Rooms are allocated on a points-based system that accounts both for academic progress and extra-curricular achievements. Though it doesn't have its own sports ground, Peterhouse does have its own squash court and a recently built gym. It also has some of Cambridge's wilder outdoor spaces known as 'The Deer Park' (no deer but many students roaming in summer). Peterhouse is well located for both the science and arts faculties and is particularly strong in the arts. It has two libraries, the Perne and the Ward, which provide plenty of quiet learning space away from the busier atmospheres of students' faculty libraries.

Queens'

Cambridge CB3 9ET   01223 335540   www.queens.cam.ac.uk
Undergraduates: 543   Postgraduates: 293   admissions@queens.cam.ac.uk

Queens' (make sure you get the apostrophe in the right place in comparison to its Oxford counterpart) is a bustling college that has a central location spanning both sides of the River Cam with the Mathematical Bridge attributed to Sir Isaac Newton joining the two. It is the third biggest of the colleges in population terms and, especially in the new courts, has a more outgoing feel than some of its calmer counterparts. Drama is popular thanks to the active BATS dramatic society and sport is strong – in the past year it has provided a number of players to Blues teams and has sports clubs covering everything from chess to water polo. It also has a well-attended biennial May Ball that has welcomed renowned bands including Kaiser Chiefs and Bastille. An eclectic mix of architecture that spans in date from the college's founding in 1448 right through to the present day allows space on site for all undergraduates to be housed for the three years of their degree and the accommodation in the Dokett building has just been reopened with en-suite facilities. Queens' is particularly strong in the sciences (thanks to a roster of bursaries and awards available in those subjects) and performs well at Tripos coming seventh in this year's Tompkins.

Robinson

Cambridge CB3 9AN   01223 339143   www.robinson.cam.ac.uk
Undergraduates: 409   Postgraduates: 125   apply@robinson.cam.ac.uk

Though occasionally ribbed for the austere redbrick architecture, Robinson students are a loyal lot and the college has made a virtue of its appearance: The Red Brick Café is envied by many other colleges' students and Brickhouse, the student theatre company makes good use of its outdoor space. The (also red brick) chapel is renowned for its fantastic acoustic and organ. It may not be the most architecturally beautiful college, but it does have a rolling programme of refurbishment that has resulted in very good facilities even if rents are not as well subsidised as some. However, there is a big focus on the quality of food and 'The Garden Restaurant' (the college's canteen) is renowned as one of the best in Cambridge. The college tends to rest in the second half of the Tompkins Table (it was 25th this year, but has been as high as 3rd) and this year nearly two thirds of the offers it made were to state school applicants. For those who want to focus on academe it is conveniently situated just behind the University Library and minutes away from the arts faculties on the Sidgwick Site and the Maths, Physics and Materials Science buildings. For those who like sport, Robinson often wields strong football, netball and rugby teams. The sports grounds are shared with Queens', Selwyn and King's College and are less than a mile from the main college site.

Selwyn

Cambridge CB3 9DG   01223 335896   www.sel.cam.ac.uk

Undergraduates: 415   Postgraduates: 102   admissions@sel.cam.ac.uk

Selwyn sits on the other side of the River Cam from the city centre and enjoys a roomy location just behind the Sidgwick Site, which makes the lecture commute an easy two-minute walk for arts and humanities students. The only gripe about its location is that it's a ten-minute or so walk to the nearest cash point and supermarket. It was among the first colleges to admit women and has a typically even gender balance – there were 62 men and 61 women in the most recent undergraduate intake. Selwyn also has one of the largest contingents of state-maintained undergraduates in the university (a roughly 70:30 ratio). All the students are accommodated for all years of their degrees in what is likely to be, thanks to an extensive refurbishment programme, an en-suite room. Academically Selwyn comes in the middle of the university's rankings – though it climbed seven places to ninth this year – but music is strong and the college choir's recent recording was a Classic FM album of the week. On the sports front, long-standing clubs known as the Hermes and Sirens fund grants for various teams and the college started the most recent May Bumps by christening a new rowing boat. The Master of Selwyn also has a dog famous both in college and out, which has featured in the QI quiz book and on BBC News.

Sidney Sussex

Cambridge CB2 3HU   01223 338872   www.sid.cam.ac.uk

Undergraduates: 373   Postgraduates: 145   admissions@sid.cam.ac.uk

Sidney Sussex, which was founded in 1596, is located, happily for students, just opposite the entrance to the city centre's main supermarket. This is not the only plus point of its central situation, however, as it is a short cycle ride in one direction to the river, a two-minute walk to the main student theatre, the ADC, and a five-minute walk to the natural science faculties. It is one of the smaller colleges in terms of population and has just celebrated 40 years of admitting women. Thanks to its size and city centre location, many students are housed off-site in one of 11 nearby hostels though there are some atmospheric rooms to be had in the college's main buildings. One of the hostels was renovated in 2016 to provide 22 new student rooms and two large kitchens. The college is a musical one with an award-winning chapel and a recently inaugurated organ. Also in the chapel, more bizarrely, is buried Oliver Cromwell's head (he was among the college's first students). The college bar is a hub for students thanks to its affordability and rowdy 'bops'. Food is also well reviewed and the college chefs scooped numerous awards in the 2017 university-wide culinary competition. Sports teams are more enthusiastic than wildly competitive and grounds are shared with Christ's, a ten-minute cycle ride away.

St Edmund's

Cambridge CB3 0BN   01223 336086   www.st-edmunds.cam.ac.uk

Undergraduates: 111   Postgraduates: 278   admissions@st-edmunds.cam.ac.uk

Having just celebrated its 50th year as a graduate college, St Edmund's (called 'Eddies' by its members) enjoys a reputation as one of Cambridge's most international colleges with a student body that, though male-heavy on the gender front, hails from as many as 85 different countries. It is also renowned for providing numerous sportsmen and women to the university's Blues teams and, this year, a team of four rowers who broke the world record for the longest continual row. St Edmund's location up on the 'hill' near Fitzwilliam and Murray Edwards gives the college a buzzing atmosphere and it is known as one of the most social of the graduate colleges. Work is still done and last year, Eddies enjoyed its best exam term record yet. Accommodation and food are on the expensive side as St Edmund's doesn't enjoy the big endowments of some of the larger colleges but there are a good variety of rooms on offer from en-suites in the recently built Brian Heap building to maisonettes a short walk from college that are available to couples and small families. Planning permission has just been granted for an extensive redevelopment of communal areas. St Edmund's is unique among Cambridge colleges for having a Catholic chapel and also takes a relaxed approach to traditions. There is no Fellow's high table in hall for example.

St Johns

Cambridge CB2 1TP   01223 338703   www.joh.cam.ac.uk
Undergraduates: 619   Postgraduates: 186   admissions@joh.cam.ac.uk

St John's and Trinity enjoy a friendly rivalry, which sparks from them both being large, rich and architecturally beautiful colleges as well as next-door neighbours. St John's is home to Cambridge's famous Bridge of Sighs and a stunning chapel whose tower is the highest building in town. Thanks to a large undergraduate body (around 600 students) St John's is a diverse place, though it is particularly renowned for its prowess on the sports field. The 'Red Boys' team is the dominant force in inter-college rugby – they have won the league for a third year in a row – and 'Maggie', as the college boat club is familiarly known, fielded the most successful men's boat in the May 'Bumps' competition. The size of St John's endowments means that it can support a wide range of activities from launching its own record label in aid of the strong music scene in college (The Gentlemen of St John's singers tour worldwide) to two new financial initiatives which aim to help those who would previously have relied on the Government's maintenance grant. For the academically ambitious, first class results are also awarded with grants from £400 to £600. Accommodation standards are high and the food in the buttery is regularly delicious and well subsidised. St John's also hosts a May Week Ball that is known as one of the most fabulous. On the night, punts fill the river near the college to watch the legendary fireworks display.

Trinity Hall

Cambridge CB2 1TJ   01223 332535   www.trinhall.cam.ac.uk
Undergraduates: 386   Postgraduates: 144   admissions@trinhall.cam.ac.uk

'Tit Hall', as Cambridge's fifth oldest college is known, is tucked behind its more grandiose neighbours, Trinity and Clare, allowing it to enjoy a less tourist-heavy river frontage. That's not to say it's not picturesque and its small size allows its 380 or so undergraduates to get to know each other quickly. It is also ideally located for a wander into town as well as short cycle rides to the Sidgwick Site for the arts faculties and the University Library. Thanks to its endowments Tit Hall is one of the richer colleges, which means that accommodation is cheap and facilities are good. A new block with double en-suite rooms called 'WYNG Gardens' opened last year and the 90 rooms at the Wychfield Site (a ten-minute walk from the main college) have recently been refurbished. The college is both sporty and musical. The chapel choir's most recent recording received gilded reviews and it has an award-winning organ scholar. It slipped to 15th in the most recent Tompkins Table (still a solid performance) and the modern Jerwood Library is a much-loved study space for students. Among those who have studied at Trinity Hall are eminent scientists Stephen Hawking and David Thouless as well as the Olympic medal-winning cyclist Emma Pooley.

Trinity

Cambridge CB2 1TQ   01223 338422   www.trin.cam.ac.uk

Undergraduates: 731   Postgraduates: 241   admissions@trin.cam.ac.uk

The largest of all Oxbridge colleges, Trinity was established in 1546 and occupies extensive grounds that span the River Cam. Particularly famous is the Wren Library, which contains everything from Shakespeare's First Folio to the earliest manuscript of Winnie-the-Pooh. Like its neighbour St John's, Trinity is incredibly well endowed (in fact it is the wealthiest of all the colleges), which allows it to provide high quality and cheap accommodation as well as lots of bursaries to its undergraduate population. The Tudor-Gothic buildings of New Court have been renovated to provide 169 student rooms and nearly half the college's accommodation is en-suite. Since 1997 Trinity has not come below eighth in the Tompkins Table and has topped it for the past seven years but there is much else besides work. A two-storey gym and netball, football, rugby and cricket pitches minutes from the main gate, mean that sports are easy to enjoy (hockey pitches, badminton, tennis and squash courts are also available) and the college punts are a popular choice on summer afternoons. The chapel is home to an active choir who recently completed a tour of Australia and Hong Kong. In 2014 the JCR was refurbished and now has a 65-inch TV with Sky Sports and Netflix. It's a wonder work gets done but students say that the college takes on a studious atmosphere in exam term. Trinity has recently expanded its access and outreach programmes and while some say it is too big and the tourists too many, others revel in the choice this allows.

Wolfson

Cambridge CB3 9BB   01223 335918   www.wolfson.cam.ac.uk

Undergraduates: 171   Postgraduates: 332   ugadministrator@wolfson.cam.ac.uk

Established as University College in 1965, Wolfson took its current name from a generous grant from the Wolfson Foundation just eight years after it was founded. It is first and foremost a college for graduate students but also welcomes 150 or so mature undergraduates each year. All are guaranteed three years of accommodation. The community is varied with students from over 80 countries and aged from 21 to 60 (the average is 25). It's a forward-thinking place with famously little distinction between fellows and students in rank (there is no 'high table' in hall for example) and a President rather than a Master. The current President is the eminent scientist Professor Jane Clarke. The 1970s buildings are not the town's most beautiful but the gardens are an oasis of calm and it is close to the River Cam's picturesque banks. It is also not far from the Sidgwick Site and the University Library though the city centre is about a 20-minute walk. On site the college has one of the university's best gyms as well as a basketball-cum-tennis court. In celebration of the college's 50th anniversary in 2015, Wolfson managed to raise £7 million in donations. Students are seeing the benefit in grants and modernisation of the college.

14 University Profiles

This chapter provides profiles of every university that appears in *The Times and Sunday Time*s league table. In addition there are profiles for the biggest supplier of part-time degrees, the Open University, and also for the two institutions which did not release data for use in the table (University College Birmingham and Wolverhampton). However, we do not have separate profiles for specialist colleges, such as the Royal College of Music (**www.rcm.ac.uk**) or institutions that only offer postgraduate degrees, such as Cranfield University (**www.cranfield.ac.uk**). Their omission is no reflection on their quality, simply a function of their particular roles. A number of additional institutions with degree-awarding powers are listed at the end of the book with their contact details.

The federal University of London (**www.london.ac.uk**) is by far Britain's biggest conventional higher education institution, with more than 120,000 students. The majority study at colleges in the capital, but such is the global prestige of the university's degrees that over 50,000 students in 180 different countries take University of London International Programmes. The university, which celebrated its 175th anniversary in 2011, consists of 18 self-governing colleges, the Institute in Paris and the School of Advanced Study, which comprises ten specialist institutes for research and postgraduate education (details at **www. sas.ac.uk**). City University joined the university in 2016. The university does not have its own entry in this chapter, but the following colleges do: Birkbeck, City, Goldsmiths, King's College London, London School of Economics and Political Science, Queen Mary, Royal Holloway, SOAS and University College London. Contact details for its other constituent colleges are given on page 568.

Guide to the profiles

The profiles contain valuable information about each university. You can find contact details, including postal address, telephone number for admission enquiries, email or web addresses for admissions and prospectus enquiries, web addresses for the university and the students' union, and the dates of forthcoming open days, where available. In addition, each profile provides information under the following headings:

» **The Times and Sunday Times rankings:** For the overall ranking, the figure in bold refers to the university's position in the 2019 *Guide* and the figure in brackets to the previous year. All the information listed below the heading is taken from the main league table. See chapter 1 for explanations and the sources of the data.

» **Undergraduates:** The number of full-time undergraduates is given first followed by part-time undergraduates (in brackets). The figures are for 2015–16, and are the most recent from the Higher Education Statistics Agency (HESA).

» **Postgraduates:** The number of full-time postgraduates is given first followed by part-time postgraduates (in brackets). The figures are for 2015–16, and are the most recent from HESA.

» **Mature students:** The percentage of undergraduate entrants who were 21 or over at the start of their studies in 2016. The figures are from UCAS.

» **International students:** The number of undergraduate overseas students (both EU and non-EU) as a percentage of full-time undergraduates. The figures are for 2015–16, and are from HESA.

» **Applications per place:** The number of applicants per place for 2016, from UCAS.

» **From state-school sector:** The number of young, full-time, first-degree entrants from state schools or colleges in 2015–16 as a percentage of total young entrants. The figures are from HESA.

» **From working-class homes:** The number of young, full-time, first-degree entrants in 2015–16 whose parental occupations are skilled, manual, semi-skilled or unskilled (NS-SEC classes 4–7) as a percentage of total young entrants. The figures are from HESA.

» **Accommodation:** The information was obtained from university accommodation services, and their help is gratefully acknowledged.

Tuition fees

Details of tuition fees for 2018–19 are given wherever possible. At the time of going to press, a number of universities had not published their international fees for 2018–19. In these cases, the fees for 2017–18 are given. Please check university websites to see if they have managed to give updated figures. Fees for 2019–20 will not be published until late summer 2018, although at universities in England, those for UK students have been limited to a maximum of £9,250 by the Government.

While EU students have been guaranteed that UK rather than International fees will apply to them if they start in 2018, no such guarantee has yet been given for students planning to start in 2019. It is of the utmost importance that you check university websites for the latest information.

Every university website gives full details of the financial and other support the university provides to its students, from scholarships and bursaries to study support and hardship funds. Some of the support will be delivered automatically but most will not, and you must study the details on the websites, including methods of applying and deadlines, to get the greatest benefit out of your university. In addition, in England the Office for Fair Access (**www.offa.org.uk**) publishes "Access Agreements" for every English university on its website. Each agreement outlines the university's plans for fees, financial support and measures being taken to widen access to that university and to encourage students to complete their courses.

University of Aberdeen

Less than a year after opening its first overseas campus, in South Korea, Aberdeen has stepped up its international activity with a new venture in Qatar, where it is the first UK university to offer bachelor's degrees. The campus in Doha, opened last October and run in partnership with a local education company, is offering its first degrees in business management and accountancy and finance but is expected to expand into Stem (science, technology, engineering and mathematics) subjects over the next four years. The university is also expanding at home, increasing its intake for the past three years, despite falling applications in 2016.

By 2019, the university will have invested £377m on its Aberdeen campuses. The latest addition is a new building for its nutrition and health research centre, the Rowett Institute, and the students' union has moved to the Hub, which has dining and retail outlets, as well as support services for accommodation and careers advice. Now well established, the futuristic Sir Duncan Rice Library, named after the principal who commissioned it, cost £57m and was chosen as one of the 12 best new buildings in Scotland.

The university is the fifth-oldest in the UK, formed from two ancient institutions, the first established in 1495. The original King's College premises are the focal point of an attractive campus with a cobbled main street and Georgian buildings about a mile from the city centre. Medicine is based at Foresterhill, a 20-minute walk away, where the university shares Europe's largest health campus with NHS Grampian, uniting researchers, scientists, clinicians and patients on one site. Buses link the two campuses with the Hillhead residential complex.

The student body is made up of 120 nationalities, with almost a third from the north of Scotland and one in six from England. Entry standards are in the top 20 in the UK, but lower offers can be made to applicants from schools with generally poor results. There is also a Children's University, which provides a range of accredited activities to encourage primary and secondary school children to get involved in educational and active extracurricular pursuits. Eight out of ten undergraduates are state-educated – rather less than the UK average for the university's course and student profiles – but about 40% are expected to receive some financial support.

New undergraduates are paired with current students, often on the same course, under the Students4Students mentoring scheme, helping them to settle in and get the most from university life. All single honours undergraduate degrees except medicine and dentistry include "enhanced study options"

King's College
Aberdeen AB24 3FX
01224 272090
study@abdn.ac.uk
www.abdn.ac.uk
www.ausa.org.uk

ABERDEEN
Edinburgh
Belfast
London
Cardiff

***The Times and The Sunday Times* Rankings**

Overall Ranking: **40** (last year: =44)

Teaching quality	78.9%	=82
Student experience	79.8%	42
Research quality	29.9%	44
Entry standards	178	15
Graduate prospects	77.6%	48
Good honours	82.6%	21
Expected completion rate	85.8%	65
Student/staff ratio	14.9	43
Services and facilities/student	£2,290	40

designed to broaden their knowledge and ensure intellectual flexibility. Students can incorporate business, computing or a language into their degree, or choose from a range of cross-disciplinary programmes. Assessors have recently praised the "transformative" effect of curriculum reforms, as well as the quality of online learning resources, personal tutoring and employability initiatives.

Given its location, the university is especially strong in disciplines related to the oil and gas industries. At its own underwater research facility, Oceanlab, at Newburgh, to the north, Aberdeen's engineers lead the world in creating systems capable of operating at depths of up to 11,000 metres. The university's expertise extends beyond these industries, however. Three-quarters of the work submitted for the 2014 Research Excellence Framework was rated as world-leading or internationally excellent. The university was placed top in the UK for research in environmental and soil science and in the top three for psychology and English.

Although the winters are long, the climate is warmer than newcomers might expect, and transport links are good. Students find the city lively and welcoming, if expensive: the JobLink service provides a good selection of part-time employment. Aberdeen was ranked as the "safest city in the UK" in 2016 by an international consulting firm which surveyed 230 cities worldwide, ranking them on a range of factors, including crime levels and policing. The region as a whole has been rated as the UK's top environment in which to live and work.

The university's ICT network has more than 1,500 computers for student use. All new undergraduates are guaranteed housing – an important benefit in a city with high rental costs. A £22m Aquatic Centre, with 50-metre pool and 10-metre diving board, opened in 2014, completing the Aberdeen Sports Village, which offers some of the best facilities at any university in the UK, including a full-size indoor football pitch.

Tuition fees

- » Fees for Scottish and EU students 2018–19 £0–£1,820
- » Fees for non-Scottish UK students 2018–19 £9,250
  (capped at £27,750 for 4-year courses and at £37,000 for 5-year courses; Medicine capped at £46,250)
- » Fees for international students 2018–19 £14,600–£18,400
  Medicine £39,000
- » For scholarship and bursary information see
  http://www.abdn.ac.uk/study/undergraduate/finance.php
- » Graduate salary £22,416

Students

Undergraduates	9,400	(560)
Postgraduates	2,620	(1,420)
Applications per place	6.5	
Overall offer rate	84.5%	
International students	26.4%	
Mature students	25.7%	
From state-sector schools	79.8%	
From working-class homes	25%	

Accommodation

University-provided places: 3,204
Percentage catered: 7%
Catered costs: £147+ per week (39 weeks)
Self-catered: £99 – £150 per week (39 weeks)
First year students are guaranteed accommodation
www.abdn.ac.uk/accommodation
studentaccom@abdn.ac.uk

Abertay University

Having reshaped its reduced portfolio of courses, with a tighter focus on its strengths, Abertay has now reviewed the entry requirements for all undergraduate programmes, identifying the minimum entry qualifications, grades and essential subjects needed. The university's contextual admissions policy allows for lower offers for applicants who attend a school where a relatively small proportion of students enter higher education, or have spent significant time in care, live in a deprived area or whose parents did not go to university.

Abertay had already introduced compulsory interdisciplinary courses for all undergraduates and launched Scotland's first accelerated degrees. The seven fast-track degrees include ethical hacking and computer arts, which can be taken in three years rather than the standard four north of the border. The final two years consist of 45 weeks rather than the usual 30. Other subjects available in this format – unique so far in Scotland – include business studies, game design and production management, sports development, and food and consumer science.

Further reforms included quicker feedback on assessed work, with students submitting work electronically and receiving their feedback and marks the same way.

Grading was simplified and students were guaranteed to have lectures and seminars in the same place at the same time every week. The changes were part of a move towards more problem- and work-based approaches to learning, focusing on real-world issues and teamwork, with less time spent in conventional lectures. All courses can be taken part-time, and new programmes aim to offer students the chance to spend at least 30% of their time in industry.

In spite of these measures, applications and enrolments fell in 2016 for the fifth year in a row. Demand for places is strongest in computer arts and games design, for which the university is best known. Undergraduates from England, Wales and Northern Ireland pay £500 more to study these subjects on top of the £8,500 tuition fee for other degrees.

Abertay introduced the UK's first degree in ethical hacking and cyber-security, and remains a leader in the field. Sony chose the university as the site for the largest teaching laboratory in Europe for its PlayStation consoles, and the university hosts the national Centre for Excellence in Computer Games Education. All games students become members of UKIE (UK Interactive Entertainment) and gain access to a bespoke programme of industry mentorship and support.

Still small, with only about 4,000 students, Abertay promises a more personal experience than undergraduates receive

---

Kydd Building
Bell Street
Dundee
DD1 1HG
01382 308 000
sro@abertay.ac.uk
www.abertay.ac.uk
www.abertaysa.com
Check website for
Open Days

The Times and The Sunday Times Rankings

Overall Ranking: **98** (last year: 85)

Teaching quality	80.3%	=64
Student experience	76.5%	=98
Research quality	5.1%	=91
Entry standards	158	=31
Graduate prospects	66.1%	103
Good honours	69.9%	77
Expected completion rate	76.9%	118
Student/staff ratio	19.9	121
Services and facilities/student	£1,842	90

at most universities. Based in the centre of Dundee, all teaching buildings are within a five-minute walk of each other. They are modern and functional, such as the innovative White Space facility, the university's flagship creative learning and working environment, where students study alongside industry professionals who are working on real commercial or broadcast projects.

New laboratories costing £3.5m opened in May, supporting teaching and research in food, forensics and biomedical science. Students were consulted on the design of the labs, which include Scotland's only Consumer Experience Laboratory for use by the university's highly-rated Division of Food and Drink.

A new degree in fitness, nutrition and health has been introduced this year, alongside another in management in the games industry, and two in human resource management. Well-qualified A-level students in all subjects are eligible for direct entry into the second year if they do not opt for an accelerated degree.

The university hosts the Dundee Academy of Sport, launched in partnership with Dundee and Angus College – a venture using sport as a vehicle for learning across the school curriculum and throughout life. There is an exercise studio on campus, which is also open to the public. The city has seen considerable investment recently, including the development of its waterfront, centred on the £80m Victoria & Albert Museum of Design, due to open this year.

The city has a large student population and the cost of living is modest. Abertay was rated the most affordable university in the UK in a study by the website GoCompare, which took account of fees, accommodation, travel and living expenses. A 500-bed student village allows all first-years to be guaranteed a place if they want one, and about 10% of students benefit from financial assistance including bursaries for students from the rest of the UK whose family income is below £34,000.

Tuition fees

» Fees for Scottish and EU students 2018–19   £0–£1,820
» Fees for non-Scottish UK students 2018–19   £8,500–£9,000
» Fees for international students 2018–19   £12,250–£14,250
» For scholarship and bursary information see http://www.abertay.ac.uk/studying/money-fees-funding
» Graduate salary   £20,000

Students		
Undergraduates	3,475	(210)
Postgraduates	175	(140)
Applications per place	5.7	
Overall offer rate	84.5%	
International students	10.2%	
Mature students	36.2%	
From state-sector schools	97.6%	
From working-class homes	33.8%	

Accommodation

University-provided places: 500
Percentage catered: 0%
Self-catered: £60 – £109 per week
First-year students are guaranteed accommodation
www.abertay.ac.uk/student-life/accommodation/

Aberystwyth University

Aberystwyth enjoyed a spectacular rise of 23 places in last year's league table, after an unprecedented turnaround in student satisfaction levels. It jumped more than 90 places on the two measures derived from the National Student Survey, from near the bottom of the table into the top 20. Improvements continued this year with a toughened-up National Student Survey helping Aber win our University of the Year for Teaching Quality award.

In common with many Welsh universities, it did not enter the Teaching Excellence Framework, but it is fifth this year on our teaching measure, as well as comfortably inside the top 50 for research.

The news of Aber's recovery is taking time to filter through to sixth forms, although a 2% decline in 2017 applications is half the UK average. The offer rate of more than 95% is among the highest in the UK, but both applications and enrolments dropped by 40% in the five years to 2016. The university's strategic plan promises further improvements in the student experience. Investment is set to double in student accommodation and in teaching and research facilities. However, the new vice-chancellor, Professor Elizabeth Treasure, is having to find savings totalling more than £11m to stave off a budget deficit.

The university blamed increasing competition for students and a drop in the number of 18-year-olds. A branch campus in Mauritius, which attracted only 40 students in its first year and lost £375,000, remains open and is described as a long-term investment.

A string of new courses have been introduced, including several in robotics, with others in biological sciences, film-making and Spanish and Latin American studies. In addition, 19 three-year science degrees are being offered as four-year programmes, including a year in industry. There is also a range of four-year integrated Master's degrees, which reach postgraduate levels of study without the need to source extra funding. A number of European and international partnerships also provide opportunities for studying abroad – for a semester or for an entire year.

Several new campus developments are planned, including a £40.5m Innovation and Enterprise Campus, financed by the European Regional Development Fund. It will feature a bio-refining centre, future food centre, analytical science laboratories and a seed processing and bio-bank facility. A new Wellbeing and Health Assessment Research Unit is also set to open in Aber's sports science department.

Scores in the 2014 Research Excellence Framework showed improvement, with the best results for the departments of international

---

Penglais
Aberystwyth
SY23 3FL
01970 622021
Ug-admissions@aber.ac.uk
www.aber.ac.uk
www.abersu.co.uk
Visiting Days:
March 3, 10, 24 2018

The Times and The Sunday Times **Rankings**

Overall Ranking: **=47** (last year: 56)

Teaching quality	86.2%	5
Student experience	84.2%	8
Research quality	28.1%	46
Entry standards	116	=105
Graduate prospects	74.3%	62
Good honours	68.5%	89
Expected completion rate	85%	=70
Student/staff ratio	16.4	=75
Services and facilities/student	£1,845	89

politics, geography and earth science, and the Institute of Biological, Environmental and Rural Sciences. The institute, which serves 1,500 undergraduate and research students, is about to begin an £8.8m programme researching resilient crops. Aber has the widest range of land-related courses in the UK and is developing an upland agricultural research centre near the town.

The attractive seaside location remains a draw for applicants, although transport links to the rest of the UK are slow. About a third of the students are from Wales, and Welsh-medium teaching is thriving, with more courses available in the language. Almost 95% of the undergraduates are state-educated – a higher proportion than the mix of subjects would imply. A Student Welcome Centre continues to offer advice on everything from money problems to learning difficulties long after undergraduates have enrolled, helping to produce one of the lowest dropout rates in Wales.

There is self-catering accommodation for more than 3,000 students, with a central hub that includes social and learning facilities. Three university libraries are complemented by the National Library of Wales, which gives free access to students. A new app brings together a range of study-related services on a single screen, allowing students to check what lectures and seminars they have, access their AberLearn virtual learning pages, look at local bus timetables and see what public computers are available.

The university's students' union (AberSU) was named the best in Wales for 2017 and has the largest entertainment venue in the region. Sports facilities are good and well used. The fitness centre has been refurbished, with new cardio and strength and conditioning equipment. There are two sports halls and outdoor facilities include a swimming pool, 400-metre running track, 50 acres of playing fields and specialist facilities for watersports. There are even facilities for students to bring their own horse.

Tuition fees

» Fees for UK/EU students 2018–19   £9,000
» Fees for international students 2018–19   £13,450–£15,000
   Medicine   £39,000
» For scholarship and bursary information see
   www.aber.ac.uk/en/student-finance/
» Graduate salary   £16,000

Students

Undergraduates	6,400	(1,285)
Postgraduates	590	(475)
Applications per place	4.8	
Overall offer rate	98.3%	
International students	12.4%	
Mature students	13.9%	
From state-sector schools	94.8%	
From working-class homes	33.8%	

Accommodation

University-provided places: 3,200
Percentage catered: 4%
Catered costs: £116+ per week
Self-catered: £85 – £127 per week
First year students are guaranteed accommodation
www.aber.ac.uk/en/accommodation

Anglia Ruskin University

Anglia Ruskin plans to open the first medical school in Essex in September 2018. The General Medical Council is yet to allocate places, but construction of a £20m building is already under way on the university's Chelmsford campus. As an avowedly regional institution, ARU hopes that half of the students will be from the east of England.

The development will be prestigious, but the expansion of degree apprenticeships, promised in a new strategy launched on the 25th anniversary of Anglia Ruskin's university status may prove to be more significant in the long run. The university already delivers the Chartered Manager Degree Apprenticeship with Barclays and has others in digital and technology solutions. Courses for nurses, software engineers and chartered surveyors will be available this autumn and "substantial" increases are promised in the coming years.

Further commitments include the integration of high-quality face-to-face and digital teaching and learning into all courses, and a personalised learning experience for students to help them reach their full potential. The university is in our top 40 for student perceptions of teaching quality, but still outside the top 100 overall. It gained a silver award in the new Teaching Excellence Framework, winning praise for its support for students at risk of dropping out and for employers' contributions to the curriculum.

Anglia Ruskin won the 2016 Duke of York Award for University Entrepreneurship, celebrating its work with 2,000 businesses and its work to instil entrepreneurial values in both students and staff. The university has an innovative scheme placing graduates with the region's small firms – usually the companies that are least likely to take on those emerging from higher education.

There are more than 35,000 students on campuses in Chelmsford, Cambridge, Peterborough, the City of London and worldwide. The numbers taking degrees have been steady since the introduction of £9,000 fees, with a big rise in applications from school-leavers in 2016. Nearly all the undergraduates attended state schools or colleges and almost 40% were from the four poorest socio-economic groups at the time of the last survey.

Each undergraduate has an adviser to help compile a degree package looking at the chosen subject from different points of view to maximise future job prospects.

The university has spent £100m on campus improvements in the past five years, adding facilities such as medical science SuperLabs, mock hospital wards, computer gaming suites and paramedic skills labs.

Bishop Hall Lane
Chelmsford CM1 1SQ
01245 493131
www.anglia.ac.uk
www.angliastudent.com
Open Days: June 9 2018
(Cambridge & Chelmsford)
Campus tours at
Chelmsford and
Cambridge every
Wednesday

The Times and The Sunday Times Rankings

Overall Ranking: **113** (last year: 108)

Teaching quality	82.1	=32
Student experience	79.5%	=47
Research quality	5.4%	=89
Entry standards	102	128
Graduate prospects	68.3%	=95
Good honours	69.4%	=83
Expected completion rate	78.9%	=110
Student/staff ratio	17.8	=99
Services and facilities/student	£1,709	102

A £45m science centre is due to open in early 2018 in Cambridge, providing a new base for students and researchers in computing and technology, psychology, forensics, animal biology and biomedical science. It will house a 200-seat bioscience laboratory, a 300-seat lecture theatre and expanded space for post-graduate students.

Anglia Ruskin was the last university to retain a polytechnic title, discarding it only in 2005. It took the name of John Ruskin, who founded the Cambridge School of Art, which evolved into one part of today's institution.

The university has a history of providing innovative courses: the BOptom (Hons) is the only qualification of its kind in the UK and the hearing aid audiology course was among the first to lead directly to registration.

The Global Sustainability Institute is building an international reputation for its research, and Anglia Ruskin is aiming to make sustainability an important part of every student's experience.

The results of the 2014 Research Excellence Framework showed that some world-leading research is undertaken in all five faculties. The best performances were in music, drama and the performing arts, where 40% of the research was found to have "outstanding" impact. Health subjects also did well, alongside media studies, geography and environmental science.

The social scene varies between campuses, all of which are within an hour of London by train.

The university offers a range of sporting facilities, including an on-campus sports centre with a well-equipped gym in Chelmsford. In Cambridge, there is also a gym on campus and work has begun on a £5m redevelopment of its nearby outdoor sports ground to add two new full-size floodlit artificial pitches, including a 3G pitch. There will be a new pavilion with changing rooms, spectator viewing and a warm-up gym plus three grass pitches for football and rugby. In Peterborough, Anglia Ruskin students have access to Vivacity's clubs. There are also leisure centres and a lido.

Tuition fees

- » Fees for UK/EU students 2018–19   £9,250
  Foundation degree   £7,500
- » Fees for international students 2018–19   £12,500–£14,500
- » For scholarship and bursary information see http://www.anglia.ac.uk/student-life/help-with-finances
- » Graduate salaries   £21,500

Students

Undergraduates	14,425	(2,845)
Postgraduates	1,775	(1,890)
Applications per place	6.7	
Overall offer rate	74.8%	
International students	9.8%	
Mature students	35.7%	
From state-sector schools	96.4%	
From working-class homes	38.9%	

Accommodation

University-provided places 2,290
Percentage catered 0%
Self-catered: £92 – £180 per week
First year students offered accommodation on first-come-first-served basis
www.anglia.ac.uk/student-life/accommodation
essexaccom@anglia.ac.uk
cambaccom@anglia.ac.uk

Arts University Bournemouth

Only four in ten applicants receive offers from the Arts University Bournemouth (AUB), making it one of the most selective institutions in the country. But plans for expansion at the university's main campus in Poole will enable it to take more students. The development will produce another 300 residential places, as well as 14,000 square metres of academic buildings and landscaping.

The new project follows £17m of improvements that were completed between 2014 and 2016. They included the opening of the first drawing studio to be built at a UK art school for 100 years. The award-winning design was the first UK building by AUB alumnus and globally renowned architect Professor Sir Peter Cook. The studio's curved design produces a softer light for drawing and was described by RIBA judges as "like a squat Buddha, ethereal and likeable".

The Photography Building, which opened in 2015 with flexible teaching spaces and IT suites, is another highlight. The Gallery showcases work by students and other contemporary artists, hosting talks, events and film nights to support the exhibition programme.

There is also an Enterprise Pavilion on campus to attract and retain new creative businesses in the southwest. The purpose-built library includes the Museum of Design in Plastics, which holds more than 12,000 artefacts of predominantly 20th and 21st-century mass-produced design and popular culture. The items are selected specifically to support the academic courses taught at Arts Bournemouth.

Laser-cutting machinery and a 3D printer feature among the hi-tech equipment available to students at AUB.

One of the big risers in our league table in the past two years, the university won the Sir Misha Black award for innovation in design education in 2016, noted for the Gallery and Drawing Studio. A new degree in drawing is planned for 2018, following the introduction of degree courses in fashion branding and communication, and creative writing.

AUB has operated as a specialist institution since 1885 and is now one of only 15 higher education institutions in the UK devoted solely to the study of art, design and media. It is the highest ranked of the five that appear in our table. There are degrees in acting, architecture, dance, event management and film production, as well as art and design subjects. The university describes its courses as having a "highly practical streak" designed to give students an edge in a competitive, creative world.

The university has a Skillset Media Academy in partnership with Bournemouth University, offering eight accredited courses such as animation and make-up for media

Wallisdown
Poole BH12 5HH
01202 363 225
admissions@aub.ac.uk
https://aub.ac.uk
www.aubsu.co.uk
Open Days 2018:
June 16

The Times and The Sunday Times **Rankings**

Overall Ranking: **51** (last year: 64)

Teaching quality	83.2%	21
Student experience	79%	=59
Research quality	2.4%	118
Entry standards	147	43
Graduate prospects	79.5%	=41
Good honours	65.5%	106
Expected completion rate	88.2%	46
Student/staff ratio	15.1	=44
Services and facilities/student	£1,731	101

and performance. The two institutions also bid successfully to become a Screen Academy, through which Skillset recognises excellence in film and the broader screen-based media. The most recent audit of the university by the Quality Assurance Agency resulted in the highest possible grade, commending the academic standards.

Only 12 staff were entered for the 2014 Research Excellence Framework, when 43% of their work was rated as world-leading or internationally excellent.

Students and staff work together on an innovative programme of professional practice and research, with different disciplines encouraged to collaborate. Many AUB staff have experience or continue to be involved in the creative industries, while the careers service provides students with subject-specific and generic advice. Industry liaison groups and visiting tutors keep the university abreast of developments in creative work and alumni return regularly as lecturers.

A low dropout rate is a point of particular pride for AUB; at just below 6%, it is half the university's benchmark figure. Seven out of ten entrants last year were expected to receive some form of financial assistance. Current support for students includes bicycle vouchers, funding for educational visits and hardship loans.

More than 700 residential places are run by the university or endorsed by it.

There is a register of approved housing at aubstudentpad.co.uk and the university runs accommodation days in July and August for current and prospective students to find potential housemates. Priority for the allocation of university places goes to overseas students and those with disabilities or medical conditions.

AUB has no sports facilities of its own but provides a subsidy for its students to access the extensive facilities and clubs at neighbouring Bournemouth University. The town of Bournemouth has a large and cosmopolitan student population and one of the most vibrant club scenes outside London. The capital is less than two hours away by regular train services.

Tuition fees

- » Fees for UK/EU students 2018-19   £9,250
  Foundation courses   £5,421
- » Fees for international students 2018-19   £16,500
  Foundation courses   £9,000-£12,900
- » For scholarship and bursary information see
  https://aub.ac.uk/plan-visit-apply/fees/
- » Graduate salary   £18,000

Students

Undergraduates	3,130	(20)
Postgraduates	65	(25)
Applications per place	6.1	
Overall offer rate	36.5%	
International students	13.7%	
Mature students	10.6%	
From state-sector schools	97.7%	
From working-class homes	30.4%	

Accommodation

University-provided places: 739
Percentage catered: 0%
Self-catered: £125 – £170 per week
https://aub.ac.uk/plan-visit-apply/accommodation
aubstudentpad.co.uk

University of the Arts London

A new Creative Attributes Framework drawn up in consultation with big employers such as John Lewis, Estée Lauder and Bafta is designed to ensure that all courses at the University of the Arts London (UAL) enable students to develop the qualities they will need to succeed in the creative industries.

The biggest art and design university in Europe, UAL has always been strong on maximising employment prospects in a notoriously uncertain field. Students have access to the largest specialist careers centre in the country for art and design, while the pioneering Emerging Artists Programme supports graduates early in their careers. Hundreds of industry professionals take part in the annual recruitment festival, providing networking opportunities and advice. The new framework adds a systematic approach to the curriculum, stressing enterprise and employability.

The university has also been investing heavily in new facilities in its six colleges. The redevelopment of the Camberwell College of Arts campus is adding new galleries, a refectory, workshops, studios and a new library, as well as a 264-room hall of residence.

A new campus is planned for London College of Fashion at the Olympic Park in Stratford, east London, forming part of the Olympicopolis arts quarter alongside the Victoria & Albert Museum and Sadler's Wells.

Another new campus is being developed for the London College of Communication, near its existing premises at Elephant and Castle, while Central Saint Martins College of Arts and Design already occupies a prizewinning building at King's Cross. The £200m King's Cross development brought Central Saint Martins together on one site for the first time, and its grade II-listed former granary was voted the world's best higher education building of the year.

UAL is among the top six institutions in the world for art and design in the QS world university subject rankings, but is yet to reach such heights either in our institutional or subject tables, which are less reliant on reputation and research strength. Indeed, it remains outside our top 100 overall. The main obstacle has been student satisfaction, which is often relatively low both in specialist art institutions and at universities in London. UAL was bottom of last year's table in the sections of the National Student Survey relating to the broader student experience.

Almost eight out of ten of the 14,000 undergraduates study art and design. They are based at colleges which continue to use their own names and enjoy considerable autonomy. Five of them – Chelsea College of Arts, the London College of Communication, Central

---

UAL 272 High Holborn
London WC1V 7EY
020 7514 6000
www.arts.ac.uk
www.arts-sa.com
For Open Days contact individual colleges

The Times and The Sunday Times **Rankings**

Overall Ranking: **115** (last year: 109)

Teaching quality	76.5	=109
Student experience	71.8%	117
Research quality	8.0%	73
Entry standards	122	=86
Graduate prospects	56.6%	126
Good honours	64.2%	108
Expected completion rate	87%	=53
Student/staff ratio	15.9	=64
Services and facilities/student	£1,644	107

Saint Martins, Camberwell College of Arts and the London College of Fashion – were part of the London Institute before forming a university in 2004. Wimbledon College of Arts joined in 2006, bringing an international reputation in theatre design and the UK's largest school of theatre.

Applications and enrolments dropped slightly in 2016 but the university is still highly selective: only 30% of applicants receive offers.

UAL performed well in the 2014 Research Excellence Framework, when 83% of the work submitted was considered world-leading or internationally excellent. All of it reached one of the top two categories for its external impact.

Perhaps more impressively for prospective applicants, half of the artists shortlisted for the 2017 Turner prize were UAL graduates, as were more than half of the designers at the 2016 London fashion week. Business of Fashion named Central Saint Martins as the best college in the world (and London College of Fashion as eighth best) for undergraduate courses in a ranking based on global impact, learning experience and long-term value.

One example of the close relationship with the creative industries is a five-year investment by fashion giant Kering to develop a joint curriculum in sustainability. All the colleges make good use of visiting lecturers, who keep students abreast of developments in their field. UAL also runs weekend classes and summer schools in an attempt to broaden the intake. One third of the undergraduates come from the four poorest socioeconomic groups, while 94% attended state schools.

The colleges vary considerably in character and facilities, although a single students' union serves them all. UAL's student hub provides a central space for students to work, socialise and share ideas, as well as hosting housing and careers services. The university has 13 residences spread around the colleges. Househunting workshops help those who have to rely on the expensive private housing market. The university owns no sports facilities, although it has arranged student discounts with a number of providers and has 25 sports clubs.

Tuition fees

» Fees for UK/EU students 2018–19	£9,250
Foundation courses from	£5,420
» Fees for international students 2017–18	£17,920
» For scholarship and bursary information see www.arts.ac.uk/study-at-ual/student-fees	
» Graduate salary	£19,000

Students

Undergraduates	14,570	(230)
Postgraduates	2,645	(760)
Applications per place	7.8	
Overall offer rate	25.9%	
International students	43.4%	
Mature students	21.4%	
From state-sector schools	93.6%	
From working-class homes	33.1%	

Accommodation

University-provided places: 3,600
Percentage catered: 0%
Self-catered: £116 – £288 per week
www.arts.ac.uk/accommodation

Aston University

Aston's popularity has soared since the introduction of £9,000 fees. By 2016 applications from school-leavers had grown by 3,000 – or 78% – in four years and enrolments by students of all ages had doubled. The main attractions are a portfolio of job-orientated degrees with work experience as standard, and consistently good graduate prospects.

The university is in the top 25 for student satisfaction with both teaching quality and the wider student experience. The same qualities helped Aston achieve gold in the government's new Teaching Excellence Framework (TEF).

A glowing testimonial from the TEF panel described "outstanding physical and digital resources that are actively and consistently used by students" and "personalised provision with the highest levels of engagement and commitment, including bookable personal tutoring sessions and a substantial number of trained student peer mentors".

The panel was also impressed with the strategic involvement of professional bodies and employers to help to embed employability skills through an integrated placement year, pre-entry masterclasses, the Talent Bank placement matching service and mentoring.

Aston's new medical school will take its first 60 students in 2018. The first cohort will be made up of international applicants and local students from families with no history of university education, who have reached the academic requirements through an access programme.

Aston has teamed up with Keypath Education to expand the range of online degrees, targeting growing markets overseas in countries such as Nigeria.

Last July the first graduates emerged with BSc (honours) in digital and technology solutions from the UK's first degree apprenticeship programme, a partnership between Aston's School of Engineering and Applied Science and Capgemini, a global consulting, technology and outsourcing company.

Aston celebrated its 50th year as a university in 2016, with a newly landscaped campus where the last of the 1970s buildings and facilities have been replaced by modern and spacious student accommodation, open green spaces and the remodelled Chancellor's Lake.

Set in the heart of Birmingham, the university focuses on business, science and technology, languages and social science, concentrating on degrees with professional placements. Seven out of ten students have a work placement, often abroad, and the target is 100% by 2020. Many later secure graduate jobs at their placement company.

Aston Triangle
Birmingham B4 7ET
0121 204 3000
apply@aston.ac.uk
www.aston.ac.uk
www.astonsu.com
Open Days 2018:
July 6

The Times and The Sunday Times Rankings

Overall Ranking: **46** (last year: 33)

Teaching quality	82.8%	25
Student experience	82%	18
Research quality	25.8%	49
Entry standards	137	=53
Graduate prospects	79.7%	38
Good honours	75.8%	47
Expected completion rate	90.5%	37
Student/staff ratio	20.9	=124
Services and facilities/student	£2,132	60

The highly-rated business school accounts for almost half of all of Aston's students and will relocate to a new central position on campus after a £19m revamp.

New degrees have been introduced in mathematics for industry, chemistry with biotechnology, and a range of dual honours programmes with English literature. In 2018, there will be more dual honours degrees with history, international business and Mandarin Chinese, biochemistry, and psychology and marketing.

The university is determined to improve the student experience and boost research performance, with the eventual aim of becoming a top ten university. Aston did well in the latest assessments of research, doubling the proportion of work in the top two categories to 80%. Life and health sciences led the way, with business and management, politics and engineering also producing good results.

New research centres in enterprise, healthy ageing, Europe, and neuroscience and child development proved their worth, and research funding is at record levels.

Aston was also one of a dozen universities to be awarded prestigious Regius professorships to celebrate the Queen's 90th birthday. Aston's is in pharmacy, another of the university's strengths.

The MyAston mobile app, used regularly by 80% of students, gives access to course materials and other information. The completion of the Aston Student Village has provided 3,000 en-suite rooms on campus, maintaining the guarantee of accommodation for all first-year students. A £215m programme of improvements includes an impressive library and the Sir Doug Ellis Woodcock Sport Centre, which features a grade II-listed swimming pool and a sports hall with indoor courts and team sports facilities. Aston's active students' union is set to be rehoused in purpose-built premises in the middle of the campus.

Tuition fees

- » Fees for UK/students 2018–19 £9,250
- » Fees for international students 2017–18 £13,300–£17,200
  2018–19 £14,300–£17,550
  Medicine £37,000
- » For scholarship and bursary information see
  www.aston.ac.uk/study/undergraduate/student-finance/
- » Graduate salary £21,909

Students

Undergraduates	9,165	(885)
Postgraduates	1,305	(1,135)
Applications per place	6.6	
Overall offer rate	84%	
International students	13.5%	
Mature students	5.1%	
From state-sector schools	93.6%	
From working-class homes	42.1%	

Accommodation

University-provided places: 3,000
Percentage catered: 0%
Self-catered: £124 – £139
First year students are guaranteed accommodation
www.aston.ac.uk/accommodation/
accom@aston.ac.uk

Bangor University

Bangor was the only university in Wales to be awarded gold in the new Teaching Excellence Framework (TEF). The panel praised the personalised support for students and strategic approach to assessment, as well as the very good physical and virtual learning resources. Welsh/English bilingual learning was also commended.

The university has always been among the leaders in the National Student Survey (one of the key drivers of the TEF rankings), regularly producing the best results in Wales. It was in the top 12 in the UK in 2016 in the sections relating to teaching quality and just outside the top 20 for the wider student experience.

Bangor has seen improvement in most elements of our table this year, moving up six places overall to more than compensate for a drop in the last edition. It is now in the top ten for student satisfaction with the organisation and management of courses, learning resources, the student voice and the learning community. It still ranks outside the top 100 for good honours and spending on student facilities, but there have been improvements in the completion rate and graduate prospects.

Applications and enrolments were steady in 2016 when 93% of school-leavers applying for a place received an offer – one of the highest proportions in the UK.

But Bangor is now planning to shed a number of academic posts in order to make savings of £8.5m a year in light of a budget deficit. It launched a review in May to determine where the savings should be made and has already closed its fine art degree.

Six new degrees were introduced, however, including Chinese as joint honours. Geography with environmental forestry and four joint law degrees are among courses on the way this year.

Bangor is among the cheapest places to study in the UK, as well as one of the safest. Much of the university estate has been redeveloped or modernised in recent years, and Bangor is in the top 20 in an international league table for its green credentials.

The university has a community focus that dates back to a campaign in the 19th century when local quarrymen put part of their weekly wages towards the establishment of a college. The School of Lifelong Learning continues the tradition with courses across north Wales and the university has built a worldwide reputation in areas such as environmental studies and ocean sciences.

Bangor finished among the top 50 universities in the 2014 Research Excellence Framework, with half of its schools rated

---

College Road
Bangor LL57 2DG
01248 383 717
applicantservices@bangor.ac.uk
www.bangor.ac.uk
www.undebbangor.com
Open Days 2018:
June & July, check website
for exact timing

***The Times and The Sunday Times* Rankings**

Overall Ranking: **55** (last year: 61)

Teaching quality	83.9%	=13
Student experience	83.4%	10
Research quality	27.2%	48
Entry standards	134	=58
Graduate prospects	69.5%	=84
Good honours	66.7%	=99
Expected completion rate	85.4%	68
Student/staff ratio	16.2	71
Services and facilities/student	£1,704	103

in the top 20 in the UK, led by leisure and tourism, languages and psychology.

The Bangor Institute of Health and Medical Research has been awarded more than £1.5m by the Welsh Government over the next two years to test the effectiveness of new healthcare treatments and services, and provide health economics research and policy support to NHS health boards.

Most students come from outside Wales, but about 20% speak Welsh and one of the halls of residence is for Welsh-speakers and those who want to learn the language. A Peer Guiding scheme arranges for second- and third-year students to mentor new arrivals and arrange social activities for them. Bangor also has a flourishing international exchange programme, which gives students the option of studying overseas for one extra year in a wide variety of destinations.

More than 95% of the students come from state schools, many of them from areas of low participation in higher education. The university's Talent Opportunities Programme, which operates in schools across north Wales, targets potential applicants from lower socio-economic groups and from families with little or no history of going to university.

There is a pioneering dyslexia service, which offers individual and group support throughout students' courses. The Study Skills Centre helps with the transition to university and provides continuing academic support. In addition, the Bangor Employability Award accredits co-curricular and extracurricular activities, such as volunteering and part-time work, that are valued by employers.

Bangor has almost 3,000 residential places – enough to guarantee accommodation to new entrants who apply by the end of July. The 600-bed student village has a cafe, shop, laundrette, student lounges, outdoor recreation and games area, a mini cinema and performance and music space. The main sports centre has 50 cardiovascular machines, a six-platform Olympic lifting area, two sports halls, an aerobics studio, cycling studio, gymnastics hall, climbing wall and squash courts.

Social life for most students is focused on the students' union. Its free clubs and societies have been voted the best in the UK for two years in succession.

Tuition fees

- » Fees for UK/U students 2018–19 £9,000
- » Fees for international students 2018–19 £12,750–£14,800
- » For scholarship and bursary information see www.bangor.ac.uk/studentfinance/info/scholarships.php.en
- » Graduate salary £17,800

Students		
Undergraduates	7.600	(640)
Postgraduates	1,405	(980)
Applications per place	4.9	
Overall offer rate	93.1%	
International students	13%	
Mature students	21.3%	
From state-sector schools	95.5%	
From working-class homes	34.9%	

Accommodation

University-provided places: 2,960

Percentage catered: 0%

Self-catered: £88 – £187 per week

First year students are guaranteed accommodation

https://www.bangor.ac.uk/studentlife/accommodation.php.en

University of Bath

Bath celebrated its 50th anniversary with the opening of the £4.5m Virgil building, a city-centre student hub and professional services building. It has a cafe and hosts student support services such as the careers service, students' union and a skills centre where students can get help to improve their writing, mathematics and statistics at drop-in sessions and tutorials.

The university's 200-acre campus is on the edge of Bath, but the new development acknowledges that – particularly beyond the first year – many students base themselves in the city, a world heritage site with a thriving social scene.

New developments for the campus include the Milner Centre for Evolution, a cross-faculty research facility for biology, health and education, opening in the spring. The university is also investing up to £3.5m developing the Sports Training Village gym, more than doubling its current capacity of 105 exercise stations and bringing in top-rate equipment early this year.

Bath, our Sports University of the Year, has outstanding facilities that include a 50-metre Olympic Legacy swimming pool, indoor running track, multipurpose sports hall, eight indoor tennis courts and indoor facilities for athletics, shooting, fencing and judo. There is even a revamped bobsleigh and skeleton start area, as used by Lizzy Yarnold, the 2014 Olympic gold medallist, and her predecessor Amy Williams.

They are among numerous graduates and elite users of the Sports Training Village to win medals at recent Olympic and Commonwealth games. But all students are encouraged to use the university's facilities through clubs for everything from ultimate Frisbee to Latin and ballroom dancing. Bath also pioneered sports scholarships a quarter of a century ago, and there will be a range of them available for 2018.

Bath has an enviable academic reputation – it is seldom far from the top ten in our league table – and employment levels are among the best in the UK, helped by strong links with business and industry. The university expanded rapidly in the early part of this decade, increasing the size of the undergraduate intake by a third in five years. Applications rose even more sharply, increasing the competition for entry to more than seven applications for each place in 2016.

However, the high-profile row over the £451,000 salary of Vice-Chancellor Dame Glynis Breakwell, which eventually resulted in her resignation, is said to have resulted in a decline in demand for 2018.

Most degree courses have a practical element, and assessors have praised the university for the work placements it

---

Claverton Down
Bath BA2 7AY
01225 383 019
Ask-admissions@bath.ac.uk
www.bath.ac.uk
www.thesubath.com
Open Days 2018:
June 22, 23,
September 15
opendays@bath.ac.uk

The Times and The Sunday Times **Rankings**
Overall Ranking: **12** (last year: 12)

Teaching quality	81.4%	45
Student experience	81.5%	24
Research quality	37.3%	24
Entry standards	186	=12
Graduate prospects	85.2%	7
Good honours	85.9%	11
Expected completion rate	94.8%	=10
Student/staff ratio	15.7	60
Services and facilities/student	£2,371	33

offers. Nearly two-thirds of undergraduates undertake a placement, either in the UK or abroad, or have a period of overseas study, as part of their course. Student entrepreneurship is actively encouraged through a number of initiatives and projects. New courses planned for 2018 include a BSc/MSci in health and exercise science, and a BSc in criminology.

Research is thriving: nearly a third of Bath's submission to the 2014 Research Excellence Framework was judged to be world-leading, with 87% in the top two categories. Projects range from developing new drugs to prolong the lives of people with breast cancer, working with Ford to develop fuel-efficient engines, to research into child poverty, which won a Queen's Anniversary prize. The research grants and contracts portfolio is worth more than £130m and there are 25 international strategic partnerships with top-ranked institutions worldwide.

Bath is a highly internationalised university, with more than 30% of students coming from outside the UK, representing more than 100 nationalities. A quarter of the undergraduates come from independent schools.

With 16,000 students, a third of whom are postgraduates, Bath remains relatively small. But it has invested £215m to improve the campus and cater for the extra students it has taken in recent years. The modern campus has pleasant grounds with a grass amphitheatre and lake, as well as conveniently placed amenities.

The Edge is the university's arts, education and events centre with a theatre, performance studio, rehearsal studios, three galleries and a cafe for students and the wider community. It is also home to the School of Management's executive education training suite. Two more academic buildings opened in 2016, one for engineering and design and the other for psychology. There is also a dedicated centre for postgraduates.

The Quads accommodation complex added 700 en-suite bedrooms in 75 flats, bringing the total number of rooms owned or managed by the university to 4,500. The new Polden student residences will add almost 300 more and will be available for those starting courses in 2018.

Students generally like the city, and many take advantage of the nightlife of nearby Bristol, which is only 15 minutes away by public transport. The popular students' union won an award for being one of the best developed and well managed in the UK.

Tuition fees

» Fees for UK/EU students 2018–19 £9,250
   Foundation courses £7,710
» Fees for international students 2018–19 £12,650–£19,800
» For scholarship and bursary information see www.bath.ac.uk/study/ug/fees/
» Graduate salary £25,000

Students

Undergraduates	11,975	(115)
Postgraduates	2,265	(1,800)
Applications per place	7.9	
Overall offer rate	80.4%	
International students	21.8%	
Mature students	2.2%	
From state-sector schools	73.5%	
From working-class homes	18.2%	

Accommodation

University-provided places: 4,545
Percentage catered: 22%
Catered costs: £100 – £210 per week
Self-catered: £70 – £180 per week
First year students are guaranteed accommodation
www.bath.ac.uk/groups/student-accommodation

Bath Spa University

Applications to Bath Spa were down by almost 16% when the official deadline passed for courses beginning last autumn. The university blames a decline in rankings – a drop of 27 places in our table last year has been followed by a 19-place fall this year – as well as national factors such as the falling number of 18-year-olds in the population. The exception is in teacher education, where applications are up by 20% for primary school training courses and 11% for secondary level.

Demand had been buoyant across the board in 2016, when fewer than 5% of places were filled through clearing and enrolments were up for the fourth year in a row. Imaginative branding as a liberal arts university has proved popular with applicants, and Bath Spa was the driving force behind the Global Academy of Liberal Arts (Gala), bringing together a diverse range of liberal arts providers from around the world.

Professor Christina Slade, who is returning to Australia after five years at the helm, repackaged Bath Spa as "the university of creativity, culture and enterprise", promising to develop critical and creative thinking skills, global awareness and digital literacy in graduates.

The academic agenda is not expected to change, but the brief for the new vice-chancellor includes a requirement to "renew the university's commitment to the student experience" – a reference, perhaps, to the sharp fall in student satisfaction that has depressed its score in national rankings. For 2018, the university is promising the option of a professional placement year for all undergraduate programmes. There will be a range of new degrees in subjects as diverse as comedy, creative music technology, furniture and product design, journalism and publishing, and jazz.

Bath Spa has a huge capital project under way, converting a former factory close to the River Avon into a new campus for the Bath School of Art and Design. Construction will start as soon as planning permission is granted for the grade II-listed building. The university has already spent £6m on specialist facilities for the school at the Sion Hill campus, within walking distance of the city centre, where there is a student village of 550 study bedrooms.

The main Newton Park campus is four miles outside the World Heritage city of Bath, in grounds landscaped by Capability Brown in the 18th century, with a handsome Georgian manor house owned by the Duchy of Cornwall as its centrepiece. Historic buildings blend sympathetically with modern facilities, following a £70m development completed in 2014. The Creative Writing Centre is housed in the 14th-century gatehouse, a scheduled ancient monument. There is also

Newton Park,
Newton St Loe,
Bath BA2 9BN
01225 875 875
admissions@bathspa.ac.uk
www.bathspa.ac.uk
www.bathspasu.co.uk
Open Days 2018:
Check website

***The Times and The Sunday Times* Rankings**

Overall Ranking: **94** (last year: 75)

Teaching quality	80%	=68
Student experience	75.8%	106
Research quality	7.9%	=74
Entry standards	120	=91
Graduate prospects	64.0%	110
Good honours	73.2%	59
Expected completion rate	85%	=70
Student/staff ratio	18.7	=111
Services and facilities/student	£1,592	111

a postgraduate centre at Corsham Court, a 16th-century manor house near Chippenham.

Bath Spa's intake is 93% state-educated, and a third were from working-class homes in the last survey. Two-thirds of the students are female, reflecting the arts and social science bias in the curriculum, and a quarter of all students are over 25.

Bath Spa was awarded silver in the government's new Teaching Excellence Framework (TEF). The panel commented on the personalised teaching, the availability of a personal tutor, peer mentoring, and independent study that provide "rigour and stretch" for students. The university's investment in physical and digital resources, supported by a team of learning technologists, "demonstrably enhances student engagement", said the assessors.

All students have the opportunity to collect a Global Citizenship award by completing a module that covers a range of cross-cutting issues with relevance to all subjects in the arts, humanities and sciences. Bath Spa offers a pre-entry year for international undergraduates with language tuition, academic instruction and information on UK history and culture, as well as the opportunity to become involved in community projects. International students now comprise 15% of the university's intake.

Bath Spa became a university only in 2005, but its constituent colleges have history going back 160 years. Alumni include Body Shop founder Anita Roddick and the Turner prizewinning painter and printmaker Sir Howard Hodgkin.

The latest research assessments in 2014 featured its best results yet, when more than half of a relatively small submission was rated as world-leading or internationally excellent, following the appointment of high-profile professors including Fay Weldon in creative writing and Gavin Turk in art and design. The university received an 86% increase in research funding as a result.

Tuition fees

» Fees for EU/UK students 2018–19 £9,250
   Foundation courses £7,950
» Fees for international students 2017–18 £12,500–£14,000
» For scholarship and bursary information see www.bathspa.ac.uk/students/student-finance/scholarships-and-funding
» Graduate salary £17,000

Students

Undergraduates	5,705	(80)
Postgraduates	955	(885)
Applications per place	5.9	
Overall offer rate	85.7%	
International students	8%	
Mature students	13%	
From state-sector schools	93.4%	
From working-class homes	33.1%	

Accommodation

University-provided places 2,262
Percentage catered 0%
Self-catered: £79 – £242 per week
www.bathspa.ac.uk/accom

University of Bedfordshire

Applications to Bedfordshire have dropped by a third and enrolments by more than a quarter in five years, but the university is planning a raft of new courses that may begin to reverse that trend. Eleven new degree courses started last autumn included public relations with a placement, media communications with languages, agricultural science, and quantity surveying and value engineering.

The 15 additions planned for 2018 are mainly in the business and management fields. They range from human resources management with law to communication and reputation management, and international tourism with events management.

Bedfordshire is also investing heavily in upgrading its facilities. A seven-floor library opened on the main campus in Luton in 2016, with 916 study spaces, laptops for loan, 530 PCs and a cafe in the £46m development. A study hub offers advice and guidance on academic and study skills.

The university has also announced plans for a £40m building for science, technology, engineering and mathematics (Stem) subjects on the Luton campus. Opening in September 2019, the new facilities will enable the university to extend its portfolio of science courses to include pharmacy, nutrition, physics, biochemistry, optometry, chemistry, geology and mechanical engineering.

The university has a campus in Bedford and a newer one in Milton Keynes, which has been developed in partnership with the local authority and is expected to have more than 500 students by 2018. The Bedford site is in a leafy setting 20 minutes' walk from the town centre, where there is a 280-seat auditorium and a students' union, as well as accommodation for 600 students.

The education and sport faculty, based in Bedford, has about 2,500 students, making it the UK's largest provider of physical education teacher training, as well as a national centre for other subjects at primary and secondary level. Another 1,000 students take subjects such as performing arts, law and business management.

However, the bulk of Bedfordshire's 14,400 students are on the university's town-centre site in Luton, where the campus has teaching and exhibition space, as well as the students' union and a careers and employment centre.

There is also a £40m student halls complex and a well-equipped media arts centre. The Putteridge Bury campus, a neo-Elizabethan mansion on the outskirts of Luton, doubles as a management centre and conference venue, while nursing and midwifery students in the growing Faculty of Health and Social Sciences are based at the Butterfield Park campus near Luton, or at the Oxford House development

University Square
Luton LU1 3JU
0300 330 0073
admissions@beds.ac.uk
www.beds.ac.uk
www.bedssu.co.uk
Open Days 2018: Luton & Bedford, April 21, 25, July 4. Bedford, June 18, 19. Aylesbury, April 28. Milton Keynes, May 2

The Times and The Sunday Times **Rankings**

Overall Ranking: **108** (last year: 121)

Teaching quality	80.1%	67
Student experience	78.9%	=62
Research quality	7%	=78
Entry standards	97	129
Graduate prospects	68.6%	94
Good honours	65.8%	=104
Expected completion rate	75.3%	122
Student/staff ratio	16.9	87
Services and facilities/student	£2,201	50

in Aylesbury, Buckinghamshire. Placements are available at a wide range of hospitals, including Stoke Mandeville, Wycombe General, Luton and Dunstable and Bedford.

Bedfordshire has been praised for its successes in widening participation, not only in enrolling students from groups that are underrepresented in higher education, but also in helping them to achieve good results. Almost all the undergraduates are state-educated and half come from the four lowest socio-economic classes.

About a third of undergraduates are aged at least 21 on entry and nearly one in five students comes from outside the EU, many taking postgraduate courses. This year's entrants from the UK, and EU undergraduates, will receive a welcome package of £450 to spend on books or university services, including £50 a year towards printing costs.

The university has enjoyed recent success in research, more than doubling the number of academics it entered for the 2014 Research Excellence Framework. It was rewarded with one of the biggest increases in funding for research at any university. Almost half of the work submitted for assessment was placed in the top two categories, with the best results for social work and social policy, health subjects and English. The university was awarded the Queen's Anniversary prize in 2014 for applied research on child exploitation, which influenced current safeguarding policy and practice.

Vocational courses include a growing portfolio of two-year foundation degrees, ranging from software development to media production and sport science, which are designed to lead on to honours degrees. Most are taught at partner colleges across the region.

Foundation years are available at a reduced fee of £6,200, with bursaries of £500 also on offer to those starting foundation year programmes. The dropout rate had been improving, but the latest projection of 16.6% is back above the national average for Bedfordshire's courses and entry qualifications.

Both Luton and Bedford have their share of pubs, clubs and restaurants, and London is 30–40 minutes away by train. Bedfordshire was 11th for its environmental record collated by the People & Planet green league. It was the second university in England to promise not to invest in the fossil-fuel industry, after a national student campaign, and is Fairtrade-accredited.

There are good sports facilities in Bedford and Luton, where there are also student discounts for non-university facilities.

Tuition fees

» Fees for EU/UK students 2018–19	£9,250
Foundation courses	£6,200
» Fees for international students 2017–18	£11,500
» For scholarship and bursary information see www.beds.ac.uk/howtoapply/money	
» Graduate salary	£21,000

Students

Undergraduates	8,585	(2,360)
Postgraduates	1,630	(1,825)
Applications per place	7.6	
Overall offer rate	80.4%	
International students	12.1%	
Mature students	46.1%	
From state-sector schools	99%	
From working-class homes	50.1%	

Accommodation

University-provided places 1,937
Percentage catered: 0%
Self-catered: £92 – £185 per week
First year students are guaranteed accommodation
www.beds.ac.uk/student-experience2/
living-at-bedfordshire/accommodation

Birkbeck, University of London

Birkbeck debuts in our league table this year because a rapid increase in full-time courses – albeit taught in the evening – makes comparisons with other universities more valid than before. However, the model contributes to a surprisingly low ranking.

Until recently, Birkbeck was exclusively part-time. It still describes itself as "London's evening university" but the option of a more intensive format that enables students to complete a degree in three years has been so popular that there was a 14% increase in applications in 2017, while other universities have struggled.

Most undergraduate programmes are now available on a full-time basis, giving students access to full student loans. A new range of one-year foundation courses in law, the arts and humanities, economics and business, psychology, biomedicine and social sciences is largely responsible for this year's growth in the demand for places. Designed as a preparation for undergraduate study, the courses provide automatic entry to an honours degree for those who pass.

The switch to full-time courses was triggered by the nationwide collapse in part-time enrolments, but the option of studying for four years, rather than three, remains open.

Birkbeck is offering degree apprenticeships in both chartered management and digital and technology solutions, and a foundation degree in laboratory science, and considers its evening study model ideally suited to more.

Birkbeck was placed in the silver category in the government's new Teaching Excellence Framework this year. The judging panel was impressed by the range of initiatives, including evening classes, that help students who would not otherwise be in higher education to graduate successfully.

Programmes supported students from diverse backgrounds, the panel said, enabling them to achieve their full potential through a curriculum which is at the forefront of research.

The university is ranked among the top 250 in the world by Times Higher Education magazine. More than 80% of its eligible academics were entered for the 2014 Research Excellence Framework and their results placed the college in the top 30 of UK institutions. Almost three-quarters of the work submitted was rated world-leading or internationally excellent, with psychology and environmental science in the top six nationally.

Founded in 1823 as a mechanics' institute, Birkbeck is part of the University of London and is based near Senate House, the university's headquarters in Bloomsbury. It has its own degree-awarding powers but, for the foreseeable future, will continue to award University of London degrees.

Malet Street
Bloomsbury
London WC1E 7HX
020 3907 0700
studentadvice@bbk.ac.uk
www.bbk.ac.uk
www.bbk.ac.uk/su
Open Days 2018:
Events throughout
year, see website

The Times and The Sunday Times **Rankings**
Overall Ranking: **122** (last year: n/a)

Teaching quality	76.7%	=107
Student experience	73.8%	115
Research quality	34.6%	35
Entry standards	104	127
Graduate prospects	73.3%	=65
Good honours	58.9%	123
Expected completion rate	68%	128
Student/staff ratio	16	=66
Services and facilities/student	£858	128

The college expanded beyond central London in 2013, sharing a five-storey building in Stratford with the University of East London. University Square Stratford is the first shared project of its kind in the capital.

Birkbeck's contribution is courses in law and business, as well as a BSc in community development and public policy, and a foundation degree in computing, information technology and web development. The building contains a 300-seat lecture theatre and teaching and learning spaces for 3,400 students.

The university's graduates enjoy high average starting salaries – among the best in the sector – partly because almost 70% are mature students, many of them returning to already successful careers. An in-house recruitment service, Birkbeck Talent, links employers with students and graduates for both employment opportunities and paid internships.

Birkbeck welcomes applications from people without traditional qualifications and continues to attract non-traditional learners of all ages and backgrounds.

Mature students tend to apply late in the application process and more than 40% of undergraduates arrive through clearing. Those who have taken A-levels or an equivalent qualification recently are made offers based on the UCAS tariff, but others are assessed by the college on the basis of interviews and/or short tests.

The My Birkbeck student centre acts as a front door to all the college's student support services, from help in choosing courses and submitting applications to information about financial support and study skills.

Almost £20m has been spent improving the college's buildings. There are new group study areas in the Torrington Square library and Birkbeck now has access to more classrooms in Senate House. The students' union has also been redeveloped and rebranded after extensive student consultation.

Bloomsbury is easily accessible by public transport and cycle routes. Most Birkbeck students already live in the capital, but full-time students looking for housing have access to University of London Housing Services. The college has an agreement with the student accommodation company Unite, which entitles full-time Birkbeck students to apply for places in its halls of residence.

Tuition fees

- » Fees for Scottish and EU students 2018–19 £9,250
  Foundation courses £7,150
- » Fees for international students 2018–19 £13,350
- » For scholarship and bursary information see www.bbk.ac.uk/student-services/financial-support
- » Graduate salary £23,000

Students

Undergraduates	2,870	(5,335)
Postgraduates	940	(3,105)
Applications per place	5.6	
Overall offer rate	n/a	
International students	7.1%	
Mature students	65.6%	
From state-sector schools	89.5%	
From working-class homes	42.8%	

Accommodation

www.bbk.ac.uk/student-services/accommodation

University of Birmingham

While other universities are worrying about whether they will fill the places on their home campuses, Birmingham is preparing to open a new one in Dubai. The first students will arrive in September 2018, taking courses in business, economics, computer science, mechanical engineering, and teaching. Other subjects will be added as the campus develops.

Professor Sir David Eastwood, the vice-chancellor, says the initiative demonstrates the university's ambition to be an outward-looking, world-class institution. Birmingham will be the only Russell Group representative among the 26 universities with a base in Dubai.

At home, the number of applications has risen for four years in a row, although there was a small dip in enrolments in 2016. The university's popularity has increased markedly since it started the trend for unconditional offers in 2013. Most subjects now operate the scheme, which guarantees places to all those who are predicted to get better than three As at A-level as long as they make Birmingham their first choice.

Prospective students also have access to an online offer calculator to give them a better idea of whether they are likely to secure a place.

The university is spending more than £600m over five years to enhance its facilities.

A £60m library opened last year and its predecessor will be knocked down to make way for the Green Heart, 12 acres of parkland at the centre of the campus. A £55m sports club also opened last year, with Birmingham's first 50-metre swimming pool, a large multisports arena, squash court complex and gym.

This summer, a new Collaborative Teaching Laboratory will revolutionise the way Stem subjects (science, technology, engineering and mathematics) are taught by giving students access to wet and dry labs, and e-labs. The university has also announced plans for a Life Sciences Park to promote the Midlands as a leading location for research and development in this area.

Birmingham was the original "redbrick" university. Its 300ft clock tower provides one of the city's best-known landmarks as it looms over the 230-acre campus in leafy Edgbaston. Dentistry is based in the city centre, while part of the School of Education is in Selly Oak, a mile from the Edgbaston campus, which has its own train station. Drama courses are also there, along with the BBC Drama Village, where there are sets used for television series.

The university did well in the 2014 Research Excellence Framework, when more than 80% of its submission was rated as world-leading or internationally excellent. Birmingham was ranked in the top five for philosophy, history, classics, theology and religion, area studies, chemical engineering,

Edgbaston
Birmingham B15 2TT
0121 414 3344
www.birmingham.ac.uk
www.guildofstudents.com
Open Days 2018:
June 22, 23,
September 15,
October 20

The Times and The Sunday Times Rankings
Overall Ranking: **15** (last year: 16)

Teaching quality	81.1%	=49
Student experience	79.7%	=43
Research quality	37.1%	26
Entry standards	167	=20
Graduate prospects	86.4%	5
Good honours	84.9%	14
Expected completion rate	94.5%	=13
Student/staff ratio	14.1	=29
Services and facilities/student	£2,665	22

and sport, exercise and rehabilitation studies. This performance has helped Birmingham maintain a position in our top 20 overall.

Students have welcomed an increased focus on employability – the university invested £5m in graduate careers services and was our University of the Year for Graduate Employability in 2015. Successful alumni offer mentoring and the university provides bursaries to support work experience and internships in the UK and overseas. Three-quarters of the undergraduates undertake work experience as part of their course.

The numbers recruited from the poorest social groups have been rising gradually. The Access to Birmingham (A2B) scheme, which encourages students from the West Midlands whose families have little or no experience of higher education to apply to university, is being extended to students in other parts of England.

Last year, students whose household income was less than £25,000 qualified for the university's Chamberlain awards of £2,000 a year, with £1,000 awards for the next band, with income up to £36,000.

Most of the halls and university flats are conveniently located in an attractive parkland setting near the main campus. There is room for nearly 5,200 students in university accommodation and plenty more in the private sector – 1,375 "endorsed" by the university although in private management.

The campus is less than three miles from the city centre, but the area has plenty of shops, pubs and restaurants. With its own nightclub on campus, there is no need to stray far, although the city is becoming increasingly popular with young people.

The sports facilities are some of the best in the country and other campus facilities are also first-rate. They include a medical practice and a comprehensive student services hub. There is also an outdoor pursuits centre by Coniston Water in the Lake District. The Active Lifestyle Programme is one of the most extensive of its kind, offering aerobic, toning and dance classes.

Tuition fees

» Fees for UK/EU students 2018–19   £9,250
» Fees for international students 2018–19   £15,720–£20,280
    Medicine & dentistry   £36,840
» For scholarship and bursary information see
    www.birmingham.ac.uk/undergraduate/fees/index.aspx
» Graduate salary   £22,500

Students

Undergraduates	20,400	(1,095)
Postgraduates	6.795	(5,540)
Applications per place	8.2	
Overall offer rate	82.3%	
International students	13.7%	
Mature students	6.6%	
From state-sector schools	80.8%	
From working-class homes	22.8%	

Accommodation

University-provided places: 6,558
Percentage catered: 25%
Catered costs: £125 – £193 per week
Self-catered: £87 – £151 per week
First year students are guaranteed accommodation
www.birmingham.ac.uk/accommodation

Birmingham City University

Birmingham City University's (BCU) degrees have been "refreshed" so students will receive the most relevant practical experience to boost their prospects in the graduate employment market. Work placements are available on most courses and employability skills are built into the curriculum through the Graduate+ scheme.

Enrolments have risen for five years in a row, increasing the size of the undergraduate intake by a quarter and, for the first time, placing BCU among the top 20 universities in terms of the volume of applications attracted.

More than 40 new or reconfigured degrees will be offered in 2018. They include four-year undergraduate master's courses in property development and planning, biomedical engineering, and business finance. New three-year degrees will include commercial photography, black studies, and video game design and production.

A new suite of courses in sport and life sciences will start this year, based in a new £41m facility at the university's City South campus, ranging from food and nutrition science, physical education and school sport, alongside sport and exercise nutrition, and sports therapy.

BCU's £260m investment in facilities also features a new conservatoire for music courses on the City Centre campus, which will open in March 2018.

Most of the university's activities will be concentrated on the two campuses after the planned closure this year of BCU's original headquarters in the northern suburb of Perry Barr. The Bournville campus offers preparatory courses for overseas students to support the university's international ambitions. These include the establishment of the Birmingham Institute of Fashion and Creative Art in Wuhan, China, in partnership with Wuhan Textile University.

The City Centre campus, close to the eventual HS2 rail terminus, houses all student support services as well as business, law, social sciences and English. The highly-regarded courses in art and design and media are also based there, and the university occupies part of the Millennium Point building, helping to create Birmingham's Eastside learning quarter.

The City South campus, in Edgbaston, has an award-winning library, IT suites, teaching facilities and recreational space.

BCU has thrived since changing its name from the University of Central England in 2007. There are strong links with business and the professions, including pioneering work in green technology, which is attracting support from national and regional partners. Students have access to learning tools such as Shareville – a virtual learning environment where students can engage with real-life scenarios.

University House
15 Bartholomew Row
Birmingham B5 5JU
0121 331 6295
admissions@bcu.ac.uk
www.bcu.ac.uk
www.bcusu.com
Open Days 2018:
March 24, June 30,
September 29

***The Times and The Sunday Times* Rankings**

Overall Ranking: **105** (last year: =93)

Teaching quality	81%	52
Student experience	77.9%	77
Research quality	4.3%	=98
Entry standards	122	=86
Graduate prospects	70.6%	77
Good honours	67.3%	=96
Expected completion rate	81.2%	96
Student/staff ratio	18.7	=111
Services and facilities/student	£1,900	87

The new STEAMhouse centre encourages collaboration between the arts, science, technology, engineering and maths (Steam) sectors. Experimental workshops focus on product development, collaborative making and societal challenges, led by industry, with subscription-based access to fabrication facilities and £2,500 grants offered to selected small firms and sole traders to cover materials for early-stage prototyping.

The university made a relatively small submission to the 2014 national research assessments, but 60% of the work reached the top two categories and almost 90% was judged to have delivered "outstanding" or "very considerable" external impact.

BCU is also introducing degree-level apprenticeships, where students spend part of their time on campus and the rest working for one of BCU's partner employers, earning a full-time wage. Initially, higher and degree apprenticeships will be available in healthcare, broadcast technology and management.

The Faculty of Business, Law and Social Sciences already offered a number of three-year professional practice courses, taught on campus for the first two years then completed and assessed in the workplace in the final year.

The university offers a range of scholarships and bursaries to encourage undergraduates to stay on for postgraduate study. In addition, all UK and EU undergraduate students starting courses in 2018 will receive at least £150 towards course materials and other costs that may be a barrier to study.

Six out of ten students come from the West Midlands, many from ethnic minorities, and 47% are from the poorest socio-economic groups. The university is working with schools in the region to encourage more young people to go on to higher education. Many students enter through the network of associated further education colleges, which run foundation and access programmes.

The prize-winning Student Academic Partners scheme spawned a formal agreement between the university and the students' union to improve the student experience. The student inquiry service, Ask, handles all questions either in person, over the phone or online.

The university owns or manages more than 2,500 residential places – enough to guarantee accommodation for first-years whose homes are more than ten miles away, if they apply before the deadline. The city's student social scene is highly rated and has become a draw for many young applicants.

Tuition fees

» Fees for UK/EU students 2018–19	£9,750
Foundation courses	£6,165
» Fees for international students 2018–19	£12,000–£19,500
Foundation courses	£8,900
» For scholarship and bursary information see www.bcu.ac.uk/student-info/finance-and-money-matters/	
» Graduate salary	£21,000

Students

Undergraduates	17,145	(2,575)
Postgraduates	1,970	(2,380)
Applications per place	7	
Overall offer rate	68.1%	
International students	8.5%	
Mature students	24.4%	
From state-sector schools	97.7%	
From working-class homes	46.9%	

Accommodation

University-provided places: 2,511
Percentage catered: 0%
Self-catered: £105 – £138 per week
First year students who live more than 10 miles away are guaranteed accommodation
www.bcu.ac.uk/student-info/accommodation

Birmingham, University College (UCB)

University College Birmingham (UCB) is unique among UK universities in having a third of its students taking further education programmes, some of them enrolling at 16. It believes that would place it at a disadvantage in league tables such as ours, so it has again instructed the Higher Education Statistics Agency not to release its data. Consequently, UCB does not appear in our main league table or any of the subject tables. Nevertheless, it was around average for overall satisfaction in the 2017 National Student Survey and was placed in the Silver category in the Teaching Excellence Framework (TEF).

The TEF panel was impressed by the strong vocational focus in UCB's curriculum design, with work placements and professional accreditation a common feature on many courses. It found that students were stretched and there were "appropriate" contact hours, personalised learning through individual and group tutorials, and effective support services.

However, the numbers starting degrees dropped by more than 20 per cent in 2016, cancelling out a rise of similar proportions a year earlier. UCB was one of only two universities in England not to charge £9,250 fees for UK and EU undergraduates in the current academic year, but it plans to charge the maximum for both Bachelor's and foundation degrees in 2018–19.

UCB chose not to change its name when full university status arrived in 2013, in order to preserve its identity. It was the largest of a dozen colleges to become universities then, with more than 5,000 higher education students and nearly 2,500 taking further education courses. The university traces its history back more than 100 years to the foundation of a Municipal Technical School offering cookery and household science courses. It has had degree awarding powers since 2007, although many degrees are still accredited by the University of Birmingham.

The core subjects are hospitality, tourism, business, sport and education. The most recent Ofsted inspection rated the further education provision as outstanding. UCB has an international reputation in hospitality and tourism, with about a third of the students coming from outside the UK. Two restaurants staffed by the university's students are open to the public, as well as to students and staff.

Based in the city centre, UCB is located close to the International Convention Centre, Symphony Hall and the Library of Birmingham, as well as the main shopping areas. The main campus is at Summer Row, five minutes' walk from New Street station. UCB is investing £100 million in new teaching

Summer Row
Birmingham B3 1JB
0121 604 1000
marketing@ucb.ac.uk
www.ucb.ac.uk
www.ucbguild.org.uk
Open Days 2018:
March 24, June 30

The Times and The Sunday Times Rankings
Data not supplied

and residential facilities. The first phase of development in Birmingham's historic Jewellery Quarter –a short walk from the main campus – opened in 2014. The second has now been granted planning permission and will open in September 2019. The new red brick building, designed to celebrate the architectural heritage of the area, will include three lecture theatres, modern teaching spaces, a high performance strengthening and conditioning suite for sports studies, a gym and a student diner.

Existing specialist teaching facilities include high-quality training kitchens, a full bakery and a £2-million Food Science and Innovation Suite. The university focuses on giving students an advantage in the highly competitive graduate job market. Many courses include full- or half-year industrial placements, including overseas opportunities in the USA, Hong Kong, Canada and Europe. As well as arranging placements, the expanded careers and employability team, hired@UCB, helps students to develop skills such as communication, teamwork, problem solving and time management.

UCB has one of the most socially diverse student bodies in the country – more than half are from a black or minority ethnic background. Student ambassadors promote further and higher education to young people from a range of backgrounds. Almost all the undergraduates are state educated and more than half come from the four poorest socio-economic groups. Retention rates have been improving, but the TEF panel commented on the below-benchmark rates for some groups.

More than 1,000 students can be accommodated in UCB's halls of residence, and accommodation can be offered to all years and programmes of study. The Maltings halls are ten minutes' walk from UCB and Cambrian Hall is only 150 yards from the main campus. Both offer among the best value in the Midlands. The Spa offers hairdressing salons, beauty therapy suites, a sports therapy clinic, a multi-gym, and a fitness assessment suite. There is also a gym and sports hall at The Maltings site, as well as a new multipurpose community hub with specialised work and dining spaces. It includes a 'beanbag' cinema area and a new dance studio.

Tuition fees

- » Fees for UK/EU students 2018–19   £9,250
  Part-time and foundation courses vary
- » Fees for international students 2017–18   £9,700
  Foundation courses   £7,600
- » For scholarship and bursary information see www.ucb.ac.uk/our-courses/ tuition-fees-and-scholarships.aspx

---

Students
Total   7,500
International   900

Accommodation
University-provided places: 1,000+
Percentage catered: 0%
Self-catered: £92 – £111 per week
www.ucb.ac.uk/accommodation/
accommodation@ucb.ac.uk

Bishop Grosseteste University

Bishop Grosseteste (BGU) was awarded gold in the government's new Teaching Excellence Framework (TEF), outperforming two thirds of the elite Russell Group universities.

The TEF panel found an outstanding learning environment and students who are engaged with developments at the forefront of research, scholarship and working practice. Course design and assessment ensures that all groups of students are challenged to achieve their full potential, the panel added.

Last year's dramatic increase in student satisfaction – the biggest at any university for teaching quality – came at the perfect moment for the TEF assessment, although there has been a small fall since, from sixth position to 15th on this measure last year. Student satisfaction with the quality of teaching remains high in the latest National Student Survey, keeping BGU in our top 20 on this measure.

However, there was a big fall in satisfaction with other areas of the student experience, such as the organisation and management of courses, and the availability and quality of learning resources. Overall, the university held its position, which remains an improvement on its early years in the table.

The university is also in the top ten for the proportion of academics holding a teaching qualification: three-quarters of the staff, compared with the national average of 44%.

BGU had been expanding its intake in pursuit of a five-year plan to double student numbers, although enrolments dropped a little in 2016. Currently one of the UK's smallest universities, it is aiming for 4,500 students by 2019. The proportion of applicants receiving offers has doubled in five years, topping 90% in the 2016 admissions cycle.

The expansion will include more mature students taking work-based courses and more from non-traditional backgrounds, as well as greater numbers of postgraduates and research students. There is scope for more international students: the data for this guide registers just 0.3% of the latest entrants as coming from overseas.

Based on a leafy campus near Lincoln's cathedral and castle, Bishop Grosseteste has been training teachers since 1862. Named after a theologian and scholar who was Bishop of Lincoln in the 13th century, BGU is still a church university within the Anglican tradition, although it welcomes students of all faiths and none.

The portfolio of courses covers a range of arts and social sciences, with more new subjects planned in the next few years, but teacher training (rated "good" by Ofsted) still dominates. Inspectors praised the high quality of training and effective partnerships

Longdales Road
Lincoln LN1 3DY
01522 583 658
enquiries@bishopg.ac.uk
www.bishopg.ac.uk
bgsu.co.uk
Open Days 2018:
June 9, July 11,
August 17

The Times and The Sunday Times Rankings
Overall Ranking: **95** (last year: 95)

Teaching quality	83.7%	15
Student experience	76.9%	=89
Research quality	2.1%	120
Entry standards	112	=114
Graduate prospects	70.9%	76
Good honours	69.2%	86
Expected completion rate	91.6%	=28
Student/staff ratio	22.3	129
Services and facilities/student	£1,299	126

between the university and schools, adding that "university tutors' involvement in current educational research provides a sharp edge to the training programme".

BGU's introduction of Early Years teaching courses has meant that, for the first time, Bishop Grosseteste is training teachers for every age group, including adults.

Most of BGU's students (60%) come from the east Midlands; 44% from Lincolnshire. Their backgrounds reflect the socioeconomic make-up of the county, with eight out of ten fulfilling one or more of the government's criteria for widening participation in university education. Almost one in five comes from an area with little tradition of higher education.

The university is divided into three schools: Teacher Development, Humanities and Social Sciences. Only 11 staff entered the 2014 Research Excellence Framework, but some work was classed as "world-leading" in the three subjects assessed: education, English and history.

The campus has been gearing up for a larger intake. The former college canteen and dining room has been turned into teaching accommodation, and a £2.2m extension has now doubled the space, creating a new landmark building for the university.

Bishop Grosseteste has launched the Lincolnshire Open Research and Innovation Centre (LORIC) to offer local businesses, public and third sector organisations a range of services, including consultancy, digitisation, Open Data mining, and analysis and research support. The service will move into a listed building close to the university campus this summer, when work on its refurbishment and modernisation is complete. The new service will complement BGU's other business support initiatives, which all receive financial support from the European Structural and Investment Funds.

A complex of flats replaced an older hall of residence and combined with the extensive refurbishment of an existing hall brought the number of campus rooms to more than 200, with another 77 rooms available off-campus.

The campus theatre has been converted to double as a cinema, the Venue, where the Lincoln Film Society is based. It is open to staff, students and the public. The library has also been extended.

The sports centre has a fitness suite and eight acres of playing fields nearby. The city of Lincoln is one of the fastest-growing in the UK, with relatively low living costs.

Tuition fees

»	Fees for UK/EU students 2018–19	£9,250
	Foundation courses	£6,935
»	Fees for international students 2017–18	£11,500
»	For scholarship and bursary information see www.bishopg.ac.uk/student/fees/funding/bursary	
»	Graduate salary	£21,000

Students

Undergraduates	1,835	(20)
Postgraduates	275	(110)
Applications per place	3.1	
Overall offer rate	90.3%	
International students	0.3%	
Mature students	41.3%	
From state-sector schools	98.3%	
From working-class homes	44%	

Accommodation

University-provided places: 217
Percentage catered: 0%
Self-catered: £101 – £126 per week
www.bishopg.ac.uk/student/accommodation

University of Bolton

A silver award in the new Teaching Excellence Framework (TEF) was "the best news Bolton has ever had", according to Professor George Holmes, the vice-chancellor. The TEF panel commended the university on an institutional culture that facilitates, recognises and rewards excellent teaching as well as providing excellent support for students from disadvantaged backgrounds.

However, Bolton remains near the bottom of our league table, despite recent improvements in student satisfaction, especially in relation to teaching quality. Bolton's relatively poor showing is down to the broader range of measures on which we rank universities, taking into account entry standards, research, degree outcomes, the dropout rate and spending per student on services and facilities.

Applications were down by more than the national average in 2017, but this followed two highly successful years and reflects the paring of the course portfolio by 21 courses.

The university has moved into Bolton Central, its new flagship building in the centre of the town, which will be used as the venue for the new Institute of Management. About 2,500 of Bolton's 11,000 students and more than 60 staff will use the five-storey building.

By the time the 2018 entrants arrive, the university will have grown further through amalgamation with Bolton College, although Bury College has dropped out of what was to have been a three-way merger.

The next few months will also see the opening of the new National Centre for Motorsport Engineering, which will host Bolton's Centre for Advanced Performance Engineering. The university has its own professional motor racing team, run in conjunction with a motor sports company, and offers degrees in automotive performance engineering and motor sport technology. Students work and learn alongside engineers and mechanics from the team, as well as the university's mechanical engineering lecturers.

Future plans include a £40m student village on council-owned land that will house 850 students, replacing two existing halls that are further from the town-centre campus and have a smaller capacity. Another collaboration with the council and the local NHS produced the Bolton One development, a £31m health, leisure and research centre on the main site, which has a sport and spinal injuries clinic as well as a multisports hall, climbing wall and 25-metre competition swimming pool. The former sports facility on campus is being transformed into a Creative Industries and Technologies Centre.

Recent developments include a £10m base for science and engineering and the formation

Deane Road
Bolton BL3 5AB
01204 903394
enquiries@bolton.ac.uk
www.bolton.ac.uk
www.boltonsu.com
Open Days 2018:
March 24, June 30

***The Times and The Sunday Times* Rankings**

Overall Ranking: **124** (last year: 124)

Teaching quality	82.1%	=32
Student experience	78.5%	71
Research quality	2.9%	114
Entry standards	114	=108
Graduate prospects	65.1%	=106
Good honours	58.7%	124
Expected completion rate	68.4%	127
Student/staff ratio	15.1	=44
Services and facilities/student	£1,272	127

of a new Health Sciences Faculty to teach biomedical sciences and subjects allied to health and dentistry. A partnership with the owners of ten dental practices in the north of England has enabled Bolton to offer a well-equipped practice and new clinical simulation facilities for degrees in advanced dental nursing and dental hygiene and therapy, as well as a Diploma of Higher Education for clinical dental technicians.

General engineering was one of two areas with most of its work rated world-leading or internationally excellent in the 2014 Research Excellence Framework. The best results were in English and almost a third of the university's submission reached the top two categories.

About 1,100 of its students are postgraduates working towards qualifications up to and including PhDs. Among the university's research resources is a Centre for Islamic Finance, which recently teamed up with St Mary's University, Twickenham, to launch the Forum for Islam-Christian Dialogue to promote greater understanding between the faiths.

The university traces its roots back 193 years to one of the country's first three mechanics institutes. The student population is among the most ethnically diverse in the UK, with about a quarter of British students coming from minority communities. More than a third of the undergraduates study part-time, a significant proportion in a period when national part-time numbers have plummeted.

Bolton exceeds all the access measures designed to widen participation in higher education: more than half of the full-time undergraduates are from working-class homes and the proportion from areas without a tradition of higher education is among the highest in the UK, at more than 20%. The downside is that the projected dropout rate is also one of the highest in the UK at 25%-plus.

Bolton has partner colleges in several Asian countries and a branch campus in the United Arab Emirates. The Ras al-Khaimah campus offers a range of undergraduate and postgraduate courses identical to those taught in the UK. The £1m development near Dubai is designed to take 700 students. Those at Bolton have the opportunity to study there for part of their degree course.

The town of Bolton has a growing range of student-orientated facilities and is only 20 minutes from Manchester by train.

Tuition fees

» Fees for UK/EU students 2018–19	£9,000
Foundation courses	£6,000
» Fees for international students 2018–19	£11,250
Foundation courses	£8,500
» For scholarship and bursary information see www.bolton.ac.uk/studentServices/ ScholarshipsAndBursaries	
» Graduate salary	£18,000

Students

Undergraduates	3,975	(1,210)
Postgraduates	410	(725)
Applications per place	4.9	
Overall offer rate	74.3%	
International students	6.2%	
Mature students	38.4%	
From state-sector schools	99.3%	
From working-class homes	52.5%	

Accommodation

University-provided places: 381
Percentage catered: 0%
Self-catered: £80 per week
www.bolton.ac.uk/accommodation

Bournemouth University

Bournemouth lost almost all the 20-place gain it made in our 2017 league table. However, the university's momentum has not stopped, with £200m invested in new buildings and equipment by the end of 2018 and more spending planned.

Construction is getting under way on the £23m Poole Gateway building on the main Talbot campus, which will provide specialist facilities for the faculties of science and technology and media and communications. The new Bournemouth Gateway building is being developed on the Lansdowne campus and will be the new home of the health and social sciences faculty and support amenities, opening in September 2019.

There are impressive facilities for the media courses that are Bournemouth's best-known provision. The university hosts the National Centre of Computer Animation and large numbers of its graduates have worked on award-winning films such as Star Wars: The Force Awakens and Ex Machina. Its state-of-the-art equipment includes a motion capture facility for real-time animation, which is used in teaching and available for use by outside companies.

There are new degrees in computer animation and games design, with others in digital creative industries and visual effects planned for 2018.

Other areas are shining too. The department of tourism and hospitality management has been designated as a Centre of Excellence in Tourism by the World Tourism Organisation, for example. Bournemouth's decision to invest £1m a year on academic appointments and the fusion of teaching and research paid off in the 2014 Research Excellence Framework, when 60% of the university's entry was judged to be world-leading or internationally excellent. It was one of the biggest proportions at any post-1992 university and a considerable improvement on previous results. The university's Fusion Investment Fund continues to promote collaborative research.

A total of 33 different professional bodies accredit Bournemouth's degrees. The university claims a number of firsts in its portfolio of courses, notably in tourism, media-related programmes and conservation. Degrees in public relations, retail management, scriptwriting and tax law were all ahead of their time.

Foundation degrees are delivered in partner colleges in Dorset, Somerset and Wiltshire, as well as on the main campus. Top-up courses are available for those who wish to turn their qualification into an honours degree. Bournemouth is also expanding postgraduate opportunities, promising up to 100 doctoral places each year until 2018, many of them fully funded.

Fern Barrow
Talbot Campus
Poole
Dorset BH12 5BB
01202 961916
futurestudents@bournemouth.ac.uk
www.bournemouth.ac.uk
www.subu.org.uk
Open Days 2018:
June 9, July 7

POOLE

The Times and The Sunday Times Rankings
Overall Ranking: **79** (last year: 62)

Teaching quality	77.6%	101
Student experience	76.5%	=98
Research quality	9%	=65
Entry standards	123	=83
Graduate prospects	70.1%	81
Good honours	77.2%	42
Expected completion rate	84.1%	=77
Student/staff ratio	16.5	=78
Services and facilities/student	£2,204	49

The university's honours degree students have the opportunity to gain work experience as part of their courses and most of them do so. Most also take advantage of personal development planning, both online and with trained staff. In addition, first-years are offered peer-assisted learning, receiving advice and mentoring from more experienced undergraduates.

The university has been increasing its use of education technology, for example to enable its part-time students to study from home or the workplace and reduce the amount of time they need to spend on campus. It has invested £6m in a new Virtual Learning Environment, which will give all students access to a range of new features and enable academics to track the performance of undergraduates, design courses, create content, and grade assignments. There is a growing emphasis on international activity, with 2,600 overseas students from 120 countries. The Global Horizons Fund helps students and staff to travel abroad for study, research or work and life experience. For international students, the new Bournemouth University International College provides preparatory courses in English and study skills.

The subject mix and an increasingly fashionable seaside location, between the world heritage Jurassic Coast and the New Forest National Park, attract more middle-class students than most post-1992 universities, although 95% of undergraduates attended state schools. The campuses are served by a subsidised bus service and students are discouraged from bringing cars.

Sports facilities have been improving following a refurbishment of the gym, with the addition of a new multipurpose large studio. The university does not own any residential accommodation, but controls 1,500 places and approves 2,000 more – enough to guarantee accommodation to first-year undergraduates.

The university finished in the top 20 in the 2016 People & Planet's league of environmental performance and has an EcoCampus Gold award as well as holding Fairtrade status.

Tuition fees

» Fees for UK/EU students 2018–19 £9,750
  Foundation courses £6,000
» Fees for international students 2018–19 £13,750
» For scholarship and bursary information see
  www.bournemouth.ac.uk/undergraduate/fees-funding/
  scholarships/
» Graduate salary £21,000

Students

Undergraduates	12,590	(2,635)
Postgraduates	1,825	(1,995)
Applications per place	5.7	
Overall offer rate	84.5%	
International students	7.8%	
Mature students	17.5%	
From state-sector schools	95%	
From working-class homes	31.4%	

Accommodation

University-provided places: 3,695
Percentage catered: 2%
Catered costs: £170 – £198 per week
Self-catered: £100 – £153 per week
First year students are guaranteed accommodation
www.bournemouth.ac.uk/why-bu/accommodation

University of Bradford

Still a small university, 50 years after its establishment, with only 11,000 students, Bradford is focusing on its strengths to grow in size and enhance its reputation. Advanced healthcare, innovative engineering and sustainable societies are the three themes of the university's academic strategy.

Bradford is bidding for a medical school to add to its highly-rated provision in nursing and pharmacy, with plans for the first 150 A-level and graduate entrants in 2019. The university is already building the Wolfson Centre for Applied Healthcare Research, beside Bradford Royal Infirmary, to work with researchers from the University of Leeds and clinicians from Bradford Teaching Hospitals NHS Foundation Trust.

The university has opened a dedicated building for optometry, part of a £260m plan to include new and upgraded teaching facilities and a large-scale refurbishment of the library, which won a Green Gown award for its insulation and natural ventilation.

The university was a pioneer of environmental initiatives in higher education, and was rated the greenest university in the UK and eighth in the world for its sustainable architecture and innovative technologies in 2015. The university's modernisation plan is keeping it at the forefront of that movement.

Bradford is the only university in the world with three buildings rated outstanding for their environmental credentials, while the Ecoversity programme pushes sustainability across all Bradford's endeavours.

Bradford's well-known Division of Peace Studies, the oldest peace studies teaching department in the world, has merged with the Centre of International Development and will launch two of the new degrees planned for 2018: BA degrees in applied peace and conflict studies, and global politics and development. Other additions to the curriculum will include sociology, criminal behaviour, international relations and a four-year integrated master's course in mathematical and computational chemistry.

Always one of the most diverse of the pre-1992 universities, Bradford draws more than half of its UK undergraduates from the four poorest socio-economic groups. Over 20% of the university's students are from overseas, many of them taught in partner institutions in Singapore, Brunei, Malaysia, Pakistan and India.

Nearer home, a number of further education colleges offer Bradford foundation degrees in areas such as public-sector administration, community justice, engineering technology and enterprise in IT. Many honours degrees offer work experience or placements, which regularly put Bradford well up the employment tables.

Bradford
BD7 1DP
01274 236 088
admissions@bradford.ac.uk
www.bradford.ac.uk
www.bradfordunisu.co.uk
Open Days 2018:
check website

The Times and The Sunday Times Rankings

Overall Ranking: **=75** (last year: 76)

Teaching quality	78.2%	=93
Student experience	79.3%	=52
Research quality	9.2%	=63
Entry standards	128	=71
Graduate prospects	80.8%	=26
Good honours	74.6%	=49
Expected completion rate	83.5%	=81
Student/staff ratio	16	=66
Services and facilities/student	£2,108	62

Other distinctive features include the highly-rated School of Management, which offers a distance-learning MBA ranked in the top ten in the world by the *Financial Times*. Overall, Bradford is recovering in our league table after slipping out of the top 80 earlier in the decade.

Recent developments include a £1.5m engineering laboratory with the latest equipment. More than £5m has been spent on modernising the biomedical science laboratories. An Integrated Learning Centre has been developed for the Faculty of Life Sciences featuring human patient simulators and facilities for studying pathology.

The university is also leading a £12m programme to create a Digital Health Zone for the city to develop new healthcare products and links with practitioners.

An online portal is available to applicants and new students to smooth their transition to higher education. Computer-assisted learning is increasing in many subjects, making use of unusually extensive IT provision and a new wireless network.

Nearly 400 of Bradford's academic staff are National Teaching Fellows, one of the highest totals at any university. While the university entered fewer than a quarter of eligible academics for the 2014 research assessments, their work produced good results: almost three-quarters reached the top two categories, with allied health, management and archaeological science producing particularly

good grades. There were also high scores for the impact of Bradford's research in archaeology, politics and management. The university was awarded the Queen's Anniversary prize for research on dementia in 2016.

The compact, lively campus is close to the city centre, with only the management school on a different site, two miles away in a 13-acre parkland setting. The sports facilities have been enhanced with the addition of a gym and climbing wall, and an improved sports hall. Bradford has now been awarded £500,000 by the Premier League and the Football Association for a sports hub for students and the local community with a floodlit, 3G football pitch, four tennis courts, refurbished changing pavilion and a conditioning suite.

Places in halls are reasonably priced and all have internet access. Rents for private housing are among the lowest in any university city. The university has particularly good provision for disabled students, who account for almost 10% of the student population.

Tuition fees

- » Fees for UK/EU students 2018–19 £9,250
  Foundation courses £6,165
- » Fees for international students 2018–19 £14,950–£18,440
  Foundation courses £11,890
- » For scholarship and bursary information see www.bradford.ac.uk/fees-and-financial-support/university-scholarships-and-support
- » Graduate salary £20,000

Students

Undergraduates	7,660	(740)
Postgraduates	775	(2,045)
Applications per place	7.3	
Overall offer rate	86.7%	
International students	12.9%	
Mature students	20.9%	
From state-sector schools	97.7%	
From working-class homes	58.3%	

Accommodation

University-provided places: 1,026
Percentage catered: 0%
Self-catered: £95 – £106 per week
First year students are guaranteed accommodation
www.bradford.ac.uk/student/accommodation/

University of Brighton

Brighton is going ahead with plans to invest £200m in its campuses over the next five years, but has adopted a new, more cautious strategy in anticipation of harder times ahead for universities after Brexit.

The university has announced the closure of its campus in Hastings and called at least a temporary halt to plans for a new library and academic building on a regeneration site in the centre of Brighton. Professor Debra Humphris, the vice-chancellor, has ruled out increasing the number of students above the current 21,000, partly to take the pressure off the local housing market.

The £17m Advanced Engineering building is now open on the Moulsecoomb campus in Brighton where much of the remaining planned development will take place. It houses the centre for advanced engineering, which has a 20-year partnership with Ricardo UK, researching low-carbon internal combustion systems. The plans include more than 800 student bedrooms in five halls of residence, a new home for the university's business school, learning and teaching spaces, a multistorey car park, gym and students' union facilities.

The Hastings campus was designed for up to 2,000 students, but had only 650 when it was deemed to be unsustainable. The existing students will complete their courses, but Hastings will then be served by Sussex Coast College, which will offer six degrees validated by Brighton through its new University Centre.

Investment will continue on the remaining campuses in Brighton and Eastbourne, where there is a modern library and extensive leisure and sports facilities. Sport science laboratories and 354 en-suite residential places have been added there, and improvements made to the learning resources centre, lecture theatres and refectory.

In central Brighton, facilities for photography, moving image and film and screen studies have been upgraded. There have also been improvements to the College of Arts and Humanities on the Grand Parade campus, which hosts the national Design Archives.

Education students, as well as those taking languages and literature courses, are taught on the Falmer site on the outskirts of Brighton, which now also boasts a £7.3m sports centre. The campus also houses the medical school, one of the first to be awarded to a post-1992 university. Run jointly with the University of Sussex, it now trains about 140 doctors a year. Its headquarters has also provided a new base for applied social sciences such as criminology and psychology.

The university is engaged in imaginative regional initiatives. It has the largest university multi-academy trust in the country, with 14 academies across Sussex and a free

Mithras House
Lewes Road
Brighton BN2 4AT
01273 644 644
enquiries@brighton.ac.uk
www.brighton.ac.uk
www.brightonsu.com
Open Days 2018:
see website

The Times and The Sunday Times Rankings

Overall Ranking: **112** (last year: 104)

Teaching quality	79.2%	=79
Student experience	76%	105
Research quality	7.9%	=74
Entry standards	119	=95
Graduate prospects	68.7%	93
Good honours	70.5%	72
Expected completion rate	82.1%	91
Student/staff ratio	17.4	=93
Services and facilities/student	£1,458	121

school in Brighton. It has also embarked on a programme of degree apprenticeships with firms in the region and is planning to expand next year in a range of sectors, from management to health and construction.

More than nine out of ten courses include a placement or the option of a sandwich year. The four-year fashion textiles degree offers work placements in America, France and Italy as well as Britain. The panel awarding Brighton silver in this year's Teaching Excellence Framework complimented the university on close working relationships with professional bodies, employers and local community groups and its personalised learning and support, particularly for students from diverse backgrounds during pre-entry and the first year.

Brighton was in the top quarter of universities for the impact of the research submitted to the 2014 national assessments. Two-thirds of its work was placed in one of the top two categories, a big improvement on 2008 when it was already among the most successful of the post-1992 universities.

The teaching facilities are designed to build real-life skills, and include a radio station and television studio, a podiatry hospital, physiotherapy clinic, flight simulator and a clinical skills and simulation suite for nursing students. Brighton is also second in the league of environmental performance for universities compiled by People & Planet.

The university's fashionable seaside location is a draw for students, who revel in Brighton's famously lively social scene. The university has a cosmopolitan atmosphere, with more international students and a larger middle-class UK intake than most post-1992 universities, although 94% of undergraduates come from state schools. Efforts to widen the intake further include well-established progression partnerships with schools in the region and cash bursaries of £500 for those with a household income of less than £25,000, with larger awards for care leavers.

Tuition fees

- » Fees for UK/EU students 2018–19 £9,250
- » Fees for international students 2018–19 £12,900–£14,040
  Medicine £29,000
- » For scholarship and bursary information see
  www.brighton.ac.uk/studying-here/fees-and-finance/
- » Graduate salary £21,700

Students		
Undergraduates	14,395	(2,775)
Postgraduates	1,680	(2,280)
Applications per place	7.8	
Overall offer rate	75.6%	
International students	11.6%	
Mature students	21.2%	
From state-sector schools	94.2%	
From working-class homes	34.2%	

Accommodation

University-provided places: 2,549
Percentage catered: 52%
Catered costs: £161 – £180 per week
Self-catered: £76 – £160 per week
All first year students are offered accommodation
www.abbrighton.ac.uk/accommodation-and-locations/

University of Bristol

A revamped curriculum launched for this academic year offers Bristol undergraduates optional enrichment courses covering innovation and enterprise, global citizenship or sustainable futures, as well as focusing on core academic skills. Bristol Futures is at the heart of a new strategy for the university, launched by Professor Hugh Brady, who became vice-chancellor in 2015.

The aim is to enable students to develop the qualities to thrive in a changing labour market. Four in five Bristol graduates go into professional jobs or on to further study.

Overall, the university has moved up another three places in the latest table and is well inside our top 20. It might have risen further if the boycott of the National Student Survey had not taken the response rate below the 50 per cent threshold required for the publication of scores, as it did at eight other universities. There was scope for improvement on Bristol's 2016 scores, which were used to compile the results in the new edition. The university remains in 95th place for satisfaction with teaching quality. It did much better in other areas, however. It is in the top five for completion and just outside the top ten for good honours.

The university is planning to remodel the centre of its main campus with a new library and a "global lounge" consolidating services for international students. Facilities for maths, engineering, biomedical sciences and geographical sciences will be upgraded. A £300m enterprise campus will be built next to Bristol Temple Meads railway station, focusing on digital technologies. It will include a new student village, but is still at the planning stage and is not expected to open until 2021–22.

The strategy also promises more support for student wellbeing and to enable students to develop personal resilience and self-reliance – a sensitive area since six students have taken their own lives in unrelated incidents in the space of a year. The university has pointed out that Bristol did not have a pattern of suicides in previous years but, after a review of support services, it has increased staffing levels and promised an additional £1m a year to boost student wellbeing.

Having added 1,600 places to its undergraduate intake over a five-year period, Bristol now has more than 16,000 undergraduates and nearly 6,000 postgraduate students – and intends to grow further. Applications were down slightly in 2017, but by half the average decline nationally.

The university draws applicants from all types of school, but despite an increase in state-educated entrants in 2015 almost 40% came from the independent sector, the highest proportion outside Oxford, Durham and St Andrews.

---

31 Great George Street
Bristol BS1 5QD
0117 394 1536
choosebristol-ug@bristol.ac.uk
www.bristol.ac.uk
www.bristolsu.org.uk
Open Days 2018:
June & September –
check website

The Times and The Sunday Times Rankings

Overall Ranking: =16 (last year: 19)

Teaching quality	n/a	
Student experience	n/a	
Research quality	47.3%	6
Entry standards	187	11
Graduate prospects	80.2%	=33
Good honours	87%	7
Expected completion rate	95.9%	=5
Student/staff ratio	13.4	24
Services and facilities/student	£2,094	66

Bristol has spent £21m on recruiting and supporting students from disadvantaged backgrounds in the past ten years, encouraging departments to make slightly lower offers to promising applicants from the bottom 40% of schools and colleges at A-level. That allowance has now been increased to two grades and Bristol will also make lower offers to five "high potential" local students. Eligibility for the scheme will be based on an assessment of potential and progress made by their head teacher, rather than examination results alone.

Bristol's place among the leading universities in the UK was confirmed in the 2014 Research Excellence Framework after entering more than 90% of its eligible staff – a higher proportion than Oxford. The assessment rated 83% of its research as world-leading or internationally excellent.

Among the many successes, geography consolidated its position as the leader in its subject, while the entire submissions in clinical medicine, health subjects, economics and sport and exercise sciences were placed in the top categories for their external impact.

Even before Bristol Futures was announced, the university had begun a £350m construction programme, partly to cater for the extra students it was recruiting. There are many new degrees in prospect, with 30 courses already under way and another eight planned for 2018, including four-year integrated master's courses in engineering and computer science.

The university has 5,500 residential places for undergraduates, who must apply by July 31 and firmly accept an offer at Bristol to be guaranteed a room. An impressive sports complex with a well-equipped gym has been developed at the heart of the university precinct, where the careers centre has also been refurbished. The students' union houses one of the city's biggest live music venues as well as a cafe, bars, a theatre and swimming pool.

Bristol has a vibrant youth culture and, as one of the country's most prosperous cities, offers job opportunities to students and graduates alike. The university merges into the centre, its famous gothic tower dominating the skyline from the junction of two of the main shopping streets.

Bristol was chosen by *The Sunday Times* this year as the best city in the UK in which to live and was also European Green Capital for 2015. Most students enjoy life there – and many stay on after graduation – although the high cost of living can be a drawback.

Tuition fees

» Fees for UK/EU students 2018–19 £9,250
» Fees for international students 2018–19 £16,500–£20,300
Dentistry £35,100, Medicine £31,800, Vet science £28,300
» For scholarship and bursary information see www.bristol.ac.uk/fees-funding/undergraduate
» Graduate salary £24,000

Students

Undergraduates	16,360	(365)
Postgraduates	3,925	(1,250)
Applications per place	8.3	
Overall offer rate	69.4%	
International students	15.2%	
Mature students	5.4%	
From state-sector schools	61.4%	
From working-class homes	14.7%	

Accommodation

University-provided places: 5,500
Percentage catered: 33%
Catered costs: £172 – £197 per week
Self-catered: £87 – £165 per week
First year students are guaranteed accommodation
www.bristol.ac.uk/accommodation/undergraduate

Brunel University London

Brunel stresses the relatively unusual combination of a single campus and a London location in its pitch to applicants. It is spending heavily to ensure that the facilities live up to expectations, with £400m already invested and another £150m planned for the current five-year period. Engineering and sports facilities will benefit from the bulk of the outlay, and a £50m learning and teaching centre is at the design stage. A new "green" building for Stem subjects (science, technology, engineering and mathematics) is already open.

The package has had mixed success in recent years. Brunel made a record number of offers in 2016 after 10% growth in applications, but ended up with almost the same number of entrants. The decline in applications in 2017 is slightly less than the national average. Some well-known figures have joined the academic staff, with Benjamin Zephaniah taking up his first academic position as chair of creative writing and Will Self joining as professor of contemporary thought. Plenty of new courses are planned for 2017 and 2018, from banking and finance to school nursing, and a foundation degree in flood and coastal engineering.

Further ahead, the university is aiming to be at the pinnacle of technological universities in the UK and in the top tier internationally. Brunel celebrated its 50th anniversary in 2016 and repeats the wording of its royal charter in its vision for 2030, promising to lead and innovate with new models of research, education and knowledge transfer, placing the needs of society at the heart of its academic activity.

Brunel is benefiting from increased research funding after a good performance in the 2014 Research Excellence Framework. More than 60% of a large submission was rated as world-leading or internationally excellent, with sport sciences achieving the best results and ranking in the top five departments in the UK. Brunel did particularly well in the new assessments of the external impact of research.

Research has been reorganised into three interdisciplinary institutes, Materials and Manufacturing; Energy Futures; and Environment, Health and Societies. The aim is to encourage the development of innovative courses and research projects. The highest-profile example has been the establishment of the first Centre for Comedy Studies Research, supported by Brunel alumni Jo Brand and Lee Mack.

Poor student satisfaction scores prevent Brunel from sitting higher in our rankings, although efforts are being made to turn the tide. The university has taken a number of steps to improve the student experience

Uxbridge
UB8 3PH
01895 265 265
course-enquiries@brunel.ac.uk
www.brunel.ac.uk
https://brunelstudents.com
Open Days 2018:
check website.
Campus tours every
Wednesday

The Times and The Sunday Times Rankings

Overall Ranking: **59** (last year: =54)

Teaching quality	77.3%	103
Student experience	78.2%	76
Research quality	25.4%	50
Entry standards	134	=58
Graduate prospects	73.1%	67
Good honours	73.4%	=57
Expected completion rate	88.6%	=44
Student/staff ratio	15.8	=61
Services and facilities/student	£2,106	63

and graduates' career prospects. The Brunel Educational Excellence Centre provides students with opportunities to enhance their academic skills and encourages innovative teaching, while the Professional Development Centre focuses on employability, bringing together the award-winning Placement and Careers Centre, Modern Foreign Languages and the Innovation Hub. The Brunel+ award adds up points from non-academic activities, so students can show employers they have useful skills beyond their degree.

The impressive library and Brunel's world-class sports facilities have accounted for much of the investment on campus, which retains the original 1960s architecture, but with the addition of striking new buildings and landscaping. The sports facilities are among the best at any university and have been used as a training base by some of the world's top athletes, including sprinters Usain Bolt and Yohan Blake.

More than 50 sports and activities clubs include American football, cheerleading, rock climbing and snowboarding, while the campus gym has four training zones. The multimillion-pound Indoor Athletics Centre on campus has a 130-metre sprint straight, pole vault, high jump and long/triple jump facilities. There is also a bespoke strength and conditioning gym for elite student athletes. Many of Brunel's sports teams compete in the premier leagues for British university and college sport. The Sports Park, just outside the campus, boasts a 400-metre athletics track with tennis and netball courts, pitches for football, rugby and hockey, and a Football Association-registered 3G pitch.

Student accommodation has been transformed as part of the campus improvements. After the refurbishment of existing halls of residence and further construction there are now more than 4,800 places for new first-year, full-time students – enough to enable Brunel to be among the few universities to guarantee accommodation even to those from the local area and those arriving through clearing, as long as they apply by the end of August. As 20% of Brunel's undergraduates enter through clearing, this is an important concession.

The university is based in Uxbridge, in northwest London, an hour or so from the West End by public transport. The campus itself is the centre of many students' social lives.

Tuition fees

»	Fees for UK/EU students 2018–19	£9,750
	Foundation courses	£6,170
»	Fees for international students 2018–19	£14,800–£18,000
	Foundation courses	£16,200–£18,000
»	For scholarship and bursary information see	
	www.brunel.ac.uk/study/undergraduate-fees-and-funding/	
»	Graduate salary	£23,000

Students

Undergraduates	9,580	(275)
Postgraduates	3,360	(950)
Applications per place	10	
Overall offer rate	81.1%	
International students	20.1%	
Mature students	11.7%	
From state-sector schools	93.8%	
From working-class homes	43.3%	

Accommodation

University-provided places: 4,816
Percentage catered: 0%
Self-catered: £88 – £206 per week
First year students are guaranteed accommodation
www.brunel.ac.uk/life/accommodation

University of Buckingham

Buckingham bucked last year's 4% downward trend in applications in spectacular fashion, with a 22% increase in demand for places. Regularly at or near the top for student satisfaction, the university was awarded gold in the first Teaching Excellence Framework results published in June.

Buckingham had the best scores in all areas of the National Student Survey in last year's guide and remains top for teaching quality scores and was *The Sunday Times* and *The Times* University of the Year for Teaching Quality in 2015.

Students value the small-group tutorial system – between eight and 20 undergraduates – and the open access to academics and teaching staff. There is also a growing market for the two-year degrees that Buckingham pioneered more than 40 years ago.

Sir Anthony Seldon, the political historian who joined as vice-chancellor in 2015 after a career in independent schools, is a critic of teaching standards and the failure to do enough to safeguard mental health at university level.

Buckingham is to become Europe's first "positive university" by using positive psychology to enable staff and students to be happier and more resilient while studying – and beyond. The programme is the brainchild of Professor Martin Seligman, the American academic who is the world's leading authority on positive psychology. All tutors will be trained in the subject and every student will have a module focussing on positive relationships, engagements, relationships, meaning and achievement.

Except in medicine, where the fees are £36,500 a year, Buckingham's UK and EU undergraduates pay a total of £25,200 for their two-year course – less than on conventional, three-year degrees, but saving a year's living costs and enabling swifter entry to the labour market. The extended academic year, which makes the university's accelerated degrees possible, demands four nine-week terms and still allows for 16 weeks off.

Undergraduates can begin courses in January, July or September. Just over half of the students are from overseas, but the proportion from Britain is growing. They have the option of a three-year degree in the humanities, and other schools are now following suit.

Students from the five counties nearest to the university – Buckinghamshire, Bedfordshire, Northamptonshire, Hertfordshire and Oxfordshire – receive an automatic reduction of £2,000 a year on their fees. Others who take out government maintenance loans of more than £5,000 qualify for bursaries of £1,100 and there are £2,000 scholarships (except in medicine) for those who achieve at least AAB at A-level.

Hunter Street
Buckingham MK18 1EG
01280 814 080
admissions@buckingham.ac.uk
www.buckingham.ac.uk
Open Days 2018:
March 10, April 19,
June 24, August 18,
October 6

The Times and The Sunday Times Rankings

Overall Ranking: =47 (last year: 41)

Teaching quality	87.2%	1
Student experience	85.9%	4
Research quality	n/a	
Entry standards	122	=86
Graduate prospects	75%	60
Good honours	62%	118
Expected completion rate	78.1%	114
Student/staff ratio	10.4	=2
Services and facilities/student	£2,185	52

For many years Britain's only private university, Buckingham is still the only one in our main league table, now well established in the top 50. It would finish higher had it been eligible for research quality assessment under the Research Excellence Framework. Buckingham has a number of research groups and more than 170 research students. It is refurbishing property to accommodate the Humanities Research Institute and plans to enter the research assessment system in future.

The very different university experience that Buckingham offers is taken up by only about 2,000 students, but current building plans, backed by a £70m fundraising programme, would allow for future expansion. The £6m Vinson Centre for liberal economics, now under construction, will also act as a social learning hub and focal point for the university, with a new lecture theatre, bookshop and public space.

A development plan for the Buckingham Riverside campus includes a new school of law, and more than 200 student bedrooms in the old Tanlaw Mill. The plans also include a sports centre and floodlit pitch for university and public use.

Buckingham's most prestigious recent development has been the opening of the UK's first private not-for-profit medical school, where 64 students arrived in 2015. The course, which has seen a 30% increase in applications in 2017, is four-and-a-half-years long. A new £8m clinical training centre opens at Milton Keynes Hospital early in 2018 and the Riverside Campus plans include an extension for the school's headquarters.

The education school is based at Whittlebury Hall, near Towcester. A minibus provides transport between the campuses. Other recent developments have included the opening of the university's first premises in London to host lectures and other activities.

The campus library and teaching space has been expanded and the main refectory refurbished as part of a rolling programme of improvements to student facilities. The main campus, which has been judged to be the safest in England, includes a bar and a fitness centre, with the Radcliffe Centre, which hosts internal and external events, nearby. The town of Buckingham is pretty but quiet, with a good selection of pubs and restaurants.

Tuition fees

»	Fees for UK/EU students 2018–19	£11,200–£12,600
		(8 or 9-term degree)
	Foundation course	£9,450
	Medicine	£36,500
»	Fees for international students 2018–19	£15,468–£17,400
	Foundation courses	£9,450
	Medicine	£36,500 (4-year course)
»	For scholarship and bursary information see www.buckingham.ac.uk/admissions/scholarships	
»	Graduate salary	£20,000

Students

Undergraduates	1,145	(65)
Postgraduates	1,105	(85)
Applications per place	8.2	
Overall offer rate	n/a	
International students	48.3%	
Mature students	23.5%	
From state-sector schools	68.4%	
From working-class homes	25%	

Accommodation

University-provided places: 550
Percentage catered: 0%
Self-catered: £89 – £196 per week
www.buckingham.ac.uk/life/accommodation

Buckinghamshire New University

There will be no scholarships or bursaries at Buckinghamshire New University for the first time in 2018–19. The university had been reviewing whether the £200,000 allocated to these programmes was money well spent and retained them for the coming academic year, but has now decided to pursue widening participation through other measures.

Only four universities enjoyed stronger growth in enrolments from the UK and EU than Bucks New's 12% increase in 2016. The university has not released figures for the current year, but has been shedding posts and suspending some courses, suggesting that it is not immune from the year's downward national trend.

The university specialises in industry-focused degree programmes and professional qualifications serving the creative and cultural industries, management and the public sector. Travel and aviation courses provide the opportunity to obtain a professional pilot's licence while studying. Bucks New offers some of the UK's only music management courses, as well as film and television production.

The university is one of the few to offer a degree in policing and is also among the leading providers of nursing qualifications in the southeast, offering adult, child and mental health pre-qualifying nursing, as well as post-registration courses. Nursing is taught in Uxbridge and there is a new and innovative campus for higher education and professional development, Aylesbury Vale, hosting programmes taught by the university and Aylesbury College.

The main campus in High Wycombe, where more than 5,000 students are based, is benefiting from more than £100m of investment over a ten-year period. Its prizewinning building, the Gateway, transformed the town-centre campus with improved teaching, social and administrative space. The complex includes a sports hall, gym, treatment rooms and sports laboratory, open to the public as well as to students.

In 2016 the university opened a Human Performance, Exercise and Wellbeing Centre, featuring a three-lane running track with 3D motion-capture technology, along with a sports injury and physiotherapy clinic.

New learning areas and informal spaces have also been added in High Wycombe, where there are now more than 400 en-suite bedrooms in a student village a short walk from the campus. This has brought the total accommodation stock to 885 residential places. New students are guaranteed a hall place if they apply by June 30.

A new centre for life sciences innovation has been backed by the Buckinghamshire Thames Valley Local Enterprise Partnership that agreed to provide £1.3m in capital

Alexandra Road
High Wycombe HP11 2JZ
03330 123 2023
admissions@bucks.ac.uk
www.bucks.ac.uk
www.bucksstudentunion.org
Open Days 2018:
June 9

The Times and The Sunday Times **Rankings**
Overall Ranking: **126** (last year: 118)

Teaching quality	78.5%	=88
Student experience	76.4%	102
Research quality	1.5%	123
Entry standards	109	=118
Graduate prospects	62%	122
Good honours	55.5%	128
Expected completion rate	77.1%	=116
Student/staff ratio	17.5	=95
Services and facilities/student	£2,047	74

funds. The facility will have bases at Stoke Mandeville Hospital and High Wycombe, developing products to help people manage their own health through medical devices and digital apps.

The university prides itself on its links with local business and private sector employers, which help to shape the curriculum as well as providing placement opportunities. The social work academy, for example, is run in partnership with Buckinghamshire county council, where the university's academics support the continuing professional development of qualified social workers and managers.

Bucks New was awarded university status in 2007. Research is focused on the needs of business, commerce and industry, along with the public and voluntary sectors. Research centres and institutes focus on nursing, policing, social work, telehealth, sport and vocational learning. However, it is near the bottom of our table for research quality, having entered only 24 staff for the 2014 Research Excellence Framework. The results play a part in the university's lowly position in our league table, which now stands in the bottom five, after a drop of eight places in the current edition. Bucks has fallen 40 places in the measure of teaching quality taken from the National Student Survey, which was its top area in the last edition of the *Guide*. There was an improvement in entry standards, but

the university is now only one place off the bottom for graduate prospects.

But the institution has been celebrating its 125th anniversary, having started life as a Science and Art School which benefited from the proceeds of a highly unpopular tax imposed on beer and spirits. The fund became so large that Parliament decided to make it available for education purposes. Buckinghamshire County Council and local fundraising fairs provided the necessary finance to build the new institution. Since then, the university has had 11 name changes and several different sites.

There are about 9,000 students, two-thirds of whom are full-time undergraduates, with 40% of them over 21 years old on entry. They all have free access to entertainment, recreational activities and sport through the university's Big Deal programme, which has been running since before the introduction of £9,000 fees.

There are clubs for 30 sports and links with professional clubs in the region. The university's gym is one of the best exercise facilities in the area, with interactive exercise equipment. High Wycombe has a range of student pubs and clubs and is within easy reach of London.

Tuition fees

» Fees for UK/EU students 2018–19	£9,250
» Fees for international students 2017–18	£10,500
» Graduate salary	£21,900

Students

Undergraduates	5,925	(1,675)
Postgraduates	330	(650)
Applications per place	5.2	
Overall offer rate	89.8%	
International students	8.6%	
Mature students	33.7%	
From state-sector schools	96.5%	
From working-class homes	46.2%	

Accommodation

University-provided places: 885
Percentage catered: 0%
Self-catered: £107 – £179 per week
First year students are guaranteed accommodation
https://www.bucks.ac.uk/life-at-bucks/accommodation

University of Cambridge

Such is the competition for places at Cambridge – the top university in our league table for the past five years – that entrance tests have now been reintroduced in addition to A-levels across the university. Some subjects had them already, but there are now pre-interview assessments in more than half of the subjects, and written tests at interview for the rest.

The change was one result of successful campaigns over a number of years to attract more applicants, especially from state schools. Almost 62% of entrants in 2015–16 were state-educated, still far below the university's benchmark but a significant improvement on previous years and a considerably greater proportion than is admitted to Oxford.

Cambridge has the highest entry standards of any UK university, demanding at least A*AA at A-level in arts subjects and A*A*A in the sciences, although candidates may be made a lower offer if their school or personal circumstances are thought to disadvantage them. There may be fewer than four applicants to each place, but only one in three receives a conditional offer. Nine out of ten entrants have at least three A grades at A-level or the equivalent.

Cambridge has dropped out of the top four in the QS world rankings and was overtaken by Oxford in Times Higher Education's equivalent, but it is widely considered the UK's pre-eminent university. It tops more than half of our subject tables and produced the best results in the 2014 Research Excellence Framework. It was awarded gold in the government's first Teaching Excellence Framework.

The university has no plans to follow the trend at other Russell Group institutions to expand the undergraduate intake, although three new degrees have been launched this year in archaeology, history and modern languages, and history and politics.

The completion of the first buildings on its colossal new North West Cambridge development will enable it to take more postgraduates. The £1bn project, which will take until 2030 to complete, will include accommodation for 2,000 postgraduates, as well as 100,000 square metres of academic and research space, 1,500 homes for university staff and another 1,500 private houses.

In the city centre, Cambridge possesses some of the most ancient and iconic buildings at any university and huge sums have been spent modernising the facilities. The £26m Maxwell Centre opened last year on the West Cambridge site where research scientists from industry occupy laboratory and desk space alongside Cambridge research groups. The university is aiming to raise £2m to create new professorships and continue developing its biomedical campus.

Cambridge Admissions Office
Fitzwilliam House
Cambridge CB2 1QY
01223 333 308
admissions@cam.ac.uk
www.cam.ac.uk
www.cusu.cam.ac.uk
Open Days 2018:
July 5, 6

The Times and The Sunday Times **Rankings**

Overall Ranking: **1** (last year: 1)

Teaching quality	n/a	
Student experience	n/a	
Research quality	57.3%	1
Entry standards	230	1
Graduate prospects	87.5%	3
Good honours	92.1%	2
Expected completion rate	98.9%	1
Student/staff ratio	11	4
Services and facilities/student	£3,510	1

Cambridge entered the most academics – 95% – for the Research Excellence Framework and 87% of their work was rated as world-leading or internationally excellent. It achieved the UK's best results in aeronautical and electronic engineering, business and management, chemistry, classics and clinical medicine.

The application system has been simplified somewhat, with candidates no longer required to complete an initial Cambridge form as well as their UCAS form. However, they are sent the Supplementary Application Questionnaire, after they have submitted their UCAS form, to cover academic experience in more detail. Applications close on October 15.

The tripos system was a forerunner of the modular degree, allowing students to change subjects (within limits) midway through their courses. Students receive a classification for each of the two parts of their degrees, based on examination outcomes at the end of their second and final years.

Choosing a college is an additional complication for those not familiar with Cambridge. Making the right choice is crucial to university life, whether you would rather live close to the centre of things or in a less hectic area, for example. Applicants can take pot luck with an open application if they prefer not to opt for a particular college but only a minority take this route. Picking a college has often been said to enhance the chances of getting a place, but statistics show it makes no difference.

The emphasis has shifted from colleges towards the centre in recent years and most teaching is now university-based rather than college-based, especially in the sciences. However, the colleges usually provide the key social groupings that sustain students through their university careers, so an open-day visit is essential to see where you feel comfortable.

Sports facilities are excellent, both at individual colleges and in the £16m sports centre, which features a large sports hall and a strength and conditioning wing.

Cambridge is not for everyone, however bright. The amount of high-quality work to be crammed into eight-week terms can prove a strain, although the projected dropout rate of 1.1% is the lowest at any university. Most students relish the experience and reap the rewards in their subsequent careers and salaries.

Tuition fees

» Fees for UK/EU students 2018–19	£9,250
» Fees for international students 2018–19	£19,197–£29,217
Medicine and veterinary medicine	£50,130
» For scholarship, bursaries and college awards see http://www.undergraduate.study.cam.ac.uk/ fees-and-finance	
» Graduate salary	£27,000

Students

Undergraduates	11,905	(315)
Postgraduates	6,380	(1,060)
Applications per place	4.9	
Overall offer rate	33.8%	
International students	20.5%	
Mature students	4.1%	
From state-sector schools	61.9%	
From working-class homes	10.2%	

Accommodation

See: www.undergraduate.study.cam.ac.uk/why-cambridge/student-life/accommodation

College websites provide accommodation details

See Chapter 13 for individual colleges

Canterbury Christ Church University

Canterbury Christ Church has received planning permission for a £150m development of its main campus. The university has bases in Chatham and Broadstairs, plus a postgraduate centre in Tunbridge Wells, but it is in Canterbury itself that it is developing its technology and engineering centre, with support from local industry and business.

There will be a specific focus on supporting skills development and careers in southeast England. There will also be a new arts facility on the Canterbury campus in September 2018 to promote employment in the creative and digital industries. Shared by the schools of media, art and design, and music and performing arts, the building will house specialist teaching facilities, including space for performance and music, design studios and the latest technology.

It is not just the buildings that are changing. Twenty new degrees have been introduced, with another six already planned for 2018, including animation, games design, music production and physiotherapy. Christ Church has also designed a range of higher and degree apprenticeship courses, offering school-leavers another route into higher education where they work full-time for an industry-leading company while also studying for a university qualification.

There are already higher and degree apprenticeships in nursing and allied health professions, and management. There are plans for others in life sciences, engineering, accountancy, law, computing, teaching, coaching and mentoring, leisure and tourism, policing and journalism.

Bucking the trend of recent years, Christ Church is moving from three terms to a new semester-based system with teaching spread over two extended periods. The university believes that this will give students more opportunity to immerse themselves in their course with in-depth study and dedicated time set aside to develop their academic, personal and employability skills. Positive feedback from the current students has helped in the design of these changes.

The university is also working with the University of Kent on proposals for a joint medical school to further support local and regional healthcare services.

The university will hope that the new developments can arrest a steady decline in applications over the past two years. Although the numbers enrolling were up slightly in 2016, there had been a 12% drop in applications since 2014. Christ Church had also dropped into the bottom 20 in our league table, mainly as a result of a decline in student satisfaction.

There are now about 17,000 students, more than half of whom come from Kent,

---

North Holmes Road
Canterbury CT1 1QU
01227 782 900
admissions@canterbury.ac.uk
www.canterbury.ac.uk
https://ccsu.co.uk
Open Days 2018:
see website

The Times and The Sunday Times **Rankings**
Overall Ranking: **111** (last year: 114)

Teaching quality	79.8%	=72
Student experience	74.9%	=111
Research quality	4.5%	97
Entry standards	113	=111
Graduate prospects	63.9%	111
Good honours	70%	=75
Expected completion rate	83.3%	=85
Student/staff ratio	16.3	=73
Services and facilities/student	£1,658	106

while nearly 1,000 of the rest are from continental Europe or further afield.

The former Church of England college achieved university status in 2005, and is one of the region's largest providers of courses and research for the public services, with teacher training courses that are highly rated by Ofsted, and strong programmes in health and social care, nursing and policing.

Seven out of ten undergraduates are female – partly the result of the subject mix, with its emphasis on health subjects and education. The university remains a Church of England foundation and has the Archbishop of Canterbury as its chancellor.

The purpose-built campus at Broadstairs offers a range of subjects, from commercial music to digital media, photography, and early childhood studies, while the recently expanded Medway site at Chatham's historic dockyard specialises in education and health programmes. The majority of students, however, are at the university's main campus at Canterbury, a world heritage site where Christ Church spent £35m on its prize-winning library and student services centre. All campuses are interconnected by a high-speed data network.

Almost half of Canterbury Christ Church's submission to the 2014 research assessments was placed in the top two categories, resulting in one of the biggest percentage increases in funding at any university.

A life sciences industry liaison laboratory opened in 2016 at Discovery Park in Sandwich, providing students with first-class facilities for science and research, and acting as an added resource for local businesses. The UK Institute for Migration Research is another high-profile addition, as is the Institute of Medical Sciences, which builds on the university's work in stem cell research and minimally invasive surgery.

Sports facilities are good for those on the Canterbury campus and there is enough residential accommodation to guarantee a place for first-year students who apply by the end of July.

Canterbury is now a thriving student centre, as the general election showed with the first Labour victory in the seat, and Christ Church contributes to the cultural life of the city with the Sidney Cooper gallery and St Gregory's Centre for Music, a historic concert venue.

Tuition fees

»	Fees for UK/EU students 2018–19	£9,250
	Foundation courses	£6,165
»	Fees for international students 2018–19	£11,500
»	For scholarship and bursary information see	
	www.canterbury.ac.uk/study-here/fees-and-funding	
»	Graduate salary	£21,500

Students

Undergraduates	10,360	(2,755)
Postgraduates	1,025	(1,915)
Applications per place	4.7	
Overall offer rate	83.7%	
International students	5.2%	
Mature students	31.3%	
From state-sector schools	97.3%	
From working-class homes	39.8%	

Accommodation

University-provided places: 1,825
Percentage catered: 0%
Self-catered: £118 – £167 per week
First year students are guaranteed accommodation
www.canterbury.ac.uk/accommodation

Cardiff University

Cardiff has overtaken Swansea by a whisker in our new league table and claimed the Welsh University of the Year title from its big rival to boot. Last year was the only occasion when Cardiff failed to rank highest of the Welsh universities.

Applications and enrolments are at record levels, it is ranked among the top 40 universities in Europe for innovation, and it was one of only 12 universities to be awarded a Regius professorship (in chemistry) to mark the Queen's 90th birthday last year.

The university is investing £600m in its estate, including £260m on student facilities. Work has begun on a £50m Centre for Student Life at the heart of the Cathays Park campus, which will provide a central hub for support services, as well as flexible social learning spaces, a 550-seat lecture theatre and shops. The centre, which is being developed in partnership with the students' union, is due to open in 2019–20.

Other projects include a new home for Cardiff's highly rated School of Journalism, Media and Cultural Studies, a hall of residence for 700 students and a £40m programme to refurbish lecture theatres, classrooms and seminar rooms.

The most recent addition was a brain imaging research centre, boasting Europe's most powerful brain scanner, which opened on the university's new £300m innovation campus. Professor Colin Riordan, Cardiff's vice-chancellor, said innovation was central to the university's strategy, as he welcomed a nine-place rise in Reuters' rankings of the most innovative universities in Europe. The university enjoyed the biggest rise in the UK in collaborative research funding last year.

Cardiff is the only member of the Russell Group of research-led universities in Wales, and the country's sole representative in the top 150 of the world rankings. It is also one of the few universities in the UK to boast two Nobel laureates on its staff.

The university increased the intake of undergraduates by another 500 in 2016, awarding places to 30% more students than at the beginning of the decade. There are now more than 30,000 students, including 6,000 from outside the UK.

The university occupies a significant part of Cardiff's civic complex around Cathays Park. The five healthcare schools at the Heath Park campus share a 53-acre site with the University Hospital of Wales. The £18m Cochrane building provides teaching and learning facilities for all healthcare schools based there. The dentistry school's dental education clinic offers students some of the UK's most modern training facilities, including a new simulation suite.

Cardiff
CF10 3AT
029 2087 4455
enquiry@cardiff.ac.uk
www.cardiff.ac.uk
www.cardiffstudents.com
Open Days 2018: April 18

Edinburgh
Belfast
London
CARDIFF

The Times and The Sunday Times Rankings

Overall Ranking: **35** (last year: 46)

Teaching quality	77.9%	=98
Student experience	78.3%	=73
Research quality	35%	34
Entry standards	157	=33
Graduate prospects	78.9%	43
Good honours	79.1%	32
Expected completion rate	93%	21
Student/staff ratio	12.9	=14
Services and facilities/student	£2,243	46

An audit by the Quality Assurance Agency complimented the university on its "powerful academic vision and well-developed and effectively articulated mission to achieve excellence in teaching and research".

One undergraduate in seven comes from an independent school – the highest proportion in Wales – but there are extensive efforts to widen participation. Bursaries of £1,000 are available to undergraduates from low-income families, and an additional £3,000 is paid to care leavers. The projected dropout rate is comfortably the lowest in Wales.

The Global Opportunities programme provides study, work and volunteering options across the world to enhance the student experience. The university has also launched a Languages for All programme, giving students the chance to learn another language alongside their chosen degree for free.

In addition, students are offered the Cardiff Award to boost their employment prospects by recognising the skills acquired from extracurricular activities, while an enterprise team helps with business start-ups, offering advice and training.

Cardiff achieved excellent results in the 2014 Research Excellence Framework, but entered only 62% of eligible staff. The entry was 12 percentage points smaller than any other Russell Group university, limiting its position in our research ranking and our wider league table. Nevertheless, 87% of the submission rated as world-leading or internationally excellent and Cardiff was in the UK's top three for the impact of its research. Civil and construction engineering was rated top in the exercise.

Library services have continued to improve, with extensive electronic resources and self-service provision to speed up the operation. Students have online access to information about their studies and social life, from reading lists to social events.

The university owns or manages almost 6,000 residential places, enabling it to guarantee a place to those making Cardiff their first choice. The main residential site at Talybont boasts a sports training village, and there is also a refurbished city-centre fitness suite and a sports ground. The students' union has been upgraded recently and, beyond the campus, Cardiff is a popular student city, relatively inexpensive and with a good range of nightlife and cultural venues.

Tuition fees

- » Fees for UK/EU students 2018–19 £9,000
- » Fees for international students 2018–19 £15,950–£19,950
  Medicine & dentistry £35,250
- » For scholarship and bursary information see
  www.cardiff.ac.uk/study/undergraduate/funding
- » Graduate salary £21,000

Students

Undergraduates	18,615	(3,290)
Postgraduates	4,745	(4,030)
Applications per place	6.6	
Overall offer rate	74.8%	
International students	17.5%	
Mature students	12.3%	
From state-sector schools	85.9%	
From working-class homes	23.8%	

Accommodation

University-provided places: 5,994
Percentage catered: 16%
Catered costs: £119 – £143 per week
Self-catered: £105 – £134 per week
First year students are guaranteed accommodation
www.cardiff.ac.uk/residences

Cardiff Metropolitan University

The university's new technologies school will welcome its first students this year, with its courses in digital media and smart technology, data science and informatics, design technology and engineering starting on Cardiff Met's Llandaff campus.

The school is expected to transfer to a new site in the city by 2020, with the university describing the scheme as a "unique collaborative approach to a global industry-education partnership".

Cardiff Met had already announced plans for a new school of media campus in the centre of the capital, in partnership with the Chinese education and media group Phoenix. The teaching and accommodation site is planned to attract 2,000 students from around the world.

A new initiative called "Cardiff Global" will be launched by the university to develop the concept of an international university rooted in Wales. Cardiff open colleges will develop partnerships with schools and further education institutes to deliver clear progression routes to university entry, promote the expansion of provision for the Welsh medium and foster civic engagement in the region.

Global academies, meanwhile, will focus on research, developing interdisciplinary and international postgraduate and research provision.

Cardiff Met has an office in China and 1,200 international students who voted the university the best in the UK for student support for six years in a row. There are also more than 6,500 students studying for Cardiff Met degrees in more than a dozen countries. These international partnerships provide an opportunity for students to spend part of their education abroad. The university has also been awarded the government's charter mark five times, the judges commenting particularly on the level of student satisfaction.

Professor Cara Aitchison, who became vice-chancellor in 2016 after moving from the University of St Mark & St John, Plymouth, said she had been attracted by Cardiff Met's strategic plan for a "growing, dynamic and ambitious university". She has already introduced an enhanced personal tutor system, promising students greater access to academic support, advice and guidance. A number of new degrees are being introduced, from fashion design and public health to dance and physical education.

In 2015 the university celebrated the 150th anniversary of the founding of the Cardiff School of Art, which eventually evolved into Cardiff Met. It adopted its present name four years earlier after a long period as the University of Wales Institute Cardiff.

---

200 Western Avenue
Llandaff
Cardiff CF5 2YB
029 2041 6010
askadmissions@cardiffmet.ac.uk
www.cardiffmet.ac.uk
www.cardiffmetsu.co.uk
Open Days 2018:
April 21 (Llandaff Campus),
April 28 (Cyncoed)

The Times and The Sunday Times **Rankings**
Overall Ranking: **90** (last year: 89)

Teaching quality	80.6%	=57
Student experience	80%	=38
Research quality	3.9%	107
Entry standards	128	=71
Graduate prospects	63.8%	112
Good honours	63.7%	=114
Expected completion rate	80.8%	=97
Student/staff ratio	17.2	91
Services and facilities/student	£2,512	30

The university had already committed £70m to improvements on its two campuses. The purpose-built art and design school is now open on the Llandaff campus, which also hosts the management school, as well as design, engineering, food science and health courses.

The Cyncoed campus, which houses education and sport, has a modern student centre and is the main centre of social activity, particularly for first-years.

The university entered only 35 academics for the 2014 Research Excellence Framework out of 381 who were eligible – only two universities entered a smaller proportion. But the small submission scored well, with 80% of the work rated in the top two categories. The university has since received a Queen's Anniversary prize for the use of design and related 3D digital scanning technologies as applied to maxillofacial reconstructive surgery.

Cardiff Met is one of Britain's leading centres for university sport, with team performances that do justice to some excellent facilities. In recent years it has had British university champions in sports ranging from archery and gymnastics to squash, weightlifting and judo. More than 300 past or present students are internationals in 30 sports.

The university's pride and joy is the £7m National Indoor Athletics Centre, but other facilities are also of high quality. As well as participating in a thriving sports club scene, about 2,000 students take sport and dance-related courses. Cardiff Met has recently completed a new sports arena, with basketball, netball and badminton courts. A 25-metre swimming pool is also being built, together with a fitness suite.

Undergraduate applications and enrolments fell for the second successive year in 2016, but the new programmes are recruiting well. Students from Wales account for two thirds of the 13,000 students, half of whom are from Cardiff or the Vale of Glamorgan.

The two sites in Cardiff are close to the city centre and linked by the Met Rider bus service during term-time. The halls of residence are a mile from the main campus on the Plas Gwyn residential campus where there are enough hall places to accommodate most first-years.

Tuition fees

» Fees for UK/EU students 2018–19 £9,000
» Fees for international students 2018–19 £12,000–£13,500
» For scholarship and bursary information see www.cardiffmet.ac.uk/study/finance/bursaries/
» Graduate salary £18,000

Students		
Undergraduates	8,595	(625)
Postgraduates	2,325	(1,035)
Applications per place	4.6	
Overall offer rate	85.6%	
International students	16.5%	
Mature students	26.8%	
From state-sector schools	96%	
From working-class homes	38.4%	

Accommodation

University-provided places: 1,548
Percentage catered: 21%
Catered costs: £153 – £174 per week
Self-catered: £110 – £130 per week
Priority is given to first year students
www.cardiffmet.ac.uk/accommodation

University of Central Lancashire

The first UK students will enrol on UCLan's medical degree in September 2018 as the university plays its part in the government's strategy to increase the number of doctors trained by a quarter by 2024.

The medical school opened in 2015 but limits on the numbers of funded undergraduate places for UK students restricted the intake initially to self-funded international students. They will continue to be charged up to £38,000 a year, but their British counterparts will pay the normal £9,250 UK fee.

UCLan offers dentistry, pharmacy and astrophysics in a surprisingly wide portfolio of more than 200 undergraduate programmes. The dental school was among the few to open in a century, while the architecture degree was the first for a decade.

As part of the university's £200m campus masterplan, a centre for engineering and innovation is due to open this year. The building will be an integrated hub for teaching, research and knowledge exchange, dedicated to reclaiming Lancashire's role as a national centre for advanced manufacturing and encouraging more women to choose a career in engineering.

Another pioneering initiative will see the first collaboration of its kind between a police force and a university. A partnership with Lancashire constabulary will involve forensic experts and students working alongside each other in new purpose-built police facilities to research, investigate and deliver forensic science services. The agreement cements plans for a forensic academy in Lancashire, based at the police headquarters, which will include research laboratories and teaching and training suites.

UCLan is in the top ten universities in the UK for the number of undergraduates it educates, despite a fall in enrolments in 2016. The university made 3,000 fewer offers, partly in order to preserve its entry standards, although it stresses that its commitment to widening participation in higher education means that it remains keen to attract entries from students with non-traditional qualifications onto a wide range of courses, including the many foundation courses designed to bring students up to the level required for an honours degree.

With more than 35,000 students, UCLan dominates the centre of Preston and brings at least £200m a year into the local economy. There are also smaller campuses in Cyprus and Mauritius. The university was the first of its peer group to appear in the QS World University Rankings. A separate rating of teaching, research and facilities by QS gave UCLan four out of five stars.

Another campus, in Burnley, gives local students the opportunity to gain qualifications without leaving home. It hosts a collaboration

---

Preston
PR1 2HE
01772 892 444
uadmissions@uclan.ac.uk
www.uclan.ac.uk
www.uclansu.co.uk
Open Days 2018:
March 24, June 13, 16

The Times and *The Sunday Times* **Rankings**

Overall Ranking: **93** (last year: =101)

Teaching quality	80.3%	=64
Student experience	77.7%	78
Research quality	5.6%	=86
Entry standards	137	=53
Graduate prospects	70%	82
Good honours	68.1%	92
Expected completion rate	79.5%	107
Student/staff ratio	16.2	=71
Services and facilities/student	£1,945	82

with Cisco Systems, an American technology firm, for advanced manufacturing incorporating robotics, computer vision, non-destructive testing and component assembly.

UCLan has long been a leader in widening participation, with 45% of its undergraduates coming from the four lowest socio-economic classes. Large numbers take external programmes delivered in further education colleges, which have been expanded this year with 16 new degrees or foundation degrees in subjects from spa management to fashion and textiles.

The university's roots go back to 1828 and it has established partnerships with a variety of high-profile organisations. There is a longstanding collaboration with Nasa, for example, the most recent research venture enabling UCLan scientists to help in the discovery of the first known system of seven Earth-size planets around a single star.

There is also sector-leading stroke research with the Department of Health, and work on nutritional science with the Bill & Melinda Gates Foundation. There was some world-leading research in all 16 subject areas that were assessed in the 2014 Research Excellence Framework. The undergraduate research internship scheme enables students from all disciplines to work on research projects for up to ten weeks.

UCLan has a strong focus on entrepreneurship and has established a range of business incubation facilities for its students and graduates. The university works with a wide variety of industrial partners and many undergraduate programmes are directly linked to them. All students can take advantage of work placements and other opportunities to enhance their employability.

The sports facilities are excellent and UCLan has nearly 50 teams in the British Universities and Colleges Sport league. Compared with Manchester or Liverpool, the security risks and cost of living are both low, yet Preston is only 50 minutes away from both cities.

Tuition fees

» Fees for UK/EU students 2010-19   £9,250
    Foundation courses   £6,400
» Fees for international students 2018-19   £12,450-£14,950
    Foundation courses   £7,350-£8,350
    Medicine   £38,000
» For scholarship and bursary information see
    http://www.uclan.ac.uk/study_here/fees_and_finance/
    bursaries_scholarships.php
» Graduate salary   £19,000

Students

Undergraduates	16,390	(3,790)
Postgraduates	1,180	(3,095)
Applications per place	6.3	
Overall offer rate	81.5%	
International students	8.6%	
Mature students	32.9%	
From state-sector schools	98.4%	
From working-class homes	45.1%	

Accommodation

University-provided places: 1,716
Percentage catered: 0%
Self-catered: £79 – £110 per week
www.uclan.ac.uk/accommodation/index.php

University of Chester

As the competition for students seeking traditional degrees intensifies, Chester is expanding its range of degree apprenticeships. Enrolments grew in 2016, despite a second successive year of declining applications. But a drop of almost 9% in those applying this year was more than twice the national average, blamed in part on the withdrawal of NHS bursaries.

The university is already running chartered manager degree apprenticeships with a number of companies, and in 2018 expects to offer the qualification in digital and technology solutions, plus several branches of engineering.

Chester received a silver award in the new Teaching Excellence Framework (TEF), praised for the wide range of activities supporting the development of employability skills. Around two thirds of undergraduates take work-based learning modules. Chester was found to have an "embedded culture of valuing, recognising and rewarding good teaching", with more than two thirds of the academic staff holding Higher Education Academy fellowships. The TEF panel also acknowledged the investment made in high-quality teaching and learning facilities as well as the university's relationship with student representatives.

A student contract of the type that is becoming universal in higher education sets out clear conditions on the offer of a place and similarly details the university's responsibilities. The student promises to "study diligently, and to attend promptly and participate appropriately at lectures, courses, classes, seminars, tutorials, work placements and other activities which form part of the programme". The university undertakes to deliver the programme to the student, but leaves itself considerable leeway beyond that.

About a quarter of the undergraduates are 21 or over on entry and two thirds are female. Nearly all are state-educated, and more than a third have working-class roots. Progression agreements guarantee interviews to students at a number of local colleges, subject to certain conditions, but there is no reduction in entry requirements.

The dropout rate had been improving, but has now slipped back slightly above the national average for Chester's courses and entry qualifications, with about one in nine students failing to complete their course.

The university more than doubled the number of submissions made to the 2014 Research Excellence Framework compared with the 2008 assessments. Some research was judged to be world-leading in all but one of the 15 subject areas.

Chester's parent institution was established in 1839 as the first purpose-built college for training teachers. William Gladstone was among the founders of the

---

Parkgate Road
Chester CH1 4BJ
01244 511 000
enquiries@chester.ac.uk
www.chester.ac.uk
www.chestersu.com
Open Days 2018:
Chester, June 2

The Times and The Sunday Times Rankings

Overall Ranking: =61 (last year: 81)

Teaching quality	82.7%	26
Student experience	79.6%	46
Research quality	4.1%	=101
Entry standards	119	=95
Graduate prospects	69.5%	=84
Good honours	64%	=109
Expected completion rate	80.7%	=100
Student/staff ratio	13.5	=25
Services and facilities/student	£2,640	23

Church of England college, which pre-dated all the English universities apart from Oxford, Cambridge, London and Durham. The link with the church remains, as does the teacher training provision, which has been rated "outstanding" by Ofsted. But by the time university status arrived in 2005 there was already a much broader range of courses.

The university increasingly operates on a regional footing after recent expansion. It opened the first undergraduate base in Shrewsbury in 2015 to add to its campuses in Warrington and Thornton, in Wirral, and four others in its home city. Like the Shrewsbury campus, the Queen's Park site in Chester is another recent addition to the university's estate. The former wartime headquarters of the army's Western Command, it now houses the business and management faculty.

The university had already opened the UK's first new engineering faculty for two decades, in the former Shell research facility at Thornton Science Park campus near Ellesmere Port.

The Parkgate Road campus, the original headquarters, is only a short walk from the centre of Chester, a 32-acre site boasting manicured gardens where recent developments include an upgraded library and sports facilities. The adjacent Riverside Innovation Centre serves new and growing businesses, including those run by entrepreneurial students and graduates.

Kingsway campus, which also has a learning resources centre, is home to the arts and media faculty. The faculties of health and social care, and education and children's services are based at Chester's historic former County Hall.

The Warrington campus, which has eight halls of residence, focuses on the creative industries and public services. It has high-quality production facilities and the university has links with the BBC in Salford, which opens up new employment opportunities for graduates. The library has tripled in size and there is a business centre for students and local firms. There is also a venue that regularly attracts up-and-coming acts.

There are extensive sports facilities at Warrington and especially on the Parkgate Road campus, which includes tennis courts, a 100-metre sprint track and a floodlit 3G multiuse sports pitch.

In keeping with the university's Christian foundation, there are chapels on two campuses and a number of other faith spaces. Students' union facilities form the basis of the social scene, but the picturesque city of Chester also has a lot to offer.

Tuition fees
- » Fees for UK/EU students 2018–19   £9,250
  Foundation courses   £8,250
- » Fees for international students 2018–19   £11,950
- » For scholarship and bursary information see www.chester.ac.uk/study/undergraduate/finance/bursaries
- » Graduate salary   £20,000

Students

Undergraduates	9,050	(1,775)
Postgraduates	1,050	(3,035)
Applications per place	6.9	
Overall offer rate	84%	
International students	4.2%	
Mature students	21.8%	
From state-sector schools	97.1%	
From working-class homes	33.9%	

Accommodation

University-provided places: 1,820
Percentage catered: 38
Catered costs: £114 – £159 per week
Self-catered: £83 – £138 per week
www.chester.ac.uk/accommodation

University of Chichester

A return to high scores in the annual National Student Survey has helped Chichester bounce back in our league table after a fall last year. Stellar performances in the survey have been the university's strong suit in rankings, alongside a dropout rate of about half the expected level, which saw Chichester crowned our University of the Year for Student Retention in both 2013 and 2016.

The university is up ten places in the new edition, thanks mainly to increases in both of our student satisfaction measures, which place it in the top 20 for each. There has been a decline in spending on student facilities but staffing levels have improved.

The independent panel that awarded Chichester silver in the government's new Teaching Excellence Framework regarded student satisfaction levels as outstanding. It found that the student experience was "tailored to the individual, maximising rates of retention, attainment and progression, with particularly outstanding support for students from disadvantaged groups".

The panel also commented favourably on how employment skills are embedded in the curriculum, although Chichester struggles in our table for employability, which relies on the proportion of graduates progressing to professional jobs or further study.

The university traces its history back to 1839 when the college that subsequently bore his name was founded in memory of William Otter, the education-minded Bishop of Chichester. It became a teacher training college for women, who still account for two thirds of the places, and eventually merged with the nearby Bognor Regis College of Education. The Chichester campus – the larger of two – continues to carry the Bishop Otter name, signifying a continuing link with the Church of England. A new academic building opened in Chichester last year and the music building has been redeveloped to offer a high-quality learning and rehearsal environment.

Still a small institution, with only 5,500 students, Chichester is planning gradual growth, mainly in Bognor Regis. An Engineering and Digital Technology Park is on the way, with facilities for an additional 500 students per year. It will include an Institute for Sustainable Enterprise and a Centre for Digital Technology, and new departments of data science and advanced engineering and design.

The £35m development, which has been part-funded through an £8m grant from the Government's Local Growth Fund, will open in September. The project has received backing from over 40 industry organisations, including Rolls-Royce and Sony, as well as small and medium-sized enterprises which

Bishop Otter Campus
College Lane
Chichester PO19 6PE
01243 816 002
admissions@chi.ac.uk
www.chi.ac.uk
www.ucsu.org.uk
Open Days 2018:
June 30, October 6, 25

The Times and The Sunday Times Rankings

Overall Ranking: **72** (last year: 82)

Teaching quality	83.9%	=13
Student experience	82.1%	17
Research quality	6.4%	82
Entry standards	122	=86
Graduate prospects	62.7%	119
Good honours	70%	=75
Expected completion rate	90.2%	39
Student/staff ratio	15.6	=55
Services and facilities/student	£1,337	125

have declared a shortage of workers with STEM skills. It will include a machine shop and fabricating and mechanical engineering laboratories, as well as a 300 square-metre film production studio, a special effects room, and a recording studio.

A tranche of new degrees is being launched in 2018 as part of the expansion plan. Creative science, mechanical engineering and materials, product design and innovation, tourism management, and 3D animation and visual effects are among 18 new offerings.

The current portfolio of 300 courses ranges from adventure education to humanistic counselling, fine art and the psychology of sport and exercise. The PE teacher training course is one of the largest in the country and is rated outstanding by Ofsted.

Chichester was granted university status among institutions that were expected to focus on teaching rather than research, but it entered a quarter of its eligible staff for the Research Excellence Framework in 2014. There were good results in music, drama and performing arts, English and sport. The Mathematics Centre, based at Bognor, has an international reputation and has become a focal point for curriculum development in Britain and elsewhere.

Residential places are roughly equally divided between the two campuses, guaranteeing places for all who make the university their first choice (nine out of ten students). There is a bus service linking the sites and students' union bars at each campus.

A £2m investment programme has improved already-excellent sports facilities. A new running track has been added on the Chichester campus along with a multiuse sports dome for netball or tennis, as well as an all-weather facility to support teaching on sports courses. The Tudor Hale Centre for Sport includes well-equipped laboratories, a fitness suite, sports injury clinic and teaching clinic. The university also runs a gifted athlete programme.

The small cathedral city of Chichester is best known for its theatre and as a yachting venue, while Bognor is said to have the longest stretch of coastline in the south, where all types of watersports are available. Both offer a good supply of private housing and some student-orientated bars. Much of the surrounding countryside has been designated an area of outstanding natural beauty.

Tuition fees

» Fees for UK/EU students 2018–19 £9,250
» Fees for international students 2017–18 £10,920–£14,450
» For scholarship and bursary information see www.chi. ac.uk/study-us/fees-finance
» Graduate salary £18,000

Students		
Undergraduates	4,270	(405)
Postgraduates	360	(485)
Applications per place	5.1	
Overall offer rate	77.9%	
International students	2.8%	
Mature students	13.8%	
From state-sector schools	95.6%	
From working-class homes	31.9%	

Accommodation

University-provided places: 1,174
Percentage catered: 36%
Catered costs: £131 – 3165 per week
Self-catered: £99 – £139 per week
First year students are guaranteed accommodation
www.chi.ac.uk/student-life/accommodation

City, University of London

City has set ambitious targets to boost the quality of its work while also increasing in size over the next ten years. With one of the largest proportions of EU and other international students of any university, it acknowledges that this will require "greater agility" as Brexit proceeds. The university is relying on its London location and committed international approach to help position it "well within" the top 300 universities in the world and the top 30 in the country.

However, a 25-place fall in our league table this year makes the top 30 seem rather distant, prompted by a slump in the proportion of graduates landing professional jobs in the latest data.

City dropped nine places to 50th in last year's table but joining the University of London in 2016 should help to underline both its location and its quality. Applications were already rising significantly when City joined – they grew by 8% in 2015. Over the next five years, growth will be focused on subjects that have momentum, particularly through new and joint degrees and shared pathways.

The university has been upgrading its facilities in preparation. A new main entrance complex opened this year, with social spaces, a coffee shop, seating areas and exhibition space. A 240-seat lecture theatre has also opened recently, along with new students' union space, informal learning and quiet study areas, cafeteria, internal courtyard and multifaith area.

Another project to transform an older university building is set to be completed in October. The renovated property will include new PC labs, social and breakout spaces, a new mezzanine balcony, improved access and external landscaping.

Other parts of City's Northampton Square campus have already been rejuvenated as part of a £150m programme. The library has been renovated, the student and careers centres have both been refurbished and the City Law School upgraded. The health sciences school moved to the main campus with new facilities, adding a biomedical and clinical skills centre.

The changes have been made with sustainability in mind; City has been in the top ten of the People & Planet green league of environmental performance for the past two years.

Once a college of advanced technology, the university now has more than a quarter of its students taking business courses, and nearly as many taking health and community subjects, with the remainder studying law, computing, mathematics, engineering, journalism and the arts. There are strong links with business and the professions.

Attaining a place in the top 20 of *The Sunday Times* and *The Times* league table on our employment measure, which records the

Northampton Square
London EC1V 0HB
020 7040 8716
ugadmissions@city.ac.uk
www.city.ac.uk
www.culsu.co.uk
Open Days 2018:
June 30, October 6

The Times and The Sunday Times Rankings

Overall Ranking: **=75** (last year: 50)

Teaching quality	76.8%	106
Student experience	77.5%	=80
Research quality	21.4%	54
Entry standards	140	49
Graduate prospects	69.4%	88
Good honours	73.6%	55
Expected completion rate	86.6%	=58
Student/staff ratio	18	105
Services and facilities/student	£2,378	32

proportion of students going into professional jobs or further study, is one of the main targets in the university's new strategy. Courses have a practical edge, and many of the staff hold professional as well as academic qualifications.

With almost ten applications for every place last year, City was one of the most selective universities in the country in 2016. It also manages higher levels of student satisfaction than most other universities in London.

The university attracts international students from more than 150 countries and many students spend a year of their course abroad. At the same time, City has a better record than most of its peer group for widening participation in higher education, with close to half of its undergraduates coming from low-income groups.

Cass Business School is one of City's great strengths, ranking among the top 50 of its kind in the world. Based in the heart of the financial district, it has built up an impressive cadre of visiting practitioner lecturers who find it conveniently located.

Its school of law was the first in the capital to offer a "one-stop shop" for legal training, from undergraduate to professional courses. The journalism department, within the arts and social sciences school, is also highly regarded and has benefited from £12m of facilities.

City entered little more than half of its eligible academics in the 2014 Research Excellence Framework, but three quarters of its submission was rated as world-leading or internationally excellent, with music and business producing the best results.

Since being redeveloped, its sports centre, located between the campus and the business school, is the largest university sports facility in central London. The 3,000 square metres of floor space at CitySport is available to students, staff and the local community. At its heart is the Saddlers Hall, which meets Sport England standards and has seating for up to 400 spectators. There is also a separate fitness area.

Tuition fees

» Fees for UK/EU students 2018–19 £9,250
» Fees for international students 2018–19 £14,280–£17,340
» For scholarship and bursary information see www.city.ac.uk/study/undergraduates/fees
» Graduate salary £24,000

Students

Undergraduates	8,860	(970)
Postgraduates	6,735	(2,435)
Applications per place	9.6	
Overall offer rate	65.8%	
International students	32.4%	
Mature students	18.6%	
From state-sector schools	92.4%	
From working-class homes	46%	

Accommodation

University-provided places: 857
Percentage catered: 4%
Catered costs: £253 – £267 per week
Self-catered: £146 – £212 per week
First year students are guaranteed accommodation
www.city.ac.uk/study/undergraduate/accommodation

Coventry University

Coventry has been perhaps the most innovative university in the UK since the introduction of £9,000 fees, providing no-frills, cheaper (university college) options while ensuring that students who choose the full university experience are among the most satisfied in the country. It remains among the top performers in the annual National Student Survey, recording outstanding scores for satisfaction with both the quality of teaching and the wider student experience.

A second satellite campus in London has opened this month, emulating the same low-cost model as the Scarborough site, finished last year, where fees are £7,100 for science and engineering courses, and £6,000 a year for classroom-based subjects. Coventry was the first provincial university to open a base in London, where it offers business courses, mainly to international students.

At the same time, the university is making the biggest investment in its history in Coventry, spending £500m on its campus. A new science and health building offers healthcare simulation facilities, an indoor running track and a biomedical sciences superlab. The university is also redeveloping a large city centre site being vacated by the council when it moves to new offices. In addition, a £73m residential development in the city centre will be available to students in September 2018, with more places to follow in 2019.

Coventry has charged up the league tables, becoming our Modern University of the Year in 2014, 2015 and 2016, as it achieved the highest position at the time by a post-1992 university. It maintained its position inside our top 50 and ahead of all except one of its peer group (Harper Adams University in Shropshire) last year – and it has repeated that trick this year, while moving up to within a whisker of its highest-ever ranking.

Coventry was one of a clutch of modern universities awarded gold in the government's new Teaching Excellence Framework (TEF), outstripping many of its longer-established counterparts in the elite Russell Group. The TEF panel found "consistently outstanding" student support services, especially for those from disadvantaged backgrounds, aiding retention and progression. There was also an exemplary approach to exposing students to the forefront of scholarship, research and professional practice, the panel said.

Applications stalled in 2016 after seven successive years of growth that brought a 50% rise in enrolments.

Undergraduates like the guaranteed return of marked work within ten days and the opportunity to make their own assessments of academics, who receive awards for excellent teaching. The Centre for Academic Writing offers advice on essays

---

Priory Street
Coventry CV1 5FB
024 7765 2222
studentenquiries@coventry.ac.uk
www.coventry.ac.uk
www.cusu.org.uk
Open Days 2018:
Contact university

The Times and The Sunday Times **Rankings**

Overall Ranking: **44** (last year: 47)

Teaching quality	84.0%	12
Student experience	84.4%	6
Research quality	3.8%	=108
Entry standards	129	=68
Graduate prospects	81.4%	25
Good honours	71.3%	67
Expected completion rate	86.9%	55
Student/staff ratio	14.6	=37
Services and facilities/student	£2,234	47

and theses, while the Maths Support Centre includes a statistics advisory service and specialist support service for dyslexics.

Coventry has halved the number of degree programmes it offers in order to focus on the most popular, successful courses. It has embraced computer-assisted learning, supported by an expanded computer network, and prioritised employability through the Add+vantage scheme. Its modules cover a wide range of skills and help students to gain work-related knowledge and prepare for a career. The International Centre for Transformational Entrepreneurship assists students and small firms to start up and grow a business.

A single-minded focus on teaching and learning showed, too, in the university's results in the Research Excellence Framework, which placed Coventry outside the top 100 on this measure. Only 13% of the eligible academics were entered for assessment, although 60% of their work was considered world-leading or internationally excellent (94% for health subjects).

Coventry is now investing £100m to increase its research capacity and performance, with new centres focusing on areas of strength. The Institute for Advanced Manufacturing and Engineering, for example, is a "faculty on the factory floor" where university researchers and Unipart engineers work together on product development.

The university traces its origins back to 1843, and has already made considerable progress rejuvenating its 33-acre campus close to the city centre. The showcase turreted library, which cost £20m, is one of the developments in a ten-year improvement programme.

A £55m engineering and computing building includes an ethical hacking lab, a former RAF Harrier jump jet and a wind tunnel built by the Mercedes Formula One team, all for use by undergraduates. The National Transport Design Centre, which opened last May, has research and teaching facilities aimed at bridging a projected shortfall in UK design skills.

The Hub contains the students' union, a music venue, plenty of informal study space, shops and restaurants. Accommodation is within walking distance of the campus and city centre. Students in Coventry welcome the relatively low cost of living there, and the city is not short of student-orientated nightlife.

Tuition fees

» Fees for UK/EU students 2018–19 £9,250
» Fees for international students 2018–19 £12,600–£14,850
» For scholarship and bursary information see www.coventry.ac.uk/study-at-coventry/student-support/finance/undergraduate-finance
» Graduate salary £21,500

Students

Undergraduates	20,870	(2,600)
Postgraduates	3,785	(2,180)
Applications per place	6.5	
Overall offer rate	80.8%	
International students	26.3%	
Mature students	17.8%	
From state-sector schools	96.7%	
From working-class homes	41.7%	

Accommodation

University-provided places: 4,360
Percentage catered: 10%
Catered costs: £142 – £151 per week
Self-catered: £113 – £123 per week
First-year students are guaranteed accommodation
www.coventry.ac.uk/accommodation

University for the Creative Arts

The University for the Creative Arts (UCA) has dropped five places in our latest table, despite recording the biggest rise at any university in the proportion of students awarded first or upper second-class degrees – more than nine percentage points. The main reason for UCA's fall was a big decline in student satisfaction – previously its greatest strength – which saw it drop 44 places on the measure compiled from the questions in the National Student Survey relating to teaching quality.

Nevertheless, at 58th in the table, UCA is still only topped by one other specialist arts university and it remains among the top ten post-1992 universities. It is in the top ten for staffing levels and the top 20 for the amount it spends per student on services and facilities.

A range of new degrees is being introduced to stimulate demand, starting this year with programmes in computer games, journalism and music production. Applications and enrolments rose in 2016, but both remained significantly lower than before the introduction of £9,000 fees. Further additions in 2018 will include creative coding and technology, interior craft and decorative art, and sports fashion and branding.

The university offers four-year degrees, incorporating a foundation year, as well as the three-year format. Students can also take a two-year foundation course that can be topped up to produce an honours degree. All students are encouraged to develop an international perspective and to collaborate with students from parallel disciplines.

UCA was awarded silver in the government's new Teaching Excellence Framework (TEF). The TEF panel praised the high levels of personalised learning, which help to develop independence. It added that course design and assessment, with good use of student feedback, allows students to be stretched. The panel said that this was reinforced by a successful partnership with the students' union.

The four campuses (Canterbury, Epsom, Farnham and Rochester) have had extensive developments including a new media building due to open in Farnham this year. There is also a new glass-blowing furnace and computer games arts studios.

Farnham is the largest campus, with more than 2,000 students taking subjects ranging from advertising, animation and computer games technology to film production, journalism, music composition and technology. An acting and performance course is based at Farnham Maltings, where students have access to a network of theatre professionals, as well as performance and rehearsal spaces.

UCA Farnham
Falkner Road
Farnham GU9 7DS
01252 892 883
enquiries@uca.ac.uk
www.uca.ac.uk
http://ucasu.com
Open Days 2018:

The Times and The Sunday Times Rankings

Overall Ranking: **58** (last year: 53)

Teaching quality	80.7%	56
Student experience	76.9%	=89
Research quality	3.4%	112
Entry standards	128	=71
Graduate prospects	61.2%	123
Good honours	72.5%	63
Expected completion rate	81.3%	95
Student/staff ratio	12.6	13
Services and facilities/student	£2,701	20

The Epsom campus specialises in fashion, graphics and music courses, and offers further education courses in general art, design and media. A new fashion styling, hair and make-up studio has been added this year.

At Rochester, a purpose-built campus overlooking the River Medway, there is a full range of art and design courses, covering fashion, photography, computer animation and jewellery making. Students taking UCA's popular television production course are based at Maidstone TV Studios, the largest independent studio complex in the UK.

Architecture is the main theme at Canterbury, a modern site close to the city centre, but there are also degrees in fine art, interior design, graphic design, and illustration and animation too. A 3D fabrication lab and games design suite are new additions. The Canterbury School of Architecture is the only such school to remain within a specialist art and design institution, encouraging collaboration between student architects, designers and fine artists.

Many staff are practitioners as well as academics, and the founding colleges, which date back to Victorian times, have produced famous graduates such as the artist Tracey Emin and the fashion designers Karen Millen and Zandra Rhodes, who is also the university's chancellor. Almost two-thirds of its small submission to the Research Excellence Framework was rated world-leading or internationally excellent and 90% reached the top two categories for its impact.

The university has signed a Creative Business Partnership with East Surrey College (ESC), which includes Reigate School of Art, allowing ESC students to benefit from early access to the progression opportunities at the University for the Creative Arts, and for eligible students to have a guaranteed conditional offer of a place without interview on the recommendation of the college. It is the first agreement of its kind that UCA has established with a further education college. The two institutions are also planning to run a summer school for GCSE leavers and pre-Foundation Art students within the local community. The benefits to ESC students could be considerable since UCA makes offers to only 70 per cent of 18-year-olds who apply for a degree place, placing it among the 30 most selective universities in our table.

Tuition fees

» Fees for UK/EU students 2018–19 £9,250
» Fees for international students 2018–19 £12,000–£15,700
» For scholarship and bursary information see www.uca.ac.uk/life-at-uca/fees/pg-financial-support
» Graduate salary £18,000

Students

Undergraduates	4,485	(15)
Postgraduates	150	(155)
Applications per place	5.3	
Overall offer rate	70.1%	
International students	12.6%	
Mature students	14.4%	
From state-sector schools	97.6%	
From working-class homes	39%	

Accommodation

University-provided places: 1,017
Percentage catered: 0%
Self-catered: £70 – £155 per week
www.uca.ac.uk/life-at-uca/accommodation

University of Cumbria

Cumbria celebrated its tenth anniversary by opening the first phase of a redevelopment of its largest campus, in Lancaster. An impressive new teaching building, which includes a 220-seat lecture theatre and social learning spaces, is part of a ten-year plan for the campus.

The university is hoping that the new facilities attract more students after five years of falling enrolments. By 2016 the numbers starting degree courses were down by almost a third on the last year before £9,000 fees were introduced. Cumbria now lies in the bottom five in our table overall after a sharp fall in student satisfaction with teaching quality this year. The university is in the bottom ten in both or our student satisfaction measures, as well as for research.

Cumbria was one of 19 universities in this guide to be awarded bronze in the government's new Teaching Excellence Framework (TEF). The university's lowly ranking in our table on measures such as graduate employment in professional jobs helps explain Cumbria's TEF rating.

Our table showed Cumbria had a low graduate employment rate in highly skilled jobs, although the university pointed out that regional job opportunities are lower than the national average. It also said that 76% of its academics hold teaching qualifications,

compared with the 44% average within universities across the UK.

The university has seven campuses, including one in London, close to Canary Wharf, to broaden the experience of its trainee teachers. There are two in Carlisle and others in Lancaster, Workington and Barrow-in-Furness, plus one of the most attractive campuses in the UK, in the Lake District setting of Ambleside. There, the university runs the country's largest programme of outdoor education courses, as well as providing a base for conservation and forestry degrees and the Institute for Leadership and Sustainability, part of the business school.

The university's headquarters are in Carlisle, where the larger of the two sites is in a parkland setting close to the River Eden. The second campus, closer to the city centre, has an innovative multimedia learning resource centre and a sports centre with a four-court sports hall and well-equipped fitness room.

The second phase of new laboratories for science, technology, engineering and maths opened last year. The extension will allow Cumbria to expand its science portfolio by offering degrees in chemistry and biomedical science, as well as providing high-quality space for teaching, research and consultancy.

The former Cumbria Institute of the Arts can trace its history in Carlisle back to 1822, eventually becoming the only specialist

---

Head Office
Fusehill Street
Carlisle CA1 2HH
01228 616 234
enquirycentre@cumbria.ac.uk
www.cumbria.ac.uk
www.ucsu.me
Open Days 2018:
June 8 (Carlisle)

The Times and The Sunday Times **Rankings**

Overall Ranking: **125** (last year: 119)

Teaching quality	75.8%	115
Student experience	70.6%	119
Research quality	1.2%	124
Entry standards	118	=100
Graduate prospects	69.1%	91
Good honours	61.2%	121
Expected completion rate	84.1%	=77
Student/staff ratio	17.8	=99
Services and facilities/student	£1,504	118

institute of the arts in the northwest and one of only a small number of such establishments in the country.

The creative arts continue to be one of the university's strengths and are earmarked for further development. They had by far the best results in the 2014 Research Excellence Framework, with 90% of the submission rated internationally excellent. Overall, though, Cumbria is just two places off the bottom of our research ranking, having entered only 27 academics in the assessment.

In Lancaster, the former St Martin's College campus is undergoing £25m of investment over a decade. A ten-minute walk from Lancaster town centre, the site now includes a gymnastics centre and fitness suite, plus extensive residential accommodation, a student centre and library.

At Furness College in Barrow, the university is a partner in both the National College for Nuclear and the new Project Academy for Sellafield, which will help provide specialist education and training in nuclear decommissioning, reprocessing and waste management.

Almost all the undergraduates are state-educated and the university has one of England's highest proportions of students from areas without a tradition of higher education. A third of the first-year students are 21 or older on entry, although only a quarter come from Cumbria itself. There are partnerships with the four further education colleges in the county to provide local higher education and the university remains one of the largest teacher training providers in England.

Cumbria has been praised for its mental health services – an increasingly important area for students - in a House of Commons report. In 2017, the university appointed two mental health case workers to work with students on its Carlisle, Lancaster and Ambleside campuses. As part of the 'Compassionate Campus' campaign, training has also been offered to all staff on suicide prevention and awareness. Nationally, there has been an increase of more than 200 per cent in the number of students leaving university due to mental health problems over the last five years. Cumbria also has a number of student quality ambassadors – students who have a particular interest or who are studying mental health nursing –working to increase awareness of mental health issues.

Tuition fees

» Fees for UK/EU students 2018–19 £9,250
  Foundation year £6,000
» Fees for international students 2018–19 £10,500–£15,500
  Foundation year £7,500
» For scholarship and bursary information see www.cumbria.ac.uk/study/student-finance/scholarships-and-bursaries
» Graduate salary £21,909

Students

Undergraduates	5,070	(1,925)
Postgraduates	805	(990)
Applications per place	5.6	
Overall offer rate	81.9%	
International students	1.8%	
Mature students	29.6%	
From state-sector schools	97.7%	
From working-class homes	41.9%	

Accommodation

University-provided places: 1,153
Percentage catered: 29%
Catered costs: £79 – £134 per week
Self-catered: £65 – £116 per week
First choice applicants are guaranteed accommodation
www.cumbria.ac.uk/student-life/accommodation

De Montfort University

De Montfort University (DMU) was one of the big winners in the Teaching Excellence Framework, its gold award coming with high praise from the assessors, who said: "De Montfort delivers consistently outstanding teaching, learning and outcomes for its students. It is of the highest quality found in the UK."

It scored particularly highly on graduate employment, with the best record in the assessment when its courses and the entry qualifications of its students were taken into account. In our league table DMU's graduate employment record is consistently among the strongest of the nine measures we use to rank UK universities and it is invariably among the top performers among the group of universities created since 1992.

Always proactive in student recruitment – DMU was the first university to advertise its courses on national television as long ago as 1993 – the university has seen the intake of undergraduates rise by more than one third in the three years to 2016. The demand for places has continued to grow, albeit at a slower pace, at a time when most institutions have been struggling to attract applicants.

About £136m has been spent on campus improvements. The latest addition is the Vijay Patel building, which has brought all art and design courses together for the first time. Its Arts Tower houses the new Leicester School of Art, while the design wing completes the spectrum of visual arts, design and architecture. The building also contains printmaking, casting and photographic facilities, as well as a food court and the Gallery, the largest display space in Leicester.

The university recently opened its new business school, based in the Great Hall of Leicester Castle. Professor Dana Brown was lured away from running the MBA programme at Oxford's Saïd Business School to be its first director, promising a school that would be responsive to the employment market, where students are exposed to leading technology and fresh ideas.

Other recent developments include a £3m renovation of the campus centre, where the students' union is based, and the creation of open parkland leading to the edge of the River Soar towards the city centre.

The DMU Global programme is intended to provide the most comprehensive curriculum of overseas study at any UK university in order to expand its students' cultural horizons and make them employable across the world. Since 2015 every undergraduate course has included at least one module that offers an international experience through a network of overseas universities and businesses. More than 1,000 students from many different courses visited

The Gateway
Leicester LE1 9BH
0116 250 6070
enquiry@dmu.ac.uk
www.dmu.ac.uk
www.demontfortsu.com/
Open Days 2018:
March 17

The Times and The Sunday Times **Rankings**

Overall Ranking: **=67** (last year: 67)

Teaching quality	81.6%	=41
Student experience	81.6%	=22
Research quality	8.9%	=68
Entry standards	111	117
Graduate prospects	80.4%	30
Good honours	67.3%	=96
Expected completion rate	83.9%	=79
Student/staff ratio	19.1	=115
Services and facilities/student	£2,177	53

New York City in 2016 as part of DMU's biggest study trip to date.

An employability award, which is available to all final-year undergraduate students, provides £100 towards the costs of securing work. For those who prefer the postgraduate route, the vice-chancellor's 2020 scholarship scheme entitles all UK and EU students who have graduated from DMU with a 2:1 or above within the previous two years to a 50% discount on the fee for a master's course.

The university also gives students the opportunity to participate in the award-winning Square Mile programme, which uses DMU's academic expertise and a network of student volunteers to offer valuable services to the local community as well as national and international projects. About 2,500 students take part in the overarching #DMUlocal initiative through course-based work placements or general volunteering.

DMU has a proud record for widening access to higher education, with more than 40% of undergraduates coming from working-class homes. The university also has a strong reputation for the support it gives to disabled students. The dropout rate has increased after several years of improvement. However, at just under 12%, it is still slightly below the expected level.

Almost 60% of the university's research was judged to be world-leading or internationally excellent in the 2014 Research Excellence Framework. There are strong links with business and industry, including partnerships with HP and Deloitte, which support innovative educational programmes, plus research collaborations.

Extensive sports facilities include an £8m leisure centre with a 25-metre swimming pool and an eight-court sports hall, while the Watershed venue also hosts indoor sport as well as activities for DMU's many student societies. Almost £1m has been spent on coaching and support for teams and there are partnerships with Leicester City football club, Leicester Tigers rugby club, Leicestershire cricket and Leicester Ladies hockey club.

The city of Leicester has become a more vibrant location, and has benefited from a £3bn regeneration project. Rents in the private sector are low and the university has more than 3,200 rooms in halls within walking distance of the city centre.

Tuition fees

» Fees for UK/EU students 2018–19 £9,250
  Foundation courses £6,000
» Fees for international students 2018–19 £12,250–£12,750
» For scholarship and bursary information see www.dmu.ac.uk/study/undergraduate-study/fees-and-funding-2018/fees-and-funding-2018.aspx
» Graduate salary £20,000

Students

Undergraduates	15,615	(1,525)
Postgraduates	1,735	(2,030)
Applications per place	5	
Overall offer rate	85.1%	
International students	8.5%	
Mature students	15.2%	
From state-sector schools	97.7%	
From working-class homes	43.1%	

Accommodation

University-provided places: 3,200
Percentage catered: 0%
Self-catered: £99 – £168 per week
First choice students are guaranteed accommodation
www.dmu.ac.uk/study/undergraduate-study/accommodation/accommodation.aspx

University of Derby

Derby was one of a dozen universities upgraded to a gold award in the Teaching Excellence Framework (TEF) when the metrics used in the exercise alone might have suggested silver. Student satisfaction with teaching quality – although marginally down this year – was the university's trump card, together with a 28-page submission that outlined Derby's new teaching and learning strategy, and its plans for technology-enhanced learning.

The university does not rank higher in our league table, however, in part due to low entry standards relative to other institutions. It is also outside our top 100 when the quality and quantity of research is taken into account. Although the first two measures were also included in the TEF judgment, Derby benefited from the system of benchmarking that makes allowance for the courses and entry qualifications at each institution.

The TEF panel highlighted the university's engagement with employers, personalised learning, engagement of students, outstanding resources and culture of excellent teaching as particular areas of strength.

Derby's success prompted a spike in visits to the university's website. Applications were down slightly in 2017, but by only half the national rate, after healthy increases in enrolments in three of the past four years. Students are attracted by the emphasis on "real-world learning", with facilities that include a simulated hospital and working radiography suite, replica crime scenes, industry-standard kitchens and a fine-dining restaurant, computer games suites, a commercial spa and salon, a law court and a 58-acre Outdoor Leadership Centre.

The university has invested £150m on its campuses. A building for science, technology, engineering and maths was completed last year, to follow a sports centre and the Derby Law School building, plus a new campus in Chesterfield for nursing, engineering, IT and business innovation.

In Derby, the Markeaton Street site hosts arts, design, engineering and technology courses, while those studying in health and social care are based at Britannia Mill, ten minutes' walk away. The university's main campus is two miles from the city centre and caters for most of the other subjects including business, computing, science, humanities, education and law.

The students' union, multifaith centre and main sports facilities are on this site, which also houses clinical skills facilities, including a purpose-built iDXA suite (where the scanner uses x-rays to provide a high-resolution digital image of full body composition and bone density). The three bases in Derby are linked

---

Kedleston Road
Derby DE22 1GB
01332 591 167
admissions@derby.ac.uk
www.derby.ac.uk
www.udsu.co.uk
Open Days 2018:
June 8, 9, 16

The Times and The Sunday Times **Rankings**
Overall Ranking: **81** (last year: 83)

Teaching quality	83.1%	22
Student experience	79.1%	=55
Research quality	2.5%	117
Entry standards	112	=114
Graduate prospects	74.1%	63
Good honours	67%	98
Expected completion rate	82.2%	=88
Student/staff ratio	14.8	=41
Services and facilities/student	£1,914	86

by free shuttle buses. The university also owns and runs the 500-seat Derby Theatre in the city centre, which houses theatre arts programmes as well as continuing as a producing theatre.

As well as its Chesterfield base, the university has a campus in Buxton that is situated in the former Devonshire Royal Hospital and offers courses in spa, outdoor recreation and hospitality management, as well as further education programmes. The listed, domed building houses a training restaurant, a beauty salon and a health spa, as well as more conventional teaching facilities. A foundation degree in spa management is also taught in London, at the London School of Beauty and Make-Up.

The university guarantees that 85% of its classes contain fewer than 30 students and that undergraduates can have access to their personal tutor whenever the need arises. The university has student representatives on all its senior management committees – another aspect of its focus on student needs.

The learning enhancement and innovation institute works with academic staff to ensure that students receive the best possible learning experience. Around half of all degree entrants qualify for an income bursary of up to £1,000 and all full-time undergraduates receive a £100 book voucher.

Derby entered only 19% of its eligible academics for the 2014 Research Excellence Framework when nearly 30% of its submission reached one of the top two categories.

Business engagement is a higher priority. The Institute for Innovation in Sustainable Engineering, for example, supports advanced manufacturing with 3D printing and advanced testing with industrial partners such as Rolls-Royce.

The university has been a pioneer of higher and degree apprenticeships, which are now running in nine subjects, from nursing to civil engineering site management, and a chartered manager degree apprenticeship that includes a BA (Hons) in leadership and business management. Foundation degrees are available in a variety of subjects, allowing students to start a course at a partner college before transferring to the university.

The university spent £30m in five years to maintain its guarantee of accommodation for all first-years, and now has almost 3,000 places. The new sports centre has a 70-station fitness gym, squash courts, sports hall, climbing wall and adjacent outdoor pitches.

Tuition fees

» Fees for UK/EU students 2018–19 £9,250
» Fees for international students 2018–19 £12,500–£13,500
» For scholarship and bursary information see www.derby.ac.uk/study/fees
» Graduate salary £21,000

Students

Undergraduates	10,255	(3,120)
Postgraduates	920	(2,005)
Applications per place	6.1	
Overall offer rate	84.2%	
International students	6.6%	
Mature students	23.5%	
From state-sector schools	97.3%	
From working-class homes	38.6%	

Accommodation

University-provided places: 2,903
Percentage catered: 0%
Self-catered: £80 – £106 per week
First year students are guaranteed accommodation
www.derby.ac.uk/campus/accommodation

University of Dundee

Two thirds of Dundee's students are from Scotland and nearly one in ten from Northern Ireland, but the university's reputation, particularly in the life sciences, has been spreading globally. International College Dundee has been established to provide an alternative entry route into degree courses and is expected to attract hundreds of additional international students. The college, on Dundee's main campus, took its first 50 students last autumn and will expand its intake in future years.

Dundee was one of only three Scottish universities to secure a gold award in the new Teaching Excellence Framework, and was our Scottish University of the Year in 2015 and 2016. Among institutions north of the border, only St Andrews and Glasgow rank higher in our league table.

Another new feature is the programme of graduate-level apprenticeships offered in partnership with business. There will be up to 70 places in the new academic year in four areas: IT management for business, IT software development, civil engineering, and engineering, design and manufacturing. Dundee is the only institution offering places across all four strands of the apprenticeship programme launched by Skills Development Scotland.

Dundee established a new business school in 2016, with a commitment to balance teaching and research, but to be research-led in virtually all areas. The university has also reoriented its humanities school in 2016 towards a liberal arts model, giving students the option of studying several different subjects throughout their degree, without the requirement to specialise in only one or two. A partnership agreement has been signed with its students' association, making a commitment to enhance student engagement, employability and representation throughout the university.

The various developments, backed up by an enhanced marketing campaign, saw undergraduate applications rise by 5% in 2017 at a time when they were falling elsewhere. They were already at record levels, allowing enrolments to rise for four years in a row.

Consistently strong graduate employment results are one important draw. Dundee sends more graduates into the professions than any other institution in Scotland, ranking eighth in our table for this. Most degrees include a career planning module and an internship option.

The university's best-known work is in the life sciences, where it has conducted pioneering research into cancer and diabetes. Dundee was the top university for biological sciences in the 2014 Research Excellence Framework and opened the £50m Discovery Centre to encourage interaction between

---

Perth Road
Dundee DD1 4HN
01382 383 838
contactus@dundee.ac.uk
www.dundee.ac.uk
www.dusa.co.uk
Open Days 2018:
June 14 (medicine),
June 15 (dentistry),
August 27

The Times and The Sunday Times **Rankings**

Overall Ranking: **23** (last year: 28)

Teaching quality	83.5%	17
Student experience	82.4%	16
Research quality	31.2%	42
Entry standards	164	=23
Graduate prospects	85.1%	8
Good honours	82.7%	20
Expected completion rate	87.6%	=50
Student/staff ratio	13.2	=18
Services and facilities/student	£2013	77

different disciplines. Other successes in the framework included civil engineering, which came in the top three in the UK, and maths and general engineering, which were both in the top ten.

The university has completed a £200m campus redevelopment designed by leading architect Sir Terry Farrell. Set in 20 acres of parkland, the medical school is one of the few components of the university outside the compact city-centre campus, although some of the nursing and midwifery students are 35 miles away in Kirkcaldy.

The highly rated design courses are taught at the Duncan of Jordanstone College of Art and Design, and the university is a key participant in the Dundee-based Victoria & Albert Museum project to improve design in Scotland.

Dundee claims that its online learning environments are among the most advanced in the UK, available via the internet and mobile phones, supporting all courses and providing specialist academic search tools. It recently invested £6m in a campus-wide network refresh, boosting wi-fi capability yet further. The new network now provides access for students to connect their Apple TV, Chromecast media player, Xbox and many other gaming and streaming devices.

Fees for students from the rest of the UK are capped at a total of £27,750 for a four-year degree, while those with a household income of less than £20,000 receive bursaries of £2,000 a year.

Dundee has a proud record in widening participation in higher education, boasting the largest increase of any university in the proportion of students admitted from the most deprived 40% of postcodes in Scotland. Applicants have access to My Dundee, an online portal giving information during the application process and in preparation for the academic year.

The city is benefiting from regeneration programmes and enjoys a cost of living that is among the lowest at any UK university city. Sports facilities are excellent and the city offers lively nightlife, while the university has one of Scotland's most active students' unions.

Tuition fees

» Fees for Scottish and EU students 2018–19   £0–£1,820
» Fees for non-Scottish UK students 2018–19   £9,250
  (capped at £27,750 for 4-year courses)
» Fees for international students 2018–19   £12,250–£16,450
  Medicine £32,000, Dentistry £43,000
» For scholarship and bursary information see
  www.dundee.ac.uk/study/scholarships
» Graduate salary   £22,000

Students

Undergraduates	8,815	(1,305)
Postgraduates	1,660	(3,130)
Applications per place	8	
Overall offer rate	56.9%	
International students	12.9%	
Mature students	31.3%	
From state-sector schools	91.5%	
From working-class homes	29.1%	

Accommodation

University-provided places: 1,587
Percentage catered: 0%
Self-catered: £122 – £144 per week
First year students are guaranteed accommodation
www.dundee.ac.uk/accommodation

Durham University

Durham has embarked on perhaps the most radical reconstruction in its history as it sets out to grow by more than 40% over the next ten years. The expansion process has already started, with the proportion of applicants receiving offers rising from below half in 2012 to almost three quarters in 2016. With six applications for every place and the seventh highest entry standards in our table, there is plenty of scope to take more, and the university is promising to maintain staffing levels as it grows.

By the time new entrants arrive in 2018, all the undergraduates will be based in Durham, with the present Stockton campus – 20 miles from Durham itself – housing a foundation college for international students. The Ogden Centre for Fundamental Physics, designed by Studio Daniel Libeskind, opened last March and £25m is being spent to upgrade the university's IT programmes.

The first project to accommodate the coming growth will be the construction of a new teaching and learning centre, close to the main library. By 2020 there will also be new buildings for mathematical sciences and computer science, plus upgraded sports facilities. Further ahead, there will be a new waterside base for the business school and remodelled and repurposed accommodation for the arts and humanities.

One of the oldest universities in England, Durham is determined to maintain its character as one of the few collegiate universities in the UK. Two additional colleges accommodating 1,000 students are part of the first phase of expansion and two existing colleges will transfer from Stockton. Undergraduates currently apply to one of 15 undergraduate colleges, all of which are mixed, and which range in size from 300 to 1,300 students.

They are the focal point of social life, although all teaching is undertaken in central academic departments. There are significant differences in atmosphere and student profile, ranging from the historic University College, housed in Durham Castle, to modern buildings on the city's outskirts such as Collingwood College, where plans are under way to establish a new 200-seat arts centre, a gym extension, an enlarged junior common room and bar conservatory, funded in large part by a £5.6m donation from Collingwood alumnus and hedge fund trader Mark Hillery.

Durham is in the top five in our league table and inside the top 100 in both the QS and Times Higher Education world rankings. Its new strategy is designed to ensure that it has the critical mass to remain competitive, especially in its strongest subjects, nationally

The Palatine Centre
Stockton Road
Durham DH1 3LE
0191 334 6128
admissions@durham.ac.uk
www.dur.ac.uk
www.durhamsu.com
Open Days 2018:
June 25, 30

The Times and The Sunday Times Rankings
Overall Ranking: **5** (last year: 4)

Teaching quality	82.5%	=27
Student experience	79.4%	=49
Research quality	39%	16
Entry standards	201	7
Graduate prospects	84.1%	=10
Good honours	89.5%	4
Expected completion rate	95.9%	=5
Student/staff ratio	14.5	=35
Services and facilities/student	£2,726	16

and globally, and maximise its contribution to the immediate northeast region.

The university has been a member of the Russell Group since 2012 and four-fifths of the work submitted to the Research Excellence Framework was considered world-leading or internationally excellent. More than a quarter of the subjects were in the top five nationally, with anthropology, archaeology, chemistry, classics, education, English, law, music, physics and theology leading the way.

The university's new strategy promises a more diverse student intake. Only Oxford and St Andrews currently take a higher proportion of undergraduates from independent schools – almost 40% in 2015. But a scheme that targets able pupils from schools in the northeast, Cumbria and West Yorkshire has helped to attract more applications from non-traditional backgrounds.

In addition to the normal open days, all those who receive an offer are invited to a special visiting day to see if Durham is for them. About 90% come from outside the northeast of England and many are coming to the region for the first time.

Sports facilities are excellent, and Durham is among the premier universities in national competitions. Its student performance programme covers 16 sports and there are national centres in cricket, fencing, lacrosse, rugby union, tennis and rowing. The university also has 12 boathouses. Three quarters of all students take part in sport on a regular basis, and Durham's College Sport programme is one of the largest intramural competitions in the UK.

About 550 teams regularly compete across 18 sports. In 2014 Durham was named Sports University of the Year by *The Sunday Times* and *The Times* and has been ranked second in the British Universities and Colleges Sport league table since 2012.

The university dominates the small cathedral city of Durham and adds considerably to the local economy. For those looking for nightlife, or just a change of scene, Newcastle is a short train journey away.

The university introduced new safety measures for those socialising in Durham after three students drowned in the River Wear after nights out in the city in the space of 14 months. A programme praised by the Royal Society for the Prevention of Accidents includes improvements to riverside lighting and barriers, safety information, late-night taxis and a revised alcohol policy.

Tuition fees

» Fees for UK/EU students 2018–19	£9,250
» Fees for international students 2018–19	£18,300–£23,100
» For scholarship and bursary information see www.dur.ac.uk/undergraduate/finance	
» Graduate salary	£25,000

Students

Undergraduates	13,050	(210)
Postgraduates	3,330	(1,215)
Applications per place	6.7	
Overall offer rate	70.7%	
International students	18%	
Mature students	5.7%	
From state-sector schools	60.5%	
From working-class homes	14.2%	

Accommodation

University-provided places: 4,413
Percentage catered: 70%
Catered costs: £189 – £200 per week
Self-catered: £132 – £144 per week
First year students are guaranteed accommodation
www.dur.ac.uk/undergraduate/live/colleges

University of East Anglia

The University of East Anglia (UEA) is the place to go if you want a first-class degree. The university has seen one of the biggest increases in firsts over the first five years of the decade and is now in the top ten on this measure. Another rise in the proportion of good honours degrees in 2016 helped UEA to move two places further up our table, to its highest-ever position of 13th. Only a decline in student satisfaction prevented the university from finishing even higher.

The university said the sustained rise in firsts was explained by an extra £20m investment over the period, with 400 more staff able to reduce the number of students per academic from 18 to 13. Students have been enrolling with better A-levels in recent years, and have benefited from peer-assisted and interactive digital learning support.

The package has certainly been successful. The numbers starting degrees are at record levels after an increase of more than a third in three years, and UEA is firmly established in our top 20. The university is planning to grow further over the next few years and extended its portfolio of science degrees in 2017.

East Anglia has been upgraded from silver to gold in the new Teaching Excellence Framework, the only university to mount an appeal successfully. The independent panel applauded UEA's support for student-led teaching awards and a "strategic approach to personalised learning which secures high levels of commitment to studies". It also found that investment in high-quality physical and digital resources has had a demonstrable impact on the learning experience.

The latest development has added a new media suite for the Faculty of Arts and Humanities, with recording and radio drama studios and edit suites. A £19m medical education and research building opened last year, as well as an Enterprise Centre. Students may be most grateful for a new "nap nook" where blackout curtains and eyeshades help them to recharge their batteries.

An online platform (#AskUEA) answers prospective students' questions about university life. However, UEA was the first university where the Competition and Markets Authority stepped in when optional modules on the highly-rated creative writing degree were made compulsory without notifying those who already had offers.

Most undergraduates have the opportunity of work experience as part of their course. An academic adviser guides all students on their options under the modular course system and monitors their progress through to graduation. The university has sharpened its focus on employability in the curriculum and introduced an internship

Norwich Research Park
Norwich NR4 7TJ
01603 591 515
admissions@uea.ac.uk
www.uea.ac.uk
https://www.uea.su/
Open Days 2018:

The Times and The Sunday Times Rankings

Overall Ranking: **13** (last year: 15)

Teaching quality	81.6%	=41
Student experience	81.6%	=22
Research quality	35.8%	32
Entry standards	157	=33
Graduate prospects	77.5%	49
Good honours	86.4%	9
Expected completion rate	89.7%	40
Student/staff ratio	13.2	=18
Services and facilities/student	£3,153	6

programme for recent graduates to work for between four and 12 weeks at a business in the eastern region.

Environmental science is UEA's flagship school. Its Climatic Research Unit and the government-funded Tyndall Centre for Climate Change Research, which has a hub in Shanghai, are among the leaders in their field and environmental science was rated in the world's top 30 for research impact. Social work and pharmacy scored even better in the 2014 Research Excellence Framework, when 82% of the university's submission in all subjects reached the top two categories.

Health studies ranks among UEA's fastest-developing areas in recent years. The £81m Quadram Institute, a new centre for food and health research, is due to open this year. The Sainsbury Centre for the Visual Arts, the Norman Foster-designed repository for a priceless collection of modern and tribal art, provides art history students with one of the greatest resources of its type on any British campus.

Two new residential buildings are part of an ambitious programme on the 320 acre campus on the outskirts of Norwich, which has been awarded a Green Flag for its high environmental standards and the quality of its facilities.

The university has also struck a deal with Alumno, a private provider of student accommodation, to add 244 new rooms in a new block in Norwich city centre. The en-suite rooms and studio flats will be available from September 2018.

A gymnastics centre has added to the excellent facilities in UEA's Sportspark. It includes an Olympic-sized swimming pool and fitness centre, five sports halls, 20 badminton courts, five squash courts, martial arts and dance studio, and a climbing wall.

Norwich, which is said to have a pub for every day of the year, has been voted one of the best small cities in the world, as well as the fourth-best location to get a tattoo, according to another survey. Others might prefer Norfolk's increasingly popular coastline and the attractive countryside beyond Norwich.

Tuition fees

» Fees for UK/EU students 2018–19 £9,250
» Fees for international students 2018–19 £15,000–£19,400
    Medicine £30,000
» For scholarship and bursary information see www.uea.ac.uk/study/undergraduate/finance/bursary-information
» Graduate salary £21,000

Students

Undergraduates	11,095	(555)
Postgraduates	2,945	(1,555)
Applications per place	6.4	
Overall offer rate	79.9%	
International students	19.5%	
Mature students	12.8%	
From state-sector schools	89.5%	
From working-class homes	25%	

Accommodation

University-provided places: 4,535
Percentage catered: 2%
Catered costs: £200 per week
Self-catered: £54 – £153 per week
First year students are guaranteed accommodation
www.uea.ac.uk/study/undergraduate/accommodation

University of East London

Applications to the University of East London (UEL) were down by a third in 2016 compared with the last year before the introduction of £9,000 fees, but the university has stopped the rot at a time when most others are experiencing a downturn. It introduced a variety of new degrees last year in subjects from events management to policing and three engineering disciplines, as well as increasing the range of degree apprenticeships it offers.

UEL has been moving away from the foot of our league table, but was still one of 20 universities placed in the bronze category in the new Teaching Excellence Framework. Little more than half of first-years arrive with A-levels and a similar proportion are 21 or older on entry, with many choosing to start courses in February rather than in the autumn. More than half of the undergraduates come from working-class homes, many from the area's large ethnic minority populations.

The university's strategic vision prioritises engagement with the local community. Indeed, UEL claims to be London's leading university for civic engagement, giving students the opportunity for personal development that is attractive to employers by working on real-life projects that benefit communities locally and around the world.

A guidance unit advises local people considering returning to education. The Legal Advice Centre provides a pro bono service, while students and graduates working in the not-for-profit Civic Architecture Office have supported initiatives ranging from local school expansions to prison rehabilitation initiatives. Staff and students are actively encouraged to undertake short and longer-term projects as part of study, research or volunteering.

Every undergraduate at UEL receives a free Samsung tablet loaded with core e-textbooks as part of the university's efforts to cater for a student population where more than half are the first in their family to experience higher education. Another £3m has been invested in new centralised "helpdesks" in the student support hubs at both Docklands and Stratford campuses.

The student charter urges undergraduates to adopt the "35-hour attitude", which means studying for at least 35 hours a week, making good use of the learning resources support and handing work in on time. UEL has also launched a centre dedicated to student success, working closely with employers to provide up-to-date information about the skills and experience they want. It helps students with employability skills training, mock job applications, internships and support with setting up businesses.

There were creditable results in the 2014 Research Excellence Framework. The amount

---

Docklands Campus
University Way
London E16 2RD
020 8223 3333
study@uel.ac.uk
www.uel.ac.uk
www.uelunion.org
Open Days 2018: June 16
(Docklands & Stratford)

The Times and The Sunday Times Rankings

Overall Ranking: **114** (last year: 123)

Teaching quality	81.3%	=46
Student experience	79.3%	=52
Research quality	7.2%	77
Entry standards	116	=105
Graduate prospects	62.1%	121
Good honours	61.7%	119
Expected completion rate	71.4%	126
Student/staff ratio	16.8	86
Services and facilities/student	£2,277	42

of world-leading research doubled compared with the 2008 assessments and 62% of the work submitted was placed in the top two categories. The university was ranked equal first in England for the impact of its psychology research.

The university has built on the legacy of the London 2012 Olympics when it hosted the United States team at the SportsDock, its £21m sports and academic centre at the Docklands campus. The waterside site, close to Canary Wharf and opposite City airport, was the first new campus in London for 50 years.

Recent projects have focused mainly on nearby Stratford, the original headquarters in UEL's days as a pioneering polytechnic. It is the location for a joint venture with Birkbeck, University of London, offering a choice of subjects including law, performing arts, dance, music and information technology as daytime or evening courses.

The Noon Centre for Equality and Diversity in Business gives extra help to black, Asian, and minority ethnic students to prepare for a successful career in business. UEL is also strong on provision for disabled students, and houses the Rix Research and Media centre for innovation and learning disability.

Almost 1,000 businesses are involved in mentoring programmes and/or a work-based learning initiative that offers accredited placements. The clinical education centre is London's only provider of clinical facilities and training in podiatry.

There are almost 1,200 bed spaces on the Docklands campus, where the rents are good value for London, but more than 20% of first-years who would like university accommodation have to be refused. Social life for many students revolves around the Docklands campus, although Stratford has more to offer since its post-Olympics transformation.

Sports facilities have improved both at Stratford and Docklands, and UEL's high-performing sports programme offers £2m in scholarships and bursaries. The sprinter Adam Gemili was the best known of several students and graduates who took part in the Rio Olympics.

Tuition fees

» Fees for UK/EU students 2018–19	£9,250
» Fees for international students 2018–19	£11,880
» For scholarship and bursary information see www.uel.ac.uk/undergraduate/fees-and-funding	
» Graduate salary	£20,000

Students

Undergraduates	9,105	(1,195)
Postgraduates	1,505	(1,820)
Applications per place	6.1	
Overall offer rate	83.1%	
International students	7%	
Mature students	42.2%	
From state-sector schools	97.3%	
From working-class homes	54.7%	

Accommodation

University-provided places: 1,170
Percentage catered: 0%
Self-catered: £138 – £182 per week
www.uel.ac.uk/accommodation

Edge Hill University

Edge Hill, our University of the Year for Student Retention, is establishing itself among the top ten post-1992 universities in our table. Its dropout rate of 8.3% over the course of a degree programme is well below the expected level of 12.4%, helping it to earn the accolade. An award-winning student finance support package rewards achievement as well as encouraging students to complete their studies rather than simply offering incentives for enrolling.

Edge Hill won a gold award when the outcomes of the new Teaching Excellence Framework (TEF) were published in the summer. Judged solely on the metrics used in the TEF the university might have expected a silver, but the assessment panel was particularly impressed by the levels of satisfaction with academic support and with assessment and feedback, the biggest bone of contention at most universities.

The university was one of only three in the northwest of England in the gold category. The TEF panel noted that "students from diverse backgrounds achieve consistently outstanding outcomes". Almost all Edge Hill's students are state-educated and one in five comes from a neighbourhood with low participation in higher education, among the highest proportions in England.

More than £250m has been invested in the 160-acre campus at Ormskirk in Lancashire, helping the university to reach the top three for its facilities and campus environment in the Times Higher Education magazine's 2016 student experience survey.

A new library and student services centre is under construction and should be open when the 2018 entrants arrive. It will be much larger than the current facility and feature a range of different study areas, social spaces and much-improved electronic facilities.

Much of the university's previous spending has been on new residences to ensure that all first-years can be guaranteed accommodation. The current project includes town houses to accommodate more second- and third-year undergraduates and postgraduates who would prefer to live on campus.

Although university status arrived only in 2005, Edge Hill has been training teachers since the 19th century. It has long since expanded into other subjects, but remains the UK's largest provider of secondary teacher training and courses for classroom assistants.

Across the university, applications and enrolments had been rising, but the withdrawal of NHS bursaries for health courses has contributed to a dip of more than 6% this year. However, applications to education programmes have shown another 5% increase and demand for biology, computer science and social science programmes remains strong.

St Helens Road
Ormskirk L39 4QP
01695 650 950
admissions@edgehill.ac.uk
www.edgehill.ac.uk
www.edgehillsu.org.uk
Open Days 2018:
June 16, August 18

The Times and The Sunday Times Rankings

Overall Ranking: **=61** (last year: 58)

Teaching quality	81.7%	=38
Student experience	79%	=59
Research quality	4.9%	=93
Entry standards	128	=71
Graduate prospects	70.4%	80
Good honours	69.4%	=83
Expected completion rate	84.2%	76
Student/staff ratio	14.2	=31
Services and facilities/student	£2,147	59

English, sport and media produced the best results in the 2014 Research Excellence Framework. Scores for all six areas in which the university submitted work showed improvement compared with the previous assessments.

A range of new degrees is planned for 2018, from food and plant science to a BSc in geo-environmental hazards, early years education, paramedic practice and global public health. All undergraduates on arts and science programmes have the option of a sandwich year in industry or a year studying abroad to enhance their learning and boost their employability.

All students have a personal tutor as well as access to counsellors and financial advice. The Solstice elearning centre is recognised officially as a national centre of excellence in teaching and learning. It has a particular focus on learning in the workplace, but is involved with curriculum development and delivery in all three of the university's faculties. Three quarters of all graduates leave with professional accreditation.

The university's flagship building, Creative Edge, houses industry-standard equipment and resources for students on media, film, animation, advertising and computing degrees. The complex is also home to the Institute for Creative Enterprise, which acts as an interface between academic research and the creative industries, giving students the opportunity to work on live television and secure work placements without leaving the campus.

Beyond Ormskirk there are seven satellite campuses in Liverpool, Manchester and other parts of the northwest to enable students to live at home.

A £30m sports centre has an eight-court sports hall, a 25-metre swimming pool, an 80-station fitness suite, aerobics studio, health suite with sauna and steam rooms, a cafe and a lounge area. The outdoor facilities include one of the largest running tracks in Europe, rugby, hockey and football pitches, an athletics field, netball and tennis courts and a "trim trail" with exercise stations.

The spacious Student Hub building houses the students' union and contains shopping and dining facilities, open-access computers and social space.

Tuition fees

- » Fees for UK/EU students 2018–19 — £9,250
  Foundation courses — £6,165
- » Fees for international students 2018–19 — £11,800
  Foundation courses — £8,600
- » For scholarship and bursary information see www.edgehill.ac.uk/study/money-matters
- » Graduate salary — £21,500

Students

Undergraduates	9,910	(2,085)
Postgraduates	1,235	(2,310)
Applications per place	6.1	
Overall offer rate	76.3%	
International students	1.4%	
Mature students	24%	
From state-sector schools	98.9%	
From working-class homes	39.1%	

Accommodation

University-provided places: 2,440
Percentage catered: 13%
Catered costs: £109 per week
Self-catered: £72 – £127 per week
First year students are guaranteed accommodation
www.edgehill.ac.uk/undergraduate/accommodation

University of Edinburgh

Edinburgh is experiencing its first change of leadership in 15 years, with Professor Peter Mathieson arriving from the University of Hong Kong. He takes over an academic establishment that is in the top 30 in the research-focused world rankings, but only fourth in Scotland in our table and well outside the top 100 in the UK for student satisfaction.

Edinburgh plans to invest £1.5bn within the next decade on new buildings and other improvements, partly, it says, in order to produce a "highly satisfied student body with a strong sense of community".

The 125-year-old students' union building will be overhauled and expanded into a new student centre, bringing together services offered by the university and its students' association. The £75m project is to be carried out in phases, starting this year with an upgrade of the existing building. The university had already announced a new personal tutor system and a peer support scheme, among other measures designed to improve the student experience.

A new recording system is being installed to enable students to access and review lecture material in their own time. The university is also investing in the use of learning analytics for course design, attainment and improving the student experience. In addition, the Edinburgh Teaching award has been developed as a two-year qualification for all staff involved in teaching and supporting learning.

Despite its consistently disappointing scores for student satisfaction with teaching quality and their wider university experience, Edinburgh remains a key draw. The demand for places is higher than ever, with the volume of applications growing by 50% in five years. The university responded by increasing the intake by 1,100 places, but it remains one of the few to make offers to less than half of its applicants.

Edinburgh's strategic vision includes a commitment to give undergraduates the opportunity to draw on expertise outside their core discipline.

Edinburgh produced Scotland's best performance in the 2014 Research Excellence Framework. More than 80% of the research submitted was judged to be world-leading or internationally excellent. Sociology, earth systems and environmental sciences, including geography, and computer science and informatics, were among the leaders in the UK.

The current research star is Professor Peter Higgs, who was awarded the 2013 Nobel prize for physics for predicting the existence of the Higgs boson, the so-called "God particle". The Higgs Centre for Theoretical Physics was established to mark the achievement.

---

33 Buccleuch Place
Edinburgh EH8 9J
0131 650 4360
Contact via website
www.ed.ac.uk
www.eusa.ed.ac.uk
Open Days 2018:
June 8, September 22,
October 6

The Times and The Sunday Times Rankings

Overall Ranking: **24** (last year: =37)

Teaching quality	75.1%	117
Student experience	75.7%	107
Research quality	43.8%	10
Entry standards	194	9
Graduate prospects	75.1%	59
Good honours	86.8%	8
Expected completion rate	92.4%	26
Student/staff ratio	12.5	=10
Services and facilities/student	£2,164	55

More than a quarter of the undergraduates come from outside the UK, while more than 2.5m learners worldwide have sampled Edinburgh's Moocs (massive open online courses). About 30% of Scottish and other UK undergraduates come from independent schools. Selection guidelines aim to look beyond grades to consider candidates' potential, giving particular weight to references and personal statements.

Measures to broaden the intake include an eight-week summer school for local teenagers and support for students in the transition to higher education. There is also a range of bursaries – some worth up to £7,250 a year – to reduce the costs to English, Welsh or Northern Irish undergraduates, who pay the full £9,250 fee for all four years of their degrees, making Edinburgh an otherwise expensive option compared with virtually all other UK universities.

The university's buildings are spread around the city, but most border the historic Old Town. The science and engineering campus is two miles to the south, where the BioQuarter is a ground-breaking collaboration between the university and public bodies to consolidate Scotland's reputation as a world leader in biomedical science.

The Appleton Tower has been refurbished for the informatics school, while the addition of 400 study spaces will significantly increase the capacity of the main library, which is now open around the clock. A new law library will offer more than 250 study spaces and enhanced computer facilities.

The university plays a prominent role in the life of the city. Scotland's oldest purpose-built concert venue – the university's St Cecilia's Hall – has recently reopened after a two-year £6.5m redevelopment. Another of the iconic buildings, the McEwan Hall, has also been renovated to become a combined ceremonial and conferencing facility.

Sports facilities are among the best in the UK and include a well-appointed outdoor centre, set in a spectacular Highland location 80 miles from Edinburgh. The university is developing a network of satellite gyms across its campuses, the first of which opened at the veterinary school at Easter Bush, seven miles out of the city.

Considerable sums have also been spent making the university more accessible to disabled students. The city is a treasure trove of cultural and recreational opportunities, and most students thrive on Edinburgh life.

Tuition fees

» Fees for Scottish and EU students 2018–19 £0–£1,820
» Fees for non-Scottish UK students 2018–19 £9,250
» Fees for international students 2018–19 £18,800–£24,600
  Medicine £32,100–£49,900
  Veterinary medicine £30,800
» For scholarship and bursary information see www.ed.ac.uk/student-funding
» Graduate salary £22,000

Students

Undergraduates	20,125	(800)
Postgraduates	7,260	(2,165)
Applications per place	10.5	
Overall offer rate	48.6%	
International students	27.2%	
Mature students	12.6%	
From state-sector schools	69.7%	
From working-class homes	18.7%	

Accommodation

University-provided places: 5,875
Percentage catered: 30%
Catered costs: £180 – £239 per week
Self-catered: £93 – £164 per week
First year students who live outside Edinburgh are guaranteed accommodation
www.accom.ed.ac.uk

Edinburgh Napier University

Plans approved by Edinburgh Napier last year will plough £84m into new teaching and research facilities across all three of its campuses. The university wants to create spaces that are more fluid than traditional classrooms to accommodate different styles of learning and teaching. There will still be lecture theatres, but their role will be reduced. Some additional facilities will be provided, but many of the new environments will be existing classrooms redesigned to promote interaction and embrace technology.

The university has spent £1m on such spaces for more than 300 students on its Merchiston campus, as well as on a new Cyber Academy training and cyber-attack simulation suite and expanded computer games laboratory. Further investment is planned to improve student social and dining areas over the next two years, delivering a new entrance, additional catering outlets and a rooftop cafe.

There are similar plans to extend the Sighthill campus to provide more social space prior to the relocation of the engineering and built environment school to the site.

Engineering is currently based at Merchiston, but the campus is to be redeveloped as a hub for computing and the creative industries. The site already has a student hub and reception area, as well

as fully soundproofed music studios and a broadcast journalism newsroom. The students' association is also based there, along with a refurbished library.

Edinburgh Napier runs Screen Academy Scotland in partnership with Edinburgh College of Art (now part of the University of Edinburgh), reflecting the university's strong reputation in film education. The creative arts produced the most successful of Edinburgh Napier's entries for the 2014 Research Excellence Framework.

The Sighthill campus houses the schools of nursing, midwifery and social care along with life, sport and social sciences. It has a five-storey learning resource centre, an environmental chamber and biomechanics laboratory, and a large simulation and clinical skills centre with mock hospital wards and a high-dependency unit.

Integrated sports facilities feature a well-equipped fitness centre and a sports hall, as well as the BT Sport Scottish Rugby Academy.

The business school, which features a glass atrium with a cyber-cafe and lecture theatres, is at the Craiglockhart campus. Once a hydropathic hotel, then a hospital to treat shell-shocked soldiers during the First World War, it features architecture that blends history and modernity. The campus also houses the War Poets Collection, an exhibition displaying the work of Siegfried Sassoon and Wilfred Owen.

---

9 Sighthill Court
Edinburgh EH11 4BN
0333 900 6040
ugadmissions@napier.ac.uk
www.napier.ac.uk
www.napierstudents.com
Open Days 2018:
Contact university

EDINBURGH
Belfast
London
Cardiff

The Times and The Sunday Times **Rankings**

Overall Ranking: **116** (last year: =93)

Teaching quality	76.5%	=109
Student experience	75.4%	108
Research quality	4.6%	=95
Entry standards	148	=41
Graduate prospects	65.7%	105
Good honours	74.4%	=52
Expected completion rate	79.2%	=108
Student/staff ratio	19.1	=115
Services and facilities/student	£1,578	113

Edinburgh Napier is planning to grow by more than 20% by 2020, adding 4,000 places, and many of the additional students will be taught outside the country, whether face-to-face or online. There are almost 4,000 international students on campus, while the same number again take courses delivered with partners in Switzerland and several Asian countries, among them China and India. The university is the largest UK provider of higher education in Hong Kong.

The demand for places has been buoyant, despite rising entry requirements. But applications dipped in 2017, partly as a result of the withdrawal of NHS bursaries for health science courses.

Many courses include a work placement, while the Confident Futures programme is said to be unique in higher education, using workshops to improve students' confidence and helping them to develop skills, attributes and attitudes that will enhance their chances of being successful both at university and in their careers.

For the growing numbers choosing to start their own businesses, Bright Red Triangle, the university's student enterprise service, offers free office space and advice to students and alumni.

Students have access to online lecture notes and study aids via Moodle, the university's virtual learning environment. The web-based system supports learning, teaching and assessment and is accessible from smartphones and tablet computers. There are fully networked libraries on each campus and a multimedia language laboratory and adaptive learning centre for students with special needs.

The modular system allows movement between courses at all levels, and the option of starting courses in January rather than September.

In order to minimise dropout rates, the university uses its students to mentor newcomers, runs bridging programmes and offers pre-term introductions to staff and information on facilities, as well as organising summer top-up courses and teaching employability skills and personal development.

Widening participation is high on the university's list of priorities. More than 2,000 students enter through "articulation routes", using their college qualifications to gain direct entry into year two or three of an Edinburgh Napier degree.

Tuition fees

» Fees for Scottish and EU students 2018–19   £0–£1,820
» Fees for non-Scottish UK students 2018–19   £9,250 (capped at £27,750 for 4-year courses and at £37,000 for 5-year courses)
» Fees for international students 2018–19   £12,350–£14,350
» For scholarship and bursary information see www.napier.ac.uk/study-with-us/bursaries
» Graduate salary   £20,000

Students		
Undergraduates	9,025	(1,335)
Postgraduates	1,065	(1,160)
Applications per place	7	
Overall offer rate	69.7%	
International students	16.4%	
Mature students	38.8%	
From state-sector schools	94%	
From working-class homes	31.1%	

Accommodation

University-provided places: 1,437
Percentage catered: 0%
Self-catered: £92 – £160 per week
First year students are guaranteed accommodation
www.napier.ac.uk/study-with-us/accommodation

University of Essex

Shortlisted for our University of the Year award, Essex has jumped to its highest ever ranking in our table. It aims to have every subject in the top 20% of its discipline and to maintain its place in our top 25 overall.

The latest in a series of big developments on Essex's 200-acre parkland campus opens this year. The £13m Science, Technology, Engineering and Maths Centre – or Stem Centre – follows a "zero carbon" business school, student centre and library extension, all of which have been completed since 2015. New sports facilities and a £10m centre for innovation will also be open by the time the 2018 entrants arrive.

The Stem Centre will include a versatile 180-seat wet laboratory for the biological sciences and a 200-seat learning space to encourage students from across the science and health faculty to work collaboratively. The building will also include social space and a cafe.

The centre for innovation will provide expertise and support for some 50 start-up and small hi-tech businesses, adding to the community of more than 20 such firms using the university's existing facilities.

The upgrade of the 1960s campus reflects a new spirit of ambition that is already attracting more students to Essex. Having spent many years trying to live it down, the university has been embracing its radical past, telling prospective applicants that it welcomes independent thinkers and "rebels with a cause". The numbers starting degrees have risen for four years in a row, increasing the intake by more than 50%.

The social sciences are Essex's greatest strength, featuring among the top 40 universities in the world in the QS rankings for both politics and sociology. It received the only Regius professorship in political science in the awards to mark the Queen's diamond jubilee.

It achieved the best results in the 2014 Research Excellence Framework in politics and was in the top ten for economics and art history. These results as a whole represented a big improvement on an already successful set of assessments in 2008. The university moved into the top 25 in our research ranking, with almost 80% of a large submission rated world-leading or internationally excellent.

The student population is unusually diverse for a pre-1992 establishment, with high proportions of mature and international students. More than a third of undergraduates are from working-class homes and 96% were state-educated.

Essex received a gold award in the new Teaching Excellence Framework, with the panel stating: "Students from all backgrounds achieve outstanding outcomes with regards

Wivenhoe Park
Colchester CO4 3SQ
01206 873 333
admit@essex.ac.uk
www.essex.ac.uk
www.essexstudent.com
Open Days 2018:
see website

***The Times and The Sunday Times* Rankings**

Overall Ranking: **22** (last year: 30)

Teaching quality	79.9%	=70
Student experience	81.3%	=26
Research quality	37.2%	25
Entry standards	130	=66
Graduate prospects	79.6%	=39
Good honours	72%	65
Expected completion rate	87.9%	49
Student/staff ratio	16	=66
Services and facilities/student	£3,262	4

to continuation and progression to highly-skilled employment or further study, notably exceeding the university's benchmark."

Essex's employability initiatives were praised by the Quality Assurance Agency. The award-winning Frontrunners scheme, established by the university and students' union, arranges on-campus, paid work experience for students. There is also an extensive internship programme and many courses offer work placement opportunities.

The Big Essex award recognises students' extracurricular activities, volunteering and work experience, while Essex Abroad supports students studying, working or volunteering overseas. Language tuition is free, and the university also does not charge fees for a full year abroad or a placement year.

The main campus near Colchester includes a four-star hotel, run by the Edge Hotel School, in Wivenhoe House, the original centrepiece of the university.

There is also a modern campus in the centre of Southend offering courses in business, health and the arts. It has an accommodation complex with a gym and fitness studio, while the Forum comprises a public and academic library, learning facilities, cafe and gallery, along with a floor reserved for student use.

In addition, the East 15 Acting School, in Loughton, is a department of the university and is offering a new degree in theatre-making from 2018. There will also be new courses on the main campus in childhood studies and speech and language therapy, both with the option of a year abroad or in employment.

Social and sporting facilities are good, with an active students' union and about 40 acres of the campus devoted to sports amenities. The new facilities will provide extra courts for badminton, basketball, netball and volleyball. The number of student sports club members has doubled to 4,000 in recent years, while another 2,400 students take part in drop-in sessions.

All new first-years are guaranteed a place in university accommodation, which has been voted among the best in the UK. Some ground-floor flats have been adapted for disabled students. All the campuses are within easy access of London, about an hour away by express train, and the surrounding north Essex coastline is among the most beautiful and atmospheric in Britain.

Tuition fees

» Fees for UK/EU students 2018–19	£9,250
» Fees for international students 2018–19	£14,020–£16,170
» For scholarship and bursary information see www.essex.ac.uk/fees-and-finance	
» Graduate salary	£18,720

Students		
Undergraduates	9,975	(815)
Postgraduates	2,030	(975)
Applications per place	6.6	
Overall offer rate	78.3%	
International students	28.2%	
Mature students	15.3%	
From state-sector schools	95.6%	
From working-class homes	38.3%	

Accommodation

University-provided places: 1,429
Percentage catered: 0%
Self-catered: £79 – £188 per week
First year students are guaranteed accommodation
www.essex.ac.uk/accommodation/default.aspx

University of Exeter

Exeter is the only university in our guide to have attracted more applications from school-leavers in each of the past ten years. It is arguably the academic establishment that has undergone the most significant change in long-term ranking over the 20-year history of this guide as well, moving from the mid-30s to a position consistently in or on the fringes of the UK top ten.

The upward trend in applications may have been interrupted this year, but only after growth of two-thirds since 2011 alone. The university has added 1,000 places to its annual intake of undergraduates in that time while also increasing its entry standards significantly.

Exeter was one of eight Russell Group universities to gain a gold award in the new Teaching Excellence Framework to add to its attractions. The awarding panel complimented the university on the contact hours and class sizes provided for students, the involvement of business, industry and professional experts in its teaching and the outstanding environment in which learning takes place.

Exeter has spent about £380m on campus improvements, expanding its facilities to cope with the growing numbers of students. The latest addition is a £1.2m digital humanities laboratory, enriching undergraduate and postgraduate teaching and research.

The main Streatham campus, close to the city centre, is one of the most attractive settings of any UK university, while the medical school, the highly rated department of sport and health sciences, and the graduate school of education are based a mile away at the St Luke's site.

The university's other base is the £100m Penryn campus in Cornwall, which has helped boost both applications and enrolments. Shared with Falmouth University, the site offers Exeter degrees in biosciences, geography, geology, clean energy, English, history, politics and mining engineering.

Always among the leading universities in the National Student Survey, Exeter also recorded much-improved results in the 2014 assessments of research. More than 80% of a large submission to the Research Excellence Framework was rated world-leading or internationally excellent, with clinical medicine, psychology and education producing particularly good results.

Exeter has since established an innovative research partnership with the University of Queensland to focus on the interdisciplinary themes of environmental sustainability, healthy ageing, and physical activity and nutrition.

There is a £30m institute for environment and sustainability at Penryn, as well as a new base there for the business school. At St Luke's, the newly refurbished South Cloisters building provides research, teaching and student study

---

Streatham Campus
Northcote House
Exeter EX4 4QJ
0300 555 6060 / 01392 723 044
ug-ad@exeter.ac.uk
www.exeter.ac.uk
www.exeterguild.org
Open Days 2018:
June 1, 2, September 8
(Exeter) June 9,
September 22 (Penryn)

The Times and The Sunday Times Rankings

Overall Ranking: **14** (last year: =9)

Teaching quality	80.6%	=57
Student experience	81.7%	=20
Research quality	38%	18
Entry standards	179	14
Graduate prospects	84.1%	=10
Good honours	85.1%	13
Expected completion rate	96.5%	7
Student/staff ratio	16.4	=75
Services and facilities/student	£2,446	31

space for the medical school, complementing its health education and research centre at the Royal Devon and Exeter Hospital.

Developments at the Streatham base have included £130m on student residences and impressive sports amenities, which include a well-equipped fitness centre. The centrepiece of the university is the Forum, which serves as a main hub and features an extended library, student services centre, technology-rich learning spaces and auditorium, along with social and retail facilities. The Exchange, a learning, teaching and research building, plays a similar role at the Penryn campus.

Almost a third of Exeter's undergraduates come from independent schools, a much higher proportion than the national average for the university's subjects and entry qualifications, although this figure has been coming down gradually.

The proportion of applicants receiving a conditional offer of a place is one of the highest rates in the UK, partly because since joining the Russell Group in 2012 the university has been attracting better-qualified applicants. Students from disadvantaged backgrounds and schools with poor results are made lower offers to encourage fair access. The dropout rate of less than 4% is also among the lowest.

The Career Zone has been expanded to increase employment support and internships, and the university's Exeter Award provides official recognition of extracurricular activities. The number of student volunteers is among the highest at any university.

Exeter's longstanding international focus is exemplified by a growing range of four-year programmes "with international study". All students are offered tuition in foreign languages and even some three-year degrees include the option of a year abroad. Career management skills are built in and students have a wide range of work experience opportunities.

A new partnership with Keypath Education, a global specialist in online higher education, heralds a drive to expand distance teaching, initially with online master's programmes in business subjects. New campus-based degrees planned for 2018 include a four-year integrated master's in maths with accounting, economics, finance or management.

More than £8m has been invested in the sports park on the main campus, adding to already outstanding leisure amenities. Exeter is one of the few UK universities to have indoor tennis facilities to national competition standards. There is no shortage of student-orientated bars and clubs in the city.

Tuition fees
» Fees for UK/EU students 2018–19   £9,250
» Fees for international students 2018–19   £16,900–£22,500
   Medicine   £33,000
» For scholarship and bursary information see
   www.exeter.ac.uk/undergraduate/money/scholarships
» Graduate salary   £22,000

Students

Undergraduates	17,270	(105)
Postgraduates	3,245	(1,050)
Applications per place	7.5	
Overall offer rate	86.4%	
International students	20.7%	
Mature students	6.8%	
From state-sector schools	68.5%	
From working-class homes	15.5%	

Accommodation

University-provided places: 5,660
Percentage catered: 20%
Catered costs: £160 – £241 per week
Self-catered: £98 – £172 per week
First year students are guaranteed accommodation
www.exeter.ac.uk/accommodation

Falmouth University

Falmouth is usually among the leading modern universities in our league table, but it dropped 17 places last year. It achieved gold in the new Teaching Excellence Framework (TEF), however, drawing praise for the personalised learning enjoyed by students. This comes partly through individual timetabling and a "data-driven approach to monitoring contact and teaching patterns".

The TEF panel also complimented the university on stretching students and ensuring they acquire the knowledge, skills and understanding that are most highly valued by employers. Evidence for those comments is provided by graduate prospects among the best for an arts-specialist institution. Falmouth is also in the top 30 for student perceptions of teaching quality and is the leading dedicated arts university. Applications and enrolments rose from 2013 to 2016, although a 12% drop this year was more than twice the national average.

Founded in 1902 as Falmouth School of Art, the university now has two campuses, which have seen more than £100m of investment. A new cafe and gallery area opened on the original Falmouth site at the end of 2016, a few months after a sports centre and nursery had been added to the Penryn base it shares with the University of Exeter.

Falmouth moved up to sixth in this year's Times Higher Education magazine student experience survey where the highest marks were for the campus environment, security and library access.

There are still fewer than 5,000 students taking a range of subjects including architecture, digital media and creative writing, as well as graphic design and fashion. The university continues to regard itself as a specialist institution, but degrees now include acting, business entrepreneurship and marketing. Some courses may carry the possibility of unconditional offers for the most promising applicants.

About 60% of the undergraduates are female, although male applicants are marginally more likely to receive an offer. Each new arrival is offered a mentor for a year to support them during their transition to university life. Falmouth has an internal teaching qualification for staff to ensure high standards in tuition, learning and assessment.

The university merged in 2008 with south Devon's Dartington College of Arts, adding a variety of performance-related courses to its portfolio. These courses are now taught at the purpose-built Academy of Music and Theatre Arts (Amata) on the Penryn site. New degrees are planned for 2018 in technical theatre arts, and theatre and performance. A unique joint students' union, FXU, serves all Falmouth students and those attending Exeter's Cornish outpost.

Woodlane
Falmouth TR11 4RH
01326 213 730
admissions@falmouth.ac.uk
www.falmouth.ac.uk
www.fxu.org
Open Days 2018:
May 19

The Times and The Sunday Times Rankings

Overall Ranking: **69** (last year: 52)

Teaching quality	82.5%	=27
Student experience	76.7%	=92
Research quality	4.6%	=95
Entry standards	124	=81
Graduate prospects	72%	=72
Good honours	73.4%	=57
Expected completion rate	86.6%	=58
Student/staff ratio	17.7	98
Services and facilities/student	£1,440	123

The Penryn site offers extensive media facilities, including a 3D printer and stereoscopic projector. Falmouth has Skillset Media Academy status for its courses. The animation and visual effects department is part of the Cross Channel Film Lab, which aims to develop innovative visual effects for use in low-budget feature film production, working on films alongside experts within the industry.

Other facilities include a 117-seat cinema, motion capture studio, video editing suites, specialist animation software and Amata, which has fully sprung Harlequin dance floors, rehearsal studios and flexible theatre space. The Exchange, based at Penryn, contains teaching and library space along with study areas, while an Academy for Innovation and Research focuses on the digital economy and sustainable design.

The Falmouth campus, near the town centre, boasts subtropical gardens and an outdoor sculpture canopy, plus studios, a library and catering facilities. An impressive building for graphic design has open-plan studios, a 130-seat lecture theatre, labs and photography spaces.

The university's "externally facing" courses include programmes that help students to set up a business while studying. The BA in business entrepreneurship uses the successful Team Academy model for teaching, prioritising practical experience and mentoring. The Falmouth Launchpad graduate entrepreneurship programme has a particular emphasis on building technology companies. There is also a focus on the "learning and leisure" market, making use of Cornwall's tourist attractions, businesses and landmarks.

There are residential places on both campuses, enabling the university to guarantee all full-time first-years accommodation as long as they apply by the published deadline. The sports centre has a gymnasium, exercise studio and multiuse games area. As befits the seaside location, there are many watersports activities. Students make full use of Cornwall's coastline and rugged moors, but there are good transport links to London and Europe. Plenty of tourist-related work is available and there is lively nightlife during the holiday season.

Tuition fees

» Fees for UK/EU students 2018–19 £9,250
  Foundation courses (at Bodmin) £6,700
» Fees for international students 2018–19 £15,000
» For scholarship and bursary information see
  www.falmouth.ac.uk/student-funding/undergraduate
» Graduate salary £16,800

Students		
Undergraduates	4,395	(20)
Postgraduates	110	(135)
Applications per place	3.6	
Overall offer rate	64.6%	
International students	8%	
Mature students	11.4%	
From state-sector schools	94.8%	
From working-class homes	27.5%	

Accommodation

University-provided places: 1,644
Percentage catered: 0%
Self-catered: £95 – £176 per week
First year students are guaranteed accommodation
www.falmouth.ac.uk/facilities/university-accommodation

University of Glasgow

The numbers starting degrees at our Scottish University of the Year are running at record levels after a dip earlier in the decade. And the signs are that the trend will continue: applications are up by more than 2% at a time when most other universities have seen the demand for places fall. The new entrants will arrive as the university embarks on one of the biggest education infrastructure projects in Scotland's history.

It has been granted planning permission for the redevelopment of the former Western Infirmary site. About £430m will be spent over the next five years as the first stage of a wider £1bn ten-year investment. The university sees this as a "pivotal step" in the creation of world-class learning and teaching, research and community facilities, which it expects to transform the west end of the city.

Work has already started on the construction of a hub for learning and teaching, with space for 3,000 students. It will contain formal and informal learning spaces, lecture theatres and technology-enhanced areas for students to work in. There will also be new buildings for the arts, social sciences, the health and wellbeing institute, and the science and engineering college, plus a research and innovation hub housing large-scale, interdisciplinary projects and incubator space for spin-out collaborations with industry.

Glasgow, which was shortlisted for our UK University of the Year title, hopes to extend its global reach, having opened a joint graduate school with Nankai University in China and set up new partnerships with institutions in Canada, Hong Kong and America. It has had a branch in Singapore for six years, working with the Singapore Institute of Technology to provide a joint engineering and mechatronics degree programme. Even on its home campus, around a quarter of the undergraduates are from outside the UK.

One of Scotland's two representatives in the Russell Group, Glasgow is in the top 100 in both the Times Higher Education and QS world rankings. It moved into the top dozen universities in the UK for research after a much-improved performance in the 2014 assessments, although it still ranks behind St Andrews in our research measure. It ranked in the UK top ten in 18 subjects, achieving best results in architecture, agriculture, veterinary science and chemistry.

The university enjoys the rare distinction of having been established by papal bull, beginning its existence in the chapter house of Glasgow Cathedral in 1451. Since 1870 it has been based on the Gilmorehill campus in the city's fashionable west end. Almost two thirds of the students still come from Scotland, many from Glasgow and the surrounding area.

University Avenue, Glasgow G12 8QQ
0141 330 2000
ruk-undergraduate-enquiries
@glasgow.ac.uk
scot-undergraduate-enquiries
@glasgow.ac.uk
www.glasgow.ac.uk
www.guu.co.uk
www.qmunion.org.uk
Open Days 2018: June 14,
August 28, October 20

The Times and The Sunday Times **Rankings**
Overall Ranking: **20** (last year: 29)

Teaching quality	79.4%	=76
Student experience	80.7%	=33
Research quality	39.9%	12
Entry standards	200	8
Graduate prospects	83%	14
Good honours	83.1%	=18
Expected completion rate	88.6%	=44
Student/staff ratio	14.6	=37
Services and facilities/student	£2,300	39

The veterinary school and outdoor sports facilities are located four miles away at Garscube. Undergraduate medical degree students undertake their clinical training in the £25m centre for teaching and learning at the Queen Elizabeth University Hospital, and there is also a campus at Dumfries, which takes liberal arts and teacher education degrees to southwest Scotland. More than £13m has been invested in improved sporting and social facilities there. In addition, £35m has been spent to create teaching and learning facilities at the redeveloped Kelvin Hall, which offer improved access to the collections of the university's art gallery and museum, the Hunterian.

Glasgow has a history of innovation: it was the first university in Britain to have a school of engineering and the first in Scotland to have a computer. More recently, it appointed Scotland's first Gaelic language officer and the country's first chair of Gaelic. The £20m Stratified Medicine Scotland Innovation Centre, at the Queen Elizabeth University Hospital involves a consortium of universities, NHS Scotland and industry partners.

Almost half of the university's applications are for arts or sciences degrees rather than specific subjects, reflecting the popularity of a flexible system that allows students to delay choosing a specialism until the end of their second year.

The university operates a number of access initiatives, including the Top-Up programme, which has been working with schools in the west of Scotland since 1999, and Talent Scholarships, which are worth £1,000 a year to academically able Scots from poor backgrounds. The Internship Hub facilitates more than 400 paid opportunities each year, including 150 on-campus internships.

Most students like the combination of campus and vibrant city, with the added bonus that Glasgow has been rated among the most cost-effective locations in which to study. Undergraduates have the choice of two students' unions, plus a sports union supporting more than 40 clubs and activities. New union facilities, including a nightclub and four cafe-bars, opened in 2015.

Tuition fees

» Fees for Scottish and EU students 2018–19   £0 – £1,820
» Fees for non-Scottish UK students 2018–19   £9,250
(capped at £27,750 for 4-year courses and at £29,570 for 5-year courses; No cap on dentistry, medicine, veterinary medicine)
» Fees for international students 2018–19   £16,650–£20,150
(Clinical programmes £42,000)
» For scholarship and bursary information see www.gla.ac.uk/scholarships
» Graduate salary   £22,500

Students

Undergraduates	17,440	(1,790)
Postgraduates	5,915	(2,070)
Applications per place	6.8	
Overall offer rate	71.4%	
International students	19.7%	
Mature students	21.9%	
From state-sector schools	84.6%	
From working-class homes	21.4%	

Accommodation

University-provided places: 3,417
Percentage catered: 7%
Catered costs: £165 – £183 per week
Self-catered: £92 – £151 per week
First year students who live beyond commuting distance are guaranteed accommodation
www.gla.ac.uk/services/accommodation/

Glasgow Caledonian University

Glasgow Caledonian (GCU) has become the first foreign university to be granted a charter to award its own degrees in New York. The powers relate to the university's portfolio of research-based master's programmes in fashion and business, launched in 2014, when GCU opened the first UK campus in the city. The university was also the first from Scotland to open a campus in London, again with fashion at its heart.

As part of Ashoka's global network of Changemaker Campuses, GCU has been striving to establish a global reputation for delivering social benefit and impact through education, research and social innovation. It helped to found the African Leadership College in Mauritius, where the first students embarked on GCU degrees this year.

In previous overseas ventures, it has co-founded the Grameen Caledonian College of Nursing in Bangladesh, set up an affiliation with an engineering college in Oman, and partnered with universities and colleges in China, India and South America.

The immediate focus, however, has been the Glasgow base, which has undergone a £32m redevelopment. It is the first campus to be named as "cycle friendly" by Cycle Scotland and is also a platinum-award-winning eco-friendly site. The centrepiece is the £30m Heart of the Campus project, which was completed in 2016 and features a striking glass reception area and atrium, a 500-seat teaching and conference facility, as well as a food mall.

GCU describes itself as the University for the Common Good, a philosophy that extends into the curriculum, focusing on four attributes to equip students to serve their communities effectively. They involve active and global citizenship, an entrepreneurial mindset, responsible leadership and self-confidence.

So far, however, satisfaction levels have failed to keep pace with rises elsewhere – and the 2017 outcomes from the National Student Survey were no exception – although there have been some good results in the barometer of international student opinion.

Widening participation in higher education has always been one of the university's main aims, and some famous names are supporting its efforts. Professor Muhammad Yunus, the Nobel laureate and anti-poverty campaigner, is the chancellor, while Sir Alex Ferguson has pledged £500,000 to a bursary programme.

The Caledonian Club works with children as young as three years old and their families in Glasgow and London. More than a third of the undergraduates are from working-class homes and about three-quarters are first in their family to attend university. The Advanced Higher Hub offers pupils in their final year at schools across Glasgow specialist

---

Cowcaddens Road
Glasgow G4 0BA
0141 331 8630
studentenquiries@gcu.ac.uk
www.gcu.ac.uk
www.gcustudents.co.uk
Open Days 2018:
see website

The Times and The Sunday Times **Rankings**

Overall Ranking: **=109** (last year: 99)

Teaching quality	76.1%	113
Student experience	74.5%	113
Research quality	7%	=78
Entry standards	165	22
Graduate prospects	69.7%	83
Good honours	74.4%	=52
Expected completion rate	82.6%	87
Student/staff ratio	19.4	119
Services and facilities/student	£1,565	115

teaching, access to GCU's facilities and preparation for university life.

The university has introduced a series of measures – such as better academic, social and financial support – for those at risk of dropping out. The projected dropout rate had risen to 10% in the latest survey, but only one of Scotland's post-1992 universities (Robert Gordon in Aberdeen) has a lower rate.

Health was one of the university's strengths in the 2014 Research Excellence Framework, which placed half of GCU's submission in the top two categories. It was in the top 20 in the UK for allied health research and did well in social work and social policy, and the built environment.

The health building brings together teaching and research facilities, including a virtual hospital. GCU is one of the largest providers of graduates to the NHS in Scotland. As the only Scottish university delivering optometry degrees, it trains 90% of the country's eye care specialists.

However, the university is best known for its fashion courses. Its British School of Fashion has partnerships with firms such as House of Fraser and Marks & Spencer, which has a design studio in GCU London and funds a scholarship programme. There are also courses in fashion business creation, luxury brand marketing and management, luxury retail management and international fashion marketing.

Across the university, more than half of the undergraduate programmes are accredited by professional bodies and 72% include work placement opportunities. The School of Engineering and Built Environment teaches three quarters of Scotland's part-time construction students, while Glasgow School for Business and Society pioneered subjects such as entrepreneurial studies and risk management and offers highly-specialised degrees, including tourism management and consumer protection.

The university's best-known graduate, Hassan Rouhani, the president of Iran, was a postgraduate student in law in the 1990s.

Student facilities include the Arc sports centre, 24-hour computer labs, an employability centre and students' association building. Residential accommodation is limited, but first-years and international students have priority in its allocation. Glasgow is a lively city with a large student population where the cost of living is reasonable.

Tuition fees

- » Fees for Scottish and EU students 2018–19   £0–£1,820
- » Fees for non-Scottish UK students 2018–19   £9,250
  (capped at £27,750 for 4-year courses)
- » Fees for international students 2018–19   £11,500
- » For scholarship and bursary information see
  www.gcu.ac.uk/study/scholarships
- » Graduate salary   £22,000

Students		
Undergraduates	11,340	(2,460)
Postgraduates	1,610	(1,170)
Applications per place	6.8	
Overall offer rate	63.7%	
International students	7%	
Mature students	38.9%	
From state-sector schools	97.3%	
From working-class homes	34.7%	

Accommodation
University-provided places: 660
Percentage catered: 0%
Self-catered: £100 – £113 per week
First year students get priority for accommodation
www.gcu.ac.uk/study/undergraduate/accommodation

University of Gloucestershire

More places will be available at Gloucestershire in 2018 and beyond as the university implements a five-year plan to grow by a third. The increased numbers will be recruited to campus programmes, but also at partner colleges, online and undertaking work-based learning. The university already offers higher apprenticeships in leadership and management, cyber-security, paraplanning and healthcare, as well as the chartered manager degree apprenticeship.

The numbers starting degrees have risen for the past three years, and most appear not to have regretted their choice. Gloucestershire is just outside the top 30 in the sections of the National Student Survey relating to both teaching quality and student experience. The results helped it attain a silver award in the new Teaching Excellence Framework, the panel commenting favourably on an integrated approach to careers, volunteering and placements that enhance student employability. It said the university's personalised method of learning encourages each student to develop a bespoke educational plan supported by personal tutors.

Gloucestershire claims to offer undergraduates more time with academics than almost any other in the UK. In most subjects, students are said to spend at least a quarter of their time in lectures, seminars or other supervised activities. The university is also implementing a new programme to enhance teaching and learning further. More than half of the academics have formal teaching qualifications, one of the highest proportions at any university. The new strategic plan promises an even higher rate as well as greater use of technology to support the learning experience, with online content available wherever possible to support face-to-face teaching.

The university has already invested heavily in its campuses. A new student village with 800 rooms has opened in Cheltenham while a business school and sports park will open this year on the Oxstalls site in Gloucester. A £1m technology suite and a £2m performing arts and events centre are among the other developments.

Gloucestershire was the first university for more than a century to have formal links with the Church of England when it achieved full university status in 2001. The three campuses are only seven miles apart so students are not as isolated as they are in some split-site institutions. The attractive main Park site is a mile from the centre of Cheltenham and houses the business, education and professional studies faculty. Art and design, and the education and public services institute are closer to the town centre at Francis Close Hall.

The Park
Cheltenham GL50 2RH
01242 714 700
enquiries@glos.ac.uk
www.glos.ac.uk
www.yourstudentsunion.com
Open Days 2018:
March 10, June 29,
July 1, September 30

The Times and The Sunday Times Rankings

Overall Ranking: **83** (last year: 71)

Teaching quality	82.1%	=32
Student experience	80.7%	=33
Research quality	3.8%	=108
Entry standards	121	90
Graduate prospects	68.8%	92
Good honours	70.9%	=68
Expected completion rate	85.7%	66
Student/staff ratio	19.1	=115
Services and facilities/student	£1,866	88

The purpose-built Oxstalls base caters for sport and exercise sciences, leisure, tourism, hospitality and event management. It also houses the Countryside and Community Research Institute, the largest rural research centre in the UK, which produced much the best results in the 2014 Research Excellence Framework. Overall, 44% of Gloucestershire's submission was rated as world-leading or internationally excellent, but fewer than 20% of the eligible staff took part.

Originally a teacher training college founded in 1847, the university offers primary and secondary teacher training courses that are rated "outstanding" by Ofsted. For other students there is a good range of work placements, which are undertaken by a third of all undergraduates. The Degreeplus initiative combines internships with additional training to improve students' future employment prospects.

Gloucestershire has a longstanding focus on green issues and again finished in the top ten in the People & Planet league for 2016 as ranked by environmental performance. There are allotments for students, diplomas in environmentalism and an International Research Institute in Sustainability that brings together researchers from around the world, undertaking work for agencies such as Unesco.

In addition to its conventional courses, the university offers a range of two-year fast-track degrees in subjects such as biology, events management and law. Gloucestershire's intake is diverse, with nearly all the undergraduates coming from state schools and more than a third from working-class homes. The projected dropout rate has improved dramatically over recent years and the latest figure of less than 8% is well below the national average for the university's subjects and entry qualifications.

Gloucestershire has a strong sporting tradition and is the only university to have a professional rugby league team. Three students were selected for the Great Britain rugby union sevens teams at the Rio Olympics. Sports facilities include a sports hall, eight grass and two all-weather pitches and a cricket pavilion. All first-year applicants are guaranteed housing in university halls or managed accommodation if they make Gloucestershire their first choice and apply by the required deadline.

Tuition fees

» Fees for UK/EU students 2018–19 £9,250
» Fees for international students 2018–19 £13,840
» For scholarship and bursary information see www.glos.ac.uk/life/finance/pages/funding.aspx
» Graduate salary £18,000

Students

Undergraduates	6,135	(360)
Postgraduates	480	(860)
Applications per place	4.2	
Overall offer rate	87.5%	
International students	4.2%	
Mature students	19.9%	
From state-sector schools	96.1%	
From working-class homes	36.4%	

Accommodation

University-provided places: 1,832
Percentage catered: 0%
Self-catered: £100 – £189 per week
First year students are guaranteed accommodation
www.glos.ac.uk/life/accommodation/pages/accomodation.aspx

Goldsmiths, University of London

The number of students starting degrees at Goldsmiths has risen for five years in a row, increasing the size of the undergraduate intake by half. There seems to be no sign of this trend reversing: applications have grown by 6% this year, with healthy increases from overseas, at a time when most universities struggled.

Popular new degree subjects include management, curating, drama and marketing, while joint honours degrees in mathematics with economics and computer science are planned for 2018.

It is Goldsmiths' traditional strength in the creative arts that remains the main attraction for students, however. It is in the top 15 universities in the world for art and design and just outside the top 20 for the performing arts in the international QS subject rankings. Alumni such as Damien Hirst and Antony Gormley are leaders in their fields. In recent years, Steve McQueen directed the Oscar-winning film 12 Years a Slave, James Blake won the Mercury prize for his album Overgrown and Laure Prouvost collected the Turner prize, making her the seventh former Goldsmiths student to receive the award.

Goldsmiths was placed in the (lowest) bronze category in the government's new Teaching Excellence Framework (TEF) this year. However, the TEF panel did concede that students had access to high-quality resources and benefited from connecting with and conducting research of relevance to local communities. The college was dragged down by low student satisfaction levels – a common problem in London – and poor graduate employment outcomes, which are a challenge in arts-dominated institutions.

The same measures prevent Goldsmiths from finishing higher in our table, with most of last year's 12-place gain lost in our latest table. It did well in the Research Excellence Framework, with 70% of its submission judged to be world-leading or internationally excellent. The best results came in communication and media studies, and the college did particularly well in the new assessments of research impact. The entire submission in music was considered world-leading in its impact.

With fewer than 9,000 students, Goldsmiths remains small for a multi-faculty university and intends to grow further in the next few years. It is based on a single campus in southeast London with a mixture of traditional and modern buildings.

The Professor Stuart Hall Building contains purpose-built media facilities such as radio and TV studios and the Ben Pimlott Building has state-of-the-art research facilities and studio space for art students. The flagship Richard Hoggart Building has been

Lewisham Way
New Cross
London SE15 6NW
020 7078 5300
Course-info@gold.ac.uk
www.gold.ac.uk
www.goldsmithssu.org
Open Days 2018:
June 16

The Times and The Sunday Times Rankings

Overall Ranking: **=63** (last year: =54)

Teaching quality	76.3%	=111
Student experience	72%	116
Research quality	33.4%	37
Entry standards	134	=58
Graduate prospects	55.4%	128
Good honours	81.3%	=22
Expected completion rate	80%	104
Student/staff ratio	14.1	=29
Services and facilities/student	£2,337	36

refurbished and its surroundings landscaped to create space for outdoor arts and events.

The refurbishment is part of a £6m programme of investment in the campus, which has excellent computing facilities. The London borough of Lewisham's first cinema for 15 years opened on campus, allowing students to watch the latest films on weekday evenings and all day at weekends for a subsidised price. A new public art gallery on the campus is due to open this year, with exhibition areas and education space.

Goldsmiths is committed to increasing recruitment from the surrounding boroughs, offering free tuition for ten Lewisham students from low-income families and other awards for those living nearby. A quarter of new undergraduates are 21 or over on entry, and there is a growing cohort of international students. Almost nine out of ten UK undergraduates are state-educated, and three in ten come from the four poorest socioeconomic groups.

There are integrated work placements on many degree courses and workshops help students to develop entrepreneurial skills. Goldsmiths also places great emphasis on equipping students with creative thinking skills. The Gold Award encourages students to develop skills that employers are looking for, while the university's higher education achievement report recognises students' co-curricular achievements.

A thriving music scene includes recitals, performances, public lectures and readings. The students' union has a strong tradition of volunteering and in recent years has won several awards for its campaigning on ethical and environmental issues.

There are about 1,400 rooms available in halls of residence, many in New Cross, and all are within a 30-minute commute of the campus. Priority for places is given to international students and new undergraduates from outside the London area. There is a well-equipped and affordable gym on campus, but the sports pitches are 30 minutes away.

Tuition fees

» Fees for UK/EU students 2018–19	£9,250
» Fees for international students 2018–19	£13,910–£20,590
» For scholarship and bursary information see www.gold.ac.uk/fees-funding	
» Graduate salary	£19,500

Students

Undergraduates	5,530	(125)
Postgraduates	1,870	(1,000)
Applications per place	6.1	
Overall offer rate	70.9%	
International students	20.2%	
Mature students	24.6%	
From state-sector schools	91.1%	
From working-class homes	30.8%	

Accommodation

University-provided places: 1,400
Percentage catered: 0%
Self-catered: £111 – £308 per week
First year students from outside London are given priority
www.gold.ac.uk/accommodation

University of Greenwich

Greenwich has registered significant increases in the proportion of students achieving good degrees and going on to graduate-level employment over the past four years. A near-trebling of the number of undergraduates taking work placements has helped, but the university remains stubbornly outside the top 100 overall.

Nevertheless, it was in the silver category in the new Teaching Excellence Framework (TEF), which takes account of the student profile in determining grades. Greenwich is one of the most socially diverse universities in the country. Only five others take a higher proportion of undergraduates from the four poorest groups, while half come from ethnic minorities and 52% are older than 21 when they start degrees.

The TEF panel praised course design and assessment practices that stretch students and ensure most make progress with their studies. It found that personalised provision secures good engagement and commitment to learning from most students, and that the university had invested in high-quality physical and digital resources to enhance learning.

For those on the spectacular main campus – a world heritage site on the banks of the Thames with buildings designed by Sir Christopher Wren – a central hub that will contain learning, recreational and office space is due to open this June after a £30m refurbishment. An enclosed courtyard will provide access to a cafe, canteen, gymnasium and basement bar.

Elsewhere in Greenwich, the prize-winning Stockwell Street development, which includes 14 landscaped roof terraces, was designed partly by the university's own specialists in architecture. There are a large architecture studio, a model-making workshop, TV and sound studios, plus the main library and other facilities.

The university has two other campuses, one of which is at Avery Hill, a Victorian mansion on the outskirts of southeast London that is the base for education, health and the social sciences. It boasts a £14m sports and teaching centre and laboratories for health courses that replicate NHS wards. The site contains a student village of 1,300 rooms alongside teaching accommodation.

At Chatham in Kent, the Medway campus houses the schools of pharmacy, science and engineering, the Natural Resources Institute, as well as nursing and some business courses. The campus, which is shared with the University of Kent, also has a new student hub in a listed building, with study spaces and a restaurant, bar and nightclub.

Average entry grades have been rising sharply but applications have dropped by 16% in two years. There was only a small fall in enrolments in 2016, however, and there are

---

Maritime Greenwich Campus
Old Royal Naval College
Greenwich SE10 9LS
020 8331 9000
courseinfo@gre.ac.uk
www.gre.ac.uk
www.suug.co.uk /
www.gkunions.co.uk
Open Days 2018: April 4,
May 2 (Medway campus);
May 23 (Greenwich)

The Times and The Sunday Times Rankings

Overall Ranking: **=109** (last year: 107)

Teaching quality	77.5%	102
Student experience	76.2%	=103
Research quality	4.9%	=93
Entry standards	133	=63
Graduate prospects	66.4%	102
Good honours	67.5%	=94
Expected completion rate	83.4%	=83
Student/staff ratio	17.8	=99
Services and facilities/student	£2,049	73

now 22,000 Greenwich students in the UK, with another 15,500 taking the university's courses in 29 other countries.

Since 2011 the number of staff with an accredited teaching qualification has increased by 40% and those with a doctorate by 20%. Greenwich has a special programme to encourage innovation in its teaching and learning, designed to produce graduates who not only have good academic knowledge but also the skills sought by employers – such as a high level of digital literacy, familiarity with new technology and expertise in social media.

It is the only university in the country to have an on-campus strategic relationship with a recruitment firm. The service, which has now been used by 2,000 students, aims to place final-year undergraduates or recent graduates in full-time, graduate-level jobs that are suited to their skills, as well as finding them high-quality internships and other opportunities along the way. The careers service team won an employability award from their peers in 2016.

The university has also been investing in research. The £18m annual income from research and consultancy is among the largest proportion at any post-1992 university.

Many of the 5,000 international students are postgraduates or research students. More than 200 academics entered the 2014 Research Excellence Framework – a considerable increase on 2008 – and 42% of their work was placed in the top two categories.

Greenwich was also in the top 20 in the 2016 People & Planet University League for environmental performance. True to the university's longstanding commitment to cut carbon emissions, a combined heat and power plant is being built to provide the Medway campus's electricity and hot water. Sports facilities are improving, with a £1.8m project adding two all-weather pitches and medical facilities at Avery Hill. Record numbers are engaging with sports clubs and societies, which enjoyed an unprecedented 38% increase in memberships in one year.

Tuition fees

» Fees for UK/EU students 2018–19 £9,250
  Foundation courses £6,165
» Fees for international students 2017–18 £11,500–£14,000
» For scholarship and bursary information see
  www.gre.ac.uk/study/finance/undergraduate/scholarships
» Graduate salary £21,258

Students

Undergraduates	13,260	(2,790)
Postgraduates	1,555	(3,045)
Applications per place	8	
Overall offer rate	74.5%	
International students	14%	
Mature students	35%	
From state-sector schools	97.4%	
From working-class homes	54%	

Accommodation

University-provided places: 2,496
Percentage catered: 0%
Self-catered: £115 – £263 per week
First year students are guaranteed accommodation
www.gre.ac.uk/accommodation

Harper Adams University

Harper Adams has climbed to the highest ranking ever held by a post-1992 university and has been awarded gold in the new Teaching Excellence Framework (TEF). The specialist agricultural institution was our Modern University of the Year in 2016 and has continued to push on, with stunning results in the toughened-up National Student Survey.

It is in the top five on both of our student satisfaction measures, as well as for its spending on student services and facilities.

The university's "strategic and inclusive approach" was praised by TEF for supporting "learning, achievement and welfare throughout the student journey, including the year in industry programme and a stretching final-year research project". The TEF panel said Harper Adams used learner support teams to good effect to ease the transition into higher education and its professional scholarship programme developed students' research skills.

Harper Adams has more than 4,500 students, but only just over half are on campus in the Shropshire countryside at any one time. The rest are on placement years or accredited part-time programmes in industry.

Degrees are offered in business, veterinary nursing and physiotherapy, land and property management, engineering and food studies, as well as agriculture. A number of courses in food science and engineering were reshaped in the Curriculum 2017 review and new degrees in applied biology, real estate and zoology are planned for 2018.

The university is investing £700,000 in teaching and learning under the Delta Project until 2019, appointing teaching fellows in each academic department and developing more video elearning.

Several courses attracted unusually high levels of satisfaction in the 2017 NSS. The honours veterinary nursing degrees, foundation veterinary nursing degrees and foundation agri-food and business degrees all scored 100 per cent for overall satisfaction. The agriculture and other agri-food and business programmes scored at least 94 per cent.

Contrary to agricultural stereotypes, most applicants and those offered places are female. About one undergraduate in six went to an independent school; almost half have a working-class background. The projected dropout rate of less than 7% is significantly lower than expected for the university's courses and entry qualifications.

Harper Adams is one of a small number of sites where the government is funding centres for innovation as part of its national strategy for agricultural technology. The university secured £5.7m of investment for the Agricultural Engineering Innovation

Edgmond
Newport TF10 8NB
01952 815 000
admissions@harper-adams.ac.uk
www.harper-adams.ac.uk
www.harpersu.com
Open Days 2018:
June 16, October 13

The Times and The Sunday Times Rankings

Overall Ranking: **33** (last year: 36)

Teaching quality	86.5%	4
Student experience	86%	3
Research quality	5.7%	85
Entry standards	133	=63
Graduate prospects	69.5%	=84
Good honours	61.4%	120
Expected completion rate	86.7%	57
Student/staff ratio	15	=44
Services and facilities/student	£3,174	5

Centre and the National Centre for Precision Farming, which have sector-leading physical and digital resources. A new suite of laboratories, funded through donations, opened in early 2017.

The university successfully completed a world first on its Hands-Free Hectare, by growing and harvesting a crop without human touch, using only automated farming techniques. The work contributed to a Queen's Anniversary Prize for Harper Adams in 2017 for innovative research in agricultural engineering. The prize-winning work also included the development of controlled traffic farming systems and support for the implementation of unmanned aerial systems. The university is already a centre of excellence for entomology teaching and research in the UK, and launched the industry-led Soil and Water Management Centre.

Harper Adams entered only 17 staff for the 2014 Research Excellence Framework – two fewer than in 2008 – but more than half of their work was considered internationally excellent or world-leading. There are links with four agricultural universities in China.

The students' union, careers service and cafe are all under one roof at the heart of the campus, where open-access computers allow students to work and socialise in the same area. The Bamford library holds one of the largest specialist land-based collections in the UK,

but the university's most prized feature is its 550-acre commercial farm, which is expanding its dairy, pig and poultry units. At its heart, Ancellor Yard is the original farm courtyard, the former home of Thomas Harper Adams, after whom the university is named.

There are more than 800 residential places on campus, with priority for first-years. A shuttle bus runs three times a day for students living in nearby Newport to get to the campus and there is free parking.

Sports facilities include a gymnasium, shooting ground, heated outdoor swimming pool, rugby, cricket, football and hockey pitches, tennis courts and an all-weather sports pitch. There is a dance/fitness studio and even a 4x4 club, as well as a rowing club that operates from nearby Shrewsbury. The setting may be rural, but the social scene is strong.

Harper Adams was rated as the top university in Times Higher Education magazine's 2017 student experience survey and was Whatuni University of the Year for the second year in a row.

Tuition fees

» Fees for UK/EU students 2018–19	£9,250
» Fees for international students 2018–19	£10,400
» For scholarship and bursary information see www.harper-adams.ac.uk/apply/finance/scholarships/internal.cfm	
» Graduate salary	£21,000

Students

Undergraduates	2,345	(2,635)
Postgraduates	115	(480)
Applications per place	4.8	
Overall offer rate	62.7%	
International students	2.7%	
Mature students	7%	
From state-sector schools	86.2%	
From working-class homes	44.4%	

Accommodation

University-provided places: 830
Percentage catered: 52%
Catered costs: £103 (shared room) – £166 per week
Self-catered: £113 – £121 per week
First year students are given priority for accommodation
www.harper-adams.ac.uk/university-life/accommodation

Heriot-Watt University

Heriot-Watt, our International University of the Year, has more than 30,000 students worldwide, only 11,000 of them on the home campus in Edinburgh. There are campuses in Dubai and Malaysia and "collaborative partners" in 150 countries, many of them offering Heriot-Watt degrees. Even a third of those studying in Scotland come from outside the country, making the university one of the most international in the UK. The Go Global programme invites undergraduates to split their studies between any or all of the university's bases.

The university is not neglecting its roots, however. It won the largest share of places in the Scottish government's Graduate Level Apprenticeships programme and will offer courses with industrial partners in IT management for business, IT software development, and engineering, design and manufacturing.

From its earliest days, the university has been committed to practical, applied learning. It traces its history back to 1821, when it was the world's first Mechanics Institute, and its name honours George Heriot and James Watt, two giants of industry and commerce.

In its modern guise, Heriot-Watt seeks to marry teaching and research in science and engineering, business and management, languages and design, a portfolio that has produced consistently good rates of graduate employment. The ambitions of the university's strategic plan require all academic staff to perform at internationally competitive levels of creativity in research, scholarship and teaching. The synergy between these goals earned Heriot-Watt silver in the new Teaching Excellence Framework.

More than 80% of the work submitted for the 2014 Research Excellence Framework was rated as world-leading or internationally excellent, and Heriot-Watt was among the leaders in the UK in mathematics, general engineering and architecture, planning and the built environment, where it made joint submissions with Edinburgh. The university did particularly well in the new assessments of the impact of research and features in the top 30 of our research ranking.

Heriot-Watt is gradually renewing the 1970s buildings on its main campus in the Edinburgh suburb of Riccarton. New halls of residence opened in 2016, as did the Learning Commons, with its extensive digital learning and study facilities.

That year also saw the opening of the £20m Lyell Centre, a main research centre for geological, petroleum and marine sciences, staffed by the university and the British Geological Survey, which has its Scottish headquarters there. A £6m refurbishment of the library was completed last summer,

Edinburgh
EH14 4AS
0131 451 3376
ugadmissions@hw.ac.uk
www.hw.ac.uk
www.hwunion.com
Open Days 2018:
September 29
(Edinburgh),
October 12 (Borders)

The Times and The Sunday Times Rankings

Overall Ranking: **39** (last year: =37)

Teaching quality	77%	105
Student experience	77.4%	82
Research quality	36.7%	28
Entry standards	167	=20
Graduate prospects	76.8%	=51
Good honours	77.4%	41
Expected completion rate	87.6%	=50
Student/staff ratio	16.6	=80
Services and facilities/student	£2,775	14

adding collaborative study spaces and more desk space.

The university also has two smaller campuses in Scotland. One in Orkney caters exclusively for postgraduates and specialises in renewable energy, while the Scottish Borders campus is 35 miles south of Edinburgh in Galashiels. It specialises in textiles, fashion and design, offering one of the few degrees in the world in menswear and the only course in Scotland in fashion communication. Heriot-Watt and Borders College share the merged campus to deliver higher and further education in a region that has been poorly served in the past.

The Dubai campus opened 12 years ago and now has 3,800 students taking business, engineering, science and technology, or textiles and design courses. Numbers in the Gulf state are expected to rise further. The purpose-built Malaysian campus, opened in 2014 near Kuala Lumpur, has space for up to 4,000 students to take degrees in science, engineering, business, mathematics and design.

The main campus in Edinburgh hosts Oriam, Scotland's national centre for performance in many sports, where world-class facilities are also available to Heriot-Watt students. The £33m centre features a Hampden Park replica pitch, outdoor synthetic and grass pitches, a nine-court sports hall, a 3G indoor pitch and fitness suite.

The university has a programme of sports scholarships, and representative teams do well. Music also thrives: there is a professional director of music and a number of music scholarships, as well as a varied programme of events.

Nine out of ten undergraduates are from state schools and colleges, while more than a quarter come from working-class homes. The projected dropout rate of 6% is better than the UK average for the university's courses and entry qualifications.

The Edinburgh halls of residence are conveniently placed and house more than 2,000 students. Regular bus services link the campus to the city centre and its wide range of nightlife and cultural events.

Tuition fees

» Fees for Scottish and EU students 2018–19   £0–£1,820
» Fees for non-Scottish UK students 2018–19   £9,250
» Fees for international students 2017–18   £13,770–£17,440
» For scholarship and bursary information see www.hw.ac.uk/study/fees/scholarships-bursaries.htm
» Graduate salary   £24,000

Students

Undergraduates	6,800	(335)
Postgraduates	2,060	(1,265)
Applications per place	6.8	
Overall offer rate	89.2%	
International students	20.6%	
Mature students	17.1%	
From state-sector schools	90.3%	
From working-class homes	26.1%	

Accommodation

University-provided places: 2,229
Percentage catered: 0%
Self-catered: £108 – £200 per week
First year students are guaranteed accommodation
www.hw.ac.uk/uk/edinburgh/accommodation.htm

University of Hertfordshire

The original "business-facing university", Hertfordshire has been commended by the Higher Education Funding Council for England for good knowledge exchange with local firms for three years in a row. It was one of a handful of universities to win the award in 2016 when it was praised for exploiting its external links to benefit both teaching and research.

The university is continuing the approach with new degree apprenticeships in business administration and information technology, teaming up with employers such as Vauxhall. There are existing programmes in construction management, and digital and technology solutions, as well as the chartered manager degree apprenticeship.

Hertfordshire has recovered slightly after dropping 15 places in our league table last year due to declines in entry standards and completion rates. It earned a silver in the new Teaching Excellence Framework, with the awards panel noting its substantial investment in physical and digital learning resources such as a £50m science building, opened at the end of 2016.

An ambitious ten-year plan is under way to provide a "distinctive campus experience … in which the dynamism of the university is embodied in its physical estate". As well as 2,500 residential places added since 2015,

still to come by 2020 are an engineering building, more teaching accommodation and a conference centre.

There have been important academic developments, too. The first students in architecture arrived in 2016, a year after pharmacy and postgraduate medicine courses were added. An innovative degree in paramedic science was Britain's first, its students using the UK's largest medical simulation centre to learn how to treat patients in emergency situations. The university has also introduced a four-year undergraduate master of optometry programme.

More than half of the academic staff hold a teaching qualification. There is a particular focus on individual development, reflected in high scores in the National Student Survey, a part of the exercise that is often ignored. More than 85% of single honours students leave with a degree that has professional accreditation or approval.

The university plays an important role in the regional economy and runs several subsidiary companies including a regional bus service, as well as offering work placements and study abroad on most courses. The student intake is diverse, with more than 40% of undergraduates from lower socio-economic groups in the last survey. The projected dropout rate has improved to 10.5%, lower than the national average for the university's subjects and entry grades.

College Lane
Hatfield AL10 9AB
01707 284 800
ask@herts.ac.uk
www.herts.ac.uk
www.hertfordshire.su
Open Days 2018:
March 17, June 16,
July 11

The Times and The Sunday Times Rankings
Overall Ranking: **89** (last year: 91)

Teaching quality	78.9%	=82
Student experience	78.6%	=68
Research quality	5.6%	=86
Entry standards	119	=95
Graduate prospects	78.8%	44
Good honours	66%	102
Expected completion rate	86.5%	60
Student/staff ratio	17.6	97
Services and facilities/student	£2,278	41

Hertfordshire has three sites, including a purpose-built £120m campus, close to the original Hatfield headquarters, which boasts some outstanding facilities. The de Havilland and College Lane bases are linked by cycle ways, footpaths and free shuttle buses. The de Havilland campus, named after the aircraft manufacturer that once occupied the grounds, has an impressive learning resources centre and sports complex.

The Hutton Hub, on the College Lane campus, has a counselling centre, students' union, pharmacy, bank and a juice bar. Also on the campus is the £10m media centre, which includes one of the region's largest art galleries and the Forum, a £38m venue with three entertainment spaces, a restaurant, cafe and multiple bars.

The Automotive Centre has upgraded the teaching facilities for its branch of engineering and an impressive number of Formula One teams have at least one Hertfordshire graduate.

The third site is the Bayfordbury campus, home to one of the UK's largest teaching observatories, plus a field centre for life and medical sciences. Bayfordbury Observatory is equipped with seven large optical individually housed telescopes, four radio telescopes and a high-definition planetarium.

The Enterprise Team helps to turn business or social enterprise ideas into successful ventures. In the 2014 Research Excellence Framework, more than half of Hertfordshire's work was placed in one of the top two categories. The best results were in history, where 45% of the submission was judged to be world-leading and all of it was given the top grade for its external impact.

Students can use the StudyNet information system for study, revision or communication, and to access university information. More than 400 different software applications are available for student use, including a Microsoft Office 365 account for the duration of their time at Hertfordshire.

The £15m Hertfordshire Sports Village includes a 110-station health and fitness centre, 25-metre pool, physiotherapy and sports injury clinic and a large multipurpose sports hall.

Tuition fees

- » Fees for UK/EU students 2018–19   £9,250
  Foundation courses   £6,165
- » Fees for international students 2018–19   £11,950
- » For scholarship and bursary information see
  www.herts.ac.uk/apply/fees-and-funding/scholarships
- » Graduate salary   £21,909

Students

Undergraduates	15,925	(3,085)
Postgraduates	1,545	(4,100)
Applications per place	7.5	
Overall offer rate	78.9%	
International students	13.5%	
Mature students	19.8%	
From state-sector schools	97.8%	
From working-class homes	42.5%	

Accommodation

University-provided places: 4,711
Percentage catered: 0%
Self-catered: £123 – £175 per week
First year students are guaranteed accommodation
www.herts.ac.uk/university-life/student-accommodation

University of the Highlands and Islands

We have removed the University of the Highlands and Islands (UHI) from our league table this year because its unique structure makes it difficult to compare on a level playing field with other higher education institutions. It has a more dispersed student body, a higher proportion of further education students and more part-time staff than most universities.

However, we still include UHI in our guide because of the outstanding resource it provides to some of the remotest places, not only in the UK, but the whole of Europe. The university is a federation of 13 colleges and research institutions spread across hundreds of miles in the Highlands and islands of Scotland, with 70 local learning centres.

The demand for places at degree level has been growing by leaps and bounds. Applications have risen for eight years in a row – by almost 25% in 2016 and by another 13% this year – while other universities are struggling to attract students. In response, the university has added 700 places to its undergraduate intake in four years.

This year's increase in applications is explained partly by the addition of nursing and also the growth in teacher training. UHI has taken over the pre-registration programmes in mental health nursing and adult nursing previously delivered by the University of Stirling in Inverness and Stornoway, and it has announced plans to develop a degree in optometry, backed by funding from the Federation of (Ophthalmic and Dispensing) Opticians Educational Trust.

A new campus at Inverness and continuing developments at its Shetland College, as well as the opening of the £6.5m Alexander Graham Bell Life Science Centre at Moray College, will enable the university to take even more students in future.

A new Academy of Sport and Wellbeing opened at the Perth College UHI campus in September 2016, with modern training facilities for students taking sport and fitness, hairdressing and beauty therapy courses.

Having added degrees in outdoor education, forestry management and marine science and robotics last year, more new programmes are planned for 2018 in food and education, creative writing and archaeology.

The students are predominantly mature and part-time, drawn mainly from the Highlands and islands. But the university has begun to recruit more young entrants – taking a record number in 2016 – as well as attracting greater numbers from the rest of Scotland, other parts of the UK and overseas. It has been adding residential places accordingly.

Students take a broad range of qualifications, from higher national certificates and diplomas to degrees and

Executive Office
12b Ness Walk
Inverness IV3 5SQ
0845 272 3600
info@uhi.ac.uk
www.uhi.ac.uk
www.hisa.uhi.ac.uk
Open Days 2018:
contact university

The Times and The Sunday Times **Rankings**
Overall Ranking: n/a
No data available

professional development awards. Teaching increasingly uses "blended" learning, combining online and face-to-face tuition, with small class sizes and extensive use of video conferencing.

The university has launched its first accelerated degree in geography, over three years rather than the usual four, but has not so far extended the option to other subjects.

The university's colleges spread from Dunoon in southwest Scotland to the village of Scalloway, the ancient capital of the Shetland Islands, in the north. Its network of campuses is much wider, however. Argyll College, for example, has 13 sites on the mainland and on islands such as Arran, Islay and Mull. Courses are also taught at more than 50 learning centres. Some colleges are relatively large in urban centres such as Perth, Elgin and Inverness. Others are smaller institutions, including some whose primary focus is research. The university insists, though, that all have a student-centred culture.

Several of the colleges are in spectacular locations. Lews Castle College UHI in Stornoway in the Outer Hebrides is set in 600 acres of parkland and claims "possibly the UK's most attractive location to study art" for its harbourside Lochmaddy campus in North Uist.

Sabhal Mor Ostaig UHI is the only Gaelic-medium college in the world, set in breathtaking scenery overlooking the Sound of Sleat on the Isle of Skye, while the Highland Theological College UHI is in Dingwall. West Highland College UHI does not even have a central campus, although its degree in adventure tourism management is taught in Fort William, close to Ben Nevis.

North Highland College UHI has an equestrian centre in Caithness, six miles from the main campus in Thurso, with international-sized outdoor and indoor arenas.

There are now more than 8,000 students taking more than 100 undergraduate courses, some completely online and many offering studies entirely in Gaelic. There are a dozen specialist research centres and an enterprise and research centre on the Inverness campus. They helped to produce some extremely good results in the 2014 Research Excellence Framework. Almost 70% of the research submitted for review was classified as world leading or internationally excellent.

Tuition fees

» Fees for Scottish and EU students 2018–19 £0 £1,820
» Fees for non-Scottish UK students 2018–19 £8,000–£9,000
» Fees for international students 2017–18 £10,500–£11,550
» For scholarship and bursary information see www.uhi.ac.uk/en/studying-at-uhi/first-steps/how-much-will-it-cost/funding-your-studies
» Graduate salary £18,000

Students

Undergraduates	5,240	(2,690)
Postgraduates	95	(390)
Applications per place	4	
Overall offer rate	75.2%	
International students	2.8%	
Mature students	46.3%	
From state-sector schools	98.7%	
From working-class homes	46.2%	

Accommodation

University-provided places: 632
Percentage catered: 0%
Self-catered: £76 – £144 per week
Check individual colleges
www.uhi.ac.uk/studying-at-uhi/first-steps/accommodation

University of Huddersfield

Huddersfield is reaping the rewards for an unwavering focus on teaching standards over a number of years. It finished in the top 20 for student satisfaction with teaching quality in the National Student Survey for the second successive year, and was awarded gold in the new Teaching Excellence Framework (TEF).

The TEF panel complimented the university on the way that effective use of learning analytics allowed targeted and timely interventions to boost students' results. It also commended an institution-wide strategy for assessment and feedback, which ensures that all students are challenged to achieve their full potential.

The university has the highest proportion of academics with a teaching qualification – they are all enrolled with the Higher Education Academy, the professional body dedicated to raising teaching standards – and an impressive number of National Teaching Fellows. Seminars, as well as lectures, are filmed so students can revisit the content later online.

Huddersfield has also been acting to improve graduate employment rates. Every undergraduate does some work experience as part of their degree course and a third take extended placements in business or industry, one of the highest proportions at any university. Many students now develop their own businesses for the work placement component of their course, taking advantage of the advice and facilities available at the university's Duke of York Young Entrepreneur Centre. Seven out of ten students leave with a professional qualification.

The university's achievements have not been reflected in the demand for places, however. The numbers starting degrees have been down for the past two years and the undergraduate intake is still considerably smaller than before the introduction of £9,000 fees. Applications were down by another 9% this year, largely because of the withdrawal of NHS funding for health science courses.

A raft of new degrees is planned for 2018, from four-year integrated master's courses in social work and health and social care to degrees in business law, digital and social media marketing and three new fashion BAs.

Huddersfield is investing £58m in teaching and research facilities, and is redeveloping a former industrial site and neighbouring land into its new Western campus. Subject to planning permission, the first project will be the £30m Barbara Hepworth building, a home for the study of art, design and architecture. It is named in honour of the West Yorkshire-born sculptor and its main frontage will overlook the Huddersfield Narrow Canal, which runs through the heart of the Queensgate campus. The university has created "pocket parks" and a landscaped

---

Queensgate
Huddersfield HD1 3DH
01484 473 969
aro@hud.ac.uk
www.hud.ac.uk
www.huddersfield.su
Open Days 2018:
June 30, September 22,
October 20

The Times and The Sunday Times **Rankings**

Overall Ranking: **65** (last year: 77)

Teaching quality	83.4%	=18
Student experience	80.8%	32
Research quality	9.4%	62
Entry standards	131	65
Graduate prospects	78.6%	45
Good honours	70.9%	=68
Expected completion rate	80.8%	=97
Student/staff ratio	18.9	114
Services and facilities/student	£1,986	80

area along the reopened canal to provide additional green space.

The £1.5m Heritage Quay archive centre serves both students and the public, and includes a Holocaust Heritage and Learning Centre.

The latest development is the £28m Oastler building for the Law School and the School of Music, Humanities and Media, which won a regional architectural prize and reached the shortlist for a national award. It brings together library, computing, sport, leisure, catering, social and meeting facilities.

Huddersfield has always been one of the most successful universities at widening participation in higher education. Almost half of the full-time undergraduates are from working-class homes and many come from areas without a tradition of higher education. The dropout rate has improved, and the latest projection of less than 13% is better than the national benchmark.

The university has a long-established reputation in textile design and engineering and traces its history to classes that first offered vocational education at Huddersfield in 1841. Even many arts and social science courses have a vocational slant at this institution.

Some of the most successful areas in the 2014 Research Excellence Framework were in the arts and social sciences. Huddersfield did well overall, entering almost a third of its academic staff for assessment and having nearly 60% of work rated world-leading

or internationally excellent. There were particularly good results in music, drama and performing arts, as well as in English, social work and social policy. Current projects include new facilities for the Institute of Railway Research, which is set to conduct research on HS2.

Most residential accommodation is concentrated in the Storthes Hall Park student village, but additional housing is available at Ashenhurst, just over a mile from the campus.

Town-gown relations are good, although students tend to base their social life around the students' union. There is easy public transport access to Leeds and Manchester for students seeking a livelier nightlife.

Tuition fees

» Fees for UK/EU students 2018–19 £9,250
» Fees for international students 2018–19   £14,000–£15,000
» For scholarship and bursary information see www.hud.ac.uk/udergraduate/fees-and-funding/ undergraduate-scholarships
» Graduate salary £20,000

Students

Undergraduates	13,025	(1,780)
Postgraduates	1,775	(2,695)
Applications per place	5.8	
Overall offer rate	83.7%	
International students	14.6%	
Mature students	31.1%	
From state-sector schools	98.7%	
From working-class homes	46.2%	

Accommodation

University-provided places: 1,666
Percentage catered: 0%
Self-catered: £75 – £111 per week
First year students are guaranteed accommodation
www.hud.ac.uk/uni-life/accommodation

University of Hull

Making offers to nine out of ten applicants enabled Hull to take more than 4,000 undergraduate entrants in 2016 for the first time since £9,000 fees were introduced. More than a third of Hull's undergraduates are local, while one in five comes from an area of low participation in higher education – many more than average for Hull's courses and entry qualifications.

New arrivals will find a university in the throes of a £200m campus development programme and a city that has benefited from its role as the 2017 UK City of Culture.

The Allam Medical Building at the heart of a £28m health campus was opened last November, with specialist teaching facilities including a mock hospital ward, operating theatre and intensive care nursing facilities. Medical students will work alongside nursing, midwifery and allied health undergraduates, as well as PhD students, advanced nurse practitioners and physician associates.

A £16m investment in sports facilities is also well under way and dining and conferencing facilities have been refurbished. The award-winning Brynmor Jones library, with its striking new atrium and revamped exterior, had its official opening in 2016 and has become the centrepiece of the main campus, while the redeveloped Middleton Hall has become a world-class concert hall with industry-standard recording and performance facilities.

The university has fallen ten places in our table this year despite an improved score for teaching quality in a much-toughened National Student Survey.

Awarding Hull silver in the new Teaching Excellence Framework (TEF) this summer, the panel commended courses that stretch students and integrate employment skills into the curriculum by working closely with industrial partners. It also said high-quality physical and digital resources in frequent use helped students to develop study and research skills.

The Curriculum 2016+ programme has been behind many of the positive features noted by the TEF panel. Charged with developing a distinctive "vision for teaching and learning", it has sought to integrate teaching skills with subject knowledge and technology to produce highly employable graduates.

The Hull Way – encouraging students to engage, debate, influence and lead, rather than receive information passively – includes extracurricular activities to help to develop the skills sought by employers. A 20-credit module on career management skills sharpens the focus on employability.

The careers service approaches undergraduates early in their time at Hull and sets up meetings with potential employers. The Enterprise Centre has a successful record

Cottingham Road
Hull HU6 7RX
01482 466 100
admissions@hull.ac.uk
www.hull.ac.uk
www.hullstudent.com
Open Days 2018:
see website

The Times and The Sunday Times Rankings

Overall Ranking: **=75** (last year: =65)

Teaching quality	79.5%	75
Student experience	77%	=87
Research quality	16.7%	55
Entry standards	126	=77
Graduate prospects	76.1%	56
Good honours	69.5%	=80
Expected completion rate	84.4%	=73
Student/staff ratio	16.5	=78
Services and facilities/student	£2,151	58

with those who would rather start their own businesses: 86 of the 137 start-ups nurtured there were active five years later, 23 of them still as tenants.

An audit by the Quality Assurance Agency made Hull one of the few universities in the latest round of reviews to receive a commendation for enhancing student learning opportunities.

A longstanding focus on Europe shows in the wide range of languages available at degree level, with the purpose-built Language Institute heavily used by students in all subjects.

Hull has long sent a steady flow of graduates into the House of Commons. The Westminster Hull Internship Programme offers a year-long placement and month-long internships for British politics and legislative studies students. The Legal Advice Centre, staffed by law students, provides guidance and advice to the public.

More than 60% of the work entered for the 2014 Research Excellence Framework was rated as world-leading or internationally excellent, although Hull made a relatively small submission for a pre-1992 university. The best results were in the allied health category where 87% of the research was awarded three or four stars, while geography and computer science also did well. Hull won a Queen's Anniversary prize for its research into slavery and played a leading role in shaping the UK's Modern Slavery Act.

The modest cost of living and ready availability of accommodation adds to Hull's attractions. The Hull Studentship provides a bursary of £1,000 in the first year of a degree course to students whose family income is below £25,000. Regardless of income, there are merit scholarships of £2,000 in the first year for students achieving at least 120 points on the UCAS tariff, while those with 152 points receive £1,000 in subsequent years as well.

Sports facilities have been upgraded recently to add football pitches on campus and improve the Sports and Fitness Centre.

There has also been a focus on improving accommodation, with 562 more places provided on campus in 2016 and 1,450 more to come through a £130m project with University Partnerships Programme.

Tuition fees

- » Fees for UK/EU students 2018–19 £9,250
  Foundation courses £6,165
- » Fees for international students 2018–19 £13,500–£16,000
  Medicine £33,000
- » For scholarship and bursary information see
  www.hull.ac.uk/Choose-Hull/Study-at-Hull/Scholarships-and-bursaries/Scholarships-and-bursaries.aspx
- » Graduate salary £20,500

Students

Undergraduates	11,515	(2,005)
Postgraduates	1,465	(1,320)
Applications per place	4.7	
Overall offer rate	89.8%	
International students	10.2%	
Mature students	25.6%	
From state-sector schools	93.4%	
From working-class homes	33.2%	

Accommodation

University-provided places: 3,328
Percentage catered: 26%
Catered costs: £94 – £143 per week
Self-catered: £99 – £124 per week
First year students are guaranteed accommodation
www.hull.ac.uk/student/accommodation-new.aspx

Imperial College London

Only Oxford and Cambridge have higher entry standards than Imperial and just over four applicants in ten receive an offer. Competition is fierce, and applications were up by 6% this year.

Imperial features in the top ten of both the QS and Times Higher Education world rankings. It was named by Reuters last year as the second most innovative university in Europe. The main blemish is in undergraduates' perceptions of teaching quality. It was in the bottom five for this in 2016, eliciting a pledge from the college's provost, Professor James Stirling, that the university would put right issues in assessment and feedback.

He will have been pleased with the immediate dividend last June of a gold award in the new Teaching Excellence Framework. The awards panel praised an "exceptionally stimulating and stretching academic, vocational and professional education that successfully challenges students to achieve their full potential".

This success followed even greater plaudits in the 2014 Research Excellence Framework, when Imperial's research was found to have greater impact on the economy and society than any other UK university's work. Of the research entered, 90% was rated as world-leading or internationally excellent overall, a performance bettered only by Cambridge.

A new 23-acre campus in White City, west London, should enable the college to make further strides. A community of research-focused businesses – many based in Imperial's new Translation and Innovation Hub – is already at work and this year researchers from the chemistry department will be the first to begin working in the Molecular Sciences Research Hub. The full development will cost a total of £3bn.

Imperial now has nine sites in London, due mainly to the expansion of its work in medicine in the 1990s. The medicine faculty is one of Europe's largest for staff and student numbers as well as its research income.

There are teaching bases attached to a number of hospitals in central and west London, while the UK's first Academic Health Science Centre, run in partnership with Imperial College Healthcare NHS Trust, aims to translate research advances into patient care. The centre was the first to be established of only five in the country, recognising international excellence in biomedical research, education and patient care.

In its first overseas venture, Imperial is also a partner in a new medical school in Singapore, run jointly with Nanyang Technological University.

The growing business school is Imperial's main venture beyond the world of science and

South Kensington Campus
Exhibition Road
London SW7 2AZ
020 7589 5111
www.imperial.ac.uk/study/
ug/apply/contact
www.imperial.ac.uk
www.imperialcollegeunion.org
Open Days 2018:
June 27, 28;
September 15

The Times and The Sunday Times Rankings

Overall Ranking: **4** (last year: 5)

Teaching quality	77.1%	104
Student experience	80.9%	31
Research quality	56.2%	2
Entry standards	222	2
Graduate prospects	90.7%	2
Good honours	88.6%	6
Expected completion rate	96.2%	4
Student/staff ratio	11.3	5
Services and facilities/student	£3,423	2

technology. It is highly rated and is accredited by the three largest and most influential business school accreditation associations worldwide. A BSc in medical biosciences with management is one of two interdisciplinary degrees to be introduced in 2018. The other, single honours medical biosciences, allows students to explore the sciences underpinning medicine and its related fields, and how they are applied in research, policy and industry.

Undergraduates in most subjects are based at the original South Kensington campus, which includes the Dyson School of Design Engineering, funded through a £12m donation from the James Dyson Foundation. As the UK's only university focusing exclusively on science, medicine, engineering and business, Imperial is unique for providing teaching and research in the full range of engineering disciplines.

More than a third of the undergraduates are from independent schools, one of the highest proportions at any university and considerably more than the benchmark calculated by the Higher Education Statistics Agency.

The Imperial bursary scheme provides support on a sliding scale for UK undergraduates with annual household incomes of up to £60,000, starting at £2,000 a year for incomes above £55,000 and rising to £5,000 where income is below £16,000 a year. About a third of the entrants are female, a proportion that has risen steadily over recent years.

Recent developments on the main campus near the South Kensington museums have included a second residential complex and refurbishments to the central library, as well as improvements to the students' union bar and nightclub. Further upgrading of the library is being phased in over several years to minimise disruption.

The students' union claims to have one of the largest selections of clubs and societies in the country. Outdoor sports facilities are remote, but a well-equipped campus sports centre offers free gym and swimming facilities, on payment of an initial joining fee.

Tuition fees

» Fees for UK/EU students 2018–19   £9,750
» Fees for international students 2018–19   £26,000–£28,650
   Medicine   £40,000
» For scholarship and bursary information see
   www.imperial.ac.uk/study/ug/fees-and-funding/
   bursaries-and-scholarships
» Graduate salary   £30,000

Students

Undergraduates	9,240	(0)
Postgraduates	6,425	(1,370)
Applications per place	7.6	
Overall offer rate	46.2%	
International students	43%	
Mature students	2.4%	
From state-sector schools	65.5%	
From working-class homes	16.2%	

Accommodation

University-provided places: 2,500
Percentage catered: 0%
Self-catered: £100 – £274 per week
First year students are guaranteed accommodation
www.imperial.ac.uk/study/campus-life/accommodation/halls/

Keele University

Applications to Keele were down by 18% – more than four times the national average – when the official deadline passed for courses starting last autumn. A planned reduction to the intake for medicine was partly responsible, but the withdrawal of NHS funding for other health degrees and the damaging impact of the Brexit vote on EU applications were contributing factors.

The absentees are missing out on a gold standard experience, according to the new Teaching Excellence Framework (TEF). The panel found an institutional culture that "demonstrably values teaching as highly as research", with outstanding levels of student engagement and excellent teaching and assessment practices resulting in a commitment to learning.

Keele was also our University of the Year for Student Experience for 2016–17 after consistently outstanding results in the annual National Student Survey. Students who come here like what they find. Keele featured in the top five both for teaching quality and the broader student experience in the 2016 survey.

The Keele student charter identifies ten "graduate attributes" that include independent thinking, synthesising information, creative problem solving, communicating clearly, and appreciating the social, environmental and global implications of all studies and activities. The university has also been at the forefront of moves to record in more detail what graduates have achieved through an annual report.

The Distinctive Keele Curriculum, introduced as the university celebrated its 50th anniversary in 2012, came in for particular praise in the TEF assessment. It covers voluntary and sporting activities, as well as the academic core, and can lead to accreditation by the Institute of Leadership and Management. Today's curriculum is a natural development for a university that was a pioneer of broad-based academic study long before it became fashionable, offering a foundation year 30 years ago. Its dual honours system, allowing exotic combinations of courses – chemistry and classics, anyone? – is taken up by 90% of students.

The TEF panel also noted the significant investment in physical and digital resources, as well as in specialist teaching spaces. A £10m redevelopment has added more teaching laboratories.

The university is aiming to grow by a third over five years, with postgraduates accounting for many of the new places. The numbers starting first degrees have risen by 25% in two years, despite falling applications. A range of new degrees in business, management and accountancy may boost numbers again in 2018.

Keele has the largest campus in the country, 600 acres of parkland near Stoke-on-Trent.

Keele
ST5 5BG
01782 734 010
admissions@keele.ac.uk
www.keele.ac.uk
www.keelesu.com
Open Days 2018:
June 16, August 19,
October 14

***The Times and The Sunday Times* Rankings**

Overall Ranking: **50** (last year: 42)

Teaching quality	82.9%	24
Student experience	83.1%	=12
Research quality	22.1%	53
Entry standards	134	=58
Graduate prospects	79.5%	=41
Good honours	67.5%	=94
Expected completion rate	90.7%	34
Student/staff ratio	13.9	28
Services and facilities/student	£2,018	76

More than £115m has been spent on the university's headquarters since the turn of the century, with additional accommodation and a social hub for both informal and formal events. A new hall of residence will open this year, the first of a series planned across the campus over the next few years.

A third of all undergraduates, as well as many postgraduates and some staff, live on a campus which includes an arboretum and has won a clutch of environmental awards. Students can grow their own fruit and vegetables on campus, and all undergraduates can take a module in sustainability or environmental studies.

Nearly all undergraduates have the option of spending a semester abroad at one of Keele's partner universities. Nine out of ten undergraduates are state-educated, but the university has been trying to broaden its intake further by offering special projects and masterclasses in local schools and bursaries for students from low-income families.

There is also an Excellence Scholarship, worth £1,000 in cash, paid to students who manage AAA at A-level (or the equivalent), regardless of household income. The projected dropout rate of 5.5% is well below the national average for the university's subjects and entry qualifications.

Keele's results in the 2014 Research Excellence Framework showed considerable improvement on the 2008 assessments. More than 70% of the work submitted was placed in the top two categories, with primary care and health sciences, pharmacy, chemistry, science and technology, the life sciences, and history scoring best. In addition, the £70m New Keele Deal, launched in 2016 with public sector organisations, is an attempt to boost innovation and low-carbon projects in Staffordshire.

The university is within an hour's drive of Manchester and Birmingham. Crime statistics suggest that Keele is the safest university campus out of six in the West Midlands. For those who live off campus, the cost of living in the Potteries and the surrounding area is relatively low.

The highly rated students' union, which has undergone a £2.7m renovation, offers entertainment on campus every night of the week during term time. It has held the Best Bar None Gold award for responsible drinking and a safe environment for five years in a row.

Upgraded sports facilities now include a full-size 3G football pitch suitable for all-weather play, along with indoor facilities.

Tuition fees

» Fees for UK/EU students 2018–19 £9,250
Foundation courses £5,500
» Fees for international students 2018–19 £13,200–£22,750
Medicine £29,000
» For scholarship and bursary information see
www.keele.ac.uk/studentfunding/bursariesscholarships
» Graduate salary £21,900

Students		
Undergraduates	7,225	(690)
Postgraduates	650	(1,560)
Applications per place	9.2	
Overall offer rate	71.9%	
International students	13.4%	
Mature students	13.3%	
From state-sector schools	91.7%	
From working-class homes	32.1%	

Accommodation
University-provided places: 3,156
Percentage catered: 0%
Self-catered: £85 – £155 per week
www.keele.ac.uk/studyatkeele/accommodation

University of Kent

Kent is one of a handful of universities in the UK to operate a college system, a feature that contributed to a gold award in the new Teaching Excellence Framework (TEF). Every student is attached to a college, although they do not select it themselves. The colleges act as the focus of social life, especially in the first year, and include academic as well as residential facilities.

Since the addition of the 800-bed Turing College in 2015 there have been six colleges in Canterbury and one on the university's Medway campus. The TEF panel saw the system as a vital element underpinning a "flexible and personalised" approach to academic support.

The panel was even more enthusiastic about Kent's "outstanding" Student Success Project, which identifies trends in results and completion rates, and acts to help those likely to fall behind. There was also praise for the university's systematic approach to embedding employability in the curriculum and providing employment placements for large numbers of students.

The package has been increasingly attractive to school-leavers, whose applications have risen by more than 15% in five years. The university has not compromised unduly on entry standards, however, and Kent has been hovering under the top 20 in our league table overall for the past three years. It is in the top 20 for staffing levels and not far behind for graduate prospects.

Kent's original low-rise campus is set in 300 acres of parkland overlooking Canterbury. A new building for mathematics, statistics and actuarial science and the Kent Business School has allowed two of the university's most successful departments to expand. Also new this year is the Wigoder law building – in part funded by a £1m donation from telecoms entrepreneur and Kent alumnus Charles Wigoder – which contains a mooting chamber, law clinic and shared working space for staff and students.

The library has been remodelled, after its extension. Previous developments include the prizewinning Colyer-Fergusson Music building and Kent School of Architecture's "crit" building where students get digital feedback on their projects.

The Medway campus, at the old Chatham naval base, is shared with Greenwich and Canterbury Christ Church universities. The Medway School of Pharmacy is the main feature of a £50m development, which now has more than 2,000 Kent students, including those in the School of Music and Fine Art. There are more than 1,000 residential places and grade II-listed former swimming baths have been converted into a student hub, incorporating facilities for the students'

Canterbury
CT2 7NZ
01227 827 272
information@kent.ac.uk
www.kent.ac.uk
www.kentunion.co.uk
Open Days 2018:
Canterbury July 7,
Medway June 23

The Times and The Sunday Times Rankings

Overall Ranking: **31** (last year: =23)

Teaching quality	78.5%	=88
Student experience	78.6%	=68
Research quality	35.2%	33
Entry standards	138	=51
Graduate prospects	82.6%	=15
Good honours	79.6%	30
Expected completion rate	90.4%	38
Student/staff ratio	13.3	=22
Services and facilities/student	£1,761	99

union, bar and other social spaces.

In addition, two historic dockyard buildings have been restored for Kent Business School, and a bistro, bar and student performance area added. The university also has a base in Tonbridge, mainly for short courses, which can be a preparation for degree-level study.

Styling itself "the UK's European university", Kent now has postgraduate sites in Brussels, Paris, Athens and Rome, as well as giving many undergraduates the option of a year abroad. There are partnerships with more than 100 European universities and nearly a quarter of Kent's staff are European. A post-Brexit world therefore poses Kent possibly an even greater challenge than most and its vice-chancellor, Dame Julia Goodfellow, has been among the most vocal in speaking out against Brexit.

She has also been busy forging new partnerships elsewhere in the world. In October 2016 Kent promised closer co-operation with Hiroshima University in Japan, which will yield joint research initiatives and staff and student exchanges. A similar deal was agreed with Kobe University the previous February.

Almost three-quarters of the work submitted for the Research Excellence Framework was judged world-leading or internationally excellent. Led by social work and social policy, music and drama, and modern languages, this stellar performance helped Kent to its highest ranking yet in our guide on this measure (33rd).

The university offers an outreach programme to more than 10,000 students in 48 partner schools and three further education colleges to encourage progression to higher education. The Kent Financial Support Package makes cash awards of £1,500 a year to state-educated students whose household income is below £42,875, if they meet other criteria such as living in social housing. There is also a range of scholarships, including music and sport.

Kent is one of the best-provided universities for accommodation, with 5,345 places in Canterbury alone. The student centre has a nightclub large enough to attract big-name bands, as well as a theatre, cinema and bars.

Some students find both Canterbury and Medway limited for social life, but campus security is good and the sports facilities include a £4.8m fitness suite, multipurpose fitness and dance studio, and an indoor tennis centre alongside the sports centre in Canterbury. The university is also a partner in the Medway Park sports centre, which has gym and swimming facilities.

Tuition fees

- » Fees for EU/UK students 2018–2019   £9,250
- » Fees for international students 2018–19   £15,200–£18,400
- » For scholarship and bursary information see https://www.kent.ac.uk/finance-student/fees/index.html
- » Graduate salaries   £20,000

Students

Undergraduates	15,075	(535)
Postgraduates	2,770	(1,285)
Applications per place	6.9	
Overall offer rate	88.4%	
International students	20.2%	
Mature students	10.4%	
From state-sector schools	93.9%	
From working-class homes	32.5%	

Accommodation

University-provided places 6,451
Percentage catered 11%
Self-catered £113 – £179 per week
Catered £129 – £208
All first year students offered accommodation
www.kent.ac.uk/accommodation

King's College London

King's may become the first UK university to open a campus in continental Europe to protect itself against the possible effects of Brexit. There has been a programme to foster collaboration with Technische Universitat Dresden in Germany since 2015, but King's is considering a physical campus there to maintain access to EU research funding and run "offshore" undergraduate programmes.

King's is already highly international, with almost 9,000 students from outside the UK and about 300 partner institutions overseas. Demand has also been rising from home students, and the numbers starting degrees are up by more than a quarter since the first year of £9,000 fees. Two thirds of school-leavers applying to King's receive an offer, compared with less than half in 2011.

One of the oldest and largest colleges in the University of London and a member of the Russell Group, King's describes itself as "the most central university in London" because four of its five campuses are within a single square mile, around the banks of the Thames. Its latest development has been the addition of Bush House, the former headquarters of the BBC World Service, opposite its Strand campus, where the new King's business school is based. It aims to make the most of its location by recruiting leading figures from business, the City, government and NGOs to share their expertise.

Opportunities for students to engage with employers were among the features that contributed to the university receiving a silver award in the government's new Teaching Excellence Framework this year. The awards panel commented on the way that students were stretched academically and the "strong research-led culture" that requires all research staff to teach. Low levels of student satisfaction, common in London, prevented King's from reaching the gold category.

The same difficulties are keeping King's out of our top 20; it was in the bottom four last year for perceptions of teaching quality and students boycotted this year's National Student Survey in sufficient numbers to prevent a score being recorded.

However, King's is in the top ten for research after 85% of the work submitted to the 2014 Research Excellence Framework was judged to be world-leading or internationally excellent. Law, education, clinical medicine and philosophy all ranked in the top three in the country and there were good results in general engineering, history, psychology and communication and media studies. Those successes led to the biggest increase in research funding of any university.

Today's researchers follow in a tradition that has seen King's play a part in many of the advances that shape modern life, including the

Strand
London WC2R 2LS
020 7848 7000
Enquire via website
www.kcl.ac.uk
www.kclsu.org
Open Days 2018:
see website, campus
tours available
year-round

The Times and The Sunday Times Rankings

Overall Ranking: **=28** (last year: 27)

Teaching quality	n/a	
Student experience	n/a	
Research quality	44%	9
Entry standards	174	16
Graduate prospects	84.1%	=10
Good honours	85.8%	12
Expected completion rate	93.6%	18
Student/staff ratio	12	9
Services and facilities/student	£2,326	38

discovery of DNA and the development of radar. Twelve of its alumni or academics have won Nobel prizes and King's is close to the top 20 in the QS World University Rankings. It is Europe's largest centre for the education of doctors, dentists and other healthcare professionals, and home to several Medical Research Council centres.

The original Strand site and the Waterloo campus house most of the non-medical departments. Nursing and midwifery and some biomedical subjects are also based at Waterloo, while medicine and dentistry are mainly at Guy's Hospital, near London Bridge, and in the St Thomas' Hospital campus, across the river from the Houses of Parliament. The Denmark Hill campus, in south London, is home to the Institute of Psychiatry, Psychology and Neuroscience, as well as more medicine and dentistry subjects.

The addition of Bush House and neighbouring buildings will enable King's to upgrade its teaching facilities. It had already expanded into the east wing of Somerset House, providing impressive new premises for the Dickson Poon School of Law, and upgraded the libraries on all the main campuses as part of a £60m programme of improvements to student facilities.

More than a quarter of the undergraduates come from independent schools, but a similar proportion are from low-income families. The access to medicine course, which attracts talented students from generally low-performing schools into medical degrees, has now been replicated for dentistry with the enhanced support dentistry programme.

There are more than 4,000 places in university-owned accommodation, as well as access to nearly 400 intercollegiate places run by the University of London. Some of the outdoor sports facilities are a long train ride from the campuses, but there are facilities for all the main sports, as well as rifle ranges, two gyms and a swimming pool.

Tuition fees

- » Fees for UK/EU students 2018–19 £9,250
- » Fees for international students 2018–19 £17,900–£23,900
  Dentistry £41,160 Medicine £34,650
- » For scholarship and bursary information see
  www.kcl.ac.uk/study/undergraduate/fees-and-funding/
  student-funding/scholarships-and-bursaries/index.aspx
- » Graduate salary £25,000

Students

Undergraduates	15,450	(2,320)
Postgraduates	7,165	(3,965)
Applications per place	8	
Overall offer rate	66.3%	
International students	27%	
Mature students	16.8%	
From state-sector schools	77.3%	
From working-class homes	26.2%	

Accommodation

University-provided places: 7,774
Percentage catered: 8%
Catered costs: £140 – £480 per week
Self-catered: £150 – £382 per week
First year students are guaranteed accommodation
www.kcl.ac.uk/study/accommodation/index.aspx

Kingston University

Kingston is preparing for life as a somewhat smaller university, with applications down by 21% in 2017. The drop is due partly to the closure of joint honours courses in the arts and social sciences and to the fall in demand for health courses experienced by most universities since the withdrawal of NHS bursaries.

But applications were already down by almost a third in five years and the university sees a smaller, but still broad-based and inclusive, intake as a natural consequence of fewer 18-year-olds and increased competition for students.

The university has also seen a parallel decline in its ranking in our table over the past 20 years, from regularly appearing among the top ten modern universities (earning a shortlisting for University of the Year in 2000 and again in 2003) to a low last year when it appeared in the bottom ten of our table for the first time.

It currently has almost 20,000 students and offered places to fewer than six out of ten applicants in 2016. It was one of 25 universities awarded bronze in the new Teaching Excellence Framework (TEF). Nevertheless, the TEF panel complimented the university on its focus on black and ethnic minority students, and a completion rate that is in line with the national average for Kingston's courses and student profile. About one in seven students drops out of a course here.

The university is still developing its portfolio of courses. Degrees in music technology, popular music, occupational therapy and others preparing graduates for the creative and cultural industries were introduced last year, as well as a degree apprenticeship in civil engineering. There are already degree apprenticeships in aircraft engineering and quality surveying, consultancy, and more may be added in 2018.

Kingston's campuses are also developing. Construction is under way on a £50m teaching building, due for completion in 2019. Its facilities will include a learning resources centre, a covered courtyard for informal gathering, performance space and new landscaping across the front of the campus. New facilities for science and technology opened last year, with innovative outreach space alongside the laboratories to show the public how cutting-edge technologies are making an impact on daily life.

The School of Art, which is rated in the top 100 in the world by QS, is being refurbished, with new academic space and an improved exterior. Its fashion degree was ranked second in the world by the Business of Fashion website in 2016. The school achieved among the best results in the 2014 Research Excellence Framework with history and English. The university entered relatively

River House
53–57 High Street
Kingston upon Thames
KT1 1LQ
0844 855 2177
admissionsops@kingston.ac.uk
www.kingston.ac.uk
www.kingstonstudents.net
Open Days 2018:
March 17, April 18,
June 6

Edinburgh
Belfast
KINGSTON UPON THAMES
Cardiff *London*

The Times and The Sunday Times Rankings

Overall Ranking: **117** (last year: 122)

Teaching quality	76.3%	=111
Student experience	76.7%	=92
Research quality	5.1%	=91
Entry standards	118	=100
Graduate prospects	63.5%	113
Good honours	67.9%	93
Expected completion rate	82.2%	=88
Student/staff ratio	17.3	92
Services and facilities/student	£2,085	67

few academics for the research exercise – only 16% of eligible staff – but 60% of the submission reached the top two categories and there was some world-leading research in each of the nine areas assessed.

Kingston has been among the top three universities for graduate start-up companies for eight years in a row, topping the rankings again for 2015–16 with 289 graduate start-ups registered in the year, 87 more than the university in second place. The Enterprise Department was established more than a decade ago, giving advice to would-be entrepreneurs in any subject and the possibility of financial support with start-ups. A career focus runs through all of Kingston's courses and the careers service won a national award in 2017 for the best strategy for preparing students for work.

The university markets itself as being in "lively, leafy London", making a virtue of its suburban, riverside location southwest of central London as well as its proximity to the bright lights. Two of its four campuses are close to Kingston town centre; another, two miles away and close to Richmond Park, is at Kingston Hill; the fourth is in Roehampton Vale, where a site once used as an aerospace factory now contains a new technology block. The university has the third-largest engineering faculty in London, with its own Learjet and a flight simulator to support its highly regarded aeronautical engineering courses.

The Faculty of Health, Social Care and Education (run jointly with St George's, University of London) now has more than 7,000 students and has won two big NHS London training contracts. There is a link with the Royal Marsden School of Cancer Nursing and Rehabilitation, enabling some students to spend up to half of their course on clinical placements working in hospital, primary care and community settings.

Kingston has one of the most ethnically mixed student populations of any UK university. More than a quarter of the places go to mature students and nearly half to those from working-class families. Most students like the university's location, although they complain about the high cost of living. More than £20m has been spent on halls of residence and a new multiuse sports building on the Kingston Hill campus is due to open soon.

Tuition fees

» Fees for UK/EU students 2018–19 £9,250
  Foundation courses £6,165
» Fees for international students 2018–19 £12,700–£15,300
» For scholarship and bursary information see www.kingston.ac.uk/undergraduate/fees-and-funding/bursaries
» Graduate salary £20,000

Students

Undergraduates	14,980	(1,295)
Postgraduates	2,480	(2,130)
Applications per place	9.2	
Overall offer rate	74.2%	
International students	13.7%	
Mature students	32.7%	
From state-sector schools	96.2%	
From working-class homes	47.3%	

Accommodation

University-provided places: 2,800
Percentage catered: 0%
Self-catered: £86 – £160 per week
First year students are guaranteed accommodation
www.kingston.ac.uk/accommodation

Lancaster University

Our University of the Year, Lancaster has not opted for expansion on the scale seen at other leading universities, but it took a record number of undergraduates in 2016. Overall it has climbed to its highest ever ranking in our table.

There was success, too, in the new Teaching Excellence Framework (TEF) where it was awarded gold. The TEF panel complimented the university on the way it makes students feel valued, supported and stretched academically. It also found a "culture of research-stimulated learning" that produced skills that are most highly valued by employers.

Having been the top university in our table from the northwest of England for more than a decade, Lancaster has also set itself the target of becoming a "global player" in both teaching and research. It is the only UK university with a presence in sub-Saharan Africa, having opened a branch campus in Ghana, and there is now a joint institute in China, with Beijing Jiaotong University, offering undergraduate programmes in computing, design, engineering and environmental science. With other partnerships in India, Pakistan, Malaysia and China, more than 2,000 students are taking a Lancaster degree overseas.

Hundreds of Lancaster students also spend part of their courses in America, Asia, Australia or Europe. The university is adding to its range of degrees incorporating a year in industry or abroad. Biology, human geography, law and international management will all be available with study abroad in 2018.

Lancaster's research grades improved substantially in the 2014 assessments, when 83% of its work was considered world-leading or internationally excellent. There were particularly good results in business and management, sociology, English and maths and statistics, and a strong performance across the board.

Lancaster was the only university in the region to receive an increase in funding because of the quality and volume of its submission. It received a Queen's Anniversary prize last year for computer analysis of world languages in print, speech and social media.

Lancaster is more successful than most research universities in widening participation among under-represented groups. Nine out of 10 undergraduates are state-educated and almost a quarter come from the four lowest socioeconomic classes. Outreach activity includes summer schools for 600 sixth-formers and college students, masterclasses for 2,000 and mentoring for 250 students.

Last year, former footballer Gary Neville, once Manchester United captain, announced that Lancaster was one of his partners in plans to open a sports university in Stretford with undergraduate courses in sports and media. A site has been identified and the first students are expected to arrive in 2019.

Bailrigg
Lancaster LA1 4YW
01524 592 028
ugadmissions@lancaster.ac.uk
www.lancaster.ac.uk
http://lusu.co.uk
Open Days 2018:
see website

The Times and The Sunday Times **Rankings**		
Overall Ranking: **6** (last year: =9)		
Teaching quality	83.4%	=18
Student experience	84.3%	7
Research quality	39.1%	15
Entry standards	159	30
Graduate prospects	84.9%	9
Good honours	77.5%	40
Expected completion rate	92.7%	=23
Student/staff ratio	13	=16
Services and facilities/student	£3,104	8

Undergraduates join one of eight residential colleges on the 560-acre parkland campus, the centre of most students' social life. Most colleges house between 800 and 900 students in self-catering accommodation. The historic city of Lancaster is a ten-minute bus ride away. Both the campus and city have been rated among the safest in the UK.

Campus developments have included eco-friendly student residences and an impressive library. Lancaster is invariably among the leaders in the National Student Housing Survey for the best university halls, taking the award six times.

The latest project is a Health Innovation Campus, a collaboration between the university, business and the NHS, next to the Bailrigg campus. The first £41m phase of the development should be completed by September 2019. There are also plans for further development of the highly rated Management School.

An award-winning building for engineering caters for undergraduate numbers that have doubled in this field. Lancaster has also brought together art, design and theatre studies with the university's public art gallery, concerts and theatre, and invested heavily in design.

The most successful university at reducing carbon emissions, Lancaster has won praise for its innovative wind turbine project, which generates about 15% of its annual electricity consumption. Its residences and other facilities have won a string of environmental awards.

The university has always championed a flexible degree structure, which allows most undergraduates to make their final choice of degree only at the end of the first year. Against the national trend for closing faculties, Lancaster reopened its chemistry department after a £26m refit and has introduced three new undergraduate degrees and several joint honours options in the subject.

The university is hugely appealing to those who love the outdoors. Some of England's most unspoilt countryside is on the university's doorstep, including the Lake District and the Forest of Bowland. The university also hosts a thriving live arts scene for the campus, the city and the region.

Sports facilities are good and conveniently placed, with a £20m sports centre on campus. Road and rail communications are good, but Lancaster is limited for off-campus nightlife.

Tuition fees
- » Fees for UK/EU students 2018–19 £9,250
- » Fees for international students 2017–18 £15,080–£19,250
  Medicine £29,170
- » For scholarship and bursary information see www.lancaster.ac.uk/study/undergraduate/fees-and-funding/scholarships-and-bursaries
- » Graduate salary £22,000

Students

Undergraduates	9,475	(25)
Postgraduates	2,275	(1,340)
Applications per place	6.4	
Overall offer rate	91.2%	
International students	29.9%	
Mature students	4.3%	
From state-sector schools	90.4%	
From working-class homes	23.9%	

Accommodation

University-provided places: 8,950
Percentage catered: 3%
Catered costs: £178 per week
Self-catered: £85 – £139 per week
First year students are guaranteed accommodation
www.lancaster.ac.uk/facilities/accommodation/undergraduates

University of Leeds

Leeds was in the top four for applications in 2016 and has maintained strong demand for places this year, although other universities have found their numbers declining. It is also one of the top five universities targeted by leading employers, according to the 2017 High Fliers graduate market survey.

The university was awarded gold in the new Teaching Excellence Framework (TEF), commended by the panel for ensuring its students take charge of their experiences with academic and co-curricular opportunities that help to prepare them for the world beyond their studies.

Our University of the Year for 2016–17 and now at an all-time high in our rankings, Leeds is second only to York in the Russell Group for student satisfaction.

It is now on the verge of the top ten in the sections of the National Student Survey dealing with the organisation and management of courses, the learning community, the student voice and the quality and availability of learning resources. The university has also improved its ranking for staffing levels and spending on student services and facilities.

More than 80% of the research assessed in the 2014 Research Excellence Framework was considered world-leading or internationally excellent, placing Leeds in the top ten in the UK in 30% of its subject areas. It is just outside the top 100 in the QS World University Rankings.

The university saw a £12m increase in research council awards during 2016/17, bringing its total to more than £50m and placing it second only to Cambridge on this measure.

Leeds is in the middle of a five-year, £520m programme of campus developments to ensure that it maintains the progress of recent years. The £26m Laidlaw library – built with a £9m contribution from Leeds alumnus Lord Laidlaw – has been designed for undergraduates and the Edward Boyle library has also been refurbished.

In the next phase of the plan, the North East Quarter project will bring together physics, computing and imaging science. Another recent venture produced the £42m Enterprise and Innovation Centre, which helps students with start-up plans and accelerates business creation and growth across the city.

The university occupies a 98-acre site within walking distance of the city centre, although much of the accommodation is further out. The student population is highly cosmopolitan, with 5,000 international students from 141 countries included in the student body of more than 31,000. Leeds also has one of the largest Study Abroad programmes in the country, with nearly 200 options from Spain to Singapore.

A new partnership agreement has been signed with Shanghai Jiao Tong University,

Woodhouse Lane
Leeds LS2 9JT
0113 343 2336
study@leeds.ac.uk
www.leeds.ac.uk
www.luu.org.uk
Open Days 2018:
June 15, 16,
September 8, October 6

***The Times and The Sunday Times* Rankings**

Overall Ranking: **10** (last year: 13)

Teaching quality	82.4%	=29
Student experience	83.3%	11
Research quality	36.8%	27
Entry standards	168	19
Graduate prospects	81.5%	=23
Good honours	84.2%	15
Expected completion rate	92.7%	=23
Student/staff ratio	13.2	=18
Services and facilities/student	£2,987	10

one of China's leading institutions, to tackle global challenges in atmospheric change, water pollution, transport and sustainable development. During 2018, the two universities will work towards founding a joint institute for environmental research, building on Leeds' strength in this area through the Priestley International Centre for Climate.

There are more than 500 undergraduate programmes, with students encouraged to take courses outside their main subject. The Leeds curriculum requires undergraduates to undertake a research project in their final year, which is intended to be seen as the "pinnacle of their academic achievement" and is weighted accordingly.

Leeds, whose staff have been consistently recognised with National Teaching Fellowships, has established a new Institute for Teaching Excellence and Innovation.

More than £2m was invested in a new lecture-capture system – one of the largest in Europe – allowing students access to video recordings so they can study at their own pace.

Leeds offers one of the biggest pots for financial support, helping one in three of its UK and EU undergraduates. The LeedsforLife service – another feature praised by the TEF panel – provides students with academic and careers advice, as well as helping to identify work placements and volunteering opportunities for five years after graduation. Leeds has more market-listed spin-outs than any other university.

More than 2,500 students volunteer in the local community and 400 of them are trained as mentors and tutors supporting schools in the region.

The rise of Leeds as a shopping and clubbing centre has added to the attractions of the university, which has more than 8,000 residential places. Sports and social facilities are first-rate, and Leeds teams regularly excel in competition. The university hosts one of six centres of cricketing excellence. It has more playing field space than any other higher education institution, while the Edge sports centre includes a 25-metre swimming pool and a huge fitness suite.

The Brownlee Centre, a £5m facility, is named after the triathlete brothers who are the university's most successful sporting alumni and train regularly there. Opened last year, it is the UK's first purpose-built triathlon training centre, located alongside a mile-long closed-loop cycling circuit for cyclists of all abilities, as well as grass pitches used regularly by students for football, rugby and other sports.

Tuition fees

» Fees for UK/EU students 2018–19   £9,250
» Fees for international students 2018–19   £17,500–£23,250
    Medicine £31,250 Dentistry £34,500
» For scholarship and bursary information see
    www.leeds.ac.uk/info/130528/funding
» Graduate salary   £21.000

Students

Undergraduates	22,995	(570)
Postgraduates	5,610	(2,610)
Applications per place	7.9	
Overall offer rate	72.9%	
International students	11.7%	
Mature students	8.3%	
From state-sector schools	79.7%	
From working-class homes	22.5%	

Accommodation

University-provided places: 8,227
Percentage catered: 14%
Catered costs: £91 – £198 per week
Self-catered: £91 – £146 per week
First year students are guaranteed accommodation
www.accommodation.leeds.ac.uk/

Leeds Beckett University

Leeds Beckett has switched from running four faculties to 13 academic schools and is investing £200m over the next seven years to create for each of them an "academic home" to reinforce a sense of community. In some cases there will be significant development; in others only refurbishments to make sure that each subject is taught in a pleasant environment conducive to collaborative academic work.

The first project will be a new building for the School of Film, Music and Performing Arts with specialist facilities such as a black box studio, Dolby Atmos cinema, three large film studios, acoustic labs and a theatre. The City campus has already had a £100m transformation, centred on the futuristic Rose Bowl lecture theatre complex next to Leeds Civic Hall, which houses the business school.

Leeds Beckett was awarded silver in the new Teaching Excellence Framework. The panel praised the opportunities for students to increase their employability by learning about professional practice through live project briefs, case studies, practice-related assessments and placements. Students were stretched, the panel said, and developed transferable and personal skills.

The reorganisation and structural reboot was badly needed. The number of students starting degrees is down by nearly 20% since 2011 and applications have dropped by almost 40%. At the same time, Leeds Beckett, which ditched its Leeds Metropolitan name in 2014, has struggled in our league table and hits the bottom ten for the first time this year.

Student satisfaction scores improved, despite the more challenging questions introduced in the 2017 National Student Survey, but the proportion of students awarded good honours declined and it was a poor year for the university's graduates in the employment market.

The university has set itself some challenging targets for improvement such as halving the chronically high dropout rate (currently running at more than one in five students and among the highest in the country) and ensuring that almost nine out of ten students are satisfied with the standard of teaching.

There are two bases in Leeds: the City campus in the heart of the centre and the Headingley campus, three miles away in 100 acres of park and woodland. The latter boasts outstanding sports facilities, including a sports arena and multiuse sports pitches, plus the Carnegie Regional Tennis Centre and teaching accommodation for education, informatics, law and business.

More than 7,000 students take part in some form of sporting activity, and the university offers a range of sports scholarships. The Athletic Union hosts 48 clubs and the 50 university teams are among the most successful in national competition, ranking 14th in last year's inter-university British

---

City Campus
Leeds LS1 3HE
0113 812 3113
admissionsenquiries@
leedsbeckett.ac.uk
www.leedsbeckett.ac.uk
www.leedsbeckettsu.co.uk
Open Days 2018: July,
check website for
exact date

The Times and The Sunday Times **Rankings**

Overall Ranking: **123** (last year: =112)

Teaching quality	79.3%	78
Student experience	79.1%	=55
Research quality	4.1%	=101
Entry standards	114	=108
Graduate prospects	62.9%	=117
Good honours	64.6%	107
Expected completion rate	75.6%	121
Student/staff ratio	19.9	=121
Services and facilities/student	£1,591	112

Universities and Colleges Sport competition.

Several recent alumni and others who use the university as their training base took part in the Rio Olympics. A basic annual sports pass costs £125. A new stand at the Headingley rugby ground has classrooms, coaching facilities and social space for use by the university and two professional clubs.

Such is the popularity of sandwich and part-time courses, only just over half of all undergraduates take conventional full-time degrees. It is intended that all Leeds Beckett students should leave the university with three graduate attributes: to be enterprising, digitally literate and have a global outlook. All undergraduate courses were redesigned with these qualities in mind and all include at least two weeks work-related learning a year.

A growing emphasis on educational technology is enhanced by 24-hour libraries, which have achieved the Customer Service Excellence standard for ten years in a row.

The university has a longstanding reputation for widening participation in higher education and runs a wide range of summer schools, attended by more than 24,000 young people a year.

The university almost doubled the number of academics it entered for the 2014 Research Excellence Framework compared with the 2008 assessments. Just over a third of their work was rated as world-leading or internationally excellent, with architecture and sports studies producing the best results. Leeds Beckett's reputation is mainly for applied research: three interdisciplinary research institutes focus on health, sport and sustainability and there are ten centres in more specialist fields.

The university has launched the Leeds Arts Research Centre (LARC), for example, bringing together creative practitioners and academics to focus on all aspects of the arts, including music, film, fine art, design and performing arts. LARC draws on staff from the School of Art, Architecture and Design and from the School of Film, Music and Performing Arts and brings together cultural historians and theorists with arts practitioners at the cutting edge of practice and research. The research centre will also provide a forum for debate and collaboration on new projects to encourage an interdisciplinary research culture at Leeds Beckett.

Leeds Beckett is benefiting from the city's growing reputation for nightlife, but it is making its own contribution with a famously lively entertainments scene. With more than 4,000 bed spaces, it means that those who accept places before clearing are guaranteed university accommodation.

Tuition fees

- » Fees for UK/EU students 2018–19 — £9,250
- » Fees for international students 2017–18 — £10,500
- » For scholarship and bursary information see www.leedsbeckett.ac.uk/undergraduate/scholarships
- » Graduate salary — £18,000

Students

Undergraduates	17,330	(4,135)
Postgraduates	1,390	(3,065)
Applications per place	5.5	
Overall offer rate	79.5%	
International students	5.2%	
Mature students	11.7%	
From state-sector schools	94.8%	
From working-class homes	35.4%	

Accommodation

University-provided places: 4,257
Percentage catered: 0%
Self-catered: £89 – £218 per week
First year students are guaranteed accommodation
www.leedsbeckett.ac.uk/accommodation

Leeds Trinity University

Leeds Trinity claims to be the only university in the UK to include at least two professional work placements – a total of 11 weeks of relevant experience – as part of every student's degree. Relationships with more than 3,000 employers give undergraduates a wide range of options.

Students receive one-to-one advice from their own placement adviser and have an intensive two-week placement preparation programme. Overseas placements are encouraged and all form part of an assessed module counting towards final degree classification.

The scheme contributed to a silver award for Leeds Trinity in the new Teaching Excellence Framework, which also commented favourably on innovative assessment and feedback practices, and excellent use of technology. Leeds Trinity's strategy for teaching and learning focuses on student-led inquiry, placing the onus on students to develop skills in order to be more employable when they graduate.

A huge improvement in student satisfaction has propelled Leeds Trinity 29 places up our league table this year, the biggest leap of any university. Despite a more exacting National Student Survey in 2017, students placed the university inside the top ten for both teaching quality and their wider student experience.

Undergraduate enrolments in 2016 were close to the previous year's, despite a drop in applications. The university broadened its portfolio of degrees last year, with 15 new offerings such as politics, sociology and exercise, health and nutrition. Another five new degrees are planned for 2018, including law, photography and physical education. The university also offers accelerated two-year degrees in education and sport, and tourism and leisure management.

Leeds Trinity is a Catholic foundation that "promotes dialogue and teaching of the Catholic church", but is not controlled by the church and welcomes students of all faiths and none. The university grew out of two Catholic teacher training colleges established in the 1960s.

Education is still the biggest subject and its Institute for Childhood and Education pools the expertise of its acclaimed departments of Primary Education, Secondary Education and Children, Young People and Families. There are also schools of Arts and Communication and Health and Social Sciences.

Leeds Trinity has just over 3,000 students on an attractive campus 20 minutes northwest of Leeds city centre, in Horsforth. Campus improvements have cost £15m so far, and another £25m investment is on the way for further developments.

Brownberrie Lane
Horsforth
Leeds LS18 5HD
0113 283 7100
admissions@leedstrinity.ac.uk
www.leedstrinity.ac.uk
www.ltsu.co.uk
Open Days 2018:
check website

The Times and The Sunday Times Rankings

Overall Ranking: **=67** (last year: 96)

Teaching quality	85.5%	6
Student experience	83.5%	9
Research quality	2%	121
Entry standards	108	=121
Graduate prospects	68%	97
Good honours	77.6%	39
Expected completion rate	86.8%	56
Student/staff ratio	21.4	127
Services and facilities/student	£1,769	97

An extension to the Learning Centre provides students with new teaching rooms, group study and social learning spaces, plus a bigger 24-hour lab and cafe. Students also have access to the Trinity Enterprise Centre if they are considering launching their own business. Its advice and facilities are available to local businesses as well as students.

Only 20 academics were entered for the 2014 Research Excellence Framework, but there were good results in communication, cultural and media studies, and library and information management. The flagship research group, the Leeds Centre for Victorian Studies, has a national and international reputation.

Nearly two-thirds of the students are female and Leeds Trinity exceeds all its national benchmarks for widening participation in higher education: more than 20% of undergraduates come from areas with little tradition of sending students to university, one of the highest proportions in the country.

The projected dropout rate has improved considerably and is now lower than the national average for Leeds Trinity's courses and entry qualifications. Among the outreach activities is a Children's University, based on the campus, which offers high-quality, innovative learning activities outside normal school hours to children aged 7–14.

The university has nearly 800 residential places, enough to guarantee accommodation to first-years as long as they apply by the end of July. A new development in 2016 added 228 beds in 29 cluster flats.

Sports facilities are good and include a 3G pitch. The university's sports centre has refurbished its fitness suite with new equipment catering for elite athletes as well as casual users.

The thriving city of Leeds with its abundant nightlife is one of the most popular with students, although Leeds Trinity's campus is not central to the social distractions on offer. On the upside, the scenic beauty of the Yorkshire Dales is close by.

Tuition fees

- » Fees for UK/EU students 2018–19 £9,250
  Foundation courses £5,000
- » Fees for international students 2017–18 £11,250
- » For scholarship and bursary information see
  www.leedstrinity.ac.uk/student-life/student-finance
- » Graduate salary £18,000

Students

Undergraduates	2,815	(50)
Postgraduates	315	(535)
Applications per place	7.4	
Overall offer rate	86.1%	
International students	1%	
Mature students	14.5%	
From state-sector schools	97.3%	
From working-class homes	42.3%	

Accommodation

University-provided places: 796
Percentage catered: 25%
Catered costs: £117 – £132 per week
Self-catered: £92 – £122 per week
First year students are guaranteed accommodation
www.leedstrinity.ac.uk/student-life/accommodation

University of Leicester

Leicester has increased its undergraduate enrolments more than any other university since £9,000 fees were introduced. Another 13% rise in 2016 enabled it to accept more than 4,000 new undergraduates for the first time, in spite of a drop in applications. Although it has slipped out of our top 30, it has good staffing levels and high spending on student services and facilities.

There has been a focus on improving the student experience, with a new student app, peer mentoring, and the filming of lectures for students to review online. The new lecture-capture system was a response to student feedback and won approval from the new Teaching Excellence Framework panel that awarded Leicester silver. The panel also congratulated the university on engaging students with current research on all its courses.

Leicester has launched the Student Lifecycle Change programme to improve services. To underline the university's commitment to teaching quality, academics can be promoted to professor or assistant professor only if they have a qualification from the Higher Education Academy.

Archaeologists at the university put the institution on the map with the discovery of the remains of Richard III beneath a Leicester car park. Not for the first time, either: Sir Alec Jeffreys discovered DNA fingerprinting here in 1984, which remains one of the great scientific strides of the 20th century. Now retired, Jeffreys remains an emeritus professor at the Department of Genetics, a star feature of the university.

Three-quarters of the work submitted to the 2014 Research Excellence Framework was rated as world-leading or internationally excellent, with the School of Museum Studies producing the best results, as it did in 2008. The results, which were also good in clinical medicine, biology, earth science and general engineering, brought a substantial increase in research funding.

Leicester also has a long-established reputation in space science, with Europe's largest university-based space research facility, including the National Space Centre. A new Space Park was announced last year for postgraduate teaching, research and tenants in the space industry. There are also plans for a life sciences park at the Charnwood site near Loughborough.

The university's main campus and much of the residential accommodation is concentrated in a leafy suburb a mile from the centre of Leicester where £6m a year is being invested in resources and facilities. The university's first overseas venture – the Leicester International Institute/Dalian University of Technology – opened last year in China. Based in Panjin, it is

---

University Road
Leicester LE1 7RH
0116 252 5281
study@le.ac.uk
www.le.ac.uk
www.leicesterunion.com
Open Days 2018:
June 9, July 6,
September 15,
October 13

The Times and The Sunday Times Rankings

Overall Ranking: **34** (last year: 25)

Teaching quality	78.1%	=96
Student experience	79.1%	=55
Research quality	31.8%	=38
Entry standards	145	44
Graduate prospects	75.7%	57
Good honours	74.7%	48
Expected completion rate	92.9%	22
Student/staff ratio	13	=16
Services and facilities/student	£2,702	19

offering degrees in English in chemistry and mechanical engineering, with mathematics to follow in 2018.

Leicester is aiming to provide the most flexible curriculum in the UK, in response to strong demand among students and prospective applicants for more choice in degree options. Undergraduates can choose single, joint or major/minor programmes. Those taking the major/minor route are able to combine a wide range of subjects, including new areas such as global studies, spending three-quarters of their time studying their principal subject and a quarter on the minor element.

The university has also introduced employability initiatives including an undergraduate internship programme with up to 500 places available each year.

The undergraduate population is among the most socially diverse of any university in our top 35. More than nine out of ten undergraduates come from state schools and 27% came from low-income families when the last survey was conducted.

Leicester has almost 4,800 bed spaces, so first-years are guaranteed a residential place as long as they apply by the end of August. Facilities at Oadby Student Village include study areas, social spaces, cinema room and bar. Many second and third-year students also live in halls, although the majority choose to live in reasonably priced private accommodation nearby.

The university has two modern sports centres, one on campus and the other at the student village. Both have a gym, swimming pool, spa, sauna and steam room, and studios. There are also floodlit tennis courts, all-weather and rugby pitches at Oadby. Students currently pay a basic membership fee of £123 a year to use the facilities.

The city of Leicester's ethnic diversity offers a rich cultural experience, and with De Montfort University also in town, students make up 12% of the population in term time. According to HSBC, it is the most affordable destination in the UK for first and second-year students.

Leicester is big enough to provide all the normal sports and entertainment opportunities, but also offers events such as one of the biggest Diwali celebrations outside India. The award-winning students' union has been refurbished and is the only one in the country to contain an O2 Academy.

Tuition fees

- » Fees for UK/EU students 2018–19 £9,250
- » Fees for international students 2017–18 £15,290–£18,855 Medicine, clinical years up to £41,945
- » For scholarship and bursary information see www.le.ac.uk/student-life/undergraduate/fees-and-funding
- » Graduate salary £21,000

Students

Undergraduates	10,765	(740)
Postgraduates	4,510	(1,810)
Applications per place	7.1	
Overall offer rate	85.9%	
International students	19.6%	
Mature students	9.1%	
From state-sector schools	91.2%	
From working-class homes	26.9%	

Accommodation

University-provided places: 4,781
Percentage catered: 14%
Catered costs: £119 – £172 per week
Self-catered: £85 – £176 per week
First year students are guaranteed accommodation
www.le.ac.uk/student-life/undergraduates/accommodation

University of Lincoln

Lincoln is consistently among the top-ranked modern (post-1992) universities in our league table, due in significant part to its success in the annual National Student Survey. A high-water mark was reached in 2016 with top-ten performances both for how students rate their teaching and their wider student experience, but Lincoln has fallen back somewhat this year.

Solid performance in the survey paved the way for Lincoln's gold award in the new Teaching Excellence Framework (TEF). The panel complimented it on a strong approach to personalised learning through highly engaged personal tutors with access to analytics to monitor students' progress proactively. It found that students were involved in the design of courses and enabled to develop their independence, understanding and skills to fulfil their full potential.

The university's popularity has been growing, particularly among school-leavers. Enrolments by 18-year-olds have risen by 35% in two years. The options for applicants have widened further with the launch last year of more than 30 foundation-year courses in science and technology to bring underqualified prospective undergraduates up to the standard required for an honours degree. Lincoln's National Centre for Food Manufacturing has also developed a new range of higher apprenticeships and degree apprenticeships for the food and drink industry.

The new School of Geography took its first intake of undergraduates this academic year. It is described by the Royal Geographical Society as "one of the most significant investments in UK university geography for a generation", and its teaching will be informed by a newly-created research centre focused on climate change, flooding and water-borne diseases.

Lincoln is investing more than £100m to upgrade its facilities and cope with additional students. Having opened the first purpose-built engineering school for 25 years, the university has added a new building to pair its strengths in engineering and computer science with the development of the new School of Mathematics and Physics.

The building triples the size of the Engineering Hub, a prize-winning collaboration with Siemens, adding a 500-seat lecture theatre. Another new building will house the schools of psychology and health and social care, providing additional teaching space, including well-equipped simulation suites for student nurses.

The TEF panel was impressed by "outstanding physical and digital resources which pervade all aspects of student experience, including state-of-the-art teaching spaces and extensive library usage with investment into the use of e-resources".

Brayford Pool
Lincoln LN6 7TS
01522 886 644
enquiries@lincoln.ac.uk
www.lincoln.ac.uk
http://lincolnsu.com
Open Days 2018:
check website

The Times and The Sunday Times Rankings

Overall Ranking: **54** (last year: 51)

Teaching quality	82.1%	=32
Student experience	81.7%	=20
Research quality	10.3%	59
Entry standards	130	=66
Graduate prospects	76.2%	55
Good honours	68.2%	=90
Expected completion rate	89.1%	43
Student/staff ratio	15.6	=55
Services and facilities/student	£1,921	84

The latest development will also house the university's Professional Development Centre, which provides training courses for medical professionals across the region, and the cross-disciplinary research centre, the Lincoln Institute for Health.

In the 2014 Research Excellence Framework, Lincoln was in the top ten in the health category. Research in agriculture, veterinary and food sciences came second in the UK and across all subjects, more than half of a large submission was considered internationally excellent or world-leading.

The university has an attractive, purpose-built campus next to a marina in the centre of Lincoln, having moved from Hull in 2001. As the University of Lincolnshire and Humberside it finished rock bottom of our 1999 league table. How times have changed.

Today there are more than 13,000 students, 18% from an area of low participation in higher education, which is significantly more than its courses and student profile would suggest. A one-stop shop provides them with careers advice, enhances their CVs, helps to gain work experience and find jobs, as well as supporting recent graduates. The university has expanded its graduate internship scheme and runs a popular summer placement programme.

Lincoln has won national recognition for its collaboration with business and industry, most notably with Siemens, which named the university as one of its global principal partners, together with Cambridge, Manchester and Newcastle. Several degrees can be taken as work-based programmes, with credit awarded for relevant aspects of the jobs. Lincoln was the first university to win a Charter Mark for exceptional student service.

The city is adapting to its student population with new bars and clubs. The campus has a £6m performing arts centre, which contains a 450-seat theatre and three large studio spaces, and there is a popular venue in a former railway engine shed.

The university either owns, manages or endorses nearly 6,000 residential places centred on the student village.

Tuition fees

» Fees for UK/EU students 2018–19 £9,250
» Fees for international students 2018–19 £13,800–£15,600
» For scholarship and bursary information see www.lincoln.ac.uk/home/studyatlincoln/undergraduatecourses/scholarships
» Graduate salary £18,500

Students

Undergraduates	10,000	(1,425)
Postgraduates	860	(1,195)
Applications per place	4.7	
Overall offer rate	90.7%	
International students	7.7%	
Mature students	10.7%	
From state-sector schools	97.2%	
From working-class homes	37.1%	

Accommodation

University-provided places: 5,686+
Percentage catered: 0%
Self-catered: £65 – £189 per week
First year students are guaranteed accommodation
www.lincoln.ac.uk/home/accommodation/

University of Liverpool

The University of Liverpool found itself the lowest ranked higher education institution in its home city – and among the bottom 20 in this guide – when the new ratings for teaching quality were published last June. The Teaching Excellence Framework (TEF) awarded Liverpool bronze based on how students rate their teaching, graduate prospects and the university's degree completion rate.

Although Liverpool is consistently near the bottom of the Russell Group of elite research-led institutions in our table, finding itself one of just three in that group awarded bronze (along with Southampton and the London School of Economics) came as a shock.

The university has dropped three places in the new edition of the *Guide*, after a big fall in staffing levels and a drop in spending on student services and facilities. Like eight other universities, most of them in the Russell Group, there was no opportunity to improve on relatively low scores for student satisfaction because a boycott of the National Student Survey took the response rate below the 50 per cent threshold for the publication of a university's results.

Whether the TEF results have an impact on future applications remains to be seen. Applications have risen to top 40,000 in 2015 and 2016 and Liverpool has added 1,000

places to the undergraduate intake.

The university is investing £600m in its city centre campus to make room for the extra students and upgrade its facilities. A ten-year development plan has already provided new and improved teaching and research space, as well as new leisure facilities and more student accommodation.

The university is also spending £70m on interdisciplinary research facilities for health and life sciences that will bring together more than 600 scientists to focus on the biggest health challenges of the 21st century. The management school has been extended, while the new Materials Innovation Factory is intended to make Liverpool a world leader in computer-aided material science by 2020.

Most students can spend a year studying in China, where Liverpool has a campus in the historic city of Suzhou, run in partnership with Xi'an Jiaotong University. There is also a collaboration with the Singapore Institute of Technology offering a criminology degree, as well as a postgraduate site in the City of London for professional courses. Other partnerships involve universities in Chile, Mexico and Spain that will allow students to complete part of their degree at one or more of these institutions.

The university is also expanding online, where it is already the largest provider of online postgraduate courses in Europe.

At 26%, the proportion of undergraduates from working-class homes is among the highest

---

Liverpool
L69 3BX
0151 794 5927
ugrecruitment@liv.ac.uk
www.liverpool.ac.uk
www.liverpoolguild.org
Open Days 2018:
June 22, 23

Belfast, Edinburgh, LIVERPOOL, London, Cardiff

The Times and The Sunday Times **Rankings**

Overall Ranking: **42** (last year: 39)

Teaching quality	n/a	
Student experience	n/a	
Research quality	31.5%	41
Entry standards	152	=39
Graduate prospects	78.5%	46
Good honours	76.7%	=43
Expected completion rate	90.6%	=35
Student/staff ratio	13.5	=25
Services and facilities/student	£2,210	48

in the Russell Group, although still slightly less than the national average for the courses and entry qualifications.

The university has committed nearly 30% of its additional fee income to support for students from lower-income backgrounds and enhanced measures to prevent students from dropping out. More than a quarter of new undergraduates qualify for support. The projected dropout rate has been improving and is now 6.5%, slightly below the expected level.

For a Russell Group university, Liverpool entered a relatively low proportion of its eligible academics in the 2014 Research Excellence Framework, which held it back in our research ranking even though 70% of the work was judged to be world-leading or internationally excellent. Chemistry produced spectacular results, with more than half of its research considered world-leading and 99% in the top two categories. Computer science and general engineering also scored particularly well.

By far the biggest spending programme, totalling £250m, has been devoted to student accommodation. More than 2,000 study bedrooms were added on the campus in two years and off-campus accommodation is being refurbished. New residences will also be built at the Greenbank site, at suburban Mossley Hill, to provide a self-contained student village.

The Guild of Students is the centre of campus social activity and the city is famously lively.

The university is heavily involved in Liverpool 2018, a ten-year anniversary of the city becoming European Capital of Culture. Part of its contribution is a celebration of ten years since the Victoria Gallery and Museum was opened to the public following restoration of the iconic Victoria Building. This was the university's 'gift' to the city of Liverpool during its year as European Capital of Culture, providing a new home for its art and heritage collections.

The indoor and outdoor sports facilities have been refurbished and a new gym has opened at the Greenbank site. A 25-metre swimming pool is open to the public as well as students.

The university has one of the largest careers resources centres in the UK and has introduced an innovative programme of "boot camps" giving new graduates opportunities for networking with employers while developing employability skills. More than £2m is being invested in student and graduate internships, most of them paid and lasting for substantial periods.

Tuition fees

» Fees for UK/EU students 2018–19   £9,750
   Foundation courses   £5,140–£7,500
» Fees for international students 2018–19   £15,750–£19,700
   Dentistry, Medicine, Veterinary   £33,600
» For scholarship and bursary information see www.liverpool.ac.uk/study/undergraduate/finance
» Graduate salary   £22,000

Students

Undergraduates	18,980	(615)
Postgraduates	3,255	(1,925)
Applications per place	7.8	
Overall offer rate	86.5%	
International students	26.7%	
Mature students	9.1%	
From state-sector schools	88.8%	
From working-class homes	25.9%	

Accommodation

University-provided places: 4,647
Percentage catered: 30%
Catered costs: £145 – £213 per week
Self-catered: £129 – £197 per week
First year students are guaranteed accommodation
www.liverpool.ac.uk/accommodation/

Liverpool Hope University

Hope boycotted league tables for several years but now admits its success in them may be one of the factors behind a rise in applications in 2017, when most universities have suffered a decline.

Although it has slipped a little in the new edition, only one university made more progress up the league table in 2017. Hope's rise of 30 places took it into the top three post-1992 universities, fuelled by outstanding levels of student satisfaction which have been maintained.

A gold award in the new Teaching Excellence Framework will be another attraction. The independent panel complimented the university on "outstanding levels of stretch provided through judicious partnerships, good curriculum design and extracurricular activities".

Undergraduates at Liverpool Hope are guaranteed small-group tutorials with a named tutor each week, and that all the teaching they receive should be informed by research. They are encouraged to register for the Service and Leadership Award, which runs alongside their degree work. Students can volunteer locally, within the region or internationally as part of Global Hope, the university's award-winning overseas charity.

New degrees in education and early childhood have been introduced and graphic design, popular music and robotics will be added for 2018. The university has moved away from modular degrees to an integrated curriculum, with a "disciplinary core" in each subject to ensure that all students have a similar experience and get a more rounded view of their subject. Most opt for combined subject degrees, choosing after the first year whether to give them equal weight or a major/minor dynamic.

Hope was formed from the merger of two Catholic and one Church of England teacher training colleges in 1980, and now sponsors an academy with the same dual-faith character. A university since 2005, it describes itself as "teaching-led, research-informed and mission-focused". The university's top priorities are student satisfaction and employability, although it includes "taking faith seriously" among its five key values.

More than half of the eligible staff were entered for the 2014 Research Excellence Framework – far more than at most post-1992 universities – and there were good results in education and theology. There are research-led seminars in the final year of degree courses to introduce undergraduates to a research culture, and all students produce a dissertation or advanced research project.

The university has increased its national recruitment profile, with nearly 60% of students now coming from beyond Merseyside.

Hope Park
Liverpool L16 9JD
0151 291 3111
enquiry@hope.ac.uk
www.hope.ac.uk
www.hopesu.com
Open Days 2018:
June 27, July 7,
September 29

The Times and The Sunday Times Rankings
Overall Ranking: **52** (last year: 49)

Teaching quality	86.9%	3
Student experience	85.8%	5
Research quality	9.2%	=63
Entry standards	117	=102
Graduate prospects	80.5%	29
Good honours	63.8%	=112
Expected completion rate	78.7%	112
Student/staff ratio	15.5	=53
Services and facilities/student	£2,080	69

However, there is still a strong commitment to the region. A new university centre has been launched in Blackburn, for example, mainly offering degrees in business and education in partnership, on the site of St Mary's College.

The Network of Hope brings university courses to sixth-form colleges in parts of the region where there is limited higher education. Hope comfortably exceeds all the official benchmarks for widening participation in higher education. More than one in five students comes from an area with little tradition of higher education – one of the highest proportions in England.

The university is concentrated on two sites in Liverpool, and there is a residential outdoor education centre in Snowdonia, North Wales. The main campus, Hope Park, is three miles from the city centre in the suburb of Childwall, while the creative and performing arts are based at the more central Creative Campus in Everton, where a performance centre houses one of only three Steinway Schools in England.

Hope has spent more than £60m in the past eight years on campus improvements. The most recent development is the £8.5m Health Sciences building, housing specialist laboratories for nutrition, genomics, cell biology and psychology, along with facilities for sport and exercise science, including a 25-metre biomechanics sprint track.

A redesigned, refurbished and extended sports hall can accommodate six courts and has a viewing gallery, squash courts, gym and fitness rooms, strength and conditioning suites and a new cafe. Work is in progress on the outdoor facilities, including a new jogging trail, 3G football pitch and tennis courts.

The 1,150 residential places are enough to guarantee accommodation for new entrants who apply before clearing. Liverpool is a popular student city and the university has partnerships with the Royal Liverpool Philharmonic Orchestra, Liverpool Tate, the National Museums Liverpool and Liverpool Sound City to develop cultural programmes.

Tuition fees
- » Fees for UK/EU students 2018–19 £9,250
- » Fees for international students 2018–19 £11,400
- » For scholarship and bursary information see www.hope.ac.uk/undergraduate/feesandfunding
- » Graduate salary £18,000

Students

Undergraduates	3,785	(150)
Postgraduates	655	(350)
Applications per place	7.1	
Overall offer rate	89.2%	
International students	1.9%	
Mature students	18.5%	
From state-sector schools	99.4%	
From working-class homes	43.2%	

Accommodation

University-provided places: 1,128
Percentage catered: 0%
Self-catered: £87 – £123 per week
First-year students who apply before clearing are guaranteed accommodation
www.hope.ac.uk/halls

Liverpool John Moores University

The £100m development that will eventually see all Liverpool John Moores (LJMU) students taught in the city centre is due for completion this year. Copperas Hill, near Lime Street station, will play a key role in regenerating a rundown part of the city. It will feature an atrium, rooftop terrace and sports facilities, as well as teaching and learning spaces.

The IM Marsh campus, four miles from the city centre, will close when Copperas Hill is ready for occupation, concentrating the university's activities in a single area. The new development is close to the Sensor City facility for industrial research, development and commercialisation, a joint venture with the University of Liverpool, continuing the establishment of a Knowledge Quarter.

LJMU has spent £180m on improved facilities in little more than ten years. Developments include the award-winning John Lennon Art and Design Building and the £25.5m life sciences building, where the world-class facilities include an indoor 70-metre running track and labs for testing cardiovascular ability, motor skills and biomechanics functions. The Redmonds Building – named after the producer and creator of Brookside, Phil Redmond – houses Liverpool Screen School, with its industry-standard TV and radio studios, the Liverpool Business School and the School of Law.

LJMU has more than recovered a 12-place drop in last year's table and was named University of the Year in the Educate North awards earlier this year. The judges noted it was the first university to receive two commendations in a single audit by the Quality Assurance Agency and praised its award-winning Centre for Entrepreneurship and degree apprenticeships scheme.

The university already offers degree apprenticeships in 11 areas, from control and automation engineering to quantity surveying and facilities management, with more in the pipeline.

A decline in student satisfaction was behind LJMU's fall in our league table, but the university has been acting to improve the student experience. Responding to feedback from the students' union, it invested £1.5m last summer to create new social spaces for students to relax, socialise and engage in "casual study". There are indoor lawns and trees, as well as IT facilities and mobile charging docks.

The university was awarded silver in the new Teaching Excellence Framework (TEF). The independent panel complimented the university on "highly effective institutional strategic drive to improve satisfaction with assessment and feedback", strong recognition of teaching excellence and a consistent commitment to student engagement.

Exchange Station
Tithebarn Street
Liverpool L2 2QP
0151 231 5090
courses@ljmu.ac.uk
www.ljmu.ac.uk
www.liverpoolsu.com
Open Days 2018:
check website

The Times and The Sunday Times Rankings

Overall Ranking: **=70** (last year: =86)

Teaching quality	82.3%	31
Student experience	81.2%	=29
Research quality	8.9%	=68
Entry standards	138	=51
Graduate prospects	72.7%	68
Good honours	74.6%	=49
Expected completion rate	83.3%	=85
Student/staff ratio	17.5	=95
Services and facilities/student	£1,557	116

The panel was impressed by LJMU's World of Work (WoW) programme, perhaps its best-known feature. The university was a pioneer of the employment-focused curriculum that has since become common in higher education. The WoW initiative involves leading companies and business organisations, encouraging undergraduates to become expert in eight transferable skills, applicable to a wide range of careers. All students are offered extensive work-related learning opportunities, both paid and voluntary, some overseas.

A Teaching and Learning Academy, launched in 2015, offers assistance from the transition from school, through university and into the workplace, while the Centre for Entrepreneurship supports students and graduates who want to start up in business, become self-employed or work freelance.

Named after the football pools millionaire and founder of Littlewoods, John Moores, the university draws more than 40% of its students from the Merseyside area. Almost all the undergraduates are state-educated and 40% come from the four poorest socioeconomic groups. A wide range of scholarships and bursaries include the John Lennon Imagine Awards, match-funded through a gift of £260,000 from Yoko Ono, helping students who have been in care or who are estranged from their parents.

A growing research reputation is a source of particular pride. More than 60% of the work submitted for the Research Excellence Framework was rated world-leading or internationally excellent – rising to 80% in physics. The university was ranked second in the UK for sports science and fourth among post-1992 universities for law and education. The physics results covered astronomy, with researchers and students using LJMU's own robotic telescope in the Canary Islands.

Liverpool has been ranked in the ten best cities in the world to visit and is also one of the UK's most affordable for students. Leisure facilities have been improving and there are discounts on theatre tickets and free access to art exhibitions and orchestral performances.

Sports facilities include an Olympic-sized swimming pool, two golf courses, fitness suites, weights rooms and all-weather football pitches. Students also have free off-peak access to 14 Lifestyles Fitness Centres across the city.

Tuition fees

»	Fees for UK/EU students 2018–19	£9,250
	Foundation courses	£7,700
»	Fees for international students 2018–19	£13,250–£14,000
	Foundation courses	£10,050
»	For scholarship and bursary information see	
	www.ljmu.ac.uk/discover/fees-and-funding	
»	Graduate salary	£20,000

Students

Undergraduates	17,105	(1,275)
Postgraduates	1,575	(1,925)
Applications per place	6.4	
Overall offer rate	80.7%	
International students	4.7%	
Mature students	17.5%	
From state-sector schools	98%	
From working-class homes	39.6%	

Accommodation

University-provided places: 3,600
Percentage catered: 0%
Self-catered: £92 – £157 per week
First year students are guaranteed accommodation
www.ljmu.ac.uk/accommodation

London Metropolitan University

London Met's £125m plan to create a single campus in Islington is under way with new facilities for the Sir John Cass School of Art, Architecture and Design, and approval for a new teaching and learning centre at the heart of the university in Holloway. The centre is due to open in 2019 and the Cass will move to Holloway in the following year. The One Campus, One Community project involves the refurbishment of existing buildings and the construction of new ones, as well as investment in technology and resources, and the adoption of a new curriculum.

Professor John Raftery, the vice-chancellor, says the revamp, which will also reduce the staff by almost 400, will "effectively create a new higher education offering in London, with a structure fit to meet the needs of its time". London Met's programme for improved student outcomes guarantees an accredited, work-related learning opportunity for all students in preparation for the graduate jobs market. Another aim is to create a better sense of community in a university that has a particularly diverse student body.

If they are successful, the changes should help to lift London Met from the bottom two in our table, where it remains this year, and out of the bronze category in the government's new Teaching Excellence Framework (TEF). An unusually negative assessment by the TEF panel said students' achievement was "notably below benchmark across a range of indicators". It acknowledged a range of positive and appropriate strategic approaches to address student satisfaction, but was concerned that comparatively few students continue their studies after graduating.

There is improvement in our latest table in graduate prospects and student satisfaction with the quality of teaching, but London Met is still last for the proportion of students awarded good honours and in the bottom five on four other measures.

The Science Centre's Superlab, one of Europe's largest teaching laboratories, has been refreshed with new audiovisual systems and the refurbished Holloway Road library has more computers, informal learning spaces and a cafe. The improvements are taking place with an eye to the environment – the university has been again shortlisted for a Green Gown sustainability award, having cut carbon emissions by half.

London Met's undergraduate intake has halved since 2011, with 3,000 fewer entrants, and applications fell for the fifth year in a row in 2016. New degrees are being introduced to stimulate demand, including criminal law, design studio practice, theatre and film production design, biology of infectious

---

166–220 Holloway Road
London N7 8DB
020 7133 4200
admissions@londonmet.ac.uk
www.londonmet.ac.uk
www.londonmetsu.org.uk
Open Days 2018:
April 18, April 25, May 2
(subject specific,
check website)

The Times and The Sunday Times **Rankings**

Overall Ranking: **128** (last year: 127)

Teaching quality	78.5%	=88
Student experience	75%	110
Research quality	3.5%	111
Entry standards	105	126
Graduate prospects	65.1%	=106
Good honours	50.2%	129
Expected completion rate	72.7%	124
Student/staff ratio	18.1	=106
Services and facilities/student	£1,417	124

disease and sport psychology, coaching and physical education. However, the university entered far fewer academics for the 2014 Research Excellence Framework than it did in the 2008 assessments: only 15% of those eligible. As a result, it slipped down our research ranking, even though half of its submission was rated as world-leading or internationally excellent, and there were particularly good scores in English and health.

Although London Met was the product of the merger in 2002 of London Guildhall and North London universities, its origins date from the mid-19th century. It has strong business links, especially in London's "Tech City", where it has a business accelerator that has been ranked in the top five in Europe. It provides regular workshops, bootcamps and an incubator programme for students thinking of setting up businesses.

The university has always offered a place for groups who are under-represented in higher education. More than a third of the students are from ethnic minorities, and the proportion of mature students is among the highest in England. More than half of the UK undergraduates come from low-income families – far above the average for the courses and entry qualifications. Student support services have been remodelled and the Pass (Peer Assisted Student Support) scheme involves successful second and third-year students coaching first-years on their course.

Undergraduates take year-long modules consisting of 30 weeks of timetabled teaching. Over a year, students will typically study four modules and receive a minimum of 60 teaching hours per module. The university is in the top ten for the amount of supervised teaching time and expects first-year students to have 12 hours of teaching a week.

Languages are a strength: London Met is one of only 22 universities in the world to be a member of the UN Language Careers Network.

The university's residential accommodation is limited, but many of its students live at home. There are fitness centres on the main campuses, and outdoor sports facilities a short Tube ride away. The competitive teams are successful and the social scene lively.

Tuition fees
- » Fees for UK/EU students 2018–19 — £9,250
- » Fees for international students 2018–19 — £11,800
- » For scholarship and bursary information see www.londonmet.ac.uk/applying/funding-your-studies
- » Graduate salary — £20,000

Students

Undergraduates	8,590	(1,360)
Postgraduates	1,275	(1,640)
Applications per place	8.9	
Overall offer rate	87.7%	
International students	10.8%	
Mature students	59.7%	
From state-sector schools	98.2%	
From working-class homes	51.4%	

Accommodation

University-provided places: 0

Self-catered: £144 – £344 per week (through external providers)
www.londonmet.ac.uk/services-and-facilities/accommodation

London School of Economics and Political Science

The LSE was the highest-profile casualty of the government's new Teaching Excellence Framework (TEF) last summer, when it received a bronze rating and attracted a barrage of criticism in the media. Low levels of student satisfaction – flagged up in last year's edition of our guide – were the main reason for the poor rating, although completion rates and graduate employment were also taken into account.

The TEF verdict came days after another official report showed LSE graduates to be the highest-paid in the country after five years, with a quarter of economics graduates earning more than £120,000. The TEF panel acknowledged that the proportion in highly-skilled jobs six months after graduation was much higher than expected, but the LSE still lost marks for its record in other types of employment.

With more than ten applications for each place – the most at any UK university – and a reputation as a world leader in the social sciences, the school did not appeal against the rating. Professor Julia Black, its interim director, said the LSE recognised that it had work to do on teaching quality, but she regretted that its graduates' "exceptional" record in highly-skilled job markets had not been taken into account.

The school is devoting an additional £11m to teaching and learning over three years, including the creation of LSE Life (praised by the TEF panel), which offers students a single source of support for their academic, personal and professional development. Also in response to student feedback, changes to assessment have been agreed and in-year exam resits are being introduced, initially for first-year undergraduates.

The LSE is just outside our top ten despite finishing bottom in both measures of student satisfaction. It was in the top four last year for completion, entry standards and research. The school is ranked among the top 25 universities in the world by Times Higher Education magazine and second for the social sciences by QS.

It attracts the highest proportion of international students at any publicly funded university. More than 30 past or present heads of state have either been LSE students or academics, as have 16 winners of the Nobel prize in economics, literature and peace.

A 3% increase in applications this year has seen the LSE buck the national trend. A new BSc in financial mathematics and statistics accounts for much of the growth, while demand in other subjects remained steady. For 2018, psychological and behavioural science will be added to the portfolio of degrees, which is already much wider than the institution's name suggests.

Houghton street
London WC2A 2AE
020 7955 6613
stu.rec@lse.ac.uk
www.lse.ac.uk
www.lsesu.com
Open Days 2018:
April & July check
website for dates

The Times and The Sunday Times **Rankings**
Overall Ranking: **11** (last year: 8)

Teaching quality	67.5%	120
Student experience	65.7%	120
Research quality	52.8%	4
Entry standards	203	5
Graduate prospects	87.1%	4
Good honours	86.1%	10
Expected completion rate	95.4%	8
Student/staff ratio	11.4	6
Services and facilities/student	£2,990	9

Dame Nemat "Minouche" Shafik, former permanent secretary at the Department for International Development, became the LSE's first female director last year. She will oversee the completion of a £120m building development to address a chronic need for more space around London's Aldwych.

The LSE had more world-leading research than any university in the 2014 Research Excellence Framework. It was the clear leader in the social sciences, with particularly good results in social work and social policy, and communication and media studies. A £10m donation from alumnus Firoz Lalji has since created an academic centre focused on Africa.

The school has a long history of political involvement, from its foundation by Beatrice and Sidney Webb, pioneers of the Fabian movement. Its international character not only gives the LSE global prestige, but also an unusual degree of financial independence: only a small proportion of its funding comes from government sources.

Almost 30% of the British undergraduates are from independent schools, one of the highest proportions in England. Substantial efforts are being made to attract a broader intake: the school is spending 60% of its additional fee income on student support and other activities to widen participation, the biggest proportion at any university.

The Norman Foster-designed redevelopment of the Lionel Robbins building houses a much-improved library: the number of books borrowed by LSE students is more than four times the national average, according to one survey.

Routes between many of the buildings have been pedestrianised, in keeping with a commitment to green issues that regularly sees the school near the top of the People & Planet league of universities' environmental performance.

London's nightspots are on the doorstep for those who can afford them and discounted student nights are easy to find. There are also more than 200 student societies. The large number of residential places for 4,600 full-time undergraduates offers a good chance of avoiding central London's high private-sector rents and there are spaces in halls for all first-years who want them.

Tuition fees

- » Fees for UK/EU students 2018–19   £9,250
- » Fees for international students 2018–19   £19,152
- » For scholarship and bursary information see www.lse.ac.uk/study-at-lse/undergraduate/fees-and-funding
- » Graduate salary   £28,500

Students		
Undergraduates	4,610	(90)
Postgraduates	5,375	(365)
Applications per place	10.9	
Overall offer rate	37.1%	
International students	48.6%	
Mature students	2.5%	
From state-sector schools	71.6%	
From working-class homes	21.1%	

Accommodation

University-provided places: 4,624
Percentage catered: 33%
Catered costs: £101 – £234 per week
Self-catered: £139 – £367
First year students are guaranteed accommodation
www.lse.ac.uk/accommodation

London South Bank University

London South Bank (LSBU) is our University of the Year for Graduate Employment, yet again challenging the most prestigious institutions both on the salaries and types of jobs secured by its graduates. It is in the top 20 for overall graduate prospects, with average salaries for those going into highly-skilled employment thousands of pounds above the national average.

For a university outside the top 100 in our table, it is a particularly impressive feat. Almost 7,000 students are sponsored by employers. The university has 1,000 employer partners and this month set up a new employment agency to help students find part-time work while they study.

LSBU's achievements stretch beyond graduate employment, however. It is one of the biggest risers in our table, moving up 14 places, with improvements in seven of the eight perforrmance indicators in our table for which there is new data.

The university received a silver rating in the government's Teaching Excellence Framework. The expert panel was impressed by the "appropriate" contact hours and consistently high levels of personalised learning for a diverse student population, provided by specialist staff and interactive learning. This produces high levels of engagement and commitment to learning and study from students, the panel said.

LSBU has adopted three core principles – student success, real world impact and access to opportunity – and was one of the first universities to embrace degree apprenticeships, where students divide their time between workplace training and higher education. Three-quarters of its students are from the capital and 40% are drawn from ethnic minorities. Many of the 13,000 undergraduates take sandwich courses but the vice-chancellor, Professor David Phoenix, would like even more to spend part of their time in industry.

The main campus is in Southwark, not far from the Southbank arts complex – although LSBU degrees are taught at a network of overseas colleges, from China to the Caribbean. At its London base, LSBU has invested more than £50m in modern teaching facilities, and developments worth £38m are in the pipeline. The Centre for Efficient and Renewable Energy in Buildings, on the main campus, is a teaching, research and demonstration resource for low-carbon technologies.

The £4m Elephant Studios @LSBU opened in 2016, with advanced technology facilities and an industry-standard theatre and rehearsal suite. Improvements to the Perry library, on the Southwark campus, and

103 Borough Road
London SE1 0AA
0800 923 8888
Course.enquiry@lsbu.ac.uk
www.lsbu.ac.uk
www.lsbu.org
Open Days 2018:
March 24, June 23

The Times and The Sunday Times Rankings

Overall Ranking: **=106** (last year: 120)

Teaching quality	79%	81
Student experience	77.5%	=80
Research quality	9%	=65
Entry standards	107	=124
Graduate prospects	82.1%	=20
Good honours	63.9%	111
Expected completion rate	74.6%	123
Student/staff ratio	17	88
Services and facilities/student	£2,248	45

the opening of a digital architecture robotics laboratory followed.

Some health students are based outside central London, at hospitals in Romford and Leytonstone, while there is a smaller satellite campus in Havering. The university is one of the main locations for training the capital's nurses and has well-regarded courses in occupational therapy and radiography.

LSBU is one of the top UK universities for knowledge transfer partnerships and was shortlisted for the Duke of York award for university entrepreneurship in the 2016 Lloyds Bank national business awards. The university entered more academics for the 2014 Research Excellence Framework than for previous assessments and scored well on the external impact of its research, with almost three-quarters of the submission placed in the top two categories on this measure.

LSBU has always given a high priority to widening participation in higher education and takes more than half of its students from the lowest socioeconomic groups – far more than other universities with similar courses and entry qualifications. The diversity of the intake is encouraged by initiatives such as after-school and Saturday clubs, and a summer festival for local people to upgrade their qualifications. However, the projected dropout rate for undergraduates is among the highest in the country and the university has struggled in the National Student Survey.

LSBU is targeting much of its fee income on providing support to help more students complete their studies in the expected time.

The student centre has brought the students' union and many support services together to make them more convenient and accessible. LSBU was the first university to receive four accreditations from the Institute of Customer Service for excellence at its accommodation service, library and learning resources, student life centre and academy of sport.

LSBU is one of the few universities in central London to have its halls of residence close by: all are less than ten minutes' walk away. A new-look sports centre opened in 2014 after a £1m makeover, with a multipurpose sports hall, therapy services and facilities that include a 40-station fitness suite and sports injury clinic. Southwark council contributed £300,000 to improve the facilities and guarantee public access. The university provides a comprehensive sports scholarship scheme.

Tuition fees

» Fees for UK/EU students 2018–19 £9,250
» Fees for international students 2017–18 £12,500–£15,100
» For scholarship and bursary information see www.lsbu.ac.uk/courses/undergraduates/fees-and-funding/scholarships
» Graduate salary £24,000

Students

Undergraduates	8,540	(4,085)
Postgraduates	1,830	(3,155)
Applications per place	10.1	
Overall offer rate	74.7%	
International students	7.7%	
Mature students	51%	
From state-sector schools	97.9%	
From working-class homes	50.7%	

Accommodation

University-provided places: 1,400
Percentage catered: 0%
Self-catered: £122 – £189 per week
First year students are guaranteed accommodation
www.lsbu.ac.uk/student-life/accommodation

Loughborough University

Loughborough has reached the top ten in our league table, continuing its remarkable progress. Only four years ago, it was outside the top 20, but some of the best student satisfaction scores in the country and the university's perennial strength in graduate prospects produced another rise in 2017, earning it runner-up spot in our University of the Year competition.

These qualities have also been reflected in Loughborough's growing popularity, particularly among school-leavers, whose applications are up by almost half since 2011. There was another 5% increase in 2017, against the national trend. New degrees in architecture and bioengineering account for part of this, but the university says there is a general rise in demand.

A gold rating in the government's new Teaching Excellence Framework (TEF) should add to Loughborough's reputation. The TEF panel found that students from all backgrounds achieve consistently outstanding outcomes, thanks to a culture of personalised learning and a comprehensive pastoral and academic tutorial programme.

Loughborough is best known for its illustrious sporting pedigree – Adam Peaty, a double gold medallist at last year's world swimming championships in Budapest, trains here – but it now has a strong academic reputation as well.

Only eight universities entered such a high proportion of their eligible staff – 88% – for the 2014 Research Excellence Framework. Almost three-quarters of their research was judged to be world-leading or internationally excellent, with sport and exercise sciences producing the best results in the UK and six other subject areas featuring in the top ten. Loughborough has since been chosen as a partner in three £10m research hubs designed to strengthen the UK's manufacturing base.

The university was only a fraction of a point off top place in the sections of this year's National Student Survey relating to the student experience and was in the top ten for teaching quality. Most subjects are available either as three-year full-time or longer sandwich degrees, which include a year in industry, and Loughborough is a leader in the use of computer-assisted assessment, offering students the chance to gauge their progress online.

However, despite high spending on student support and outreach activities, Loughborough misses all its access benchmarks: fewer than a quarter of the undergraduates were from working-class homes when this was last surveyed and only one in 15 from areas of low participation in higher education.

The university's campus has seen a series of developments in recent years. The West

---

Epinal Way
Loughborough LE11 3TU
01509 223 522
admissions@lboro.ac.uk
www.lboro.ac.uk
www.lsu.co.uk
Open days 2018:
June 29, 30
September 21, 22

The Times and The Sunday Times Rankings

Overall Ranking: =7 (last year: 11)

Teaching quality	84.4%	9
Student experience	86.9%	2
Research quality	36.3%	=30
Entry standards	157	=33
Graduate prospects	82.3%	19
Good honours	80.7%	28
Expected completion rate	93.4%	19
Student/staff ratio	14.2	=31
Services and facilities/student	£2,864	11

Park teaching hub opened in 2016, with five lecture theatres, two seminar rooms and a central learning and exhibition zone. Work has been completed on STEMLab, which houses science and engineering laboratories, workshops, computer-aided design and prototyping facilities and a design studio. This will enable Loughborough to launch degrees in biochemistry, bioengineering, biological sciences and natural sciences in 2018.

The university is strong in art and design and remains a key centre for engineering, with more than 2,800 students in a £20m integrated engineering complex. The Science and Enterprise Park, which is home to almost 70 companies, has the BAE-sponsored Systems Engineering Innovation Centre as its centrepiece. The university has a London campus for postgraduates, in the Queen Elizabeth Olympic Park, which focuses on research and innovation.

Student sports facilities at Loughborough are the best this side of the Atlantic and include a £5.6m health and fitness centre and a sports hall providing space for badminton, basketball, netball and volleyball. The university hosts a National Centre for Sport and Exercise Medicine, one of three in the UK.

There is a 50-metre swimming pool on campus, national academies for cricket and tennis, a gymnastics centre and a high-performance training centre for athletics. The university also hosts the UK's only centre for disability sport and carries out research at its Sports Technology Institute. The programme of sports scholarships is the largest at any UK university.

Loughborough has almost 6,000 residential places and has announced plans for another 600 in a £70m development that is due to open in 2019. It will include sport-specific accommodation for athletes to cement its status as one of the country's best training environments for elite athletes.

Social activity is concentrated on a prize-winning students' union which is among the most popular in the country with its members. The university is close to the centre of Loughborough and both Leicester and Nottingham are within easy reach.

Tuition fees

- » Fees for UK/EU students 2018–19 £9,250
- » Fees for international students 2018–19 £16,400–£20,500
- » For scholarship and bursary information see www.lboro.ac.uk/study/undergraduate/fees-finance
- » Graduate salary £25,000

Students

Undergraduates	12,525	(195)
Postgraduates	2,690	(1,535)
Applications per place	7.8	
Overall offer rate	79.3%	
International students	10%	
Mature students	3.2%	
From state-sector schools	82.1%	
From working-class homes	21.9%	

Accommodation

University-provided places: 5,812
Percentage catered: 41%
Catered costs: £152 – £189 per week
Self-catered: £86 – £162 per week
First year students are guaranteed accommodation
www.lboro.ac.uk/accommodation

University of Manchester

Everything at Manchester is on a big scale. The university has the most applications, more than 1,000 degree programmes, the largest student population (almost 40,000) and now claims to be making the biggest investment in facilities undertaken by any UK university.

Already, £750m has been spent on improvements to the main campus and other facilities, and a further £1bn is planned by 2022. The current phase of the masterplan includes the £350m Manchester Engineering Campus Development (MECD), new facilities for the Alliance Manchester Business School and a student village that will eventually have 3,000 rooms.

The eventual aim is to create a single "world-class" campus that the university hopes will help it to secure a place among the top 25 research universities in the world. It has only nine places to go in the QS World University Rankings, although a little further by other international measures.

In our league table, with its focus on undergraduate study, Manchester remains outside the top 20 despite a rise of seven places this year. Student satisfaction has been its Achilles heel. The undergraduates, in common with those at some other Russell Group universities, boycotted the National Student Survey in sufficient numbers to prevent ratings being published last year but the 2016 results left Manchester outside the top 100 for perceptions of teaching quality.

Those results were a factor in the university being limited to silver in the new Teaching Excellence Framework. Nevertheless, it is in our top 20 for graduate prospects, entry standards, research and its high degree completion rate. The TEF panel acknowledged the investment taking place and was impressed by the way that students were stretched, enabling them to progress and develop transferable and professional skills.

More than 80% of the work submitted to the 2014 Research Excellence Framework was considered world-leading or internationally excellent, although the university entered a lower proportion of its academics than many of its Russell Group peers.

The first projects in the campus masterplan, which opened in 2015, were the Manchester Cancer Research Centre and the National Graphene Institute. The latter continues the work of Professors Andre Geim and Kostya Novoselov, who won the Nobel prize for physics in 2010, taking Manchester's all-time complement of laureates to 25.

The Whitworth art gallery was refurbished and has won several awards. It was named the Art Fund's museum of the year in 2015. The remodelling and refurbishment of the university's business school is due to be completed this year, adding a new library and

Oxford Road
Manchester M13 9PL
0161 275 2077
study@manchester.ac.uk
www.manchester.ac.uk
http://manchesterstudentsuniuon.com
Open Days 2018:
June 22, 23 September 29

The Times and The Sunday Times **Rankings**

Overall Ranking: **25** (last year: 32)

Teaching quality	n/a	
Student experience	n/a	
Research quality	39.8%	13
Entry standards	170	17
Graduate prospects	82.5%	18
Good honours	78.4%	35
Expected completion rate	93.1%	20
Student/staff ratio	13.3	=22
Services and facilities/student	£2,700	21

spaces for teaching and research. There will also be a 19-storey hotel development and an executive education centre. The MECD, which will house four engineering schools and two research institutes, is due to open in 2020 on the Oxford Road campus.

Other developments include the Graphene Engineering Innovation Centre and the Sir Henry Royce Institute for Advanced Materials Research, a £235m project that features prominently in the government's Northern Powerhouse initiative. Manchester was awarded a Regius Professorship of materials to mark the Queen's 90th birthday.

Outstanding teaching is one of the key goals in the university's strategy. The £24m Alan Gilbert Learning Commons provides more than 1,000 flexible learning spaces, high-quality IT facilities and a hub for student-centred activities and learning support services. The Learning Through Research programme funds undergraduates to work with researchers.

Manchester has been trying to broaden its intake, with a particular focus on increasing recruitment from the city and its surrounding area. The university admits more low-income students than most others in the Russell Group and is close to the national benchmarks for widening participation.

The university has also been developing its offer beyond the curriculum. One project saw 8,000 students take part in a sustainability challenge, designing a fictional university as part of the Ethical Grand Challenges programme. The Stellify initiative encourages students to take up a range of activities to broaden their horizons.

Employers in *The Times'* top 100 companies named Manchester among their top two recruiting grounds for 2016–17 – an important accolade when some firms limit their recruiting visits – and they also rate the careers service highly.

Manchester's famed youth culture, plentiful accommodation and the university's position at the heart of a huge student population remain great attractions for applicants. There are first-rate sports facilities and the university's teams frequently rank near the top of the British Universities and Colleges Sport leagues.

Tuition fees

- » Fees for UK/EU students 2018–19 £9,250
- » Fees for international students 2018–19 £18,000–£22,000
  Dentistry, Medicine £40,000
- » For scholarship and bursary information see www.manchester.ac.uk/study/undergraduate/student-finance
- » Graduate salary £21,900

Students

Undergraduates	27,195	(440)
Postgraduates	8,815	(3,250)
Applications per place	8.3	
Overall offer rate	72.4%	
International students	25.2%	
Mature students	9.4%	
From state-sector schools	82.2%	
From working-class homes	21.5%	

Accommodation

University-provided places: 8,091
Percentage catered: 28%
Catered costs: £130 – £141 per week
Self-catered: £95 – £142 per week
First year students are guaranteed accommodation
www.accommodation.manchester.ac.uk

Manchester Metropolitan University

Manchester Metropolitan (MMU) claims to be the leading provider of the UK's degree apprenticeships, promising yet more growth at the country's second biggest university. Applications to traditional degrees were down slightly in 2016, but only the neighbouring University of Manchester has more than its 38,000 students.

There are degree apprenticeships for solicitors, digital marketers and chartered managers, as well as for those studying chemical science and digital and technology solutions. Students are based in the workplace, paid throughout the programme and not charged tuition fees. Professor Malcolm Press, the vice-chancellor, has said MMU is poised to meet the exponential growth in demand for degree apprenticeships that he expects to see in the near future.

In the meantime, the university has continued its yo-yo pattern of recent years in our league table. An eight-place drop in the latest edition has brought at least a temporary end to three years of progress, in which it gained 30 places. A decline in student satisfaction is largely responsible.

The university was given a silver rating in the government's new Teaching Excellence Framework (TEF) this year. The TEF panel praised the inclusive curriculum for providing high levels of support for a diverse student population, the use of learning analytics and high levels of engagement with employers.

Entry standards are higher than at most post-1992 universities. More than 1,000 courses are offered in more than 70 subjects, more of them professionally accredited than at any other university and many involving work placements.

Less than a quarter of its academics were entered for the 2014 Research Excellence Framework but almost two-thirds of the work submitted was rated world-leading or internationally excellent. Health, art and design, and English produced the best results. The poet laureate, Professor Carol Ann Duffy, is creative director of the English department's writing school.

Fashion and media are two of the areas earmarked for expansion at MMU. The Manchester Fashion Institute is a multidisciplinary partnership that is intended to be an international hub connecting education, research and enterprise, while the university also has the lead role in the new International Screen School Manchester, whose industry advisory board will be co-chaired by the film director Danny Boyle. The school will provide a range of courses for more than 1,000 students a year.

MMU is also planning a new independent, international medical school in partnership

---

All Saints Building
All Saints
Manchester M15 6BH
0161 247 6969
manmetuni@mmu.ac.uk
www.mmu.ac.uk
www.theunionmmu.org
Open Days 2018:
check website

***The Times and The Sunday Times* Rankings**

Overall Ranking: **80** (last year: =72)

Teaching quality	79.2%	=79
Student experience	78.3%	=73
Research quality	7.5%	76
Entry standards	134	=58
Graduate prospects	69.5%	=84
Good honours	68.9%	=87
Expected completion rate	83.9%	=79
Student/staff ratio	15.6	=55
Services and facilities/student	£2,084	68

with the University of Manchester and the University of Salford.

The university has embarked on a £200m development plan for its campuses. It has been given planning permission for a new arts and media building for acting and drama, creative writing, journalism and the university language centre, and has announced plans for a £4m technology hub for Manchester companies working on carbon-neutral hydrogen fuel cells. The university consistently finishes in the top three of the People & Planet league measuring environmental performance.

The Birley Fields campus and the original All Saints campus are close to each other in the city. A £75m business school and science and engineering buildings have been added at All Saints in recent years. The Brooks Building, at Birley Fields, which hosts the education and health faculties, won an award for regeneration, while the new Manchester School of Art and the students' union building were recognised by the Royal Institute of British Architects.

The Cheshire campus at Crewe, 35 miles south of Manchester, currently serves 800 trainee teachers and 3,000 other students taking contemporary arts, including drama, music and dance, and sports science. But the university said last year that it planned to withdraw from that campus in 2019 because student numbers there had fallen by 45%

over five years. The university trains more teachers than any other and its courses are rated outstanding by Ofsted.

MMU has a longstanding commitment to extending access to higher education. Its First Generation scheme targets young people who would be the first in their family to go to university, providing financial, professional and personal support throughout their studies and into their careers.

Almost two-thirds of MMU graduates stay and work in the northwest. The Talent Match service, backed by the Greater Manchester Chamber of Commerce, helps to match skilled graduates to the needs of local employers.

All first-years who request accommodation can be housed, with priority going to disabled students and those who live furthest from Manchester. The university's sports facilities are good and the city's attractions do no harm to recruitment levels.

Tuition fees

» Fees for UK/EU students 2018–19 £9,250
» Fees for international students 2018–19 £13,500–£16,500
» For scholarship and bursary information see www.mmu.ac.uk/study/undergraduate/money-matters
» Graduate salary £18,500

Students

Undergraduates	25,110	(1,725)
Postgraduates	2,435	(3,215)
Applications per place	7.3	
Overall offer rate	80.6%	
International students	5.9%	
Mature students	15.1%	
From state-sector schools	96.8%	
From working-class homes	41.5%	

Accommodation

University-provided places: 5,135
Percentage catered: 0%
Self-catered: £106 – £205 per week
First year students are guaranteed accommodation
www.mmu.ac.uk/accommodation

Middlesex University

Middlesex has suffered one of the biggest falls in our table – 17 places – wiping out the gains it made in the previous edition. An unusually poor year for graduate prospects, which left the university in the bottom five on this measure, was largely responsible. There was a dip, too, in student satisfaction, although Middlesex is close to the top five for the amount it spends on student services and facilities.

The university had better news from the government's Teaching Excellence Framework (TEF), which uses older data than this guide. Middlesex was placed in the silver category and drew praise for its students' progress to highly-skilled employment. The TEF panel commented favourably on the tailored employability support system for the diverse student body as well as the embedding of employability within and alongside programmes of study.

The number of students starting degrees at Middlesex has shot up by nearly 1,000 – an increase of almost 39% – in the past two years. Demand should be stimulated further by the launch of a raft of foundation-year courses to bring students up to the standard required to enter degree courses, as well as a number of degrees in biochemistry.

A growing population on its north London campus is outnumbered by those taking Middlesex courses outside the UK. There are branch campuses in Mauritius, Dubai and Malta, and partner colleges on five continents. Middlesex was the first overseas university in Malta and opened a new campus in Mauritius last year, while the Dubai site has 2,500 students.

The new Mauritius campus, developed in partnership with a private firm, will accommodate up to 2,000 students and includes a sports complex with a 50m Olympic-sized swimming pool, football and rugby pitches, and a gym and fitness centre.

Altogether, 38,000 students are taking Middlesex courses or engaging in research, including more than 1,300 undergraduates in London from other EU countries, the product of a longstanding focus on Europe.

A new university strategy for the next five years brands Middlesex as a 'University for Skills', promising distinctive practice-based learning and embracing the value and power of diversity. It claims a reputation for the university as one that combines academic rigour with meeting practical needs. One example is the UK's first Cyber Factory training facility, which trains students to design, develop and maintain the smart factories and smart cities of the future. Installed by Festo, a leading international supplier of automation technology, the factory teaches disciplines that do not yet exist in the workplace, but will be sought after in the near future.

The university has invested more than £200m

The Burroughs
Hendon
London NW4 4BT
020 8411 5555
enquiries@mdx.ac.uk
www.mdx.ac.uk
www.mdxsu.com
Open Days 2018:
check website

The Times and The Sunday Times **Rankings**
Overall Ranking: **91** (last year: 74)

Teaching quality	78.1%	=96
Student experience	77.2%	=83
Research quality	9.7%	61
Entry standards	117	=102
Graduate prospects	59.2%	125
Good honours	65.9%	103
Expected completion rate	77.6%	115
Student/staff ratio	16.6	=80
Services and facilities/student	£3,140	7

concentrating its diverse activities on an impressive campus in Hendon and attracting 150 new academics. It has a new building with specialist teaching rooms for the faculty of science and technology and the faculty of the arts and creative industries. There have also been additional wet labs for biology sciences, and new facilities for media teaching and rehearsal space.

The campus also has a new library, well-equipped biomedical and technology labs, modern classrooms and lecture theatres, a high-end TV production studio, and art and design workshop spaces. An £80m centre for art, design and media, has won a string of accolades. It includes TV studios and flexible performance and exhibition spaces.

Undergraduates are sent a free e-book at the start of every module. The university's flexible course system allows students to start some courses in January if they prefer not to wait until autumn, and offers the option of an extra five-week session in the summer to try out new subjects or add to their credits. There is a range of work-based courses that allow participants to gain recognition and academic credit for learning in the workplace. The conventional degrees are also focused on future employment, many including work placements or the option of a sandwich year.

More than a third of the eligible staff at Middlesex were entered for the 2014 Research Excellence Framework, and 58% of their work was placed in one of the top two categories. Art and design produced the best results, with three quarters of the research assessed as world-leading or internationally excellent.

Almost all of the British students are state educated, more than half coming from the four poorest socioeconomic groups. Middlesex does not offer bursaries for undergraduates from low-income homes, believing that outreach and retention activities are more effective at broadening the intake and improving completion rates.

Three-quarters of the full-time students on the main campus are from London, many of them returning to education after a spell at work. There are about 1,200 residential places on or near the campus, including 630 in a privately-run development near Wembley stadium, with more to come in the next few years. Priority in their allocation is given to international students and other first-years whose first choice is Middlesex and who live outside London.

Sports facilities have been improving and include a well-equipped fitness pod at Hendon with a gym and multipurpose outdoor courts.

Tuition fees

» Fees for UK/EU students 2018–19 £9,250
» Fees for international students 2018–19 £11,500
» For scholarship and bursary information see www.mdx.ac.uk/life-at-middlesex/support-services/finance/scholarships-and-bursaries
» Graduate salary £20,000

Students

Undergraduates	12,885	(1,555)
Postgraduates	1,780	(2,890)
Applications per place	7.2	
Overall offer rate	76.8%	
International students	19.1%	
Mature students	25.9%	
From state-sector schools	98.3%	
From working-class homes	56.3%	

Accommodation

University-provided places: 1,119
Percentage catered: 0%
Self-catered: £138 – £176 per week
First year students from outside London are given priority
www.mdx.ac.uk/life-at-middlesex/accommodation

Newcastle University

Newcastle has enjoyed one of the biggest rises in applications of any university choosing to reveal a figure for 2017. The 6.3% increase is partly due to the addition of popular new degrees in pharmacy, and sport and exercise science, but the demand for places has been rising for most of the decade. There was a 22% increase in enrolments in 2016 alone.

A gold rating in the new Teaching Excellence Framework (TEF) will add to the university's attractions. The TEF panel was impressed by "exceptional" support for students, including tailored provision for the disabled.

The introduction of pharmacy makes Newcastle one of the few universities to offer courses and research in medicine, dentistry, biomedical sciences, psychology and pharmacy. The transfer of Durham University's courses in medicine and pharmacy will boost Newcastle's numbers by 2,000 students and staff. The two institutions previously had a joint programme where Durham's medics spent their first two years on its Stockton campus before moving to Newcastle for the remainder of their course.

Newcastle was also the first UK university to open an overseas medical school offering full degrees in medicine, in Johor, Malaysia. There is also an association with the Singapore Institute of Technology, providing degrees under the rubric of Newcastle University Singapore.

The university's home campus is in the heart of a city that frequently wins the popular vote for student life. A £75m student village, with 1,300 en-suite bedrooms in six blocks, will be ready for students starting courses this year. Next year will see the opening of a £30m extension of the sports centre with an eight-court sports hall, four squash courts, a strength and conditioning suite and two exercise studios.

Buildings have already opened for physics, music and medicine, science and engineering laboratories have been upgraded, and disabled access improved. The refurbished library, with 24-hour opening during term-time, is the only one in the UK to have been awarded five Charter Marks in a row for excellent customer service.

By far the biggest development, however, is the £350m Science Central project, run in partnership with the city council. It will house the new National Innovation Centre for Ageing, the National Innovation Centre for Data and the National Centre for Energy Systems Integration. The university's £58m Urban Sciences building opened on the site last year, providing a new home for the 1,395 staff and students in the School of Computing Science, focusing on digitally-enabled urban sustainability.

Newcastle upon Tyne
NE1 7RU
0191 208 3333
www.ncl.ac.uk
enquiries via website
www.nusu.co.uk
Open Days 2018:
June 29, 30
September 15

The Times and The Sunday Times **Rankings**

Overall Ranking: **26** (last year: 22)

Teaching quality	80.5%	=60
Student experience	81.2%	=29
Research quality	37.7%	=21
Entry standards	163	=26
Graduate prospects	80.7%	28
Good honours	81%	=26
Expected completion rate	93.9%	17
Student/staff ratio	14.6	=37
Services and facilities/student	£2,097	65

The university is also investing £34m in a learning and teaching centre at Science Central. Opening in 2019, the new centre will contain state-of-the-art learning facilities for more than 2,000 students across three floors, with a 750-seat auditorium. Unusually for a Russell Group university, Newcastle also has a longstanding reputation for agriculture, which benefits from two farms in Northumberland.

A third campus, on the site of the former Newcastle General Hospital, focuses on research into ageing and is another element of the university's lead role in turning Newcastle into one of the six officially designated "science cities". The university also has a campus in London, in partnership with INTO, the company that runs a teaching and accommodation complex on the Newcastle campus to prepare international students for undergraduate and graduate courses. Newcastle University London offers courses from the triple-accredited business school for the international market.

Nearly all degrees now include the opportunity to spend up to a year in the workplace. The award-winning ncl+ initiative encourages all students to develop employability skills through extracurricular activities. Students commit to at least 70 hours of activity, and the award will appear on their Higher Education Achievement Report.

Almost 80% of the entry for the 2014 Research Excellence Framework was judged to be world-leading or internationally excellent, with neuroscience, English language and literature, and computing science rated as leading departments in the UK.

Newcastle is popular with students from independent schools, who took up almost a quarter of the places in 2015, but the university was among the first in its peer group to mount substantial programmes to attract more students from non-traditional backgrounds. It now leads a national access programme. The students' union has been refurbished and a student forum created alongside it as a central outdoor social space. University accommodation is plentiful, and the campus hosts an independent theatre, museum and art gallery. The Hatton Gallery has just reopened after a £3.7m refurbishment.

Tuition fees

» Fees for UK/EU students 2018–19   £9,250
» Fees for international students 2018–19   £16,200–£21,000
    Dentistry £35,200 Medicine £32,000
» For scholarship and bursary information see
    www.ncl.ac.uk/undergraduate/finance/scholarships
» Graduate salary   £22,000

Students

Undergraduates	17,680	(45)
Postgraduates	4,565	(1,505)
Applications per place	6.3	
Overall offer rate	88.3%	
International students	19.3%	
Mature students	6.6%	
From state-sector schools	76.5%	
From working-class homes	20.3%	

Accommodation

University-provided places: 4,664
Percentage catered: 17%
Catered costs: £140 – £167 per week
Self-catered: £84 – £161 per week
First year students are guaranteed accommodation
www.ncl.ac.uk/accommodation/contact

Newman University

Newman has dropped nine places – and into the bottom ten – in our league table after a decline in graduate-level employment and a second successive fall in student satisfaction. Only four years ago it was in the top 15 in our analysis of the National Student Survey and almost 50 places higher in the table.

In other respects, however, it is thriving. The numbers starting degrees are up by a quarter compared with the last year before £9,000 fees and there was a 4% increase in applications for courses beginning last autumn, in sharp contrast to the decline at most institutions in its peer group.

The university received a silver rating in the new Teaching Excellence Framework. The awards panel said students were "acquiring knowledge, skills and attributes that are valued by employers through work placements, volunteering support and enterprise opportunities and which proactively embed career skills into the curriculum".

Newman was also named among the top three universities in a calculation carried out by The Economist of graduate salaries compared with their expected levels, given students' backgrounds, qualifications and subjects. The authors acknowledged that part of the explanation lay in the high proportion of Newman students going into teaching and other public service jobs where employment levels are high and early-career salaries competitive. Nevertheless, they estimated that an average salary of £24,300 five years after graduation was £2,800 more than expected.

There are still fewer than 3,000 students, but the university is investing £22m in new accommodation and teaching space. The recently opened halls of residence provide 108 en-suite bedrooms and open-plan living spaces. A new library and entrance building were among the other recent additions to the campus at Bartley Green, about eight miles southwest of Birmingham city centre.

A new integrated foundation year for students aiming for degrees in the social sciences but lacking the necessary qualifications should help continue Newman's recent growth. For the moment, however, it will have to do without new entrants from outside the EU. The Home Office suspended the university's licence to sponsor international students because more than 10% of applicants – only two students in Newman's case – had been refused visas.

Newman was one of three Catholic foundations among the crop of institutions awarded university status in 2012. It takes its name from the 19th-century cardinal John Henry Newman, the author of The Idea of the University. His vision of a community of scholars guides the institution, which was established in 1968 as a teacher training college,

Genners Lane
Bartley Green
Birmingham B32 3NT
0121 476 1181
admissions@newman.ac.uk
www.newman.ac.uk
Open Days 2018:
June 23, July 7,
October 13

The Times and The Sunday Times Rankings

Overall Ranking: **121** (last year: =112)

Teaching quality	78.9%	=82
Student experience	76.2%	=103
Research quality	2.8%	115
Entry standards	117	=102
Graduate prospects	63.4%	=114
Good honours	62.8%	117
Expected completion rate	78.6%	113
Student/staff ratio	16.1	=69
Services and facilities/student	£1,627	108

but now has a wider portfolio of degrees, mainly in the social sciences and humanities.

The cardinal's influence is evident in the small class sizes and teaching style adopted by the university, which stresses its Catholic affiliation, but also its commitment to be inclusive in its recruitment and subsequent activities.

The campus is in a quiet residential area with views over the Bartley reservoir and the Worcestershire countryside beyond. The modern buildings are arranged around a series of inner quadrangles of lawns and trees. All full-time degrees include work placements, some of which are abroad, and undergraduates can opt to study at a partner university in Europe or further afield. There is also a range of part-time courses and foundation degrees, most of which are taught at Newman rather than partner colleges.

The university previously received one of eight national awards to improve the use of technology in learning and teaching. The successful bid drew on a project designed to boost the university's own students' digital literacy, part of a larger initiative called "Newman in the Digital Age".

Only 23 academics were entered for the Research Excellence Framework, but that was twice as many as were put forward for the previous assessments. Education and history produced the best results, but less than a third of the university's research was placed in the top two categories. Newman does not employ staff for research alone, in order to ensure that students have regular contact with active researchers.

Three-quarters of the undergraduates are female, almost all of them state-educated and more than half come from working-class homes.

Halls of residence are close to the teaching areas and library, with first-year students taking priority in their allocation. The refurbished fitness suite and performance room have improved sports facilities that already included an artificial sports pitch, sports hall, gymnasium and squash courts. Birmingham city centre has an abundance of cultural venues and student-orientated nightlife.

Tuition fees

- » Fees for Scottish and EU students 2018–19 £9,250
- » Fees for international students 2018–19 n/a
- » For scholarship and bursary information see www.newman.ac.uk/scholarships/2951
- » Graduate salary £19,000

Students

Undergraduates	1,825	(430)
Postgraduates	275	(285)
Applications per place	6.1	
Overall offer rate	86.6%	
International students	0.4%	
Mature students	30.7%	
From state-sector schools	99.6%	
From working-class homes	56.2%	

Accommodation

University-provided places: 192
Percentage catered: 0%
Self-catered: £100 – £135 per week
www.newman.ac.uk/accommodation

University of Northampton

Students starting courses in 2018 will be the first to experience Northampton's new £330m Waterside campus. The university is moving out of its two existing sites to occupy a 58-acre brownfield site a few minutes' walk from the town centre, where construction has been taking place since 2015.

The campus will provide academic facilities for 15,000 students, residential accommodation for 1,000 and leisure facilities open to the community. Its development has been funded mainly through a £231.5m bond guaranteed by the Treasury – the first time the government has made a university such a guarantee.

The centrepiece will be the four-storey Learning Commons, where most teaching will take place, and a new library will be open around the clock. A Creative Hub will house laboratories and specialist teaching spaces for the sciences and creative disciplines, and the student village will include a 32-bed hotel and community facilities including a multi-faith chaplaincy, bank, convenience store and health centre.

An energy centre that will reduce the university's emissions dramatically by using woodchip biomass and gas to service all its buildings is already open, while a grade II listed engine shed close to the Waterside site has been restored to house the students' union. Some residential accommodation on the old Park and Avenue campuses will remain open temporarily to maximise the options available to students.

The project typifies the ambitious nature of a university, which was the first in the UK to be named a "Changemaker Campus" by the Ashoka global network of social entrepreneurs and has since been ranked top in the country for social enterprise. Every student has the opportunity to work in a social enterprise as part of their course, developing new entrepreneurial skills to make them more employable. This may involve a work placement, volunteering or participating in one of the university's social or economic partnerships.

Northampton was given a gold rating in the new Teaching Excellence Framework (TEF), despite falling below its benchmark for highly-skilled graduate employment. It was in the bottom five for graduate prospects in our table last year – the most recent data considered in the TEF – although it has improved in the current edition. The TEF panel was impressed by "an embedded approach to the involvement of students in research, scholarship and professional practice, with strengths in community-based research and scholarship and sector-leading work on social enterprise".

Although it was awarded university status only in 2005, Northampton traces its

---

Boughton Green Road
Northampton NN2 7AL
0300 303 2772
study@northampton.ac.uk
www.northampton.ac.uk
www.northamptonunion.com
Open Days 2018:
check website

The Times and The Sunday Times **Rankings**
Overall Ranking: **97** (last year: 97)

Teaching quality	79.8%	=72
Student experience	77%	=87
Research quality	3.2%	113
Entry standards	108	=121
Graduate prospects	63.4%	=114
Good honours	69.4%	=83
Expected completion rate	83.4%	=83
Student/staff ratio	18.5	110
Services and facilities/student	£2,577	27

history back to the 13th century. Henry III dissolved the original institution, allegedly because his bishops thought it posed a threat to Oxford. The modern university originated in an amalgamation of the town's colleges of education, nursing, technology and art. It has a particular focus on training for the region's public services. Business is the most popular area, but teacher training and health subjects are not far behind. The university is the region's largest provider of teachers and healthcare professionals.

The university also backs the iCon building in Daventry, which provides a base for green businesses, and it co-sponsors a University Technical College in the town, as it does at the nearby Silverstone motor racing circuit.

Northampton takes its mission to widen participation in higher education seriously: almost all the undergraduates are state-educated and four out of ten come from working-class homes, more than the national average for the university's courses and entry qualifications.

The university entered a quarter of its eligible staff for the 2014 Research Excellence Framework. Only 30% of its research was placed in the top two categories, but there was an outstanding result in history, where two-thirds of the work was considered world-leading or internationally excellent.

Sports enthusiasts are well catered for, with professional rugby union, football and first-class cricket on the doorstep, plus Silverstone for motor racing. The university's new sports facilities will include three multi-use games areas and a floodlit all-weather pitch. The university has also announced a multiuse sports dome, designed to Sport England dimensions, suitable for a variety of sports, including football, badminton and netball. The sports dome will be used for teaching, as well as recreational use, with two sports performance labs and teaching rooms.

The town has a number of student-orientated bars, and the new campus will add to the leisure facilities. Both London and Birmingham are about an hour away by train.

Tuition fees

» Fees for UK/EU students 2018–19 £9,250
» Fees for international students 2018–19 £12,000–£21,300
» For scholarship and bursary information see www.northampton.ac.uk/study/fees-and-funding/
» Graduate salary £20,000

Students

Undergraduates	9,010	(1,655)
Postgraduates	570	(1,750)
Applications per place	6	
Overall offer rate	76.6%	
International students	9.2%	
Mature students	26.9%	
From state-sector schools	96.8%	
From working-class homes	40.2%	

Accommodation

University-provided places: 2,097
Percentage catered: 0%
Self-catered: £67 – £151 per week
www.northampton.ac.uk/study/student-life/accommodation

Northumbria University

Northumbria has shown that the Brexit vote need not be the obstacle to recruiting EU students that other universities fear. It did not disclose how many UK students applied in 2017, but a new strategy on the Continent has produced a rise of 50% in EU applications for degree courses, in contrast to the 5% decline across the UK.

Overall enrolments have been steady over recent years, as is the university's position in our table this year. Student satisfaction with teaching has declined, but graduate prospects have improved and there has been much higher spending on facilities and services. It is aiming eventually for the top 30.

Northumbria was awarded silver in the government's new Teaching Excellence Framework. The panel praised the university for helping students to enjoy their studies and achieve high attainment through a range of academic and personal support services, graduate start-up and careers assistance. High-quality physical and digital resources were used effectively both in teaching and by students, it said.

The university is investing £52m in its City campus to improve the student experience. A new Student Central zone around the students' union and library will bring together services such as the careers, welfare and international support. Two more developments are on the way, for computing and information sciences and architecture and built environment, as well as renovations of two of the university's original main buildings. Laboratories for engineering, physics, maths and computer science have been upgraded and there are plans for new studios for architecture and the built environment.

Northumbria is the biggest university in the northeast of England. It has already spent £200m on its city centre headquarters and the Coach Lane campus, three miles away, which has a sports centre and a clinical skills centre, where students learn in simulated hospital environments. There is also a base in the City of London, mainly for postgraduates.

About half of the students are from the northeast, but numbers drawn from other parts of the UK have been rising. There are more than 3,000 international students on campus and another 3,600 taking Northumbria courses overseas. There is a design school in Jakarta, Indonesia, established with Binus International university, and Northumbria has been chosen to deliver a new degree in nursing in Malta to address the island's shortage of nurses.

More than a third of the UK undergraduates were from the four lowest socioeconomic classes when this was last surveyed. Free one-day taster courses run throughout the year to give prospective

Ellison Building
Newcastle upon Tyne
NE1 8ST
0191 349 5600
er.admissions@northumbria.ac.uk
www.northumbria.ac.uk
www.mynsu.co.uk
Open Days 2018:
check website

The Times and The Sunday Times Rankings

Overall Ranking: **66** (last year: =65)

Teaching quality	80%	=68
Student experience	79.5%	=47
Research quality	9%	=65
Entry standards	144	45
Graduate prospects	72.5%	=69
Good honours	74.6%	=49
Expected completion rate	86.1%	=62
Student/staff ratio	17.1	=89
Services and facilities/student	£1,944	83

students an idea of what university life would be like and there are bursaries of £800 a year for applicants from the poorest homes.

More than 560 employers sponsor undergraduate programmes – one of the highest rates in the UK – and accreditation comes from 60 professional bodies. The university was one of the pioneers of degree apprenticeships and now has programmes in five areas: business leadership and management, quantity surveying, digital and technology solutions, real estate and building surveying.

Northumbria is also among the leading universities for graduate start-ups, its companies boasting the highest turnover in the UK for 2015–16. At £69.2m, this was almost £25m more than the second-placed institution.

All Northumbria's teacher training programmes have been rated "outstanding" by Ofsted for 15 years in a row. The university also more than doubled the numbers entered for the 2014 Research Excellence Framework compared with the 2008 assessments while improving the results; 60% of the work was judged to be world-leading or internationally excellent

The sports facilities are good, and Northumbria has been in the top ten of the British Universities and Colleges Sport league table since 2013–14. The £30m sports centre includes a swimming pool, climbing wall and 3,000-seat indoor arena. There is also a generous sport scholarship scheme.

The university reinforced its reputation for women's football last year when it was named as one of eight FA Women's High Performance Football Centres.

Most first-years are offered places in university accommodation, which was placed in the top three in the 2014 Student Housing Survey. There are now more than 4,000 rooms available, including almost 1,000 en-suite bedrooms in nearby Gateshead, where there are fitness facilities and a multiuse games area. There is a plentiful supply of privately rented flats and houses in Newcastle upon Tyne, a magnet city for students.

Tuition fees

» Fees for UK/EU students 2018–19   £9,250
» Fees for international students 2018–19   £13,000–£15,000
» For scholarship and bursary information see www.northumbria.ac.uk/study-at-northumbria/fees-funding/
» Graduate salary   £21,500

Students

Undergraduates	18,770	(3,645)
Postgraduates	2,375	(2,375)
Applications per place	5.1	
Overall offer rate	82.2%	
International students	8.8%	
Mature students	19.5%	
From state-sector schools	94.4%	
From working-class homes	37.2%	

Accommodation

University-provided places: 4,000+
Percentage catered: 8%
Catered costs: £112 per week
Self-catered: £75 – £165 per week
First year students are guaranteed accommodation
www.northumbria.ac.uk/study-at-northumbria/accommodation/

Norwich University of the Arts

Norwich University of the Arts (NUA) is opening new buildings in 2018 to cope with rising demand for its courses. Enrolments are up by almost a quarter since university status arrived in 2012 and there are 1,000 more applications. The university has now added three degrees in computer games design and development and will introduce "year 0" courses this year in subjects such as photography and illustration to bring students up to the standard required for degree-level study.

The Sir John Hurt film studio, named after the university's late chancellor, has already opened in a recently renovated building in the city centre that also houses the architecture school. The renovation, which in 2016 won an award from the Royal Institute of British Architects, represented the first stage of a £10m development plan, enabling NUA to double in size.

A gold in the new Teaching Excellence Framework (TEF) should help it achieve this ambition. A glowing endorsement by the TEF panel found that course design and assessment practices encouraged experimentation, creative risk-taking and team-working, providing "outstanding levels of stretch for students". It added that investment in high-quality physical and digital resources had produced a learning environment that is enriched by collaborative working, with staff who are professional practitioners in their own right, alongside frequent sessions provided by visiting lecturers and industry professionals.

NUA has also regained all the ground it lost the previous year in our table – and more – with a 28-place rise in the new edition. A big increase in student satisfaction with the quality of teaching and much-improved graduate prospects have taken the university back into the top half of the table, in a creditable 60th place.

Unlike the other arts universities, NUA makes a virtue of focusing entirely on the arts, design and media rather than venturing into business or the humanities and social sciences.

The institution traces its history back to 1845 when the Norwich School of Design was established by the artists and followers of the Norwich school of painters, the only provincial British group with an international reputation for landscape painting. Former tutors include the artists Lucian Freud, Michael Andrews and Leslie Davenport.

The campus is concentrated on the pedestrianised centre of Norwich, from the 13th-century Garth, which is now the photography centre, to the Monastery Media Lab, claimed by NUA to be a "world-class" digital design centre, and St Georges, where the traditional high ceilings and huge windows

---

Francis House
3–7 Redwell Street
Norwich NR2 4SN
01603 610 561
admissions@nua.ac.uk
www.nua.ac.uk
www.nuasu.co.uk
Open Days 2018:
check website

The Times and The Sunday Times Rankings

Overall Ranking: **60** (last year: 88)

Teaching quality	84.1%	=10
Student experience	79.1%	=55
Research quality	5.6%	=86
Entry standards	135	57
Graduate prospects	66.8%	100
Good honours	70.8%	70
Expected completion rate	82%	92
Student/staff ratio	17.1	=89
Services and facilities/student	£1,806	96

make it an ideal setting for fine art. The university's public art gallery enables students to showcase their work and gain experience curating and organising exhibitions, while the library houses the largest specialist art, design and media collection in the eastern region.

The Ideas Factory – also praised by the TEF panel – provides supported facilities to help graduates with the development of new digital businesses. It also hosts the university's Digital User Research Lab and its creative agency, which provides opportunities for students to work on commercial projects with local, national and international organisations. Recent clients include the BBC and Norwich airport.

There are still only 18 BA degrees and 2,000 students, 62% of whom are female. Approaching 40% of the undergraduates come from working-class homes and the projected dropout rate is much lower than the national average for its courses and entry qualifications. Most courses include units of self-managed learning and exploration that allow students to concentrate on areas of particular interest.

More than half of the work submitted to the 2014 Research Excellence Framework was judged to be world leading or internationally excellent, with 90% placed in the top two categories for its impact on the broader cultural and economic landscape.

NUA has its own art materials shop, which sells basic and specialist art supplies at discounted prices. Individual studio space is provided for all full-time students in the faculties of art and design, while students in the media faculty have access to digital workstations. Workshops for everything from digital video editing to laser cutting provide specialised resources and are staffed by experienced professionals, including graduates and practising artists.

The university has a little over 300 residential places located in the city centre, enough for four out of five new entrants wanting accommodation. NUA does not have its own sports facilities, but its students have access to the University of East Anglia's Sportspark, which boasts some of the best amenities in the higher education system, including an Olympic-sized swimming pool. The city is attractive and popular with students while consistently rated one of the safest and "greenest" cities in the UK.

Tuition fees

» Fees for UK/EU students 2018–19	£9,250
» Fees for international students 2018–19	£13,700
» For scholarship and bursary information see www.nua.ac.uk/study/finance	
» Graduate salary	£17,000

Students

Undergraduates	1,920	(0)
Postgraduates	25	(55)
Applications per place	4.1	
Overall offer rate	61.4%	
International students	6.5%	
Mature students	10%	
From state-sector schools	97.2%	
From working-class homes	37.6%	

Accommodation

University-provided places: 305
Percentage catered: 0%
Self-catered: £96 – £145 per week
www.nua.ac.uk/study/accommodation/

University of Nottingham

Nottingham launched a £200m research fund the day after it had received a gold rating in the Teaching Excellence Framework (TEF), helping the university earn a second successive shortlisting for our University of the Year award.

In a year of high achievement, Nottingham also moved further up our top 20, was once again named among graduate employers' favourite recruiting grounds, and featured as the top Russell Group university in a calculation carried out by The Economist of average graduate salaries in comparison with their expected levels, taking account of background, qualifications and subjects.

It is a satisfying legacy for Sir David Greenaway, who retired last year after 20 years as vice-chancellor or pro vice-chancellor. His successor, Professor Shearer West, formerly provost and deputy vice-chancellor of the University of Sheffield, is the first woman to hold the role.

The new research fund is the biggest at any UK university. The investment will be spread over five years and is expected to leverage more funding from industry, government and philanthropists. It will focus on six diverse areas, from modern slavery, future food and green chemicals to precision imaging, propulsion and smart industrial systems.

The university has a strong research base on which to build, with two Nobel prizes since the millennium for work carried out at Nottingham in medicine and economics. More than 80% of the work entered for the 2014 Research Excellence Framework was rated as world-leading or internationally excellent. The university was in the UK's top ten in half of the 32 subject areas in which it made submissions.

Nottingham's efforts to prepare students for the employment market – it was our University of the Year for Graduate Employment in 2017 – contributed to its TEF rating. The independent panel found high levels of monitored contact time, a culture of personalised learning that ensures all students are challenged to achieve their full potential and exceptionally high student engagement with advanced technology-enhanced learning.

Applications rose significantly in the previous two years, although they dipped in 2017, as they have all over the UK. Nottingham has award-winning campuses in China and Malaysia, as well as 330 acres of parkland in its home city that is one of the most attractive university settings in Britain. With undergraduates encouraged to transfer between campuses and more than 7,000 international students in Nottingham, the university markets itself as a global institution. It is well inside the top 100 universities in the world in the QS rankings, with 21 subjects in the top 100.

University Park
Nottingham NG7 2RD
0115 951 5559
undergraduate-enquiries@
nottingham.ac.uk
www.nottingham.ac.uk
www.su.nottingham.ac.uk
Open Days 2018:
June 29, 30,
September 14, 15

The Times and The Sunday Times Rankings

Overall Ranking: **18** (last year: 20)

Teaching quality	80.6%	=57
Student experience	80.1%	37
Research quality	37.8%	20
Entry standards	164	=23
Graduate prospects	83.3%	13
Good honours	83.1%	=18
Expected completion rate	94%	16
Student/staff ratio	13.8	27
Services and facilities/student	£2,345	34

A £21m redevelopment of the science and engineering library was opened last year, and a new teaching building will be ready for students arriving in 2018, part of a £40m programme for new and refurbished teaching spaces. There has been considerable investment, too, on the Jubilee campus, which houses the schools of business, computer science and education, as well as 750 residential places.

The Centre for Sustainable Chemistry, part-funded by GlaxoSmithKline, is housed in a carbon-neutral building that is the first of its kind in the UK. The school of medicine is also close to University Park, with a £4.5m facility for nursing located at the Royal Derby Hospital, while the biosciences and veterinary schools are at Sutton Bonington, about 12 miles south of the city in a rural setting.

The university's purpose-built campuses in China and Malaysia both have echoes of Nottingham's distinctive clock tower and are centres of research as well as teaching. With 6,000 students at Ningbo in China and almost 5,000 half an hour's drive from Kuala Lumpur, both are well established. They bring Nottingham's total student population to more than 44,000, making it one of the largest UK institutions.

Since last autumn, undergraduates across the full range of disciplines have been able to undertake a placement year as part of their studies. The Nottingham Advantage award also offers extracurricular modules, as well as providing scores of internships for graduates, who enjoy lifetime access to the careers service.

The two main campuses in Nottingham are within three miles of the city centre, which has a good selection of student-orientated clubs. However, halls of residence and the students' union tend to be the centre of social life for students, especially in the first year. The newly completed David Ross Sports Centre, a £40m campus complex, has a host of facilities including a 60-metre indoor sprint track, hydrotherapy pool and 200-station fitness suite. Other provision includes a water-based hockey pitch and 25-metre pool. Nottingham is in the top four in the British Universities and Colleges Sport leagues.

Tuition fees

»	Fees for UK/EU students 2018–19	£9,250
»	Fees for international students 2018–19	£16,350–£21,060
	Foundation courses	£14,700
	Medicine	£22,170
»	For scholarship and bursary information see www.nottingham.ac.uk/studentservices/support/ financialsupport/bursariesandscholarships/index.aspx	
»	Graduate salary	£22,000

Students

Undergraduates	23,170	(770)
Postgraduates	5,420	(2,765)
Applications per place	7.7	
Overall offer rate	79.1%	
International students	17%	
Mature students	11.7%	
From state-sector schools	79.2%	
From working-class homes	20.3%	

Accommodation

University-provided places: 7,488
Percentage catered: 50%
Catered costs: £156 – £223 per week
Self-catered: £99 – £166 per week
First year students are guaranteed accommodation
www.nottingham.ac.uk/accommodation/accommodation. aspx

Nottingham Trent University

Exceptional levels of student satisfaction have catapulted Nottingham Trent University (NTU) into the top 50, placing it among the top three post-1992 universities in this year's table. Our Modern University of the Year is up ten places on last year to its highest position yet and is in the top ten for perceptions of teaching quality.

The same qualities helped NTU achieve a gold award in the new Teaching Excellence Framework. The independent panel acknowledged the "considerable investment" in the university's employability team and the provision of high-quality work placements for all students. There is "exemplary engagement with employers who contribute to curriculum development in a way which demonstrably enhances students' employability", the panel added.

The university has invested £421m on improvements since 2003 across its three campuses. The libraries have been given a fresh look, historic buildings revamped and new ones built. The award-winning students' union has new social and leisure spaces and extensive additional accommodation has been provided on the main City site. Now the Clifton base, five miles from the centre of Nottingham, is being redeveloped with two new teaching buildings and landscaped outdoor spaces, as well as a developing student village.

The next phase will be at NTU's Brackenhurst campus, the base for the animal, rural and environmental sciences school, 14 miles from the city. As well as the new environment centre, which will contain the main teaching facilities, a 200-seat lecture theatre and exhibition space, there will be a separate building to house a reception area. Construction is due to begin this year for completion by the end of 2019.

NTU is also investing more than £10m to improve its facilities for Stem (science, technology, engineering and mathematics) disciplines. A new suite of degrees in biomedical, electronic and sport engineering was launched for this academic year.

The university is in the top ten for the number of students on year-long work placements, a format that it is doubly keen to promote since establishing that it transforms the job prospects of students from poor backgrounds in particular. A third of the undergraduates come from working-class homes and more than nine out of ten were state-educated.

Most courses now include a work placement of at least four weeks. NTU is also aiming to offer all its students an "international learning experience", which may involve a study or work placement abroad, learning a foreign language or studying another culture or country.

---

50 Shakespeare Street
Nottingham NG1 4FQ
0115 941 8418
admissions@ntu.ac.uk
www.ntu.ac.uk
www.trentstudents.org
Open Days 2018:
March 24

The Times and The Sunday Times **Rankings**

Overall Ranking: =47 (last year: 57)

Teaching quality	84.8%	8
Student experience	83.1%	=12
Research quality	6.5%	81
Entry standards	136	56
Graduate prospects	76.7%	=53
Good honours	69.9%	=77
Expected completion rate	87.4%	52
Student/staff ratio	15.8	=61
Services and facilities/student	£2,061	71

Art and design, architecture, law, business and the social sciences are taught at the City site, while science and technology, education and the humanities are based at Clifton. The Brackenhurst campus includes one of the region's best-equipped equestrian centres, with a purpose-built indoor riding area, as well as 340 residential places.

NTU now has about 27,000 students, including 3,000 from outside the UK. It is best known for fashion and other creative arts, but also boasts one of the UK's biggest law schools, offering legal practice courses for both solicitors and barristers as well as degrees. Many courses are sponsored by employers. A Trailblazer Apprenticeship in management, for example, gives students a degree and Chartered Institute of Management Accountants qualification in four years, with fees and salary paid by a company.

The university is also building on a long and distinguished history in teacher education with the launch of the Nottingham Institute of Education, a centre of excellence that is intended to align teaching and research expertise more effectively from the early years to higher education. An extensive research programme previously attracted an £8m donation – thought to be the largest to a post-1992 university – to advance the university's work in cancer diagnosis and therapy.

More than half of the research submitted to the 2014 Research Excellence Framework was considered world-leading or internationally excellent. The best results were in health subjects and general engineering where more than 80% of the work was placed in the top two categories. The university has since won a Queen's Anniversary prize for new technologies for food safety and security and aviation security.

NTU has a strong sporting reputation, frequently reaching the top 20 in the British Universities and Colleges Sport leagues. The Lee Westwood Sports Centre includes a 100-station gym, sports halls, studios and a nutrition training centre, while the outdoor facilities include an Olympic-standard hockey pitch.

Social life varies between campuses, but all have access to the city's lively cultural and clubbing scene. A bus service links the main campuses and the city's tram system serves the university.

Tuition fees

» Fees for UK/EU students 2018–19 £9,250
» Fees for international students 2018–19 £13,450
» For scholarship and bursary information see www.ntu.ac.uk/study-and-courses/undergraduate/fees-and-finance/bursaries-and-scholarships
» Graduate salary £19,200

Students

Undergraduates	21,520	(1,325)
Postgraduates	2,235	(2,845)
Applications per place	6	
Overall offer rate	86.7%	
International students	7.7%	
Mature students	10.7%	
From state-sector schools	93.7%	
From working-class homes	33.1%	

Accommodation

University-provided places: 4,754
Percentage catered: 0%
Self-catered: £99 – £158 per week
First year students are guaranteed accommodation
www.ntu.ac.uk/accommodation

The Open University

The Open University is conducting a root and branch review of its activities to reduce an annual budget of £420m by almost a quarter. Up to £70m will be reinvested in a programme to transform the OU into a "digital-first institution", while the rest of the savings will be required to secure the university's future after funding changes and the national collapse in part-time student recruitment.

Under the plans, the OU's curriculum will be streamlined and unpopular courses closed. Peter Horrocks, the vice-chancellor, said: "The OU will still be the OU. We will retain our core mission of offering higher education to all, regardless of background or previous qualifications. But we will be delivering it in a different way, matching future needs to future technology."

The OU's technology will be updated and its staff retrained so that it can become what Horrocks describes as a "university of the cloud", rather than the 1960s vision of a "university of the air". Seven regional offices are already closing, as the university reversed several years of deficits.

Although still by far the biggest university in the UK, with more than 170,000 students, the OU has seen enrolments drop by a third in less than a decade. However, it is arguably the world's most highly regarded distance learning institution, a model for universities on every continent.

Based in Milton Keynes, Buckinghamshire, the OU does not appear in our league table because the absence of on-campus undergraduates makes it unsuitable for comparison with conventional universities on some of the measures used. There are no entrance requirements, for example, and no need for physical student facilities.

On those measures where a comparison is possible, the OU generally performs well. For many years, it featured at or near the top of the National Student Survey, although it was only just in the top 50 for overall satisfaction in 2017.

The university's academics also have a proud research record: 72% of the OU's submission for the 2014 Research Excellence Framework was considered world-leading or internationally excellent.

In keeping with its new digital focus, the OU hosts FutureLearn, a consortium of leading universities and cultural organisations such as the British Museum and the British Council, offering Moocs (massive open online courses). They are now available in a wide range of subjects, some offering credits towards OU degrees.

The OU has not stopped offering new degrees of its own, however. Recent additions include economics and history and a combined science, technology, engineering

Walton Hall
Milton Keynes
MK7 6AA
0300 303 5303
general-enquiries@open.ac.uk
www.open.ac.uk

***The Times and The Sunday Times* Rankings**
Not applicable

and mathematics BSc. Criminology and music will be added to the portfolio this year.

In an attempt to revitalise part-time higher education, the university has launched the Pearl website (Part-Time Education for Adults Returning to Learn), providing information on the opportunities for adults to increase their skills and progress in their chosen careers.

The OU has also started a joint apprenticeship service with the consultant KPMG giving information to employers, and launched higher apprenticeship programmes for healthcare practitioner assistants and chartered managers, as well as in digital and technical solutions.

Undergraduate fees are £5,728 for the equivalent of full-time study in 2017–8, the cheapest at any university and eligible for a tuition fee loan. The OU provides fee waivers for students from poor backgrounds through its Widening Access and Success programme.

In addition to degrees in a named subject, the OU also awards "Open" bachelor degrees, where the syllabus is designed by the students combining a number of modules. Assessment is by both continual assessment and examination or, for some modules, a main assignment. Except in fast-moving areas such as computing, there is no limit on the time taken to complete a degree.

More than 5,000 part-time associate lecturers (tutors) guide students through

degrees. The OU's "supported open learning" system allows students to work where they choose — at home, in the workplace or at a library or study centre. They have contact with fellow students at tutorials, day schools or through online conferencing and electronic forums, social networks and informal study groups.

Three in ten students are under 25 years old and three-quarters work either full or part-time while studying. More than 60% of undergraduates are female and most live in the UK, but there are now 15,000 students in other countries. The OU offers special support for disabled students and currently has more than 20,000 students with disabilities.

Tuition fees

» Fees for UK/EU students 2018–19: Scotland, Wales, Northern Ireland £1,916. England £5,728 – fees paid per module of 30 or 60 credits.
» Fees for international students 2018–19   £5,728
  For further fee information see
  www.open.ac.uk/courses/fees-and-funding

Students

Undergraduates	0 (119,155)
Postgraduates	250 (7,220)

Accommodation

Not applicable

University of Oxford

Oxford is rated as the top university in the world in Times Higher Education's research-dominated ranking, but it remains second, behind Cambridge, in our table. Like several Russell Group universities, its students boycotted the National Student Survey, but Oxford has ground to make up on its ancient rival in graduate prospects, completion, spending on student services, entry standards and research.

The university was awarded gold in the new Teaching Excellence Framework. The independent panel raved about Oxford's collegiate system and the small-group tutorials, as well as the opportunities for students to engage as active researchers, with the possibility in some cases of co-publishing with world-leading academics. The only negative comments concerned satisfaction levels among disadvantaged students and the immediate prospects for black and ethnic-minority graduates.

Applications have risen for the past two years and are running at record levels, but there have been barely any more places available. Fewer than a quarter of 18-year-olds applying to Oxford in 2016 received an offer – the lowest proportion in the UK and significantly less than at Cambridge. But Oxford made offers to its highest recorded number of state-school applicants in 2017, nudging 60%.

Last year, it also released sample questions from the notoriously oblique interviews that are the cause of the greatest anxiety for many applicants. They are still available on the section of the university's website devoted to admissions.

Candidates must apply by mid-October and it is not possible to apply to both Oxford and Cambridge. There are written tests for some subjects and you may be asked to submit samples of work. Certain subjects now demand two A* grades and another A at A-level and 99% of successful candidates achieve at least three As at A-level or their equivalent.

The prize is a place at the oldest and probably the most famous university in the world, with 51 Nobel prize-winners and 27 British prime ministers among its alumni and former academics.

In the 2014 Research Excellence Framework, Oxford achieved the best results in the UK in nine subject areas and 87% of its submission was rated as world-leading or internationally excellent, but it entered 87% of eligible staff, compared with 95% at Cambridge. Oxford has since won a Queen's Anniversary prize for collaborations between engineering and medical technology.

Selection is in the hands of the 30 undergraduate colleges, which vary considerably in their approach. Sound advice

---

University Offices
Wellington Square
Oxford OX1 2JD
01865 288 000
undergraduate.admissions@ox.ac.uk
www.ox.ac.uk
www.ousu.org
Open Days 2018:
June 27, 28
September 14

The Times and The Sunday Times Rankings

Overall Ranking: **2** (last year: 2)

Teaching quality	n/a	
Student experience	n/a	
Research quality	53.1%	3
Entry standards	221	3
Graduate prospects	85.3%	6
Good honours	92.8%	1
Expected completion rate	98.2%	2
Student/staff ratio	10.3	1
Services and facilities/student	£3,334	3

on colleges' academic strengths and social factors is essential for applicants to give themselves the best chance of winning a place and finding a setting in which they can thrive. A minority of candidates opt to go straight into the admissions pool without expressing a preference for a particular college. The choice is particularly important for arts and social science students, whose tuition is based in college. Science and technology are taught mainly in central facilities. All subjects operate on eight-week terms and assess students entirely on final examinations, a system some find too pressurised.

Oxford continues to try to broaden its intake, mounting 3,000 outreach events involving 72% of all UK schools with a sixth form, but it still admitted the lowest proportion of undergraduates from state schools and colleges in 2015. The university offers the most generous financial support in UK higher education for students from poor backgrounds. Nearly a quarter of all students receive some support. Those from the lowest-income families receive support totalling at least £3,700 a year.

The career prospects for graduates are stellar. Five years after graduation their salaries average almost £43,000 – even more than their backgrounds, qualifications and subjects would suggest, according to The Economist.

A new programme, the Student Consultancy, is sending students to work with local firms on strategy or business problems. The Foundry, a Victorian warehouse and former comedy club, opened last summer, helping students and alumni with their own start-up plans.

Oxford's facilities are being improved and expanded, with the aid of a £200m loan from the European Investment Bank, the largest it has made to a university. A new building has opened for the physics department, with high-quality laboratory and teaching space, and last summer the historic Duke Humfrey's Library, part of the world-famous Bodleian Library network, was renovated. The Iffley Road sports complex is being upgraded, too, with a new gym and sports hall, complementing college amenities.

Applications for admission close on October 15.

Tuition fees
» Fees for UK/EU students 2018–19 £9,250
» Fees for international students 2018–19 (including college fees of £7,570) £23,800–£31,455
Medicine £26,190–£36,007 (clinical years)
» For scholarship and bursary information see www.ox.ac.uk/admissions/undergraduate/fees-and-funding/fees-funding-and-scholarships
» Graduate salary £25,000

Students

Undergraduates	11,320	(3,395)
Postgraduates	8,110	(2,035)
Applications per place	6.1	
Overall offer rate	24.7%	
International students	15.6%	
Mature students	3.5%	
From state-sector schools	55.7%	
From working-class homes	10%	

Accommodation
www.ox.ac.uk/students/life/accommodation
www.ox.ac.uk/admissions/undergraduate/colleges/college-listing

Also see Chapter 13 for information about individual colleges

Oxford Brookes University

Oxford Brookes has dropped another 15 places in our league table, making a decline of almost 30 places in two years. Staffing levels and spending on student services have improved since the last edition, but there has been a fall of five percentage points in the sections of the National Student Survey relating to teaching quality and eight points on the broader student experience over two years, leaving the university outside the top 80.

Brookes received a silver award in the Teaching Excellence Framework, however. The independent panel noted that there had been high levels of investment in physical and digital resources, which are valued by students, and a "developing" focus on graduate prospects for employment or further study.

Brookes is the UK's only representative in QS's ranking of the top 50 universities in the world that are less than 50 years old. There has been a growing focus on its international profile, notably through a global partnership with the Association of Chartered Certified Accountants, which gives the institution far more students than any other UK university – at least 200,000 – taking its qualifications in other countries.

At home, the university is two years into a £220m development programme. It moved into a new campus for nursing on a business park in Swindon in 2016, and opened a bio-imaging unit on the main Headington campus in Oxford for its biological light and electron microscopes. A new business school on the same site is now open, next to collaborative teaching and social learning spaces.

The Harcourt Hill campus, which houses the education school, is being refurbished and acquiring a teaching and learning hub, while the sports facilities are upgraded. The Wheatley campus, which is the base for engineering and technology, is also being refurbished, with the library and student centre being redesigned after feedback from students and staff, adding recreational space and a gym.

Another innovative collaboration was launched last year, combining education, clinical practice and research across the nursing, midwifery and allied health professions. The Oxford School of Nursing and Midwifery is a partnership between the university, Oxford University Hospitals NHS Foundation Trust and Oxford Health NHS Foundation Trust, under the umbrella of the Oxford Academic Health Science Centre. Brookes offers probably the most valuable bursary at any UK university, in the shape of the Tessa Jane Evans bursary for nursing, worth £30,000 over three years to three candidates from low-income households.

In 2015 the university celebrated the 150th anniversary of its establishment as the

---

Headington Campus
OX3 0BP
01865 483 040
admissions@brookes.ac.uk
www.brookes.ac.uk
www.brookesunion.org.uk
Open Days 2018:
June 30 (Oxford);
March 24, June 23
(Swindon for
nursing etc)

The Times and The Sunday Times **Rankings**

Overall Ranking: **84** (last year: 69)

Teaching quality	78.2%	=93
Student experience	77.2%	=83
Research quality	11.4%	58
Entry standards	129	=68
Graduate prospects	72.5%	=69
Good honours	73%	61
Expected completion rate	89.7%	=40
Student/staff ratio	16.6	=80
Services and facilities/student	£1,623	109

Oxford School of Art. There is a tradition of innovation that dates back to its time as a polytechnic, when it pioneered the modular degree system that has swept British higher education. The latest example is the grade point average (GPA) system that gives students a more accurate assessment of their work. Students still receive the traditional degree classification as well, but all their marks from the first year onwards now count towards their GPA.

The university excelled in the 2014 Research Excellence Framework when it entered more academics than most of its peer group and still saw almost 60% of its work rated as world-leading or internationally excellent. There were particularly good results in architecture, English and history. The overall performance produced a 41% rise in research funding, among the top ten increases in England.

Brookes is particularly popular with independent schools, which provide more than a quarter of the undergraduates, by far the highest proportion among the post-1992 non-specialist universities and three times the national average for the university's subjects and entry grades. The institution has been trying to attract more students from state schools and has targeted areas in Oxfordshire and the wider region.

Brookes ID, launched for the current academic year, enables students to track their progress in a wide range of co-curricular activities and receive recognition of their achievements through a purpose-built app. Those who develop in multiple areas will be recognised through an annual awards ceremony.

The impressive sports facilities include a 25-metre swimming pool and nine-hole golf course. Brookes is particularly strong in rowing, and Dame Katherine Grainger, silver medallist at the Rio Olympics after her gold in London in 2012, is chancellor of the university. Its cricketers combine with Oxford University to take on county teams. The students' union runs one of the biggest entertainment venues in Oxford, a city that can be expensive, but which offers enough to satisfy most people who study there.

Tuition fees

» Fees for UK/EU students 2018–19	£9,250
Foundation courses	£7,200
» Fees for international students 2018–19	£13,150–£14,000
» For scholarship and bursary information see https://www.brookes.ac.uk/international/fees-and-funding/scholarships-and-financial-support	
» Graduate salaries	£21,909

Students

Undergraduates	12,185	(1,715)
Postgraduates	1,720	(2,220)
Applications per place	6.8	
Overall offer rate	80.5%	
International students	15.6%	
Mature students	25.3%	
From state-sector schools	72.9%	
From working-class homes	27.9%	

Accommodation

University-provided places: 5,454
Percentage catered: 3%
Catered costs: £147 per week
Self-catered: £81 – £175 per week
First year students are guaranteed accommodation
www.brookes.ac.uk/studying-at-brookes/accommodation

Plymouth University

Private companies are building so much student accommodation in Plymouth it has been predicted that some of it will become "high-rise ghost towns" with few tenants, a situation alarming city councillors. Two new blocks for more than 500 students are now open and another with 600 bedrooms is planned, even though the university has warned that it is not expecting to expand. With 2,800 places already on the institution's approved list, students could find themselves in a buyer's market.

The university is concentrating its investment on academic developments. The newly-opened £17m Derriford research facility, brings together medical, dental and biomedical research under one roof. The university is also opening a new school of nursing in Exeter, adding to its provision in Plymouth and Truro.

Other developments include the creation of the Plymouth Conservatoire, with the university working alongside the Theatre Royal Plymouth across a range of performing arts degrees. Plymouth is also launching the Tamar Engineering Project, designed to increase the number of students moving into engineering, providing successful applicants from priority backgrounds with one-to-one mentoring from an industry professional, a financial award of £3,000 and a £1,500 course fee-waiver per year of study.

Such activity came too late to save Plymouth from a bronze rating in the new Teaching Excellence Framework. The panel acknowledged the university's efforts to enhance satisfaction and outcomes for part-time students and its continuing initiatives to improve graduate prospects, as well as the significant investment in physical and digital learning resources. But its record on graduate employment and part-time students' satisfaction levels pulled it down.

Plymouth has also dropped six places in our table, wiping out the gains made in the last edition. Satisfaction scores have declined by more than the national average, especially in relation to the broad student experience where questions in the National Student Survey are more challenging this year.

However, only two post-1992 universities produced better results in the 2014 Research Excellence Framework and the Times Higher Education magazine ranks it among the 70 best universities in the world that are less than 50 years old. Plymouth entered a far larger proportion of its academics for the framework than most of its peer group and still saw nearly two-thirds of its research judged world-leading or internationally excellent.

Plymouth is the only post-1992 university with its own medical school since ending its partnership with the University of Exeter

Drake Circus
Plymouth PL4 8AA
01752 585 858
prospectus@plymouth.ac.uk
www.plymouth.ac.uk
www.upsu.com
Open Days 2018:
April 28, June 27

The Times and The Sunday Times Rankings

Overall Ranking: =86 (last year: 80)

Teaching quality	80.9%	=53
Student experience	79.7%	=43
Research quality	15.9%	57
Entry standards	125	80
Graduate prospects	71.5%	74
Good honours	70.6%	71
Expected completion rate	84.5%	72
Student/staff ratio	16.1	=69
Services and facilities/student	£1,659	105

in the management of the former Peninsula College of Medicine and Dentistry. The school had an initial entry of only 75 students taking medicine, although Plymouth kept all 50 of Peninsula's places in dentistry. It has already expanded to more than 300 students through an increase in core numbers and the addition of degrees in biomedical and healthcare sciences. The university is the largest provider of nursing, midwifery and health professional education and training in the region.

With about 27,000 students, Plymouth is the largest higher education institution in Devon and Cornwall, and was the first university to be awarded Regional Growth Fund money to promote economic development. It has declared an intention to become "the enterprise university, truly 'business-engaging' and delivering outstanding economic, social and cultural benefits". Plymouth has one of the country's top ten business incubation facilities, part of its managed portfolio of £100m of incubation and innovation assets.

The undergraduate intake reflects Plymouth's position as the working-class hub of the southwest, with more than 92% of students state-educated and more than a third from the poorest social classes when last surveyed. About 12,000 students undertake work-based learning or placements with employability skills embedded throughout the curriculum, while the Plymouth award recognises extracurricular achievements. There are also 17 partner colleges across the southwest delivering the university's degrees, as well as others in Greece, Switzerland, Hong Kong, Sri Lanka and Singapore.

University amenities include the medical and wellbeing centres and a student village. Upgraded facilities for watersports and an £850,000 fitness centre have added to the sports provision, while a range of sports scholarships and bursaries support high-flyers. The university has a partnership with Plymouth Albion rugby club to promote and support sport in the city and was one of the investors in the £46m-plus Plymouth Life Centre. The city centre is not short of student-orientated nightlife.

Tuition fees

» Fees for UK/EU students 2018–19 £9,250
» Fees for international students 2018–19 £13,000
  Dentistry and Medicine £18,600–£34,500
» For scholarship and bursary information see www.plymouth.ac.uk/study/fees/scholarships-and-bursaries-and-fees
» Graduate salary £21,400

Students

Undergraduates	17,215	(2,860)
Postgraduates	1,315	(1,760)
Applications per place	4.8	
Overall offer rate	87.8%	
International students	7.7%	
Mature students	23.3%	
From state-sector schools	93.9%	
From working-class homes	31.9%	

Accommodation

University-provided places: 3,060
Percentage catered: 0%
Self-catered: £97 – £168 per week
First year students are guaranteed accommodation
www.plymouth.ac.uk/student-life/services/accommodation

Plymouth Marjon University

Declines in student satisfaction and graduate prospects have cancelled out most of the progress that the newly renamed Plymouth Marjon University made in our table last year. It has dropped into the bottom ten and is well inside it for the proportion of leavers in professional jobs or further study six months after graduation.

The Plymouth-based university was given a silver rating, however, in the Teaching Excellence Framework (TEF), which used older statistics than those in our table, as well as allowing for the backgrounds of undergraduates.

The TEF panel found "appropriate levels of contact time on courses, and a personalised approach to delivery that promotes good engagement". Course design and assessment practices ensured that students were stretched, it said.

Marjon was also placed top of an index of social mobility for the graduate-level jobs secured by students recruited from poorer backgrounds, although this has not been updated recently. Nearly all the undergraduates are state-educated and nearly 40% come from the four lowest socioeconomic groups.

Applications have dropped by a third since the last year before £9,000 fees were introduced. The numbers starting courses have also fallen, but only by 10%, thanks partly to a much higher offer rate.

The university has adopted Plymouth Marjon as its trading name, ditching the cumbersome official moniker, University of St Mark and St John, Plymouth, for the title by which it has long been popularly known. It has launched a dozen new degrees, as it pursues its plan for considerable expansion over the coming decade. They range from a foundation degree in theology to a four-year integrated master's in osteopathic medicine. They also include a new law degree, one in musical theatre and one in forensic criminology.

Marjon suffers in our table for a decision not to take part in the 2014 Research Excellence Framework, which leaves it last in our rankings for research quality. It was the only publicly funded university for more than 20 years to submit no work for the official assessments of research. A new research strategy has reversed the policy, but the fruits of this will not be measured until 2021 when the next research assessments are due.

Established in the 1840s as a Church of England teacher training college in London, with the son of poet Samuel Taylor Coleridge as its first principal, the university describes itself as "arguably the third-oldest higher education institution in England". The College of St Mark and St John only moved to Plymouth in 1973.

Still officially a Church of England voluntary institution, it was one of several

---

Derriford Road
Plymouth PL6 8BH
01752 636 890
admissions@marjon.ac.uk
www.marjon.ac.uk
www.marjonsu.com
Open Day 2018:
June 9

The Times and The Sunday Times **Rankings**

Overall Ranking: =119 (last year: 105)

Teaching quality	81.5%	44
Student experience	78.7%	=66
Research quality	0%	127
Entry standards	137	=53
Graduate prospects	59.9%	124
Good honours	58.2%	125
Expected completion rate	80.7%	=100
Student/staff ratio	21.3	126
Services and facilities/student	£1,995	=78

religious foundations among the universities awarded that status in 2012. The attractive modern Chaplaincy Centre is at the heart of the campus, but there is less emphasis on religion in the new university's promotional material than at some of its counterparts.

The university is located on the expanding north side of Plymouth, close to the Dartmoor National Park and within easy reach of the sea. The green agenda extends to an on-campus duck pond and nature trail. A new student-centred hub opens this autumn, as a one-stop shop for student support services such as learning support, employability and career development, counselling, placement support and financial advice. It also contains a new bar that will double as a cafe and social space during the day.

Every course includes core personal development training where students work in small tutorial groups and have individual coaching.

Marjon lists sport at the top of its list of specialisms, followed by education, languages, journalism and the creative arts. Recent campus developments have included extensive refurbishment of the library to provide a new social learning space. New sports science labs include a climate chamber, a Bod Pod body-composition tracking system and an anti-gravity treadmill.

The university has also opened Plymouth Studio School on its campus for 14–19-year-olds focusing on careers in sport, sport coaching and development or sport management.

Teacher training remains strong, with Ofsted giving an outstanding rating for the leadership and management of courses that run in four counties, as well as in Cyprus and Germany.

Sports facilities are extremely good: there is a floodlit 3G pitch, climbing wall, 25-metre indoor swimming pool and well-equipped gym, as well as a rehabilitation clinic. A second all-weather hockey pitch is on the way.

There are residential places on campus for 456 students between seven halls of residence and 38 village houses, where rents compare favourably with most universities. First-year students are guaranteed places and encouraged to take them up while they make the transition to higher education. Those living on campus may only bring a car in exceptional circumstances, but the lively city centre is a short bus ride from the campus.

Tuition fees

» Fees for UK/EU students 2018–19 £9,250
   Foundation courses £6,000
» Fees for international students 2018–19 £10,500–£11,000
» For scholarship and bursary information see www.marjon.ac.uk/student-life/student-support/student-funding-advice
» Graduate salary £16,500

Students		
Undergraduates	1,855	(145)
Postgraduates	225	(140)
Applications per place	3.4	
Overall offer rate	86.5%	
International students	1.5%	
Mature students	33.8%	
From state-sector schools	97.3%	
From working-class homes	37%	

Accommodation

University-provided places: 456
Percentage catered: 64%
Catered costs: £95 – £110 per week
Self-catered: £90 – £110 per week
First year students are guaranteed accommodation
www.marjon.ac.uk/student-life/accommodation

University of Portsmouth

Portsmouth is the top university in the country for boosting the salaries of graduates, if their backgrounds, qualifications and subjects are taken into account, according to The Economist. Although the average salary of Portsmouth graduates was only £26,168 five years into their careers, compared with £45,950 for their London School of Economics counterparts, the magazine calculated that this was £3,093 more than might have been expected. The advantages enjoyed by LSE graduates might have been expected to produce £609 more.

In our table, the university is on the verge of the top 30 (and level with Southampton) for employment and further study six months after graduating. Overall, Portsmouth is up six places and close to the top 50, with only five post-1992 universities ahead of it. There have been big improvements in graduate prospects and in spending on student services.

The university achieved a gold rating in the Teaching Excellence Framework (TEF) this year. The independent panel found "optimum" levels of student engagement and commitment to learning that was secured through excellent and integrated teaching and assessment practices. The TEF also said that industry-leading physical and digital resources provided real and simulated

learning opportunities, which were used by students to develop their independence and confidence, enhancing learning and progression.

The TEF rating may help revive applications to Portsmouth, which have fallen for the past two years. They dropped in 2017 in line with the national average. An increased offer rate helped the university to achieve a record level of enrolments in 2016.

Portsmouth is placing its hopes for the future on giving students the hands-on experience needed to succeed in their chosen careers. Recent developments enable students to dispense medicines for a high-street pharmacy in the university's dispensary, treat NHS patients in its dental clinic, access the same data and analytics as City traders in its Bloomberg suite, work alongside police officers in a forensic centre and develop skills in a professional-standard interpreter training suite.

New courses this autumn include adult nursing and optometry, taught in the university's Centre for Simulation in Health and Care. Health subjects led the way to a good performance by Portsmouth in the 2014 Research Excellence Framework. Almost two-thirds of the research was rated world-leading or internationally excellent. The best results came in dentistry, nursing and pharmacy, and in physics, with about 90% of the submission reaching the top two categories.

Academic Registry
University House
Portsmouth PO1 2UP
023 9284 5566
admissions@port.ac.uk
www.port.ac.uk
www.upsu.net
Open Days 2018:
check website

The Times and The Sunday Times Rankings

Overall Ranking: **53** (last year: 59)

Teaching quality	82.4%	=29
Student experience	81.3%	=26
Research quality	8.6%	71
Entry standards	124	=81
Graduate prospects	80.3%	=31
Good honours	73.9%	54
Expected completion rate	86%	64
Student/staff ratio	15.4	=49
Services and facilities/student	£2,159	56

The Future Technology Centre gives engineering students hands-on experience of specialist technology. Innovation engineering courses will use the facilities to teach engineering fundamentals, combined with projects that address problems in health, humanitarianism and the environment.

The university has stepped up its support for students and their wellbeing. Academic staff, including personal tutors, have been trained in awareness of mental health issues and how best to support their students. It uses an app to promote communication between students and wellbeing services.

Teaching in all subjects is concentrated on the Guildhall campus in the centre of Portsmouth, with most residential accommodation nearby. The campus has undergone much redevelopment, with the library remodelled to provide more access to study spaces and IT equipment. About 700 self-issue laptops are available via laptop lockers located around the campus.

Portsmouth has one of the country's largest language departments, teaching six languages to degree level and offering free language courses to all students. About 1,000 students go abroad for part of their course, and at least as many come from the Continent. The university is an official centre of teaching and research about the EU and has 3,000 international students from further afield.

A number of subjects now offer common first years, with specialisation in later years, allowing students to select final degree programmes that suit their skills and interests.

A £6.5m student centre caters for the multicultural population of the university and includes alcohol-free areas.

Sport, exercise and fitness facilities include gyms, dance studios and a sports hall. The university's seafront location provides an excellent base for watersports and nearly £1m was invested in an all-weather pitch suitable for football, rugby, lacrosse and American football.

Many students live in Southsea, which has a vibrant social scene and quirky shops. A new hall of residence for 2017–18 enables Portsmouth to guarantee accommodation to all new students who apply in time and make the university their firm choice.

Tuition fees
- » Fees for UK/EU students 2018–19 £9,250
- » Fees for international students 2018–19 £13,200–£15,100
  Dental therapy £25,400
- » For scholarship and bursary information see www.port.ac.uk/application-fees-and-funding/undergraduate-fees-and-funding
- » Graduate salary £20,500

Students

Undergraduates	16,825	(1,920)
Postgraduates	1,695	(1,620)
Applications per place	5.4	
Overall offer rate	96.3%	
International students	14.8%	
Mature students	12.7%	
From state-sector schools	96.9%	
From working-class homes	32.9%	

Accommodation

University-provided places: 4,290
Percentage catered: 14%
Catered costs: £107 – £157 per week
Self-catered: £89 – £148 per week
First year students are guaranteed accommodation
www.port.ac.uk/accommodation

Queen Margaret University

Queen Margaret University (QMU) would have climbed up our table this year had it not been for a disastrous performance in the National Student Survey. The proportion of final-year undergraduates satisfied with teaching quality has fallen by more than five percentage points, leaving the university in the bottom three on this measure. In the sections relating to the broader student experience, the decline was an almost unprecedented 12 percentage points.

In other respects, the university has made good progress, especially on graduate prospects, where the proportion of leavers in professional employment or further study six months after graduation is up by almost 20 percentage points and QMU is on the verge of the top 50. Overall, the university is within a single place of last year's position, just outside the top 100, and applications for courses last year were up by an impressive 9%, at a time when most institutions faced falling demand for places.

In common with several other Scottish institutions, QMU did not enter the Teaching Excellence Framework (TEF). But the university retains a focus on some of the priorities shared by the TEF. Its Strategy 150, setting targets up to QMU's 150th anniversary in 2025, says: "A student-centred approach is integral to our strategy and we will continue to nurture our culture of providing personalised support."

This is done partly through the university's Centre for Academic Practice, which provides support both for those who teach and study at QMU. It seeks to "optimise learning" through the convergence of research and technological advancements. QMU has three "flagship areas" for teaching and research: health and rehabilitation, creativity and culture, and sustainable business. It expects to add others, such as food and drink, in the next few years. It has launched the Scottish Centre for Food Development and Innovation and has a partnership with the Edinburgh New Town Cookery School, run by a QMU graduate, to support students on its international hospitality management degree.

The university is providing more work placements in partnership with organisations such as Ryder Cup Europe and has a highly successful employer mentoring scheme. The programme matches third and fourth-year students with experienced professionals who have relevant industry experience.

Named after Saint Margaret, the 11th-century Queen of Scotland, the institution dates from 1875 and was originally a cookery school for women. The university moved into an impressive, modern campus, designed in consultation with the students, in the seaside

---

University Drive
Edinburgh EH21 6UU
0131 474 0000
admissions@qmu.ac.uk
www.qmu.ac.uk
www.qmusu.org.uk
Open Days 2018:
September 22,
October 6

The Times and The Sunday Times **Rankings**

Overall Ranking: **=102** (last year: =101)

Teaching quality	74.9%	118
Student experience	71.3%	118
Research quality	6.6%	80
Entry standards	139	50
Graduate prospects	76.7%	=53
Good honours	77.8%	38
Expected completion rate	79.2%	=108
Student/staff ratio	18.1	=106
Services and facilities/student	£1,569	114

town of Musselburgh, to the southeast of Edinburgh, when it was awarded university status ten years ago.

The campus is one of the most environmentally sustainable in the UK, exceeding current standards. Sustainability is a top priority in the curriculum as well as in the way the university operates.

It has more than 6,000 students, three-quarters of them female, divided between two schools: arts, social sciences and management, and health sciences. The university promises "inter-professional" teaching and research to encourage the professions to work better together.

Health is an area of particular strength: QMU has the broadest range of allied health courses in Scotland, from dietetics, podiatry and audiology to art therapy, music therapy and health psychology.

Research ratings improved considerably in the 2014 Research Excellence Framework. Although only 22% of the eligible staff were entered, almost 60% of their work was considered world-leading or internationally excellent. Renowned for its research in speech and language sciences, QMU saw 92% of its work in this area rated in the top two categories, placing the university second in the UK and first in Scotland.

It has launched new centres for research and knowledge exchange, which place academics in direct contact with business, industry and the health profession. The Business Gateway on campus promotes entrepreneurship and offers support and advice to student and graduate start-ups.

The campus is located next to Musselburgh train station, from where Edinburgh city centre is less than ten minutes away. There are 800 residential places on campus, about 300 of them larger, premier rooms with double beds and more space. As part of its accommodation service, QMU offers the ResLife programme, run with the sports centre and students' union, that includes a range of social, educational, recreational and cultural activities to help students settle in and learn new skills.

Tuition fees

- » Fees for Scottish and EU students 2018–19   £0–£1,820
- » Fees for non-Scottish UK students 2018–19   £7,000
- » Fees for international students 2018–19   £12,000–£13,000
  Medicine   £39,000
- » For scholarship and bursary information see www.qmu.ac.uk/study-here/fees-and-funding/undergraduate-funding
- » Graduate salary   £18,720

Students

Undergraduates	3,005	(650)
Postgraduates	560	(1,065)
Applications per place	7.5	
Overall offer rate	54.7%	
International students	17.4%	
Mature students	29.8%	
From state-sector schools	95.8%	
From working-class homes	34.4%	

Accommodation

University-provided places: 800
Percentage catered: 0%
Self-catered: £104 – £120 per week
First year students are guaranteed accommodation
www.qmu.ac.uk/accommodation/

Queen Mary, University of London

Queen Mary, University of London (QMUL) has introduced a new degree structure to improve students' networking and communication skills, and provide experience outside their subject. The QMUL Model will account for 10% of a student's degree, covering activities such as work experience, volunteering in the community, overseas travel, project work with local businesses and other organisations, learning a language and taking modules from other subjects.

The university sees the system as a new approach to degree-level study, enabling students to broaden their skills as part of their course. The new modules, which will count towards students' degree classifications, will be compulsory in the first year. Students will choose from a range of options, in consultation with their personal tutor, in subsequent years.

The initiative came too late to be considered in the government's Teaching Excellence Framework (TEF) this summer, in which QMUL received a silver rating. The TEF panel was impressed by the quality of its coaching programmes, mentoring schemes and employer engagement that help students gain highly skilled employment.

Like other London institutions, QMUL is hampered in our table (and the TEF) by low student satisfaction scores. It is in the bottom 20 for teaching quality, the score derived from the National Student Survey, in contrast to a top-20 place for research and a top-ten ranking for staffing levels.

Overall, it dropped three places in the latest table and out of the top 40.

QMUL does not suffer from the dispersed nature of other London institutions, with most of its 17,000 undergraduates both taught and housed on a self-contained campus in the fashionable East End. The medical faculty at Barts and the London School of Medicine and Dentistry is based in Whitechapel.

The university's undergraduate intake has grown by almost half since it joined the Russell Group in 2012. Sixteen new degrees were launched last year, mainly in engineering, economics and maths. QMUL is adding more options to study abroad, enabling students to apply for a degree that includes this element at the outset, rather than having to apply during their course, as they have had to up to now.

Students can now study at Queen Mary's new medical school in Malta, which closely matches the London programme. The venture, taught by QMUL staff, will add to the university's 5,500 international students.

QMUL also has also established a joint research institute with China's Northwestern Polytechnic University (NPU), focusing on the modern equivalent of the Silk Road,

Mile End Road
London E1 4NS
020 7882 5511
admissions@qmul.ac.uk
www.qmul.ac.uk
www.qmsu.org
Open days 2018:
June 22, 23, October 6

The Times and The Sunday Times **Rankings**

Overall Ranking: **43** (last year: 40)

Teaching quality	76%	114
Student experience	76.8%	91
Research quality	37.9%	19
Entry standards	155	36
Graduate prospects	73.6%	64
Good honours	76.6%	45
Expected completion rate	91.6%	=28
Student/staff ratio	12.5	=10
Services and facilities/student	£2,604	26

the One Belt and One Road initiative. Collaboration between the two universities includes two BEng programmes in materials science and engineering, and polymers materials science and engineering. Courses are jointly taught in English by NPU and Queen Mary staff at NPU's campuses in Xi'an, in China's Shaanxi province. Successful students will be awarded a degree from both universities.

Improvements to the Mile End campus that have cost almost £100m are nearing completion. A new graduate centre that opened this year also provides new premises for the school of economics and finance. The People's Palace, which brought education to the Victorian masses, is still QMUL's most recognisable feature and has been restored to host cultural events.

The medical school, which is rated in the top 100 in the world by QS, is based in the £45m Blizard Building. The Whitechapel campus houses the Centre of the Cell, the first science education centre in the world to be located in working biomedical research laboratories.

Medicine and the other health subjects did well in the 2014 Research Excellence Framework, but the university's best results came in the humanities. About 95% of the research in linguistics and in music, drama and the performing arts was rated as world-leading or internationally excellent, while more than 85% of QMUL's entire submission reached the top two categories.

Most lectures are filmed and made available online to allow students to go back over parts that they may not have understood.

The university has by far the highest proportion of undergraduates from working-class homes in the Russell Group – more than a third. Many come from London's ethnic minority groups. There are bursaries worth £1,571 a year for students whose household income is less than £25,000, or £1,256 where income is below £42,600.

For Mile End students, social life centres on the campus, which features a refurbished students' union. A subsidised health and fitness centre has improved the sports facilities. Students welcome the relatively low prices in east London, and their proximity to the lively youth culture of Shoreditch, Brick Lane and Spitalfields. Queen Mary students can use the sports facilities at the Queen Elizabeth Olympic Park, including the Copper Box arena and the Aquatic Centre's swimming pool.

Tuition fees

- » Fees for UK/EU students 2018–19 £9,250
- » Fees for international students 2018–19 £15,400–£21,500 Dentistry £33,750 Medicine £34,300
- » For scholarship and bursary information see www.qmul.ac.uk/undergraduate/feesandfunding/bursaries
- » Graduate salary £24,000

Students

Undergraduates	12,375	(10)
Postgraduates	3,590	(1,160)
Applications per place	8.2	
Overall offer rate	76.9%	
International students	23.8%	
Mature students	9.8%	
From state-sector schools	88.7%	
From working-class homes	37%	

Accommodation

University-provided places: 1,500
Percentage catered: 0%
Self-catered: £129 – £172 per week
First year students from outside London are given priority
www.residences.qmul.ac.uk

Queen's University, Belfast

The return of Queen's to our top 30 was short-lived, with the university falling 12 places in the table this year. It has not been able to maintain the exceptional level of satisfaction with the student experience demonstrated in the 2016 National Student Survey and there have been marginal declines in other areas.

Queen's has ambitious plans for the future, however. It has invested £350m in campus improvements over the past ten years and is planning to spend the same again in the next ten. A computer science hub to support expansion in the subject, a £20m School of Law building and the Wellcome-Wolfson Institute for Experimental Medicine have all opened in the past year. A new school of biological sciences and city-centre accommodation for 1,200 students will follow in 2018.

The university has launched no fewer than 20 new degrees, mainly in the biological sciences, pharmacy and music. Those in the biological sciences are four-year master's degrees, providing high-level research skills and workplace experience with access to undergraduate student support.

Applications and enrolments have been running at record levels for the past four years. Uncertainty over fee levels,

with no devolved government in place for Northern Ireland, has not helped this year's recruitment. Yet a 2% decline in applications was half the UK average.

A member of the Russell Group, Queen's is recognised as Northern Ireland's premier university, with graduates in senior positions in many of the province's top 100 companies. It is based in an attractive part of south Belfast, with easy access to the city centre. Almost 100 of the university's buildings are listed, complemented by recent developments such as the £50m McClay Library, which has won national awards.

Queen's is in our top 15 for research after entering 95% of its academics for the 2014 Research Excellence Framework, a proportion matched only by Cambridge. In the large submission, 77% of the research was considered world-leading or internationally excellent and 14 subject areas were ranked in the UK's top 20.

The university has since won a Queen's Anniversary prize for research and technology transfer in cyber-security, and has been awarded Northern Ireland's first Regius professorship in electronics and computer engineering.

It has established four global research institutes in food security; health sciences; electronics, communications and information technology; and global peace, security and justice. Queen's claims to be the UK's top university for the commercialisation of

---

University Road
Belfast BT7 1NN
028 9097 3838
admissions@qub.ac.uk
www.qub.ac.uk
www.qubsu.org
Open Days 2018:
check website

The Times and The Sunday Times Rankings

Overall Ranking: **38** (last year: 26)

Teaching quality	79.9%	=70
Student experience	79.7%	=43
Research quality	39.7%	14
Entry standards	153	=37
Graduate prospects	79.9%	36
Good honours	77.9%	37
Expected completion rate	91.2%	=31
Student/staff ratio	15.6	=55
Services and facilities/student	£2,171	54

intellectual property and the establishment of knowledge transfer partnerships, of which it has about 350.

Non-denominational teaching is enshrined in a charter that has guaranteed student representation and equal rights for women since 1908. Queen's was one of four university colleges for the whole of Ireland in the 19th century, and still draws students from all over the island. However, the majority come from Northern Ireland and Queen's suffers in the comparison of entry grades because relatively few sixth-formers in the province take four A-levels.

The university has 1,800 international students and is a favourite destination for American Fulbright scholars. It is among the top ten universities in Europe for the number of students who go on work placements abroad as part of the Erasmus scheme. Undergraduates are encouraged to take language programmes via online tuition from any computer in the university. IT facilities are good: Queen's was the first institution to meet the national target of providing at least one computer workstation for every five undergraduate students.

The university's cinema, art gallery and theatre are open to students and the wider community alike. The much-improved city centre is not short of nightlife, but the Queen's social scene is concentrated on the students' union and the surrounding area.

Belfast student rents were rated the cheapest among UK cities in one recent report, and the university will own, manage or endorse 4,000 rooms when its new development opens.

Sports facilities include pitches for rugby, football and Gaelic sport, climbing walls and squash courts. The Physical Education Centre provides physiotherapy, sports massage and podiatry, and there is a boathouse for rowers on the River Lagan. An elite athlete programme offers up to £8,000 of support for leading performers.

Tuition fees

» Fees for Northern Ireland/EU students 2018–19 £4,160
» Fees for other UK students 2018–19 £9,250
» Fees for international students 2018–19 £15,550–£19,500
 Medicine (clinical years) £37,695
» For scholarship and bursary information see
 www.qub.ac.uk/study/undergraduate/
 fees-and-scholarships
» Graduate salary £21,000

Students		
Undergraduates	15,055	(3,905)
Postgraduates	2,905	(2,005)
Applications per place	7.1	
Overall offer rate	85.2%	
International students	8.2%	
Mature students	18.2%	
From state-sector schools	98.4%	
From working-class homes	31.9%	

Accommodation
University-provided places: 2,886
Percentage catered: 16%
Catered costs: £113 – £156 per week
Self-catered: £73 – £165 per week
First year students are guaranteed accommodation
www.qub.ac.uk/about/campus-and-facilities/accommodation

University of Reading

Reading was forced by the Advertising Standards Authority to withdraw a claim on its website that it was among the top 1% of the world's universities. Since it is ranked in the top 200 both by QS and Times Higher Education, the claim was almost certainly accurate, but the university had to admit it could not prove it because not all universities are ranked. In the UK, it is in the top 25% and only a decline in student satisfaction prevented it from gaining a place in our top 30 this year.

The university was awarded silver in the government's Teaching Excellence Framework last year. The awards panel found high-quality physical and digital resources, with particularly consistent use of the virtual learning environment and effective integration of student support services with academic provision. There was consistent engagement of students with developments from the forefront of research, scholarship and practice, the panel added.

Teaching and learning facilities have been at the forefront of a £200m investment programme, with many of the developments a response to student feedback. Work has started on a health and life sciences building that will house one of the largest teaching labs in the UK and bring together a school that is currently spread across the main Whiteknights campus. More teaching and learning space is being added at the Henley Business School to meet increasing demand there and there will be a new home for the school of architecture.

A new annual £1m capital fund has been set up to improve the student experience, with the successful projects chosen by student union officers. The first six projects, for 2018, include an extension of the filming of lectures, relaxation zones and lockers, a student union app and a new 4G sports pitch. In the longer term, there are plans to improve the quads at the centre of the main campus to create a more vibrant focal point for the university.

A second project will create an integrated series of routes that facilitate safe and enjoyable walking and cycling on the campus. The £35m refurbishment of the URS building is on hold as the university reconsiders its plans following a decision by Historic England to list it.

Reading's 2026: Transform programme is intended to help the university become a "larger, vibrant and more sustainable institution" by its centenary year. The university's offer rate has declined since the introduction of £9,000 fees and both applications and enrolments have been steady in recent years.

Originally Oxford University's extension college, Reading was one of only two universities established between the two world wars. Its main campus, which has won a series of Green Gown environmental awards,

---

Whiteknights
PO Box 217
Reading RG6 6AH
0118 378 8372
www.reading.ac.uk
(enquire via website)
www.rusu.co.uk
Open Days 2018:
June 15, 16

Edinburgh
Belfast
Cardiff London
READING

The Times and The Sunday Times **Rankings**

Overall Ranking: **32** (last year: 31)

Teaching quality	78.2%	=93
Student experience	77.2%	=83
Research quality	36.5%	29
Entry standards	142	47
Graduate prospects	75.6%	58
Good honours	81.2%	24
Expected completion rate	91.5%	30
Student/staff ratio	14.4	34
Services and facilities/student	£2,344	35

is set in 320 acres of parkland on the outskirts of Reading. There is a second site in Reading, and the university also owns about 2,000 acres of farmland at nearby Sonning and Shinfield, where the renowned Centre for Dairy Research is located.

The former Henley Management College – now the university's business school – occupies an attractive site on the banks of the river at Henley-on-Thames. It houses postgraduate and executive programmes, while undergraduates are taught on the Whiteknights campus.

Reading also has a campus in Malaysia, which is expected to have 2,000 students by 2020. Located at Iskandar, on the southern tip of Malaysia, the site is shared with Newcastle and Southampton universities, which specialise in different disciplines.

About a fifth of Reading's undergraduates come from outside the UK, many of them are attracted by its global reputation for courses and research in agriculture and development. All undergraduates have the opportunity to go on work placements as part of their course, as well as taking career-management skills modules that contribute credits towards their degree classification.

Reading's online learning support system, which provides advice, exercises and information, has been bought by other universities and colleges. Sessions are delivered by academics and careers advisers, with input from alumni and leading employers.

Reading recorded a strong performance in the 2014 Research Excellence Framework (REF), in which real estate, planning and construction management were among the leading players. The school of architecture will help the university to capitalise on a strong reputation in the built environment. Reading entered more academics for assessment than most of its peers and saw almost 80% of its research rated as world-leading or internationally excellent.

The halls of residence are either on or within easy walking distance of the main campus and the large students' union has been voted among the best in Britain. There are more than 50 sports clubs and representative teams have a good record in inter-university competitions. Water sports are strong, with off-campus boathouses on the Thames and a sailing and canoeing club nearby.

The town may not be the most fashionable, but Reading has plenty of nightlife and an award-winning shopping centre, although the cost of living is high. Students who live off campus can make use of the free bus service to take them to the town centre.

Tuition fees

» Fees for UK/EU students 2018–19 £9,250
» Fees for international students 2018–19 £16,070–£19,330
» For scholarship and bursary information see www.reading.ac.uk/ready-to-study/fees-and-funding.aspx
» Graduate salary £21,500

Students

Undergraduates	10,230	(85)
Postgraduates	2,870	(1,790)
Applications per place	6.7	
Overall offer rate	89.4%	
International students	20.5%	
Mature students	7.9%	
From state-sector schools	87.4%	
From working-class homes	27.3%	

Accommodation

University-provided places: 4,982
Percentage catered: 18%
Catered costs: £143 – £180 per week
Self-catered: £116 – £200 per week
First year students are guaranteed accommodation
www.reading.ac.uk/ready-to-study/accommodation.aspx

Robert Gordon University

Robert Gordon University (RGU) was one of only five Scottish universities to enter the government's new Teaching Excellence Framework (TEF) and was rewarded with a gold rating. The panel was impressed by the range of opportunities for students to develop knowledge, skills and understanding that are most highly valued by employers, and to engage "consistently and frequently" with developments at the forefront of professional practice.

High graduate employment levels have been RGU's greatest strength since the time, at the start of the decade, when it was the leading post-1992 university in our table. It is still in the top 50 on this measure, but that compares with a place in the top 20 in our 2016 guide – and for many years before that – when the North Sea oil and gas industry was at its peak.

In spite of that, RGU was among the five leading universities in the UK – and top in Scotland – in The Economist's comparison of graduate salaries against the levels that might have been expected, allowing for backgrounds, subjects and prior qualifications. An already impressive average of £28,858 five years after graduation was £2,703 more than the researchers would have expected.

Overall, the university has moved up four places in this year's table but, at 82nd, it is 30 places lower than in its heyday. Entry standards were already the highest at any modern university and, like other universities in Scotland, RGU has benefited from the recalculation of Scottish qualifications in UCAS's new entry tariff. It now features in the top 25 in our table on this measure.

Applications have been falling but an increased offer rate has helped to ensure that the numbers starting degrees have grown for the past two years. One obvious attraction is a system of work placements, lasting up to a year, that has become the norm for all the university's degrees.

A £135m capital programme has been completed, bringing the university together on one site for the first time. All teaching now takes place on the Garthdee campus, on the southwest side of Aberdeen, overlooking the River Dee. A new building for the Scott Sutherland School of Architecture and Built Environment was the last piece of the jigsaw, although there will be further improvements after the sale of part of the university's historic city centre site.

A striking green glass library tower with spectacular views over the river and city has become a landmark at the heart of the campus. Previous developments included specialist facilities for the faculty of health and social care. The Aberdeen Business School, designed by Norman Foster, has been upgraded with new teaching and student

---

Garthdee House
Garthdee Road
Aberdeen AB10 7QB
01224 262 728
UGOffice@rgu.ac.uk
www.rgu.ac.uk
www.rguunion.co.uk
Open Days 2018:
check website

The Times and The Sunday Times **Rankings**

Overall Ranking: **82** (last year: =86)

Teaching quality	80.5%	=60
Student experience	78.6%	=68
Research quality	4%	=104
Entry standards	164	=23
Graduate prospects	77.8%	47
Good honours	69.5%	=80
Expected completion rate	85.1%	69
Student/staff ratio	18.1	=106
Services and facilities/student	£1,474	120

learning spaces and an open-plan area with IT access, group study areas, and exhibition and seminar space.

Named after an 18th-century philanthropist, RGU has a pedigree in education that goes back more than 250 years. The university has invested heavily in research, but made a relatively small submission to the 2014 Research Excellence Framework. More than 40% of the work assessed was placed in the top two categories, with the best results in health subjects and communication and media studies.

Nearly three quarters of the undergraduates either attend the business school or take courses in health and social care. Although the creative industries are a growth area, the university is still best known for its links with offshore industries. The RGU Oil and Gas Institute has a training simulator, providing a full-scale reproduction of an offshore platform.

Efforts to extend access to RGU beyond the normal higher education catchment have produced a diverse student population, with almost a third of undergraduates coming from working-class homes and 92% from state schools or colleges. There is a strong focus on new technology, including an award-winning virtual campus. The Moodle system, used by students on campus and others engaged in distance learning, provides teaching, online forums and options for submitting work electronically.

Aberdeen is a long way to go for students from some parts of the UK, but train and air links are excellent, and the city regularly features in top 10s for quality of life.

Researchers from the university have been working with Aberdeen City Council and other partners to develop innovative ways of integrating technology into the city's infrastructure, to improve the lives of residents. They have provided expertise in areas such as architecture and the built environment, creative and cultural business and computing. RGU is establishing a digital 'hub' at Garthdee, which will bring together equipment and expertise from across the university.

The sports and leisure facilities include a centre of excellence for hockey, a swimming pool and gyms. Although renting in the private sector can be expensive, RGU has enough residential places to accommodate first-years from outside the area.

Tuition fees

» Fees for Scottish and EU students 2018–19 £0 £1,820
» Fees for non-Scottish UK students 2018–19 £6,750–£9,000
» Fees for international students 2018–19 £12,360–£15,760
» For scholarship and bursary information see www.rgu.ac.uk/future-students/finance-and-scholarships/scholarships
» Graduate salary £22,000

Students		
Undergraduates	7,630	(1,365)
Postgraduates	1,425	(2,330)
Applications per place	4.7	
Overall offer rate	79.6%	
International students	14.1%	
Mature students	31%	
From state-sector schools	92.1%	
From working-class homes	32%	

Accommodation

University-provided places: 1,766
Percentage catered: 0%
Self-catered: £103 – £156 per week
First year students from outside the area are guaranteed accommodation
www.rgu.ac.uk/student-life/accommodation

University of Roehampton

Roehampton is one of the few universities whose female graduates earn more than their male counterparts, five years into a career. Seven out of ten undergraduates are female and, as graduates, their earnings are higher in every subject except psychology by an average of £1,700 a year, according to new data released in the summer based on graduates' tax records.

The gender gap in recruitment reflects the domination of education, the arts and social sciences in the portfolio of degrees, and persists in spite of a much higher offer rate for male applicants. Overall, the numbers starting degrees have been rising gradually since £9,000 fees were introduced.

The university is making no apology for bucking the national trend for men to be paid more than women. Its oldest college, Whitelands, which celebrated its 175th anniversary in 2016, claims to have been the first in the country to open higher education to women.

All four colleges maintain some of the traditional ethos of their religious foundations: the Anglican Whitelands, the Roman Catholic Digby Stuart, the Methodist Southlands, and the Froebel, which follows the humanist teachings of Frederick Froebel. Students need not follow any of these denominations to enrol in the colleges, whose leisure facilities and bars are open to all members of the university. Roehampton also has a Jewish resource centre and Muslim prayer rooms.

A new library with 300,000 books and 1,200 study spaces, which is open to the public as well as students, is now the centrepiece of Roehampton's attractive parkland campus in southwest London where all four colleges are based.

Drama space has been upgraded and new computer suites added, and students' union facilities have been enhanced to cater for the increased number of students on campus. Another 359 student rooms and a conference centre were added in 2016.

Roehampton outperformed all post-1992 universities in the 2014 Research Excellence Framework, entering two-thirds of its eligible academics for assessment and still finding 66% of its work rated as world-leading or internationally excellent. The university had the most highly rated dance department in the UK, with 94% of research placed in the top two categories, while the results in education and English were among the best in London. Its successes produced a 40% increase in funding for research.

The university was given a bronze rating in the Teaching Excellence Framework (TEF), although its panel acknowledged that the involvement of employers ensured that

---

Grove House
Roehampton Lane
London SW15 5PJ
enquiries@roehampton.ac.uk
www.roehampton.ac.uk
www.roehamptonstudent.com
Open Days 2018:
March 15 (dance only)

The Times and The Sunday Times **Rankings**

Overall Ranking: **74** (last year: 78)

Teaching quality	76.7%	=107
Student experience	76.6%	=95
Research quality	24.5%	51
Entry standards	108	=121
Graduate prospects	69.3%	=89
Good honours	68.2%	=90
Expected completion rate	82.2%	=88
Student/staff ratio	14.3	33
Services and facilities/student	£2,126	61

programmes were contemporary. Course design and assessment practices mean that most students are stretched and acquire knowledge, skills and understanding that employers value, the panel added.

Education courses still account for a quarter of the students, although the university long ago diversified its offer at degree level. The law school welcomed its first students in 2015 and operates a legal advice clinic for the local community. International partnerships include an agreement with the EU Business School to offer Roehampton-accredited degrees to students across the Continent.

The Quality Assurance Agency complimented Roehampton on the accessibility of academic staff to students and the positive ways in which they responded to student needs.

Almost all of the undergraduates are state-educated, with 43% coming from working-class homes when this was last surveyed. The university does not offer bursaries to students from poor backgrounds, other than for care leavers, so only those winning scholarships will receive financial support on entry.

Another residential development, 20 minutes from the main campus by public transport at Vauxhall, features a swimming pool and other facilities and has brought the number of residential places to more than 2,300. The university is now able to guarantee accommodation for UK students who make

Roehampton their firm choice and apply by the end of May. International applicants have until the end of July.

While rents are not cheap in the private sector, students like the proximity of central London and the lively and attractive suburbs around Roehampton.

The sports facilities on campus have been enhanced, with a new gym, football pitches, running track and multiuse games area. The sport performance and rehabilitation centre provides well-equipped laboratory facilities and performance coaching.

Tuition fees

» Fees for UK/EU students 2018–19	£9,250
» Fees for international students 2018–19	£13,520
» For scholarship and bursary information see www.roehampton.ac.uk/finance/scholarships	
» Graduate salary	£20,592

Students

Undergraduates	6,885	(165)
Postgraduates	1,005	(695)
Applications per place	4.7	
Overall offer rate	91.3%	
International students	8.5%	
Mature students	15.3%	
From state-sector schools	96.2%	
From working-class homes	43%	

Accommodation

University-provided places: 2,325
Percentage catered: 0%
Self-catered: £117 – £174 per week
First year students are guaranteed accommodation
www.roehampton.ac.uk/accommodation

Royal Agricultural University

The Royal Agricultural University (RAU) has fallen more than 20 places in our new table, making a decline of 35 places in two years. A dramatic decrease in graduate prospects is the biggest factor in the latest drop, which leaves the university just outside the bottom 20 on this measure after ranking 50th for graduate jobs the previous year.

The number of students starting degrees at the RAU has almost doubled in 10 years, however, and applications for 2017 were up by another 5.7%, against the national trend. Two new degrees have boosted the demand for places, but the upwards swing was already established when university status was awarded in 2012.

Assessors in the new Teaching Excellence Framework placed the RAU in the silver category, commenting favourably on the high-quality rural estate and specialist facilities. The panel was impressed by the employer-informed course design, work placements and extracurricular opportunities for students to develop skills and attributes valued by businesses.

The links with agri-tech companies will be further enhanced by the opening of new workshops at the university's Rural Innovation Centre to research, create and test their products. The development is part of the Farm491 project, named after the number of hectares (about 1,200 acres) available here for research and testing. A "growth hub" will follow later this year on the main campus, providing business development and support networks, strategy and advisory services.

RAU was founded in 1845 as the Royal Agricultural College (the institution was the first of its type in the English-speaking world) on the initiative of the Fairford and Cirencester Farmers' Club, which was concerned at the lack of government support for education, particularly in relation to agriculture. Subsequently, every monarch since Queen Victoria has visited at least once.

Now operating as the RAU, it is sometimes described as the "Oxbridge of the countryside" because of its privileged intake and beautiful campus near Cirencester, in the Cotswolds. It is the only university in our table to recruit the majority of its undergraduates from independent schools, although almost a third also came from the four poorest socioeconomic groups when this was last surveyed.

Its size — with only 1,200 students it is the smallest publicly funded university — makes for exaggerated swings in the statistics. There are only a dozen honours degrees and four top-up courses for students who have completed foundation degrees, as well as a growing portfolio of master's courses.

An equine management and science school was established in 2014, joining those

Stroud Road
Cirencester GL7 6JS
01285 889 912
admissions@rau.ac.uk
www.rau.ac.uk
www.rau.ac.uk/university-life/
social/student-union
Open Days 2018:
April 9, June 25,
September 10

The Times and The Sunday Times **Rankings**

Overall Ranking: =86 (last year: 63)

Teaching quality	78.4%	=91
Student experience	78.8%	=64
Research quality	1.1%	125
Entry standards	114	=108
Graduate prospects	64.5%	108
Good honours	68.9%	=87
Expected completion rate	94.5%	=13
Student/staff ratio	21.8	128
Services and facilities/student	£2,705	18

focused on agriculture, food and the environment; business and entrepreneurship; and real estate and land management.

However, the university has one of the lowest scores for research. Only 12 staff were entered for the 2014 Research Excellence Framework — a quarter of those with research contracts — and just 7% of their work was placed in the top two categories.

The two university farms are both close to the campus. Coates Manor Farm focuses on arable farming, while Harnhill Farm is an example of an integrated livestock and cropping system. In addition, there is an equestrian centre providing stabling and livery facilities, and students also have access to a large dairy complex. All are run as commercial enterprises.

All business, equine and agriculture courses include a 20-week work placement. There is an extensive network of student placement sponsors in the UK and overseas, and part-time work is available both in the university and in nearby Cirencester. RAU has been rated within the top ten UK universities and colleges for its Enterprise activities.

On campus, there is a well-stocked library and computer suites, as well as specialist laboratories. The virtual learning environment ensures that all teaching materials are available online 24 hours a day.

The small numbers and countryside setting encourage a collegiate atmosphere.

The campus is the centre of social activities, including four balls each year. There are eight halls of residence on campus for undergraduates, with enough rooms for most first-years to be offered a place. Private rentals are available in Cirencester and the surrounding area.

Sport plays an important part in student life and, in addition to the normal range, there are clubs for polo, clay-pigeon shooting, beagling and team chasing (a cross-country equestrian sport). There are ample opportunities to explore the Cotswold countryside and London is only 90 minutes away by train.

The number of female students has been rising consistently and has almost reached parity with the men, while 15% are from outside the UK. The RAU also delivers degree courses in Hong Kong and mainland China.

Tuition fees

» Fees for UK/EU students 2018–19   £9,250
» Fees for international students 2018–19   £10,000
» For scholarship and bursary information see
   www.rau.ac.uk/study/undergraduate/fees-and-funding
» Graduate salary   £22,000

Students

Undergraduates	930	(35)
Postgraduates	225	(10)
Applications per place	3.4	
Overall offer rate	n/a	
International students	7.3%	
Mature students	16.7%	
From state-sector schools	46.8%	
From working-class homes	29.9%	

Accommodation

University-provided places: 360
Percentage catered: 75%
Catered costs: £110 – £223 per week
Self-catered: £131
First year students are given priority for accommodation
www.rau.ac.uk/university-life/accommodation

Royal Holloway, University of London

Royal Holloway claims to have one of the most beautiful campuses in the world, offering students a safe environment in Egham, Surrey, that is about 40 minutes by train from central London. Students seem to agree: satisfaction levels are the best in the University of London, and it is in the UK's top 30 for research.

London's "campus in the country", as Royal Holloway is known, has been growing in popularity. Almost nine out of ten school-leavers who apply receive at least a conditional offer of a place, and there have been gradual increases in enrolments for four years in a row.

Although applications have been running at record levels, there are still only 10,000 students. This mark is likely to be passed in the near future, with 15 new degrees being launched last year and the same again for 2018. Law, engineering and computer science were the main areas for 2017, while translation studies, ecology and conservation, classical archaeology and ancient history, drama with film, and American literature and creative writing follow this year. There is also a flexible new modern languages degree, which allows students to study one or more languages rather than having to specialise.

Royal Holloway received a silver rating in the new Teaching Excellence Framework.

The judging panel was impressed by the level of investment in elearning facilities and said students were engaged with developments from the forefront of research, scholarship and professional practice.

The 135-acre woodland campus near Windsor Great Park is dominated by the iconic Founder's Building, which was modelled on a French chateau and opened in 1886 by Queen Victoria. The facilities have been upgraded, with a new library and student services centre opening at the heart of the campus, with landscaped and pedestrianised spaces around it. The library provides seating for 1,150 and different zones to accommodate silent, social, creative and collaborative study, and there is a careers and recruitment hub as well as a shop, cafe and bank.

A science building is due to open during this academic year, with multifunctional laboratories and space for Royal Holloway's new electronic engineering department. One aim is to attract more female students into science and engineering – an appropriate brief for a college that was founded for women only. The gender balance is now roughly equal.

About 15% of the undergraduates come from independent schools, but the proportion from working-class homes is close to the national average for its courses and entry qualifications. There is a range of bursaries for undergraduates from low-income households and some for postgraduates so that students

---

Egham Hill
Egham TW20 0EX
01784 414 944
study@royalholloway.ac.uk
www.royalholloway.ac.uk
www.su.rhul.ac.uk
Open Days 2018:
check website

The Times and The Sunday Times Rankings		
Overall Ranking: =28 (last year: 34)		
Teaching quality	81.2%	48
Student experience	80%	=38
Research quality	36.3%	=30
Entry standards	148	=41
Graduate prospects	72%	=72
Good honours	76%	46
Expected completion rate	91%	33
Student/staff ratio	14.8	=41
Services and facilities/student	£2,265	44

who graduate with large debts are not deterred from continuing their studies.

More than 80% of the work assessed in the 2014 Research Excellence Framework was judged to be world-leading or internationally excellent, placing Royal Holloway in the top 30% on this measure in our table. Geography achieved the best results in England, while earth sciences, psychology, mathematics, music, media arts, and drama and theatre were all in their respective top 10s.

Royal Holloway has also been chosen as one of the government's eight centres of excellence in cyber-security research.

The Royal Holloway Passport, intended to enhance graduates' employability, recognises the additional skills that students gain from extracurricular activities. An advanced skills programme, covering information technology, communication skills and foreign languages, further encourages breadth of study. The university offers a number of edegrees and promotes numerous opportunities to study abroad, building on the international flavour of the campus and its links with institutions such as New York, Sydney and Yale universities.

New halls of residence have opened as part of a plan to add 600 study bedrooms to the already extensive stock of accommodation. First-year undergraduates are guaranteed a place, as long as they apply by early June with Royal Holloway as their firm choice. The 56 new townhouses include communal space and are surrounded by mature trees and green spaces.

Sports facilities are good and Royal Holloway has had considerable success with its award scheme for talented athletes. A thriving community action programme involves more than 1,000 students volunteering with various local organisations and charities. The recently refurbished students' union is the centre of the university's social life, putting on entertainment and activities every day of the week.

Tuition fees

» Fees for UK/EU students 2018–19 £9,250
» Fees for international students 2018–19 £16,500–£18,900
» For scholarship and bursary information see www.royalholloway.ac.uk/studyhere/undergraduate/feesandfunding/bursariesandscholarships/index.aspx
» Graduate salary £20,000

Students

Undergraduates	7,095	(380)
Postgraduates	1,790	(725)
Applications per place	7.1	
Overall offer rate	88.8%	
International students	26.4%	
Mature students	7%	
From state-sector schools	84.4%	
From working-class homes	28.4%	

Accommodation

University-provided places: 3,546
Percentage catered: 7%
Catered costs: £102 (30 weeks only) – £141 (meals extra)
Self-catered: £169 – £177 (30 weeks only)
First year students are guaranteed accommodation
www.royalholloway.ac.uk/studyhere/accommodation

University of St Andrews

As a perennial leader in the National Student Survey, it was no surprise to find St Andrews among the handful of Scottish universities entering the new Teaching Excellence Framework and coming out with a gold rating. The independent panel praised the "exemplary" teaching, and a learning and teaching environment of the highest quality.

The panel added that a culture of rigour within a research-intensive environment stimulates optimum levels of enthusiasm among students. Another good year for student satisfaction has helped St Andrews retain third position in our table, 17 places ahead of its nearest challenger in Scotland.

It is second in the table for student satisfaction with teaching quality and top in the assessment of their broader academic experience, helping St Andrews to win our University of the Year for Student Experience award. Applications are running at record levels, but only a few more places have been made available.

The offer rate has increased in the past four years, but still fewer than half of all applicants received offers in 2016. Eleven new degrees have been introduced, more than half of which offer direct entry into the second year of extended master's courses. They range from maths and statistics to geography combined with Persian.

Four out of ten undergraduates are international students, much the largest group coming from America, often on study abroad programmes. Another 30% arrive from south of the border, even though – together with Edinburgh – St Andrews has the highest fees in the UK for undergraduates from England, Wales or Northern Ireland. They pay £9,250 a year for each of the four years of a degree, whereas most Scottish universities cap fees at the three-year cost to bring them in line with England. Bursaries are available for students from low-income families. Scots and other EU students continue to pay nothing.

The university celebrated its 600th anniversary in 2013 and is Scotland's oldest higher education institution and the third oldest in the English-speaking world. Its reputation has always rested above all on the humanities: St Andrews boasts Europe's first Centre for Syrian Studies, an Institute of Iranian Studies and a Centre for Peace and Conflict Studies.

St Andrews has the UK's largest medieval history department and has added film studies and sustainable development. It has also taken over the running of the town's Byre Theatre, which is used as teaching space by day while continuing to offer productions in the evenings and at weekends. The university is also planning a new £8m music centre with rehearsal and teaching spaces, recording suite and library.

St Katharine's West
16 The Scores
St Andrews
KY16 9AX
01334 462 150
student.recruitment@st-andrews.ac.uk
www.st-andrews.co.uk
www.yourunion.net
Open Days 2018:
March 7, April 4, 11, 18

The Times and The Sunday Times **Rankings**

Overall Ranking: **3** (last year: 3)

Teaching quality	87%	2
Student experience	87.1%	1
Research quality	40.4%	11
Entry standards	209	4
Graduate prospects	81.9%	22
Good honours	91.1%	3
Expected completion rate	96.4%	3
Student/staff ratio	11.6	=7
Services and facilities/student	£2,635	24

However, St Andrews has also been investing heavily in the sciences, which produced some of the best results in the 2014 Research Excellence Framework, when more than 70% of its submission reached the top two categories. Classics and history of art scored particularly well, but more than 90% of two joint submissions with Edinburgh in chemistry and physics was rated world-leading or internationally excellent.

A £3.7m physics facility opened in 2015, while an ultra-low vibration laboratory is the most advanced in the UK and one of a handful worldwide. The £45m Medical and Biological Sciences building was one of the first in the UK to integrate research facilities for the medical school with the other sciences.

The university has the largest operational optical telescope in Britain and has invested £25m in an award-winning green energy centre at the Eden Campus, four miles outside St Andrews, which pumps hot water to heat university buildings. More than 350 staff are to relocate to the campus in 2018.

The town of St Andrews is steeped in history, as well as being the centre of the golfing world. The university accounts for about half of its 18,000 inhabitants. Among the many traditions are academic "families", in which third or fourth-year students help new undergraduates ("bejants" and "bejantines") to adjust to academic life.

Nearly half of the students live in university-owned accommodation, with first-year undergraduates guaranteed a hall place provided they apply by the end of June. More than 40% of the UK undergraduates come from independent schools.

The university is in the middle of a £100m fundraising campaign, £13m of which is to support bright students who would otherwise be unable to attend St Andrews.

Most students enjoy a lively social life in a tight-knit community. The university has been carrying out a £14m redevelopment of its sports centre, with a new sports hall, larger and better-equipped fitness suite, and an indoor tennis centre. It is also investing £70m in new and refurbished residences to provide an additional 900 student beds. The university already owns or endorses 4,000 accommodation places.

Tuition fees

- » Fees for Scottish and EU students 2018–19 £0–£1,820
- » Fees for non-Scottish UK students 2018–19 £9,250
- » Fees for international students 2018–19 £21,290
  Medicine £30,080
- » For scholarship and bursary information see www.st-andrews.ac.uk/scholarships
- » Graduate salary £24,000

Students

Undergraduates	7,150	(885)
Postgraduates	2,390	(320)
Applications per place	9.4	
Overall offer rate	54.7%	
International students	41.4%	
Mature students	2.7%	
From state-sector schools	56.7%	
From working-class homes	14.2%	

Accommodation

University-provided places: 4,004
Percentage catered: 54%
Catered costs: £175 – £215 per week
Self-catered: £103 – £171 per week
First year students are guaranteed accommodation
www.st-andrews.ac.uk/accommodation/

St George's, University of London

Of the students graduating from St George's, 95% go straight into highly-skilled employment – the highest proportion in our table. But other universities' medical schools are even more successful on this measure and with a slightly lower three-year average, St George's received just a bronze rating in the government's new Teaching Excellence Framework (TEF).

Student dissatisfaction with assessment and feedback was an even bigger problem in the TEF – and also in our table, which has seen St George's fall 27 places in two years. The school remains in the bottom ten in both of the measures derived from the National Student Survey. Nevertheless, the TEF panel gave credit for an "embedded institutional culture that rewards excellent teaching, and promotes inclusivity among staff and students".

St George's is the only free-standing medical school in the University of London and the only one in our table. Courses cover the full range of biomedical and healthcare sciences, and not just medicine. With almost 6,000 students, it is one of the biggest medical schools in the country and increased its intake of undergraduates in 2016. Recent growth has come mainly in areas other than medicine,

where numbers are centrally controlled. There is a joint provision with Kingston University in nursing, physiotherapy and radiology, as well as degrees in biomedical sciences and anatomy.

St George's became the first university to advertise in advance that it would have places in medicine available in clearing in 2016 and it did the same last summer. The medical school was not short of candidates in either year – only half of those applying receive offers – but it says using clearing is the "fairest way for us to get high-quality students".

St George's has done more than most medical schools to broaden its intake. Its adjusted criteria scheme reduces the entry requirements by two A-level grades for anyone applying from a non-selective state school whose results are in the bottom 20% nationally. The scheme applies to medicine, biomedical science, physiotherapy and healthcare science. A shadowing scheme offers sixth-formers from Wandsworth and Merton state schools the opportunity to accompany a doctor or other healthcare professional at St George's or Queen Mary's Hospital. Three out of ten undergraduates come from low-income households – well above average for the courses and entry qualifications.

A new biomedical science curriculum was launched this year to broaden students' career options and allow them to graduate with degree titles reflecting their chosen

---

Cranmer Terrace
Tooting
London SW17 0RE
020 8725 2333
study@sgul.ac.uk
www.sgul.ac.uk
www.sgsu.org.uk
Open days 2018:
March 21, June 23,
September 29

The Times and The Sunday Times Rankings

Overall Ranking: **=75** (last year: 70)

Teaching quality	74.3%	119
Student experience	75.3%	109
Research quality	22.2%	52
Entry standards	162	28
Graduate prospects	93.6%	1
Good honours	72.4%	64
Expected completion rate	94.6%	12
Student/staff ratio	12.5	=10
Services and facilities/student	£2,552	28

specialism. There is also a new occupational therapy degree, which promises small group teaching and close contact with occupational therapists working in the local area.

The medical school was founded at Hyde Park Corner in London. Edward Jenner was a student there before performing the first smallpox vaccination. The hide of the cow he used in his original experiment remains at St George's, which moved to Tooting, south London, in the 1970s. The university shares a clinical environment with St George's Hospital, one of the busiest in the capital.

St George's has a strong research record, which includes the invention of the first endocardial cardiac pacemaker and pioneering work on in vitro fertilisation. Only Imperial College London scored more highly for the external impact of its work in the 2014 Research Excellence Framework (REF). Overall, 70% of the work submitted for the REF was considered world-leading or internationally excellent.

Three research institutes focus on biomedical and scientific discovery, advancing the prevention and treatment of disease in the fields of population health, heart disease and infection.

The campus includes a preparatory centre for international students that is run jointly by St George's and the Into foundation. The university offers a four-year graduate entry bachelor of surgery degree in Cyprus,

at the University of Nicosia, where the first students graduated in 2015. St George's was the first UK institution to launch the MBBS Graduate Entry Programme (GEP), a four-year fast-track medical degree course open to graduates in any discipline, which has become a popular route into the medical profession.

The university has almost 500 residential places, the most recent development adding 150 single study bedrooms 15 minutes' walk from the campus. The sports centre is on campus and teams compete in regional and national competitions, Tooting Lido's open-air pool is not far away and the West End is less than half an hour by Tube for shopping and nightlife excursions.

Tuition fees

- » Fees for UK/EU students 2018–19 £9,250
- » Fees for international students 2018–19 £13,500–£17,000
  Medicine £32,500
- » For scholarship and bursary information see
  www.sgul.ac.uk/study/undergraduate/fees-and-funding/grants-and-bursaries
- » Graduate salary £24,000

Students

Undergraduates	2,645	(2,445)
Postgraduates	180	(655)
Applications per place	12.5	
Overall offer rate	49.9%	
International students	8.2%	
Mature students	27%	
From state-sector schools	79.6%	
From working-class homes	30.4%	

Accommodation

University-provided places: 486
Percentage catered: 0%
Self-catered: £160 – £170 per week (39 weeks)
Priority is given to first-year and international students
www.sgul.ac.uk/study/accommodation

St Mary's University, Twickenham

St Mary's appears (just) inside the top 100 in our table after a rise of 16 places more than cancelled out a decline of similar proportions last year. A big increase in spending on student services and improved graduate prospects are largely responsible.

The university also achieved a silver rating in the new Teaching Excellence Framework. The independent panel noted that high-quality resources are much appreciated by students and enhance their learning, while good staffing levels also facilitate personalised and small-group working.

St Mary's is the largest Catholic university in the UK, one of three created in recent years. It has appointed a series of high-profile visiting professors, including Mary McAleese, the former president of Ireland, Sir Vince Cable, now leader of the Liberal Democrats, Sir Clive Woodward, who coached England to the 2003 rugby World Cup, and Cherie Blair QC. Ruth Kelly, education secretary under former prime minister Tony Blair, has become pro vice-chancellor of research and enterprise.

The numbers starting degree courses dropped a little in 2016, but only in comparison with a record year for recruitment. Applications have been steady, but are yet to regain the level seen in the last year before £9,000 fees were introduced.

Historically, the focus at St Mary's has been on teacher training. It was founded in Hammersmith in 1850 by the Catholic poor schools committee to meet the need for teachers for the growing numbers of poor Catholic children.

A third of the students are still training to teach, but it is the university's sporting prowess that has captured headlines. Its students and alumni at the Rio Olympics won six medals, three of them gold, and would have finished in the top 30 in the medal table. They were led by Sir Mo Farah, a graduate of St Mary's, after whom its track is now named and who has a scholarship programme for promising young athletes at the university.

Since its move to Twickenham in 1925, the spectacular Strawberry Hill House has been its centrepiece. The building was designed as a gothic fantasy by Horace Walpole, the son of Britain's first prime minister. Leased from the university by a trust, the property has now been restored and is open to the public.

The campus occupies 35 acres of gardens and parkland close to the Thames, with a variety of modern teaching and residential accommodation. Additional sports facilities are located in neighbouring Teddington.

Developments have included a £6m library and a computer suite with the latest Apple MacPro workstations, offering

Waldegrave Road
Strawberry Hill
Twickenham TW1 4SX
020 8240 4000
admit@stmarys.ac.uk
www.stmarys.ac.uk
www.stmaryssu.co.uk
Open Days 2018:
check website

The Times and The Sunday Times **Rankings**

Overall Ranking: **99** (last year: 116)

Teaching quality	80.9%	=53
Student experience	80.2%	36
Research quality	4%	=104
Entry standards	123	=83
Graduate prospects	73.3%	=65
Good honours	59.7%	122
Expected completion rate	80.5%	102
Student/staff ratio	17.9	=102
Services and facilities/student	£1,593	110

students 24-hour access to professional-grade technologies.

A new "community building" has been added in the centre of Twickenham, with theatre space, six multifunction studio rooms and a large conservatory area with a cafe. The Exchange will offer training courses for local residents and firms, as well as providing more teaching space for students.

St Mary's has a continued commitment to training teachers for Catholic and other Christian schools, although it admits students of all faiths and none. Its first stated objective is "to be a distinctive institution within UK higher education, providing a unique experience for our students and staff by virtue of our values and identity as a Catholic university." Its researchers have formed a Forum for Islam-Christian Dialogue with those at the Centre for Islamic Finance at the University of Bolton.

There are nearly 500 undergraduate degree combinations across four schools covering sport, health and applied science; education, theology and leadership; management and social sciences; and the arts and humanities.

Nine new degrees are planned for 2018, mainly in combinations of marketing, communications, management and politics.

The university has a small, but growing cohort of international students and has joined the US-based Common Application system, used by more than 500 universities around the world, to attract more.

Almost 40% of the UK undergraduates are from working-class homes and the university has a number of outreach schemes designed to broaden the intake further. The e-mentoring scheme, in which current students help selected groups of school pupils throughout the academic year, has received excellent feedback from participants. Other initiatives provide academic support and monitor the progress of under-represented groups once they begin courses.

Most students like the combination of an attractive setting in southwest London that is only half an hour from Waterloo by train. The £8.5m sports centre is good enough to have attracted teams from Japan and China during last year's World Athletics championships.

Tuition fees

- » Fees for UK/EU students 2018–19 £9,250
  Foundation courses £4,625–£6,000
- » Fees for international students 2018–19 £11,220
- » For scholarship and bursary information see www.stmarys.ac.uk/student-finance/scholarships/scholarships.aspx
- » Graduate salary £20,000

Students

Undergraduates	3,710	(405)
Postgraduates	465	(950)
Applications per place	5.2	
Overall offer rate	91.7%	
International students	5.9%	
Mature students	18.8%	
From state-sector schools	96.3%	
From working-class homes	38.8%	

Accommodation

University-provided places: 710
Percentage catered: 100%
Catered costs: £132 – £224 per week
First year students are guaranteed accommodation
www.stmarys.ac.uk/student-life/accommodation/

University of Salford

Having already narrowed the range of subjects it offers to focus on its strengths, Salford has decided to concentrate its activities on four Industry Collaboration Zones: engineering and environments, health and wellbeing, digital and creative, and sport. The university describes the change as a "bold departure from traditional structures and models of learning".

Students will operate closely with academics and industrial partners on work-based projects, applying their learning and skills in real-world environments. New subjects will be introduced to fit the structure.

Salford's initial pruning of the curriculum has been successful, with applications rising for three years in a row and the numbers starting degrees growing by a third since 2012. The university has also gone up ten places in our table this year, although it remains the lowest-ranked pre-1992 institution.

However, these successes did not extend to the new Teaching Excellence Framework (TEF), in which Salford was awarded bronze. The university said the low grade reflected the historic position on graduate employment, rather than recent improvements. Our new table updates the TEF data and puts Salford in the middle reaches for graduate jobs, with just over seven in ten students progressing to professional jobs or further study within six months of leaving.

The TEF panel acknowledged "excellent" targeted investment in buildings and facilities, however, and the introduction of extensive support for Salford's diverse student population. Innovative learning materials respond to different learning styles, the panel said.

Campus developments have been considerable. The New Adelphi, a flagship building at the gateway to the site, opened last year. It will be the main social hub and the teaching centre for art, performance, and design and technology students. It includes a 350-seat theatre, industry-standard TV, radio and music studios, as well as exhibition space and cafe and bar areas.

The other big project for teaching and learning was a £30m development in MediaCityUK, in Salford Quays, where there are opportunities to work with BBC staff and other media professionals using the latest equipment, studios and laboratories. In addition, Salford has invested more than £80m in the Peel Park Quarter, with 1,367 residential places on campus and impressive student facilities.

Two of the three campuses border the River Irwell and are within walking distance of Manchester city centre. One is for the 5,000 health students, and includes practice clinics, hospital ward facilities and a human performance laboratory. The School of

---

The Crescent
Salford
Greater Manchester
M5 4WT
0161 295 4545
www.salford.ac.uk
enquire via website
www.salfordstudents.com
Open Days 2018:
June 23

The Times and *The Sunday Times* **Rankings**		
Overall Ranking: **88** (last year: 98)		
Teaching quality	81.1%	=49
Student experience	79%	=59
Research quality	8.3%	72
Entry standards	127	76
Graduate prospects	71.1%	75
Good honours	73.1%	60
Expected completion rate	81.5%	94
Student/staff ratio	16.6	=80
Services and facilities/student	£1,814	=93

Nursing, Midwifery, Social Work and Social Sciences received outstanding ratings from its regulatory body, while the health sciences school has an international reputation for the treatment of sports injuries.

Salford is also planning a private medical school in partnership with Manchester and Manchester Metropolitan universities, and has opened a branch campus in Bahrain. Salford is the first UK university to have a campus in the Gulf state, offering degrees in engineering, quantity surveying and computer science under the rubric of the British College of Bahrain.

The medical school, which will cater for international students, is a longer-term project and part of Salford's plans for "considerable" growth in the next five years.

Engineering is the university's traditional strength, attracting many of the 3,000-plus international students. However, its business school has been the main point of growth, as well as winning awards for innovation and the delivery of its courses via a mix of traditional teaching and innovation projects.

Two-thirds of Salford's courses – and all those in the business school – offer work placements, some of which are abroad. Almost all count towards degree classifications.

The university does well on the government's access measures: more than 40% of undergraduates come from working-class homes and one in five is from an area that sends few students to higher education. The dropout rate has been improving and is now close to the national average for the subjects and students' qualifications.

The university entered only a third of its eligible academics for the 2014 Research Excellence Framework, but more than half of their work was found to be world-leading or internationally excellent.

Salford's location is one of its main selling points, with Manchester a prime draw for students. The residential accommodation is all within ten minutes' walk of the main campus. The new Peel Park development has communal areas including a cinema room, gym, TV and games room and group study lounges.

The neighbouring sports centre, which has been refurbished recently, has a swimming pool, squash courts, sports hall and four fitness suites.

Tuition fees

» Fees for UK/EU students 2018–19 £9,250
» Fees for international students 2018–19 £8,225–£14,400
» For scholarship and bursary information see www.salford.ac.uk/askus/our-services/money-matters/bursaries-and-scholarships
» Graduate salary £21,000

Students

Undergraduates	14,685	(1,040)
Postgraduates	2,665	(2,125)
Applications per place	6.3	
Overall offer rate	74.4%	
International students	9.6%	
Mature students	27.1%	
From state-sector schools	98.1%	
From working-class homes	42.2%	

Accommodation

University-provided places: 2,400
Percentage catered: 0%
Self-catered: £93 – £143 per week
www.salford.ac.uk/study/life-at-salford/accommodation

University of Sheffield

The numbers starting traditional degree courses at Sheffield are running at record levels, after four consecutive increases. But, uniquely for a Russell Group university, the first priority in its strategy for education and the student experience is to offer the best degree apprenticeships in the UK.

Hundreds of apprentices are at work with Boeing at the university's Advanced Manufacturing Research Centre, with the option of taking undergraduate and master's degrees. Another 90 apprentices started studying for degrees in integrated materials and rail engineering last year, in a joint programme with Sheffield Hallam University.

Sheffield already has a more diverse undergraduate population than most of its peers, with more than 86% from state schools or colleges and the proportion from areas of low participation in higher education above average for its courses and entry qualifications. It sees the development of new pathways into higher education as part of its role as a modern civic university.

The university was awarded silver in the new Teaching Excellence Framework. The panel said students learn in a research-led environment that engages them by combining academic rigour and disciplinary knowledge with real-world connections. It was impressed, too, by targeted programmes including volunteering, internships for graduates in the area and a programme to support students in gaining work experience with local businesses.

Sheffield remains one position outside our top 20 and is among the universities whose students boycotted the National Student Survey in sufficient numbers to prevent a score being released this year to assess teaching quality and the wider student experience. However, *Which?* and *Times Higher Education* have placed it near the top of their own surveys of the student experience.

The striking £81m Diamond engineering building — the university's biggest single development — caters for the growing number of students in one of Sheffield's key strengths. The aluminium-clad structure has 19 specialist laboratories and 1,000 study spaces.

The highly rated engineering faculty, which has 4,000 students, had already opened the £21m Pam Liversidge building, named after one of UK's leading female engineers, and will add more laboratories, offices and social space this year.

The main university precinct now stretches into an almost unbroken mile-long "campus" that ends not far from the city centre. Previous developments have seen the conversion of the former Jessop Hospital into a new centre for the arts and humanities and the renovation of the original university

---

Western Bank
Sheffield S10 2TN
0114 222 2000
shefapply@sheffield.ac.uk
www.sheffield.ac.uk
http://su.sheffield.ac.uk
Open Days 2018:
check website

***The Times and The Sunday Times* Rankings**

Overall Ranking: **21** (last year: 24)

Teaching quality	n/a	
Student experience	n/a	
Research quality	37.6%	23
Entry standards	161	29
Graduate prospects	82.6%	=15
Good honours	80%	29
Expected completion rate	94.4%	15
Student/staff ratio	14.6	=37
Services and facilities/student	£2,276	43

library and the Arts Tower, which remains the tallest university building in the country more than 50 years after it opened. The £23m Information Commons operates 24 hours a day throughout the year and has been refurbished over the summer.

Eighty-five per cent of the research submitted to the Research Excellence Framework was considered world-leading or internationally excellent, with biomedical sciences, control and systems engineering, history and politics all in the top three in the UK. But the university entered a smaller proportion of its academics than most of its peers in the Russell Group.

Sheffield is among the 100 leading universities in the world, according to the QS rankings, and attracts more than 8,000 students from outside the UK. It also remains comfortably inside the top 20 favourite recruiting grounds for *The Times*'s 100 leading employers, according to the 2017 graduate market survey by High Fliers.

Most university flats and halls of residence are within walking distance, in the suburbs on the affluent west side of Sheffield. The Endcliffe student village caters for 3,500 students in a mix of refurbished Victorian houses and new flats, while Ranmoor village houses more than 1,000 students in self-catering apartments, which include some family accommodation and studios. Private housing is reasonably priced in student areas close to the university.

The excellent sports facilities close to the main university precinct include five floodlit synthetic pitches, a large fitness centre with more than 150 pieces of equipment, a swimming pool with sauna and steam rooms, sports hall, fitness studio, multipurpose activity room, four squash courts and a bouldering wall.

The 45 acres of grass pitches for rugby, football and cricket are a bus ride away. Sheffield has one of the biggest programmes of internal leagues at any university and elite sport is thriving. Three of its alumni won either a gold or a silver at the Rio Olympics.

The famously lively social scene is based on the recently extended students' union. The city has plenty of student-orientated bars and clubs, and town-gown relations are much better than in most main university centres.

Tuition fees

» Fees for UK/EU students 2018–19 £9,250
» Fees for international students 2018–19 £16,800–£21,450
  Foundation courses £15,430–£17,620
  Medicine £35,500 (clinical years 2017–18)
» For scholarship and bursary information see www.sheffield.ac.uk/undergraduate/finance
» Graduate salary £22,000

Students

Undergraduates	18,720	(835)
Postgraduates	6,330	(2,040)
Applications per place	7.1	
Overall offer rate	84.6%	
International students	20.1%	
Mature students	9%	
From state-sector schools	86.9%	
From working-class homes	21.2%	

Accommodation

University-provided places: 6,128
Percentage catered: 6%
Catered costs: £143 – £168 per week
Self-catered: £102 – £165 per week
First year students are guaranteed accommodation
www.sheffield.ac.uk/accommodation

Sheffield Hallam University

Already one of the UK's biggest higher education institutions, with more than 31,000 students, Sheffield Hallam is aiming to be "the world's leading applied university", building on strong links with business and industry and its position as an "anchor institution" in the regeneration of the local economy. To achieve this, a new strategy promises to look radically at the way the university works, be innovative and respond quickly to new opportunities.

Hallam, which developed its reputation as one of the country's top technical institutions while still a polytechnic, is up nine places in our new table, thanks mainly to greater satisfaction with teaching quality and a much higher proportion of students achieving good honours. It was given a silver rating in the government's new Teaching Excellence Framework (TEF), which was chaired by Professor Chris Husbands, the university's vice-chancellor.

Husbands was not involved in the decision, but the TEF panel complimented the university on an exemplary commitment to the Sheffield area and support for students to be retained in the region through considerable employability activities. It also found strong evidence of the impact on learning and progression of the university's consistent approach to curriculum and assessment design.

Two-thirds of the students come from within 40 miles of Sheffield. Applications are currently nearly 10,000 down on the level of 2011, the last year before £9,000 fees were introduced, but the numbers embarking on degrees are back to that year's level.

Hallam continues on a £110m project to transform parts of the city centre through the creation of innovative new learning and research facilities. A two-year refurbishment of the science, technology, engineering and maths (Stem) facilities has upgraded the chemistry laboratories and engineering equipment, adding a spectacular atrium that houses galleries, collaborative spaces, social learning and access to the train station.

A new £30m building houses the Sheffield Institute of Education, which has more than 150 academic staff and 5,000 students, making it one of the country's largest providers of teacher training. The conversion of the city's former head post office provided a new home for the Sheffield Institute of Arts, bringing art and design courses under the same roof.

Meanwhile, the university's Advanced Wellbeing Research Centre (AWRC) is the centrepiece of Sheffield's Olympic Legacy Park, a venture between the university, the city council and Sheffield Teaching Hospitals NHS Foundation Trust, set in the city's advanced manufacturing innovation district.

Hallam claims that the AWRC is the most advanced research and development

---

City Campus
Howard Street
Sheffield S1 1WB
0114 225 5555
admissions@shu.ac.uk
www.shu.ac.uk
www.hallamstudentsunion.com
Open Days 2018:
check website

The Times and The Sunday Times Rankings

Overall Ranking: **=70** (last year: 79)

Teaching quality	82%	36
Student experience	80%	=38
Research quality	5.4%	=89
Entry standards	120	=91
Graduate prospects	69.3%	=89
Good honours	73.5%	56
Expected completion rate	86.1%	=62
Student/staff ratio	16.6	=80
Services and facilities/student	£2,101	64

centre for physical activity in the world and is developing a longer-term plan for a health innovation campus on the site.

The university is also collaborating with the University of Sheffield on a new programme of degree apprenticeships in engineering. Hallam is one of the largest providers of degree apprenticeships and the two Sheffield universities are the "anchor institutions" for regeneration in the city and the wider region, developing a 25-year prospectus for a post-industrial economy.

Previous developments focused mainly on the City campus, near Sheffield's central shopping area. Business and management courses, which account for the biggest share of places, have their own city-centre headquarters, as does the students' union, which took over the spectacular, but ill-fated National Centre for Popular Music.

Business and industry are closely involved in the development of Hallam's courses and more than half of the undergraduates take work placements. The university gives a full fee waiver for those who take a complete year out. More than 200 specialist flexible courses mix part-time study, distance learning and work-based learning and more than 3,500 businesses work with the university on activities including knowledge exchange and placements.

Hallam exceeds all its access benchmarks and the projected dropout rate is lower than the national average for its courses and entry.

qualifications. The university also has a growing international dimension, with large cohorts taught in partner institutions in Malaysia and other Asian countries, as well as almost 4,000 who go to Sheffield from outside the EU.

Unlike many big post-1992 universities, Hallam guarantees accommodation for first-years, although the large local intake means that many students live at home. The university does not own its own accommodation, but has more than 5,000 rooms at its disposal through private providers. Transport in the city is excellent, with well-run bus and tram services.

Sports facilities are supplemented by those provided by the city for the 1991 World Student Games. The impressive swimming complex, for example, is on the university's doorstep.

The university has taken over the management of Sheffield's only athletics stadium, which will be among the facilities used for Bucs (British Universities and Colleges Sport) events. The redeveloped facility is available to community groups, schools and local clubs, as well as students.

Tuition fees

» Fees for UK/EU students 2018–19   £9,250
» Fees for international students 2018–19   £12,750–£14,750
» For scholarship and bursary information see www.shu.ac.uk/study-here/fees-and-finance/undergraduate
» Graduate salary   £21,000

Students		
Undergraduates	21,750	(2,960)
Postgraduates	3,350	(3,425)
Applications per place	5.6	
Overall offer rate	78%	
International students	5.2%	
Mature students	18.2%	
From state-sector schools	96.7%	
From working-class homes	40.8%	

Accommodation

University-provided places: 5,100
Percentage catered: 0%
Self-catered: £83 – £135 per week
First year students are guaranteed accommodation
www.shu.ac.uk/accommodation

SOAS University of London

More than 90% of applicants – the highest proportion at any university in our top 40 – receive at least a conditional offer from SOAS, the School of Oriental and African Studies. A range of new degree programmes helped the school to a fourth year of rising applications, bucking the national trend. But there are still only 6,000 students, little more than half of them undergraduates.

SOAS has been celebrating its centenary by moving into the north block of Senate House, the headquarters of the University of London. The five-floor development has brought the school together on a single site for the first time in many years. It includes a new student hub, hosting services such as accommodation, counselling, student finance and careers, and a plaza under a double-curvature glass canopy.

The centrepiece of the Bloomsbury precinct is an airy building with gallery space as well as teaching accommodation, a gift from the Sultan of Brunei. The library is one of the UK's five National Research Libraries and holds 1.5m volumes, periodicals and audiovisual materials in 400 languages, attracting scholars from around the world.

More than 40% of the university's degree programmes offer students the opportunity to spend a year at one of the school's many partner universities in Africa and Asia.

SOAS appealed unsuccessfully against its bronze rating (the lowest grade) in the government's new Teaching Excellence Framework, believing that the figures used to measure retention and employment did not reflect the changes the school had made recently. Big increases in student satisfaction and completion contributed to a rise of nine places in our table last year.

As one of nine universities where a student boycott of the National Student Survey took the response rate below the 50 per cent threshold for the publication of results, there was no opportunity to continue the improvement in satisfaction levels in the latest table. But a further increase in the completion rate went some way to compensating for a big fall in spending on student services and facilities.

Centenary celebrations took place in 2016–17 with alumni in India, Nigeria, the United Arab Emirates, Hong Kong and the United States, reflecting the global prestige that the school enjoys. As the only higher education institution in the UK specialising in the study of Africa, Asia and the Middle East, its teaching and research concerns two-thirds of the world's population. It is led by Baroness Amos, who was the UK's first black woman cabinet minister and the first black woman to lead a British university.

Thornhaugh Street
Russell Square
London WC1H 0XG
020 7898 4700
study@soas.ac.uk
www.soas.ac.uk
http://soasunion.org
Open days 2018:
June 13, October 20

The Times and The Sunday Times **Rankings**

Overall Ranking: **=36** (last year: 35)

Teaching quality	n/a	
Student experience	n/a	
Research quality	27.9%	47
Entry standards	153	=37
Graduate prospects	70.5%	=78
Good honours	81%	=26
Expected completion rate	85.5%	67
Student/staff ratio	11.6	=7
Services and facilities/student	£2,050	72

A £20m gift from a graduate with a passion for southeast Asian art is funding new posts, building development and scholarships for Asian students to go to London.

SOAS has also established a new partnership with the education centre of the China Guardian, one of China's largest art institutions, and the Art Institute of Chicago to deliver new courses on Chinese art.

Two-thirds of students are from Britain and the rest of the EU. Almost a fifth of the British undergraduates come from independent schools, but more than one in three are from the four poorest socioeconomic groups.

The school devotes much of its fee income to outreach activities and bursaries. Among the current schemes is the SOAS excellence bursary, which consists of more than 300 awards of at least £2,250, targeted at those with household incomes below £25,000.

The university has a much wider portfolio of courses than its name would suggest, offering more than 400 degree combinations and 100 postgraduate programmes. Degrees are available in familiar subjects such as law, history, music and the social sciences, with an emphasis that reflects the SOAS ethos.

There is also a more limited portfolio of foundation programmes and language courses. About 45% of undergraduates take a language as part of their degree and the school has introduced a language entitlement programme that offers one term of a non-accredited SOAS Language Centre course free of charge.

The £6.5m Library Transformation Project added more language laboratories, music studios, discussion and research rooms, and gallery space.

SOAS is in the top 40 in the QS world rankings for the arts and humanities, which led the way in the 2014 Research Excellence Framework. Music, drama and the performing arts produced the best results in a submission in which two-thirds of the work was rated world-leading or internationally excellent.

There is no separate students' union building but students have their own social space, bar and catering facilities. The former University of London Union — now a student centre — is close at hand, with a swimming pool, gym and bars.

More than 1,100 residential places are available within 20 minutes' walk of the school. However, SOAS has few of its own sports facilities and the outdoor pitches are remote. Students tend to be highly committed and are often politically active, and many return to positions of influence in their own country.

Tuition fees

»	Fees for UK/EU students 2018–19	£9,250
»	Fees for international students 2018–19	£16,907
»	For scholarship and bursary information see www.soas.ac.uk/registry/scholarships	
»	Graduate salary	£22,000

Students

Undergraduates	3,165	(55)
Postgraduates	1,700	(1,150)
Applications per place	6.6	
Overall offer rate	91.5%	
International students	37.1%	
Mature students	17%	
From state-sector schools	80.6%	
From working-class homes	35.7%	

Accommodation

University-provided places: 1,123
Percentage catered: 7%
Catered costs: £143 – £267 per week
Self-catered: £147 – £273 per week
www.soas.ac.uk/accommodation/

University of South Wales

The University of South Wales (USW) is "streamlining" its operations to ensure that it remains financially sound in the face of rising costs and greater competition for students. Applications and enrolments have fallen in both years since the merged institution (created in 2013 from the former University of Glamorgan and the University of Wales, Newport) began handling its own admissions, and the university is making pre-emptive cuts in staffing and other budgets.

USW is one of five Welsh universities reviewing their activities but it has not announced any course closures. On the contrary, ten new degrees are planned for 2018, including counselling and therapeutic practice, sports journalism and sustainable hotel management.

One of USW's five campuses, at Carleon, near Newport, closed in 2016 as an efficiency measure, with investment focusing instead on the £60m Newport Knowledge Quarter and the ATRiuM campus for the creative industries, in the centre of Cardiff.

The largest campus is in Pontypridd, 10 miles outside Cardiff, where two sites cater mainly for science, engineering and health subjects. Developments there include a law school, upgraded laboratories and the £6m learning resource centre.

USW is one of Wales's two largest universities, with almost 30,000 students, and the University of South Wales Group extends its reach further. It includes the Royal Welsh College of Music and Drama and Merthyr Tydfil College, while a strategic alliance brings in further education colleges throughout southeast Wales. The alliance covers 38 campuses, providing 98,000 learners with advice and structured progression routes from further education to university.

About half of USW's own students are full-time undergraduates and of these, a quarter are at least 21 years old on entry. Three-quarters are from Wales and more than one in five come from an area of low participation in higher education.

Like several universities in Wales, USW did not enter the government's new Teaching Excellence Framework, but it has fallen four places in our table and into the bottom ten. There has been improvement in graduate prospects and spending on student services, but the completion rate and student satisfaction levels have declined.

There was a relatively small submission for the 2014 Research Excellence Framework, but half of the work was considered world-leading or internationally excellent. The best results came in a joint submission with Cardiff Metropolitan and Trinity St David universities in art and design, and in sport and exercise science, and social work and social policy.

Pontypridd
CF37 1DL
03455 76 0101
www.southwales.ac.uk
enquire via website
www.uswsu.com
Open Days 2018:
April 18 (information fair)

Edinburgh
Belfast
PONTYPRIDD NEWPORT
CARDIFF London

The Times and The Sunday Times Rankings
Overall Ranking: **=119** (last year: 115)

Teaching quality	77.9%	=98
Student experience	74.2%	114
Research quality	4%	=104
Entry standards	128	=71
Graduate prospects	62.4%	120
Good honours	66.5%	101
Expected completion rate	80.8%	=97
Student/staff ratio	17.9	=102
Services and facilities/student	£1,810	95

USW is a significant player in the arts at its Cardiff campus, too, notably through its internationally acclaimed film school, whose graduates include double-Bafta winner Asif Kapadia, and Justin Kerrigan, director of the cult movie Human Traffic.

The university offers industry-standard animation facilities and one of the UK's oldest photography schools. The original ATRiuM building, next to the BBC headquarters, hosts law and accounting and finance courses, as well as the Cardiff school of creative and cultural industries. The new ATRiuM 2B facility, completed in 2016, replicates industry workspaces across the creative sector. It has advertising, television, film set design and fashion facilities plus rehearsal spaces and dance and photographic studios. Further provision includes an animation render farm and recording studios.

A focus on employability extends to other simulated learning facilities including a moot courtroom, TV studios, stock exchange trading room, hospital wards, and a scene-of-crime house.

Aircraft maintenance and engineering students benefit from two on-campus working aircraft hangars complete with aircraft. USW is the only UK university to have a partnership with British Airways, which enables students to graduate with an EASA pilot's licence as well as a degree.

A partnership with the Celtic Manor Resort will give students on USW's new BA (Hons) hotel and hospitality management course first-hand experience of working in the industry. The course will combine weekly practical exposure with classroom lectures, designed to support student learning and help people be "industry ready" at the end of the three-year degree.

New facilities at USW Sport Park include a specialist centre for strength and conditioning with 12 lifting platforms and providing a high-performance environment for aspiring athletes. A full-size 3G indoor football pitch will be the only one in Wales and one of five in the UK. The park is used by both the public and professional sport teams, including the British Lions and international teams, as well as Cardiff City FC. South Wales also hosts one of six centres of excellence in cricket.

USW has a good record in student competitions, especially in rugby, football and golf. Sports scholarships are available.

The city of Newport is undergoing a £2bn regeneration programme and has plenty of clubs and entertainment venues, including Friars Walk, but students in search of serious cultural or clubbing activity tend to gravitate to nearby Cardiff.

Tuition fees

- » Fees for UK/EU students 2018–19 — £9,000
- » Fees for international students 2018–19 — £12,300
- » For scholarship and bursary information see www.southwales.ac.uk/study/fees-and-funding/undergraduate
- » Graduate salary — £20,000

Students

Undergraduates	14,940	(5,900)
Postgraduates	1,730	(2,695)
Applications per place	4.8	
Overall offer rate	83.4%	
International students	9.5%	
Mature students	24.7%	
From state-sector schools	97.6%	
From working-class homes	42%	

Accommodation

University-provided places: 1,825
Percentage catered: 0%
Self-catered: £92 – £161 per week
www.southwales.ac.uk/accommodation

University of Southampton

Southampton led the criticism of the government's Teaching Excellence Framework (TEF) after becoming one of three Russell Group universities placed in the lowest category last year. Sir Christopher Snowden, Southampton's vice-chancellor, insisted there was "no logic" in the university's bronze rating and argued that the process was "fundamentally flawed".

The TEF panel complimented the university on an innovative approach to the curriculum and acknowledged that it was taking steps to improve student satisfaction with assessment and feedback, but an appeal against the rating — which could only be on procedural grounds — was rejected.

Southampton attracted the biggest increase in demand for undergraduate places at any university in 2016, with 5,000 more applications. But it actually took fewer new entrants than in the previous year, as it began to raise entry requirements.

The university has adopted a new strategy, which includes reaching the top ten in national rankings, but has travelled sharply in the opposite direction in our table this year. Its ranking of 30th is down nine places, due in part to a fall of 40 places in satisfaction with the student experience, reinforcing some of the issues highlighted by the TEF.

Southampton has launched no fewer than 45 new degrees this academic year, most of them four-year integrated master's courses in engineering and technology, with an industrial placement year. Another 15 are planned for 2018 in similar areas, including ship science, aeronautics and astronautics, and acoustical engineering.

The university performed well in the 2014 Research Excellence Framework (REF) and is in our top seven for research quality. The best REF results came in physics, chemistry, health subjects, environmental science, psychology, electronic engineering and music, drama and performing arts.

There are also strengths in computer science, where Sir Tim Berners-Lee, inventor of the worldwide web, is a professor and Dame Wendy Hall is a Regius professor in the subject.

A £300m public bond issued this year will allow the university to invest further in facilities and infrastructure. Recent developments include the £140m Boldrewood Innovation Campus, developed jointly with Lloyd's Register — said to be the largest business-university relationship of its kind in the UK —and five new residential blocks with 350 en-suite bedrooms.

Current projects include a £25m Centre for Cancer Immunology, already under way and funded entirely through donations; the National Linear Infrastructure Laboratory,

---

University Road
Highfield
Southampton SO17 1BJ
023 8059 9699
enquiry@southampton.ac.uk
www.southampton.ac.uk
www.susu.org
Open Days 2018:
July 6, 7,
September 8,9,
October 13

Edinburgh
Belfast
Cardiff London
SOUTHAMPTON

***The Times and The Sunday Times* Rankings**
Overall Ranking: **30** (last year: 21)

Teaching quality	78.4%	=91
Student experience	77.1%	86
Research quality	44.9%	7
Entry standards	152	=39
Graduate prospects	80.3%	=31
Good honours	78.5%	=33
Expected completion rate	91.2%	=31
Student/staff ratio	13.2	=18
Services and facilities/student	£2,190	51

which is due to open in 2018; and a teaching and learning centre, scheduled to open in 2019. The famous submersible vessel Boaty McBoatface found a new home at the university last year.

The university has campuses in Southampton and Winchester, as well as one in Malaysia dedicated to engineering. The main Highfield campus is in an attractive green location two miles from the city centre. The nearby Avenue campus is home to most of the humanities departments, while clinical medicine is based at Southampton General Hospital.

Winchester School of Art has been part of the university since 1996, while other sites include the National Oceanography Centre Southampton, which is based in the revitalised dock area.

At the university's branch campus in Malaysia, undergraduates can study for two years before finishing their degree in Southampton.

Southampton is just outside the top 100 in the QS global rankings and the proportion of income derived from research is among the highest in Britain. It has 8,000 international students and a growing number of those from the UK spend time at one of the partner institutions in 54 countries.

The flexible undergraduate curriculum sees some subjects offering a "major-minor" structure that allows students to spend 25% of their time on a subject other than their original degree choice. There are also interdisciplinary modules that are designed to give students a broader perspective.

Almost 86% of the students were state educated, one of the highest proportions in the Russell Group. Students act as ambassadors, associates and mentors in local schools and colleges as part of the university's efforts to broaden its intake.

The latest developments have brought the number of residential places to more than 7,000. Sports facilities are first-class, with an indoor sports complex next to the students' union and a 25-metre pool. There are several gyms, outdoor grass and synthetic pitches.

Tuition fees

- » Fees for UK/EU students 2018–19 £9,250
- » Fees for international students 2018–19 £16,536–£20,320
  - Foundation courses (Stem subjects) £17,700
  - Medicine (clinical years) £40,230
- » For scholarship and bursary information see www.southampton.ac.uk/uni-life/fees-funding.page
- » Graduate salary £22,000

Students

Undergraduates	17,270	(215)
Postgraduates	5,910	(1,480)
Applications per place	8.7	
Overall offer rate	82.2%	
International students	18.2%	
Mature students	12.8%	
From state-sector schools	85.6%	
From working-class homes	23.1%	

Accommodation

University-provided places: 7,014
Percentage catered: 9%
Catered costs: £136 – £178 per week
Self-catered: £105 – £299 per week
First-year students are guaranteed accommodation
www.southampton.ac.uk/accommodation

Southampton Solent University

Southampton Solent is up ten places in our table this year, and just into the top 100. The graduate employment rate, which was the main cause of a bronze rating in the Teaching Excellence Framework (TEF), has improved from 57% to 64% of graduates in 2017 getting professional-level jobs or going into further study, and the university is close to the top 50 for staffing levels.

The TEF panel complimented the university on an inclusive curriculum and effective student support, as well as on its strong employer relationships. But in the three years under consideration, fewer than 60% of leavers found graduate-level jobs or continued their studies within six months of graduating.

Despite this, Solent is in the top ten universities for graduate start-ups, assisting in the launch of 110 in 2015–16. It was also close to the top ten in an added-value ranking of graduate salaries five years into their careers, calculated by The Economist and taking account of students' backgrounds, subjects and prior qualifications. Although the average for Solent graduates was less than £25,000, this was at least £1,500 more than the researchers would have expected. Students wishing to set up their own businesses or become freelancers are offered rent-free offices and are supported by the Solent Entrepreneur Programme. They have access to the university's creative agency, Solent Creatives, and the Re:So store, the first fully student-operated retail outlet in a UK shopping centre.

The university's support for students, which includes a Graduate Associate Scheme providing employment for more than 50 recent graduates, was identified as an example of best practice by the Quality Assurance Agency.

Applications dropped in 2016, after a strong performance in 2015, and the numbers starting courses were 1,000 lower than they were in the last year before £9,000 fees were introduced, a fall of more than 30%.

New degrees have been launched in music management, renewable energy engineering and hospitality and tourism. The main campus is close to the city centre, where the £33m Spark building opened last year. It has 40 hi-tech teaching spaces accommodating 1,500 at any one time, with furniture that is designed to promote more interaction with students.

A number of smaller developments have included a specialist facility for sports and exercise therapy, laboratories for applied human nutrition and biomedical sciences, a building for the art design school and facilities for courses in computer games, computer networking and audio production.

East Park Terrace
Southampton SO14 0YN
023 8201 5066
admissions@solent.ac.uk
www.solent.ac.uk
www.solentsu.co.uk
Open Days 2018:
March 10, April 14

The Times and The Sunday Times **Rankings**

Overall Ranking: **=100** (last year: =110)

Teaching quality	79.4%	=76
Student experience	77.6%	79
Research quality	0.5%	126
Entry standards	109	=118
Graduate prospects	64.1%	109
Good honours	69.7%	79
Expected completion rate	77.1%	=116
Student/staff ratio	15.5	=53
Services and facilities/student	£1,995	=78

A newly-opened virtual-reality suite supports a number of courses. But the next big project in the £100m investment at East Park Terrace will be a £28m sports building that is due to open in 2019. It will provide two sports halls, gymnasiums, fitness suites and teaching facilities, and be used by students in subjects such as media, journalism and photography, as well as sport.

There is strong demand for places in marine and maritime-based courses, which benefit from a world-renowned training and research facility for the superyacht, shipping and offshore oil industries. The university is UK higher education's premier yachting institution, with a student team that previously won the student World Cup and triumphed in the national championships four times in six years, plus alumni who have gone on to win Olympic and Paralympic gold medals.

The industry-focused Solent curriculum embraces a wide range of disciplines, however, including business, technology, the creative industries and sport. The university is a Skillset Media Academy-accredited centre of excellence in television production, broadcast journalism, screenwriting and performance, with expertise in live event broadcast, studio and post-production.

Solent recruits mainly in London and the south of England, but about 1,500 come from outside the UK. The university finished bottom of those that entered the 2014 Research Excellence Framework. It entered the lowest proportion of eligible academics, at only 7%, and none of its research was placed in the top two categories for its external impact.

Football facilities accredited by the Football Association are used by the city's Premier League team. The Lawrie McMenemy Centre for Football Research is helping to cement the university's reputation for academic study of the sport and, having assumed responsibility for sport development in the city, Solent has also become the country's largest provider of coaching education.

The existing sports facilities include a sports hall and fitness suite on campus and outdoor pitches, tennis and netball courts four miles away. There are more than 2,300 places in six halls of residence, enough to guarantee accommodation to first-years who apply by the end of June.

Tuition fees

» Fees for UK/EU students 2018–19 £9,250
» Fees for international students 2018–19 £11,000–£12,500
» For scholarship and bursary information see www.solent.ac.uk/funding
» Graduate salary £18,000

Students

Undergraduates	9,390	(1,495)
Postgraduates	175	(230)
Applications per place	5.7	
Overall offer rate	88.2%	
International students	14.7%	
Mature students	18.7%	
From state-sector schools	97.7%	
From working-class homes	43.8%	

Accommodation

University-provided places: 2,190
Percentage catered: 0%
Self-catered: £88 – £145 per week
First year students are guaranteed accommodation
www.solent.ac.uk/studying-at-solent/accommodation

Staffordshire University

Staffordshire is one of two universities sharing the biggest rise in this year's guide — 29 places — taking it to its highest position to date and into the top half of the table for the first time. The main factor behind its rise has been an astonishing improvement in graduate prospects of more than 20 percentage points, which has taken it from inside the bottom ten into the top 40 on this measure.

The improvement came too late to give the university a chance of improving on a silver rating in the Teaching Excellence Framework (TEF), which uses figures stretching back to 2012–13. It was well below its employment "benchmarks" in those years, although the TEF panel commented favourably on the introduction of a number of initiatives to develop graduate employability skills, close the regional skills gap and provide opportunities for employment and further study.

The panel was also impressed by Staffordshire's campus transformation project, which has seen the university shut its base in Stafford to transfer most of its activities to Stoke-on-Trent. Only the highly-rated nursing and midwifery programmes and other health-related courses will remain in Stafford, on a different site.

As well as saving money, the aim was to improve the student experience and create an award-winning, teaching-led university with a focus on employability, enterprise and entrepreneurialism.

Staffordshire's new configuration may help to arrest a 35% decline in applications that began when the £9,000 fees arrived in 2012. The reduction in actual enrolments has been much lower, and the university reports that the transfer of its flagship computing courses to Stoke has coincided with a 28% increase in the proportion of those receiving offers taking up places at the university.

The main campus is at the heart of Stoke's University Quarter project, which forms a gateway to the city for anyone arriving at its main train station. An £80m investment programme has involved upgrading a number of buildings, expanding the university library, extending student accommodation and improving the public spaces.

Two satellite campuses have survived the reorganisation. Primary teacher training programmes are based at Lichfield, where there is an integrated further and higher education centre, developed in partnership with South Staffordshire College.

The other site is in Shrewsbury, Shropshire, where nursing and midwifery students are based in the Royal Shrewsbury Hospital.

Staffordshire's overall strategy has the title of the "connected university" and is committed to widening participation, promoting social mobility and connecting its

---

College Road
University Quarter
Stoke-on-Trent ST4 2DE
01782 294 400
enquiries@staffs.ac.uk
www.staffs.ac.uk
www.staffsunion.com
Open Days 2018:
March 10 (Stafford)

The Times and The Sunday Times **Rankings**

Overall Ranking: **=63** (last year: 92)

Teaching quality	84.1%	=10
Student experience	80.3%	35
Research quality	16.5%	56
Entry standards	115	107
Graduate prospects	79.8%	37
Good honours	65.8%	104
Expected completion rate	76%	120
Student/staff ratio	15.2	=47
Services and facilities/student	£1,766	98

communities. There is particular emphasis on academic enrichment through subject clubs and passport progression schemes, links with regional businesses and communities and the creation of accessible courses.

New degrees are planned for 2018 in early childhood studies with special education needs and disability, e-sports and the reintroduction of chemistry, building on the success of forensic science.

The university is also playing a leading role in the delivery of degree and higher apprenticeships, working with employers such as Vodafone and the NHS, and claims the largest number of higher apprentices at any university in England. Staffordshire was among the first institutions to offer a BSc in computer science and more recently has been a pioneer of two-year fast-track degrees, which are available in accounting and finance, business management, English and law.

With almost half of the UK undergraduates coming from working-class homes and approaching a quarter from areas of low participation in higher education, Staffordshire exceeds all the benchmarks for the breadth of its intake. The dropout rate remains stubbornly high, however, and is well above expected levels, with close to one in four students (22.6%) failing to complete their courses.

Staffordshire increased the size and scope of its submission to the 2014 Research Excellence Framework, compared with previous research assessments, but still entered only 91 academics. The best results were in sport and exercise sciences, although all of the university's research in psychology was placed in the top two categories for its external impact.

Stoke is not the liveliest city of its size, but the University Quarter is attracting more social and leisure facilities, and there is a lively and active students' union.

Sports facilities are good and will see more investment as numbers on the Stoke campus rise. The university has launched Team Staffs Sports Elite scholarships and spent £1.25m refurbishing the sports centre, adding new studio spaces and tripling the capacity of the gym.

Until now, the 1,200-plus residential places have been enough to satisfy all first-year students requiring accommodation, but no guarantees are offered.

Tuition fees

» Fees for UK/EU students 2018–19	£9,250
» Fees for international students 2018–19	£11,100
» For scholarship and bursary information see www.staffs.ac.uk/undergraduate/funding	
» Graduate salary	£20,000

Students

Undergraduates	8,650	(4,950)
Postgraduates	790	(1,470)
Applications per place	5.4	
Overall offer rate	82.3%	
International students	3.8%	
Mature students	34.2%	
From state-sector schools	98.8%	
From working-class homes	47.6%	

Accommodation

University-provided places: 1,241
Percentage catered: 0%
Self-catered: £118 – £25 per week
www.staffs.ac.uk/student-life/living-here/accommodation

University of Stirling

Applications to Stirling have risen for five years in a row, including the current admissions cycle, when the UK total has been down. But the university cut the number of offers it made in 2016 and enrolled 20% fewer undergraduates.

Stirling is aiming to be in the UK's top 25 universities by 2021 and a rise in entry standards might help it achieve that target. In our latest table, the university has lost two of the seven places it gained the previous year. Lower rankings for student satisfaction are largely responsible.

Like most Scottish universities, Stirling did not enter the Teaching Excellence Framework. It features among Times Higher Education's top 50 universities under 50 years old. Stirling was also awarded the maximum five stars in the QS global rating system, which covers teaching, graduate employability, internationalisation and inclusiveness.

The university, which celebrated its 50th anniversary last year, has 14,000 students. They share one of the most attractive campuses in the UK, 330 acres of parkland around a loch at the foot of the Ochil Hills. A number of the original 1960s structures — notably the Pathfoot Building — have listed status, partly due to the way they blend into their outstanding surroundings. There are two other campuses: one for nurses and midwives in Inverness and a Western Isles site in Stornoway.

One target in the university's strategy is to raise its income by £50m and an increase in the number of international students will contribute to this. A new international study hub, the INTO Academic Centre, opened on the main campus last year, offering preparatory courses for students hoping to take degrees at Stirling.

A new virtual learning environment has been introduced to improve students' access to course and campus information. Lectures are being filmed to make them accessible online.

Almost three quarters of the work submitted by the university to the 2014 Research Excellence Framework was judged to be world-leading or internationally excellent. The best results were in agriculture, veterinary and food science, where Stirling was ranked fourth in the UK. It was also top in Scotland for health sciences and third for psychology.

Stirling is particularly well provided with sports facilities, having been designated Scotland's University for Sporting Excellence. The campus is home to national swimming and tennis centres, as well as a golf course and a football academy.

The sports centre has been refurbished and has a central gym, strength and conditioning areas and a cycle studio. The university runs an international sports scholarship

Stirling
FK9 4LA
01786 467 044
admissions@stir.ac.uk
www.stir.ac.uk
www.stirlingstudentsunion.com
Open Days 2018:
check website

STIRLING
Edinburgh
Belfast
London
Cardiff

***The Times and The Sunday Times* Rankings**

Overall Ranking: **45** (last year: 43)

Teaching quality	79.7%	74
Student experience	76.6%	=95
Research quality	30.5%	43
Entry standards	158	=31
Graduate prospects	74.8%	61
Good honours	81.3%	=22
Expected completion rate	87%	=53
Student/staff ratio	15.8	=61
Services and facilities/student	£1,814	=93

programme and manages Winning Students, the national sport scholarship programme for students across Scotland.

Academic facilities include a modernised library and dedicated study zone. The university also has a chaplaincy that is open to students and staff of all faiths.

Stirling was the British pioneer of the semester system, which has become popular throughout higher education. The academic year is divided into two blocks of 15 weeks with short mid-semester breaks. Students have the option of starting courses in January, rather than September, and can choose subjects from across all five faculties. Degrees in sport business management and sustainable events management are being introduced in 2018.

Undergraduates can switch the direction of their studies, in consultation with their academic adviser, as their interests develop. They can also speed up their progress on a summer academic programme, which squeezes a full semester's teaching into July and August. Full-time students are not allowed to use the programme to reduce the length of their course, but part-timers can.

Two-thirds of the university's students are from Scotland and the remainder come from more than 100 countries. International exchanges are common, with many of Stirling's students going to American, Asian and European universities.

There are 3,000 residential places after a £38m expansion of student accommodation. The Student Hub team assists with inquiries and provides support services.

There is a lively social scene based on the students' union. It has a social space that can be transformed into a nightclub venue or an area for society meetings and study groups.

The MacRobert Arts Centre has a full programme of cultural activities, while the surrounding countryside offers its own attractions for walkers and climbers. The campus has been described by police as one of the safest in Britain and there is a safe taxi scheme. A counselling and wellbeing service offers support for mental and emotional health, and there is a disability service to help students.

Tuition fees

» Fees for Scottish and EU students 2018–19 £0–£1,820
» Fees for non-Scottish UK students 2018–19 £9,250 (capped at £27,750 for 4-year courses)
» Fees for international students 2018–19 £12,140–£14,460
» For scholarship and bursary information see www.stir.ac.uk/undergraduate-study/financial-information
» Graduate salary £21,400

Students

Undergraduates	8,020	(565)
Postgraduates	1,955	(1,295)
Applications per place	10.9	
Overall offer rate	36.1%	
International students	11.2%	
Mature students	30.8%	
From state-sector schools	94.4%	
From working-class homes	32.1%	

Accommodation

University-provided places: 3,000
Percentage catered: 0%
Self-catered: £84 – £163 per week
First year students are given priority
www.stir.ac.uk/campus-life/accommodation/

University of Strathclyde Glasgow

Only five universities, including Oxford and Cambridge, recruit better qualified students than Strathclyde Glasgow. Like other universities north of the border, it has benefited from the uprating of Scottish qualifications in the new UCAS tariff – used for the first time in this year's Good University Guide – but its entrants now have higher average grades than those at Glasgow or Edinburgh.

The trend has helped Strathclyde to a rise of seven places in our table, where it remains just outside the top 40. The university achieved its customary high score for graduate prospects, with 80% of leavers finding highly-skilled jobs or continuing their studies within six months of graduation, but it is in the bottom ten for staffing levels.

The high grades certainly have not put off applicants. A surge in applications in 2015 was followed by another significant increase. Although fewer than half received offers, the intake of undergraduates has still grown by almost 38% in five years.

Nor has Strathclyde's commitment to widening participation in higher education suffered unduly. More than nine out of ten undergraduates are state-educated – far above the UK average for its courses and entry grades – and more than a quarter were from working-class homes, when this was last surveyed. The Learning in Later Life programme is one of Scotland's most successful routes to education for older people.

Strathclyde, which now adds Glasgow to its name, is the third largest university in Scotland, with more than 21,000 students. It emphasises the mission it has had since its establishment in 1796 – to be a "place of useful learning" – and is aiming to be one of the world's leading technological universities.

Like most Scottish universities, Strathclyde did not enter the new Teaching Excellence Framework, but it excelled in the Research Excellence Framework, which took the university close to the top 20 in our research ranking.

Almost 80% of an exceptionally large submission was rated world-leading or internationally excellent. The university was top in the UK for physics and top in Scotland for business, among a clutch of eye-catching performances. It is the European partner for South Korea's global research and commercialisation programme.

The university is investing nearly £600m in campus improvements over the current decade. Approval has been given for a £30m sports facility and a teaching and learning hub at the heart of the campus. Research buildings and the award-winning Strathclyde Business School have been refurbished, while £20m is to be spent on a heat and power

McCance Building
16 Richmond Street
Glasgow G1 1XQ
0141 548 4400
ugenquiries@strath.ac.uk
www.strath.ac.uk
www.strathstudents.com
Open Days 2018:
check website

The Times and The Sunday Times Rankings

Overall Ranking: **41** (last year: 48)

Teaching quality	78.9%	=82
Student experience	78.3%	=73
Research quality	37.7%	=21
Entry standards	202	6
Graduate prospects	80%	35
Good honours	79.2%	31
Expected completion rate	88%	=47
Student/staff ratio	19.7	120
Services and facilities/student	£1,839	91

system that will cut the university's carbon emissions by half.

The £89m Technology and Innovation Centre, the largest in the UK, is the most striking project completed so far.

All courses are taught on the city-centre John Anderson campus, with the faculty of humanities and social sciences at its heart, enabling staff to work more closely with colleagues in research and teaching. Away from the campus, the Advanced Forming Research Centre, a research partnership with international engineering firms, operates near Glasgow airport.

The business school, rated among the top 40 in Europe by the *Financial Times*, is one of Strathclyde's greatest strengths. It is among the largest in Europe and one of only 74 in the world to be "triple accredited" by the main international bodies. The school has international centres in Europe, the Gulf and Southeast Asia.

The engineering faculty is the largest in Scotland and home to Europe's biggest university electrical power engineering and energy research grouping.

Strathclyde Enterprise Pathway allows students to develop, enhance and test their transferable skills, while alumni and businesses in the Strathclyde 100 network support emerging entrepreneurs. Since 2005, the university has helped to launch more than 150 spin-out companies.

There is a student village on the main campus with 1,400 rooms and about 600 residential places in the nearby Merchant City. The union building attracts students from all over Glasgow. Proximity to a vibrant and celebrated music scene is a plus, and the city has numerous other cultural attractions.

On the sporting side, Strathclyde Glasgow was the only training venue in Scotland for the London 2012 Olympics, and the university's students and alumni made up 5% of Team Scotland in the 2014 Commonwealth Games. The new Sport, Health and Wellbeing complex is expected to open in the summer of 2019.

Tuition fees

» Fees for Scottish and EU students 2018–19   £0–£1,820
» Fees for non-Scottish UK students 2018–19   £9,250
  (capped at £27,750 for 4-year courses except MPharm £37,000)
» Fees for international students 2018–19   £14,050–£19,800
» For scholarship and bursary information see
  www.strath.ac.uk/studywithus/universityfunding
» Graduate salary   £22,500

Students

Undergraduates	12,860	(2,105)
Postgraduates	4,060	(2,445)
Applications per place	7	
Overall offer rate	63.8%	
International students	12.1%	
Mature students	32.5%	
From state-sector schools	91.6%	
From working-class homes	25.9%	

Accommodation

University-provided places: 2,000
Percentage catered: 0%
Self-catered: £106 – £137 per week
First year students from outside Glasgow are guaranteed accommodation
www.strath.ac.uk/studywithus/accommodation/

University of Suffolk

Suffolk has slipped to the bottom of the table in its second year in our ranking. But having secured independent university status only in 2016, it is still being judged largely on data that measured its performance when it was a satellite of the universities of East Anglia (UEA) and Essex.

The university is competitive in several areas, but no score could be compiled for the 2014 Research Excellence Framework and less than a third of the UK average was spent on student services in the two years before independence arrived.

Richard Lister, the vice-chancellor, says that many of the initiatives Suffolk has made in the past year will only bear fruit many years into the future. Becoming independent merely provided "a place on the starting line" and too much should not be expected immediately.

The Ipswich-based university has developed a new academic strategy and set up a foundation board with a philanthropic role. It launched ten new degrees in 2017, as well as three degree apprenticeships, in digital and technology solutions, management and healthcare. There is also a new package for international students coming to the UK on Study Abroad programmes.

However, Suffolk still received a bronze rating in the new Teaching Excellence Framework (TEF) because it was "substantially" below its benchmarks for student satisfaction and graduate employment. It also performs poorly on both measures in our league table. The TEF panel did acknowledge the contribution of employers to course design and found a "developing approach to the creation of research and practice-based communities of staff enabling students to benefit by exposure to scholarship, research and professional practice".

Founded in 2007 as University Campus Suffolk, it was expected to take 20 years to become an independent university, but was granted the power to award degrees in 2015 and the privy council agreed to confer the full university title shortly afterwards. UEA and Essex will continue to work with the new university.

There are 5,000 students on the Waterfront campus and at smaller bases in Bury St Edmunds, Lowestoft, Great Yarmouth and Otley. The target is between 6,500 and 7,000 students by 2020. Applications increased this year when some universities — particularly those with similar entry grades to Suffolk's — suffered a sharp decline.

Having completed a renovation of the library, Suffolk has refurbished one of its main teaching buildings, adding specialist facilities for psychology, computer games design, network and software engineering. The Atrium also houses the Ipswich

---

Waterfront Building
Neptune Quay
Ipswich IP4 1QJ
01473 338 348
admissions@uos.ac.uk
www.uos.ac.uk
www.uosunion.org
Open Days 2018:
March 6, April 21,
July 7

The Times and The Sunday Times Rankings
Overall Ranking: **129** (last year: 126)

Teaching quality	77.7%	100
Student experience	74.9%	=111
Research quality	n/a	
Entry standards	113	=111
Graduate prospects	65.9%	104
Good honours	56.9%	126
Expected completion rate	72.5%	125
Student/staff ratio	19.2	118
Services and facilities/student	£683	129

Waterfront Innovation Centre for business and entrepreneurial activities.

The university is a partner in the Ipswich Vision, a collaborative project to create a successful town centre. Its new strategy sees Suffolk as a distinctive "community impact" institution, with a focus more on science, technology, engineering and mathematics.

A partnership with Ipswich Town football club is typical of the university's community approach. A suite of football sports science and coaching courses cover coaching, performance analysis, sports performance physiology, sports psychology, and strength and conditioning. The four-year master's courses include placements at Ipswich Town.

Further afield, Suffolk has established links with the Maastricht School of Management, the No 2 business school in Holland, to offer an executive MBA. The two institutions will deliver the qualification jointly, and will offer students the chance to spend part of the course in America, at Suffolk University in Boston.

Undergraduate courses are tailored to the employment market and include a range of foundation degrees, which will expand in 2018, with the addition of practical life sciences. There are more than 100 undergraduate course options, with offerings in business, computing, engineering, healthcare, psychology and sport.

Four out of ten students are over 25 when they start their courses, most of them coming from the region. The proportion of students from working class homes, at 45%, is higher than average for the university's courses and entry grades, while the percentage from areas of low participation in higher education is among the highest in the country, at almost 27%.

Suffolk has been devoting a larger-than-average share of its fee income to student support, more than half of its spending going on cash bursaries for students from under-represented backgrounds.

Student satisfaction was high in the early years of the National Student Survey, but has dropped sharply in the past two years, with Suffolk in the bottom ten now for the broad student experience.

Many students live at home but there is a privately operated hall of residence for 700 students close to the campus in Ipswich. The university accredits other accommodation in the town and in its other locations.

Tuition fees

» Fees for UK/EU students 2018–19   £9,250
    Foundation courses   £8,220
» Fees for international students 2018–19   £11,500–£13,000
» For scholarship and bursary information see www.uos.ac.uk/content/student-finance
» Graduate salary   £21,500

Students

Undergraduates	3,610	(1,030)
Postgraduates	70	(320)
Applications per place	3.6	
Overall offer rate	72.4%	
International students	2.2%	
Mature students	56.8%	
From state-sector schools	98.9%	
From working-class homes	44.8%	

Accommodation

University-provided places: 708
Percentage catered: 0%
Self-catered: £70 – £160 per week
www.uos.ac.uk/content/accommodation

University of Sunderland

Sunderland's applications have dropped by 44% since 2011, the final year before £9,000 fees, and by 12% in 2016 alone. But the decline in the numbers actually enrolling is much less severe, partly because of a higher offer rate.

About a quarter of the 13,000 students are from outside the UK, placing Sunderland among the ten universities where the biggest share of income comes from international fees. The university also opened a campus in Hong Kong this year.

Sunderland is one of the top institutions in our table for widening participation in higher education. About 58% of its UK undergraduates come from households with a combined income of less than £25,000 a year and almost 30% are from (often local) areas that send few students to university — the highest proportion in the country.

There is generous financial support for students from poor backgrounds, which includes £600 towards public transport costs or university rents, as well as various scholarships. A separate scheme operates on the university's London campus.

Sunderland's open access policy produces predictably low entry scores, close to the bottom ten universities. But Sunderland has recorded its second successive rise in our table, moving up four places with better rankings for student satisfaction and more students achieving good honours.

The university received a silver rating in the new Teaching Excellence Framework this year. The awards panel said students' academic experiences were tailored to the individual, with personalised support available. It also praised the exposure of students to professional practice through engagement with industrial and community partners, and the engagement with employers in course development.

A range of new degrees is being launched both in Sunderland and on the London site, near Canary Wharf, which focuses on business, tourism and nursing degrees, as well as postgraduate programmes. The additions in Sunderland include social media management, screen performance and the chartered manager degree apprenticeship, which leads to a BA in management and professional practice. The new offerings in London include banking and finance, and four-year programmes with a foundation year in events management, and international tourism and hospitality.

The university's extended school of nursing is the first in the UK to be linked directly to a school of pharmacy. The school, on the original City campus in Sunderland, has received approval this year to work with three more partner NHS trusts, after the investment of

---

City Campus
Chester Road
Sunderland SR1 3SD
0191 515 2000
020 7531 7333 (London campus)
Student.helpline@sunderland.ac.uk
www.sunderland.ac.uk
www.sunderlandsu.co.uk
Open Days 2018:
March 14 (Sunderland)

The Times and The Sunday Times **Rankings**
Overall Ranking: **96** (last year: 100)

Teaching quality	80.2%	66
Student experience	78.9%	=62
Research quality	5.8%	=83
Entry standards	112	=114
Graduate prospects	68.3%	=95
Good honours	63.7%	=114
Expected completion rate	76.3%	119
Student/staff ratio	15.4	=49
Services and facilities/student	£2,064	70

£3.5m in facilities, including a mock patient transfer suite with a functioning ambulance and a positive pressure isolation unit.

A second base in Sunderland, the Sir Tom Cowie campus, occupies 24 acres on the banks of the Wear. It is built around a 7th-century abbey described as one of Britain's first universities and incorporates the National Glass Centre, a heritage centre for the glass industry.

The campus also houses the business school and has a media centre with excellent television and video production facilities. New facilities have been added for engineering.

Provision for disabled students is excellent, with trained support staff in the libraries and in every academic school, and special modules to help dyslexics. The main campus houses the North East Regional Assessment Centre, which monitors the requirements of students with disabilities and specific learning difficulties. There is special provision in the halls of residence.

Many students take work placements with multinational companies that have been attracted to the northeast and have links with the university. Nissan, in nearby Washington, for example, helped to design a course in mechanical engineering.

Less than a third of the work submitted for the 2014 Research Excellence Framework reached the top two categories, but the university entered almost 40% of the eligible academics, a much higher proportion than most of its peers. There was some world-leading research in 10 of the 13 subjects in which it submitted work.

The city of Sunderland is fiercely proud of its identity and has the advantage of a riverside and coastal location. There is a £12m student village and leisure facilities are good: the city has a 50-metre swimming pool and a dry ski slope, as well as Europe's biggest climbing wall and a theatre showing West End productions.

The — whisper it — more extensive attractions of Newcastle are less than half an hour away by Metro or bus.

Tuition fees

» Fees for UK/EU students 2018–19	£9,250
» Fees for international students 2018–19	£11,000
» For scholarship and bursary information see www.sunderland.ac.uk/about/your-finances/scholarships-discounts-and-specialised-grants	
» Graduate salary	£22,416

Students

Undergraduates	9,180	(1,395)
Postgraduates	1,545	(875)
Applications per place	4.5	
Overall offer rate	87.9%	
International students	20.5%	
Mature students	40%	
From state-sector schools	98.5%	
From working-class homes	44.9%	

Accommodation

University-provided places: 1,136
Percentage catered: 0%
Self-catered: £72 – £98 per week
First year students are guaranteed accommodation
www.sunderland.ac.uk/about/accommodation

University of Surrey

Surrey — our University of the Year in 2015 — has seen the biggest rise in first-class degrees of any university, the proportion more than doubling, from 19% to more than 40%, in the first five years of the decade. Surrey has moved up 26 places in our table based on the proportion of firsts and 2:1s awarded — our league table measure — over the same period.

The university said the trend reflected enhanced educational provision and better-qualified entrants. A second successive decline in student satisfaction is the main reason for this year's fall in Surrey's overall ranking. Unusually, the university is outside our top 50 for graduate prospects, normally one of its main strengths.

Surrey received a gold rating in the Teaching Excellence Framework (TEF), however. A glowing reference from the TEF panel complimented the university on "innovative and personalised provision that secures the highest levels of engagement and encourages a high degree of commitment to learning and study". It found high levels of teaching excellence and an effective approach to the development of professional skills and employability.

Applications have declined this year, but only after a record number in 2016 when there was an increase of almost 20%, which the university attributes partly to its league table performance (and, dare we say it, our University of the Year award). The numbers starting degrees have never been higher, almost reaching 3,000 for the first time last year.

They are likely to rise again in 2019, when Surrey hopes to open a medical school. Its curriculum would seek to give doctors greater digital skills to deliver personalised medicine.

Four new degrees have been launched as part of Surrey's Innovation for Health initiative, combining health or biomedicine with data science and electronic engineering. They will make use of the £12.5m Innovation for Health Learning Laboratory that opened last year.

Surrey tops our table for food science for the third year in a row, and the university was awarded a Queen's Anniversary Prize in 2017 for its work informing public policy on food and nutrition, which includes pioneering research in obesity, diabetes, osteoporosis, vitamin D, iodine and food labelling.

Surrey has been among the most proactive universities in recent years. The £45m veterinary school, which opened in 2015, was only the second to be established in half a century. The campus in Guildford has been extended and another opened in Dalian, China, in partnership with the Dongbei University of Finance and Economics. The 5G Innovation Centre brings together Surrey's researchers with global players in mobile telecommunications.

Senate House
Guildford GU2 7XH
01483 682 222
admissions@surrey.ac.uk
www.surrey.ac.uk
www.ussu.co.uk
Open Days 2018:
June 22, 23,
September 15,
October 13

The Times and The Sunday Times **Rankings**

Overall Ranking: **19** (last year: 14)

Teaching quality	81.7%	=38
Student experience	81.4%	25
Research quality	29.7%	45
Entry standards	169	18
Graduate prospects	76.8%	=51
Good honours	83.6%	16
Expected completion rate	90.6%	=35
Student/staff ratio	15.4	=49
Services and facilities/student	£2,734	15

Almost 80% of the work submitted to the 2014 Research Excellence Framework was rated world-leading or internationally excellent. The best results were in nursing and other health subjects.

The university has been awarded £1million by the Leverhulme Trust to establish the world's first doctoral training centre for quantum biology. Students will work on projects from photosynthesis to nanotechnology.

Professor Max Lu, the vice-chancellor, is keen to develop Surrey's international reputation. The university has a high proportion of students from outside the UK — over a quarter — and more than half of its research publications have an international partner.

All students are encouraged to take a free course in a European language alongside their degree, in a programme known as the Global Graduate Award. Undergraduates in most subjects undertake work placements of one year, or several shorter periods, often abroad. As a result, most degrees last four years.

Large numbers take engineering and science subjects but the university also has other strengths, notably in business and the sector-leading school of hospitality and tourism management. SurreyLearn, a virtual learning environment, allows students to work with others on their courses online and to take part in discussions and blogs, as well as allowing lecturers to set coursework and interact with undergraduates.

The Surrey campus is ten minutes' walk from the centre of Guildford. Developments since 2000 have cost £400m. The Surrey Research Park, a centre for science and engineering, is one of the largest in the UK to be owned, funded and managed by its host university.

Another 500 residential places will be available on the Manor Park campus, which is effectively an extension of the university's Stag Hill headquarters, by September 2018. A further 700 rooms will be added in the following year, taking the total on the campus to almost 3,000 – enough to guarantee places for new entrants.

The £36m Surrey Sports Park has extensive indoor and outdoor facilities. The main campus is the centre of social life, although Guildford has plenty of retail, cultural and recreational facilities. The proximity of London (35 minutes by train) is an attraction to many students, although it helps account for the high cost of renting in the private sector.

Tuition fees

» Fees for UK/EU students 2018–19 £9,250
» Fees for international students 2018–19 £15,800–£20,500
  Veterinary Medicine £31,500
» For scholarship and bursary information see www.surrey.ac.uk/fees-and-funding/scholarships-and-bursaries

---

Students

Undergraduates	10,095	(900)
Postgraduates	2,705	(1,350)
Applications per place	9.4	
Overall offer rate	68.1%	
International students	21.9%	
Mature students	11.5%	
From state-sector schools	92.1%	
From working-class homes	28.6%	

Accommodation

University-provided places: 5,147
Percentage catered: 0%
Self-catered: £71 – £170 per week
First year students are guaranteed accommodation
www.surrey.ac.uk/accommodation

University of Sussex

Sussex has dropped nine places in our new table, taking the university out of the elite top 20. It could not sustain last year's outstanding graduate outcomes, falling almost 30 places in our ranking for this measure, and there has been a significant decline in satisfaction with the broader student experience.

Applications have never been healthier, however, growing by a quarter in 2016 alone. The intake of undergraduates was 1,000 higher than at the time £9,000 fees were introduced, as Sussex pursued a target of 18,000 students by 2018. It is sufficiently close to that mark, with more than 15,000 students, that the university was content to match last year's enrolment and avoid clearing this summer.

Sussex was placed in the silver category in the Teaching Excellence Framework. The independent panel praised an "outstanding" employment strategy, underpinned by curriculums designed to develop transferable employment skills. Students were frequently exposed to, and engaged in, cutting-edge research, the panel added, and significant investment in the university estate boosted the quality of learning.

The university has invested £150m in ten years regenerating the campus in the Brighton suburb of Falmer. New teaching laboratories in the school of engineering and informatics are the latest addition. A £29m academic building includes lecture theatres, study and teaching space, and a social centre, while the Attenborough Centre is an interdisciplinary arts hub for the university and the wider community.

The aim of increasing student numbers was to provide opportunities for a more diverse range of students and achieve the "critical mass" that Sussex considers necessary to strengthen the interdisciplinary approach that has been its hallmark since the 1960s, engage with partners and be internationally competitive in research. Three-quarters of the work submitted for the Research Excellence Framework was judged to be world-leading or internationally excellent, and Sussex was among the leaders in English, psychology, history and geography.

There is excellence in a variety of subjects: Sussex researchers have made significant advances in quantum computing recently, for example. The university is ranked top in the world for development studies and has launched a sustainability research programme headed by the former chief scientist at the UN Environment Programme. There are research centres on adoption, corruption, Middle East studies and consciousness science.

International development with geography will be offered both as a three-year BSc and a four-year integrated master's degree in 2018. The university has a growing

Sussex House
Falmer
Brighton BN1 9RH
01273 876 787
ug.enquiries@sussex.ac.uk
www.sussex.ac.uk
www.sussexstudent.com
Open Days 2018:
check website

The Times and The Sunday Times **Rankings**

Overall Ranking: **27** (last year: 18)

Teaching quality	78.8%	86
Student experience	79.4%	=49
Research quality	31.8%	=38
Entry standards	141	48
Graduate prospects	80.2%	=33
Good honours	78.5%	=33
Expected completion rate	92.7%	=23
Student/staff ratio	16.3	=73
Services and facilities/student	£2,710	17

range of four-year degrees, across the arts, sciences, engineering and technology, with access to student loans and leading to a master's qualification.

Arts and social science students account for the biggest share of places, but the physical and life sciences are not far behind, while a successful joint medical school is shared with neighbouring Brighton University, and split between the Royal Sussex County Hospital and the two universities' Falmer campuses.

Except on accredited courses, undergraduates are encouraged to study outside their core area. They can take a language or an elective in another subject, leading to a major/minor degree and opening up opportunities to study abroad. There are two 12-week teaching periods, punctuated by mid-year assessment – a pattern that the university believes improves the way students learn and are assessed.

Support includes a work-study programme to help students earn money, funded work placements and three years' aftercare for graduates to help them find a career that suits them. The Sussex Plus programme documents and credits students' extracurricular skills, while Startup Sussex supports creative business ideas and social projects.

Sussex has extensive bursary and scholarship schemes to broaden its intake, focusing particularly on candidates with no family experience of higher education. A prize-winning scheme supports them with rent reductions and scholarships. There is also a new scholarship scheme for up to 50 Syrian refugees to receive intensive English language tuition for between five and 28 weeks.

A quarter of the students come from outside the EU and the university has performed consistently well in the International Student Barometer, which gauges overseas students' satisfaction. Together with other first-years, they are guaranteed one of the 5,350 places in university-managed accommodation that has been expanded and upgraded in recent years.

The campus is located within the South Downs National Park, with excellent transport links to the city. There is no shortage of social events on campus and Brighton has plenty to offer.

The university's sporting facilities are good and sports scholarships are available to outstanding athletes, including basketball and hockey players.

Tuition fees

» Fees for UK/EU students 2018–19 £9,250
» Fees for international students 2018–19 £15,500 – £19,200
  Medicine £29,000
» For scholarship and bursary information see
  www.sussex.ac.uk/study/undergraduate/
  fees-and-scholarships/undergraduate-scholarships
» Graduate salary £20,000

Students

Undergraduates	10,935	(0)
Postgraduates	3,530	(690)
Applications per place	5.7	
Overall offer rate	92.3%	
International students	26.1%	
Mature students	11.9%	
From state-sector schools	88%	
From working-class homes	22.5%	

Accommodation

University-provided places: 5,350
Percentage catered: 0%
Self-catered: £99 – £153 per week
First year students are guaranteed accommodation
www.susesx.ac.uk/study/accommodation

Swansea University

Swansea has gone up seven places in our table this year, but may still be frustrated with the result. That is because, having overtaken Cardiff for the first time to become the leading university in Wales in 2016 — and winning our inaugural Welsh University of the Year award, to boot — it has finished three points behind its great rival in this new edition.

In other respects, the university could hardly be more successful. A new campus opened two years ago, applications and enrolments are at record levels and Swansea registered the biggest rise in income at any university in the latest survey. Now in the top 40, It has never been higher in our table.

The numbers starting degrees have grown by almost 70% since 2012, although Swansea has not been immune from the downturn in applications this year. Nine new degrees took their first students last autumn, when chemistry was reintroduced as a BSc and four-year integrated master's degree, taught in new laboratories.

Swansea was given a silver rating in the new Teaching Excellence Framework, whose panel said that high-quality personalised learning was embedded across the university, with a tutorial system, a specialised centre and attendance monitoring providing high levels of engagement and commitment to learning and study.

The second phase of the Bay Campus is due to open in September 2018 and includes a £31m "computational foundry", which has the aim of turning Swansea and the surrounding region into a global destination for computational scientists. It is part of a £522m capital plan that includes the continuing redevelopment of the original Singleton Park site.

The £450m, 65-acre Bay Campus is among the only ones in the UK with direct access to a beach. It is home to the engineering college and management school and houses about 1,500 students in new halls of residence, relieving pressure on the original base five miles along the coast.

Swansea's focus is on applied research with industry; the new Engineering Quarter houses two research institutes where there are collaborations with Rolls- Royce, Airbus and Tata Steel.

Singleton Park occupies a prime position at the gateway to the Gower peninsula, the UK's first area of outstanding natural beauty. About £72m has already been invested in new facilities, and the new programme includes improvements to the library and upgraded laboratories and other teaching facilities.

Swansea's strongest suit in our table continues to be the prospects for its graduates, where it is now inside the top 20. More than four in five graduates land professional-level jobs or go on to further study. The Employability Academy provides paid

---

Singleton Park
Swansea SA2 8PP
01792 205 678
admissions@swansea.ac.uk
www.swansea.ac.uk
www.swansea-union.co.uk
Open Days 2018:
June 16, October 13, 27

The Times and The Sunday Times **Rankings**

Overall Ranking: **=36** (last year: =44)

Teaching quality	81.1%	=49
Student experience	81.3%	=26
Research quality	33.7%	36
Entry standards	129	=68
Graduate prospects	82.6%	=15
Good honours	78%	36
Expected completion rate	89.6%	42
Student/staff ratio	15.2	=47
Services and facilities/student	£2,336	37

internships and co-ordinates a variety of career support activities.

Four-fifths of the work submitted for the 2014 Research Excellence Framework was assessed as world-leading or internationally excellent, with health subjects, English and general engineering doing particularly well. Swansea University Medical School is one of the UK's fastest-growing.

Undergraduates are encouraged to stray outside their specialist area in their first year. Many degrees include opportunities to work abroad or study at one of more than 100 partner institutions worldwide. Only 28% of undergraduates came from working-class homes when this was last surveyed, significantly less that the UK average for the university's subjects and entry grades, but the projected dropout rate is much better than Swansea's benchmark figure.

The department of adult and continuing education teaches mature students throughout the valleys and elsewhere in South Wales, while the South West Wales Reaching Wider Partnership targets areas of deprivation. Swansea has good provision for disabled students, whose needs are addressed through an assessment and training centre.

The £20m sports village was used as a training facility by the New Zealand and Canada squads during the 2015 rugby World Cup. It has an athletics track, grass and all-weather pitches, squash and tennis courts,

plus the indoor athletics training centre and 80-station gym. The adjacent Wales National Pool has 50-metre and 25-metre pools and is a designated Welsh high-performance centre.

The 360 Beach and Watersports Centre is the only university-operated facility of its kind in the UK, while Swansea also has grass and 3G pitches a few miles away at its Fairwood development, built in partnership with Swansea City football club. The Bay campus has a sports hall, gym and two outdoor multiuse areas.

The university has one of the best ratios of computers available for student use at any UK institution and there are about 5,000 residential places, enough to guarantee places to new entrants who apply by the end of June with Swansea as their firm choice. The city has a good range of leisure facilities and Cardiff is less than an hour away by train for those looking for a change of scene.

Tuition fees

» Fees for UK/EU students 2018–19 £9,000
» Fees for international students 2018–19 £13,700–£17,950
  Medicine £35,700
» For scholarship and bursary information see
  www.swansea.ac.uk/scholarships
» Graduate salary £20,500

Students

Undergraduates	12,910	(1,770)
Postgraduates	1,920	(850)
Applications per place	5.7	
Overall offer rate	90.7%	
International students	14.2%	
Mature students	11.3%	
From state-sector schools	91.9%	
From working-class homes	27.9%	

Accommodation

University-provided places: 5,000
Percentage catered: 4%
Catered costs: £128 – £133 per week
Self-catered: £89 – £143 per week
First year students are guaranteed accommodation
www.swansea.ac.uk/accommodation

Teesside University

Teesside has launched no fewer than 40 new undergraduate programmes in this academic year. These range from a four-year integrated master's course in computer games design to an innovative suite of Higher National Certificate and diploma courses in home construction, developed with television architect George Clarke, that lead from sub-degree to postgraduate level.

There is also a growing range of higher and degree apprenticeships, which are now available or under development for more than a dozen roles, from laboratory scientist to registered nurse and power engineer.

The developments follow the adoption of a new learning and teaching strategy, which promises to employ Teesside's strength in digital technology to enrich the student experience. DigitalCity Innovation, the university's centre for digital excellence and entrepreneurship, has helped in the creation of hundreds of new companies and contributed to a Queen's Anniversary prize for the university's services to business and enterprise.

Teesside was given a silver rating in the government's new Teaching Excellence Framework. The awards panel was impressed by a "comprehensive and well-received investment in high-quality physical and digital resources" and the innovative and well-resourced support for the development of employability. In particular, the panel praised the investment in internships, which encourage progression to highly-skilled employment.

The university has gone up nine places and into the top 100 in our table this year. It has reached the top 40 for graduate prospects after rising more than 50 places on this measure, offsetting a sharp decline in student satisfaction.

The university supports the career development of its graduates for a minimum of two years after graduation and is expanding paid work placements as part of a student's course. The Get Ahead scheme provides three-month paid internships and training for graduates, as well as helping to provide summer placements for second-year students.

Teesside is well known for its commitment to widening access to higher education. Only one university has a higher proportion of undergraduates from areas of low participation in higher education, and the share of places going to students from the four poorest socioeconomic groups is significantly higher than average for its courses and entry qualifications.

More than 8,000 of the 18,500 students are part-time – a much larger proportion than at most universities since the decline of part-time higher education nationally – and over 6,000 are taking courses below degree level. Two-thirds are from the northeast and about four in ten are 21 or over on entry.

Middlesbrough
TS1 3BX
01642 738 181
enquiries@tees.ac.uk
www.tees.ac.uk
www.tees-su.org.uk
Open Days 2018:
March 24, June 16

Belfast
Edinburgh
MIDDLESBROUGH
London
Cardiff

The Times and The Sunday Times Rankings

Overall Ranking: **92** (last year: =101)

Teaching quality	81.3%	=46
Student experience	76.7%	=92
Research quality	3.6%	110
Entry standards	119	=95
Graduate prospects	79.6%	=39
Good honours	63.8%	=112
Expected completion rate	79.8%	=105
Student/staff ratio	16.6	=80
Services and facilities/student	£2,152	57

Applications have been steady over several years and the numbers starting courses have risen, in line with the university's strategy. The 11,000 health students are by far the largest group in the university, while design and computer animation and gaming are generally regarded as the other main strengths. The relaunched Teesside University Business School has a range of new undergraduate and postgraduate courses.

Only 14% of Teesside's eligible academics were entered for the 2014 Research Excellence Framework, but almost 60% of their work was considered world-leading or internationally excellent – twice as much as in the previous research assessments. Social work and social policy, history and health subjects produced the best results.

Teesside has spent £270m on campus improvements over recent years, mainly at its base in Middlesbrough town centre. Work is currently taking place on the £22m National Horizons Centre, a new biosciences research, education and training facility at the university's second campus, in Darlington. A new £300m masterplan will continue this investment over the next ten years.

Priorities include a new hub for student services, a teaching and conferencing centre, central laboratory facilities, a digital production facility and a new business school. Further investment is planned in the campus public realm to create more open spaces and residential accommodation will also be improved and extended.

The main campus has shops, bars, cafes and restaurants on the doorstep, and the students' union has been rated among the top ten in the country. The internationally renowned contemporary art gallery Mima (Middlesbrough Institute of Modern Art), a member of the Plus Tate Network, is now part of the university.

The cost of living is another attraction: rents in the private sector are among the cheapest in the UK and there are almost 1,000 residential places on campus.

The Olympia sports complex has a large 500-spectator capacity sports hall among its facilities. There is a £2.75m health and fitness centre, and the university also has a watersports centre on the River Tees.

Tuition fees

- » Fees for UK/EU students 2018–19   £9,250
  Foundation courses   £6,150
- » Fees for international students 2018–19   £11,825
  Foundation courses   £9,750
- » For scholarship and bursary information see www.tees.ac.uk/sections/fulltime/scholarships.cfm
- » Graduate salary   £21,000

Students

Undergraduates	9,455	(6,880)
Postgraduates	745	(1,490)
Applications per place	4.5	
Overall offer rate	76.5%	
International students	4.1%	
Mature students	38.3%	
From state-sector schools	98.9%	
From working-class homes	45.7%	

Accommodation

University-provided places: 1,004
Percentage catered: 0%
Self-catered: £58 – £115 per week
www.tees.ac.uk/accommodation

University of Wales, Trinity St David

The University of Wales Trinity Saint David (UWTSD) is back in our league table for the first time in five years, after a boycott of all rankings.

It returns in a familiar position, just outside the top 100, but with contrasting performances on the different measures. UWTSD is well inside the top 20 for student satisfaction with teaching quality, but bottom for graduate prospects and close to the bottom ten for research and entry standards.

UWTSD was one of six Welsh universities to enter the Teaching Excellence Framework and the only one to emerge with the lowest bronze rating. The awards panel did like the university's small classes and culture of personalised learning, which helps to ensure students are effectively supported and challenged to achieve their full potential.

The panel also said Welsh medium and Welsh-language education is deployed in ways that support, stretch and challenge students.

There are fewer than 10,000 students, even after the merger of Trinity Saint David with Swansea Metropolitan University. Applications declined in 2016 when there was a 16% fall in the numbers starting courses. Twenty new degrees have been launched in subjects as diverse as advocacy, international sports management, architecture, mental health and personal training.

The first phase of a £300m Swansea Waterfront Innovation Quarter in the city's SA1 area is due to be ready when students arrive in September. The initial development will house the faculties of architecture, computing and engineering, education and communities, as well as a new library.

The project will see UWTSD co-locating and collaborating with professional partners to enable its students to engage with employers as part of their studies and to provide opportunities for its graduates. A second phase, covering a further 18,000 square metres, is due for completion in 2021 for academic and business use.

Core student services and the students' union will be located alongside sports and leisure facilities, and there will also be community and commercial amenities. The 19-acre campus will complement the university's existing £30m investment in a Cultural Quarter for the city.

Two mergers in three years created UWTSD. The first saw the former Trinity University College, Camarthen, come together with the University of Wales Lampeter 23 miles away. Only Oxford and Cambridge were awarding degrees before St David's College, Lampeter, which eventually became the smallest publicly funded university in Europe.

Carmarthen Campus
Carmarthen SA31 3EP
0300 500 5054
admissions@uwtsd.ac.uk
www.uwtsd.ac.uk
www.tsdsu.co.uk
Open Days 2018: June 30 (Carmarthen and Lampeter), August 18 (all campuses), September 15 (Carmarthen), September 8 (Lampeter), June 23, September 22 (Swansea)

The Times and The Sunday Times Rankings

Overall Ranking: **104** (last year: n/a)

Teaching quality	83.6%	16
Student experience	78.7%	=66
Research quality	2.6%	116
Entry standards	109	=118
Graduate prospects	53%	129
Good honours	66.7%	=99
Expected completion rate	78.9%	=110
Student/staff ratio	15.4	=49
Services and facilities/student	£2,043	75

The university now offers students the choice of a rural or urban experience, from the green campuses of Lampeter and Carmarthen to the urban surroundings of Swansea, following the merger with Swansea Met. There is also a London campus, near the Oval cricket ground, for international students taking business, management and IT degrees.

In addition, a group structure connects UWTSD with two large further education colleges in southwest Wales, Coleg Ceredigion and Coleg Sir Gar, in Carmarthenshire.

With a long history in teacher training, the university has established Yr Athrofa, the Institute of Education, to operate on the Carmarthen and Swansea campuses. The aim is to produce a new and innovative approach to teacher education, with the university and partner schools jointly responsible for the construction and delivery of all training programmes.

It has also welcomed the first cohort of students to its new Academy of Sinology in Lampeter, a partnership with the Chin Kung Multicultural Educational Foundation, which is based in Hong Kong.

A new centre for outdoor education has opened, a mile from the Carmarthen campus on the All Wales coastal walking path. Another new centre will open later this year on the Carmarthen campus, hosting S4C, Wales's national broadcaster, and a number of other companies and organisations in the creative and digital industries. The centre will also provide a space for graduate start-up companies linked to the university's programmes.

The UWTSD Lampeter campus continues to make a virtue of its small size by stressing its friendly atmosphere and intimate teaching style. Based on an ancient castle and modelled on an Oxbridge college, it offers subjects including anthropology, archaeology, Chinese, classics and philosophy.

The Carmarthen campus was established in 1848 to train teachers. It now offers a range of other programmes in the creative and performing arts, as well as a growing portfolio within the School of Sport, Health and Outdoor Education.

The Swansea campus began life as a college of art in 1853, and became part of UWTSD in 2013. Its automotive engineering courses — especially those focused on motor sport — are its best-known feature, but there has been strong demand for places on a variety of vocationally orientated courses.

Tuition fees

- » Fees for UK/EU students 2018–19 £9,000
  Foundation courses (STEM) £7,000
- » Fees for international students 2017–18 £10,400–£14,900
- » For scholarship and bursary information see www.uwtsd.ac.uk/bursaries
- » Graduate salary £17,500

Students		
Undergraduates	6,040	(2,380)
Postgraduates	650	(855)
Applications per place	3.7	
Overall offer rate	85.5%	
International students	5.7%	
Mature students	39.8%	
From state-sector schools	98.9%	
From working-class homes	42.4%	

Accommodation

University-provided places: 1,118
Percentage catered: 17%
Catered costs: £4,074 annually
Self-catered: £64 – £91
First year students are given first chance to apply
www.uwtsd.ac.uk/accommodation

Ulster University

Both applications and enrolments grew at Ulster in 2016, but this is likely to come to at least a temporary halt after the closure of the modern languages department and the withdrawal of a number of other courses. The university previously said that it expected to shed 1,200 places over three years to cope with cuts in its government grant.

Ulster has fallen five places in our new table, making a 16-place decline in two years. There have been improvements in entry standards, completion rates and the proportion of students achieving good honours, but they were outweighed by declines in the remaining areas, including student satisfaction.

New degrees have been launched, however, in football coaching and business management, and ceramics, jewellery and silversmithing, as well as one in applied pharmaceutical science for students taking a higher apprenticeship. The coaching degree is a partnership with the Irish Football Association and will be delivered partly at the national football stadium, at Windsor Park, Belfast.

Ulster also hopes to open a medical school on its Magee campus in Londonderry. If the bid is successful, the first 80 students will join in September 2019. In the longer term, the university expects to increase the number of undergraduates on the campus by more than 2,500 to 6,000. A new central teaching block is opening, although its main purpose is to upgrade the current facilities rather than catering for more students.

The university also upgraded its teaching facilities and has opened a new sports centre on its Coleraine campus. But the main capital development is in Belfast's Cathedral Quarter where a £250m campus is taking shape. The 12,450 students at Jordanstown, the university's biggest site, will move to the new development in 2019. Only the High Performance Sports Centre, which houses the Sports Institute Northern Ireland, will remain in Jordanstown, using the outdoor and indoor sprint tracks, sports science and sports medicine facilities, which will still be available to students.

At present, Belfast concentrates on art and design, architecture, hospitality event management, photography and digital animation. Jordanstown will remain the location for courses starting in 2018 in business and management, the built environment, computing and engineering, health and sport sciences, and social sciences. The third campus, at Coleraine, on Northern Ireland's north coast, offers environmental and life sciences, humanities, media, film and journalism and tourism management. A £6.5m media centre there has been rated as one of the most impressive in the UK by the National Council

Cromore Road
Coleraine BT52 1SA
028 9036 8821
study@ulster.ac.uk
www.ulster.ac.uk
http://uusu.org
Open Days 2018:
check website

COLERAINE Edinburgh
Belfast
London
Cardiff

***The Times and The Sunday Times* Rankings**

Overall Ranking: **73** (last year: 68)

Teaching quality	80.5%	=60
Student experience	79.2%	54
Research quality	31.8%	=38
Entry standards	126	=77
Graduate prospects	67.8%	98
Good honours	71.6%	66
Expected completion rate	83.5%	=81
Student/staff ratio	18.8	113
Services and facilities/student	£1,835	92

for the Training of Journalists. The BBC has a studio in the centre, which includes a high-definition television studio, the largest multimedia newsroom on the island of Ireland, high-definition editing suites and five satellite feeds.

The Coleraine campus is also home to the Centre for Molecular Biosciences, which produced the most highly rated work in the 2014 Research Excellence Framework. More than 70% of Ulster's submission was considered world-leading or internationally excellent, with law and nursing and health science producing outstanding results, too. The university has since been awarded almost £20m in research funding from an EU cross-border scheme for projects in health and life sciences and renewable energy. The largest share will go to a personalised medicine programme.

Magee has a focus on the creative and performing arts, nursing and social work, computing, business and management, and social sciences. Its expansion will focus on computer science, engineering and creative technologies. There is already a Centre for Stratified Medicine near the campus, at Altnagelvin Area Hospital.

Ulster has branch campuses in London and Birmingham where it offers courses in business, computing and engineering in partnership with the QA Higher Education, a private organisation that also delivers apprenticeships and training programmes.

Most courses now include the option of a year-long work placement.

Neither of the universities in Northern Ireland entered the Teaching Excellence Framework, but Ulster features in Times Higher Education magazine's top 150 universities in the world that are less than 50 years old. Business links are strong, and the university is ranked in the top seven in the UK for the volume of knowledge transfer it undertakes.

All undergraduates are from state schools and more than 45% come from working-class backgrounds. The university's award-winning sports outreach programme has been particularly successful. Accommodation is guaranteed for all first-year students on all four campuses and private sector rents are low by UK standards. There are students' union facilities at every location, but social life inevitably varies by campus.

Tuition fees

» Fees for Northern Ireland and EU students 2018–19 £4,160
» Fees for students from England, Scotland, Wales 2018–19 £9,250
» Fees for international students 2018–19 £13,240
  Foundation courses £8,820
» For scholarship and bursary information see www.ulster.ac.uk/apply/fees-and-funding/scholarships
» Graduate salary £19,200

Students

Undergraduates	15,905	(3,965)
Postgraduates	1,800	(3,490)
Applications per place	6.3	
Overall offer rate	85.5%	
International students	6.1%	
Mature students	21.9%	
From state-sector schools	100%	
From working-class homes	44.6%	

Accommodation

University-provided places: 2,100
Percentage catered: 0%
Self-catered: £73 – £146 per week
First year students are guaranteed accommodation
www.ulster.ac.uk/accommodation

University College London

University College London (UCL) is adopting a new "connected curriculum" to ensure that every student gets the opportunity to engage in research. It is part of a five-year strategy to improve teaching and learning, focusing first on assessment and feedback, which has been the greatest source of dissatisfaction among undergraduates.

Its students boycotted the National Student Survey (NSS) last year but their perceptions of teaching quality have been in the bottom ten in our table in recent years and ensured that UCL was restricted to silver in the new Teaching Excellence Framework (TEF). Students have been recruited as UCL ChangeMakers in departments with low NSS scores to investigate what undergraduates would like and advise on new types of assessment.

The TEF panel found a "wide array of exceptional learning resources, both physical and digital" and complimented UCL on a highly successful approach to supporting students into employment or further study. The college is in our top five for graduate prospects, as well as being second for staffing levels. With a median salary of £25,000 six months after graduating, UCL graduates are among the best paid in the UK. Just three universities have higher-earning graduates.

Overall, UCL is joint seventh in our table, one of the academic powerhouses of UK higher education with 29 Nobel prize-winners to its name. It is also in the top seven universities in the world in the QS rankings, which place more emphasis on research. Such was the quality and quantity of UCL's submission to the 2014 Research Excellence Framework that only Oxford has received a higher research grant subsequently.

More than 90% of the eligible academics were entered for assessment and more than 80% of their work was rated as world-leading or internationally excellent. UCL had the most world-leading research in medicine and the biological sciences, the largest volume of research in maths, science, technology and engineering, and the biggest share of top grades in the social sciences.

It was one of the Russell Group universities to take advantage of the ending of restrictions on the number of UK students it could recruit. Offers are now made to more than 60% of school-leavers who apply, compared with less than 40% in the year before £9,000 fees were introduced. Almost 800 places have been added to the intake in that time – a rise of nearly 40% – and applications were up by almost 6% in 2017, when most universities saw the demand for places decline.

About £1.2bn is being invested over ten years to implement the Transforming UCL

Gower Street
London WC1E 6BT
020 3370 1214
020 3108 8520 (International)
study@ucl.ac.uk
international@ucl.ac.uk
www.ucl.ac.uk
http://uclu.org
Open Days 2018:
check website

Edinburgh
Belfast
Cardiff
LONDON

The Times and The Sunday Times Rankings

Overall Ranking: **=7** (last year: 6)

Teaching quality	n/a	
Student experience	n/a	
Research quality	51%	5
Entry standards	193	10
Graduate prospects	82.1%	=20
Good honours	88.8%	5
Expected completion rate	94.8%	=10
Student/staff ratio	10.4	=2
Services and facilities/student	£2,805	13

programme, which includes a new campus in Stratford, east London, at the Queen Elizabeth Olympic Park, as well as upgrading existing campuses. UCL East will bring together expertise in areas such as creativity and material culture, future global cities, and experimental engineering. It is the largest capital investment programme UCL has undertaken since building its original Bloomsbury campus. The refurbished and extended Astor College halls are due to reopen in September and a new student centre is scheduled to open three months later.

A new School of Management opened at Canary Wharf in 2016 and there is a recently developed archaeology and conservation campus in Qatar. The medical school, with several associated teaching hospitals, is among the UK's biggest. UCL was a founding partner in the Francis Crick Institute in the capital, which is carrying out leading-edge research to advance understanding of health and disease.

Comfortably the largest of the University of London's colleges, UCL has more than 37,000 students. Concerted attempts are being made to broaden the undergraduate intake with summer schools, outreach activities and campus-based programmes. But the share of places going to independent school students remains among the highest in Britain, at almost a third.

UCL has a history of pioneering subjects that have become commonplace in higher education: modern languages, geography and fine arts among them. Students are required to have a foreign language GCSE at grade C or above, although they are allowed to reach this standard during their degree if they have not taken a language at school. In future, British sign language will be accepted under this requirement.

Close to the West End and with its own theatre and recreational facilities, UCL offers plenty of leisure options. Students also have access to the facilities of the student centre in the former University of London union building in Bloomsbury. Residential accommodation is plentiful and of a good standard. Indoor sports and fitness facilities are close at hand, but the main outdoor pitches, though good enough to attract professional football clubs, are in Hertfordshire.

Tuition fees

» Fees for UK/EU students 2018–19   £9,250
» Fees for international students 2018–19   £17,890–£26,430
    Medicine   £33,650
» For scholarship and bursary information see
    www.ucl.ac.uk/prospective-students/scholarships
» Graduate salary   £25,000

Students

Undergraduates	16,755	(1,155)
Postgraduates	12,960	(6,265)
Applications per place	7.6	
Overall offer rate	63%	
International students	39.7%	
Mature students	6.9%	
From state-sector schools	68.4%	
From working-class homes	19%	

Accommodation

University-provided places: 4,556
Percentage catered: 18%
Catered costs: £154 – £222 per week
Self-catered: £103 – £125 per week
First year students are guaranteed accommodation
www.ucl.ac.uk/prospective-students/accommodation

University of Warwick

Warwick has never been out of our top ten and was last year's favourite choice of recruiters in *The Times*'s top 100 employers seeking the best graduates. Although down two places in our new table, it is close to the top 50 in the QS World University Rankings and received a gold rating in the new Teaching Excellence Framework (TEF).

The TEF panel said the extent to which students were stretched both within and beyond the curriculum was "exemplary". There were high-quality physical and digital resources, and a focus on research-informed teaching.

Warwick — our University of the Year in 2014 — has expanded its undergraduate intake by almost 30% since 2012, the first year of £9,000 fees. There are now 15,000 undergraduates in a total student population of more than 25,000 but, with almost eight applications to a place, the university remains one of the most selective.

A £250m investment programme is under way on Warwick's campus, three miles south of Coventry. A new teaching building has opened, with 250 and 500-seat lecture theatres and social learning spaces. A purpose-built building for the arts faculty has been approved and work has begun on a new £27m mathematical sciences building. In addition, a three-year extension and refurbishment of the Arts Centre has started.

The £150m Centre for National Automotive Innovation, where research engineers from car manufacturers will work closely with Warwick Manufacturing Group (WMG), is nearing completion. The centre is part-funded by the government as well as by Jaguar Land Rover and Tata Motors. It will include the world's most adaptable driving simulator for research on driverless cars. WMG is also planning a Cycling Innovation and Technology Hub to provide a "catalyst for business to accelerate technological innovation within the UK cycling industry".

Almost 90% of the work submitted for the 2014 Research Excellence Framework was rated as world-leading or internationally excellent, confirming Warwick's place among the top ten universities for research. English and computer science produced the best results, but Warwick ranked in the UK's top ten in 14 different subject areas.

The university has reconfigured its research around its "Global Research Priorities" programme, which focuses on key areas of international significance. Current themes include energy, connecting cultures, food security, global governance, individual behaviour and innovative manufacturing. A new unit for cancer research brings together experts in maths, physics and engineering to research new treatments using digital technologies. The university was awarded £14.5m to establish an Advanced Steel

Undergraduate Admissions Office
University House
Coventry CV4 8UW
ugadmissions@warwick.ac.uk
www.warwick.ac.uk
www.warwicksu.com
Open Days 2018:
check website

The Times and The Sunday Times Rankings

Overall Ranking: **9** (last year: 7)

Teaching quality	78.6%	87
Student experience	79.4%	=49
Research quality	44.6%	8
Entry standards	186	=12
Graduate prospects	80.8%	=26
Good honours	83.4%	17
Expected completion rate	95.1%	9
Student/staff ratio	12.9	=14
Services and facilities/student	£2,605	25

Research Centre and is among six Midlands universities sharing £60m for energy research.

There is a centre for history students in Venice and a close partnership with Monash University in Melbourne. The business school launched a London base in the Shard in 2015 and Warwick has received approval to open a campus in California. The ambitious project involves a partnership with a non-profit-making trust to create a campus for 6,000 students near Sacramento, in the north of the state. The first postgraduates will arrive in 2018.

The first phase of a £30m extension to Warwick Business School has already opened, making it one of the largest business schools in the UK. There is also a thriving graduate-entry medical school — recently extended — with more than 2,000 students. At the undergraduate level, Warwick is also one of the few leading universities to have embraced two and three-year foundation degrees.

There is a smaller proportion of independent school students than at most Russell Group universities — less than a quarter — although this does not translate into large numbers of working-class undergraduates. The university has introduced a "student lifecycle" approach to widening participation, helping non-traditional students from before the application stage through to employment or postgraduate study. The scheme includes bursaries of up to £3,000 a year for those from families with a combined income of less than £35,000.

The 750-acre campus has a wide range of residential accommodation — soon to be increased when some of the original halls are demolished to make way for flats for nearly 800 students — and there is an off-campus study facility for the many students living in nearby Leamington Spa. The campus sports facilities are both extensive and conveniently placed, and include a running track, an indoor climbing centre and an indoor tennis centre. The main sports centre and gym have been upgraded recently and further investment in sports amenities is planned.

Coventry has a growing range of student-orientated facilities and good travel links to London and other parts of the country.

Tuition fees

- » Fees for UK/EU students 2018–19 — £9,250
- » Fees for international students 2018–19 — £18,330–£23,380
  Medicine (clinical years) — £37,290
- » For scholarship and bursary information see https://warwick.ac.uk/services/academicoffice/funding/fundingyourstudies/warwickusb
- » Graduate salary — £25,000

Students

Undergraduates	13,590	(1,785)
Postgraduates	5,605	(3,680)
Applications per place	7.8	
Overall offer rate	83.2%	
International students	25.5%	
Mature students	6.4%	
From state-sector schools	77.1%	
From working-class homes	19.3%	

Accommodation

University-provided places: 6,786
Percentage catered: 0%
Self-catered: £72 – £176 per week
First year students are guaranteed accommodation
www.warwick.ac.uk/study/undergraduate/campuslife/accommodation

University of West London

After registering the biggest rise in last year's table the University of West London (UWL) has jumped another 28 places in the current edition. The combined rise of 65 places is almost unprecedented, and has taken UWL from near the foot of the table well into the top half.

A big rise in student satisfaction with teaching quality is the biggest contributor this year. UWL is now in the top seven on this key measure, having been in the bottom 15 only two years ago, when the level of satisfaction was more than eight percentage points lower.

The transformation is extraordinary for a university that was once at risk of closure under its previous title of Thames Valley University. Its recent success has coincided with the opening of the £150m Future campus.

The first phase was called the Heartspace because of its central location on the university's Ealing campus and provides a vibrant social area for students and staff. The opening of the Paul Hamlyn Library followed, stretching across all four floors of the campus. The 24-hour social learning area has a variety of study spaces, 40 PC desks and a Mac lab.

Other new facilities include a concrete testing lab, an architecture studio, music practice rooms and a performance space. A refurbished students' union with a modern bar area, cafe and gym opened in 2013. The project has seen UWL move into the top 20 for spending on student facilities.

The campus had already seen significant investment, as the university opted for the narrower geographical focus implied when it dropped the title of Thames Valley University. The Slough campus closed and most activities were concentrated on the institution's original base, as UWL set about becoming the country's leading university for employer engagement, with an accent on the creative industries and entrepreneurship.

The university was given a silver rating in the Teaching Excellence Framework (TEF) last year. The panel acknowledged UWL's strategic approach to course design and assessment practices, one which is highly valued by employers and which stretches, challenges and supports students.

The university offers students guaranteed work placements, in-study financial support and employment prospects that improved considerably in the latest survey and compare favourably with its peer group. Undergraduates have access to an award-winning student portal, which combines academic study with social networking.

Further investment will see the university open the Westmont Enterprise Hub, where students and west London companies will be able to collaborate on business projects, providing an economic stimulus for the local area and opportunities for students to learn from visiting professionals.

St Mary's Road
Ealing
London W5 5RF
0800 036 8888
Undergraduate.admissions@uwl.ac.uk
www.uwl.ac.uk
www.uwlsu.com
Open Days 2018:
April 21, June 20,
July 7, August 18

The Times and The Sunday Times Rankings

Overall Ranking: **56** (last year: 84)

Teaching quality	85.3%	7
Student experience	82.9%	14
Research quality	1.6%	122
Entry standards	119	=95
Graduate prospects	70.5%	=78
Good honours	69.5%	=80
Expected completion rate	79.8%	=105
Student/staff ratio	15.6	=55
Services and facilities/student	£2,837	12

The Reading campus, which houses the Berkshire Institute of Health, is within walking distance of the station and focuses entirely on nursing, midwifery and healthcare. It has recently opened a £1m high-tech simulation centre to replicate hospital and healthcare settings for students. The landmark Paragon building in Brentford, not far from the Ealing campus, remains the headquarters of one of the largest healthcare faculties in Britain, with top-quality ratings for nursing and midwifery.

Many UWL degrees include the option of a foundation year and there is a portfolio of two-year foundation degrees.

Approaching half of the students are 21 or more on entry, and about 60% are female. Nearly 50% of the undergraduates come from low-income families, but UWL's projected dropout rate of almost 19% is significantly worse than the national average for its courses and entry qualifications.

The university is ethnically diverse, with only 45% of the undergraduates of white, UK origin. There are means-tested scholarships and bursaries to support full-time undergraduates whose household income is below £25,000 and fee waivers for part-time students where income is £42,875 or less.

The university has specialist scholarships and bursaries for each of the academic schools, funded by alumni. These are available for students with high academic entry grades or demonstrating outstanding applied skills.

Among UWL's strengths is the London Geller College of Hospitality and Tourism, which is recognised by the Académie Culinaire de France for its culinary arts programmes, while the London College of Music, which is part of the university, has some of the longest-established music technology courses in the country.

However, the university is in the bottom five of our research ranking after entering only 13% of eligible academics for the 2014 Research Excellence Framework. A quarter of its submission was judged to be world-leading or internationally excellent, the best results coming in communication and media studies.

The town centre sites in Ealing and Brentford are linked by a free bus service. Almost half of UWL's students are from the capital or Berkshire.

The Paragon has more than 800 residential places, but those relying on private housing find the cost of living high.

The gym is reserved for student use, and facilities are about to improve with a new sports centre featuring a large gym and multipurpose sports hall under development.

Tuition fees

» Fees for UK/EU students 2018–19 £9,250
» Fees for international students 2018–19 £11,500–£12,000
» For scholarship and bursary information see www.uwl.ac.uk/students/undergraduate/scholarships-and-bursaries
» Graduate salary £21,000

Students

Undergraduates	7,355	(1,695)
Postgraduates	480	(875)
Applications per place	7.5	
Overall offer rate	71.1%	
International students	13.7%	
Mature students	52.5%	
From state-sector schools	96.9%	
From working-class homes	49.9%	

Accommodation

University-provided places: 839
Percentage catered: 0%
Self-catered: £152 – £207 per week
www.uwl.ac.uk/students/support-services-for-students/accommodation

University of the West of England

Applications to the University of the West of England (UWE Bristol) have fallen significantly over recent years, but the university has managed to reverse this trend and buck the national one in 2017. While other universities were suffering a 4% drop in demand, applications to UWE Bristol were up by 10%.

The university attributes the turnaround to its £300m investment in buildings and facilities, and partnerships with thousands of businesses and other organisations that enable its graduates to be "work ready" when they complete degrees.

UWE Bristol is up three places in our table, and remains among the top ten post-1992 universities. It received a silver rating in the Teaching Excellence Framework. The independent panel praised the extensive links with employers the development of student enterprise skills. It found an extensive set of activities to support personalised learning, meeting the diverse needs of different student groups.

Already the biggest higher education institution in the region, the university's campus masterplan is intended to ensure that it is competitive in teaching, research and student facilities, but has the option of taking more students in future. It has just opened a £50m building on the main Frenchay campus for the business and law schools, and there are also film studios with industry-standard production and post-production facilities for animation, photography and filmmaking students at Bower Ashton. This will be followed in 2018 by another building to house design studios and other facilities.

There has been investment, too, at the Glenside campus, with upgraded suites for radiotherapy and simulated hospital wards. But plans for a 20,000-seat stadium to be shared with Bristol Rovers, on land bought to extend the Frenchay site, appear to have foundered after the club's new owners withdrew from negotiations.

The three sites in Bristol are mainly in the north of the city, with regional centres near hospitals in Gloucester and Bath that concentrate on nursing and allied health professions. The main campus, four miles from the city centre, has already doubled in size and seen a number of improvements, including the opening of the UK's largest robotic laboratory and the biggest exhibition and conference centre in the region.

Hartpury College, near Gloucester, is an associate faculty of the university, specialising in agriculture, equine studies and other land-based courses. The university's degrees are also taught in a growing number of institutions overseas. UWE Bristol's own

Frenchay Campus
Coldharbour Lane
Bristol BS16 1QY
0117 328 3333
admissions@uwe.ac.uk
www.uwe.ac.uk
www.thestudentunion.co.uk
Open afternoons 2018:
March 14 (Glenside campus), March 28, April 18 (Frenchay)

The Times and The Sunday Times Rankings

Overall Ranking: **57** (last year: 60)

Teaching quality	83%	23
Student experience	82.8%	15
Research quality	8.8%	70
Entry standards	126	=77
Graduate prospects	77.1%	50
Good honours	72.6%	62
Expected completion rate	84.4%	=73
Student/staff ratio	18.1	=106
Services and facilities/student	£2,544	29

international college, run in partnership with the Kaplan group, provides preparatory courses for students from outside the UK coming to Bristol.

UWE Bristol launched more than a dozen new degrees last autumn, in subjects ranging from business management to film studies, healthcare science and marketing communications management. Business computing and music degrees are planned for 2018.

More than half of the students come from the West Country and the university has broadened its intake in recent years. The proportion of independent school entrants has dropped to about 6%, and the share of places going to students from working-class homes has increased. About a quarter of UK undergraduates receive some financial support from the university.

More than 60% of the work submitted for assessment in the 2014 Research Excellence Framework was rated as world-leading or internationally excellent. Health subjects and communication and media studies produced the best results. Law received a commendation from the Legal Practice Board and UWE Bristol is one of just four universities recognised by the Chartered Society of Forensic Sciences for the quality of courses in the subject.

The careers and employment service runs an innovative web-based jobs and placement service with the local chamber of commerce.

UWE Bristol Futures awards certificates for extracurricular activities and encourages students to acquire skills that will help in the employment market. The university also has one of the largest internship programmes at any UK institution and graduates can apply to access the Centre for Graduate Enterprise to launch businesses in an incubator hub at Frenchay.

Bristol is a hugely popular student centre: an attractive and lively city, although not cheap. The university owns or endorses more than 4,700 residential places, and a £23m development provided 561 additional rooms for the start of this academic year. The UWE Bristol sports complex has a 70-station fitness suite, as well as outdoor facilities. The separate Wallscourt Farm Gym is designed for elite athletes.

Tuition fees

» Fees for UK/EU students 2018–19 £9,250
  Foundation courses £7,500
» Fees for International students 2018–19 £12,500–£13,000
» For scholarship and bursary information see
  www.uwe.ac.uk/students/feesandfunding.aspx
» Graduate salary £21,500

Students

Undergraduates	18,395	(2,670)
Postgraduates	1,990	(4,665)
Applications per place	5.2	
Overall offer rate	74.7%	
International students	10.8%	
Mature students	25.2%	
From state-sector schools	93.8%	
From working-class homes	30.2%	

Accommodation

University-provided places: 4,738
Percentage catered: 0%
Self-catered: £95 – £174 per week
First year students are guaranteed accommodation
www.uwe.ac.uk/students/accommodation

University of the West of Scotland

University of the West of Scotland's (UWS) new Lanarkshire campus will take its first students in 2018, maintaining a presence in Hamilton, the base for one of the two partners in the merger that formed the university in 2007. That link was at risk because UWS could not upgrade the former Bell College premises in the town centre, but the new EcoCampus, two miles away, will provide a gleaming new home for 4,300 students.

A three-storey "street atrium" will link the university's three main buildings on the Hamilton International Technology Park, housing advanced teaching and learning spaces and a students' union. There will also be new student residences on the campus, which will be one of the UK's greenest educational environments, with carbon-neutral buildings set in almost 40 acres of woodland.

The university's headquarters will remain in Paisley, where there has been significant investment in improving student facilities and expanding the residential accommodation. The campus also has an atrium as its centrepiece, a flexible learning area with interactive technology, meeting spaces and a cafe that is open to staff, students and members of the public. The Hub, a location for student services, was added in 2016.

Another £81m was invested in a modern campus for 2,300 students in Ayr and there is also one in Dumfries, which is operated in partnership with the University of Glasgow and Dumfries and Galloway College.

UWS has entered the top 100 universities for the first time since its establishment ten years ago after a second successive rise in our table. Like other universities north of the border, it has benefited from the uprating of Scottish secondary qualifications in the UCAS tariff, but there has also been a big increase in spending on student services and a rise of five percentage points in the proportion of students achieving good honours.

In common with the majority of universities in Scotland, UWS did not enter the Teaching Excellence Framework. But it is just outside the top 40 for student satisfaction with teaching quality for the second successive year, and has improved its scores for completion and graduate prospects this year.

The university was the product of a merger between the University of Paisley and Bell College in Hamilton, institutions serving two less than prosperous towns in areas of low participation in higher education. Almost all UWS's students are state-educated and 40% are from working-class homes. Applications dipped a little in 2016 but recovered last year, with UWS registering an increase at a time of falling demand for places elsewhere in Scotland and the rest of the UK.

Paisley Campus
Paisley PA1 2BE
0800 027 1000
ask@uws.ac.uk
www.uws.ac.uk
www.sauws.org.uk
Open Days 2018:
check website

PAISLEY
Edinburgh
Belfast
London
Cardiff

***The Times and The Sunday Times* Rankings**

Overall Ranking: **=100** (last year: 106)

Teaching quality	81.6%	=41
Student experience	76.6%	=95
Research quality	4.3%	=98
Entry standards	143	46
Graduate prospects	72.1%	71
Good honours	70.2%	74
Expected completion rate	80.1%	103
Student/staff ratio	20.2	123
Services and facilities/student	£1,747	100

UWS is among the largest modern universities in Scotland, with more than 15,000 students. They include almost 1,500 international students, mainly from other EU countries. The university opened a London campus in 2015 and already has more than 1,000 students there. The site, in Southwark, offers undergraduate and postgraduate courses in business, health, music, quality management, project management, and education.

The attractive Dumfries campus has 550 UWS students, while the Ayr campus is shared with Scotland's Rural College and has a prize-winning library with flexible space. A £12m investment in information technology across all campuses is being phased in.

Many students either take sandwich degrees or have work placements built into their courses. A number of new degrees have been launched across the university, in business, law, education, sport and politics. There are close links with business and industry, plus all students are offered hands-on computer training. UWS was the first UK university to be approved by tech giants such as Microsoft and Cisco, and it is also in Microsoft's IT Academy Programme. A games development laboratory, supported by Sony, was part of a £300,000 investment in multimedia and games facilities.

The School of Health, Nursing and Midwifery is the largest north of the border, and for the third year in a row the university performs well in our table for education. Health subjects produced much the best results in the 2014 Research Excellence Framework, when 44% of its submission reached one of the top two categories.

UWS is aiming to become Scotland's most "student-focused" university. It has a formal Student Partnership Agreement with the students' association, which won NUS Scotland's Higher Education Students' Association of the Year award for 2016. The university has only 860 residential places, ahead of the opening of the Lanarkshire campus, but its high proportion of home-based students means that up to now this has been enough to satisfy all new entrants requiring accommodation.

Tuition fees

» Fees for Scottish and EU students 2018–19   £0–£1,820
» Fees for non-Scottish UK students 2018–19   £0,460
   (capped at £27,750 for 4-year courses)
» Fees for international students 2018–19   £10,600–£13,800
» For scholarship and bursary information see
   www.uws.ac.uk/money-fees-funding/
   undergraduate-fees-funding/
» Graduate salary   £22,000

Students

Undergraduates	10,785	(2,630)
Postgraduates	1,180	(965)
Applications per place	5.6	
Overall offer rate	68.8%	
International students	6.9%	
Mature students	55.6%	
From state-sector schools	98.7%	
From working-class homes	40.6%	

Accommodation

University-provided places: 859
Percentage catered: 0%
Self-catered: £75 – £142 per week
www.uws.ac.uk/accommodation

University of Westminster

Westminster is up 11 places in our latest table, but still outside the overall top 100. Its score for graduate prospects has improved this year but the university, in common with many other London-based institutions, is held back by low student satisfaction levels.

This was behind a bronze rating in the government's new Teaching Excellence Framework. An unusually brief commentary by the awarding panel praised the consistent support for students at risk of dropping out and acknowledged a strategic approach and commitment to improving employment and entrepreneurship.

Grants worth more than £3m were awarded by the Quintin Hogg Trust in 2017 to improve the student experience at Westminster. The 30 successful projects included student field trips, educational events, academic research, and the improvement of facilities, including the development of smart learning spaces. Each project was designed to enhance students' experience, as well as improving their employability prospects. One of the most successful projects was FAB FEST, a week-long fabrication festival which enabled students from Westminster and across the world to design 50 pavilions under supervision and mentoring from industry experts and with the help of Fabrication Laboratory Westminster.

All the university's courses were reviewed as part of its Learning Futures programme, which came into operation in 2016. The structure of undergraduate programmes changed to promote deeper learning through year-long modules, weaving work-related skills into degrees. There is support for employability and international mobility, and awards for students' extracurricular activities aim to recognise outstanding contributions of benefit to the public.

Applications dropped by 5,000 in two years up to 2016 and the number of students starting degrees was down by 20% over the same period. New degrees in theatre studies, with creative writing or English literature, have taken their first students, and foundation year courses will be introduced this year in a number of subjects for students who lack the necessary qualifications for degree-level study.

More than 6,000 international students include almost 2,000 from the EU. Westminster's courses are also taught in nine overseas countries, from Sri Lanka to Uzbekistan, a characteristic which won the university a Queen's Award for Enterprise. Expanding the opportunities for students to study or work abroad is one of the main planks of the university's global engagement strategy.

Westminster promises a "dynamic synergy" between the creative arts and design,

---

309 Regent Street
London W1B 2HW
020 7911 5000
course-enquiries@
westminster.ac.uk
www.westminster.ac.uk
www.uwsu.com
Open Days 2018:
March 10, June 20

The Times and The Sunday Times **Rankings**

Overall Ranking: **=106** (last year: 117)

Teaching quality	75.5%	116
Student experience	76.5%	=98
Research quality	9.8%	60
Entry standards	123	=83
Graduate prospects	67.2%	99
Good honours	70.4%	73
Expected completion rate	81.7%	93
Student/staff ratio	17.9	=102
Services and facilities/student	£1,917	85

architecture and the built environment, science and technology, business, law, and the social sciences and humanities. Its ultimate aim is to be the leading "practice-informed" university. It works with a network of more than 3,000 companies and encourages all students to undertake a work placement which can form part of their degree.

Almost half of the UK undergraduates are from the four poorest socioeconomic groups and the numbers from ethnic minorities are among the highest at any university. The projected dropout rate has been improving and is now lower than average for Westminster's courses and entry qualifications.

Almost two thirds of the work submitted for the 2014 Research Excellence Framework was judged to be world leading or excellent, albeit with less than 30% of the eligible staff entered for assessment. Westminster was among the leading universities for communication and media studies, and there were even better results in art and design, as well as a good performance in English. The university has since established the Westminster Institute for Advanced Studies to foster interdisciplinary and independent critical thinking, supporting research in the sciences and humanities.

Westminster traces its history back to 1838, when it became the UK's first polytechnic. The headquarters building, near the BBC's Broadcasting House, houses social sciences, humanities and languages. The university offers one of the widest ranges of language teaching of any British institution and partners SOAS, University of London, in leading the "routes into languages" programme to encourage more people to learn a language.

The university has invested in its buildings and facilities. The business school was selected as a centre of excellence in 2013 by the Chartered Institute for Securities and Investment – one of only 12 centres worldwide. But Westminster is perhaps best known for its media, arts and design faculty, based in Harrow.

There is no guarantee of accommodation for new entrants, even as Westminster has expanded its stock of student rooms over recent years. Most students will have to brave the capital's inflated private market at some stage. A living expenses support scheme helps those who get into financial difficulties during the academic year.

The Harrow campus is lively socially but students based at other sites tend to be spread around London. Sports facilities are also dispersed, with playing fields and a boathouse in Chiswick and a gym on Regent Street.

Tuition fees

» Fees for UK/EU students 2018–19   £9,250
» Fees for international students 2018–19   £12,750
» For scholarship and bursary information see
  www.westminster.ac.uk/study/fees-and-funding
» Graduate salary   £21,000

Students

Undergraduates	13,255	(2,780)
Postgraduates	2,090	(2,070)
Applications per place	8	
Overall offer rate	78.8%	
International students	26.8%	
Mature students	19.8%	
From state-sector schools	96.6%	
From working-class homes	49.3%	

Accommodation

University-provided places: 1,664
Percentage catered: 0%
Self-catered: £135 – £270 per week
www.westminster.ac.uk/study/prospective-students/
student-accommodation

University of Winchester

Winchester has fallen 13 places in our new table, making a decline of more than 20 places in two years. The main cause is lower student satisfaction — until recently its biggest strength — particularly where teaching quality is concerned. The university has dropped more than 50 places over the two years, from the verge of the top ten, on this measure.

There was a silver rating, however, in the new Teaching Excellence Framework (TEF), which uses older data than this guide. The TEF panel was impressed by the "appropriate" contact hours, tutorials and buddy schemes that produce personalised learning and high levels of commitment from students. Most students are stretched sufficiently to make progress, and acquire knowledge, skills and understanding that are valued by employers, the panel added.

Applications had grown for three years in a row, but were down by almost 9% in 2017 after the closure of some courses and their replacement by others that the university expects to take time to become established. The 17 new degrees included anthropology, economics, mathematics, and music and sound production. A dozen more will be launched for 2018, including applied drama, computer-aided design, digital media development, and policing and criminal investigation.

The numbers starting courses have risen gradually every year since before £9,000 fees were introduced. There are now more than 7,500 students, twice as many as when university status was awarded in 2005. Winchester was one the first universities to appoint its own ombudsman to handle complaints.

Winchester has also been investing in research and held its own in the 2014 Research Excellence Framework. Almost 45% of its work was considered world-leading or internationally excellent, with communications and history producing the best results. The university has since established a Centre for English Identity and Politics, run by John Denham, the former Labour universities secretary.

An animal welfare facility was added in 2016, while a sport and exercise research centre was established in 2015 to mark the 175th anniversary of the original institution's foundation. It was then a Church of England foundation for teacher training and was known as King Alfred College until 2004.

The university is still best known for its education courses, which Ofsted rates as outstanding, although they no longer dominate in terms of student numbers. Other degrees span business, arts, humanities, health and social care, and social science. There are also degree apprenticeships in digital and technology solutions, with partner employers such as Fujitsu, Transactor Global Solutions and OceanWise.

Sparkford Road
Winchester SO22 4NR
01962 827 234
course.enquiries@winchester.ac.uk
www.winchester.ac.uk
www.winchesterstudents.co.uk
Open Days 2018:
check website

The Times and *The Sunday Times* Rankings

Overall Ranking: **85** (last year: =72)

Teaching quality	80.4%	63
Student experience	78.4%	72
Research quality	5.8%	=83
Entry standards	113	=111
Graduate prospects	63.1%	116
Good honours	76.7%	=43
Expected completion rate	88%	=47
Student/staff ratio	15.9	=64
Services and facilities/student	£1,533	117

Undergraduates can take advantage of exchange schemes with a number of American universities, as well as others in Japan and across Europe. The number of international students has trebled in the current decade and now accounts for almost 7% of the intake.

The compact site is on a wooded hillside overlooking the cathedral city, a ten-minute walk away. The campus is well equipped, with theatrical performance spaces, sports hall and fitness suite supplemented by the Winchester Sports stadium. Open to locals as well as students, the stadium has a 400-metre, eight-lane athletics track with supporting facilities for field events and a floodlit all-weather pitch.

An award-winning extension to the library added 450 study spaces and extra computers, while a modern learning and teaching building significantly improved the facilities for lectures and independent study. The Victorian chapel has been restored and extended in the past year to include a small side chapel and a social and meeting space.

The West Downs campus, which is only a short walk away, is the base for the business school and the location for a student village of more than 700 rooms. There is also a gallery that is open to the public and a centre for research and knowledge exchange.

Two other complexes adjacent to the King Alfred campus bring the number of residential places close to 2,000, but UK entrants must apply by the end of May, with Winchester as their firm choice, to be guaranteed accommodation. The newest student village includes a large gym, which is available for use by local residents as well as students and staff.

Students value the close-knit atmosphere and find the city is livelier than its staid image might suggest, with a number of bars catering to their tastes. Southampton is not far for those who hanker after the attractions of a bigger city and London is only an hour away by train.

Tuition fees

» Fees for UK/EU students 2018–19 £9,250
» Fees for international students 2018–19 £12,950
» For scholarship and bursary information see www.winchester.ac.uk/accommodation-and-winchester-life/scholarships-bursaries-and-awards/
» Graduate salary £21,000

Students

Undergraduates	5,760	(365)
Postgraduates	345	(1,070)
Applications per place	4.8	
Overall offer rate	89.7%	
International students	7.2%	
Mature students	16.4%	
From state-sector schools	95.9%	
From working-class homes	30.4%	

Accommodation

University-provided places: 1,991
Percentage catered: 5%
Catered costs: £154 per week
Self-catered: £80 – £140 per week
First year students are guaranteed accommodation
www.winchester.ac.uk/accommodation-and-winchester-life

University of Wolverhampton

Wolverhampton has declined to release any data for use in league tables since 2009, when it finished just outside the top 100. Its intake of undergraduates has dropped by more than 1,000 since then, despite raising the offer rate from less than 60 per cent to almost 85 per cent in 2016. The university is one of only two to maintain a boycott this year. As a result, Wolverhampton is missing from both the main ranking and all the subject tables.

A statement on its website says that tables such as ours disadvantage universities like Wolverhampton and do not represent a fair picture of their strengths, although its governors have empowered the Vice-Chancellor, Professor Geoff Layer, to reverse this policy at an appropriate time, based on the university's estimated position. It has refused to disclose more information on the decision, in spite of a ruling by the Information Commissioner.

The university was placed in the bronze category in the Teaching Excellence Framework because it missed its benchmarks for student satisfaction and highly-skilled graduate employment. However, the TEF panel noted that there had been extensive investment in physical and digital learning resources, and that course design – often informed by employers – together with work placements, internships and enterprise opportunities, ensure most students acquire knowledge and skills that are valued by employers. Scores have been rising in the National Student Survey. The 2017 survey showed another increase in overall satisfaction, although Wolverhampton was back in the bottom 30 universities.

The university is in the midst of a £250-million investment programme, the biggest in its history, to drive economic growth for the benefit of students and the wider region. The five-year project includes new buildings and facilities, as well as investment in teaching, research and skills training. An £18-million building for the business school opened in 2015 and impressive new engineering facilities are being provided in Telford and Wolverhampton. New courses have been launched in automotive and motorsport engineering, electronic and telecommunications engineering, chemical engineering and, most recently, aerospace engineering.

A new science centre, the Rosalind Franklin Building, opened fully in 2015. The most ambitious project will see the £100-million redevelopment of the derelict Springfield Brewery site in the city, to create a new campus for construction and the built environment. The new West Midlands Construction University Technical College (UTC) is already open, an Elite Centre for Manufacturing Skills is under construction

Wulfruna Street
Wolverhampton WV1 1LY
01902 321 000
enquiries@wlv.ac.uk
www.wlv.ac.uk
www.wolvesunion.org
Open Days 2018:
April 21, June 16,
August 18

***The Times and The Sunday Times* Rankings**
Data not supplied

and the university's School of Architecture and the Built Environment will complete a range of provision that will provide skills and education from the age of 14, through to undergraduate and postgraduate courses and executive education.

The university has also signed an agreement to deliver higher education courses in education, leadership and management, travel and tourism, hospitality and computing on a 50-acre campus in Stafford bought by the Chinese-based New Beacon Group from Staffordshire University. The centre was officially opened last year and the first students, recruited directly from China and locally in Staffordshire, began courses in January.

There are already three bases in the West Midlands: the original site in the centre of Wolverhampton, a campus in Walsall dedicated to sport and performance, as well as education and part of the School of Health and Wellbeing, and a purpose-built campus at Telford, in Shropshire, which focuses on business and engineering.

Research mainly serves the needs of business and industry, as well as underpinning teaching. By far the best REF results were in information science, where almost 90 per cent of the research submitted was considered world-leading or internationally excellent.

Wolverhampton's success in widening participation in higher education is such that only one university (Bradford) had a higher proportion of undergraduates coming from working-class homes when this was last surveyed. Almost all the students are from state schools and one in five comes from an area of low participation. The university draws two-thirds of its 20,000 students from the West Midlands. The university is leading a regional scheme to encourage young people to consider higher education.

Student facilities improved with the redevelopment of the students' union on the City Campus and the opening of a new union bar on the Walsall Campus. There is a 350-bed student village and sports facilities, including a Sports Science and Medicine Centre which was used to train Olympic contenders. The Performance Hub, in Walsall, the university's centre for performing arts, has exceptional facilities for music, dance and drama. The city of Wolverhampton has a growing nightlife, and the university was voted the friendliest in the West Midlands by former students.

Tuition fees

- » Fees for UK/EU students 2018–19 £9,250
  Foundation courses £6,165
- » Fees for international students 2018–19 £11,700
- » For scholarship and bursary information see
  www.wlv.ac.uk/study-here/money-matters/
  financial-support

Students

Undergraduates	13,068	(3,652)
Postgraduates	11,352	(3,068)

Accommodation

University-provided places: 1,350+
Percentage catered: 0%
Self-catered: £85 – £102 per week
https://www.wlv.ac.uk/study-here/accommodation/
where-can-I-live/

University of Worcester

The numbers of students starting degrees are at record levels, up by nearly a quarter since the first year of £9,000 fees. There are now about 10,500 students, and a raft of new degrees have taken their first undergraduates. They include five integrated master's courses in biological sciences, which take four years and give access to student loans. Degrees in the business school have also been reorganised, with a new offer of 23 programmes at undergraduate level.

A new law school opened last year, with mock courtroom, jury room and a number of seminar rooms. Its portfolio of courses has been extended to include LLBs in law with criminology and law with forensic psychology.

Worcester was awarded a silver in the new Teaching Excellence Framework last year. The panel said that the teaching encourages high levels of student engagement and commitment, with "excellent" levels of contact time, and schemes that involve students in the enhancement of their learning experience.

Yet the gains that Worcester made last year, with a ten-place rise in our table, have been more than wiped out in this year's edition. No area has seen a big decline, but the university's ranking is lower in five of the eight measures with new data.

Plans have been submitted for an Art House, which will create new teaching facilities for art and illustration. The art deco building, with a distinctive clock tower, was built in 1939 as a car showroom and should be converted by the time students arrive in September 2018.

Originally a post-war emergency teacher training college, the university remains strong in education and in nursing and midwifery. It is the partner university for the National Childbirth Trust, delivering all of the latter's antenatal training.

There are three teaching campuses, less than a mile from each other and all close to the centre of Worcester. The main St John's base occupies a parkland site 15 minutes' walk from the city centre. It includes science facilities, the National Pollen and Aerobiology Research Unit, the digital arts centre and drama studio.

The City campus largely occupies the historic buildings of the former Worcester Royal Infirmary. It includes teaching, residential and conference facilities and is the site of Worcester Business School. Almost next door is the university's spectacular library and history centre, the award-winning Hive, which was the first joint public and university library to open in Britain.

The other star facility is a 2,000-seat indoor sporting arena, which is one of only two specialist sports venues in the UK

Henwick Grove
Worcester WR2 6AJ
01905 855 111
admissions@worc.ac.uk
www.worcester.ac.uk
www.worcsu.com
Open Days 2018:
March 25, June 24

The Times and *The Sunday Times* Rankings

Overall Ranking: =102 (last year: 90)

Teaching quality	81.7%	=38
Student experience	80%	=38
Research quality	4.3%	=98
Entry standards	120	=91
Graduate prospects	66.5%	101
Good honours	63%	116
Expected completion rate	84.3%	75
Student/staff ratio	16.4	=75
Services and facilities/student	£1,450	122

designed specifically for wheelchair athletes as well as the able-bodied. The arena is on the Riverside campus, which is being developed as an International Centre for Inclusive Sport and Health to include a new cricket centre in partnership with Worcestershire county cricket club.

The university has also added the Lakeside campus, a ten-minute drive from the main campus, which has sports pitches and a lake that has been adapted for a range of inclusive watersports and other outdoor activities. The university's commitment to disability sports extends to the UK's first disability sport degree.

Worcester was one of the most improved universities in the 2014 Research Excellence Framework compared with previous assessments: it went up 20 places in our research ranking, partly because it entered five times as many academics as in 2008. A third of the work was considered world leading or internationally excellent, with history and art and design achieving the best scores.

More than a third of the undergraduates come from working-class homes and the projected dropout rate is better than average for Worcester's subjects and entry standards. The university has long-established projects working with primary schools to try to broaden the intake further.

The Reach programme gives students access to ebooks, stationery, art supplies, digital equipment, or other course-specific equipment at discounted prices. New undergraduates paying full fees will receive £100 bursaries to spend through the scheme. There are excellent links with local businesses and students have access to an extensive "earn as you learn" scheme.

An active students union acts as a social hub and the university has 1,400 residential places on the St John's and City campuses, enough to guarantee accommodation to new entrants. The cathedral city is not large, but is safer than many university locations, and has its share of pubs and clubs that cater for a growing student clientele.

Tuition fees

- » Fees for UK/EU students 2018–19 £9,250
  Foundation courses £8,200
- » Fees for international students 2018–19 £12,100
- » For scholarship and bursary information see
  www.worcester.ac.uk/your-home/scholarships.html
- » Graduate salary £18,000

Students

Undergraduates	7,590	(1,275)
Postgraduates	570	(1,020)
Applications per place	5.3	
Overall offer rate	72.1%	
International students	5.4%	
Mature students	35.2%	
From state-sector schools	97.4%	
From working-class homes	36.9%	

Accommodation

University-provided places: 1,400
Percentage catered: 0%
Self-catered: £91 – £149 per week
First year students are guaranteed accommodation
www.worcester.ac.uk/your-home/living-in-halls.html

Wrexham Glyndŵr University

Glyndŵr remains three places from the bottom of our table, but it is in the top 40 for student satisfaction with teaching, feedback and academic support. It had the highest score in Wales in the 2017 National Student Survey (NSS) for undergraduates feeling that they had been challenged to produce their best work.

That was also one of the features identified by the independent panel that gave Glyndŵr a silver rating in the Teaching Excellence Framework. The university achieved particularly good scores for its part-time courses and the panel was impressed by the high levels of interaction with industry, business and the public sector. It commented favourably on the quality of work-based learning and on a curriculum that matched the region's priorities.

However, the university has the third-highest projected dropout rate in the table — with a quarter of all recruits not expected to complete their degree — and is in the bottom ten for staffing levels, with more than 20 students per academic.

It has only just retained its place in the top 100 in the sections of the NSS dealing with the broad student experience, in contrast to the high levels of satisfaction with teaching quality.

Glyndŵr is celebrating its tenth anniversary as a university this year. It took the name of the 15th-century Welsh prince Owain Glyndŵr, who championed the establishment of universities in Wales, after a long campaign of its own for university status. Undergraduate recruitment improved significantly in 2016 after a decline in the previous year as Glyndŵr closed its London campus.

New degrees have been launched in more than 20 subjects, many of them with the option of a foundation year for those lacking the qualifications needed for degree-level study. They range from animation and game art to policing, automation engineering and football coaching.

The main campus is on the outskirts of Wrexham, with a second base for the school of art in the town centre. There are two further sites at Northop, in Flintshire, and St Asaph, in Denbighshire.

There are now 6,600 students, of whom almost 3,000 are part-time undergraduates. The university has introduced bursaries worth up to 40% of the tuition fee for part-time students living in Wales this autumn. Nearly all the undergraduates are state-educated, with almost half of them coming from the four poorest socioeconomic groups, far more than average for the university's subjects and entry grades.

Glyndŵr also has the largest proportion of disabled students in Wales and has a dedicated

---

Mold Road
Wrexham LL11 2AW
01978 293 439
enquiries@glyndwr.ac.uk
www.glyndwr.ac.uk
www.wrexhamglyndwrsu.org.uk
Open Days 2018:
March 3

The Times and The Sunday Times Rankings		
Overall Ranking: **127** (last year: 125)		
Teaching quality	81.9%	37
Student experience	76.5%	=98
Research quality	2.3%	119
Entry standards	107	=124
Graduate prospects	62.9%	=117
Good honours	64%	=109
Expected completion rate	67.7%	=129
Student/staff ratio	20.9	=124
Services and facilities/student	£1,490	119

centre that assesses students' needs before they embark on a course.

Northop hosts the university's rural campus, specialising in courses on animal studies and biodiversity, where students have access to a small-animals care unit and an equine centre. The St Asaph campus houses Glyndŵr Innovations, a research centre that brings together academia and industry, focusing on high-level optoelectronics technology.

There is also an Advanced Composite Training and Development Centre, at Broughton, in partnership with Airbus, which has a large plant nearby. Research carried out there will help to improve the efficiency of aircraft and feed into the university's engineering courses.

Glyndŵr entered only 34 academics for the 2014 Research Excellence Framework, but a third of their work was judged to be internationally excellent, with some world-leading.

The Campus 2025 strategy promises a number of developments over the next eight years beginning with an upgrade of the catering facilities.

The full strategy includes an overhaul of the Wrexham campus to include new student accommodation, car parking, upgraded academic and research rooms and conversion of buildings, including an upgrade of the main entrance. The university is proud of its green policies and won an award from the British Astronomy Society for fitting specialised lamps which shine downwards, reducing light pollution in the surrounding area.

Glyndŵr has embarked on a series of academic developments, including two-year fast-track degrees and four-year master's degrees in art and design, and computing.

The Centre for the Creative Industries hosts the regional home of BBC Cymru Wales as well as providing high-quality studios for the university's television degree. Other facilities include a recording studio that is available around the clock, a Chinese medicine clinic, crime scene labs, computer game development labs, flight simulator and supersonic wind tunnel.

A high proportion of the students are local, many living at home, which eases the pressure on residential accommodation. Wrexham is not without nightlife and there has been a £90,000 upgrade of the students' union, which won a national award for its education activities.

Tuition fees

» Fees for UK/EU students 2018–19 £9,000
» Fees for international students 2018–19 £11,750
» For scholarship and bursary information see www.glyndwr.ac.uk/en/feesandstudentfinance
» Graduate salary £18,000

Students		
Undergraduates	3,155	(2,850)
Postgraduates	175	(475)
Applications per place	4.2	
Overall offer rate	84%	
International students	14%	
Mature students	62.2%	
From state-sector schools	99.7%	
From working-class homes	46.2%	

Accommodation

University-provided places: 233
Percentage catered: 0%
Self-catered: £86 – £97 per week
First year students are given priority for accommodation
www.glyndwr.ac.uk/en/accommodation

University of York

Students arriving at York in 2018 will be enrolled on a new personal development programme designed in partnership with leading graduate employers to boost their career prospects. Undergraduates will engage with employers early in their studies and receive help to find work experience, placements, internships and volunteering during the remainder of their university career.

The university claims that the York Futures programme represents a first for the UK because of its comprehensive nature. Degree modules have been designed to develop the skills that will boost employability, and careers advice will be delivered through the 29 academic departments.

From this year, every undergraduate has the option of a placement year, usually taken after the second year of a degree. Students are also studying abroad in growing numbers, spending between a fortnight and a year at leading universities in Europe, the United States, China, South Africa and Brazil. There is free language and cultural tuition as part of the programme.

The university's overall position in our table, well inside the top 20, is up one place compared with last year. Even ahead of the introduction of the new employment programme, its graduate prospects show considerable improvement, with an increase of four percentage points in the proportion of leavers in professional employment or further study six months after graduation.

York remains inside the top 20 nationally for student satisfaction with both the quality of the teaching they find here and their wider student experience. It is the only member of the elite Russell Group of research-led universities to achieve this feat.

Yet the university was ranked silver in the government's Teaching Excellence Framework, published for the first time last year. The independent judging panel reported excellent levels of intellectual stimulation and an "embedded strategic approach to teaching and learning". Individual supervision, resident college tutors and peer mentors ensured that personalised support was available for all students, it added.

York appealed its rating, a spokesman saying: "We do not believe that the silver rating reflects the teaching excellence offered here at York." The appeal was not successful, however.

All students join one of the nine colleges – small, distinct communities based on the two linked campuses. They combine academic and social roles and provide a network of support, events and activities. Some departments have their headquarters in one of the colleges, but the student communities are a mix of disciplines, years and sexes.

York has invested £750m on its estate since deciding that the university was too

Heslington
York YO10 5DD
01904 324 0000
Ug-admissions@york.ac.uk
www.york.ac.uk
www.yusu.org
Open Days 2018:
June 29, July 1,
September 15,16

The Times and The Sunday Times Rankings
Overall Ranking: **=16** (last year: 17)

Teaching quality	83.4%	=18
Student experience	81.8%	19
Research quality	38.3%	17
Entry standards	163	=26
Graduate prospects	81.5%	=23
Good honours	81.2%	=24
Expected completion rate	92.3%	27
Student/staff ratio	14.5	=35
Services and facilities/student	£1,982	81

small to maximise its research capability and satisfy the demand for its places. The student population has grown by 50% since and the undergraduate intake continues to expand.

Campus developments have included new colleges, teaching and learning space, laboratories, research facilities and a new sport village. The Piazza Learning Centre, features a 350-seat auditorium and more than 30 flexible learning spaces. It will be followed later this year by a new medical centre and shops for Campus East. The International Pathway College, which opened in 2016 offering preparatory programmes for overseas students, will be based in the Piazza building.

The university is also investing £500,000 in enhanced mental health services, having carried out a review following five student suicides in a single year. The initiative includes digital campaigns and events on the benefits of sleep, effective studying methods and how to identify signs of distress and where to seek appropriate help.

A member of the Russell Group since 2012, the university is situated within walking distance of York's historic city centre, where archaeology and medieval studies are based in suitably medieval buildings. Every student has a supervisor responsible for their academic and personal welfare, and support for studies alongside the main curriculum includes access to foreign language tuition and mathematics and writing study skills centres.

York lost ground on some of its competitors in the 2014 Research Excellence Framework, when it submitted a lower proportion of its academics for assessment than most of the leading universities. Nevertheless, more than 80% of the research was considered world leading or internationally excellent, and York was in the top ten for the impact of its research. Eight departments were ranked in the top five for their subject and the university remains in the top 20 both for research quality and overall.

The free Festival of Ideas, run by the university, is the largest of its type in the UK and cultural events abound on campus and in the city. Campus life is lively and there are television and radio stations, student newspapers and magazines. In town there are plenty of pubs and a strong music scene.

The £12m York Sports Village features a 25-metre pool, learner pool, 100-station gym, full-size 3G pitch and three further five-a-side pitches. The university has the only velodrome in Yorkshire, a 1km cycling track and an athletics track.

Tuition fees

- » Fees for UK/EU students 2018–19 — £9,250
- » Fees for international students 2018–19 — £16,620–£20,910
  Medicine — £33,000
- » For scholarship and bursary information see www.york.ac.uk/study/undergraduate/fees-funding
- » Graduate salary — £21,500

Students

Undergraduates	12.165	(930)
Postgraduates	3,045	(1,020)
Applications per place	7	
Overall offer rate	80.5%	
International students	12.6%	
Mature students	8.4%	
From state-sector schools	81.2%	
From working-class homes	19.6%	

Accommodation

University-provided places: 6,055
Percentage catered: 16%
Catered costs: £124 – £179 per week
Self-catered: £106 – £153 per week
First year students are guaranteed accommodation
www.york.ac.uk/study/accommodation/undergraduate

York St John University

York St John (YSJ) enjoyed the biggest increase in first-year enrolments of any university in 2016 and has come close to repeating the feat this year. While other universities have struggled to attract applications, it has seen a rise of almost 14%.

The university attributes this increase to dramatic diversification in its portfolio of courses, having reorganised into nine academic schools. Eighteen new degrees have been launched, six of them in management, three in police studies and others in subjects such as sport and exercise science, and working in the wider children's workforce.

Professor Karen Stanton, the vice-chancellor, said the increases reflected the university's investment in new facilities and excellent teaching, and were in line with its ambitious growth strategy. The aim is to have 7,300 students by 2020, compared with almost 6,500 at present, and to be "the best of England's small universities".

League tables will be one of the measures of this, but York St John has dropped eight places in ours, compounding a larger fall last year. It is now close to the bottom ten and is in this year's bottom three for graduate prospects.

Low rates of graduate employment in highly-skilled jobs also contributed to a bronze rating in the Teaching Excellence Framework. However, the independent panel commented favourably on a scheme that involves undergraduates in research and on the "dialogue days" involving students and staff. It also reported innovative measures to support vulnerable students with high support needs, including those experiencing mental health difficulties.

YSJ continues to charge the lowest fees in England – only £4,000 in the next academic year – for its foundation degrees in education and theology. But the courses are for a limited range of mature students without traditional qualifications; the fees for all honours courses are £9,250.

The university's mission statement says its provision is "shaped" by the York St John's church foundation that dates back to 1841, although it welcomes students of all beliefs. The then Diocesan Training School opened with just one pupil on the register, in whose honour the students' union is named. Full university status arrived in 2006.

Divided between York and Ripon for most of its existence, the university now concentrates all its activities on York. The 11-acre site faces York Minster across the city walls and is a five-minute walk from the city centre. The campus has undergone a £100m transformation over the past ten years.

The Fountains Learning Centre has 530 computer workstations, multimedia group-

Lord Mayor's Walk
York YO31 7EX
01904 876 598
admissions@yorksj.ac.uk
www.yorksj.ac.uk
http://ysjsu.com
Open Days 2018:
July 2, 18

The Times and The Sunday Times **Rankings**

Overall Ranking: **118** (last year: =110)

Teaching quality	80.8%	55
Student experience	78.8%	=64
Research quality	4.1%	=101
Entry standards	120	=91
Graduate prospects	55.8%	127
Good honours	56.4%	127
Expected completion rate	86.4%	61
Student/staff ratio	17.4	=93
Services and facilities/student	£1,692	104

work facilities, a stock of books, 24-hour access to self-service facilities, an internet cafe and lecture theatre. Nearby De Grey Court serves the health and life sciences. York Business School is the biggest school, having overtaken education and theology, as well as health and life sciences. It is offering a chartered manager degree apprenticeship, as well as conventional degrees.

Almost two-thirds of the students are female and there is a growing cohort of international students. More than 96% of the UK undergraduates attended state schools or colleges, and one in six comes from an area of low participation in higher education – well above average for YSJ's courses and entry qualifications.

UK students receive financial support through the YSJ Aspire card, which gives access to discounted course materials through a dedicated website.

Psychology produced the best results in the 2014 research assessments, when 30% of research was regarded as world-leading or internationally excellent. A new research strategy to promote interdisciplinary research, building on current areas of expertise, is aimed at producing further improvement in the 2021 exercise.

The university's 57-acre sports facility, Nestlé Rowntree Park, just a 15-minute walk from campus, includes a 3G pitch for rugby and football, a synthetic pitch for hockey and small-sided games, netball and tennis courts, as well as grass pitches, a sprint track and a bowling green. A separate sports facility offers a gym, changing rooms and conference and teaching space. On campus, there is also a sports hall, a climbing wall, basketball and netball courts, indoor football facilities and cricket nets.

Social life for many students centres on the active students' union. York itself is home to a growing range of clubs as well as, supposedly, a pub for every day of the year. Relatively high numbers of local mature students ease the pressure on residential accommodation. As a result, first-years who want to live in university-owned accommodation are guaranteed places.

Tuition fees

- » Fees for UK/EU students 2018–19 £9,250
  Foundation degrees £4,000
- » Fees for international students 2018–19 £12,500–£14,000
- » For scholarship and bursary information see www.yorksj.ac.uk/student-services/funding-advice/money-advice/bursaries--scholarships/
- » Graduate salary £18,000

Students		
Undergraduates	4,800	(470)
Postgraduates	385	(330)
Applications per place	4.9	
Overall offer rate	78.7%	
International students	6.3%	
Mature students	7.9%	
From state-sector schools	96.1%	
From working-class homes	34.9%	

Accommodation

University-provided places: 1,902
Percentage catered: 0%
Self-catered: £89 – £173 per week
First year students are guaranteed accommodation
www.yorksj.ac.uk/study/accommodation/

Specialist and Private Institutions

1 Specialist colleges of the University of London

This listing gives contact details for specialist degree-awarding colleges within the University of London not listed elsewhere within the book. Those marked * are members of GuildHE (www.guildhe.ac.uk). Fees are given for UK/EU undergraduates for a single year of study.

Courtauld Institute of Art
Somerset House Strand
London WC2R 0RN
020 7848 2645
www.courtauld.ac.uk
Fees 2018–19: £9,250

London Business School
Regent's Park London NW1 4SA
020 7000 7000
www.london.edu
Postgraduate only

London School of Hygiene and Tropical Medicine
Keppel Street
London WC1E 7HT
020 7299 4646
www.lshtm.ac.uk
Postgraduate medical courses

Royal Academy of Music
Marylebone Road London NW1 5HT
020 7873 7373
www.ram.ac.uk
Fees 2018–19: £9,250

Royal Central School of Speech and Drama*
Eton Avenue
London NW3 3HY
020 7722 8183
www.cssd.ac.uk
Fees 2018–19: £9,250

Royal Veterinary College
Royal College Street London NW1 0TU
020 7468 5147
www. rvc.ac.uk
Fees 2018–19: £9,250

University of London Institute in Paris
9–11 rue de Constantine
75340 Paris Cedex 07, France
(+33) 1 44 11 73 83
https://ulip.london.ac.uk
Degrees offered in conjunction with Queen Mary and Royal Holloway colleges
Fees 2018–19: £9,250

2 Specialist colleges and private institutions

This listing gives contact details for other degree-awarding higher education institutions not mentioned elsewhere within the book. All the institutions listed below offer degree courses, some providing a wide range of courses while others are specialist colleges with a small intake. Those marked * are members of GuildHE (www.guildhe.ac.uk). Fees are given for UK/EU undergraduates for a single year of study.

BPP University
6th floor, Boulton House
Chorlton Street, Manchester M1 3HY
    Campuses in Abingdon, Birmingham,
    Bristol, Cambridge, Leeds, Liverpool,
    London, Manchester.
03331 224 359
www.bpp.com/bpp-university
Fees 2018–19: £13,500 (two-year course);
£9,000 (three-year course)

Conservatoire for Dance and Drama
Comprised of:
    Bristol Old Vic Theatre School Central
    School of Ballet
    London Academy of Music and Dramatic
    Art (LAMDA)
    London Contemporary Dance School,
    National Centre for Circus Arts,
    Northern School of Contemporary
    Dance, Rambert School of Ballet and
    Contemporary Dance, Royal Academy of
    Dramatic Art (RADA)
    Tavistock House, Tavistock Square
    London WC1H 9JJ
020 7387 5101
www.cdd.ac.uk
Fees 2018–19: £9,250

Dyson Institute of Engineering and Technology
Tetbury Hill Malmesbury
Wiltshire SN16 0RP
dysoninstitute@dyson.com
www.dysoninstitute.com
Paid degree courses – no fees

Glasgow School of Art
167 Renfrew Street, Glasgow G3 6RQ
0141 353 4500
www.gsa.ac.uk
Fees 2018–19: Scotland / EU, no fee,
RUK £9,250

Guildhall School of Music and Drama
Silk Street, Barbican,
London EC2Y 8DT
020 7628 2571
www.gsmd.ac.uk
Fees 2018–19: £9,250

The University of Law
Birmingham, Bristol, Chester, Exeter,
Guildford, Leeds, London (Bloomsbury and
Moorgate), Manchester
0800 289997
www.law.ac.uk
Fees 2018–19: £12,500 (two-year course)
£9,250 (three-year course)

Leeds College of Art*
Blenheim Walk,
Leeds LS2 9AQ
0113 202 8000
www.leeds-art.ac.uk
Fees 2018–19: £9,250

Liverpool Institute for Performing Arts*
Mount Street,
Liverpool L1 9HF
0151 330 3000
www.lipa.ac.uk
Fees 2018–19: £9,250

The London Institute of Banking and Finance
4–9 Burgate Lane
Canterbury, Kent CT1 2XJ
01227 818609
Student campus:
   25 Lovat Lane, London EC3R 8EB
020 7337 6293
www.libf.ac.uk
Fees 2018–19: £6,000

New College of the Humanities
19 Bedford Square,
London WC1B 3HH
020 7637 4550
www.nchlondon.ac.uk
Fees 2018–19: £9,250

Pearson College
80 Strand,
London WC2R 0RL
0203 7334 456
www.pearsoncollegelondon.ac.uk
Fees (2017): £9,000

Plymouth College of Art*
Tavistock Place,
Plymouth PL4 8AT
01752 203434
www.plymouthart.ac.uk
Fees 2018–19: £9,250

Ravensbourne*
6 Penrose Way,
Greenwich Peninsula,
London SE10 0EW
020 3040 3040
www.ravensbourne.ac.uk
Fees 2018–19: £9,250

Regent's University London*
Inner Circle,
Regent's Park, London NW1 4NS
020 7487 7505
www.regents.ac.uk
Fees 2018–19: £16,400

Rose Bruford College of Theatre and Performance*
Lamorbey Park,
Burnt Oak Lane,
Sidcup, Kent DA15 9DF
020 8308 2600
www.bruford.ac.uk
Fees 2018–19: £9,250

Royal College of Music
Prince Consort Road,
London SW7 2BS
020 7591 4300
www.rcm.ac.uk
Fees 2018–19: £9,250

Royal Conservatoire of Scotland
100 Renfrew Street,
Glasgow G2 3DB
0141 332 4101
www.rcs.ac.uk
Fees 2018–19: Scotland/EU, no fee;
RUK £9,000

Royal Northern College of Music
124 Oxford Road,
Manchester M13 9RD
0161 907 5200
www.rncm.ac.uk
Fees 2018–19: £9,250

Royal Welsh College of Music and Drama
Castle Grounds, Cathays Park,
Cardiff CF10 3ER
029 2034 2854
www.rwcmd.ac.uk
Fees 2018–19: £9,000

St Mary's University College*
191 Falls Road, Belfast BT12 6FE
028 9032 7678
www.stmarys-belfast.ac.uk
Fees 2018–19: £4,030; RUK £9,250

Scotland's Rural College
Campuses at Aberdeen, Ayr, Cupar,
Dumfries, Ecclesmachan, near Broxburn,
Edinburgh
0800 269453
www.sruc.ac.uk
Fees 2018–19: Scotland/EU, no fee;
RUK £6,950

Stranmillis University College
Stranmillis Road, Belfast BT9 5DY
028 9038 1271
www.stran.ac.uk
Fees 2018–19: £4,030; RUK £9,250

Trinity Laban Conservatoire of Music and Dance
Music Faculty: King Charles Court
Old Royal Naval College,
Greenwich, London SE10 9JF 020 8305 4444
Dance Faculty: Laban Building, Creekside
London SE8 3DZ
020 8305 9400
www.trinitylaban.ac.uk
Fees 2018–19: £9,250

UCFB (University College of Football Business)
Burnley FC Turf Moor
Harry Potts Way Burnley
Lancashire BB10 4BX
Wembley Stadium
London HA9 0WS
(also has a Manchester campus)
033322 06860
www.ucfb.com
Fees 2018–19: £9,250

Writtle University College*
Lordship Lane,
Writtle, Chelmsford, Essex CM1 3RR
01245 424200
www.writtle.ac.uk
Fees 2018–19: £9,250

Index